Local and Urban Governance

Series Editor

Carlos Nunes Silva, Institute of Geography and Spatial Planning, University of Lisbon, Lisbon, Portugal

This series contains research studies with policy relevance in the field of sub-national territorial governance, at the micro, local and regional levels, as well as on its connections with national and supranational tiers. The series is multidisciplinary and brings together innovative research from different areas within the Social Sciences and Humanities. The series is open for theoretical, methodological and empirical ground breaking contributions. Books included in this series explore the new modes of territorial governance, new perspectives and new research methodologies. The aim is to present advances in Governance Studies to scholars and researchers in universities and research organizations, and to policy makers worldwide. The series includes monographs, edited volumes and textbooks. Book proposals and final manuscripts are peer-reviewed.

The areas covered in the series include but are not limited to the following subjects:

- Local and regional government
- Urban and metropolitan governance
- Multi-level territorial governance
- Post-colonial local governance
- Municipal merger reforms
- Inter-municipal cooperation
- Decentralized cooperation
- Governance of spatial planning
- Strategic spatial planning
- Citizen participation in local policies
- Local governance, spatial justice and the right to the city
- Local public services
- Local economic development policies
- Entrepreneurialism and municipal public enterprises
- Local government finance
- Local government and sustainable development
- Anthropocene and green local governance
- Climate change and local governance
- Smart local governance

The series is intended for geographers, planners, political scientists, sociologists, lawyers, historians, urban anthropologists and economists.

More information about this series at http://www.springer.com/series/16129

Keith Hoggart

A Contrived Countryside

The Governance of Rural Housing in England
1900–74

 Springer

Keith Hoggart (iD)
Department of Geography
King's College London
London, UK

ISSN 2524-5449   ISSN 2524-5457   (electronic)
Local and Urban Governance
ISBN 978-3-030-62650-1   ISBN 978-3-030-62651-8   (eBook)
https://doi.org/10.1007/978-3-030-62651-8

This Springer imprint is published by the registered company Springer Nature Switzerland AG
The registered company address is: Gewerbestrasse 11, 6330 Cham, Switzerland

For Linda, for the past 30 some years and more

Preface

The prompts for this book go back to graduate student days, particularly reading Richard Crossman's (1975) diary on his years as Minister of Housing and Local Government. Crossman's diaries provoked outrage and debate as they differed from the usual run of self-congratulatory political accounts, which seemed to focus on 'explaining' uncomfortable 'realities' accompanied by huge dollops of gloss on personal involvement in 'key' political decisions or events. Published posthumously, Crossman offered a day-by-day, blow-by-blow account of life as a minister. With the first volume emerging just five years after he left the Cabinet, they offered a glimpse behind the politician's façade and manufactured 'truths' of a politically inspired press. At a time when graduate schools in geography were swirling with numerous theses using increasingly sophisticated statistical methods to 'explain' corporate and government actions, my interest peaked with Crossman's insight on cross-departmental skirmishes, restricted vision amongst Westminster politicians and Whitehall mandarins, and the highly subjective, often self-seeking and commonly visionless drivers behind politicians' actions. This dissonance between mainstream academic writing and the 'realities' of policymaking has stayed with me since. It drew me to a project that would access material exploring the internal arguments and priority setting in government agencies.

Having worked on both rural and urban projects, one frustration with both was the way many studies were grounded locally. The national context in which local events were played out often received little reference or if acknowledged came forth principally through exploring how specific policies impacted on localities. In this regard I was fortunate in having spent a considerable time outside Britain when younger, which drew me to an appreciation of national contexts. This awareness induced contributions exploring similarities (and differences) in outcomes across diverse settings (Hoggart 1991; Hoggart et al. 1995), as well as consideration of rural–urban distinction and differentiation within the countryside (Hoggart 1988, 1990). All this strengthened the conviction that rural researchers need to pay careful attention to the broader economic, political and social networks of the localities they investigate. To paraphrase Goodwin-Hawkins (2015), a focus on 'the local' carries within it the risk that researchers are captured by the idealisations many of their informants articulate.

The seriousness of this issue derives from the relatively small number of researchers focusing on the countryside in so-called advanced economies. There is so much we do not know and so much needs exploration that the rural literature is frequently reliant on a small number of outputs for its insight. This was the case when this project started, resulting in an initial focus on how working-class housing options are influenced by landowner employers and the in-migrant service classes. A concentration on housing was also spurred by a belief not enough was known about this core rural necessity. In this context, I was surprised by a colleague telling me my 2003 review of the field offered a different, interesting perspective. I trust this volume will kindle similar curiosity.

London, UK   Keith Hoggart

Acknowledgements

Research costs for travel and accommodation for this book were covered by the British Academy. I should like to thank the Academy for support to enable data collection to be completed. Other contributions for which I am grateful include the many archivists and librarians at the Bedfordshire, Hertfordshire and Norfolk county record offices, The National Archives and the British Library. Their quiet dedication and helpful assistance made completing this project more enjoyable and much easier. Colleagues and fellow researchers whose inputs have made innumerable contributions to this work, often without them knowing how important and in what ways they have been an influence, all deserve my thanks. I am obliged to Carlos Nuñes Silva for drawing my attention to the Springer series as an outlet for this book, as well as to Solomon George of Springer for his helpful advice and technical support in preparing the manuscript. My partner, Linda Newson, has as ever enabled me to maintain a semblance of sanity in this mad world, as well as reviving me when I despair over the ineptitude of leaders, national and local. She has contributed in so many ways that I am not able to capture their true value or breadth in words. Good cheer, strong support and depth of encouragement have stretched beyond realms I deserve.

Contents

About the Author

Keith Hoggart is emeritus professor of geography at King's College London. His research has focused on links between housing, migration and social change in rural areas, with policymaking and the governance of local socio-economic change as key interests. Professor Hoggart is the author/co-author of eight books/research monographs and has edited/co-edited seven books. He graduated from the University of Salford, was a Commonwealth scholar at the University of Toronto and completed his PhD at King's College London. Professor Hoggart has been Fulbright scholar at the University of Maryland and Temple University, and visiting researcher at the University of California, Berkeley. He was head of King's Department of Geography and its School of Social Science and Public Policy, and was a King's vice principal from 2005 to 2013.

Abbreviations

ARDCM	Ampthill Rural District Council Meeting
ARDCHCM	Ampthill Rural District Council Housing Committee Meeting
ARDCHPBuCM	Ampthill Rural District Council Housing, Planning and Building Committee Meeting
ARDCHPByCM	Ampthill Rural District Council Housing, Planning and Byelaws Committee Meeting
ARDCMOHar	Ampthill Rural District Council Annual Report of the Medical Officer of Health
AUDCHBCM	Ampthill Urban District Council Housing and Building Committee Meeting
AUDCM	Ampthill Urban District Council Meeting
AUDCMOHar	Ampthill Urban District Council Annual Report of the Medical Officer of Health
B&BR	Beds and Bucks Reporter
B&NEHG	Buntingford and North-East Herts Gazette
BC&BG	Biggleswade Chronicle and Bedfordshire Gazette
BiRDCM	Biggleswade Rural District Council Meeting
BiRDCHCM	Biggleswade Rural District Council Housing Committee Meeting
BiRDCHECM	Biggleswade Rural District Council Housing Executive Committee Meeting
BiRDCHLCM	Biggleswade Rural District Council Housing Letting Committee Meeting
BiRDCTPCM	Biggleswade Rural District Council Town Planning Committee Meeting
BiUDCM	Biggleswade Urban District Council Meeting
BrRDCM	Braughing Rural District Council Meeting
BrRDCECM	Braughing Rural District Council Estates Committee Meeting
BrRDCFCM	Braughing Rural District Council Finance Committee Meeting
BrRDCFGPCM	Braughing Rural District Council Finance and General Purposes Committee Meeting

BrRDCHCM	Braughing Rural District Council Housing Committee Meeting
BrRDCJFHCM	Braughing Rural District Council Joint Finance and Housing Committee Meeting
BrRDCPHHCM	Braughing Rural District Council Public Health and Housing Committee Meeting
BRO	Bedfordshire Record Office
BuRDCM	Buntingford Rural District Council Meeting
CB	County Borough (city)
CHAC	Central Housing Advisory Committee
CPRE	Council for the Protection of Rural England
D&FT	Dereham and Fakenham Times
DoE	Department of the Environment
EDP	Eastern Daily Press
ERDCM	Erpingham Rural District Council Meeting
ERDCHCM	Erpingham Rural District Council Housing Committee Meeting
FakPost	Fakenham Post
GLC	Greater London Council
H&EO	Herts and Essex Observer
H&FP	Holt and Fakenham Post
H&PBG	Hatfield and Potters Bar Gazette
HA&SAT	Herts Advertiser and St Albans Times
HaRDCM	Hadham Rural District Council Meeting
HCH	House of Commons Official Report (Hansard)
HertsMerc	Herts Mercury
HM&CP	Hertfordshire Mercury and County Press
HMC&WP	Holt, Melton Constable and Wells Post
HRA	Housing Revenue Account
HtRDCM	Hatfield Rural District Council Meeting
HtRDCH&TPCM	Hatfield Rural District Council Housing and Town Planning Committee Meeting
HtRDCHCM	Hatfield Rural District Council Housing Committee Meeting
HtRDCJMHF	Hatfield Rural District Council Special Meeting of Housing and Town Planning and Finance, Establishment and General Purposes Committees
HRO	Hertfordshire Record Office
LCC	London County Council
LGB	Local Government Board
MAF	Ministry of Agriculture and Fisheries
MB	Municipal Borough
MHLG	Ministry of Housing and Local Government
MTCP	Ministry of Town and Country Planning
MOA	Mass Observation Archive (University of Sussex)
MoH	Ministry of Health
MP	Member of Parliament
NBC	North Beds Courier

NBC&BR	North Beds Courier and Biggleswade Record
NBC&SN&DN	North Beds Courier and St Neots and District News
NFU	National Farmers' Union
NHS	National Health Service
NM&PWJ	Norwich Mercury and People's Weekly Journal
NNN	North Norfolk News
NorfChron	Norfolk Chronicle
NRO	Norfolk Record Office
NUAW	National Union of Agricultural Workers
NWP&ENS	North Walsham Post and East Norfolk Standard
ONS	Office of National Statistics
PM	The Prime Minister
PWLB	Public Works Loan Board
RDC	Rural District Council
RDCA	Rural District Councils' Association
SaUDCM	Sandy Urban District Council Meeting
SmRDCM	Smallburgh Rural District Council Meeting
SmRDCHCM	Smallburgh Rural District Council Housing Committee Meeting
T&WT	Thetford and Watton Times
TNA	The National Archives
UDC	Urban District Council
UDCA	Urban District Councils' Association
W&DR	Woburn and District Reporter
WR&WSR	Woburn Reporter and Woburn Sands Record
WRDCM	Walsingham Rural District Council Meeting
WRDCHCM	Walsingham Rural District Council Housing Committee Meeting
YarmInd	Yarmouth Independent

List of Figures

List of Tables

Chapter 1
Governance and Rural Transformation: An Investigative Approach

Abstract Outlining the initial prompts for undertaking this research, this chapter examines arguments that working-class housing in the English countryside has been restricted by landowner employers and service-class in-migrants who seek an imagined bucolic rurality. These drivers of restraint on the housing options of those not able to afford home ownership are deemed insufficient to capture the magnitude of rural housing deficiencies. Given their limited resources, pathways to housing improvement for the low-paid depended on public policy interventions. Explaining why the book explores housing conditions across eight decades, with a focus on England, attention is drawn to insufficient knowledge about key contributions to the rural housing drama; not simply rural council actions but also construction firm and national government involvement. Offering an account of the analytical framework utilised in the volume, the chapter draws out the rationale for selecting seven rural districts for primary attention, while indicating that conclusions are based on insight from a variety of national and local information sources. These ensure equal attention is devoted to decision criteria and policy action nationally and locally.

Keywords Landowner vested interests · Service-class in-migrants · Local–central government relations · Study areas · Data sources

This book explores how failings in the governance of housing deprived longstanding rural residents of better accommodation and fostered conditions conducive to the service-class 'capture' of the English countryside (Newby 1980; Cloke and Thrift 1990; Murdoch 1995).[1] The time span for this investigation extends into the

---

[1]The literature refers to a (relatively) recent 'middle-class' takeover of the countryside (e.g. Murdoch 1995) but the middle-classes have been strongly represented in rural areas for a long time, as with farmers and small business owners. Even as primary sector roles declined, new petit bourgeois occupations, as in the holiday trades, filled gaps (e.g. Vince 1952). The idea of 'middle-class capture' refers to new middle-class occupations. It distinguishes what Perkin (1989, p.82) called the 'business strata' of the middle-class, with its long history in the countryside, and a 'professional strata' (or 'service-class') comprised of professionals and managers-owners of large enterprises. The service-classes have been attributed with greater workplace autonomy, easier promotion prospects, higher remuneration and relatively secure careers. Commonly linked to regular job changes and geographical mobility, these attributes mean the service-classes are well-placed to

© Springer Nature Switzerland AG 2021
K. Hoggart, *A Contrived Countryside*, Local and Urban Governance,
https://doi.org/10.1007/978-3-030-62651-8_1

mid-1970s, for by then, even in the so-called 'deep countryside', the fundamental traits of this seizure were grounded and clearly visible. At this time, analysts saw in-migration and burgeoning economic buoyancy penetrating beyond metropolitan catchments into the wider countryside (e.g. Fielding 1982; Cross 1990). This adjusted conceptualisation of rural dynamics moved accounts away from themes of decline, depopulation and despondency (e.g. Mitchell 1950; Saville 1957; Hodge and Whitby 1981), towards new agitations over social tension, conflict and deprivation amongst longstanding residents (Connell 1978; Duckers and Davies 1990; Derounian 1993). At a basic level, the contrast between the two eras highlighted a past in which claims on rural housing were assumed to have fallen and a late-twentieth-century intensification in demand for rural living. In public policy terms, this introduced a new emphasis. Early in the century, government attention largely responded to the public health consequences of housing deficiencies. Late in the century '… new rural housing problems are frequently caused by increased wealth rather than deprivation' (Rogers 1976, p.96). Yet, key drivers within these two eras changed little; at heart the core shortcoming was limited options for those unable to buy their own home. What did change was the context in which this dynamic was played out. By the 1970s, absolute housing shortages in England were at an end (Holmans 1987, pp.91–93). But for the countryside, previous stock surpluses had been reincarnated into deficits. This book examines how the intervention of public agencies in rural housing markets up to the 1970s resulted in missed opportunities to address often dire housing circumstances for the less advantaged. It thereby articulates the transformation of rural housing from a state of near desperation into a service-class playground.

From a governance perspective, a conviction in this volume is the inappropriateness of conceptualising the countryside as separate from its urban counterpart; viz. of inverting the regular fallacy in urban studies of assuming 'the urban' is 'the nation'. Both these interpretive lenses proffer diminished accounts of locality and nation. Interactions between the two require elaboration to enrich understanding of ground-level occurrences. As Shucksmith et al. (1996, p.18) summarised, locality studies give depth but this must be contextualised by appreciating interplays with wider economic, political and social processes: 'Locality studies are often able to get behind the myths and assumptions about the areas they study. However, a strong sense of what is special about a particular locality also hinders putting that locality into the broader matrix. Consequently, this level of analysis is often lacking'. Such shortfalls have been especially evident in the rural housing literature, given a paucity of investigations, especially for the first three-quarters of the twentieth-century. The faintness of research over this period (and for decades later) is captured in the way reviews of rural housing studies covered similar issues and reference the same publications, perhaps with marginal updates to reflect the reviewer's predilections

---

achieve life goals (Savage et al. 1992; Goldthorpe 1995). This group, not an expansion of the petit bourgeoisie, has forged service-class capture, not just by increasing numbers but also by a 'take-over' of village activities and the conditioning of longstanding residents' behaviour (Perry et al. 1986; Rapport 1993).

(e.g. Rogers 1976; Robinson 1992; Hoggart 2003). Not surprisingly, given the slimness of published work, mainstream insights were heavily influenced by a few key studies. Amongst these, two strands stand out. Both identified a key role for local governance. Both help perpetuate the 'exceptionalist myth' that rural housing conditions were principally determined in the countryside.

The first research thread came to prominence following investigations by Newby and colleagues on East Anglia (e.g. Rose et al. 1976; Newby et al. 1978; Saunders et al. 1978). The quality of this research rightly made a profound impression on rural studies. They highlighted how farmer 'control' of rural councils was used to foster farmer dominance in the workplace, as farm labourers were dependent on their employers for housing given rural councils erected little alternative accommodation. A lost job could mean a lost home; a potent retardant on demands for better wages or working conditions.[2] Of course, there was unevenness in the employment of farm labourers, with areas dominated by small family farms having less employees, while regional divergence in farm commodity production, in the skill-sets required for products, and in labour market competition, induced disparate farmer proclivities to supply cottages (Gasson 1975; Grigg 1987). But even where farm-worker numbers were low, rural housing authorities, viz. the rural district councils (RDCs), were dominated by councillors with farming, clergy, small shop-keeper and similar backgrounds (Springall 1936; Pedley 1942; Bealey et al. 1965; Newby et al. 1978). This gave rural councils a petit bourgeois tone, with local policies open to distortion to support farmer interests (e.g. Gilg and Kelly 1997). Beyond their farming ties, rural councils were described as non-interventionist, tax averse and disinclined to support the low-paid (e.g. Bennett 1914; Hollis 1987, p.390). Hence: 'Economy was the watchword, and councillors were more concerned to keep down the [property tax] rates than to accept any expensive responsibility for replacing notorious slums with new council houses' (Mingay 1990, p.121; also Eley 1973; Shucksmith and Henderson 1995; Read 2003). From across the British Isles, investigators have revealed how deferential social environments depressed rural initiative, especially in more 'peripheral' zones (Caird and Moisley 1961; Kendall 1963; Johnson 1972; Madgwick et al. 1973; Dyer 1978; Bird 1982). Enclaves with a strong non-farm economic base were often exceptions (e.g. Ryder 1984; Pooley 1996), although numerically they accounted for few rural districts. Even so, such councils indicated that, where there was a will, there was a way. By implication, the message was that weak responses to inadequate housing resulted from rural leader (in)action.

This interpretation matched long dominant rural themes, wherein rural societies were caricatured as isolated, socially backward, and dependent on cities for innovation (Redfield 1947; Berry 1970; Fischer 1975). As the twentieth-century

---

[2] As Benson (1989, pp.83-84) noted, in the nineteenth-century, employer-owned dwellings reinforced control over workers in various industries, but in the twentieth-century, tied accommodation withered, retaining potency largely in agriculture and mining. For Danziger (1988, p.158), not until 1976 legislation were farm-workers effectively freed from fear of home loss at the 'virtual whim' of their employer.

progressed, this vision became less tenable (Pahl 1966; Newby 1980). Even early in the century, Mackinder (1907, p.258) gave notice of its limitations:

> … all southeastern England is a single urban community; for steam and electricity are changing our geographical conceptions … East Anglia and the West of England possess a certain independence by virtue of their comparatively remote position, but, for various reasons, even they belong effectively to Metropolitan England. (also Horn 1984, p.234; Beard 1989, p.43; Howkins 2003, p.57, p.62)

These effects were more intense closer to London and other metropolitan centres, as studies of single villages and counties highlight (e.g. Hooson 1958; Bell 1994; Burchardt 2012). Yet, the outward march of metropolitan influence was sufficient for Taylor (1965, pp.167–68) to hold that, between 1911 and 1951: 'All England became suburban except for the slums at one extreme and the Pennine moors at the other'. With in-migrant newcomers wresting control or at least disrupting prior social practices (Masser and Stroud 1965; Perry et al. 1986; Rapport 1993), explaining rural (in)action as a consequence of 'isolated' local elite predispositions lost potency as the century progressed. Alongside their social and landscape imprints on villages (e.g. Pahl 1965; Radford 1970; Ambrose 1974; Connell 1978), incoming service-class residents created a new rural power nexus (sometimes allied with longstanding leaders; e.g. Sturzaker and Shucksmith 2011). As various studies articulated, the general disposition within newcomer circles was to resist housing expansion, especially but not solely if this was targeted at working-class occupants (Masser and Stroud 1965; Buller and Lowe 1982; Cloke and Thrift 1990; Sturzaker 2010).

In this regard, the English land-use planning system played into newcomers' hands, as it gave opportunities to village residents to create delay and impose building conditions that heightened costs and so enhanced exclusivity. But while service-class lobbying could manifest itself in oppositional movements, greater effects could result from influencing planning direction (Gilg and Kelly 1997; Sturzaker 2010) or creating expectations of resistance that dissuaded development applications (Buller and Hoggart 1986). With land-use planning policies favouring house-building in larger villages and small towns (Moseley 1974; Cloke 1979), building restraint in smaller, more attractive villages created a price premium for older dwellings, especially in areas of special landscape designation (Shucksmith 1981; Clark 1982; Cloke 1983). For sure, looseness of fit existed between building permissions and planning policies; as investigations of planning applications have shown (Blacksell and Gilg 1977; Anderson 1981; Preece 1981). But these disparities were not sufficient to disrupt geographical concentrations in house-building, which intensified dissonance between supply and demand, so diminishing housing affordability, especially in small villages (Shucksmith 1991; Bramley and Smart 1995). As Radford (1970, p.17) summarised for the Midlands:

> … houses in villages are often auctioned, and it is extremely frustrating for the existing villagers to stand no chance in out-bidding the wealthier potential newcomers. Where new or existing buildings are sold by private treaty, the asking price is probably such as not to make it possible for the existing population even to consider purchase.

In combination, housing markets and land-use planning have been portrayed as weakening prospects of the less well-endowed acquiring rural homes (Dunn et al. 1981; Shucksmith 1990; Satsangi et al. 2010). If country living was to continue for the working-classes, some form of social housing was necessary.

One reason for caution in ascribing weight to this vision is that it might misrepresent earlier decades of the century. It has potency today, when building restrictions heighten demand for rural homes (Satsangi et al. 2010), but what about when demand for country living was muted? Note, for example, that the service-class presence in rural England was lower than its urban counterpart up to the 1970s. Even in South-East England, where metropolitan links were strongest, service-class percentages fell below urban equivalents until the 1980s, and into the 1990s for the rest of rural England (Hoggart 1997). A further cause for doubt is the complex make-up of social classes. For one, many working-class rural (and urban) residents have partners in a different class, while occupational mobility, alongside transitions from rural-to-urban living (and vice versa), indicate dynamism in local social class habitation (e.g. Hoggart 2007). All this adds weight to the prospect that, earlier in the century, service-class 'capture' was not a defining force.

Yet, for most of the century, housing conditions in rural England left much to be desired. Indeed, by the Second World War, when demand for improved food production intensified, the neglect of the countryside was obvious. Then rural areas needed to be attractive places to live to entice workers back to the land. In this quest, better housing was critical. The 1942 Scott Committee concurred: 'The improvement of rural housing is an essential prerequisite to the re-establishment of a contented countryside'.[3] But if the countryside was not content, and service-class capture lay in the future, should housing deficiencies be laid at the door of local leaders? Reasons for caution in supporting this view arise because other contributors to rural housing outcomes have been insufficiently investigated. As a start, few have studied rural building firms. You search high and low for studies of rural house builders in the early decades of the twentieth-century, except as subdued items in glossy volumes on architecture or design.[4] Most attention given to rural construction has centred on the outskirts of towns, often involving large firms (e.g. Fleming 1984; Rydin 1985). How far this represents small operations away from towns is a moot point. For one, at least since the nineteenth-century, larger builders secured higher returns on their work, making them more profitable (Burnett 1986, pp.34–35). For another, builders in smaller places had higher costs (e.g. Shucksmith 1981, p.35; Shucksmith and Henderson 1995, p.2). This suggests small rural builders operated in a different market from larger companies. This is important, for, as Ball

---

[3] TNA HLG37/48 'Summary of Report to the Scott Committee', undated c1942. This report was published as Ministry of Works and Planning (1942).

[4] The summary of Satsangi and co-workers (2010, pp.111–13) is instructive. They found little in the literature on builders in villages. Larger firms became more influential in the later decades of the century, partly because construction was concentrated on fewer companies (Wellings 2006) and partly because rural areas (beyond 'suburbanisation') became more attractive when land-use planning favoured bigger sites in larger settlements.

(1983, Ch3) noted, the construction sector had disproportionately small operations (40% of firms employed fewer than 25 workers even in the late-1970s). As small, local companies dominated rural building (MoH 1944), it is difficult to anticipate impacts on housing production from insight on large companies functioning at city or cross-county levels. Is it realistic to assume building firms responded quickly to rural council requests for more houses, or for small private builders to gear up for surges in home ownership demand, in a sector renowned for irregular, sectional demand fluctuation (e.g. Bowley 1937; Barras and Ferguson 1985)? All in all, given the dominance of large firms, and their influence on government policy (e.g. Dunleavy 1981), is it reasonable to assume small builders walked through more treacle than their larger kin? Our lack of knowledge on rural builders undermines understanding of rural housing circumstances.

The same applies for national impacts on local housing policies. Within the rural literature, for most of the twentieth-century, this weakness applied for the public sector and for private housing.[5] Yet, national policies have been critical to both sectors. This might seem self-evident for the public sector, but impacts on private housing have been significant. Most directly, building for private owners benefited from direct public subsidies, as for new-build under the 1923 Housing Act (Bowley 1945) and from home improvement grants, which date back to 1926 in rural areas (e.g. Martin 1938; Adamson 1974). Also important were indirect government interventions. Hence, it is difficult to disentangle what Humphries (1987, p.325) described as primarily a private sector inter-war housing boom, which has been widely accepted as the backbone of British economic recovery at this time (Richardson 1967), from government strategies that positioned the state as facilitator for private economic actions (Booth 1987). Adherence to what McKibbon (McKibbin 2010, pp.88–89) charged were failed government policies, did at least reduce, and then sustain, low interest rates, which supported building society growth that fuelled owner-occupied house-building (Bellman 1928; Marshall 1968). This does not detract from the enormous efforts building societies made themselves (Mowat 1955; Swenarton and Taylor 1985; Scott and Newton 2012), but their involvement was state-supported through tax concessions (Pugh 2008, p.64) and loan guarantees that unlocked builder caution over buyer ability to pay (Connor 1936, p.7; Merrett 1982, p.81). Further incentives to home ownership had existed since 1889, when councils were allowed to grant home purchase loans, offering mortgages to those building societies thought marginal (Niner 1975; Duncan 1976). Home purchase was additionally encouraged through tax reductions for mortgages (Holmans 2000) and later by shared ownership and other low-cost mortgage schemes (Richmond 1987). State subsidies and other supports for housing associations added a further element to a

---

[5] Almost all publicly owned housing was built for councils. After 1945, some was for New Town Development Corporations. A few rural councils, like Hatfield, could nominate applicants on their waiting list for new town dwellings. A small portion of public sector dwellings were owned by other state institutions, like government departments. Where there was clarity in the records, this book refers to 'council' or 'new town' dwellings. In other cases 'public sector' has been used, even though most dwellings would be council-owned.

multi-faceted, fluctuating and inevitably complicated state support system for the private sector (Best 1991). If we accept that teasing out governmental impacts on private housing is complex, this should prompt questions about the lack of rural investigations of the relationship.

But what about understanding public sector activity? Here commentators on the countryside have been prone to 'draw down' national policies, assuming national canons were implemented by rural councils (unless timidity or self-interest encouraged sloth). This interpretation matches the worldview that: 'Local government in Britain, for all its trappings of democracy and autonomy, can usefully be viewed as a decentralised administrative mechanism for carrying out the bidding of central government' (Foley 1972, p.20). Indeed, even for cities, analysts charge local policies largely mirror national trends:

> … when the separate performance of all the leading actors on the local stage have been weighed and appraised, it appears that the leading part in the city's [Birmingham's] housing drama has often been played by the central government on the one hand, and by general economic conditions on the other. In fact, for all the heat and flurry surrounding the house-building issue, for all the hard words in council debates and the contumely hurled by each party at the other, for all the activity of citizen organisations, and for all the power and influence of city architects and engineers, the city's housing record is remarkably like that of other large provincial cities. (Newton 1976, p.200; also Finnigan 1984)

Policy arenas like housing, where most costs are capital investments, have long been integral to national economic policy (Ball 1980), which encouraged national control over local action (e.g. Layton 1961; MacGregor-Reid 1977). Yet Cullingworth's (1966) analysis of housing policy emphasised that the mechanisms available to ministries meant the national government's role in housing policy was 'remarkably weak'. This was because councils were able to interpret national legislation differently; as in determining what were local 'housing needs' or what was a 'reasonable' response to them. For Ball (1980, p.116), within councils, '… defiance is active, but not so as to bring the full weight of the law onto their heads'. Not surprisingly, national '… departments do not trust all the local authorities' (Griffith 1966, p.54). These observations on local–national relations come from some of the most widely respected researchers and commentators of the time. Their vision probably came with a heavy city-focused lens, but there are few empirical rural investigations to contradict their insight. Those investigations that exist tend to focus on single legislative Acts, one policy issue or one point in time (e.g. Phillips and Williams 1982; Forrest and Murie 1992; Long 2005).[6] Such studies are welcome, but together they represent too thin a menu to give general rural insights. This is important given the regularity with which commentators have charged that rural

---

[6] More attention to rural housing emerged late in the twentieth-century partly because legislation was controversial, such as tenants' Right-to-Buy their homes under the 1980 Housing Act (Beazley et al. 1980; Chaney and Sherwood 2000) or the dispersal of council portfolios (Long 2005). Another reason was growing tension over interactions between land-use planning (particularly greenfield sites), conservation and house-building (e.g. Bishop 1998; Gallent and Bell 2000; Adams and Watkins 2002).

issues are neglected in national housing policies (e.g. Rogers 1976; Lawton and Pooley 1992). Perhaps this is so, but if so we need to articulate how this has been manifest and what its consequences have been. One intention in this volume is to investigate whether claims of rural neglect have substance.

1.1 Key Themes

At core, this book is concerned with the physical fabric of rural housing, as expressed in availability and quality. Complementing this emphasis is attention to the social dimension of housing; which, in the form of access and cost, recruited most attention in the literature up to the 1980s (e.g. Dunn et al. 1981; Shucksmith 1981; Clark 1982; Phillips and Williams 1982). The structure of the book incorporates perspectives on rural housing that are under-represented in the literature. For example, one element that distinguishes this volume is the way rural housing is investigated. As a starting point, take Rogers (1987) observation that the rural housing literature up to the mid-1980s demonstrated a sequence of flirtations with specific issues, which captured the imagination briefly before falling to the next fad; second homes, tied cottages, housing deprivation, public sector shortcomings and counterurbanisation all had limited top spots. Studies generally focused on specific issues, often for a single housing tenure. Wide-ranging assessments of the changing housing stock were few and far between. Dunn et al. (1981) came close to providing a broader empirical account, although they focused on access to dwellings; not on how housing numbers and quality evolved to favour service-class 'capture'. What Dunn and associates did provide was a valuable exploration of the difficulties many rural residents faced in securing homes; drawing out how access varied by place and by socio-economic standing. Where this volume extends their contribution is by identifying what led to the differential access they identified. How was the English countryside transformed from over-abundant poor quality dwellings into 1970s shortages, yet with continued deprivation? To grasp what produced this transfiguration requires focusing on stock changes, in terms of what generated and thwarted efforts to add numbers, what drove the composition of the stock (such as bedroom numbers and household amenities), what decided the distribution of new-build, demolition and home improvement, and how occupants shifted over time. Put simply, how and why did the actions of private agents and government organisations conspire to change the rural housing scene from over- to under-supply? Integral to any answer must be how the housing stock was 'managed', not simply in limiting losses or extending dwelling utility through improvement, but also in determining the access of social groups.[7]

---

[7] Alongside Dunn et al. (1981), occupant access and mobility have been investigated for the public sector (Phillips and Williams 1982; Forrest and Murie 1992) and for agricultural tied cottages (Fletcher 1969; Gasson 1975; Jones 1975).

For much of the twentieth-century, the rural literature has been timid in address-ing such questions. Rural commentators have signified important roles for house builders and for the financing of construction; yet few examined their role pre-1970. More recently, the attraction of rural living and the role of big construction firms have increased, which has provoked more research on rural building and finance (Rydin 1985; Short et al. 1986; Adams and Watkins 2002). For earlier decades, the literature offered thin gruel. Consequently, knowledge of the rural housing scene was weakened. Nowhere was this more apparent than for housing conditions. This was brought starkly to policy-makers' attention with the first national Housing Condition Survey (MHLG 1968). Despite repeated claims by policy-makers that poor housing was primarily a large city problem (e.g. Spencer 1970, p.77; Wilson 1971, p.526; Crossman 1975, p.44), and with spending commitments targeting cit-ies, the 1967 survey found 11.3% of the housing stock in conurbation and 'other urban' areas were unfit for human habitation, whereas the supposedly 'less needy' countryside had 13.3% of its stock unfit. Further, while rural districts accounted for 20.5% of all dwellings included in the national survey, amongst those requiring the highest expenditure on repairs (over £1000), the rural share was 34.2%. Policies based on weak evidence not unexpectedly figure as a theme in this volume.

As well as deficient data, failure to understand rural housing problems has derived from the narrow focus of investigations. Too regularly, research has focused on 'management' of the stock, without due regard to how and why stock volumes and qualities change. To understand these features it is not enough to explore them in situ. They also need contextualising with comparative analysis. Like their urban counterparts, rural analysts have often explicitly or implicitly sought explanations within localities, without comparison with other contexts. Such attributions also characterise the worldviews of national policy-makers. In 1900–1908, for example, the Local Government Board's Medical Officer of Health blamed continuing rural housing problems on no rural desire to address them (Wilding 1972, p.3). Such claims of rural distinctiveness were around 60 years later, as in Sharpe's (1973, pp.2–3) observation that:

> What remains of genuinely rural local government in most industrial societies seems to be a profoundly different animal to the urban variety. What may be said for one is almost cer-tain to be wrong for the other and in many ways rural local government never quite seems like local government in the classical sense.

Prompting doubt over this assertion is Grant's (1977, p.5) message that there is '… a general lack of studies of the distinctiveness of rural politics in Britain'. Without comparing rural actions with other areas, can claims to rural distinctiveness be justi-fied? Even if they existed, is it correct to assert that rural–urban differences neces-sarily resulted from action by rural-based agents? Suggesting this might not be the case, Astor and Rowntree (1939, p.213) charged that, for 1919–1939 slum rehous-ing and home improvement campaigns, national neglect of rural areas was critical. Lawton and Pooley (1992, p.261) put the point in a wider context, concluding that, in the first half of the twentieth-century, '… living conditions in the countryside suffered because of the urban bias of most legislation which failed to take account of rural needs'. Potentially, 'rural difference' was the flipside of urban prioritisation?[8] Of course, this assumes rural areas are 'different', when analysts have identified common strands in rural and urban housing (e.g. Cullingford and Openshaw 1982; Bramley and Smart 1995). Gains from comparative analysis have been well-illustrated in cross-national investigations. These reveal shared traits, signify uniqueness and, over time, highlight impacts of learning, the spread of good practice and changes in the public mood (e.g. Barlow and Duncan 1994; Harloe 1995; Doling 1997). Without a comparative framework, it is easier to misjudge tendencies as place-specific, to downplay wider trends, to miss learning from others and to caricature knock-on effects. This is not to suggest rural and urban are the same. How can they be, given diversity within both the rural and the urban realms (e.g. Hoggart 1990; Murdoch et al. 2003)? What it does point to is the potential for deeper understanding by comparing actions, reactions and outcomes.

A further distinction between this book and most rural housing investigations is attention to the evolution of government policies and market conditions. Research has given us valuable insight into the governance of rural housing, but this has tended to focus on a single point in time (e.g. Dunn et al. 1981). By contrast, this book investigates housing conditions as an accumulation of actions. This is achieved by using archival, official and statistical records at local and national levels. The framework underlying this approach is that, to understand service-class 'capture', requires identifying how private and public sector initiatives in one era led to particular outcomes down the line. This approach is not new. It was popularised by Massey (1984), whose geological metaphor articulated how social conditions at one time create a 'layer' with which emergent social tendencies fuse. Current outcomes result not simply from the character and intensity of new practices but also from the strength and attributes of previous social formations. An illustration is Pfeffer's (1983) account of the search for profit amongst large landowners in the USA. He shows how this shared driving force produced different social formations across regions as landholders adjusted to dissimilar local conditions. Hence, in the Midwest, the emergence of new settler territories, at a time when it was difficult to attract workers owing to abundant city employment, induced landowners to profit from land sales to small owner-occupying farmers. By contrast, in the South, the abolition of slavery at end of the Civil War saw many seeking employment with few resources, leading plantation owners to offer 'assistance' to a new class of tenant farmers, who paid for their land through share-cropping, so perpetuating discriminations by creating a dependent workforce with few alternatives. Then, in California, favourable allocations by Washington legislators saw gigantic former Spanish ranches become estates. This created a different prospect for profit-making, given a small local workforce and difficulties attracting migrants from elsewhere in the USA. To circumvent limitations, landowners developed an agricultural economy based on importing temporary workers from areas of economic distress (China, then

---

[8] For more recent times, Forrest and Murie (1992, p.63) held that housing policies affecting rural areas were '… developed as responses to the urban stereotype'.

Japan, Oklahoma and Mexico). The impetus behind these scenarios was the same – to maximise profit – but the outcomes were very different.

This perspective underscores the elongated time-frame adopted here. But the approach differs from the clunky descriptions of many housing studies. Cole (2006, p.286) neatly captured the problem with such investigations:

> Historical analysis of Britain's housing policy ... has often been founded on chronologies of legislation and/or review of the key 'events' in each housing tenure, the kind of 'history by numbers' decried in other contexts by writers such as Carr, Hobsbawm and Taylor. It has rarely strayed towards an analysis focused on primary evidence about specific moments, movements, ideas or epochs so that surprising discoveries can challenge conventional wisdom, and in the process present a more provocative view of how housing systems can change and new policies emerge.

Rather than a blow-by-blow account of periods dominated by Acts of Parliament, this volume asks critical questions about the production of housing outcomes. The interrogations demanded show how varied opportunities and constraints, between places and over time, coalesced to create uneven housing results. Fundamental to processes producing these outcomes were the priorities of local and national agencies, including uneven emphasis on private and public solutions, demand for different dwelling types, and varied capacities amongst enablers and providers to achieve goals. In exploring these forces of change, chapters have been organised along thematic lines. This results in chapters centring on specific themes, with primary illustrations taken from different eras, accompanied by reference to whether key trace elements were shared with other time periods. The early chapters focus on fundamental underpinnings to state involvement in housing; living conditions, pressures for state action and uneven demand for accommodation. These chapters take their principal time frame as the inter-war decades. The chapters that follow focus more on mechanisms of state intervention. Early state actions are covered principally in the first block of chapters, so as to illustrate early responses to housing deficiencies. The second block is grounded more in the post-1945 world. Organised in this way, similar topics, like slum clearance, public subsidies and upgrading the existing stock, are viewed in different places from dissimilar perspectives.

1.2 Chapter Organisation

As the starting point, this volume provides a baseline account of housing conditions in the countryside early in the twentieth-century. Like cities and other urban centres, early decades saw very different rural housing conditions than in the 1970s. For one, across the nation, only around 10% of homes were owner-occupied, with less than 1% in the public sector. Close to 90% were privately rented (DoE 1977, p.38). The housing stock at the time was in an appalling state by today's standards (Gauldie 1974; Daunton 1983; Mingay 1990). Responses to dwelling deficiencies were feeble. After First World War, private builders and landlords saw little profit in housing (Simon 1933, p.6; Dale 1980, p.201), while state authorities, on which even private operatives pinned hope (Orbach 1977, p.71), were not convinced intervention was legitimate or necessary (Wilding 1972, p.3; Morgan and Morgan 1980, p.73). What provoked the state from slumber was fear of civil insurrection (which at times reared its head; Beavan 2006), made more urgent by the realisation that the First World War had trained hundreds of thousands in armed combat, alongside gratitude over working-class war-time sacrifices (Dowie 1975; Bedale 1980; Swenarton 1981). The resulting 1919 Housing, Town Planning, Etc. Act transformed British housing policy (Orbach 1977; Swenarton 1981). Additional to introducing significant Treasury subsidies for new dwellings, local councils were directed to survey housing needs and respond to them. That the intensity of national interventions fluctuated after this has been much commented upon (e.g. Lowe 1978), but housing failures required continued state involvement leading to a string of Parliamentary Acts (see Merrett 1979, 1982; Burnett 1986; Harloe 1995). Chapter 2 notes how this legislative evolution gave little succour to private rental. It declined markedly, leaving council (or more broadly public sector) tenancies and owner-occupation as dominant tenures late in the century. Effectively, for those who could not become home owners, council tenancies were the best chance of better housing. The council sector consequently forms a key focus for this book. In identifying need for rural council-building, this chapter, and those that follow, explore accounts of housing conditions, alongside debates and deliberations within rural councils and national ministries. Drawing on these sources, Chap. 2 explores conditions in the run-up to the 1919 Act, what created these conditions, and how they varied geographically.

Against this backcloth, rural priorities for housing are investigated in Chap. 3. Here the precepts of 'rural exceptionalism' are explored. Did rural leaders act distinctively, with weaker and slower housing responses (e.g. Jennings 1971); and, if they did, why? This chapter analyses the fiscal, political and social environments in which rural housing decisions were made. This is a tale in which reluctance to commit to housing improvement was evident (e.g. Crotch 1901; Sherwood 1996; Read 2003; Linsley 2005). Yet many city leaders also resisted council-building, most especially when propertied interests were reluctant to pay to ease working-class deprivations (on Oldham, North Shields, Manchester and Nottingham, see Bedale 1980; Byrne 1980; Dale 1980; Smith et al. 1986). Phillips and Williams (1982, p.34) speculated that a cause for less rural council homes was political party control; with higher building rates linked to Labour control (Hoggart 1987), which was rare in rural England (Grant 1977). Put another way, were farmer-dominated rural districts, which are commonly accused of resisting housing improvement for the low-paid (Newby 1987), little different from propertied interests in cities? Perhaps what was played out was not an articulation of rural distinctiveness but class-based political decisions. Potentially, changes in rural housing owed little to rural exceptionalism. Exploring one possibility is the centrepiece of Chap. 4.

The core issue for Chap. 4 is whether demand for housing improvement (extra units and quality gains) was so depressed in rural England that tepid rural action should have been the norm. Marshall (1968) presented this view, arguing that low rural building rates were tied to population losses and low incomes, which generated slight demand for housing advancement. Springall (1936) and Tilley (1947) also linked slow engagement with Housing Acts to rural depopulation. Significantly, some influential accounts, like that of Saville (1957), helped to create an impression of rural areas in which, except near larger towns, the dominant demographic trend was stagnation or depopulation (e.g. Astor and Rowntree 1939; Drudy 1978). Many official reports suggest a vicious circle operated, with poor quality housing adding to reasons for outmigration (e.g. MoH 1939, p.94; Association of County Sanitary Officers 1952, p.5). Yet, without denying its existence in some places, recent studies cast doubt on the generality of population decline. For one, rural populations could be dynamic (e.g. Williams 1963; Goodwin-Hawkins 2015), with rural in-migration starting much sooner than today's policy-makers or academics often acknowledge (e.g. Pooley and Turnbull 1998; Burchardt 2012). Some analysts go further, arguing claims about rural depopulation are exaggerated (Moseley 1980). Howkins (2006, p.15), for instance, reported that, even in the inter-war years, using the same area boundaries to compare trends, rural populations rose. For example, in Staffordshire and Warwickshire, the depopulation of previous decades was reversed in the 1930s (Howkins 2003, p.100). But population numbers alone might not generate housing demand. Also critical is an ability to pay. Here a rural 'peculiarity' was dwellings with low or no rent attached to farm employment (Green 1920; Mingay 1986). This was not the bounty it might seem for two reasons: first, because, from the 1870s, agricultural estates suffered substantial income losses (Duke of Bedford 1897; Barnes 1993; Howkins 2003), with consequences for dwelling maintenance and cottage provision (Mackintosh 1936; Kendall 1963); and, second, because, outside these low rent arrangements, rural housing charges could be disproportionately high (e.g. Benson 1989, p.78). With rural wages generally low (Newby 1972; Howkins and Verdon 2009), even population growth might not have created demand for accommodation uplifts. As Wilding (1972, p.4) explained:

> As there was no hope of profitable terms or commercial rents in most rural areas, private enterprise was unlikely to do any building. It was because this gap between an economic rent and the rent the rural worker could pay was so obvious, that concern centred on rural housing.

Might insufficiency of demand have been a primary dampener on rural housing change over most of the twentieth-century? Chapter 4 investigates the prospect.

In Chap. 5 the central question is whether institutions prominent in rural housing drives had the capacity to meet expectations placed on them. In the case of local government, were resources sufficient? Early in the century, national governments were less committed to equalising local revenue capacities than in later decades (Newton 1980); resulting in a close relationship between local fiscal resources and policy commitments (e.g. Powell 1995). In this context, rural councils fared badly. The Ministry of Health's annual reports illustrate this. Thus, in 1924 urban districts had rateable values four times those of rural councils (MoH 1924, p.76), yet just seven years later the ratio was six-to-one (MoH 1931, p.180). At this time, rural councils only received one-fifth of the national subsidies of urban districts

(Registrar-General 1929, p.10). For sure, the breadth of rural and urban responsibilities was different (RDCA 1966), but there was no question that rural resources were '… an undoubted handicap to the proper administration of rural housing' (MoH 1944, p.25). Not surprisingly, rural councils had insufficient staff to manage housing programmes; with only 42 of 416 rural councils employing a housing manager by the late-1930s (MoH 1938, p.15). Capacity shortfalls extended beyond the public sector, with rural house builders unable to respond to calls for more housing-building. Linsley (2005, p.186) captured the tone of contemporary assessments in the MP for East Norfolk's letter to the Minister of Health (9 December 1924): 'The village builders in most parts of Norfolk are very small men and it is more or less useless to rely on them for any considerable progress'.[9] Some 30 years later, the Minister of Housing and Local Government, and later Prime Minister, Harold Macmillan (1969, p.405), showed expectations had not changed: 'No one seemed to pay any regard to the possibility of rapidly attracting the small builders and filling up small vacant plots in a village or town not suitable for large-scale development'. That Macmillan was credited with getting the best out of small builders (Turner 1994, p.81), possibly suggests their performance owed more to the framework they were allowed to operate within rather than any absolute shortfall. But analysts have rarely wrestled analytically with evidence on rural builders. Chapter 5 explores whether capacity was an issue driving housing outcomes, alongside circumstances that eased or lessened housing stock gains.

The question of national intervention is central to Chap. 6. As already noted, some see close alignment between national and local housing trends (Newton 1976; Finnigan 1984), with shifts in local emphasis following national legislation (e.g. Dickens et al. 1985, pp.187–88). This is despite claims of substantial council discretion in defining local housing needs, in management practices, in improvement grant policies, etc. (Cullingworth 1966; Bassett and Short 1980). Indeed, while local–national relations vary across functional sectors, and between capital and current spending (MacGregor-Reid 1977, p.180; Cullingworth 1979, p.12), analysts have asserted that national policy direction is weak for housing (Cullingworth 1966; Murie et al. 1976). Given an aversion within the British state to the 'territorial politics' of many European countries (Tarrow et al. 1978), national ministries have always been heavily dependent on 'independent' councils to implement their policies (this also impacted on privately owned homes; Sharp 1969). You might ask, does substantial local autonomy not give substance to the 'rural exceptionalism' case? At one level, it does. At another, it leaves large holes in our understanding of housing prospects. Note, for example, how many commentators ascribe political rather than economic (or other) rationalities for trends in housing (e.g. Layton 1961; Murie et al. 1976; McKay and Cox 1979). Evidence of a critical national role in transforming housing programmes is not difficult to find. Start with the 1919 Act. This cannot be disentangled from national fears over the re-emergence of political radicalism following the dampening of class antagonism in the First World War. In

---

[9] Original source TNA HLG48/859.

this political context, a national 'Homes Fit for Heroes' campaign led to the 1919 Act, with new rehousing responsibilities for councils and pressure to participate in building schemes (Orbach 1977; Swenarton 1981; Olechnowicz 1997). After the Second World War, we see similar national impositions on local government, as with the 1945–1951 Labour government pushing building for councils rather than private owners, with the 1951–1955 Conservative government reinforcing this emphasis for electoral gain (Eatwell 1979; Morgan 1984; Campbell 1987). In both scenarios, national direction often rubbed against local priorities. This fed tendencies for local implementation to thwart or distort national goals (e.g. Pressman and Wildavsky 1984; Rocke 1987; Gilg and Kelly 1997).

This not only arose from priority differences. It also emerged from dissimilar understandings of problems and knowledge about them. Take Linsley's (2005, p.135) account of Blofield RDC, whose housing plans were reduced by 163 dwellings in 1921 because the Ministry[10] weaken criteria for identifying 'unfit houses', so enabling the Ministry to ignore estimates of unfitness it regarded as generous. The basis on which Whitehall mandarins made sweeping assumptions of this kind is little explored in the literature on local–national government relations. Its potency was illustrated in the mid-1960s by the then minister for housing, who was 'delighted' by a head of department's account of the Ministry of Power, which:

> … had the facts about every pit in the country at their fingertips and we ought to have the facts about every local authority's building programme at our fingertips too. He is quite right. Under the Dame [Evelyn Sharp, Permanent Secretary], intelligence and information were never organised in the Ministry. (Crossman 1975, p.514)

On this point politician and civil servant might have agreed, for Evelyn Sharp (1969, p.79) held that, with around 1200 housing authorities in England, it was no use pretending the Ministry knew enough about local housing to judge comparative needs. She even admitted the Ministry was inadequately provided with information on the state of housing (p.71); although the tenor of this 'complaint' can be questioned, given the implied message that data deficiencies were someone else's problem, not that of the Ministry she headed. To be fair, though, even economic statistics, which, given the scale of government intervention in the economy, required quality data, were seriously deficient for most of the twentieth-century (Cairncross and Watts 1989; O'Hara 2007). If this was so for economic data, no surprise information on the countryside was a long way short of desirable (Hill 2003). In effect, national agencies made detailed interventions in housing with limited knowledge of local conditions. How these intercessions impacted on rural housing occupies our attention in Chap. 6.

---

[10] The Ministry of Health (MoH) was the primary government department overseeing housing following the abolition of the Local Government Board (LGB) in 1919. In 1951 it was superseded by the Ministry of Local Government and Planning, which had its name changed to the Ministry of Housing and Local Government (MHLG) later that year. Housing was placed under the newly formed Department of the Environment (DoE) in 1970. Throughout this book, the expression 'the Ministry' refers to the primary Whitehall department for housing legislation and its enactment at the time.

The main thrust of Chap. 7 then swings towards mechanics for implementing policies. In broad terms, Chap. 6 examines national policy direction and its impact on housing outcomes. In Chap. 7, the focus is more on how far councils were able to impose their priorities on policy outcomes. Even if there was unanimity over policy direction between councils and Whitehall, numerous studies indicate that council action could be hindered by the bureaucratic procedures of national agencies (in urban and rural locales; e.g. Bullock 1989). Take the case of Penshurst in Kent, where local leaders sought permission under the 1890 Housing of the Working Classes Act to construct six houses, only for the Local Government Board to call three public inquiries, occupying five years from start to finish, before the houses were completed in 1900 (Crotch 1901, p.114, p.125). One feature of this book is the way it brings into focus the importance of delay in housing performance. The deferral of building starts, adjustments to funding regimes and the shortening of building schemes all diluted housing programmes, leading to under-performance against council ambitions. A finger can be pointed at national authorities over this but they are only one part of complex processes that bore down on achievement. In Chap. 7, for instance, we look at ways in which the search for sites for house-building often caused delay; and even redirected building from one settlement to another. Interactions between the multitude of forces that impacted on housing construction come into play here, as this chapter examines how local and national considerations combined to produce particular within-district housing distributions.

This leads to the final chapter. For some decades we have been instructed to accept that the world is speeding up; that the pace of change is accelerating (Toffler 1970). We might quibble over relative magnitudes of change in the past, and point out that politicians are wired to stress policy impacts (persuading electorates they have achieved), while academics emphasise newness (PhDs should be 'original'; Hoggart and Paniagua 2001). Even with such caveats, there is no doubt globalisation tendencies have marked cultural, economic, political and social moments. Such trans-local forces are recognised in rural research in globalised agricultural production (LeHeron 1994; Tanaka et al. 1999), new strands in rural manufacturing (Keeble et al. 1992; Townsend 1993) and the demographic revitalisation of rural peripheries (Perry et al. 1986; Cross 1990). In the final chapter, insights from earlier chapters are placed in the context of wider themes in English society. Chapter 8 acknowledges that local and national inputs generate local outcomes, not simply because national processes structure local options but also because national mores are carried into local perspectives. There is no direct translation downward in this process. Both local and national actors have agency (Urry 1987; Dickens 1988). Nevertheless, especially in as centralised a state as the United Kingdom, it is remiss not to anticipate heavy national colouring in local outcomes. No process is inevitable but, like national housing markets themselves (Harloe 1995), tracing English rural housing change brings to the fore a unity between the local and the national.

1.3 Investigative Approach

The primary geographical emphasis of this volume is rural England. More commonly investigators have taken England and Wales as the focus. The decision to concentrate on England came from a conviction that both countries merit treatment in their own right. Combining them can confuse rather than elucidate. The point is illustrated by examining census statistics for 1971; close to the end of period investigated here. Then, looking only at rural districts, 13.0% of English counties had more than one-tenth of their workforce employed as farmers, whereas in Wales 71.4% of counties were so placed. Ratchet up to one-fifth of the workforce and the values were 2.2% and 28.6%. For housing, the per cent of households in the three main tenures were compared relative to the mean average for England and Wales.[11] In England, 17.8% of counties had rural districts with owner-occupation levels at more than one standard deviation above the England and Wales mean average, with the same percentage one deviation below the mean. In Wales, the values were zero and 7.7%. For public sector housing, the English values were again the same with 11.1% removed from the national mean by more than one standard deviation, both negatively and positively, whereas in Wales concentrations in this tenure were more likely (23.1% above and 7.7% below). If anything, the reverse applied for private rental, with a reasonable balance in England (17.8% and 13.3%) but a lopsided distribution in Wales (zero above and 30.8% below). More starkly, in 4.4% of English counties the RDC population fell over 1961–1971, compared with 46.2% in Wales. Clearly, different economic and demographic dynamics were at play. This is drawn out in some fine studies of single Welsh localities (Frankenberg 1957; Emmett 1964; Madgwick et al. 1973), and in broader analyses of the Principality (e.g. Bollom 1978; Wenger 1980; Cloke 1984). The issues and problems that confront policy-makers over rural Wales have often not been the centre of attention for rural England. Indeed, a strong case can be made that, by examining England and Wales together, trends in rural England have been distorted by images that over-play the significance of farming and demographic decline, and downplay dissimilarities in rural housing markets.

This does not mean this investigation covers all rural England. A considerable portion of the volume centres on national policy but it is critical to understand the interaction of the national and the local. Hence, a group of rural districts received detailed attention. At the outset of the project, the template for analysis came from insight on large-scale landowners resisting housing provision for low-paid workers (e.g. Saunders et al. 1978), coupled with service-class opposition to (any but especially council) new housing in villages (e.g. Sturzaker 2010). Combining these strands pointed to selecting locales for investigation at varied distances from

---

[11] The three tenures were owner-occupation, public sector tenancy and private rental tenancy. For each, percentages across all rural districts in each county were compared with the mean average figure for RDCs in all counties in England and Wales. This comparison used 'z' scores, so differences across tenures were standardised against the national mean average of each.

London, to include places that at any one point in time were differentially positioned as regards waves of demographic (and other) outflows from London (Warnes
1991), while also ensuring study districts had significant employment on the land.
Norfolk and Suffolk had previously been identified as counties where farmer-
dominated districts reluctantly provided council-housing (e.g. Rose et al. 1976;
Newby et al. 1978). These counties are also distant from London, so slower service-
class inroads were expected. Nearer to London, Berkshire, Buckinghamshire,
Hertfordshire and Surrey offered the opposite end of the spectrum, with early residential in-flows from London (Bourne 1912; Hooson 1958; Connell 1978; Murdoch
and Marsden 1994; Burchardt 2012). A further consideration was the possibility
that trends might need exploring later than 1974 (viz. after the reorganisation of
non-metropolitan local government in England). In the end, this was not deemed
necessary, but it did favour the selection of districts in which post-1974 local authorities were an amalgamation of complete pre-1974 councils.

1.3.1   Investigated Districts

These guidelines resulted in the selection of seven pre-1974 rural districts. In
Norfolk, the councils that merged to form North Norfolk in 1974 were selected
(Fig. 1.1). They comprised three pre-1974 rural districts (Erpingham, Smallburgh
and Walsingham), plus four small urban districts (Cromer, North Walsham,
Sheringham and Wells-next-the-Sea, only one with more than 5000 residents in
1921 and only two so placed in 1971). At around 120 miles from London to the
largest settlement in the rural districts (Fakenham), and 140 miles from the most
distant town (North Walsham), this was a 'traditional countryside' zone.
Employment-wise, the area had more working in agriculture than the national norm,
especially amongst employees, with few service-class residents even by 1971, and
with a localised labour market, as indicated by relatively low levels of work outside
districts (Table 1.1). Norfolk was not a county dominated by huge landed estates in
the past, being middle-ranked in this regard, with around 20% of its land owned by
estates of more than 10,000 acres in the 1870s. This was modest compared with
front-runners like Northumberland and Rutland (both over 50%), but higher than
Essex, Kent, Middlesex and Surrey, with under or around 10% (Beckett 1986). But
North Norfolk did have more large estates than the rest of the county (Wade-Martins
1994, p.122). Not all such estates were in the districts investigated here but
Walsingham contained much of the Earl of Leicester's Holkham Estate (43,000
acres; Barnes 1993, p.16) and the Astleys (later Lord Hastings) Melton Estate (over
12,000 acres; Wade-Martins 1980, p.7). Additionally, the north of the county had
some substantial agricultural operations. As an example, William Womack Ringer
was farming 7000 acres and employing 200 workers in north-west Norfolk in the
1920s (Howkins 2003, p.80).

    Selected as an 'intermediate' location, in that the impress of London was antici-
pated to be later in the century, today's Central Bedfordshire District was selected.

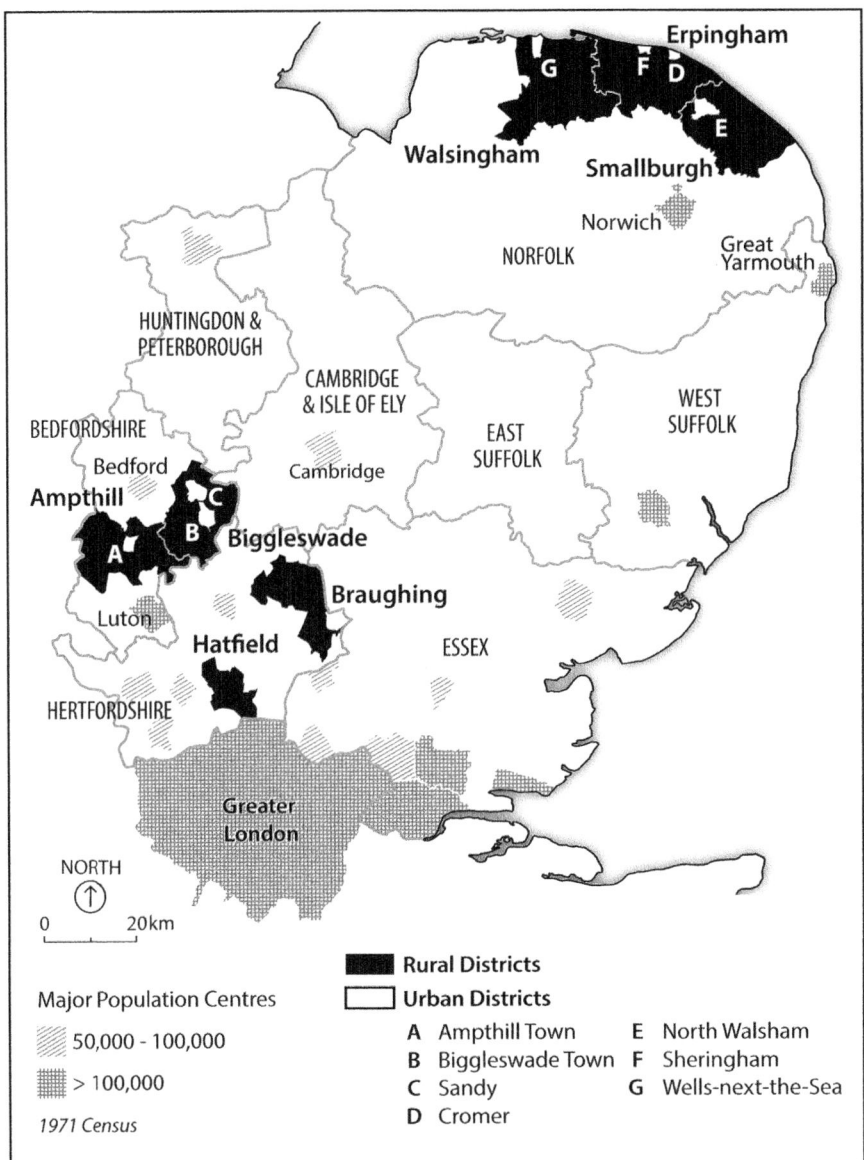

Fig. 1.1 Location of primary investigated districts

This lies around 50 miles north of central London. Before 1974, the area was covered by two rural councils (Ampthill and Biggleswade) and three urban ones
(Ampthill, Biggleswade and Sandy, one over 5000 inhabitants in 1921, all at this
level in 1971, if only just so for two of them). The analysis in this book largely
focuses on rural districts but allied urban centres are given some attention. One

Table 1.1 Employment characteristics of heads of households in investigated rural districts, 1971

	% workforce							Resident and non-resident workers in district per 100 residents
	Farmers	Farm-workers	Armed forces	Manual workers (excluding farm-workers)	Small enterprise owners-managers	Service-class	% employed residents working outside the RDC	
Hertfordshire								
Hatfield	0.8	1.1	0.1	37.7	15.1	15.5	46.5	43.4
Braughing	6.6	9.8	0.0	36.1	11.1	14.9	50.8	26.6
Bedfordshire								
Ampthill	3.8	5.2	1.0	45.5	9.7	11.9	59.2	25.3
Biggleswade	6.1	7.1	9.0	40.2	8.3	9.1	48.1	27.8
Norfolk								
Erpingham	5.6	15.7	0.5	37.3	13.2	5.2	40.3	24.3
Smallburgh	9.2	16.1	3.7	34.2	10.4	6.4	39.7	29.1
Walsingham	9.3	18.1	6.8	32.8	9.2	3.8	18.8	39.6
All English RDCs								
	6.2	4.8	2.5	41.2	10.5	10.6	51.7	28.1

Source: Computed from Registrar-General (2002)
Note: These computations exclude poorly specified occupations in census returns. These figures were computed using Socio-Economic Group (SEG) data, so they provide approximation for categories. The 'service-class' is comprised of owners-managers of large establishments plus professional workers

reason is that, in both Bedfordshire and Norfolk, these 'towns' had smaller populations than larger villages in the investigated rural districts by 1971. To avoid confusion, while Bedfordshire is the only investigated county where rural and urban authorities had the same name, rural districts are referred to by name alone throughout this book, while their urban counterparts have the attached label 'Town' or 'UDC'. Like Norfolk, the rural districts in Bedfordshire had extensive holdings by a few landowners, although again in the middle-rank for counties (Beckett 1986). However, the break-up of estates began earlier in Bedfordshire than in most English counties (Godber 1969, p.550), perhaps spurred by the Duke of Bedford (over 33,589 acres in 1873), who used an upturn in the market to sell close to half his estate in 1909 (Thompson 1963, p.202). Some estates disintegrated rather than terminated through cold calculation, as owners lost interest (Grayson 1992), died or experienced financial problems (Houfe 1995). Even so, the Duke's Bedford Settled Estate was important in Ampthill in the 1970s (and beyond). In this regard, Ampthill differed from Biggleswade, which had no 'great family' dominance (Kennett 1978, p.97). In agricultural terms, Biggleswade was distinguished more by its profitable market gardening (Beavington 1975). It also benefited from military investment, such as the Henlow Air Force base (Table 1.1) and, with Ampthill, has long been a major production centre for brick-making (Kennett 1978, pp.113–15). All this provided a more mixed occupational make-up than North Norfolk (Table 1.1), with villagers also engaged in significant commuting to proximate urban centres in Bedfordshire (like Luton) and Hertfordshire (such as Letchworth). Further separating the Bedfordshire districts from their Norfolk counterparts was their settlement structure. This was marked by proportionately fewer small parishes and the growing importance, demographically and numerically, of larger villages (Table 1.2).

Hertfordshire was selected to provide a sweep of districts at varying distances from the north of London. Hertfordshire abuts Greater London, losing small parts of its territory to the capital when London government was reorganised in 1965 (Ruck and Rhodes 1970). Compared with Bedfordshire and Norfolk, Hertfordshire has longstanding commuter links with the capital (Hooson 1958). Signifying early commuting ties, when the railway arrived at Much Hadham (1871 population 1318, in what became Braughing) organisers brought 130 day-trippers by a special train to attend the 1877 promotion of an 80-acre site laid-out for housing and weekend chalets (Smalley 1995, p.25). This is a noteworthy example, for Much Hadham is in east Hertfordshire. As Bailey (1978, p.28) explained: 'The social distinctions in the county are most marked along a south-west to north-east axis. One end is dominated by posh residential villages and new towns, and the other is relatively unspoilt agricultural territory'. Initially, my intention was to select a part of Hertfordshire comprised of whole pre-1974 districts. But to capture this east–west divide, rural districts were selected in each. Table 1.1 highlights the patterning, with Braughing in the east not far removed from North Norfolk as regards indicators of 'traditional rurality', like the importance of agricultural and small business employment; although its features are laced with London commuter overtures, as in a relatively high service-class presence. These two strands were present in previous administrative arrangements, as Braughing was only created in 1935, largely by merging Hadham RDC to the south, with stronger London ties, and the agriculture-centred Buntingford RDC to the north. To accompany Braughing, Hatfield was selected from the county's western, commuter-dominated territory. Early in the twentieth-century, Hatfield was an unusual RDC, in that Old Hatfield parish (or Bishop's Hatfield) was a small market town (1921 population 5695), which was bigger than some UDCs in the county (comparable with more). With a total 1921 population of 9072, the RDC covered three more rural parishes, giving a mix of rurality and urbanity within London's shadow. Following the Second World War, the district was transformed when part of it was designated a new town (Clapson 1998). In this regard, Hatfield highlighted a particular dimension of rural change, as national direction brought substantial change, not just in growth but in working-class inflows from London. In this regard, Hatfield characterised much of Hertfordshire, which had seen early new settlements (Letchworth and Welwyn Garden City) as well as formal later London overspill (Elstree, Hemel Hempstead and Stevenage). In numbers, by 1971 just one of the 11 RDCs in the county had proportionately fewer households in public sector dwellings than the English rural average (22.1%), whereas half of Bedfordshire's RDCs and 66.7% in Norfolk were so placed. Some districts, like Braughing, were close enough to the national average to be seen as

Table 1.2 Per cent of parishes of different population sizes in investigated rural districts by county, 1921–1971

| Population | Per cent of parishes by size category at each census | | | | | | | | | | | | | | |
| | Hertfordshire | | | | | Bedfordshire | | | | | Norfolk | | | | |
	1921	1931	1951	1961	1971	1921	1931	1951	1961	1971	1921	1931	1951	1961	1971
3000 plus	4.3	8.7	13.0	13.0	17.4	1.9	1.9	3.7	7.4	13.0	0.0	0.0	0.9	1.7	0.9
2000–4999	4.3	0.0	0.0	0.0	0.0	3.7	3.7	9.3	7.4	11.1	1.7	0.9	0.9	0.9	0.9
1000–1999	4.3	8.7	8.7	8.7	13.0	20.4	20.4	16.7	13.0	18.5	2.6	1.7	8.5	6.0	6.8
500–999	39.1	34.8	26.1	26.1	17.4	22.2	22.2	24.1	27.8	20.4	23.9	24.8	24.8	19.7	21.4
Under 500	47.8	47.8	52.2	52.2	52.2	51.9	51.9	46.3	44.4	37.0	71.8	72.6	65.0	71.8	70.1

Source: Computed from county reports in the population censuses

Note: The 'parishes' used were those in 1971, with parish mergers in earlier decades aggregated to 1971 boundaries as far as possible. (One parish, Thursford (Walsingham) merged and then de-merged with Fulmodeston, with no entry for Thursford in 1961 though there was in 1971. Fulmodeston was grouped with Thursford as one 'parish' throughout.) Parishes in a district in 1921 which had relocated to another district by 1971 were excluded, while parishes 'imported' from elsewhere by 1971 were included for all years. This produced 194 parishes in the seven investigated RDCs. Acreages across census periods were overwhelmingly the same. Counting a 1% deviation in area across census periods as effectively representing the same area (many additions or subtractions had no population effects), the percentage of parishes with larger adjustments were 1.0% for 1921–1931, 13.4% for 1931–1951, 1.5% for 1951–1961 and 3.6% for 1961–1971. There were 38 acreage changes over 1.0% during 1921–1971. Comparing populations for the same date at the relevant two censuses (with old boundaries and new), only five changes altered a parish's population category between census dates (two up, three down). Four of the five were over 1931–1951 and one 1961–1971. Using 1971 parishes throughout underplays the low populations of former parishes. For instance, while this table includes 38 parishes for Walsingham across all census years, there were 54 parishes at the 1921 census (the smallest had only two residents). Overwhelmingly, boundary adjustments that created 1971 parishes came through the merging of whole parishes

near equivalents, but six, including Hatfield, had more than 30% in this tenure; well above the national figure. Hatfield was different from the other districts investigated, for while it was officially a rural district up to 1974, by 1971 three of its four parishes had populations over 5000, testifying to the growth pressures it experienced, with the fourth (Essendon) exhibiting 'rural characteristics' akin to many Braughing parishes. Hence, in Table 1.2, the top two rows for Hertfordshire represent three of the four Hatfield parishes (only Buntingford in Braughing breaks into this group, and then only in 1971), while the lower three rows essentially refer to Braughing, save for Essendon which had 500–999 inhabitants throughout. Both districts had significant landed estates in the past but there was little mainstream housing engagement by estates in the period investigated.

Giving a sense of how these rural districts fitted into the diversity of rural England, there was a slight under-representation of owner-occupation alongside higher levels of private rental (Table 1.3). The latter arose in part from the continued importance of landed estates in some districts. For council tenancies, most districts were close to the rural average, with two some way above and one somewhat below. Later chapters examine growth in these districts over a longer period but it is worth noting patterns over 1961–1971, the last complete census decade in the period investigated. Then there was faster growth in household numbers than for the whole of England, but rates tended to be lower than the national rural average, despite

Table 1.3 Household expansion and housing tenure in investigated rural districts, 1961–1971

	% household growth 1961–1971	% households by tenure in 1971		
		Owner-occupied	Council or new town	Private rental
	Hertfordshire			
Hatfield	20.3	42.1	47.9	10.0
Braughing	23.6	49.6	22.8	27.6
	Bedfordshire			
Ampthill	32.5	56.7	20.9	22.3
Biggleswade	36.5	47.2	28.6	24.3
	Norfolk			
Erpingham	7.6	53.6	16.8	29.6
Smallburgh	16.4	50.6	23.4	26.0
Walsingham	0.4	38.6	23.0	38.4
	England			
All English rural districts	23.9	56.7	22.1	21.3
All England	12.8	50.1	28.0	21.9

Source: Computed from county reports in the population censuses

Note: For 1961–1971, these districts either saw no change in boundaries, or changes affected less than 0.1% of their acreage. Only Biggleswade had a larger figure, with expansion at over 1%. Comparison of the three Biggleswade parishes affected shows 6028 inhabitants in 1961 using 1961 boundaries and 5913 for the same year using their 1971 boundaries. With a 1961 population of 27,278, the loss of 115 inhabitants owing to boundary changes makes a marginal impact on the figures above

investigated districts being weighted towards southern and eastern counties. One reason was the performance of the Hertfordshire districts. That they grew proportionately less in the 1960s than their Bedfordshire counterparts was due to the outward expansion of London impacts not imposing themselves on Bedfordshire until the 1960s, at a time when green belt restrictions dampened dynamism in Hertfordshire. Overall, then, there is breadth to the districts investigated. A few councils cannot capture the diversity of rural experience, but the range used here offers enough to highlight trends and dissimilarities in local–national relations.

1.3.2   Data Sources

To bring these to the forefront required accessing, organising, interpreting and presenting information to articulate significant messages. Focusing on a 75-year period, which started 120 years ago, necessitated heavy dependence on written documents. Five key data sources were used. The first was statistical evidence, such as the census and other official reports. As noted at points in this text, such records are flawed. At one level, they are hemmed in by a tendency to cover non-controversial topics or to measure issues in a manner amenable to repeatable measurement (Hakim 1982), but not necessarily as a valid (let us say 'accurate') representation of what they seek to measure. Thus, writing in 2020, when there is a hue and cry over immigration volumes into and out of the UK, debates are devoid of statistics we can have faith in.[12] This claim might take some by surprise, but the history of British official statistics is pockmarked with data falling far short of requirements (Hindess 1973; Irvine and Evans 1979; Slattery 1986). Illustrative examples include census records on housing tenure only beginning to be collected in 1961 (Benjamin 1970), statistics on industrialised building methods only being kept from 1964, long after government pressure on councils to prioritise their use (Holmans 1987, p.116), and, after more than a century of political (let alone literary and religious) recognition of the appalling physical condition of much of the housing stock (Gauldie 1974; Daunton 1983), in the first national housing condition survey being delayed until 1967; the results of which shone bright light on errors in government knowledge of the housing scene (MHLG 1968). Take such bundles of deficits and transpose them into a rural setting. What you uncover are shortfalls derived from sparse coverage, weak delineation, avoidance through definitional fiat and partial reporting (Hill 2003); all of which magnify deficiencies dramatically.

Consequently, other sources were explored. One was *Hansard* Parliamentary debates. This is an under-used resource in rural studies. Its availability online now stretches back for longer than the period examined here,[13] even if analysts must

---

[12] For instance: 'Fight against illegal immigration hindered by lack of reliable figures', *The Times* 17 June 2020, p.6.

[13] https://api.parliament.uk/historic-hansard/volumes/5C/index.html covers 1909–81 debates and reports in the House of Commons.

check online figures against physical volumes as the transcription process is at times quirky. The online source nevertheless offers easy access to powerful information, for Members of Parliament (MPs) ask questions of governments, with responses often as statistical tabulations; sometimes with breakdowns, such as data for rural districts alone, which are not available in published sources. Of course, there are frustrations using *Hansard*. Often, ministers fail to state the time period covered by presented figures, resulting in differences across reports that seem inconsistent but might simply be due to dissimilar start or end dates (as for calendar and financial years). Other times reports fail to specify the geographical remit for statistics (or, for our purposes, commonly only offer figures for England and Wales, from which England alone cannot be disentangled). As *Hansard* captures 'political' messages, there is also a tendency for requests for 'factual' information to be answered with anecdotes or evasions. British politicians are not alone in using such deflections in political statements (e.g. on Ronald Reagan's indulgences see Green and MacColl 1987). But political scientists have long known that such non-responses, as with government inaction, can illuminate political intentions, public fears and policy biases as much as direct action (e.g. Salamon and van Evera 1973; White 1976; Nivola 1978; Simpson 1996). In this regard, the role of *Hansard* as a purveyor of statistical information is surpassed by its articulation of political rationalities and mindsets (at least in their 'public' displays). While *Hansard* records come with political manicuring, the tidying up of MP contributions to debates falls short of the multi-stage, full-facial reconstructions that official reports go through before they enter the public realm. In this regard, analysis of full debates in Parliament potentially offers much.

Even more can be extracted from exploration of interactions between politicians and mandarins when devising and implementing policy. To tap into such insight, a third key data source was files in the National Archives. There are some excellent guides when starting projects using National Archives' files (e.g. Alford et al. 1992; Land et al. 1992; Bridgen and Lowe 1998). One reason such guides are initially valuable is the volume of material that is available. This includes communications within and between ministries, details of transfigurations as official documents go through revision before public exposure, demonstrations through correspondence of how national officials justified actions to councils, as well as how councils sought to change ministry positions. Additionally, there are many items on single councils, companies or organisations, alongside statistical accounts for internal consumption. Often collected for administrative reasons rather than public presentation, such records can be exceptional sources. By way of comparison, in investigating inter-war council house-building, both Marshall (1968) and Jennings (1971) were able to access ministry card indexes on every council in England and Wales to generate a national picture of housing construction. My enquiries on these cards produced the response their location was unknown, assumed destroyed. Departmental records it seems are less durable than those in the National Archives. Of course, there is a major issue over which files are sent to the National Archives (Holmes 1981;

Knightsbridge 1983), for a huge amount of ministry material is 'lost' or discarded.[14] There are even suggestions that some records are deliberately removed, by politicians or others, in order to guard against political or social embarrassment (e.g. Bailey 2012). However, with the amount of paper that crosses ministry desks over the years, it is reasonable to expect many attempts to exclude material come unstuck due to the number of files on a single topic. In this investigation, the same document with different commentaries was found regularly, casting a different light on the same issue. No doubt the material is not as complete as some would like but what is significant about the records is the way they get 'behind the scenes', exposing concerns, goals, hopes and irritations in government circles.

In this regard documents in the National Archives offered more than local government records. For the seven rural districts explored, alongside a less detailed exploration of urban districts, council documents covering the whole period investigated were analysed. These were illuminating and frustrating. Themes raised their head as significant issues only to disappear completely in the minutes a short time later. It was not uncommon for reports to make no clear point, or for significant issues to be hidden in the way they were described. Having spent many years on university committees, they reminded me too readily of insecure chairing, where minutes are bland in the extreme to hide controversies, limit possibilities of challenge, or even give so vague a report on unwelcome decisions that they can be wriggled out of later. Take, by way of illustration, the following 1952 entry from Ampthill Town minutes: 'Land for Housing: A circular letter was received from the Beds County Council enquiring as to this Councils [sic] building programme during the next three years. It was resolved to recommend that the Clerk be instructed to reply giving the particulars asked for'.[15] Likely this was not controversial but passages that fail to expose council policy were too common. Searching for years either side of such minutes sometimes did not lift the fog. In this volume, the reader will experience some of the products of such reportage. It might be seen in accounts on council activities that run for very short or interrupted time periods, for council records regularly dipped in and out of topics, frustrating efforts to identify trends,[16] with consistent information on the same theme often absent, sometimes even over

---

[14] Take the recent 'discovery' of reports from the Supreme Headquarters Allied Expeditionary Force on the 1944 D-Day landings, which were given by HQ members to a secretary in appreciation of her work, acquired by a military history collector, then put up for auction (*The Times* 11 March 2020, p.12). The 'disappearance' of national records like this is regularly revealed in auction house catalogues.

[15] BRO UDA9/2 AUDCHBCM 16 October 1952.

[16] For example, reports on awarded home improvement grants were common but when they were not included in minutes did this mean no awards were made? Annual summaries of activity were rare. An exception was medical officer of health annual reports for some councils, although they covered limited items; additional to which county record offices often did not hold them (although partial accounts might appear in council minutes). Holdings in the British Library were a saviour for some councils.

short periods of time.[17] The records were a long way from ideal but they offered a wealth of information, as this volume will demonstrate.

The value of these records is enhanced by other information on council activities. MacFarlane (1977) is instructive here in reminding us that even full transcription of documents is not necessarily satisfactory, as it is not uncommon to return to documents to check ambiguities. This is not simply when documents are hand-written but also for printed material. A difficulty in working with series like council minutes is that they are so extensive that note-taking might not capture the context of a commentary, or coverage lapses mean the significance of entries in earlier (or later) meetings are not picked up. In this context, other sources help fill gaps. Most helpful for this investigation were local newspapers. Newspaper articles should come with health warnings, as journalists' reports are written to sell newspapers not to provide an historical record (Stewart and Kamins 1993). In my experience with the British national press this can lead to the same information being distorted to the point where evidence is lost in the quest to make political points (Curran and Seaton 1988). Local newspapers are somewhat different. This does not mean they are not without political bias but their limited circulation (and staffing), perhaps aided by the non-party political composition of most small councils (Grant 1977), combines to yield more 'factual' accounts of council activities. This can reach the point of blandness on occasion, but local newspapers commonly provided information missing in council minutes. Some of this might seem minor in context. An example would be if council records did not state the name of a company providing a new waterworks but the newspaper report did. On many, many occasions, newspaper accounts offered 'facts' council records omitted; even if council records were generally more detailed. More importantly, newspaper articles cited arguments by proponents and opponents of council motions, which rarely occurred in council records (except when reporting decisions made by Ministry officials). Newspapers consequently often added insight on debate in council chambers and on the rationale for council actions in a more pointed manner than council records exposed.

For the above, the reader should have a sense of the breadth of the analysis that follows. In geographical terms, national archives and statistical accounts give a broad context for housing change in rural (and urban) England. In indicating how these sources detail housing change, material supporting the points made are mainly listed as footnotes. Except where text is cited verbatim, these references almost universally should have 'for example' in front of them, as more documents support the points made; longer lists are employed to demonstrate breadth over the decades, across districts or in different contexts. Seven rural districts provide the bulk of

---

[17]As an illustration, when reporting on contracts for council-building, minutes might omit the name of the builder, where the firm was located, even how many houses were to be built (and their attributes, like bedroom numbers, floor space, bungalows or houses, etc.), the value of the contract or where homes were to be built. If the builder failed to erect the dwellings, this would not necessarily be reported. It might be picked up if an identical contract was issued months or even years later, which could (sometimes) be cross-referenced with dwelling completion numbers by place. Other times, builder contract details and reasons for builder non-completion were revealed in detail.

evidence provided, with three counties focused on, to explore whether neighbouring councils exhibited similar traits, as well as how dissimilarities in urban influence and landowner involvement impacted on housing performance. Combining the various information sources employed, alongside insight from different contexts, yielded a complex, intriguing tale of English rural housing.

References

Adams D, Watkins C (2002) Greenfields, brownfields and housing development. Blackwell, Oxford

Adamson S (1974) The politics of improvement grants: a survey of local authority procedures for implementing housing improvement grants. Town Plan Rev 45:375–386

Alford BWE, Lowe R, Rollings N (1992) Economic planning 1943–1951: a guide to documents in the Public Record Office. HMSO, London

Ambrose PJ (1974) The quiet revolution: social change in a Sussex Village 1871–1971. Chatto & Windus, London

Anderson MA (1981) Planning policies and development control in the Sussex Downs AONB. Town Plan Rev 52:5–25

Association of County Sanitary Officers (1952) Housing: second interim report on the housing survey in rural areas (England and Wales). Norwich

Astor V, Rowntree BS (1939) British agriculture: the principles of future policy. Penguin, Harmondsworth

Bailey BJ (1978) Portrait of Hertfordshire. Robert Hale, London

Bailey C (2012) The secret rooms. Penguin, London

Ball ID (1980) Urban investment controls in Britain. In: Ashford DE (ed) National resources and urban policy. Croom Helm, London, pp 115–142

Ball M (1983) Housing policy and economic power: the political economy of owner occupation. Methuen, London

Barlow J, Duncan SS (1994) Success and failure in housing provision: European systems compared. Pergamon, Oxford

Barnes P (1993) Norfolk landowners since 1880. University of East Anglia Centre of East Anglian Studies, Norwich

Barras R, Ferguson D (1985) A spectral analysis of building cycles in Britain. Environ Plan A17:1369–1391

Bassett KA, Short JR (1980) Housing and residential structure. Routledge & Kegan Paul, London

Bealey F, Blondel J, McCann WP (1965) Constituency politics: a study of Newcastle-under-Lyme. Faber & Faber, London

Beard M (1989) English landed society in the twentieth century. Routledge, London

Beavan B (2006) Challenges to civic governance in post-war England: the peace day disturbances of 1919. Urban Hist 33:369–392

Beavington F (1975) The development of market gardening in Bedfordshire 1799–1939. Agric Hist Rev 23:23–47

Beazley M, Gavin D, Gillon S, Raine C, Staunton M (1980) The sale of council houses in rural areas: a case study of south Oxfordshire. Working Paper 44. Oxford Polytechnic Department of Town Planning, Oxford

Beckett JV (1986) The aristocracy in England 1660–1914. Blackwell, Oxford

Bedale J (1980) Property relations and housing policy: Oldham in the late nineteenth century and early twentieth century. In: Melling J (ed) Housing, social policy and the state. Croom Helm, London, pp 37–72

Bell MM (1994) Childerley: nature and morality in a Country Village. University of Chicago Press, Chicago

Bellman H (1928) The silent revolution: the influence of the building societies on the modern housing problem. Methuen, London

Benjamin B (1970) The population census. Heinemann, London

Bennett EN (1914) Problems of village life. Williams & Norgate, London

Benson J (1989) The working class in Britain, 1850–1939. Longman, Harlow

Berry BJL (1970) Commuting patterns: labour market participation and regional potential. Growth Chang 1(4):3–10

Best R (1991) Housing associations 1890–1990. In: Lowe S, Hughes D (eds) A new century of social housing. Leicester University Press, Leicester, pp 142–158

Bird SE (1982) The impact of private estate ownership on social development in a Scottish rural community. Sociol Rural 22:43–55

Bishop KD (1998) Countryside conservation and the new right. In: Allmendiger P, Thomas H (eds) Urban planning and the new right. Routledge, London, pp 186–210

Blacksell M, Gilg AW (1977) Planning control in an area of outstanding natural beauty. Soc Econ Adm 11:206–215

Bollom C (1978) Attitudes and second homes in rural Wales. University of Wales Press, Cardiff

Booth A (1987) A managed economy? Econ Hist Rev 40:499–522

Bourne G [pseudonym for Sturt, G] (1912) Change in the village, 1955 edition. Duckworth, London

Bowley M (1937) Fluctuations in house-building and the trade cycle. Rev Econ Stud 4:167–181

Bowley M (1945) Housing and the state 1919–1944. Allen & Unwin, London

Bramley G, Smart G (1995) Rural incomes and housing affordability. Rural Development Commission, Salisbury

Bridgen P, Lowe R (1998) Welfare policy under the Conservatives 1951–1964. HMSO, London

Buller HJ, Hoggart K (1986) Nondecision-making and community power: the case of residential development control in rural areas. Prog Plan 25:133–203

Buller HJ, Lowe PD (1982) Politics and class in rural preservation: a study of the Suffolk Preservation Society. In: Moseley MJ (ed) Power, planning and people in rural East Anglia. University of East Anglia Centre for East Anglian Studies, Norwich, pp 21–41

Bullock N (1989) Fragments of a post-war utopia: housing in Finsbury 1945–51. Urban Stud 26:46–58

Burchardt J (2012) Historicizing counterurbanization: in-migration and the construction of rural space in Berkshire (UK), 1901–51. J Hist Geogr 38:155–166

Burnett J (1986) A social history of housing 1815–1985, 2nd edn. Methuen, London

Byrne DS (1980) The standard of council housing in inter-war North Shields – a case study on the politics of reproduction. In: Melling J (ed) Housing, social policy and the state. Croom Helm, London, pp 168–193

Caird JB, Moisley HA (1961) Leadership and innovation in the crofting communities of the outer Hebrides. Sociol Rev 9:85–102

Cairncross A, Watts N (1989) The economic section 1939–1961: a study in economic advising. Routledge, London

Campbell J (1987) Nye Bevan: a biography. Hodder & Stoughton, London

Chaney P, Sherwood K (2000) The resale of right to buy dwellings: a case study of migration and social change in rural England. J Rural Stud 16:79–94

Clapson M (1998) Invincible green suburbs, brave new towns: social change and urban dispersal in postwar England. Manchester University Press, Manchester

Clark G (1982) Housing and planning in the countryside. Wiley, Chichester

Cloke PJ (1979) Key settlements in rural areas. Methuen, London

Cloke PJ (1983) An introduction to rural settlement planning. Methuen, London

Cloke PJ (1984, ed) Wheels within Wales: rural transport and accessibility issues in the principality. St David's University College Centre for Rural Transport, Lampeter

Cloke PJ, Thrift NJ (1990) Class and change in rural Britain. In: Marsden TK, Lowe PD, Whatmore SJ (eds) Rural restructuring: global processes and their responses. David Fulton, London, pp 165–181

Cole I (2006) Hidden from history? housing studies, the perpetual present and the case of social housing in Britain. Hous Stud 21:283–295

Connell J (1978) The end of tradition: country life in central Surrey. Routledge & Kegan Paul, London

Connor LR (1936) Urban housing in England and Wales. J R Stat Soc 94:1–65

Cross DFW (1990) Counterurbanization in England and Wales. Avebury, Aldershot

Crossman R (1975) The diaries of a Cabinet Minister: volume one – Minister of Housing 1964–66. Hamish Hamilton and Jonathan Cape, London

Crotch WW (1901) The cottage homes of England: the case against the housing system in rural districts, 2nd edn. P.S. King & Son, London

Cullingford D, Openshaw S (1982) Identifying areas of rural deprivation using social area analysis. Reg Stud 16:409–418

Cullingworth JB (1966) Housing and local government in England and Wales. Allen & Unwin, London

Cullingworth JB (1979) Essays on housing policy. Allen & Unwin, London

Curran J, Seaton J (1988) Power without responsibility: the press and broadcasting in Britain, 3rd edn. Routledge, London

Dale J (1980) Class struggle, social policy and state structure: central-local relations and housing policy, 1919–1939. In: Melling J (ed) Housing, social policy and the state. Croom Helm, London, pp 194–223

Danziger R (1988) Political powerlessness: agricultural workers in post-war England. Manchester University Press, Manchester

Daunton MJ (1983) House and home in the Victorian city: working-class housing 1850–1914. Edward Arnold, London

Department of the Environment (1977) Housing policy: technical volume 1. HMSO, London

Derounian J (1993) Another country: real life beyond rose cottage. National Council for Voluntary Organizations, London

Dickens P (1988) One nation? social change and the politics of locality. Pluto Press, London

Dickens P, Duncan SS, Goodwin M, Gray F (1985) Housing, states and localities. Methuen, London

Doling J (1997) Comparative housing policy: government and housing in advanced industrialized countries. Macmillan. Basingstoke

Dowie JA (1975) 1919–20 is in need of attention. Econ Hist Rev 28:429–450

Drudy PJ (1978) Depopulation in a prosperous agricultural region. Reg Stud 12:49–60

Duckers N, Davies H (1990) A place in the country. Michael Joseph, London

Duke of Bedford (1897) A great agricultural estate: being the story of the origin and administration of Woburn and Thorney. John Murray, London

Duncan SS (1976) The allocation of mortgages and the formation of housing sub-markets. Area 8:307–316

Dunleavy PJ (1981) The politics of mass housing in Britain 1945–75. Clarendon, Oxford

Dunn MC, Rawson M, Rogers A (1981) Rural housing: competition and choice. Allen & Unwin, London

Dyer MC (1978) Leadership in a rural Scottish county. In: Jones GW, Norton A (eds) Political leadership in local government. University of Birmingham Institute of Local Government Studies, Birmingham, pp 30–50

Eatwell R (1979) The 1945–1951 Labour government. Batsford, London

Eley AW (1973) The passing of independence: the story of a rural district council. Occasional Paper 1. Bradwell Abbey Field Centre for the Study of Archaeology, Natural History & Environmental Studies, Milton Keynes

Emmett I (1964) A north Wales village: a social anthropological study. Routledge & Kegan Paul, London

Fielding AJ (1982) Counterurbanization in Western Europe. Prog Plan 17:1–52

Finnigan R (1984) Council housing in Leeds 1919–1939: social policy and urban change. In: Daunton MJ (ed) Councillors and tenants. Leicester University Press, Leicester, pp 102–153

Fischer CS (1975) Toward a subcultural theory of urbanism. Am J Sociol 80:1319–1341

Fleming SC (1984) Housebuilders in an area of growth: negotiating the built environment in central Berkshire. Geographical Paper 84. University of Reading, Reading

Fletcher P (1969) The agricultural housing problem. Soc Econ Adm 3:155–166

Foley DL (1972) Governing the London region. University of California Press, Berkeley

Forrest R, Murie A (1992) Change on a rural council estate: an analysis of dwelling histories. J Rural Stud 8:53–65

Frankenberg R (1957) Village on the border: a social study of religion, politics and football in a north Wales community. Cohen & West, London

Gallent N, Bell P (2000) Planning exceptions in rural England: past, present and future. Plan Pract Res 15:375–384

Gasson RM (1975) The provision of tied cottages. Occasional Paper 4. University of Cambridge Department of Land Economy, Cambridge

Gauldie E (1974) Cruel habitations: a history of working-class housing 1780–1918. Allen & Unwin, London

Gilg AW, Kelly M (1997) Rural planning in practice: the case of agricultural dwellings. Prog Plan 47:75–157

Godber J (1969) History of Bedfordshire 1066–1888. Bedfordshire County Council, Bedford

Goldthorpe JH (1995) The service class revisited. In: Butler T, Savage M (eds) Social change and the middle classes. UCL Press, London, pp 313–329

Goodwin-Hawkins B (2015) Mobilities and the English village: moving beyond fixity in rural West Yorkshire. Sociol Rural 55:167–181

Grant W (1977) Independent local politics in England and Wales. Saxon House, Farnborough

Grayson WC (1992) Chicksands: a millenium history. Shefford Press, Shefford

Green FE (1920) A history of the English agricultural Labourer 1870–1920. P.S. King & Co., London

Green M, MacColl G (1987) Reagan's reign of error, rev edn. Pantheon, New York

Griffith JAG (1966) Central departments and local government. Allen & Unwin, London

Grigg DB (1987) Farm size in England and Wales from early Victorian times to the present. Agric Hist Rev 35:179–189

Hakim C (1982) Secondary analysis in social research. Allen & Unwin, London

Harloe M (1995) The people's home? social rented housing in Europe and America. Blackwell, Oxford

Hill BE (2003) Rural data and rural statistics. Economic & Social Research Council, Swindon

Hindess B (1973) The use of official statistics in sociology. Macmillan, Basingstoke

Hodge I, Whitby MC (1981) Rural employment: trends, options, choices. Methuen, London

Hoggart K (1987) Does politics matter? redistributive policies in English cities 1949–74. Br J Polit Sci 17:359–371

Hoggart K (1990) Let's do away with rural. J Rural Stud 6:245–257

Hoggart K (1997) The middle classes in rural England 1971–1991. J Rural Stud 13:253–273

Hoggart K (2003) England. In: Gallent N, Shucksmith DM, Tewdwr-Jones M (eds) Housing in the European countryside: rural pressure and policy in Western Europe. Routledge, London, pp 153–167

Hoggart K (2007) The diluted working classes of rural England and Wales. J Rural Stud 23:305–317

Hoggart K, Paniagua A (2001) What rural restructuring? J Rural Stud 17:41–62

Hollis P (1987) Ladies elect: women in English local government 1865–1914. Clarendon, Oxford

Holmans AE (1987) Housing policy in Britain: a history. Croom Helm, London

Holmans AE (2000) Housing. In: Halsey AH, Webb J (eds) Twentieth-century British social trends. Macmillan, Basingstoke, pp 469–510

Holmes C (1981) Government files and privileged access. Soc Hist 7:333–350

Hooson DJM (1958) The recent growth of population and industry in Hertfordshire. Trans Inst Br Geogr (25):197–208

Horn P (1984) The changing countryside in Victorian and Edwardian England and Wales. Athlone, London

Houfe S (1995) Bedfordshire. Pimlico, London

Howkins A (2003) The death of rural England: a social history of the countryside since 1900. Routledge, London

Howkins A (2006) Death or rebirth? English rural society, 1920–1940. In: Brassey P, Burchardt J, Thompson L (eds) The English countryside between the wars: regeneration or decline? Boydell, Woodbridge, pp 10–25

Howkins A, Verdon N (2009) The state and the farm worker: the evolution of the minimum wage in agriculture in England and Wales, 1909–24. Agric Hist Rev 57:257–274

Humphries J (1987) Inter-war house building, cheap money and building societies: the housing boom revisited. Bus Hist 29:325–345

Irvine J, Evans J (eds) (1979) Demystifying social statistics. Pluto, London

Jennings JH (1971) Geographical implications of the municipal housing programme in England and Wales 1919–39. Urban Stud 8:121–138

Johnson RW (1972) The nationalisation of English rural politics: Norfolk South West, 1945–1970. Parliam Aff 26:8–55

Jones A (1975) Rural housing: the agricultural tied cottage. Occasional Paper in Social Administration 56. Bell, London

Keeble DE, Tyler P, Broom G, Lewis J (1992) Business success in the countryside. HMSO, London

Kendall D (1963) Portrait of a disappearing English village. Sociol Rural 3:157–165

Kennett DH (1978) Portrait of Bedfordshire. Robert Hale, London

Knightsbridge AAH (1983) National archives policy. J Soc Arch 8:213–223

Land A, Lowe R, Whiteside N (1992) The development of the welfare state 1939–1951. HMSO, London

Lawton R, Pooley CG (1992) Britain 1740–1950: an historical geography. Edward Arnold, London

Layton E (1961) Building by local authorities. Allen & Unwin, London

LeHeron R (1994) Globalized agriculture: political choice. Pergamon, Oxford

Linsley B (2005) Homes for heroes: housing legislation and its effects on housing in rural Norfolk 1918–1939. PhD thesis University of East Anglia

Long IE (2005) Fiscal conservatism versus local paternalism: divergent experiences of public housing decline in rural areas of England during the 1980s. J Rural Stud 21:111–129

Lowe R (1978) The erosion of state intervention in Britain, 1917–24. Econ Hist Rev 31:270–286

MacFarlane A (1977) Reconstructing historical communities. Cambridge University Press, Cambridge

MacGregor-Reid G (1977) Expenditure and finance 1939–74. In: Marshall JD (ed) The history of Lancashire County Council. Martin Robertson, London, pp 156–193

Mackinder HJ (1907) Britain and the British seas, 2nd edn. Clarendon, Oxford

Mackintosh JM (1936) Rural housing. Northamptonshire County Council, Northampton

Macmillan H (1969) Tides of fortune 1945–1955. Macmillan, London

Madgwick PJ, Griffiths N, Walker V (1973) The politics of rural Wales: a study of Cardiganshire. Hutchinson, London

Marshall JL (1968) The pattern of housebuilding in the inter-war period in England and Wales. Scottish J Polit Econ 15:184–205

Martin JG (1938) Memorandum upon the Housing (Rural Workers) Acts 1926 to 1938. National Housing & Town Planning Council, London

Masser FI, Stroud DC (1965) The metropolitan village. Town Plan Rev 36:111–124

Massey DB (1984) Spatial divisions of labour. Macmillan, London

McKay DH, Cox AW (1979) The politics of urban change. Croom Helm, London

McKibbin R (2010) Parties and people: England 1914–1951. Oxford University Press, Oxford

Merrett S (1979) State housing in Britain. Routledge & Kegan Paul, London

Merrett S (1982) Owner-occupation in Britain. Routledge & Kegan Paul, London

Mingay GE (1986) The transformation of Britain 1830–1939. Routledge & Kegan Paul, London

Mingay GE (1990) The rural slum. In: Gaskell SM (ed) Slums. Leicester University Press, Leicester, pp 92–143

Ministry of Health (1924) Fifth annual report, 1923–1924. Cmd 2218. HMSO, London

Ministry of Health (1931) Twelfth annual report, 1930–1931. Cmd 3937. HMSO, London

Ministry of Health (1938) The management of municipal housing estates. HMSO, London

Ministry of Health (1939) Twentieth annual report, 1938–1939. Cmd 6089. HMSO, London

Ministry of Health (1944) Rural housing: third report of the Rural Housing Sub-Committee of the Central Housing Advisory Committee. HMSO, London

Ministry of Housing & Local Government (1968) Housing condition survey: England and Wales, 1967. Econ Trends 175:87–99

Ministry of Works & Planning (1942) Report of the Committee on Land Utilisation in Rural Areas. Cmd 6378. Scott Report. HMSO, London

Mitchell GD (1950) Depopulation and rural social structure. Sociol Rev 42:69–85

Morgan KO (1984) Labour in power, 1945–1951. Clarendon, Oxford

Morgan KO, Morgan J (1980) Portrait of a progressive: the political career of Christopher, Viscount Addison. Clarendon, Oxford

Moseley MJ (1974) Growth centres in spatial planning. Pergamon, Oxford

Moseley MJ (1980) Rural development and its relevance to the inner city debate. Inner City in Context Report 7. Social Science Research Council, London

Mowat CL (1955) Britain between the wars, 1918–1940. Methuen, London

Murdoch J (1995) Middle class territory? some remarks on the use of class analysis in rural studies. Environ Plan A27:1213–1230

Murdoch J, Marsden TK (1994) Reconstituting rurality. UCL Press, London

Murdoch J, Lowe PD, Ward N, Marsden TK (2003) The differentiated countryside. Routledge, London

Murie A, Niner P, Watson CJ (1976) Housing policy and the housing system. Allen & Unwin, London

Newby HE (1972) The low earnings of agricultural workers. J Agric Econ 23:15–24

Newby HE (1980) Urbanization and the rural class structure. In: Buttel FH, Newby HE (eds) The rural sociology of the advanced societies. Croom Helm, London, pp 255–279

Newby HE (1987) Country life: a social history of rural England. Weidenfeld & Nicolson, London

Newby HE, Bell C, Rose D, Saunders P (1978) Property, paternalism and power. Hutchinson, London

Newton K (1976) Second city politics: democratic processes and decision-making in Birmingham. Oxford University Press, Oxford

Newton K (1980) Central government grants, territorial justice and local democracy in post-war Britain. In: Ashford DE (ed) Financing urban government in the welfare state. Croom Helm, London, pp 97–118

Niner P (1975) Local authority housing policy and practice - a case study approach. Occasional Paper 31. University of Birmingham Centre for Urban & Regional Studies, Birmingham

Nivola PS (1978) Distributing a municipal service: a case study of housing inspection. J Polit 40:59–81

O'Hara G (2007) Towards a new Bradshaw? economic statistics and the British state in the 1950s and 1960s. Econ Hist Rev 60:1–34

Olechnowicz A (1997) Working class housing in England between the wars. Clarendon, Oxford

Orbach LF (1977) Homes for heroes: a study of the evolution of British public housing 1915–1921. Seeley Service & Co., London

Pahl RE (1965) Urbs in rure: the metropolitan fringe in Hertfordshire. Geographical Paper 2. London School of Economics, London

Pahl RE (1966) The rural-urban continuum. Sociol Rural 6:299–329

Pedley WH (1942) Labour on the land: a study of the developments between the two great wars. P.S. King & Staples, London

Perkin H (1989) The rise of professional society: England since 1880. Routledge, London

Perry R, Dean K, Brown B (1986) Counterurbanization: international case studies of socio-economic change in rural areas. Geo Books, Norwich

Pfeffer MJ (1983) Social origins of three systems of farm production in the United States. Rural Sociol 48:540–562

Phillips DR, Williams AM (1982) Rural housing and the public sector. Gower, Farnborough

Pooley GC (1996) Local authority housing: origins and development. The Historical Association, London

Pooley CG, Turnbull J (1998) Migration and mobility in Britain since the eighteenth century. UCL Press, London

Powell M (1995) Did politics matter? municipal public health expenditure in the 1930s. Urban Hist 22:360–379

Preece RA (1981) Patterns of development in the Cotswolds area of outstanding natural beauty. Research Paper 27. University of Oxford School of Geography, Oxford

Pressman JL, Wildavsky A (1984) Implementation: how great expectations in Washington are dashed in Oakland; or, why It's amazing that federal programs work at all, this being a saga of the Economic Development Administration as told by two sympathetic observers who seek to build morals on a foundation. University of California Press, Berkeley

Pugh M (2008) 'We danced all night': a social history of Britain between the wars. Bodley Head, London

Radford E (1970) The new villagers: urban pressure on rural areas in Worcestershire. Frank Cass, London

Rapport N (1993) Diverse world-views in an English village. Edinburgh University Press, Edinburgh

Read B (2003) Henley rural: the history of a rural district council in Oxfordshire 1894–1932. ELSP, Bradford-on-Avon

Redfield R (1947) The folk society. Am J Sociol 52:293–308

Registrar-General (1929) Local Government Act, 1929: part VI and the second, third, fourth and fifth schedules. Memorandum LGA 17. HMSO, London

Registrar-General (2002) 1971 census aggregate data. UK Data Service. https://doi.org/10.5257/census/aggregate-1971-1

Richardson HW (1967) Economic recovery in Britain 1932–39. Weidenfeld & Nicolson, London

Richmond P (1987) The social implications of state housing provision in rural areas. In: Lockhart DG, Ilbery BW (eds) The future of the British rural landscape. Geo Books, Norwich, pp 137–156

Robinson GM (1992) The provision of rural housing: policies in the United Kingdom. In: Bowler IR, Bryant CR, Nellis MD (eds) Contemporary rural systems in transition: volume two – economy and society. CAB International, Wallingford, pp 110–126

Rocke T (1987) Implementation of rural housing policy. In: Cloke PJ (ed) Rural planning: policy into action? Harper & Row, London, pp 164–184

Rogers AW (1976) Rural housing. In: Cherry GE (ed) Rural planning problems. Leonard Hill, London, pp 85–121

Rogers AW (1987) Issues in English rural housing: an assessment and prospect. In: MacGregor BD, Robertson DS, Shucksmith DM (eds) Rural housing in Scotland. Aberdeen University Press, Aberdeen, pp 147–153

Rose D, Saunders P, Newby HE, Bell C (1976) Ideologies of property. Sociol Rev 24:699–730

Ruck SK, Rhodes G (1970) The government of Greater London. Allen & Unwin, London

Rural District Councils' Association (1966) Evidence of the Rural District Councils' Association to the Royal Commission on Local Government in England. HMSO, London

Ryder R (1984) Council house building in county Durham 1900–39. In: Daunton MJ (ed) Councillors and tenants. Leicester University Press, Leicester, pp 40–100

Rydin Y (1985) Residential development and the planning system. Prog Plan 24:1–69

Salamon LM, van Evera S (1973) Fear, apathy and discrimination: a test of three explanations of political participation. Am Polit Sci Rev 67:1288–1306

Satsangi M, Gallent N, Bevan M (2010) The rural housing question. Policy Press, Bristol

Saunders P, Newby HE, Bell C, Rose D (1978) Rural community and rural community power. In: Newby HE (ed) International perspectives in rural sociology. Wiley, Chichester, pp 55–85

Savage M, Barlow J, Dickens P, Fielding AJ (1992) Property, bureaucracy and culture: middle-class formation in contemporary Britain. Routledge, London

Saville J (1957) Rural depopulation in England and Wales. Routledge & Kegan Paul, London, pp 1851–1951

Scott P, Newton LA (2012) Advertising, promotion, and the rise of a national building society movement in interwar Britain. Bus Hist 54:399–423

Sharp E (1969) The Ministry of Housing and Local Government. Allen & Unwin, London

Sharpe LJ (1973) American democracy reconsidered: part one. Br J Polit Sci 3:1–28

Sherwood KB (1996) Housing provision and population change in the countryside 1919–1939: some evidence from Northamptonshire. East Midland Geogr 19(2):43–58

Short JR, Fleming S, Witt SJG (1986) Housebuilding, planning and community action: the production and negotiation of the built environment. Routledge & Kegan Paul, London

Shucksmith M (1981) No homes for locals? Gower, Farnborough

Shucksmith M (1990) Housebuilding in Britain's countryside. Routledge, London

Shucksmith M (1991) Still no homes for locals? affordable housing and planning controls in rural areas. In: Champion AG, Watkins C (eds) People in the countryside. Paul Chapman, London, pp 53–66

Shucksmith M, Henderson M (1995) A classification of rural housing markets in England. HMSO, London

Shucksmith M, Roberts D, Scott D, Chapman P, Conway E (1996) Disadvantage in rural areas. Rural Development Commission, Salisbury

Simon ED (1933) The anti-slum campaign. Longmans, Green & Co., London

Simpson S (1996) Non-response to the 1991 census: the effect of ethnic group enumeration. In: Coleman D, Salt J (eds) Ethnicity in the 1991 census. HMSO, London, pp 63–79

Slattery M (1986) Official statistics. Tavistock, London

Smalley B (1995) A short history of Much Hadham. self-published volume, Much Hadham

Smith R, Whysall P, Beuvrin C (1986) Local authority inertia in housing improvement 1890–1914: a Nottingham study. Town Plan Rev 57:404–424

Spencer K (1970) Housing and socially deprived families. In: Holman R (ed) Socially deprived families in Britain. Bedford Square Press, London, pp 51–108

Springall LM (1936) Labouring life in Norfolk villages 1834–1914. Allen & Unwin, London

Stewart DW, Kamins MA (1993) Secondary research: information sources and methods, 2nd edn. Sage, Newbury Park

Sturzaker J (2010) The exercise of power to limit the development of new housing in the English countryside. Environ Plan A42:1001–1016

Sturzaker J, Shucksmith M (2011) Planning for housing in rural England: discursive power and spatial exclusion. Town Plan Rev 82:169–193

Swenarton M (1981) Homes fit for heroes: the politics and architecture of early state housing in Britain. Heinemann, London

Swenarton M, Taylor S (1985) The scale and nature of the growth of owner-occupation in Britain between the wars. Econ Hist Rev 38:373–392

Tanaka K, Juska A, Busch L (1999) Globalization of agricultural production and research: the case of the rape-seed sector. Sociol Rural 39:54–77

Tarrow S, Katzenstein PJ, Graziano L (1978, eds) Territorial politics in industrial nations. Praeger, New York

Taylor AJP (1965) English history 1914–1945. Clarendon, Oxford

Thompson FML (1963) English landed society in the nineteenth century. Routledge & Kegan Paul, London

Tilley MF (1947) Housing the country worker. Faber & Faber, London

Toffler A (1970) Future shock. Bodley Head, London

Townsend AR (1993) The urban-rural cycle in the Thatcher growth years. Trans Inst Br Geogr 18:207–221

Turner J (1994) Macmillan. Longman, Harlow

Urry J (1987) Society, space and locality. Environ Plann D 5:435–444

Vince SWE (1952) Reflections on the structure and distribution of rural population in England and Wales, 1921–31. Trans Inst Br Geogr 18:53–76

Wade-Martins S (1980) A great estate at work: the Holkham estate and its inhabitants in the nineteenth century. Cambridge University Press, Cambridge

Wade-Martins P (ed) (1994) An historical atlas of Norfolk, 2nd edn. Norfolk Museums Service, Norwich

Warnes AM (1991) London's population trends: metropolitan area or megalopolis? In: Hoggart K, Green DR (eds) London: a new metropolitan geography. Edward Arnold, London, pp 156–175

Wellings F (2006) British housebuilders: history and analysis. Blackwell, Oxford

Wenger GC (1980) Mid-Wales: deprivation or development. University of Wales Press, Cardiff

White LT (1976) Local autonomy in China during the cultural revolution: the theoretical uses of an atypical case. Am Polit Sci Rev 70:479–491

Wilding P (1972) Towards Exchequer subsidies for housing 1906–1914. Soc Econ Adm 6(1):3–18

Williams WM (1963) A West Country village, Ashworthy: family, kinship and land. Routledge & Kegan Paul, London

Wilson H (1971) The Labour government, 1964–1970: a personal record. Weidenfeld & Nicolson and Michael Joseph, London

Chapter 2
Provoking 1919 and Beyond: Housing Conditions in Rural England

Abstract Providing a baseline for appreciating the dire state of rural housing early in the twentieth-century, this chapter explores the circumstances that provoked the British state to intervene in 1919 with a major programme of local government new-build for the working-classes. Health improvements, fear of social unrest, inaction by private builders and political party competition all made contributions to state involvement, which extended well beyond 1919 as alternatives to municipal provision lacked favour. The state was drawn to intervene as its earlier actions had diminished incentives amongst private landlords to build or even upgrade properties. But addressing poor housing conditions was not made easy because concepts central to evaluations were contested, and counts of accommodation deficiencies were influenced by capacities to respond to them. For national authorities, serious information gaps made assessment of relative needs problematical. Using the limited information that is available, rural housing conditions in 1971 are explored. This reveals diversity in rural housing circumstances, distinguishing traditional agrarian-based districts from others, as well as pointing to conditions in rural deficits that were not so dissimilar from those in cities.

Keywords Private rental decline · 1919 Housing Act · Housing conditions · Rural-urban divergence · Rural diversity

As its subtitle signifies, this chapter is concerned with housing circumstances in rural England or rather with understanding assessments of housing conditions against which state interventions were made. Readers might baulk at attributing a focal position to the state when the private sector was a major contributor to the housing stock, but this chapter illustrates how the state was central to rural housing. Later chapters highlight the state's crucial contribution to private and public sector responses. To make the point, the chapter starts by exploring how deficiencies in the dwelling stock promoted direct state intervention in housing. The impetus for involvement fluctuated over time, but the imprint of the state was strong. This is evident in the array of housing responsibilities given to local government. Yet, even armed with permission to intervene, both councils and government were aware of persistent housing distress. This chapter examines this disorder. There is no claim that definitive messages on rural ailments will be made, for a key point in the

© Springer Nature Switzerland AG 2021
K. Hoggart, *A Contrived Countryside*, Local and Urban Governance,
https://doi.org/10.1007/978-3-030-62651-8_2

analysis is exemplifying how the interpretive gaze of policy-makers induced arbitrary, or ideologically inspired, assessments. The tools were available for securing more surety over housing circumstances, but these were not utilised in a coordinated manner. Policy-makers lacked rigorous evidence on which to base housing polices. Worse still, from a rural perspective, the data on which policy-makers relied disguised the depth of rural ills. In the 1960s, policy-makers were rudely awakened to errors in the oft-proclaimed opinion that poor housing was a city phenomenon (Yelling 2000, pp.244–45). Consequently, the brush-strokes that cross the canvass of this chapter do not paint sharp distinctions between housing divergences, in their intra-rural geography or in rural–urban contrasts. Rather, they bring to the fore the highly political nature of the demarcation and description of housing.

2.1   Conceptualising Housing Conditions

At its most basic, a critical divide exists between housing circumstances regarded somehow as satisfactory and those deemed unsatisfactory. At this juncture, graduations of 'satisfactoriness' are not critical, for while both residents and state officials might be committed to improving housing standards, most state intervention and public concern focused on failure to meet valued criteria. One measurement formalisation of such criteria was the 12-point scheme recommended by the Standards for Fitness of Habitation Sub-Committee in 1946 (MHLG 1966, p.11). These criteria reflect mainstream thinking over the twentieth-century. The 12 points specified that a dwelling should:

(a) be in a good state of repair and substantially free from damp
(b) have each room properly lighted and ventilated
(c) have an adequate supply of wholesome water inside the dwelling
(d) have an efficient, adequate means of supplying hot water
(e) have an internal WC, if practicable, or a readily accessible external one
(f) have a fixed bath or shower in a bathroom
(g) have a sink or sinks, with suitable arrangements for disposing of waste water
(h) have a proper drainage system
(i) have adequate points for gas or electric lighting in each room
(j) have adequate facilities for heating
(k) have satisfactory facilities for storing, preparing and cooking food
(l) have proper provision for storing fuel

Cursory examination of the list reveals its subjective nature, given imprecision over words like 'adequate', 'proper', 'satisfactory' and 'good'. No matter how compelling the list is intuitively, its arbitrary features are exemplified when attention is drawn to what is missing. Immediately striking is the focus on individual dwellings. In effect, standards for accommodation are portrayed as the physical condition of the building (points a, b, k and l), the availability of water and sewerage facilities (c, g and h), the supply of heat and light (b, d, i and j) and access to other household amenities (e, f, g and k). The new 1966 Ministry standard for housing went beyond these dimensions by emphasising that satisfactory living required the environment surrounding dwellings to be wholesome, as well as placing more weight on the internal arrangement of rooms, doors and storage facilities (MHLG 1966). These considerations were not wholly new, as they were embedded in earlier housing legislation. The environmental context of a dwelling, for instance, was highlighted in slum clearance and area improvement policies in the 1930s (e.g. MoH 1931b). Also relevant is the failure of the 12 points to include dwelling availability and usage. Yet significant housing concerns in the twentieth-century revolved around home occupancy, as shown in efforts to reduce overcrowding (MoH 1935) or multi-family occupancy (MHLG 1965), while the first major Treasury contributions to housing improvement were prompted as much by numerical shortage as by poor quality (Ministry of Reconstruction 1918b).

None of this suggests an objective assessment of housing circumstances. There are many aspects to such calculations, and a variety of ways of measuring each dimension; none is non-contentious. This is important because bundles of indicators are not neutral. Inclusion or exclusion emphasises or diminishes traits in housing environments; and traits are not uniform geographically or socially. As a consequence, assessments of poor housing, or good housing, depend upon the measures used in their evaluation. In this regard, Humphrys's (1968) insight was significant in noting that the UK census only records 6 of the 12 points in the Sub-Committee's scale. This has had a telling impact on images of rural housing deprivation. For the present, the key points to gasp are: first, that policy-makers were aware of the subjective nature of housing assessments; and, second, that acknowledged dimensions of housing stress were known to interact in significant ways with other housing traits. It would be easy to indulge the reader with a swath of examples of policy-maker awareness of this subjectivity. A few illustrations from public utterances and internal ministry communications illustrate the point. Capturing the essence, the 1922 Minister of Health, Alfred Mond, held that: 'It is a matter of argument how many houses are fit or unfit'.[1] The General Inspector at the Ministry made the same point a decade later with reference to Linton RDC:

> I do not mean that the existing standard in Linton is 'definitely not insanitary'. There is no definiteness about it, there are infinite gradations of sanitariness, and no line which is at all definite can be drawn dividing the sanitary from the insanitary houses.[2]

For the 1952 minister for housing, Harold Macmillan, there was no '… means of making a reliable estimate short of a detailed survey' to identify dwellings capable of being made fit for habitation at reasonable cost.[3] Yet, both the 1954 and 1957

---

[1] HCH 26 July 1922, Vol.157, col.441.

[2] TNA HLG40/19 Letter to E.C.H. Salmon, 10 November 1931.

[3] HCH 27 November 1952, Vol.508, col.95W. Reference to the 'reasonableness' of improvement costs was central to interpretations of whether dwellings were unfit. This had been so for some time (e.g. HCH 23 September 1943, Vol.392, col.379). On condemned houses, for the MHLG: 'Perhaps the easiest definition—for our purposes—would be this. They are houses which the

Housing Acts (followed by their 1969 equivalent) looked for consistent evaluations by promoting 'universal' criteria for dwelling unfitness (English et al. 1976, p.25).[4] This objective would comply with earlier Rural Housing Sub-Committee recommendations, which reported council difficulties determining unfitness, noting that rural councils would appreciate guidance (MoH 1944a, p.30). That this was not easy to provide was suggested when the government tried to generate 'objective' standards for unfit dwellings in 1965.[5] While promoting more objective measures, the MHLG (1966) recognised that 'unfitness' was multidimensional, as a 1973 minister for housing asserted when claiming there was '… no single definition by which houses can be classified as substandard'.[6]

It was not simply that dissimilar weights might be applied to measures of housing distress but that potential indicators interact. For example, following Alfred Mond's comment cited above, he went on:

> With regard to questions of effective demand, I do not want to enter into controversy at the present time, but a great deal can be said on the question of what effective demand means. It depends very much upon the figures put down by the local authority and the medical officer of health.

This was in response to questions about the scale of housing stress, which Mond disputed. He questioned unfitness numbers, and linked 'demand' for housing to council assessments, which Richard Crossman, the minister for housing four decades later concurred with:

> I am well aware of the remarkable variations in the standards of local authorities in their definition of a slum. Every effort will be made to remedy that, but it would be a great mistake merely to rely on a national survey. I want the collaboration of the local authorities, and they all have their own methods of reviewing their problems.[7]

Contradicting this wholesome message, the Ministry itself admitted that: 'Until 1967 the Government had to rely upon local authorities' own estimates of the number of slums in their areas. Some of these estimates were rather rough, and different authorities naturally applied different standards' (MHLG 1968a, p.1). This variability meant official counts could be well off the mark:

> In 1955 local authorities estimated there were 850,000 slums in England and Wales and they demolished 516,000 of them in the ten years 1955–64. But a fresh survey in 1965 estimated there were then some 770,000 slums, an increase over the ten years of 436,000. Local authorities tend to put in their estimates only those houses which they think they can

---

owner cannot put into a decent state of repair even with aid of the additional rents proposed, and cannot even be made "habitable" by the local authorities' (TNA CAB129/58 CP(53)24 'Houses Old and New', 22 January 1953).

[4] HCH 26 November 1963, Vol.685, col.68-69; HCH 4 May 1971, Vol.816, col.339W.

[5] HCH 29 June 1965, Vol.715, col.39W.

[6] HCH 11 December 1973, Vol.866, col.108W.

[7] HCH 24 November 1964, Vol.702, col.1074.

demolish in a reasonable time. It is known that in Glasgow alone there are some 200,000 slums compared with the 11,000 declared by the Corporation.[8]

Evidence on this was clear. As early as 1918, the Cabinet was aware that: 'The clearance of slum areas and the closing of slum houses cannot be effectively undertaken unless there is sufficient alternative accommodation for those inhabitants who are displaced'.[9] Almost 25 years later, Sheringham's Medical Officer of Health similarly claimed that rigid adherence to Ministry instructions on unfit houses would close all villages as so many houses would have to be pulled down.[10] Likewise, in Ampthill: 'The Housing Manager pointed out that it was estimated that there were 423 unfit houses in the district awaiting action under the Housing Act 1957, but little progress could be made in this direction until such time as alternative accommodation could be provided'.[11] But were rural councils in a position to act? The case of Biggleswade in 1952 illustrates tension over this prospect, for when the Medical Officer of Health reported dire living conditions, recommending a survey be undertaken, this was voted down by the Council, as: '… little purpose would be served by such a survey. It would take the Council all its time to keep up with the present applications and demolitions without finding a lot more unsatisfactory property'.[12] Despite official knowledge of manicured and manipulated local numbers, ministers repeatedly laid responsibility for assessing deficiencies on councils.[13]

This practice gave ministers and Whitehall officials wriggle room to respond to council numbers. Internal ministry reports identified uneven application of standards and challenged the commitment of councils to the task: '… in some districts through complacency or lack of interest, the authority had neglected to include many houses which should have been condemned'.[14] Official reports referred to 'marked variations' in standards (MoH 1944a, p.26), with clear biases in coverage that poorly served rural districts: 'Few of the smaller authorities seem to have any real idea of the condition of their housing stock. Larger authorities seem better informed but can seldom produce precise information'.[15] Yet ministers and officials pontificated over aggregated totals from council assessments, giving the impression they were 'gospel', with bold statements on where unfitness was most pronounced or less of a concern (see MHLG annual reports; e.g. MHLG 1956, p.6).

---

[8] TNA HLG118/413 'The Housing Programme in the 1970s', undated c1966.

[9] TNA CAB24/44 'Note on the Urgent Need for the Commencement of a Large Housing Programme Immediately After the War', 11 March 1918, pp.1-2.

[10] *NNN* 22 February 1957, p.1.

[11] BRO RDAM1/28 ARDCHPBuCM 14 June 1972, p.7. This sentiment was common, as in Hatfield (*HM&CP* 27 January 1923, p.9), East Anglia and the south Midlands (TNA HLG37/47 Rural Housing Sub-Committee. 'Notes on Visits to East Anglia and South Midlands') and amongst ministers for housing (e.g. HCH 24 March 1953, Vol.513, col.641).

[12] *NBC&BR* 30 September 1952, p.2.

[13] A view held up to 1974 (e.g. HCH 17 October 1973, Vol.861, col.183).

[14] TNA HLG37/47 Rural Housing Sub-Committee 'Notes on Visits to East Anglia and South Midlands', undated c1943.

[15] TNA HLG118/558 'Housing Improvement', undated c1966, p.1.

On other occasions, recognising statistical insight came from uncertain quarters, expressions of frustration and even exasperation surrounded local numbers, which were deemed insufficient or exaggerated, depending (at least in part) on political disposition. Take, by way of illustration, commentary around the 1931 Housing (Rural Authorities) Act. This had been promoted to address previous legislative shortcomings that saw few new working-class homes in the countryside.[16] Rural council requests for new houses under this Act failed to impress its sponsor, John Tudor Walters, who did not regard them '… as a true measure of rural need'.[17] Yet, other officials were infuriated by the 'generosity' of new-build proposals, as for Norfolk:

> … the Norfolk County Council, for instance, after assuring the General Inspector of their intention to carry out a detailed investigation into local conditions, have produced a document which is almost useless for our purposes. We have reason to suspect, too, that certain other County Councils have endorsed applications without any close examination of their merits.[18]

Suspicions that submissions had not been challenged were permeated with the fiscal mood of the time, which favoured fiscal retrenchment (Committee on National Expenditure 1931; MoH 1932b). That councils were swept along with the ethos of retrenchment was exemplified in applications for only 7229 new dwellings (MoH 1932a, p.109),[19] despite the Act being an emergency project of 40,000 to address shortages.[20] The Treasury was opposed to committing the required resources, and Tudor Waters recognised the scheme might be postponed or implemented by instalment.[21] The outcome, as exemplified by the investigated Norfolk rural districts, was that Erpingham applied for 66 dwellings, the County Council supported 66, the Ministry's own inspector recommended 66, but the allocation was 22. For Smallburgh, the equivalent numbers were 62, 62, 46 and 20, with 84, 84, 50 and 22 for Walsingham.[22] The cull helped reduce the programme from 40,000 to less than 2000 dwellings. This might come across as no surprise given fiscal concerns at the time. The real issue is that councils, the County Council and Ministry inspectors all

---

[16] TNA HLG29/180 'Notes on Meeting to Discuss Tudor Walters' Scheme', 15 April 1931; TNA CAB24/221 CP104(31) 'Rural Housing', 23 April 1931; CP127(31) 'Rural Housing', 15 May 1931.

[17] TNA HLG40/20 Rural Housing Advisory Committee. 'Notes by J. Tudor Walters for Consideration of the Committee', undated c1932.

[18] TNA HLG40/19 Letter to A.P. Hughes-Gibb from Rural Housing Advisory Committee Secretary, 24 October 1931; Letter to F. Collin Brown, 24 October 1931.

[19] Applications came from 145 councils but 27 withdrew their bids, while 14 were deemed not to satisfy conditions of the Act, so less than 7,000 dwellings were eventually applied for (MoH 1933a, p.99).

[20] TNA CAB24/221 CP104(31) 'Rural Housing', 23 April 1931, p.5.

[21] TNA HLG40/30 Letter from Hilton Young to Neville Chamberlain, 1 December 1931; Reply, 7 December 1931.

[22] The figures are all from TNA HLG40/20 'Particulars of Tenders Received and Approved by 26 November 1932'.

agreed higher numbers were needed. They identified greater housing deficits than this programme addressed. The government's follow-up response was zero. There were no further instalments for the programme, with attention shifting to slum clearance and the alleviation of overcrowding by 1933. The additional houses promised to address shortages were not sanctioned. When it suited the government, and its ideological predilections, 'evidence' of housing need could be laid aside.

Adding a further twist to assessments of local housing conditions were nudges from local citizens. Thus, when writing to the Minister of Health in 1930, the Minister of Agriculture referred to:

> … the provision in Section 35(4) of the Housing Act, 1930, where any four voters in the rural area may call for an enquiry by the Ministry of Health if this Section is not being operated. The feeling [at a meeting of the Society of Labour Party Candidates] was expressed that there might be a possibility of victimisation of voters in this connection.[23]

Homes tied to employment induced unwillingness to complain.[24] Rural councils were further hemmed in by the limited resources of private landlords. One example was revealed in a 1935 solicitor's letter to Braughing about Mrs Clay's reluctance to 'turn out' her tenants:

> … the damp course is prohibited. The houses are not damp and this cannot reasonably be required. A very large number of the houses in this village, in fact most of the houses, both cottages and large houses, have no damp courses. If your Council is going to demand the damp course to be put in all houses, and surely you cannot treat Mrs Clay's cottages differently to other people's cottages and houses, you may well start to work and repair the bulk of the village. This demand therefore we consider unreasonable and cannot entertain it.[25]

More generally, for the Rural Housing Sub-Committee:

> … several local authorities who appeared to be diligent in carrying out their duties under the Housing Acts expressed reluctance to take action in respect of certain old unsatisfactory houses because they were incapable of satisfactory reconstruction save at very great expense and their demolition would deprive the owner-occupiers and working-class owners of the savings of a lifetime.[26]

These examples are from the 1930s, but change came slowly. Only in 1954 did national authorities give guidance on common standards for assessing poor quality accommodation (English et al. 1976, p.25). Decades later: '… local authorities' returns on unfit houses were frequently strongly influenced by their views about how many such houses they can in fact deal with, and so cannot be treated as if they were "objective" measures of the number of unfit houses' (Holmans 1987, p.77). In

---

[23] TNA MAF48/207 Letter from C. Addison, MAF, to A. Greenwood, MoH, October 1930.

[24] Worker deference to employers' wishes was common social practice in agricultural areas (Newby 1975). That deference was expected well into the twentieth-century was exemplified by instances like the Duke of Norfolk contacting Conservative Central Office for instructions on how to tell his tenants to vote in the 1955 General Election (Williams 2012, p.111).

[25] HRO RDC3/31/1 Letter from Hare and Son, Much Hadham, to Braughing Clerk, 26 July 1935.

[26] TNA HLG37/43 'Report on Local Investigations in Wiltshire, Bedfordshire, Derbyshire and Anglesey', undated c1936, p.5.

the 1970s, the Ministry was still of the view that rural councils '… operate a very much lower standard of fitness than the towns'. Indeed, the depth of distrust in local evaluations was such that: '… it is unlikely that any formal approach would produce useful information'.[27] What was known was that housing conditions for the working-classes were often poor. Despite this, officials and politicians continued to rely on local estimates of deficiencies when pronouncing on the scale and distribution of national shortcomings.

2.2   Prompts for State Intervention

Even if numbers were not precise, it was difficult to avoid appalling housing conditions in the countryside early in the century. This understanding was encapsulated in Hollis's (1987, p. 388) reference to the '… cliché that housing in rural England was worse than in the East End, decorated though it was by roses'. Numerous accounts bring this reality to light (Green 1920; Shears 1936; Tilley 1947; Mingay 1990). Core messages were repeated in official reports, both nationally (e.g. Land Enquiry Committee 1913) and locally (e.g. Thresh 1891; Mackintosh 1936). That bad housing was a nation-wide phenomenon led to the 1909 Housing and Town Planning Act requirement that councils appoint 'permanent', professional medical officers of health to check accommodation standards (Booth and Huxley 2012). This was a response to severe past lapses, as the MP for Ilkeston explained in 1908:

> In a town of say 20,000 inhabitants or a large rural district of 10,000 or 15,000 inhabitants the local authority depended for all their information upon the sanitary inspector and the medical officer of health. These two officers held their posts by yearly tenure, and the consequence was that, if they were active in exposing the bad condition of local habitations, when they came up for election next year they were dropped …[28]

With property ownership requirements limiting the electorate, this outcome was predictable given that landlords owned 90% of homes (Benson 1989, p.73). With most councillors coming from the same propertied classes as landlords (Pedley 1942, p.131; Horn 1984, p.187), investigators like Crotch (1901, p.7) called for independent surveys, noting one study of 78 villages by 'a London Association' which graded nearly a quarter of the 4179 cottages assessed as 'bad' or 'extremely bad'. As councils began systematic surveys, the character of 'bad' housing became better known:

> Not only are the cottages too few but a large number are of quite insufficient size and in many of them a person of ordinary stature could not stand erect. The bedrooms are too often metre spaces in the roof, ill-lighted and unventilated … The foundations of these Cottages are nearly always damp, the floor frequently of bricks or tiles laid on the earth and set in mortar, is often below the level of the adjoining ground. The closet accommodation is generally a privy or a dilapidated wooden structure badly floored, dirty and ill-lighted. The

---

[27] TNA HLG118/1392 'Unfit Houses in Rural Districts', undated c1970, p.1.
[28] HCH 12 May 1908, Vol.188, col.978.

drains, if any exist, are old and leaky, with traps of an obsolete and faulty type. What wonder if the owner hesitates to spend 2 or 3 years' rent in putting such places into repair! It would be better to burn them. (Biggleswade RDC 1914, pp.12–14)

Fifteen years later, Walsingham recorded cottage floors two feet below the surrounding land, roofs sagging, walls bulging, and dwellings '… in such a bad state that the rain penetrates, causing the houses to be very damp'. Further, 'In practically every house the windows are too small, and will not open, so that the inhabitants are unable to secure an adequate amount for sunlight and fresh air. Many of the houses have insufficient land attached to them to enable the tenants to dispose of excreta in an efficient manner'.[29] Move forward a decade and little had changed, as in Swaffham, where shortage were compounded by the 'decayed and unsound' condition of existing dwellings, with dampness rising through broken brick floors, lack of light and ventilation through inadequate size and openings of windows, low ceilings, sunken roofs, unventilated food storage, insufficient ground for disposal of refuse, and, in many cases, contaminated water.[30]

The 1919 Housing, Town Planning, Etc. Act was the first major state intervention to address such conditions, raising expectations of more aggressive attacks on housing deficiencies (Orbach 1977; Swenarton 1981; Olechnowicz, 1997). More strenuous inspections of 'suspect' homes were to be matched with census-like surveys of local conditions. These were sometimes explicitly required by national authorities, as with identifying slums for clearance under the 1930 Housing Act (MoH 1933b), overcrowding for the 1935 Act (MoH 1935) and new dwelling needs after the Second World War (MoH 1944c). Surveys articulated the generality of deep-seated inadequacies. In a 1935 Northamptonshire census, for instance, 20.3% of more than 25,000 inspected rural homes were condemned (Mackintosh 1936, p.114), while a New Forest survey found 36.4% unfit for habitation with a further 29.7% needing reconditioning.[31] After the Second World War, following inter-war decades when building for private owners dominated (Swenarton and Taylor 1985; Humphries 1987), official commentaries found:

> Much of the rural housing is old, out-of-date and unhygienic compared by modern standards. Most of it was built for poorly-paid agricultural workers, and little improvement was made between the Wars, for house construction took place largely in and around the towns. Tied cottages when in poor condition (a common feature apparently) are most unpopular amongst farm labourers and many authorities favour their replacement by some other system of dwelling allocation. Further the traditional low rents of many country cottages are not conducive to making extensive improvements to the dwellings.[32]

No surprise that post-1945 rural (and national) housing inadequacies were high on the political agenda. Councils were required to undertake rural housing surveys,

---

[29] NRO DC19/6/16 WRDCM 10 October 1928, p.69. Little had changed in Walsingham since 1920, when 1,220 cottages required demolition; 30.0% of the district's dwellings at the 1921 census (NRO DC19/6/8 WRDCM 14 April 1920, p.72 in binding).

[30] *YarmInd* 17 July 1937, p.17.

[31] TNA HLG37/44 'NUAW Memorandum on Rural Housing', October 1936.

[32] TNA HLG125/9 'Rural Decline', 20 May 1949, p.5.

with fears over food production giving urgency to addressing shortages (MoH 1944a, c). These surveys told a sorry tale of countryside living. Members of Parliament seemed to compete in detailing deficiencies in their constituencies. In Norfolk South-West, only 28.2% of dwellings were fit in all respects, with 24.5% needing demolition.[33] But there was significant geographical divergence, as in dissimilar RDC scores for Horncastle (4.8% fit in all respects, while 9.0% needed demolishing),[34] Uckfield (1.2% and 18.0%),[35] Ploughley (33.0% and 5.4%)[36] and Blackburn (11.0% and 16.9%).[37] These surveys showed that many, many dwellings were neither wholly fit nor required pulling down. Variety existed regionally and locally. Table 2.1 illustrates this for three counties. There was disparity not only across rural districts but also between proximate places (as found more recently by Shucksmith and Henderson 1995). In Hertfordshire, for example, there was a staggering contrast between Braughing, where only 11.7% of dwellings were deemed fit for occupation in all respects, and Watford RDC, where 90.4% secured this rating.[38] Overall rural housing distress was uncomfortably high. Responses to these deficits continued to be insufficient, despite record additions to the national housing stock in the 1950s and 1960s.[39] Thus, in 1967, English RDC declarations listed 75,000 unfit dwellings, whereas the first national housing condition survey projected a total closer to 400,000 (MHLG 1968b). The national survey was undertaken by inspectors with considerable experience evaluating structural conditions, with meetings

Table 2.1 Housing conditions in rural Bedfordshire, Hertfordshire and Norfolk, January 1948

County	% dwellings fit in all respects[a]	% dwellings needing minor repairs	% dwellings needing major repairs	% dwellings unfit for human habitation	Range across RDCs in % fit in all respects	Range across RDCs in % unfit for human habitation
Hertfordshire	43.4	16.2	30.1	10.3	11.2–90.4	3.3–27.2
Bedfordshire	36.4	38.7	19.8	5.2	18.4–76.3	2.9–8.5
Norfolk	35.0	19.0	22.9	16.0	9.0–77.4	4.7–27.8

Source: TNA HLG40/47 'Rural Housing Survey Records. Progress up to 31 January 1948 Region 4'
Note: [a]This figure includes dwellings reconditioned under the Housing (Rural Workers) Act

[33] HCH 21 October 1946, Vol.427, col.1397.

[34] HCH 25 March 1947, Vol.435, col.1102.

[35] TNA HLG37/52 RW12 'Memorandum from Mr Monks', undated c1946.

[36] TNA HLG37/52 RW42 'Proposed Tour of Selected Areas', undated c1946.

[37] TNA HLG101/418 'Blackburn RDC. Survey of Houses Occupied by or Suitable for Occupation by the Working-Classes', 1948.

[38] TNA HLG40/47 Rural Housing Survey Records 1946-47. 'Progress to 31 January 1947: Region 4'.

[39] Examine HCH 11 March 1946, Vol.420, col.163W-64W; HCH 20 January 1967, Vol.739, col.143W-45W; HCH 24 March 1970, Vol.798, col.337W-38W.

between inspectors, close alignment with Ministry specialists and checks on judgements to minimise errors. Contrasting their estimates with council figures showed local authorities in conurbations reported around 75% of unfitness recorded in the national survey, but values were only 36.9% in other urban areas and 18.8% in rural districts. These divergences were known long before the 1967 survey, as official reports signalled (e.g. MoH 1944a, p.26). Recognition of rural neglect had produced a series of special enquiries into their housing problems (MoH 1936b, 1937b, 1939b, 1944a, 1947), while broader rural investigations made pointed housing recommendations (e.g. Ministry of Works and Planning 1942; MTCP 1947). Why was rural housing in such a troubled state?

2.2.1   Private Rental Decline

A primary impetus behind the 1919 Housing, Town Planning, Etc. Act, was private sector failure. Official estimates on housing tenures for 1914 place 89.6% of all dwellings in private rental, with 10.1% owner-occupied and 0.2% in the public sector (DoE 1977, p.38). The England and Wales private rental figure had dropped to 57.9% by 1938 (owner-occupied 32.5% and 9.6% public sector), then again to 19.3% of households in 1971 (52.6% owner-occupiers and 28.7% public sector tenants). Linked to these huge changes were steps to mitigate shortages and poor quality. These started in earnest after 1919, when it was recognised private builders had not overseen sufficient improvement. Building to a conviction state intervention was necessary, a multitude of reports attested to private builder shortcomings. Thus, local reports in the 1910s confirmed that, for housing, 'private enterprise is non-existent'[40] or showed no prospect of meeting demand.[41] Senior national figures warned not to expect change after the First World War. Hence, according to Hayes Fisher, the 1918 Local Government Board (LGB) President:

> Private enterprise very naturally builds for profit. What will be the cost of building houses after the War? We do not know exactly, but it will be, I believe, prohibitive, and no profit can be derived from building, looking to the rents which the working-classes are likely to be able or willing to pay … I see nothing to entice the private builder on to the ground which he has already left. I have discussed this question with groups of private builders, and I have received no encouragement whatever from them to suppose that the private builder is going to build any dwellings for the working-classes …[42]

Stated numerically, Fisher explained that of 1806 councils, only three definitely believed private enterprise would build required volumes.[43] Various explanations were given. For rural areas, increased taxation, which was perceived to target landed

---

[40] TNA HLG1/845 'Report of Inquiry by Harry Stewart', 7 July 1913.

[41] TNA HLG1/972 'Report on Happisburgh and Horning', 1911.

[42] HCH 2 May 1918, Vol.105, col.1732-33.

[43] HCH 28 October 1918, Vol.110, col.1199.

estates hard, was seen to deprive employers of funds.[44] For others, bad housing was rife long before 1910s tax rises, so a better explanation was high building costs producing unaffordable rents. Builder and landlord inaction was reinforced when rent restrictions were introduced in 1915:

> Repairs are attended to in a dilatory manner and cottages which might be kept in commission are gradually allowed to go out of occupation. It does not pay owners radically to improve their cottages, and many owners would gladly close them as soon as they can induce the local authority either to find or provide alternative housing accommodation. The owners' reasons for not attempting repairs are generally that the rents are too low; and that the cost of building high, the latter owing to the long distances materials have to be carted, sometimes as much as from two to three miles, and also to lack of competition amongst the builders.[45]

Little had changed by 1924 when: '… the present day cost is such that working-class houses cannot be produced in an economically satisfactory basis, such as would induce the investment of capital, unless a subsidy is provided by the State' (National House Building Committee 1924, p.8). The result was both housing shortage and an increasingly derelict stock: '… not only is it a question of lack of houses as far as new houses are concerned, but a large number of houses that are already occupied are unfit for habitation really, and there is a great need for a really big building scheme for rural districts of this country'.[46] A decade later, the situation saw no change, with the Rural District Councils' Association concluding that '… private enterprise can be left out of account in considering the provision for agricultural needs'.[47]

A strategic rethink was required. Thus, having pushed for an end to 1919 Act subsidies (new approvals ceased in 1921), the Minister of Health changed tack in 1922 to argue that he had '… been reluctantly forced to the conclusion that some further state assistance is necessary to bridge the transition period before ordinary economic conditions are restored'.[48] Despite his reluctance, and irrespective of how 'ordinary' economic conditions became, state support for housing entered the policy mainstream for the rest of the twentieth-century (Burnett 1986; Merrett 1979, 1982). But, unlike other countries (Harloe 1995), state support principally benefited owner-occupiers and public sector tenants. Rent restrictions continued for decades in various manifestations, with regular complaints from landlords that rents left little room for maintenance and repairs. Official reports considered abolishing rent

---

[44] For example, HCH 15 March 1912, Vol.35, col.1462.

[45] TNA HLG40/38 'Memo from H.A. Chapman to Tudor Owen on visits to Hereford and Oxfordshire', undated c1926.

[46] TNA MAF48/206 TUC General Council. 'Deputation to Ministers of Health and Agriculture Minutes', 9 March 1926, p.21.

[47] TNA HLG37/45 Rural Housing Sub-Committee. 'RDCA Submission', undated c1936. The message was reiterated in the County Councils' Association's submission (same TNA file).

[48] TNA HLG68/29 'Housing', 10 August 1922.

restraint (MoH 1931c, 1937a, 1946a), Cabinet committees explored it,[49] and limits on some rents were eased in 1933, 1938 (Mowat 1955, p.165) and 1957 (Simmonds 2002). But, as Self (2006, p.89) put it:

> … on one hand, it was politically impossible to repeal rent restrictions because the acute shortage of houses would immediately produce a catastrophic increase in rents. On the other hand, however, by removing all prospect of a reasonable profit, rent controls acted as a major disincentive to speculative builders and investors who might otherwise have entered the market to satisfy the demand for low cost working-class housing for rent.

The reality that confronted the Cabinet was that many dwellings were in such a bad condition that closing orders had been placed against them '… but have not been put into operation because of the absence of alternative accommodation in the neighbourhood'.[50] Yet, policy-makers were not inclined to introduce supportive legislation, as landlords lacked political support (Merrett 1982; Daunton 1984; Cannadine 1990, p.122). Little backing might be expected from the political Left, given the unpopularity of the landlord class. But the political Right was similarly restricted, with added complications for the Conservative Party, which had traditionally favoured large property interests (Tylecote 1982; Perkin 1989; Cannadine 1990). A 'solution' for the 1930s was eased by the availability of building society funds. With weak demand from other investors, funds could be redirected into housing (Swenarton and Taylor 1985; Humphries 1987; Scott and Newton 2012). Yet few inter-war private homes were built for rent (Marshall 1968). Even after the return of a Conservative government in 1951, the priority was council homes and owner-occupation, dampening prospects that rent restraints would weaken,[51] despite growing rent disparities as restrictions eased.[52] As reported to Cabinet in 1953:

> In the climate of an expanding programme of new Housing, we can—and must—now turn our energies to the problem of the maintenance and repair of old houses. We cannot, therefore, avoid the nettle of 'rent restriction'. But we must emphasise that this is *not* a question of giving a larger 'net' return to the owners of house-property. We are concerned with preserving a great national asset. Moreover, we ought to deny that rents or 'rent restriction' has much to do with the clamour about the houses falling down; being abandoned by their owners; slums or near-slums. Most of the houses which are as bad as this are houses that ought to have fallen down or been pulled down long ago … No increase in rents, under any of the schemes suggested by anyone, would make them an economic proposition for the owner—except perhaps for the 'worst' type of 'slum landlord' or 'speculator'.[53]

---

[49] For example, TNA CAB24/294 CP14(38) Committee on Rent Restrictions Acts and Rating Revaluation, 27 January 1938; TNA CAB129/43 CP(50)273 'Rent Restrictions Acts', 15 November 1950.

[50] TNA CAB27/309 CP30(26) Committee on Rural Housing and Slum Areas, 1926, p.1.

[51] For example, TNA T227/805 CC(52)99 'Conclusions. Housing Programme', 20 November 1952.

[52] As Minister of Health, Aneurin Bevan, put it: 'There are quite a number of anomalies arising out of the Rent Restrictions Acts, but I can hold out no prospect of immediate legislation' (HCH 11 March 1948, Vol.448, col.1423).

[53] TNA CAB129/58 CP(53)24 'Houses – Old and New', 22 January 1953.

Decontrol was to come under the 1957 Rent Act, but this would offer landlords too little, too late, to halt decline. None of this meant a fall in private rental was inevitable. This arose because other tenures were prioritised. With private rental opportunities higher in the countryside than in towns (Bevan and Sanderling 1996), a rural complication was the depressing of agricultural labourers' wages as cheap food for urban voters and support for farmers were prioritised (Bowers 1985; Chase 1993; Howkins and Verdon 2009), which meant farm-workers were unable to pay new-build or improved dwelling rents. With low wages encouraging outmigration (Pedley 1942; Drudy and Wallace 1971; Drudy 1978), the culmination of policy biases was landlord property sales and dwelling dilapidation (e.g. Kendall 1963). So, while there was no *fait accompli* when 1915 rent restrictions came, in the absence of political support, for private rental, the train had left the station. Rental properties were lost in large numbers through sale and demolition (Table 2.2). With council housing providing better quality accommodation, accompanied as this was by higher rents, from the 1950s private rental tenants were disproportionately drawn from the low-paid (Bentham 1986, p.160). Private rental had the poorest accommodation, as seen in the proportion of unfit dwellings in owner-occupation (30.3%) falling well below its share of the housing stock in the late-1960s (50.8%), with public sector dwellings faring better (3.9% and 27.1%),[54] whereas other tenures,

Table 2.2 Change in the housing stock by tenure in England and Wales, 1914–1975 (millions)

	Owner-occupied	Council or new town	Private rental	Total
	1914–1938			
New build	+1.8	+1.1	+0.9	+3.8
Purchase(+)/sale(−)	+1.1	0.0	−1.1	0.0
Demolition/use change	0.0	0.0	−0.3	−0.3
Net	+2.9	+1.1	−0.5	+3.5
	1938–1960			
New build	+1.3	+2.3	+0.1	+3.7
Purchase(+)/sale(−)	+1.5	+0.2**	−1.7	0.0
Demolition/use change ***	−0.1	0.0	−0.4	−0.5
Net	+2.7	+2.5	−2.0	+3.2
	1960–1975			
New build	+2.6	+1.6	+0.3	+4.5
Purchase(+)/sale(−)	+1.1	+0.1	−1.2	0.0
Demolition/use change	−0.2	−0.1****	−0.8	−1.1
Net	+3.5	+1.6	−1.7	+3.4

Source: DoE (1977, p.39)
Note: '0.0' negligible; ** mainly requisitioned in the Second World War and subsequently purchased; *** includes 0.2 million destroyed by enemy action; and, **** mainly temporary post-1945 prefabricated dwellings

---

[54] This divergence was acknowledged locally, as Biggleswade councillor Gurney explained: 'The most respectable houses in the village were those belonging to the RDC' (*BC&BG* 23 March 1962, p.15).

which comprised 21.4% of the stock, accounted for 60.9% of unfitness (MHLG 1968a, p.18).[55]

2.2.2 Societal Pressures

Alongside private sector failings, demand for better homes provoked state intervention. The conundrum was that:

> In many cases it is clear that the people are able to pay a larger rent if more suitable premises were obtainable, and in many parts of the district the urgency of the need of more and better cottages cannot be doubted. The burning questions here, as elsewhere, are: can these be supplied at a remunerative rental, and is private enterprise sufficient to meet the demand? (Biggleswade RDC 1914, p.12)

Acceptance of state involvement had grown despite ideological aversion to 'interference' with the private sector. These ideological dispositions would last for decades, as in 1940s councils expressing uncertainty over the legality of applying Public Health Acts to unfit housing, with an expectation that local magistrates would refuse to close dwellings, 'especially in farming areas'.[56] But a transformation in national thinking was evident after the First World War, with more responsibility for housing placed on the state's shoulders. Hence, national agents felt justified in intervening if councils were slow in implementing building programmes. Bedford Town, for instance, was decreed in default of its responsibilities, when no new dwellings were started despite at least 400 being needed. The Ministry took over the Town's scheme in 1920 and started negotiations to buy sites, while making clear that costs would be borne by the Council.[57] Saffron Walden RDC faced similar Ministry condemnation:

> The Ministry of Health decided that these houses were to be built. They told the Council that unless they prepared a scheme they would put it into the hands of the County Council and if the County Council refused to do it the Ministry would do it themselves, and that the Council, instead of receiving any subsidy from the Ministry, would be charged the full extra expenses on the rates.[58]

Four main encouragements lay behind such extensions of state operations.

---

[55] These percentages exclude dwellings closed under the Housing Acts. These comprised 0.7% of the housing stock.

[56] TNA HLG101/258A Circular 2090. 'Postponement of Demolition of Unfit Houses. Note of Interview', 27 March 1940.

[57] HCH 22 April 1920, Vol.128, col.594W-95W. Cromer also incurred the Ministry's wrath, arguing workers could only afford annual rents of £20, not the £26 the Ministry wanted. This led to the warning: 'The Ministry had got the town of Cromer very carefully under observation and said that if they did not soon get the scheme going the Ministry would come down and build the houses themselves' (FakPost 17 September 1920, p.7).

[58] H&EO 23 April 1921, p.3.

The first was apparent in nineteenth-century legislation on state oversight, such as the 1875 Public Health Act, which awarded councils the authority to promote decent sanitary conditions.[59] Medical opinion at the time associated poor housing with disease, such that an 'intimate and close connection' was drawn between tuberculosis and unsatisfactory living arrangements (Savage 1919, p.160). Fears over the impact of inadequate accommodation extended long after 1919, and were subject to medical officer of health reports for decades. For instance, Ampthill reports broke down tuberculosis numbers by parish in every year from 1921 to 1963. The incidence of infection fell over time but not so as to terminate district-wide tabulations up to the Council's demise in 1974. Thus, from the 1920s, when the annual average was 26.8 cases for the district, tuberculosis numbers in the decades to the 1970s averaged 17.1, 15.3, 15.8, 9.7 and 3.5.[60] Given inter-war inclinations to leave health care to private providers, charities and wealthy municipalities (Powell 1995), cynicism over government commitment to improving housing for health reasons was not unreasonable. Nevertheless, interventions gave regular indications of this driving force. As one example, slum clearance under the 1930 Housing Act was justified when dwelling deficiencies '… are dangerous or injurious to the health of the inhabitants of the building' (Kirby 1979, p.3). A change in the political orientation of the ruling government did not change this rationale, as captured when Hilton Young, the 1933 Minister of Health, explained that slum clearance subsidies were essential as:

> This is work that will earn a large return in health, and will save public money now spent in the cure and alleviation of disease and ill-health. It will earn a large return in happiness and content. It passes indeed all the tests of work that a nation cannot afford to neglect, even in times of great financial stringency … [61]

That health gains continued to capture the imagination of analysts, commentators and policy-makers is apparent in the photographs of Don McCullin (2007), in academic research (Shanks and Smith 1992; Haynes and Gale 2000), and in commissioned reports (Townsend and Davidson 1982).

While associations between health and housing were on the political agenda well before and long after 1919 legislation, social unrest provided a more immediate prompt for the 1919 Act. The literature is well served by studies on this second reason for an enhanced state role (e.g. Swenarton 1981). Those hoping for a return to the laissez-faire days before 1914 soon had their wishes disabused. The Ministry

---

[59] The first Public Health Act was passed in 1848. It was followed in 1851 with legislation on lodging houses, with the 1868 'Torrens Act' enabling action against houses unfit for human habitation, while the 1875–1879 'Cross Acts' allowed insanitary areas to be reconstructed. Most of these Acts were consolidated in the 1890 Act (amended in 1909), which allowed councils to build their own dwellings (MoH 1931b).

[60] Figures exclude the parish of Toddington, which left the RDC in 1933 to become part of Luton RDC, and were computed for all available years in each decade. Between 1921 and 1973, only 1937, 1940, 1946, 1949 and 1950 were not available.

[61] TNA HLG48/686 Letter from Minister of Health to the Chancellor of the Exchequer, 3 March 1933.

of Reconstruction (1918a, p.3) warned that rents would rise quickly after the War unless steps were taken to remedy housing shortages, with the Committee on the Increase of Rent and Mortgage Interest (War Restrictions) Acts (1920, p.3) holding that tenant organisations and landlords believed public opinion would not accept rent rises if rent restrictions lapsed. The dilemma was spelt out in a 1918 Cabinet paper:

> Closely connected with the foregoing are the effects of bad housing upon *Industrial Unrest*. In seven out of the eight districts' reports of the Royal Commission on Industrial Unrest, attention is drawn to the fact of insufficient and bad housing being a cause of unrest … Of course the most important reason is that homes must be provided for the returning soldiers and sailors … To let them come from horrible water-logged trenches to something little better than a pigsty here would indeed be criminal on the part of ourselves, and would be a negation of all we have said during this War, that we can never repay these men for what they have done for us.[62]

For Orbach (1977, p.48): 'If the Russian Revolution seemed impossible in a civilised country like England the Cabinet was not persuaded of this entirely'. Tory grandees certainly had the jitters: 'Bonar Law so often referred to the need to arm stockbrokers that the Cabinet Secretary had visions of militant stockbrokers manning the barricades' (Hinton 1983, p.109).

This was due both to city activism and countryside agitation. Thus, late-1919 Cabinet papers emphasised that: 'Discontent regarding the lack of houses shows no abatement', before proceeding to note: 'The delay in starting building operations in other parts of the country, especially in rural districts, is having a deplorable result'.[63] Slip forward another nine months and, besides industrial discontent, officials thought: 'Scarcely less serious is the unrest among the agricultural workers, who have taken kindly to the revolutionary propaganda of the extremists. The unrest may culminate in a strike during the harvest'.[64] Adding detail:

> There has been a very remarkable development in the membership of the Agricultural Labourers' Union, from approximately 23,000 in 1915 to over 160,000 in 1920. Apart from the fact that the increase in wages threatens to absorb the entire profits of many farmers, the propaganda of the Union is giving a strongly revolutionary bias to labourers in the rural districts. Some kind of counter propaganda seems urgently to be required. The teaching of the Union has given rise, in some districts, to a talk of seizing the land, and a well-informed correspondent states that in remote villages in Suffolk he found the farm hands talking of a strike during the forthcoming harvest, and declaring that if their demands are not conceded they will seize and occupy the land themselves. It will be remembered that at the recent Conference in Leicester nationalisation of the land was advocated … [and] 10,000 Essex farm workers have already balloted in favour of a strike …[65]

---

[62] TNA CAB24/44 GT3877 'Note on the Urgent Need for the Commencement of a Large Housing Programme Immediately After the War', 11 March 1918, p.3.

[63] TNA CAB24/88 GT8144 'Report on Revolutionary Organisations in the UK', 11 September 1919, p.125, p.127-3.

[64] TNA CAB24/107 CP1049 'Report on Revolutionary Organisations in the UK', 17 June 1920, p.1.

[65] TNA CAB24/107 CP1049 'Report on Revolutionary Organisations in the UK', 17 June 1920, p.4.

Widespread support for farm-worker action was evinced in many public meetings, such as the 2000 attendees at a May 1919 Agricultural Labourers' Union and Rural Workers' League meeting at Fakenham (1921 population 2966).[66] But national and local fears of rebellion were short-lived. Social disquiet rumbled on, in the eyes of some until the General Strike of 1926 (Seaman 1966), but the end of the post-war boom in 1921 dampened agitation as unemployment rose, wages fell and fiscal retrenchment bit hard (Taylor 1965; Branson 1975; Pugh 2008). Where agricultural unionism was stronger, wage reductions and work-hour extensions did fuel discontent, with strikes by Norfolk farm-workers in 1923 symbolising misgivings (Newby 1977; Howkins 1985; Danziger 1988). More generally, social unrest after the War discomforted the leaders of the two main pre-1914 political parties, by suggesting that an electorate might swing towards more revolutionary or at least socialist sentiments.

Although manifest during and after the First World War, as Perkin (1989, p.192) noted, social unrest had a longer gestation. Lloyd George expected massive industrial disruption before 1919, but it was delayed by war. In this regard, social disharmony provided a characteristic prompt in the story of housing legislation, which Orbach (1997, p.46) portrayed as '… the story of the permanent adoption of solutions to what was conceived as a temporary problem'. But temporary problems need something to sustain their effect, whether repeated incidences or more fundamental drivers. This came from changed political circumstances, which provided a third encouragement for more state intervention. In particular, as the years rolled forward, the Liberal Party declined as a political force and the Labour Party garnered increased support. The Cabinet did not take its eyes off this rising force. By late-1919, for instance, more numerous Labour candidates in local elections were noted.[67] This influenced government thinking, given the anticipation that '… the recent Elections had resulted in filling the municipalities with Labour members, who would resolutely refuse to hand over their [housing] schemes to private enterprise'.[68] Labour was reported to have cultivated demobbed armed forces personnel, even allotting them candidatures for a General Election.[69] The significance of Labour's rise, even though it would take decades to win a majority election, came from Conservative fears over the policy impact of electoral loss. Agitation amongst Conservative supporters was visible when Labour secured minority rule in 1924, as with the fabricated Zinoviev letter, which contributed to Labour's loss in the second 1924 General Election (Chester et al. 1967), and 1931 scare stories that Labour would use Post Office savings to support depleted unemployment payments (Calder 1969; Spalding 2018). Yet Labour's standing was not strong in the 1930s. This was evident in its victory at the 1945 General Election, when success owed much to

---

[66] *FakPost* 9 May 1919, p.6.

[67] For example, TNA CAB24/89 CP1049 'Report on Revolutionary Organisations in the UK', 25 September 1919, p.95-1, p.97-3.

[68] TNA CAB23/18 7(19) Cabinet Conclusions, 14 November 1919, p.3.

[69] TNA CAB24/97 CP521 'Report from the Ministry of Labour for Week Ending 28 January 1920', p.58.

disenchantment with the 'undiluted' market forces that heralded 1930s inequality increases and mass unemployment (Martin 1988; Dunford 1995), rather than trust in the Party (Fielding 1992; Mortimer 1993). Commentaries on Labour from the 1920s to the 1950s abound but they portray a cautious, non-doctrinaire leadership (Miliband 1961; Campbell 1987; Addison 1994), that sought competent, pragmatic management, taking steps like nationalisation for reasons of efficiency not ideology (Guttsman 1968; Calder 1969; Hinton 1988), while not challenging elite institutions or practices (Owen 2007; Gardiner 2010; McKibbin 2010). Yet, as various analysts have explored, Conservative politicians were preoccupied with Labour's electoral threat, despite thin policy differences (Smith 1992; Pugh 2008; McKibbin 2010).[70]

Faced with economic downturn in 1920, the then government had reverted to type, slashing expenditure and terminating building under the 1919 Act. Construction by councils plummeted, from 85,976 completions in 1922 to 25,241 in 1923, then to 14,544 in 1924.[71] The private sector did not take up the slack, despite falling construction costs,[72] so housing shortages in 1923 were worse than in 1919 (Bowley 1945, p.23). Chamberlain's 1923 Housing Act sought to boost private construction through builder subsidies. Councils required special application to use the Act. Only one in 20 did so (Jennings 1971). Even builders reported that 1923 Act subsidies were insufficient to erect working-class rental units (National House Building Committee 1924, p.8). The short-lived minority Labour government of 1924 provided a new slant, both because its 1924 Housing (Financial Provisions) Act limited public subsidies to rental properties and because the Act was accompanied by agreement with construction companies on long-term orders, accompanied by commitments to build homes and train workers (Clarke 1924; MoH 1924; Lyman 1957). This so-called Wheatley Act was the first to acknowledge that 'the housing supply problem' was not short term but required long-term investment and solution (MoH 1924). Labour's approach was significant in that the 1923 Act continued to operate. The joint running of the two Acts after 1924 helped to lubricate diversity in council responses, with public support available for renters and owner-occupiers. The soon reinstated Conservative administration returned the compliment by retaining 1924 Act subsidies. This signified how decisive the 1924 Act was in British housing policy, for there was nothing inevitable about a large council housing sector (Holmans 1987, p.85). Its retention by the Conservative government bore testament to the political weakness of private landlords and signalled awareness amongst Conservatives that state housing for the low-paid was for the long haul. This did not mean commitments could not be watered down. Subventions were reduced in 1927, but over 1925–1927, these Acts funded 206,766 council and 230,336 private sector

---

[70] Fear over 1945 General Election outcomes reintroduced the scare-mongering of earlier decades, as with Winston Churchill's claim that Labour needed a British Gestapo to implement its policies (Fielding 1992, p.631).

[71] HCH 11 March 1946, Vol.420, col.161W-62W.

[72] Building costs per sq.ft. were 23% higher in 1920 than in 1919 but 43% below 1919 levels by 1922 (MoH 1944b, p.51).

dwellings. Over the same period, unsubsidised private completions were 162,737.[73] The two major political parties had begun a journey whereby private and public sector options addressed shortfalls in housing numbers and standards. Encased in this pursuit was acknowledgement, if at times reluctant, that without subsidies new dwellings were unaffordable for those unable to buy a home. For rural districts, the 1924 Act was highly symbolic in this regard, as it granted, for the first time, larger subsidies for new homes in agricultural parishes.[74] Yet the two Acts betrayed their political origins in their construction histories. By 1936, when the 1923 and 1924 Acts had ceased operations, only 7.1% of rural dwellings under the 1923 Act were owned by councils, whereas 93.1% were for the 1924 Act.[75]

The retention of the 1924 Act by the 1924–1929 Conservatives points to a recurring theme in housing policy. In times of close electoral competition, policy strands were often shared in Conservative and Labour thinking. Thus, for 1951–1955, the Conservatives continued Labour's prioritisation of new council homes, while in 1964 Labour retained the Conservative's high-rise programme, as well as a strong commitment to owner-occupation (Crossman 1975). As examined later, when political parties felt electorally advantaged, a stronger ideological tone was evident. When electoral competition was tight, governments also faced pressure from local associations, who feared losing votes through housing policies. Note, for instance, considerable local lobbying around 1954, as the Conservative government began to shrink council-building.[76] For the countryside, insofar as electoral competition impacted on housing policy, this was disadvantageous. Fluctuating around the mark across censuses, the rural population was about one-fifth of the English total between 1921 and 1971. With tranches adjacent to towns, which policy-makers could subsume under 'suburbanisation',[77] the demographic weight calling for housing attention in 'deep rural' areas was slight. In these circumstances, if there were distinctive rural needs, would national policy-makers appreciate them? Internal documents from 1945 suggest Ministry of Agriculture officials were not convinced:

---

[73] HCH 11 March 1946, Vol.420, col.161W-62W.

[74] When first implemented, compared with the general £9 per dwelling annual Treasury subsidy, new-build in agricultural parishes received £12/10/0d. Both lasted for 40 years. For dwellings erected after 30 September 1927, subsidies were reduced to £7/10/0d and £11, respectively.

[75] TNA HLG37/43 'Rural Districts. Houses Completed Since the Armistice', August 1936.

[76] See TNA HLG101/812 Letter from Warrington RDC, 8 January 1954; Letter from Conservative Research Department, 28 January 1954; Letter from H. Brabin, Conservative and Unionist Central Office, 10 February 1954; Letter from Conservative Association Woking Division, 28 June 1954; Letter from the Earl of Woolton, 10 September 1957.

[77] Following Flowerdew and Boyle (1992), 'suburbanisation' has been used in this volume to capture urban-centred relocations into the countryside; little more than 'spillover' from more densely to less densely settled zones in urban commuter belts. This phrasing has been preferred, as it helps distinguish urban spillover from moves to the 'deep countryside'; albeit improved transport and communications shrank the territory justifying the latter moniker as the century progressed. Hence, by the 1970s, rural Bedfordshire had '… a suburban feel about much of the development in villages' (Kennett 1978, p.118).

> It was suggested that the Ministry of Health did not appreciate the special needs of rural and particularly of agricultural housing. They took the line that houses should be built on the spot by the labour on the spot; and that priority in selecting tenants could not be given on any grounds but those of housing need. Mr. Bevan [Minister of Health] was understood to feel that the Ministerial Housing Committee was too large for dealing with anything other than broad policy issues; and he had set up a small informal Committee from which this department was excluded.[78]

That said, special subsidies for agricultural parishes under the 1924 Act did acknowledge special rural conditions (viz. inability to pay). Special rural measures also characterised the 1931 Housing (Rural Authorities) Act (Linsley 2005, pp.254–59) and the 1938 Housing (Financial Provisions) Act (Martin 1938), although both were curtailed by fiscal retrenchment or the Second World War. Further acknowledgement of rural distinctiveness was found in the 1926 Housing (Rural Workers) Act, which introduced improvement grants, decades before they were available for towns. There was, then, some legislative attention towards the countryside in the first half of the century, but, as we see later, with relatively little effect.

Perhaps in this regard, the 1946 Housing (Financial and Miscellaneous Provisions) Act stands a little apart, as it offered enhanced rural support alongside prioritisation for farm-worker homes (MoH 1946b). This emerged as an element in the fourth factor behind more active state housing provision and regulation. This owed its origins to anxiety over national security and economic performance. Nervousness of this kind was evident as early as the 1919 Act, with Cabinet concerns that shortages and poor quality dwellings might make demobbed soldiers unwilling to return or move to the countryside, when the nation needed higher farm production.[79] At this time, no special allowance was awarded for rural house-building, although the 1924 Act gave some redress. By 1946, a string of official reports had exposed difficulties emanating from poor rural housing (MoH 1936b, 1937b, 1944a; Ministry of Works and Planning 1942). Spurred by apprehension over negative trade balances, during the late-1940s, building in mining and agricultural areas was supported but construction in other areas was trimmed.[80] Like backing farmers immediately after the First World War (Penning-Rowsell 1997), this special status did not last long, but demonstrated a willingness to favour places or economic sectors critical to the national economy. A local manifestation of this prioritisation occurred in Hatfield (1931 population 11,001), when the 'shouldering out' of the de Havilland Aircraft Company from Edgware led to a 1930s' relocation to the district.[81] This generated increasing demand for 'key worker' housing,[82] fol-

---

[78] TNA MAF234/10 'Agricultural Aspects of Housing Policy. Notes of a Policy Meeting', 14 November 1945.

[79] For example, TNA CAB24/44 GT3877 'Note on the Urgent Need for the Commencement of a Large Housing Programme Immediately After the War', 11 March 1918, p.5.

[80] TNA CAB129/20 CP(47)236 'Balance of Payments. Housing', 22 August 1947.

[81] *HM&CP* 26 January 1934, p.15.

[82] Early indications were reported in *H&PBG* 26 September 1947, p.1 and HRO RDC7/1/14 HtRDCM 5 December 1950, p.189. In 1955, after the new town was created as an independent unit

lowed by rapid population growth through in-migration (with 23,334 residents in 1951 and 45,143 in 1971), with around 70 per cent of total employment in Hatfield coming from this one firm in the mid-1950s (Hooson 1958, p.202). Backing for key worker accommodation after 1945 was expressed regularly in internal communications within ministries and in government statements.[83] More broadly, national priorities found expression in the new and expanding town programmes, with a New Town Development Corporation for parts of Hatfield from 1947.[84] More dispersed new homes for key workers came later across a range of rural districts and small towns. Illustrative, from the 1950s up to the 1970s, were Biggleswade,[85] Biggleswade Town,[86] Sandy[87] and Walsingham.[88] So, more than half the rural districts investigated here benefited in one way or another from key worker initiatives, excluding general 1945–1951 support for more dwellings for farm-workers. The bias towards the southeastern quadrant of England in the investigated councils impacts on this pattern (especially given London overspill demands), but this does not lessen the point that state agencies encouraged local house-building to support the national economy.

2.3   Specifying Local Responsibilities

Whatever the provocations for state intervention, discussion within government circles towards the end of the First World War leaned towards a temporary state role, with expectations of a return to private sector dominance.[89] Anticipated shortages of

---

[83] occupying part of Hatfield RDC, 1,163 dwellings had been built by the New Town Corporation, covering half the demand of workers employed by de Havilland (*H&PBG* 1 April 1955, p.1).

[83] TNA CAB129/20 CP(47)249 'Priority of Housing for Miners, Agricultural Workers and Key Workers in the Development Areas', 5 September 1947; TNA T227/808 Letter to Duncan Sandys, MHLG, from Peter Thorneycroft, 10 February 1955; also Harold Macmillan, the relevant minister, at HCH 20 July 1954, Vol.530, col.1148.

[84] HRO RDC7/1/13 HtRDCM 30 October 1947, p.238.

[85] There are numerous examples here. Early cases were six houses for Messrs James Garnar and Sons Ltd. at Potton (BRO RDBwM1/23 BiRDCM 6 August 1952, p.145) and two for Messrs F.W. Braybrooke (Potton) Ltd. (*NBC&BR* 25 November 1952, p.2).

[86] *BC&BG* 21 September 1962, p.1.

[87] *BC&BG* 21 April 1967, p.9.

[88] NRO DC19/6/32 WRDCM 20 May 1970.

[89] TNA RECO1/472 'Rural Housing 1917'. Those believing the private sector would soon respond to housing difficulties held that state intervention was due to the war but would soon end (Bowley 1945, p.15). Thus, Neville Chamberlain's 1923 Act was introduced on an assumed two-year lifespan (Lyman 1957, p.110; Self 2006, p.90). This applied to expectations for house-building and rent restrictions. 'Temporary' might be an elastic concept but the duration of interventions stretched even generous interpretations, with rent restrictions effectively lasting without major alteration from 1915 until 1957 (Seaman 1966, p.120), despite tinkering in 1933 and 1938 (Mowat 1955, p.165).

building materials, alongside what was then seen as massive Treasury funding, justified 'emergency' national intervention, especially given the scale of housing shortages. Councils were to be active players, given their local knowledge, with initial
proposals allocating housing responsibilities to county councils and large urban
authorities, but not to smaller urban or rural districts.[90] In the end, lower tier districts
were made housing authorities. Nevertheless, with estimates that as many as
500,000 new houses were needed,[91] costs were beyond district councils without
substantial aid. Hence, under the 1919 Act, the Treasury covered the bulk of the
state's costs.[92] The critical role of councils came through identifying and responding
to local needs. This was a legal requirement placed on them. It marked a key change
with the past. As the Ministry of Health (1944b, p.7) later described it: 'The Act of
1919 transformed the optional power into an obligation on local authorities to provide for the whole of the working-class need for their district so far as it was not
likely to be met by other agencies'. Able to build homes under the 1890 Housing of
the Working Classes Act, the feebleness of this Act compared to its 1919 equivalent
was captured by the MP for Stafford:

> The average building by local authorities between the time the Act was passed in 1890 and
> the beginning of the War was only 1000 houses a year; an absolutely infinitesimal number.
> It was not half the number of houses that were built by the co-operative building societies,
> who built 38,000 working men's houses in the period that the local authorities built 18,000.[93]

For Bowley (1945, p.17): 'The Act of 1890 had made it possible to open the door to
the introduction of state provision of housing, and state responsibility for housing
conditions. In 1919 the door was kicked wide open' (also MoH 1920, p.11; 1944b,
p.7). Tension was inevitable over so fundamental a change in expectations. Desires
to see the private sector restored to its 'rightful' place did not wither. Its continued
importance was seen in the 1919 Housing (Additional Powers) Act, which awarded
lump sums if builders erected homes for private owners. The fact this support was
considered necessary further testified to the depressed state of private building. In
all, 39,186 dwellings were erected under this Act by 1923–1924 compared with
169,526 under the Housing, Town Planning, Etc. Act (MoH 1939a, p.253).[94] The

---

[90] TNA CAB24/50 GT4485 'Housing. Note by the Minister of Reconstruction', 2 May 1918.

[91] TNA CAB23/18 7(19) Cabinet Conclusions, 14 November 1919, p.2.

[92] The Treasury met the annual cost of housing loans, minus rents paid, with councils contributing
one penny per (£) pound of the rateable value of each dwelling built. Indicating the significance of
Treasury inputs for rural areas, Linsley (2005, p.65) noted that Depwade RDC identified a need for
300 new dwellings, but planned to build less than a quarter of them until Treasury funding was
confirmed, when its programme was raised to 316.

[93] HCH 7 April 1919, Vol.114, col.1799.

[94] The line separating these two Acts was not absolute but the Acts were largely sector specific. The
Housing (Additional Powers) Act was solely for private-owner dwellings, whereas the Housing,
Town Planning, Etc. Act accounted for 171,054 council and 4,545 private-owner homes by 1930
(HCH 29 January 1931, Vol.247, col.1172W-73W). 'Private-owners' included public utility com-
panies (PUCs), many of which later transitioned into today's housing associations. PUCs could not
receive rate contributions on new houses, which contributed to their weak engagement with the Act
(Malpass 2000). Private building could be curtailed by councils if there were local labour short-

1923 Housing Act proffered another attempted kick-start for private building, although some analysts concluded that it took the best part of a decade for private building to recover after the 1914–1918 war (Ravetz 2001, p.77). For rural areas especially, symbols of how critical state intervention was are not hard to find. As former Minister of Health, Arthur Greenwood, reported in 1933, 23 out of every 24 homes built for farm-workers between 1924 and 1932 received state subsidies.[95] The 1919 Act was only a first step in a widening and deepening of state regulation and action.[96]

Friction generated by the passing of the 1919 Act was not limited to concern over private and public contributions. It also raised questions about the roles of local and national government. Under *ultra vires*, councils acted illegally unless they could trace authority for an action to national legislation. At the edges, some councils acted first, with national permission following (e.g. Swann 1972). More commonly, the government came down on councils that 'went rogue' over national priorities (e.g. Skinner and Langdon 1974; Branson 1979; Parkinson 1985). Between these 'extremes', the 'norm' was cooperation (Griffith 1966; Keith-Lucas and Richards 1978; Rhodes 1981). This enabled national politicians to maintain the polite 'fiction' that councils were autonomous. The claim repeated regularly in official documents and in House of Commons debates was that national authorities did not interfere with local discretion. Yet national agents were not timid to enforce their aims. We have already noted the Bedford Town example under the 1919 Act. That the 'centre' wanted compliance, despite so-called local autonomy, was made clear by the DoE's Parliamentary Under-Secretary in 1972:

> Local authorities have some statutory duties imposed upon them by Parliament, and it is the duty of local authorities to comply with them. They cannot pick and choose between statutory duties and decide to abide by some which they like and not to carry out those which they do not. Local authorities have a duty to abide by all statutory obligations placed upon them. [97]

So, councils had flexibility to identify and respond to local needs, but this was subject to direction from Whitehall. In the jargon of the 1919 Act, councils had a 'duty' to prepare and submit to the Minister a housing scheme; not just in 1919, but 'thereafter as occasion arises' (MoH 1920, p.11). It requires too much space to list the

---

ages, although council authority on such interventions was weak (HCH 5 August 1920, Vol.133, col.395). While no data were collected at the time on new no-subsidy private homes, estimates suggest that around 30,000 were built over 1919-22. This meant that around 30% more private homes were built with subsidy than without, with total new-build for private-owners close to half that for councils (HCH 11 March 1946, Vol.420, col.161W-62W).

[95] HCH 28 February 1933, Vol.275, col.204.

[96] Throughout this book, rather than complicating descriptions with constant caveats over the '1919 Act', this expression is taken to encompass both the Housing, Town Planning, Etc. Act and the Housing (Additional Powers) Act. That one was directed largely at council provision, the other solely at private, presented a mixture that was no different from many Acts. The 1923 Housing Act promoted building for private-owners but a few councils used it, with the reverse occurring for the 1924 Act, to offer two examples.

[97] HCH 20 December 1972, Vol.848, col.1326-27.

responsibilities imposed on councils over time. The breadth of their duties should be grasped. Alongside surveying homes to ensure that they met reasonable living standards, under 1919 (and earlier) legislation, councils could insist that dwellings were improved or closed. The 1925 Housing Act then specified that acceptable dwelling standards included '… water supply, closet accommodation, drainage, housing inspection, fixing numbers of persons who can live in a dwelling, cleansing and decorating, securing adequate lighting, prevention of fires, etc.', while the 1930 Housing Act allowed the demolition of insanitary dwellings or where whole areas were deemed '… dangerous or injurious to the health of the inhabitants by reason of disrepair or sanitary defects' (MoH 1931b, pp.3–5; also Clarke 1931). Over time, more layers were added. Often, however, the Ministry 'encouraged' rather than enforced, as with the temporary housing programme after 1945 (Ministry of Works 1945) or high-rise construction in the 1950s–1960s.[98] Yet the core stated expectation over the first three-quarters of the century was clear:

> Housing is a local function requiring control by persons intimately acquainted with the circumstances of the districts and the requirements of the community and of individuals … Housing schemes are essentially a local charge and whilst in the past added rate burdens were a deterrent, the generous subsidies now available have removed this difficulty.[99]

But if the 'difficulty' really had gone, why was rural housing so inadequate across the decades?

2.4 Divergence in Housing Conditions

When seeking to identify the geography of housing conditions, problems arise with the reliability of official accounts. On the one side, local authority reports were suspect, as they often limited detections at levels councils were willing to react to. On the other side, when councils reported deficiencies, governments could challenge assessments or even bar local action. As such, reports on housing circumstances need approaching with scepticism. Most evidently, caution is required over uneven coverage and variation across dimensions of housing need. Take as a starting point the 12 points articulated as desirable standards for dwellings (MHLG 1966). Examined closely, these 12 can be folded into two dimensions. They overlap for sure, but in essence, they relate, first, to the physical fabric of a building and, second, to the facilities that ease comfortable living. The state of repair of a building, freedom from damp, and the adequacy of natural lighting and air circulation are essentially physical conditions. The availability of water, electricity, gas, storage, cooking, washing and drainage occupy the domain of facilities. These amenities might be deficient in physically sound buildings, just as they might be available as a dwelling collapses around its inhabitants. But, important as these two 'dimensions' might be,

---

[98] TNA CAB129/110 C(62)145 'Housing', 2 October 1962.
[99] TNA HLG37/48 Rural Housing Sub-Committee. 'Work of RDCs on Housing', undated c1943.

on their own, they do not capture housing situations adequately. More difficult to measure, and subject to political dispute, even heroic assumptions, is a further dimension, which is the sufficiency of accommodation numbers.

2.4.1 Housing Supply

Assessing supply volumes raises similar problems to evaluating unfit dwellings. Despite statutory obligations, housing shortage estimates have long been contested. This has been apparent over recent decades in assessments of homelessness (Niner 1989). Evans and Duncan (1988), for example, found that only half of councils accepted residents of statutorily unfit dwellings as effectively homeless, with less than a fifth acknowledging that young, single people could be homeless. Influential reports indicated significant 'hidden' shortages, such as unwillingly sharing a home with parents or 'camping out' on friends' settees, which made evaluations of homelessness difficult technically and contested politically (Greve et al. 1971). For sure, in the latter decades of the twentieth-century, homelessness became a controversial issue, given that household numbers had fallen below dwelling counts (Table 2.3), which sharpened criticisms of housing market failure. With more general shortages earlier in the century, homelessness was less prominent in political dialogue; what drove policy more was increasing numbers to reduce shortage. Unfortunately, as Hayes Fisher made clear in 1917, there were no reliable estimates of shortfalls.[100]

The Registrar-General did attempt an approximation by using the number of newly married women to indicate changing housing demand. Adding guestimates for growth in the number of widows–widowers and single persons wanting homes, estimates were refined, but the process was still political. Thus, despite rates of new marriages far outstripping new construction levels, early in the century ministers

Table 2.3 Dwelling stock and household numbers in England and Wales, 1911–1971 (000s)

	Increase in dwellings	Increase in households	Dwellings relative to households
1911–1921	228	796	−508
1921–1931	1421	1494	−73
1931–1938	2000	1070	+930
1938–1951	1130	1960	−830
1951–1961	2116	1385	+731
1961–1971	2378	2055	+323

Source: DoE (1977, p.22)

---

[100] HCH 28 June 1917, Vol.95, col.548W. For similar government statements, see Kingsley Wood (HCH 4 April 1927, Vol.204, col.1682) and Ernest Marples (HCH 27 May 1952, Vol.501, col.137W).

downplayed the merits of marriage volumes as an indicator of housing demand.[101] Certainly, it offered an incomplete estimation, as no allowance was made for affordability.[102] Bowley (1941) offered some perspective on this shortcoming, when using marriage rates to compute 1921–1931 housing 'requirements' against building volumes. She reported that 'more rural' counties, like Cornwall, Herefordshire, Norfolk and Suffolk, lay at one extreme with the lowest 'demand' for new housing, while prosperous counties in the South-East and the Midlands had the highest. This was not unexpected given the geography of inter-war economic change (Richardson 1967; Ward 1988). When compared with building volumes, however, it was rural counties, like Herefordshire, Lincolnshire, Rutland, Westmorland and Wiltshire, alongside the more urbanised Derbyshire, which saw the biggest gaps between demand and supply. Moreover, while Bowley saw council contributions as generally too small to satisfy demand, the combination of private and council efforts fell below expanding family numbers (perhaps contributing to ministers disliking demand estimates based on new marriages). This particularly applied to the council sector, for while private-owner building was short on requirements, its distribution did follow demand increases. Rates of council-building, by contrast, differed little across the nation. As a consequence, council provision was particularly low where demand was highest, especially around London and adjoining counties. Exploring other data sources, Bowley posited that peaks in unsatisfied council demand were found where tenant costs were high. These might be due to high building costs fuelling rent charges or high non-housing tenant costs, such as those associated with added transport charges on suburban council estates (Benson 1989; Olechnowicz 1997; Gardiner 2010). Given the nature of national support, Bowley (1941, p.70) concluded that: '… unless the level of working-class incomes is sufficiently above that in other towns to compensate for these higher costs, either the local authorities will require a larger subsidy per house from the Treasury, or the number of houses they build will most probably be particularly inadequate'. The Registrar-General's method of assessing housing demand was modest, with more sophistication needed, but it highlighted what became well established in later decades, that building volumes were insufficient to meet demand, especially where tenant costs were high relative to incomes (Bowley 1945). Such divergence between wages and building costs could occur in low-remuneration rural regimes or in high-cost city locations. In both, the least well-off were disadvantaged, restricting council housing effectively to the wealthier segment of the working-class (Pooley and Irish 1984; Benson 1989; Jones 2010).

Offering an alternative version for assessing housing shortages, the Inter-Departmental Committee on Rent Restrictions (MoH 1937a, p.27) submitted that

---

[101] Neville Chamberlain's response on marriages as a housing indicator are at HCH 14 March 1923, Vol.161, col.1592W; 4 March 1925, Vol.181, col.473W.

[102] As research on hidden homelessness reveals, housing costs reduced the potentially accessible stock, leading to many couples unwillingly sharing homes with parents (e.g. Bottle et al. 1974).

overcrowding identified working-class housing shortage.[103] This suggestion arose following nation-wide surveys to identify overcrowding for the 1935 Housing Act. This legislation introduced subsidies and authority for councils to alleviate dwelling over-occupation. For these surveys, councils were given little discretion (White 1977). To create equivalent tabulations across the nation, homes suspected of over-crowding on a first visit were revisited to measure room sizes.[104] But what was overcrowding? Opposition politicians charged that government designations for overcrowded dwellings were too tough.[105] The accusation was that the fewer over-crowded homes identified, the lower the need for new dwellings (hence less Treasury payments). For White (1977, p.89), the standard for designating homes as over-crowded enabled the government to exaggerate the adequacy of house-building for the working-classes. For our purposes, an additional consideration was the impact on where new dwellings were seen to be required. Official overcrowding rates for families were 7.0% for the City and metropolitan boroughs of London, 4.2% for county boroughs (CBs), 3.0% for other urban centres (UDCs-MBs) and 2.9% for RDCs (MoH 1936c, p.xvii). The message that rural districts needed few new homes fed into government thinking, as a 1936 memo to the Minister of Health on agricul-tural families captured: 'The amount of statutory overcrowding in the agricultural districts altogether is not great and I believe that the amount found to exist among the agricultural population in those districts will be quite trifling when compared with the total amount of overcrowding'.[106] This view contrasted with earlier state-ments by John Burns, then LGB President, who in 1908 took the *Estates Gazette* at its word that '... it has been said practically with full truth that there is not a spare

---

[103] Two Committee members thought overcrowding an inappropriate indicator of housing shortage. As the literature on street-level bureaucrats shows, when faced with housing shortage, municipal inspectors face a dilemma if they instruct landlords to improve properties, as they might evict ten-ants rather than incur expense (Nivola 1978; Lipsky 1980). In rural England, such occurrences were reported across the decades by councils (e.g. Biggleswade RDC 1914, p.12), by worker organisations (TNA HLG37/44 'NUAW Memorandum on Rural Housing', October 1936), and via internal ministry investigations, as with Chard RDC reporting that landlords neglected old dwell-ings in order to 'invite' a closing order so they could evict tenants and sell properties (TNA HLG118/1392 'Unfit Houses in Rural Districts', undated c1970). Since councils had a statutory duty to address housing distress, they could move overcrowded families into council dwellings, resulting in more overcrowding in council homes than others. Thus, the 1935 Housing Act surveys recorded an overcrowding rate of 4.3% in English council homes and 2.7% for other tenures (MoH 1936c, p.33). One reason for overcrowding was that three-bedroomed homes were the 'norm' for councils, with only 2.5–3.0% of council dwellings having four or more bedrooms (HCH 26 January 1954, Vol.522, col.223W-24W; MHLG 1967, p.65). Hence, overcrowding amongst smaller families might be alleviated within the existing stock, but larger families might remain overcrowded after a move, although council accommodation otherwise provided better household amenities and lower rates of unfitness than other tenures (e.g. MHLG 1968b, p.94).

[104] Despite this intention: 'The surveys vary in quality. Some are as exact as possible, every room in every working-class house has been measured; others have the entries relating to unmeasured houses properly adjusted on a basis suggested by the experience of the houses which have been measured ...' (MoH 1936c, p.ix).

[105] See Arthur Greenwood at HCH 30 January 1935, Vol.297, col.386.

[106] TNA HLG40/2 'Memo to the Minister from J.W.', 30 September 1936.

cottage in England'.[107] Of course, much might have happened between 1908 and the mid-1930s, but housing output was depressed before 1914 and inter-war rural council additions lagged well behind towns, adding only 18.9% inter-war to rural numbers compared with 30.2% for urban (MoH 1944a, p.61). Perhaps no surprises when Whitehall was informed in 1929 that: '... the increase in tied cottages, whether let by farmers or not, is due to the shortage of houses in the country and the difficulty could, of course, be got over if it were possible rapidly to increase the number of available houses in the country for agricultural workers'.[108] Rural districts, it seemed, had fewer overcrowded dwellings, but they also had substantial housing stock shortfalls.

One reason for inter-war reluctance to recognise numerical shortage was a belief in 'filtering-up' processes (Harris 2012), whereby those moving into new homes freed up dwellings for those of lesser means. This understanding lay behind the regressive subsidies of Chamberlain's 1923 Housing Act (Bowley 1945), offering aid only to the better-off was justified as the poor would benefit 'down the line'. That this idea had deep flaws in assuming vacated houses would be suitable for poorer households in terms of size, layout, location and cost did not seem to trouble policy-makers.[109] Others were less generous, as with the Council for Research on Housing Construction (1934, p.14), which criticised the 1930 Act's slum clearance subsidies as: '... misused, in a theory of 'filtering-up', which has never worked more than very incompletely and, since the slump, has scarcely worked at all'. Official sources at the time were prone to agree:

> ... there has been discouragingly little improvement in the worst cases of overcrowding and unhealthy conditions. The conclusion was inescapable that the general filtering up process had been retarded by certain factors, for which perhaps insufficient allowance had been made, and the indirect method of improving the housing of the poorest classes had to this extent fallen short of expectation. (MoH 1931a, p.99; also MoH 1931c, p.23)

The Ministry reaffirmed this conclusion a few years later when commenting on the 1930 Act: 'Experience has shown that reliance for a solution cannot be placed upon indirect influences such as "filtering up" into new accommodation' (MoH 1933b, p.1). But the Cabinet sought to justify this reliance. In 1934, for example, a report was tabled on a study of 709 new dwellings in six towns in which 694 household movement chains were explored, from which 364 working-class families improved their housing circumstances. This led to the conclusion that: '... there is no reason to suppose that private enterprise cannot now be relied upon to provide in due course all that is necessary in the way of ordinary housing for persons in receipt of normal wages'.[110] Unfortunately, this account was silent on the economic circumstances of

---

[107] HCH 12 May 1908, Vol.188, col.945.

[108] TNA MAF48/207 'Tied Cottages', 18 November 1929.

[109] Filtering was not just problematical within private housing but also in the council sector (see Thomas 1966; Bird 1976).

[110] TNA CAB24/247 CP12(34) 'Housing Policy', 1 February 1934, p.10, p.8. Some details were published in MoH (1934, p.151).

those down the transfer chain, ducked the issue of insufficient new dwellings and
ignored location. Both at the time, as Marshall (1968) reported for slum clearance,
and more recently, as Phillips and Williams (1982, p.91) showed for rural areas,
options were constrained for the low-paid when available units were 'inconvenient'
locationally. Better-off workers might be prepared to travel but for the low-paid,
especially in rural areas, where turnover rates were traditionally lower (Pacione
1980; Forrest and Murie 1992; DTZ Pieda Consulting 1998), this was often not
viable (Connor 1936; Burnett 1986; Clapson 1998). Over the years, state intervention saw a nibbling away of housing shortages, but the changes occurring were
complex. Thus, in the mid-1960s, it was predicted that: 'By 1970 there will be a
surplus of houses compared with families but the surplus will be entirely unfit or
unimprovable houses'.[111]

2.4.2   The Physical Fabric of Dwellings

National statements on the desirability of a vigorous response to unfit homes
abound. To justify government intervention, statistics on the incidence of bad housing were regularly reported. Yet, measurement of housing quality was insecure.
Indicative of the uncertainty, in 1933, the Rural Housing Sub-Committee of the
Central Housing Advisory Committee noted that 33,500 unfit dwellings existed in
rural districts; by 1939, the number was 67,900 (MoH 1944a, p.11). Such changes
might be put down to learning or gaining familiarity with what 'unfitness' meant,
which the MoH (1936a, p.86) conveniently assumed was the cause for the adjustment. But this explanation is difficult to sustain when set against uneven fitness
levels. Consider, for instance, the implications of a 1957 MHLG memo:

> The fact that the London estimate of unfit houses is only 20,000 as against Manchester's
> figure of 68,000 is due to several reasons. First and probably most important, the LCC and
> the Metropolitan Boroughs deliberately limited their returns to their first five years' pro-
> gramme: they are expected to return a roughly comparable figure for the second five years'
> programme. Manchester, on the other hand, had every reason not to minimise their
> problem ...[112]

For rural districts, such discrepancies were problematical, as they were handled differently from towns, with action against unfit dwellings largely beyond the oversight of the Ministry:

> Orders submitted by rural district councils differed little over the country as a whole. They
> were fewer in proportion than those from urban areas since, although the number of unfit
> houses in rural areas is estimated at about 16 per cent of the national total, single properties,

---

[111] TNA HLG118/413 'The Housing Programme 1966-70', undated c1966. Ministers repeated this
message again and again in the late-1960s (e.g. HCH 25 March 1969, Vol.780, col.1262; HCH 16
December 1969, Vol.793, col.1115), sometimes with the assertion that shortages were most profound in cities (HCH 14 October 1969, Vol.788, col.181–82).

[112] TNA HLG101/778 'Memo to Mr Phillips from Miss Fox', 6 March 1957.

which comprise the bulk of the rural problem, are dealt with by demolitions and closing orders under Part II of the Housing Act, 1957, and do not fall within the Minister's jurisdiction. (MHLG 1957, p.9)

Then, there was the question of what to do about unfit dwellings. Suspend 'reality' for a moment, and assume that measurement captured differences in quality. This still leaves unanswered what was done to reduce poor quality. Suggesting rural districts did well in this regard, the pace of rural demolitions in the late-1930s (83.3%) was higher than in towns (74.6%), or it was at least for units in clearance areas. However, unfit rural houses were not as geographically concentrated as in towns. For 1938, for example, 57.4% of recorded unfit rural dwellings were outside designated clearance areas (MoH 1939a, p.96), a pattern that persisted for decades, as shown by only 11.1% of 1967 unfit dwellings in English clearance zones being in rural districts, compared with 41.8% outside these zones (MHLG 1968a, p.17). The significance of this is twofold: first, there was uncertainty over the magnitude of the problem at hand; and, second, the Ministry did not have a grip on overseeing rural district actions. Hence, official statements regularly noted that Whitehall only recorded demolition figures if a programme was Ministry overviewed.[113] Amidst the murk that hid the state of play, the Dennington Report on standards of housing fitness eventually recommended that detailed information be collected on the physical condition of the housing stock (MHLG 1966). This led to the 1967 Housing Condition Survey. The broad trends this revealed demonstrated deep flaws in previous pronouncements about the distribution of bad housing, with proportionately fewer unfit houses in conurbations and in the North (MHLG 1968b).

2.4.3   Household Amenities

The message is that on two of the three key dimensions of housing deficiency, namely shortage and physical unfitness, government mechanisms failed to determine the 'reality' of national shortcomings (let alone regional or local ones). Arguably, this was a lesser problem for the third housing dimension, namely, dwelling amenities. For sure, even here, there were deficiencies in data gathering, with the main source of information coming from decennial censuses, which up to 1931 only recorded room occupancy levels. The 1951 Census gave more, with records of households lacking or sharing a piped water supply, a cooking stove, a kitchen sink, a WC and a fixed bath. Rising expectations refined these measures over time, with 1961 distinguishing between cold and hot water supplies, while dropping cooking stove and kitchen sink entries. By 1971, cold water supply was not recorded, with flush WCs noted rather than any WC. Amenities were also reported in 1971 by housing tenure. Data inadequacies there were but the census did enable comparison

---

[113] For example: Kingsley Wood (HCH 3 March 1938, Vol.322, col.1278); Reginald Bevins (HCH 23 June 1959, Vol.607, col.115W).

across councils (Knox 1975) and within them (Cullingford and Openshaw 1982). Yet, these records had a less attractive side. In particular, they presented easily measurable (or at least available) housing indicators, which focused attention on housing amenities, to the detriment of understanding shortages and physical conditions. This applied to academic investigations and research by public officials, as with a landmark study by officers in the Ministry with responsibilities for housing. They claimed '… that in bulk and severity in relation to total housing stock the [obsolescent housing] problem is concentrated in ten major urban areas' (Burnett and Scott 1962, p.35). Given such messages from within the Ministry, perhaps it is no surprise that the official government view was:

> At one end of the scale, there are many rural areas and small towns where most cases of acute housing need that require local authority assistance have already been met, or very nearly so. At the other end, there are the big cities and towns where large unsatisfied demands of all kinds still persist, and where a high level of building by the authorities concerned will continue to be necessary for years to come. (MHLG 1961, p.5)

Yet, the Burnett and Scott conclusion derived largely from four indicators, plus commentary on what were known to be unreliable estimates of dwelling unfitness. Their indicators – the proportion of dwellings with three or less rooms, households with no fixed bath, households without exclusive use of a WC, and dwellings with a rating for property taxes at £13 or less – suggest that bad-quality housing meant small (cheaper) houses, alongside some amenity deficiencies. By implication, provision was undesirable for single elderly or young people, or even couples. This is not what many understand as inadequate housing. Yet, in the absence of better data, and despite questionable assumptions on what constituted poor accommodation, Burnett and Scott at least sought proxy measures to unlock insight on housing deprivation. For this, they merit commendation. However, their amenity indicators were not persuasive in detecting unfit dwellings. When, through the 1967 Housing Condition Survey, comparison with the physical condition of dwellings was made, dwellings decreed unfit for habitation did have less basic housing amenities, with 76.9% lacking an inside WC and 72.1% having no fixed bath. However, while the absolute proportion of dwellings in conurbations without an inside WC (32.8%) or fixed bath (34.5%) looked huge, these numbers were less horrifying placed beside the stock of conurbation dwellings (33.9%). The contrast fell far short of justifying a fixation with city deprivation (the relevant rural values were 18.6%, 19.9% and 20.5%; MHLG 1968b, p.98).

Yet, the convenience of focusing on amenity measures became a major feature in commentaries on poor housing. Insufficient coverage and inconsistent interpretation led to little insight on other dimensions of housing distress, so easily measurable amenity and occupancy indicators dominated reports on housing conditions, leading to the conclusion that bad housing was principally a city problem.[114] This

---

[114] This view featured regularly in ministerial statements. In 1963, the 38 councils recognised in 1955 as having 'serious' slum clearance problems were raised to 50; none a rural district (HCH 31 July 1963, Vol.682, col.105W). In 1966, the government prioritised 130 councils for house-build-

claim needs exploring, for, even given data inadequacies, amenity measures did expose issues about rural–urban differences.

2.4.4   Rural–Urban Disparities

It is pertinent to note rural–urban divergence across housing tenures. Tenure was not collected in national censuses until 1961, with links to local housing amenities added in 1971. The 1971 evidence gave clear pointers on private rental decline. Government estimates for England and Wales indicate the market share of this tenure fell from 45% to 17% from 1951–1973, compared with a 28%–52% rise in owner-occupation and gains from 18%–31% for the public sector.[115] Investigations of this declining role already exist (Harloe 1985), a few on rural areas (Bowler and Lewis 1987; Bevan and Sanderling 1996; Hancock 2002).[116] Disputes over causation there might be, but it is generally acknowledged that landlords thought rents too low to justify new-build or dwelling improvements.[117] Lower standards of accommodation resulted. For example, in England, the rate for exclusive use of hot water, a fixed bath or shower and an inside WC in 1971 was 89.4% under owner-occupation, 92.0% for council or new town dwellings and 55.9% for private rental. This unevenness might have had a minimal effect on rural–city contrasts, for private rental covered near identical shares of rural and city housing markets (21.3% for RDCs and 21.2% for county boroughs).[118] Yet high owner-occupation might have led to poorer rural amenities (56.7% of rural homes were owner-occupied against 45.6% in county boroughs, with the public sector at 22.1% and 33.1%, respectively). However, rural districts had superior amenities within tenures. Compared to exclusive amenity access in county boroughs of 85.5% (owner-occupation), 90.1% (public sector) and 46.2% (private rental), rural districts recorded 91.3%, 93.3% and 74.0%. For private rental, perhaps one reason was a stronger rural association with dwellings tied to

---

ing, with rural districts again having no presence (HCH 11 May 1966, Vol.728, col.96W-97W), as was the case when the list was revised (HCH 30 January 1967, Vol.740, col.27W-28W).

[115] HCH 10 April 1974, Vol.872, col.175W-76W. The values for 1951 do not add to 100 because accommodation rented with business premises was counted as 'other tenure'. Adding this category to private rental in 1951 meant the drop was from 53% to 17% for the period.

[116] Rural studies of private rental are slightly more numerous if housing associations are included (Richmond 1984; Cloke and Edwards 1985; Hoggart and Henderson 2005).

[117] For example, TNA HLG40/38 'Memo from H.A. Chapman to Tudor Owen on Visits to Hereford and Oxfordshire', undated c1926; TNA T227/805 'Scheme for Increases in Rents to Promote Repairs', undated c1953; HCH 22 March 1965, Vol.709, col.72-73.

[118] County boroughs (CBs) were essentially non-London cities. London's position was so different from county boroughs in general that it has been excluded from most comparisons as its inclusion distorts contrasts between rural districts and the cities nearest to them. For example, on tenure, 34.3% of London households lived in private rental in 1971 compared with 21.2% in CBs, with 25.0% and 31.3% in public sector homes and 40.6% and 45.6%, respectively, in owner-occupation. When London is included in 'city' figures in this volume, this is indicated clearly.

paid employment.[119] This might seem a strange comment, given antipathy towards tied accommodation (Fletcher 1969; Newby 1977), but evidence shows these units were more likely improved and better endowed than other rental options (Giles and Cowie 1960; Fletcher 1969). In part, this was because these homes were increasingly needed for skilled farm-workers (Newby 1972; Gasson 1975). Enhanced rural rental conditions might have also stemmed from more military bases in the countryside, as well as the homes of many farmers coming with a rented business.[120] If we added these contributions together, potentially, the gap between rural districts and smaller urban centres was breached. But the rural–city gap was large for private rental amenities, which fed into wider city–rural divergences.

This statement appears to contradict Carr-Saunders and associates' (1958, p.44) view that, for housing amenities, '... towns are generally better off than rural areas'. But the Carr-Saunders group was not writing about 1971. The most systematic evidence available to them would have been the 1951 census. As Table 2.4 shows, at that time data supported their conclusion. Despite this, even then official reports constructed an agenda about a concentration of unfit houses in cities, with the fact London had few reported unfit dwellings dismissed as '... no doubt partly due to the destruction of much slum property by enemy action during the War' (MHLG 1956, p.6). Over time, though, significant change occurred. Modification to variables describing housing amenities does not allow strict comparison across censuses, although density of occupation offers less definitional transposition, even if it only captures one living standard. Nonetheless, if the intention is comprehension of changing housing circumstances, this provides the longest time-span for

Table 2.4 Percent of households with/without named household amenities by English local government category, 1951

	London	CBs	UDCs-MBs	RDCs
Lack piped water	0.6	1.9	2.7	20.2
Lack or share piped water	26.7	15.9	13.4	26.8
Lack a fixed bath	33.0	37.6	31.6	46.1
Lack or share a fixed bath	51.5	45.2	37.5	48.3
Lack a WC	0.3	1.0	3.4	34.0
Lack or share a WC	28.5	16.5	13.5	37.5
Exclusive use of five basic amenities	44.4	52.2	60.1	45.6

Source: Computed from county reports in the 1951 population census
Note: 'London' was taken to be the counties of London and Middlesex

---

[119] This tenure category was distinguished in the 1961 census, when 12.3% of rural households lived in dwellings by virtue of their employment (a further 3.4% in dwellings rented with a farm or business), with equivalent CB values of 2.1% and 0.8%, respectively.

[120] For 1971, the English workforce in the armed forces was 3.9% for rural districts, compared with 0.8% for CBs and 1.3% for other urban areas. For farmers, 30% wholly rented their operation in 1971, which most likely came with accommodation, while 24% were part-owners, part-renters, for which the proportion renting a home was probably much smaller (Bowler 1992, p.100). Farmers constituted 5.7% of the male RDC workforce in 1971.

Table 2.5 Percentage of the English population in private residences living at 1.5 or more persons a room by local government category, 1931, 1951 and 1971

	London	CBs	UDCs-MBs	RDCs
1971	5.0	3.9	1.9	1.5
1951	10.2	10.4	7.3	7.7
1931	17.6	14.7	14.0	11.0

Source: Computed from county reports in the population censuses
Note: For 1931 and 1951 'London' was taken to be the counties of London and Middlesex. In 1971 the Greater London area was used

Table 2.6 Percent of households with/without named housing attributes by English local government category, 1971

	London	CBs	UDCs-MBs	RDCs
Exclusive use of three basic household amenities	75.7	78.2	86.3	87.4
Lack or share hot water supply	13.2	9.7	5.9	6.5
Lack or share a bath	19.4	14.0	8.7	8.3
Lack or share a flush WC	11.7	4.6	2.6	4.3
Sharing a dwelling	13.4	3.4	1.7	0.5

Source: Computed from county reports of the 1971 population census
Note: In 1971 the three basic amenities were hot water, a fixed bath or shower and an inside WC

comparisons using censuses. This temporal vision reveals transparent improvement over time (Table 2.5), with less rural housing stress on this dimension than in cities. Yet, while improvement occurred, there was divergence in rural trajectories and in end-conditions.

Alongside density of occupation, at first glance household amenities in rural England in 1971 looked superior to those in cities (Table 2.6). For smaller towns (UDCs-MBs), though, there was little to distinguish rural and urban. Further, the starkest contrast between city and countryside was for households sharing a dwelling. This represents one aspect of living conditions but only one. We see this when the absence of facilities is tabulated (Table 2.7). Thus, the disparity of 11.1% between London and rural districts in the proportion of households without exclusive access to a bath or shower drops to 1.4% for complete absence rather than exclusive access. Few might question a preference for sole access over sharing, but sharing might be preferred to absence, and it was sharing, not no supply that lay at the heart of rural–city differences (compare Tables 2.6 and 2.7). At one level, both the absence and the sharing of facilities was a 'management' issue, assuming building fabrics had a robustness that enabled improvement. Both absence and sharing could be improved through management if sufficient physically sound homes were available. 'Management' interventions will concern us when we examine home improvement policies but, for the present, the message to take forward is of relatively insignificant rural–urban disparities in the absence of amenities by 1971.

This stark statement should be investigated before we move on. A key reason is that the contexts of urban and rural residence varied. To explore this, housing indicators for all 1971 English districts were analysed. An area classification was

Table 2.7 Percent of households lacking key amenities by English local government category, 1971

	London	CBs	UDCs-MBs	RDCs
Lack a hot water supply	7.7	7.4	4.7	6.1
Lack a bath or shower	9.1	10.5	7.0	7.7
Lack a flush WC	0.2	0.3	0.5	3.5

Source: Computed from county reports of the 1971 population census

Table 2.8 Percent of districts by commuting – service-class type within English local government categories, 1971

		Local government category			
Service-class type	Out-commuting type	London	CBs	UDCs-MBs	RDCs
High-ranked	High relative volume	15.2	1.3	7.5	13.1
	Moderate relative volume	12.1	0.0	8.7	9.3
	Low relative volume	3.0	0.0	1.9	0.2
Mid-ranked	High relative volume	24.2	0.0	11.8	15.6
	Moderate relative volume	30.3	12.7	24.4	37.1
	Low relative volume	0.0	59.5	19.5	6.1
Low-ranked	High relative volume	3.0	0.0	5.9	0.2
	Moderate relative volume	15.1	10.1	11.4	11.7
	Low relative volume	0.0	16.5	8.7	6.6
All districts		100.0	100.0	100.0	100.0

Source: Computed from Registrar-General (2002)
Note: The source only provided data by basic Socio-Economic Group (SEG) for heads of household, which is not as fine-tuned as some other sources (including county reports of the population census). The service-class was computed as the percentage of heads of households (excluded if occupation was unclear) in the three SEG grades 'managers-owners of large establishments', 'self-employed professionals' and 'professional employees'. Commuting volumes were the percentage of employed residents in a district who worked outside the district. Across the 1198 English districts mean averages and standard deviations for both measures were computed. High-ranked (high volume) districts were those with values 0.75 standard deviations above the mean average for all districts, middle-level standings lay between −0.75 and +0.75 standard deviations from the mean, and low standing were below −0.75 standard deviations away

developed that focused on the potential importance of service-class and external influences on rural housing (Chap. 1). As described in Table 2.8, this typology exposed high, moderate and low dependence on non-local jobs, alongside uneven service-class compositions in each district. A significant proportion of districts, across all local government categories, were mid-ranked on a commuting – service-class scale,[121] but the essential point for the typology was identifying dissimilar

---

[121] This is what would occur if the distribution of values followed a normal curve. However, the process of classification requires the imposition of 'arbitrary' cut-off points on continuous variables. Using above or below 0.75 standard deviations from the mean as a cut-off is not common but service-class inflows into rural zones were lower and less widespread in 1971 than in later decades (Hoggart 1997), which favoured a less stringent cut-off. Using 1.0 standard deviations gave only 13 (out of 410) districts in the 'low out-commuting – low service-class' group, while the middling group (mid-ranked for both) contained 55.4% of all districts. So 'bulky' a centre-ground

rural contexts to see how far housing conditions varied. Wide-ranging service-class impacts on the countryside might be of relatively recent origin (Cloke and Thrift 1990; Murdoch 1995), but broader intrusions from wealthier (and sometimes less affluent) urbanites have a longer pedigree. For instance, as early as 1900, Biggleswade's Peel Estate had accommodation difficulties for labourers owing to demand from nearby towns,[122] Savage (1915, p.135) reported rural cottage insufficiency over at least 30 years because those living in towns 'rediscovered' the countryside, while the 1919 Runton Women's Village Council drew Erpingham's attention to houses suitable for villagers rented to those coming from far away for holidays or weekends.[123] Pressing the Cabinet on the issue of rural diversity, in 1918, the President of the Board of Agriculture was clear:

> The 657 Rural Districts of England and Wales, though classed as rural under the Public Health Acts, are not necessarily rural in conditions: still less are they of necessity predominantly agricultural in character. If in Rural Districts houses are required for a residential or industrial population, the satisfaction of that demand cannot be treated, and ought not to be treated, as a supply of agricultural cottages. The two different needs should be clearly and sharply distinguished, just as in the past the needs have been almost entirely met from two different sources. Speculative builders have supplied the one; agricultural landowners have supplied the other.[124]

By 1921, rural parts of counties like Surrey were '… already within the orbit of a newer suburban world where the traditional "norms" of agricultural society were considered unimportant in reality, even if the incomers saw themselves as living in a rural idyll of parson and squire' (Howkins 2003, p.57). Inter-war, urban interest in the countryside increased, although perhaps not concern for its economic well-being (Lowerson 1980; Sheail 1981; Moore-Colyer 1999). Even so, by the late-1930s, official agencies were questioning the meaning of 'rural', noting distinctions between more agricultural and more semi-industrial or residential territories.[125] Such were the impacts that some RDCs adjacent to towns built no council homes, whereas in other districts, standards of accommodation were low, with private enterprise not active (MoH 1944a, p.25). The taxonomy used here to explore divergence across the rural realm was designed to elucidate such trends. Given area

---

surrounded by small numbers at the 'edges' downplayed rural diversity. Using the 0.75 cut-off saw numbers at the 'extremes' increase to 27 districts for the lowest ranked districts on both variables and to 54 for the highest ranked, while the middling group covered 37.1% of all districts. Using one cut-off or the other did not alter conclusions. For instance, the percent of households with exclusive access to three basic household amenities in RDCs with the highest service-class and commuting scores fell if a 1.0 cut-off was used (from 91.3% to 91.1%), as it did for districts with the lowest scores on both dimensions (from 87.4% to 86.7%). Similarly, for households in private rental, values were 16.5% and 16.0% (highest scoring) and 32.6% and 35.0% (lowest scoring). The numbers changed slightly but the distributions deviated little.

[122] BRO X344/93 Letter from John Willmot to Viscount Peel, 18 April 1900.

[123] *NWP&ENS* 24 January 1919, p.4.

[124] TNA CAB24/43 GT3724 'Rural Housing', 25 February 1918, p.1.

[125] TNA HLG37/44 'Evidence of Neville Hobson, RDCA Executive Council Member', undated c1936, p.1.

classifications approach categorisation from dissimilar viewpoints (Craig 1985; Shucksmith and Henderson 1995), there is no sense that the scheme adopted here is the 'right' one. Its advantages lie in its conceptual simplicity and its alignment with key themes in this investigation. Significantly, however, as Table 2.8 demonstrates, rural districts were dispersed across varied combinations of service-class densities and commuter belt dependencies. Comparable urban centres existed, although more amongst smaller places than county boroughs or London.

What Table 2.9 highlights is the manner in which the commuting – service-class categories were linked to dissimilar socio-economic attributes. Very evidently, districts with a high service-class presence exhibited signs of more wealth, as signified by superior housing conditions and an occupational make-up of more small business owners and fewer manual workers. No surprise, exactly half the rural districts with high out-commuting and service-class numbers were in either Cheshire or counties bordering Greater London, as were 44.7% with high service-class but moderate commuting scores (more if you include Hampshire and Sussex in London's commuter field). Yet, service-class volumes were sufficiently meagre that they did not 'decide' housing conditions.[126] Rather, the service-classes appear to have been drawn to rural areas with better accommodation. They might contribute to upgrading existing dwellings (Phillips 2005) but, as private estates on village edges testified (Crichton 1964; Popplestone 1967; Radford 1970; Ambrose 1974), incomers often purchased new(er) homes in larger settlements (Cloke 1979; Herington and Evans 1979).[127] Common images about service-class in-migrants note the attractions of quality-of-life considerations, of area 'amenity', of separation from the 'vices' of cities and of an expected comforting new lifestyle (Perry et al. 1986; Hughes 1997). In other words, with consumption styles attributed to the countryside, although how far these were specifically rural merits questioning (Halfacree 1994, 2004). But associations between service-class growth and rurality came in different forms. Evidence indicates movement into small villages often had housing motives and involved short distance transfers (Herington and Evans 1979; Dunn et al. 1981; Glasser 2002), possibly from within the same district or a neighbouring area. Longer distance migration had thinner volumes and was often employment-related (e.g. Findlay et al. 1999; DTZ Pieda Consulting 1998). These movements might be directed towards the rurality of a district with a new home on a 'suburban' estate. 'Rurality' could have dissimilar meanings for different types of residential relocation.

Even so, Table 2.9 reveals that a strong service-class presence at the district level was aligned with distinctive housing profiles compared with more traditionally 'isolated' rural zones (viz. generally lower commuting links, smaller in size and with

---

[126] The mean average percentage for heads of household in the workforce in the service-classes was 9.3% for the 1,198 English districts, with the standard deviation at 4.7%, so to be in the group of 'high ranked' service-class districts only required a 12.8% district share of the workforce.

[127] I am aware of little research on this point but note Walford's (2001, pp.332–33) evidence on mid-Wales that 70% of migrant households moved into a home newer than the one they had left. While this conclusion was not specific to the service-class, it offers an intriguing pointer.

Table 2.9 Diversity across English rural districts by commuting – service-class type, 1971

	High service-class		Middle-rank service-class			Low service-class	
	High out-commuting	Moderate out-commuting	High out-commuting	Moderate out-commuting	Less out-commuting	Moderate out-commuting	Less out-commuting
Percent of households							
Exclusive use of three basic amenities	91.3	89.6	87.5	87.0	84.1	80.7	84.7
Lack or share bath or shower	5.7	7.1	7.6	8.9	10.9	12.7	10.8
Lack or share inside WC	7.3	8.7	11.2	11.0	13.6	17.3	12.8
Percent heads of households employed							
Farmers	3.5	4.5	4.0	7.4	14.0	9.0	14.8
Farm labourers	2.5	3.7	3.1	5.7	7.2	8.4	9.7
Non-farm manual	35.1	36.3	48.8	40.2	36.1	50.8	33.8
Armed Forces personnel	1.3	1.5	1.1	3.4	4.6	3.1	7.8
Small business owners-managers	13.5	12.1	9.3	10.1	9.1	6.8	9.4
Service-class	16.7	14.8	9.7	9.0	7.1	4.2	4.8
Percent of economically active residents (excluding those sick)							
Seeking work	2.5	2.6	3.2	3.1	3.1	4.4	3.3
Percent all employed residents							
Work outside the district	64.9	49.8	64.0	45.7	23.6	41.5	23.0
Percent of heads of household in-migrants to district							
In previous five years	27.8	27.0	26.3	23.1	15.6	15.0	16.4
District populations							
Average population size	33,459	30,504	30,652	21,356	13,256	18,928	11,814
% aged 0–14 years	13.8	14.0	14.3	13.6	13.2	13.9	13.2
% aged 65 or more	14.4	14.7	14.5	16.5	17.7	16.6	17.1

(continued)

Table 2.9 (continued)

| | High service-class | | Middle-rank service-class | | | Low service-class | |
	High out-commuting	Moderate out-commuting	High out-commuting	Moderate out-commuting	Less out-commuting	Moderate out-commuting	Less out-commuting
% women aged 15 plus in paid work	29.9	29.2	29.0	27.2	26.3	25.2	24.7
% employed women working at least 30 hours a week	57.5	57.7	60.9	59.8	61.0	62.9	60.9

Source: Computed from Registrar-General (2002)

Note: Service-class – commuting types had to represent more than one district for inclusion. The smallest shown had 25 districts

more in agriculture). As well as low service-class numbers, such 'traditional' districts had low rates of in-migration, some with notable armed forces numbers and
generally poorer housing (Table 2.9). These districts fell into three different 'camps'.
Two were distinguished by low levels of out-commuting but had either low or moderate service-class numbers, while the third had moderate out-commuting but few
service-class residents. This last group stood apart from the others, as it constituted
a category with a strong working-class base but with few farm-workers (Table 2.9).
The four counties with its largest representations were Cornwall, Lincolnshire,
Norfolk and Yorkshire's West Riding. This gives a clue to the mixed character of
this group. It contained districts with a stronger manufacturing or mining component, as with Easington, Sedgefield (both Durham), Blackwell, Clowne (both
Derbyshire), Hemsworth and Thorne (West Riding), all of which had 70% or more
of their workforces as manual non-farm, or East Dean (Gloucestershire c60%),
Goole (West Riding), Isle of Axholme (Lincolnshire) and St Austell (Cornwall, last
three c50%). Yet, the category also contained districts with a more characteristically
agricultural look, like Erpingham, some with high farm-worker numbers (like
Boston and Spalding in Lincolnshire, both over 30% of the workforce) but others
with low representations (Liskeard in Cornwall and Worksop in Nottinghamshire
with under 10%). This was a mixed group, then, with some 'industrial' components.[128] This was not so for the two categories with the least out-commuting. Both
might be characterised as 'traditionally rural', with 56% of districts in the moderate
service-class category found in Devon, Shropshire and Yorkshire's North Riding,
and just under half in the low service-class category in Cornwall, Northumberland,
Westmorland and the North Riding. Looking within counties, the main distinction
between the two low-commuting categories was location, with districts holding less
service-class residents tending to be in more peripheral zones, such as North
Cornwall or the Pennines, rather than lowland farming areas. The difference was not
large, leaving a sense of gradation rather than distinction. The main separation was
with the group with a stronger 'industrial' component.

A point to take from this is that high service-class populations were not necessarily linked to high out-commuting (see London in Table 2.8). This is not surprising
in conurbations, where journeys to work and other social interactions create complex flows, which often cross administrative boundaries within an urban aggrega-
tion. Perhaps popular imagery focuses on suburban to central city commuting, but
the reality of city networks is more complicated, with 'districts' sending and receiving substantial numbers (Herington 1984). Even in rural areas, commuting has been
driven less by single-city targets than is often assumed, with many dispersed or
multi-centred configurations (Champion et al. 1987; Henderson and Hoggart 2003).
Yet understanding commuting behaviour requires attention to reporting units. Cities
are generally larger than small towns and villages, and contain more job openings,
especially as key foci for the organisation of economic activity (Berry 1970; Hodge

---

[128] Increasing the standard deviation scores from 0.75 to 1.0 halved the number of districts in this
group but left unchanged the three counties with the most members, with the 'industrial' tone of
the group remaining.

and Whitby 1981). As they offer less local work opportunities, proportionately more outflows should emanate from rural than from urban areas. But neither cities nor rural districts are equal in size. In 1971, for example, the smallest county borough in England had just 33,175 inhabitants (Canterbury), whereas the largest had 1,014,664 (Birmingham). City centres in conurbations helped raise the average size of England's 79 county boroughs to 169,710 inhabitants. This was not far off Basildon (Essex), the largest UDC-MB at 129,308, with the largest RDC at 102,547 (Meriden, Warwickshire). On average, UDCs-MBs (22,783) and RDCs (23,798) had fewer inhabitants than cities, as both contained districts with few residents (the smallest were Eye MB in Suffolk with 1655 and Masham RDC in North Yorkshire with 1471). We might expect commuting externally to have been greater in Masham than in Meriden. Yet, the lowest rate of out-commuting was in smaller places, with rural districts with low out-commuting volumes having a mean average 1971 population of just 12,672. Moderate out-commuting districts averaged 22,327 and areas with the highest out-commuting 31,696. Rather than smaller districts having higher outflows, the reverse occurred. This cannot be divorced from underlying socio-economic conditions. If anything, places with substantial service-class numbers relied more heavily on external job opportunities, as did some districts with mid-level service-class volumes. This was relevant in distinguishing the three counties receiving most attention in this investigation (Table 2.10). Proximity to London put rural and urban Hertfordshire in a different position for both service-class compositions and out-commuting than Norfolk, with Bedfordshire in an intermediate

Table 2.10 Number of districts by commuting – service-class type in rural and urban Bedfordshire, Hertfordshire and Norfolk, 1971

		Hertfordshire		Bedfordshire		Norfolk	
Service-class type	Commuting type	Urban centres	Rural districts	Urban centres	Rural districts	Urban centres	Rural districts
High-ranked	High relative volume	6	7	1			
	Moderate relative volume	8	2	1			1
	Low relative volume	1					
Mid-ranked	High relative volume	1	1	1	2		3
	Moderate relative volume	3	1	3	1	5	4
	Low relative volume	3		3		6	
Low-ranked	Moderate relative volume					1	6
	Low relative volume					4	1

Source: Computed from Registrar-General (2002)

Note: There were no 'low service-class, high-commuting districts' in the three counties

position. In Table 2.10, the two investigated districts in Hertfordshire (Braughing and Hatfield) had high service-class standing with middling commuting (Hatfield having many local jobs; Table 1.1). In Bedfordshire, Ampthill and Biggleswade were not adjacent to a large town, with Ampthill moderate on service-classes but high on out-commuting, while Biggleswade was mid-ranked for both. In Norfolk, Walsingham was in the group with the lowest service-class and commuting volumes (Table 1.1). Erpingham and Smallburgh had little to distinguish them, with both having moderate commuting volumes, although they fell just either side of the cut-off for service-class numbers with Erpingham falling in the lowest group and Smallburgh the middle. Hence, these districts offer a range of contexts in which to explore the evolution of housing conditions.

Before turning to this, further insight on the national scene is merited. Tables 2.6 and 2.7 make the point that there were few differences by 1971 in housing amenities in rural districts and in smaller urban centres. Table 2.11 reinforces the point using the single indicator of exclusive access to three basic amenities. 'Controlling' for dissimilarities in service-class and commuting circumstances reveals little to distinguish rural districts from smaller urban centres in the same commuter–service-class category, although a good part of the divergence between cities and the countryside came from unevenness in the sharing of dwellings (Table 2.6). Looking at a broader range of housing conditions, Table 2.12 reinforces the point that the real rural–urban gap in amenities was between London and the countryside. Conditions in other cities and towns were not so far apart from rural districts. This is a point to retain for later, as priorities for housing investment regularly failed to acknowledge proximity in the circumstances of most urban environments and the countryside.

Where obvious rural–urban disparity existed was in housing tenure. Perhaps surprisingly, there was an exception to this, which was for owner-occupation (Table 2.13). Variability here was linked more to service-class composition than country or town residence, with higher ownership, if anything, found in urban centres across service-class – commuting types. In fact, where service-class incidence was high, rates of public sector tenancy were little different, being as high or higher

Table 2.11 Percent of households with exclusive use of basic household amenities by local government category and commuting – service-class type, 1971

Service-class type	Commuting type	London	CBs	UDCs-MBs	RDCs
High-ranked	High relative volume	83.4		93.3	91.3
	Moderate relative volume	81.5		90.0	89.6
Mid-ranked	High relative volume	71.8		87.7	87.5
	Moderate relative volume	79.5	82.6	86.3	87.0
	Low relative volume		79.4	86.2	84.1
Low-ranked	Moderate relative volume	66.8	75.0	78.3	80.7
	Low relative volume		73.4	84.7	84.7

Source: Computed from Registrar-General (2002)

Note: Service-class – commuting types had to represent more than one district for inclusion. The lowest shown was in London with four districts

Table 2.12 Percent of households with/without named housing attributes by English local government category in low service-class, moderate out-commuting districts, 1971

	London	CBs	UDCs-MBs	RDCs
Exclusive use of three basic household amenities	66.8	75.0	78.3	80.7
Lack or share hot water supply	18.7	10.4	7.0	9.5
Lack or share a bath	26.2	15.5	12.6	12.7
Lack or share an inside WC	24.7	23.7	20.2	17.3
Sharing a dwelling	15.0	1.5	0.4	0.3

Source: Computed from Registrar-General (2002)

Table 2.13 Percent of households by tenure in English rural districts by commuting – service-class type, 1971

		Owner-occupied		Public sector tenants		Private rental tenants	
Service-class type	Commuting type	RDCs	UDCs-MBs	RDCs	UDCs-MBs	RDCs	UDCs-MBs
High-ranked	High relative volume	64.5	69.9	19.0	16.4	16.5	13.7
	Moderate relative volume	59.1	60.6	21.2	21.1	19.6	18.3
Mid-ranked	High relative volume	58.8	58.7	24.2	28.5	17.0	12.8
	Moderate relative volume	55.6	55.8	20.9	27.5	23.5	16.7
	Low relative volume	47.5	51.5	21.7	31.5	30.8	17.0
Low-ranked	Moderate relative volume	44.1	43.6	29.4	37.8	26.5	18.6
	Low relative volume	47.9	49.3	19.6	34.5	32.6	16.1

Source: Computed from Registrar-General (2002)
Note: Service-class – commuting types had to represent more than one district for inclusion. This comparison is limited to UDCs-MBs as CBs did not appear for many of the service-class – commuting categories (Table 2.8)

in rural than in urban districts.[129] Associations between rurality and low public sector housing were evident where out-commuting was low, particularly if there were few service-class workers (viz. in 'traditional farming areas'). Notably, though, the rural and urban districts that comprised these low-commuting districts came from different parts of England. The concentration of the highest-ranked service-class rural districts around London and in Cheshire has already been noted. This was also the case for UDCs-MBs, for which 56.9% in this class were in these counties. But

---

[129] This comment is restricted to contrasts with boroughs and UDCs, as local authorities with high representations for the service-classes were singularly absent in county boroughs (Table 2.8). London boroughs in the top category for the service-classes also saw fewer public sector homes than RDCs, with 4–5% less in the housing stock.

for the lowest-ranked commuting districts, rural–urban distributions were different. The lowest out-commuting districts in 'peripheral' zones (bottom row in Table 2.13) were most populous in Cornwall, Northumberland, Westmorland and the North Riding, whereas comparable urban concentrations were in different counties; Devon and Wiltshire alone accounted for just over a third of relevant UDCs-MBs. Urban 'isolationism' did not occur in the midst of similarly placed RDCs, for only 11.1% of low-ranked RDCs were in these counties. In low-ranked service-class centres with some 'industrial' tones (moderate out-commuting), the divergence was even sharper, with 58.4% of UDC-MBs in 'old industrial' counties like Derbyshire, Durham, Lancashire, and Yorkshire's West Riding (which only accounted for 18.8% of RDCs in this category). That the core of this urban group had a strong manual worker, 'old industrial and mining' tone is captured in the importance of public sector tenancy, with 68.8% in the urban group having household compositions above the national average of 28.0% for this tenancy. The 'industrial' component of the rural district counterpart was weaker, with 29.2% above the national average. Some of these looked similar to their urban cousins (e.g. Ryder 1979, 1984), but only 6.3% of these RDCs had more than 40% of households as public sector tenants compared with the urban figure of 33.8%. The message then is the same across virtually all the contexts in Table 2.13, namely there was little to distinguish rural from urban for owner-occupation within categories, but rural districts generally had less public sector rental and more private rental, albeit for areas with more service-class residents, rental differences were minor, while areas with little out-commuting relied more heavily on private rental.[130] On average, living conditions were better where the service-class composition was higher and, 'independently', where districts were more integrated through commuting into the wider economy. These patterns draw attention to the peculiarity of what have often been called 'traditional rural districts', with their substantial reliance on agriculture, their generally small size, little in-migration and weighty reliance on private rental. These districts were primarily distinguished in Table 2.9 by their slight engagement with external employment, viz. by their relative 'isolation'. Thus, while rural districts were not so different from urban centres of a similar size, where local government units had more proximate responsibilities and resources (RDCs and UDCs-MBs; Tables 2.11 and 2.12), within rural (and urban) districts, there were disparities in local circumstances.

As the three counties focused on occupied different positions as regards commuting and service-class representations (Table 2.10), they might be expected to reveal dissimilar housing conditions. At one level, this was true. While, for

---

[130] In agricultural counties, much of this private rental was tied accommodation. In 1961, RDCs in the 'agricultural counties' of Lincolnshire, Norfolk and Suffolk had 16.3%, 14.2% and 16.0% of all households, respectively, living in such dwellings. By comparison, the three 'peripheral or upland counties' of Cornwall, Devon and the North Riding scored 7.5%, 10.0% and 13.6%. Even in 1961, the agricultural counties provided more council homes, with RDC shares at 19.9%, 19.1% and 18.4%, respectively, compared with 11.5%, 13.6% and 14.1% for RDCs in the three 'peripheral or upland' counties.

owner-occupied dwellings, there were no sharp divides, there was a downward gradation in quality indicators from the county with the highest service-class occupancy (Hertfordshire) through the middle-ranked county (Bedfordshire) to the lowest ranked (Norfolk), with rural districts, especially those away from large towns in Norfolk, generally recording poorer conditions than urban centres (Table 2.14). This effect was perhaps less pronounced for public sector dwellings, although Norfolk again stood apart with generally poorer rural household amenities. Significantly, for both Bedfordshire and Hertfordshire, little separated urban from rural in the availability of public sector homes, whereas in Norfolk, rural provision was well below urban. But it was private rental where the greatest differences in amenities existed. How this is interpreted depends on the measures focused on. If exclusive access to three basic amenities is taken as a single indicator, then rural districts had superior amenities than their urban counterparts by some way (Table 2.14). If specific facilities, like access to a bath or shower, are looked at, the same point holds, provided attention is directed at exclusive access. But a focus on the absence of basic facilities reveals little rural–urban differentiation. As at the national level, by 1971, the primary distinction between the rural and the urban came from more shared facilities in urban centres than in the countryside.

2.5   Contributing to Contrivance

For the 75 years investigated in this book, a dominant housing condition was shortage. For Whitehead (1997, p.8), the central policy emphasis over this period was increasing numbers. Only in the 1970s were there more dwellings than households. This was an improvement on a technical 1951 deficit of more than 700,000 dwellings, which was itself a serious under-estimate (Cullingworth 1960, p.8). Yet, faced with shortfalls, the policy response was weak. Numerically, this was seen in 1970s' 'surpluses' being comprised of dwellings that fell below acceptable standards.[131] Then, there were multiple homes meeting these standards owned by single households. How many second homes there were is unclear, as data were not collected systematically, but worrying geographical concentrations were acknowledged, with home acquisitions by urban residents heightening rural difficulties from early in the Century.[132] Of course, supply problems were also socially concentrated, especially amongst the less well-paid. Writing about 1939, but pointing to earlier and later tendencies, Mowat (1955, p.509) observed that: 'For the more prosperous families of the working-class, and for the middle-class, there need no longer be a housing problem'. Householders might grumble about design or fittings, they might prefer

---

[131] As expected in the 1960s (e.g. TNA CAB129/132 C(67)125 'Public Expenditure. Proposed Adjustments', 7 July 1967, p.2).

[132] Government estimates in 1972 put second home ownership at 1%, which was small relatively but significant for a nation with housing shortages. Locally there were concentrations, as with 11% in the Lake District (Clark 1982) and over 20% in north Norfolk (Coleman 1982).

Table 2.14 Housing diversity in rural districts of Bedfordshire, Hertfordshire and Norfolk, 1971

	Hertfordshire		Bedfordshire			Norfolk		
	Urban	Rural commuter	Urban	Rural commuter	Rural other	Urban	Rural commuter	Rural other
Owner-occupied								
% with exclusive use of three basic amenities	94.6	95.6	92.4	91.0	91.0	84.6	91.7	82.4
% lack a bath or shower	2.5	2.7	3.4	6.1	6.3	9.6	5.7	13.6
% lack or share a bath or shower	3.0	3.0	4.5	6.4	6.5	10.0	5.8	13.8
% lack a flush WC	0.2	0.9	0.1	2.9	1.8	0.7	3.9	9.8
% lack or share a flush WC	1.2	1.5	1.2	3.9	2.3	1.3	4.1	10.3
% of all households in this tenure	48.3	47.5	60.0	59.5	52.0	40.4	69.8	50.4
Public sector tenants								
% with exclusive use of three basic amenities	97.0	96.9	93.0	95.6	89.1	90.5	86.4	88.2
% lack a bath or shower	0.8	0.5	1.8	1.7	1.8	1.6	10.5	6.9
% lack or share a bath or shower	1.4	0.9	2.1	3.4	2.5	1.9	10.6	7.2
% lack a flush WC	0.0	0.0	0.1	0.5	1.1	0.1	9.8	5.9
% lack or share a flush WC	0.4	0.3	0.3	1.4	1.4	0.2	9.8	6.0
% of all households in this tenure	38.4	37.2	22.6	21.8	24.7	40.0	14.3	21.5
Private rental tenants								
% with exclusive use of three basic amenities	65.3	80.1	54.6	70.6	68.0	54.9	67.3	65.6
% lack a bath or shower	16.9	11.5	21.7	20.4	25.9	31.1	26.4	29.3
% lack or share a bath or shower	28.1	14.6	36.6	21.3	26.8	37.7	27.3	29.8
% lack a flush WC	0.4	2.9	0.4	7.7	8.8	1.2	18.6	22.0
% lack or share a flush WC	11.8	6.4	15.2	9.5	10.3	8.5	19.6	22.9

(continued)

Table 2.14 (continued)

	Hertfordshire		Bedfordshire			Norfolk		
	Urban	Rural commuter	Urban	Rural commuter	Rural other	Urban	Rural commuter	Rural other
% of all households in this tenure	13.3	15.3	17.4	18.7	23.3	19.5	15.9	28.1

Source: Computed from county reports of the 1971 population census

Note: 'Urban' districts were county boroughs, boroughs and urban district councils. 'Rural commuter' districts were those immediately adjacent to the largest towns in the county (Bedford, Great Yarmouth, Luton and Norwich), with all rural districts in Hertfordshire taken to be in commuter territory, given London's proximity and the county's numerous urban centres. All the adjacent districts in Bedfordshire and Norfolk were high volume out-commuting areas. They account for every district in Norfolk of this kind and two of the three in Bedfordshire

dwellings above their pay grade or fret about threatened changes to their neighbourhood, but they benefited overall from national housing mechanisms geared to address the wants of the better-paid (LeGrand 1982). A multitude of failings in housing production and maintenance came to light over the decades, but the real spur to change arose following the First Word War. Despite different reactions to the peculiarities of that time, government responses across Europe shared many features. In particular, there was an early prioritisation of building new homes for those who could pay for them, alongside a steep rise in government intervention (Harloe 1995, Ch.2). In many countries, social housing institutions became closely integrated into state procedures and practices, which placed Britain apart as local government had primacy in substituting for private sector shortcomings. For rural areas, this function was critical, for, throughout the inter-war years, private builders shunned virtually all but 'suburbanising' involvements in the countryside.[133] That the whole nation started the century with a housing stock almost wholly in private ownership mattered little. Owner-occupation was out of reach for the less materially wealthy,[134] while private rental trended towards poor-quality and a dwindling stock (Harloe 1985). Whether responses to this were through direct state action or indirect support and regulation was not critical, as the experiences of other European nations showed (Doling 1997; Golland 1998). What was essential was that there was clarity

---

[133] TNA HLG37/44 'Evidence of Neville Hobson, RDCA Executive Council Member', undated c1936, pp.4-5; TNA HLG40/26 'Rural Housing', 5 November 1942.

[134] Gardiner (2010, p.304) held that only one-fifth of working-class households could afford owner-occupation in 1939, which was less than in 1915, although organisations supporting working-class home purchases were well established (Samy 2012). The issue was often not monthly payments but high deposits, which were 20–30% until improved credit arrangements brought reductions in the 1930s (Scott 2008a), which increased working-class interest (Benson 1989; Wellings 2006). While it could be cheaper to buy a new suburban home than rent in the late-1930s (Scott 2008a, p.9), extra costs from suburban living and unforgiving commitments to owner-occupation brought strains on household budgets that required extra jobs or limits on family size (e.g. Scott 2008b). 'For all its benefits, home ownership was an ideal to which most working people could scarcely begin to aspire' (Bowley 1945, p.175; Benson 1989, p.77).

over the nature and magnitude of dwelling deficiencies, and that they were responded to effectively.

This chapter has been written to lay down foundations for what is to follow. The central issues were to highlight what underscored national convictions that the state had to intervene in housing as never before, drawing out the responsibilities laid on local government for this task, and highlighting how rural areas were integral to intervention impulses. But as many failed government actions bear witness (e.g. Hall 1980), it is easy to pontificate on the need for action but if effective solutions are sought, this requires accurate information on the problem at hand and an under-standing of the processes through which amelioration can take place (e.g. Pressman and Wildavsky 1984). On these grounds, responding to housing deficiencies is not a straightforward task. For one, there are a variety of dimensions to the concept of housing inadequacy. For another, as the remainder of this book indicates, respond-ing to them is coloured by political blinkers. Concepts like 'non-affordability', 'need', 'necessity' and 'available resources' are politically charged. At core, though, even those of different political persuasion commonly accept basic principles about housing deficiencies. Disagreement arises over their scale and how to respond to them. Variance of opinion can draw on the best information available or it can stay rooted in ideology, ignoring the 'reality' of the circumstances public policy seeks to address. One aim of this chapter was to draw attention to shortcomings in the data governments relied on to make decisions about priorities. This theme is considered in more detail in Chap. 6 but has a particular relevance here, as these deficiencies fed into understandings about the magnitude of rural housing problems. In particu-lar, weak specification and/or measurement of housing traits like 'shortage' and 'poor physical condition' worked against effective rural policy responses. Thin data favoured undue reliance on readily available indicators, like household amenities. The absence of adequate information might have left policy-makers in the dark, but the inconvenience this created pales beside the discomforts and health problems associated with living in damp, ill-ventilated and otherwise deficient homes.[135] Yet, not until 1967 was systematic evidence collected on the physical fabric of dwell-ings, despite awareness that council numbers on unfitness were massaged by politi-cally inspired interpretations of 'achievability' and 'affordability'.[136] Throughout the decades, ministers repeatedly asserted that securing information on housing

---

[135] As an illustration, when 170 houses were inspected in the village of Braughing in 1921, 90 had water on the premises, it was within 100 yards for 70, and for 10 more than 100 yards away (HRO 6/1/5 HaRDCM 7 July 1921, p.130). A similar survey for the smaller village of Furneux Pelham recorded 22 with water on the premises, 34 within 100 yards and 21 farther away (HRO 6/1/5 HaRDCM 6 October 1921, p.146).

[136] Harold Macmillan illustrated the point when asserting that: '... since the outbreak of the last War very little has been done in slum clearance, because of the tremendous pressure of housing needs and the unwillingness of authorities to turn out people who already had houses, however bad' (HCH 24 March 1953, Vol.513, col.641).

conditions was too costly to merit the effort.[137] Decisions on investment were consequently based on limited government knowledge.

Adding to the insight others have offered (Dunn et al. 1981; Cullingford and Openshaw 1982; Shucksmith and Henderson 1995), this chapter has cautioned that there was no single 'rural housing' problem. There were also some wafer-thin distinctions between rural and urban. In some contexts, rural–urban contrasts were sharp (as with manufacturing-mining districts and more 'peripheral or upland' rural equivalents), but in others there was little between them (as in places with service-class concentrations). Where disparity existed, some researchers have linked weak rural housing commitments to differences in local political party control (as in public sector provision; Phillips and Williams 1982, p.35; Shucksmith and Henderson 1995, p.21). Indications from this chapter cast doubt on this assertion. The same applies to assumptions that those employing more farm-workers thwart alternative housing options (e.g. Rose et al. 1976). Such claims suggest that local socio-economic and political leaders contrive to create a rural landscape to perpetuate their vested interests. What this chapter starts to demonstrate is that attempts at contrivance did not only operate at the local level. As later chapters explore, convenient assumptions about bad housing concentrations in cities helped justify policies that worked to the detriment of rural districts. In the same way, lack of precision over what was 'housing shortage' and the failure to measure 'physical deficiencies' reliably contributed to a void in national policy-makers' understanding of rural difficulties. That local policy-makers were not immune from similar contrivances should not be doubted. But the magnitude of housing divergence across rural districts should point us towards exploring why they occurred. This is what we now turn to, starting with an exploration of how the locally influential responded to housing conditions. When engaging with this analysis, the reader should carry forward the message that, whatever local leaders sought to achieve, they operated within a national environment characterised by loose concepts and slack measurement. If local leaders were looking to contrive a particular rural world, they had to contend with national worldviews that favoured outcomes in which rural areas played a small part. Any engineering by one side had to interact with machinations on the other, and one was a much bigger player than the other.

---

[137] House of Commons statements on this include: Alfred Mond (HCH 5 July 1922, Vol.156, col.393W-94W); Neville Chamberlain (HCH 14 March 1923, Vol.161, col.1542); Kingsley Wood (HCH 11 March 1925, Vol.181, col.1323); and, Harold Macmillan (HCH 27 November 1952, Vol.508, col.95W).

References

Addison P (1994) The road to 1945: British politics and the Second World War, rev edn. Pimlico, London

Ambrose PJ (1974) The quiet revolution: social change in a Sussex Village 1871–1971. Chatto & Windus, London

Benson J (1989) The working class in Britain, 1850–1939. Longman, Harlow

Bentham GC (1986) Socio-tenurial polarization in the United Kingdom, 1953–83: the income evidence. Urban Stud 23:157–162

Berry BJL (1970) Commuting patterns: labour market participation and regional potential. Growth Chang 1(4):3–10

Bevan M, Sanderling L (1996) Private renting in rural areas. University of York Centre for Housing Policy, York

Biggleswade Rural District Council (1914) Annual report of the medical officer of health and sanitary inspector 1913. Biggleswade

Bird H (1976) Residential mobility and preference patterns in the public sector of the housing market. Trans Inst Br Geogr 1:20–33

Booth P, Huxley M (2012) 1909 and all that: reflections on the Housing, Town Planning, Etc. Act 1909. Plan Perspect 27:267–283

Bottle B, McNicholas T, Mulheirn L, Ormrod D, Ruddock J (1974) Homelessness in Kent. Shelter, London

Bowers JK (1985) British agricultural policy since the Second World War. Agric Hist Rev 33:66–76

Bowler IR (1992) The agricultural significance of farm size and land tenure. In: Bowler IR (ed) The geography of agriculture in developed market economies. Routledge, London, pp 85–108

Bowler IR, Lewis GJ (1987) The decline of private rented housing in rural areas: a case study of estate villages in Northamptonshire. In: Lockhart D, Ilbery BW (eds) The future of the British rural landscape. Geo Books, Norwich, pp 115–136

Bowley M (1941) Local authorities and housing subsidies since 1919. Manch Sch 12:57–79

Bowley M (1945) Housing and the state 1919–1944. Allen & Unwin, London

Branson N (1975) Britain in the nineteen twenties. Weidenfeld & Nicolson, London

Branson N (1979) Poplarism 1919–25: George Lansbury and the councillors' revolt. Lawrence & Wishart, London

Burnett J (1986) A social history of housing 1815–1985, 2nd edn. Methuen, London

Burnett FT, Scott SF (1962) A survey of housing conditions in the urban areas of England and Wales 1960. Sociol Rev 10:35–79

Calder A (1969) The people's war: Britain 1939–1945. Pimlico, London

Campbell J (1987) Nye Bevan: a biography. Hodder & Stoughton, London

Cannadine D (1990) The decline and fall of the British aristocracy. Yale University Press, New Haven

Carr-Saunders AM, Jones DC, Moser CA (1958) A survey of social conditions in England and Wales. Clarendon, Oxford

Champion AG, Green AE, Owen DW, Ellin DJ, Coombes MG (1987) Changing places: Britain's demographic, economic and social complexion. Edward Arnold, London

Chase M (1993) 'Nothing less than a revolution?': Labour's agricultural policy In J. Fyrth (ed) Labour's high noon: the government and the economy 1945–51. Lawrence & Wishart, London, pp78–95

Chester L, Fay S, Young H (1967) The Zinoviev letter. Heinemann, London

Clapson M (1998) Invincible green suburbs, brave new towns: social change and urban dispersal in postwar England. Manchester University Press, Manchester

Clark G (1982) Housing and planning in the countryside. Wiley, Chichester

Clarke JJ (1924) The new Housing Act, 1924. Town Plan Rev 11(2):119–127

Clarke JJ (1931) Slums and the Housing Act, 1930. Town Plan Rev 14(3):163–193

Cloke PJ (1979) Key settlements in rural areas. Methuen, London

Cloke PJ, Edwards G (1985) Rural housing associations and the rented sector market: a mid-Wales case study. Cambria 12(2):139–153

Cloke PJ, Thrift NJ (1990) Class and change in rural Britain. In: Marsden TK, Lowe PD, Whatmore SJ (eds) Rural restructuring: global processes and their responses. David Fulton, London, pp 165–181

Coleman R (1982) Second homes in north Norfolk. In: Moseley MJ (ed) Power, planning and people in rural East Anglia. University of East Anglia Centre for East Anglian Studies, Norwich, pp 97–117

Committee on National Expenditure (1931) Report. Cmd 3920. HMSO, London

Committee on the Increase of Rent & Mortgage Interest (War Restrictions) Acts (1920) Report. Cmd 658. HMSO, London

Connor LR (1936) Urban housing in England and Wales. J R Stat Soc 94:1–65

Council for Research on Housing Construction (1934) Slum clearance and rehousing: the first report of the Council for Research on Housing Construction. P.S. King & Son, London

Craig J (1985) A 1981 socio-economic classification of local and health authorities of Great Britain. OPCS Studies in Medical & Population Subjects 48. HMSO, London

Crichton RM (1964) Commuters' village: a study of community and commuters in the Berkshire village of Stratford Mortimer. David & Charles, Dawlish

Crossman R (1975) The diaries of a Cabinet Minister: volume one – Minister of Housing 1964–66. Hamish Hamilton and Jonathan Cape, London

Crotch WW (1901) The cottage homes of England: the case against the housing system in rural districts, 2nd edn. P.S. King & Son, London

Cullingford D, Openshaw S (1982) Identifying areas of rural deprivation using social area analysis. Reg Stud 16:409–418

Cullingworth JB (1960) Household formation in England and Wales. Town Plan Rev 31:5–26

Danziger R (1988) Political powerlessness: agricultural workers in post-war England. Manchester University Press, Manchester

Daunton MJ (1984) Introduction. In: Daunton MJ (ed) Councillors and tenants. Leicester University Press, Leicester, pp 1–38

Department of the Environment (1977) Housing policy: technical volume 1. HMSO, London

Doling J (1997) Comparative housing policy: government and housing in advanced industrialized countries. Macmillan, Basingstoke

Drudy PJ (1978) Depopulation in a prosperous agricultural region. Reg Stud 12:49–60

Drudy PJ, Wallace DB (1971) Towards a development programme for remote rural areas: a case study in north Norfolk. Reg Stud 5:281–288

Dunford M (1995) Metropolitan polarization, the north-south divide and socio-spatial inequality in Britain: a long-term perspective. Eur Urb Reg Stud 2:145–170

Dunn MC, Rawson M, Rogers A (1981) Rural housing: competition and choice. Allen & Unwin, London

English J, Madigan R, Norman P (1976) Slum clearance: the social and administrative context in England and Wales. Croom Helm, London

Evans A, Duncan S (1988) Responding to homelessness: local authority policy and practice. HMSO, London

Fielding S (1992) What did 'the people' want? the meaning of the 1945 General Election. Hist J 35:623–639

Findlay AM, Short D, Stockdale A (1999) Migration impacts in rural England. Countryside Agency Publications, Wetherby

Fletcher P (1969) The agricultural housing problem. Soc Econ Adm 3:155–166

Flowerdew R, Boyle PJ (1992) Migration trends for the West Midlands: suburbanisation, counterurbanisation or rural depopulation. In: Stillwell J, Rees PH, Boden P (eds) Migration processes and patterns: volume two. Belhaven, London, pp 144–116

Forrest R, Murie A (1992) Change on a rural council estate: an analysis of dwelling histories. J Rural Stud 8:53–65

Gardiner J (2010) The thirties: an intimate history. Harper Press, London

Gasson RM (1975) The provision of tied cottages. Occasional paper 4. University of Cambridge Department of Land Economy, Cambridge

Giles AK, Cowie WJG (1960) Some social and economic aspects of agricultural workers' accommodation. J Agric Econ 14(2):147–169

Glasser ME (2002) Migration through time: a residence history analysis of a rural population. PhD thesis University of Leicester

Golland A (1998) Systems of housing supply and housing production in Europe: a comparison of the United Kingdom, The Netherlands and Germany. Ashgate, Aldershot

Green FE (1920) A history of the English agricultural labourer 1870–1920. P.S. King & Co., London

Greve J, Page D, Greve S (1971) Homelessness in London. Scottish Academic Press, Edinburgh

Griffith JAG (1966) Central departments and local government. Allen & Unwin, London

Guttsman WL (1968) The British political elite. MacGibbon & Kee, London

Halfacree KH (1994) The importance of 'the rural' in the constitution of counterurbanization: evidence from England in the 1980s. Sociol Rural 34:164–189

Halfacree KH (2004) Rethinking 'rurality'. In: Champion AG (ed) New forms of urbanization: beyond the urban-rural dichotomy. Ashgate, Aldershot, pp 285–304

Hall PG (1980) Great planning disasters. Weidenfield & Nicolson, London

Hancock P (2002) The private rental sector in rural areas. In: Lowe S, Hughes D (eds) The private rented sector in a new century. Policy Press, Bristol, pp 65–77

Harloe M (1985) Private rented housing in the United States and Europe. Routledge, London

Harloe M (1995) The people's home? social rented housing in Europe and America. Blackwell, Oxford

Harris R (2012) 'Ragged urchins play on marquetry floors': the discourse of filtering is reconstructed, 1920s–1950s. Hous Policy Debate 22:463–482

Haynes RM, Gale S (2000) Deprivation and poor health in rural areas: inequalities hidden by averages. Health Place 6:275–285

Henderson SR, Hoggart K (2003) Ruralities and gender divisions of labour in Eastern England. Sociol Rural 43:349–378

Herington J (1984) The outer city. Harper & Row, London

Herington J, Evans DM (1979) The spatial pattern of movement in 'key' and 'non-key' settlements. Working Paper 3. Loughborough University Department of Geography, Loughborough

Hinton J (1983) Labour and socialism: a history of the British labour movement 1867–1974. Wheatsheaf, Brighton

Hinton J (1988) Self-help and socialism: the squatters' movement of 1946. Hist Work J 25:100–126

Hodge I, Whitby MC (1981) Rural employment: trends, options, choices. Methuen, London

Hoggart K (1997) The middle classes in rural England 1971–1991. J Rural Stud 13:253–273

Hoggart K, Henderson SR (2005) Excluding exceptions: housing non-affordability and the oppression of environmental sustainability? J Rural Stud 21:181–196

Hollis P (1987) Ladies elect: women in English local government 1865–1914. Clarendon, Oxford

Holmans AE (1987) Housing policy in Britain: a history. Croom Helm, London

Hooson DJM (1958) The recent growth of population and industry in Hertfordshire. Trans Inst Br Geogr 25:197–208

Horn P (1984) The changing countryside in Victorian and Edwardian England and Wales. Athlone, London

Howkins A (1985) Poor labouring men: rural radicalism in Norfolk 1870–1923. Routledge, London

Howkins A (2003) The death of rural England: a social history of the countryside since 1900. Routledge, London

Howkins A, Verdon N (2009) The state and the farm worker: the evolution of the minimum wage in agriculture in England and Wales, 1909–24. Agric Hist Rev 57:257–274

Hughes A (1997) Rurality and 'cultures of womanhood'. In: Cloke PJ, Little J (eds) Contested countryside cultures. Routledge, London, pp 123–137

Humphries J (1987) Inter-war house building, cheap money and building societies: the housing boom revisited. Bus Hist 29:325–345

Humphrys G (1968) A map of housing quality in the United Kingdom. Trans Inst Br Geogr 43:31–36

Jennings JH (1971) Geographical implications of the municipal housing programme in England and Wales 1919–39. Urban Stud 8:121–138

Jones B (2010) Slum clearance, privatization and residualisation: the practices and politics of council housing in mid-twentieth-century England. Twent Century Br Hist 21:510–539

Keith-Lucas B, Richards PG (1978) A history of local government in the twentieth century. Allen & Unwin, London

Kendall D (1963) Portrait of a disappearing English village. Sociol Rural 3:157–165

Kennett DH (1978) Portrait of Bedfordshire. Robert Hale, London

Kirby DA (1979) Slum housing and residential renewal: the case of urban Britain. Longman, London

Knox PL (1975) Social well-being: a spatial perspective. Oxford University Press, Oxford

Land Enquiry Committee (1913) The land - volume one: rural, 3rd edn. Hodder & Stoughton, London

LeGrand J (1982) The strategy of equality: redistribution and the social services. Allen & Unwin, London

Linsley B (2005) Homes for heroes: housing legislation and its effects on housing in rural Norfolk 1918–1939. PhD thesis University of East Anglia

Lipsky M (1980) Street-level bureaucracy. Russell Sage Foundation, New York

Lowerson J (1980) Battles for the countryside. In: Gloversmith F (ed) Class, culture and social change: a new view of the 1930s. Harvester, Brighton, pp 258–280

Lyman RW (1957) The first Labour government 1924. Chapman & Hall, London

Mackintosh JM (1936) Rural housing. Northamptonshire County Council, Northampton

Malpass P (2000) Public utility societies and the Housing and Town Planning Act, 1919: a re-examination of the introduction of state-subsidized housing in Britain. Plan Perspect 15:377–392

Marshall JL (1968) The pattern of housebuilding in the inter-war period in England and Wales. Scott J Polit Econ 15:184–205

Martin JG (1938) Memorandum upon the Housing (Financial Provisions) Act, 1938 (revised November 1938). National Housing & Town Planning Council, London

Martin RL (1988) The political economy of Britain's north-south divide. Trans Inst Br Geogr 13:389–418

McCullin D (2007) In England. Jonathan Cape, London

McKibbin R (2010) Parties and people: England 1914–1951. Oxford University Press, Oxford

Merrett S (1979) State housing in Britain. Routledge & Kegan Paul, London

Merrett S (1982) Owner-occupation in Britain. Routledge & Kegan Paul, London

Miliband R (1961) Parliamentary socialism: a study in the politics of Labour. Merlin Press, London

Mingay GE (1990) The rural slum. In: Gaskell SM (ed) Slums. Leicester University Press, Leicester, pp 92–143

Ministry of Health (1920) First annual report, 1919–1920: part II – housing and town planning. Cmd 917. HMSO, London

Ministry of Health (1924) Circular to local authorities on the Housing (Financial Provisions) Act, 1924. Circular 520. HMSO, London

Ministry of Health (1931a) Twelfth annual report, 1930–1931. Cmd 3937. HMSO, London

Ministry of Health (1931b) Model byelaws issued from the Ministry of Health: XIIIc improvement areas. HMSO, London

Ministry of Health (1931c) Report of the Inter-Departmental Committee on the Rent Restrictions Acts. Cmd 3911. HMSO, London

Ministry of Health (1932a) Thirteenth annual report, 1931–1932. Cmd 4113. HMSO, London

Ministry of Health (1932b) Report of the Committee on Local Expenditure (England and Wales). Cmd 4200. HMSO, London

Ministry of Health (1933a) Fourteenth annual report, 1932–1933. Cmd 4372. HMSO, London

Ministry of Health (1933b) Housing Act, 1930: part I. Circular 1331. HMSO, London

Ministry of Health (1934) Fifteenth annual report, 1933–1934. Cmd 4664. HMSO, London

Ministry of Health (1935) Sixteenth annual report, 1934–1935. Cmd 4978. HMSO, London

Ministry of Health (1936a) Seventeenth annual report, 1935–1936. Cmd 5287. HMSO, London

Ministry of Health (1936b) Rural housing; report of the Central Housing Advisory Committee. HMSO, London

Ministry of Health (1936c) Housing Act, 1935: report on the overcrowding survey in England and Wales 1936. HMSO, London

Ministry of Health (1937a) Report of the Inter-Departmental Committee on the Rent Restrictions Acts. Cmd 5621. HMSO, London

Ministry of Health (1937b) Rural housing: second report of the Rural Housing Sub-Committee of the Central Housing Advisory Committee. HMSO, London

Ministry of Health (1939a) Twentieth annual report, 1938–1939. Cmd 6089. HMSO, London

Ministry of Health (1939b) The demolition of individual unfit houses in rural areas: report of the Demolition Procedure Sub-Committee of the Central Housing Advisory Committee. HMSO, London

Ministry of Health (1944a) Rural housing: third report of the Rural Housing Sub-Committee of the Central Housing Advisory Committee. HMSO, London

Ministry of Health (1944b) Private enterprise housing: report of the Private Enterprise Sub-Committee of the Central Housing Advisory Committee of the Ministry of Health. HMSO, London

Ministry of Health (1944c) Rural housing. Circular 64/44. HMSO, London

Ministry of Health (1946a) Rent control in England and Wales. HMSO, London

Ministry of Health (1946b) Housing (Financial and Miscellaneous Provisions) Act, 1946. Circular 118/46. HMSO, London

Ministry of Health (1947) Reconditioning in rural areas: fourth report of the Rural Housing Sub-Committee of the Central Housing Advisory Committee. HMSO, London

Ministry of Housing & Local Government (1956) Report of the Ministry of Housing and Local Government for the Year 1955. Cmd 9876. HMSO, London

Ministry of Housing & Local Government (1957) Report of the Ministry of Housing and Local Government for the Year 1956. Cmnd 193. HMSO, London

Ministry of Housing & Local Government (1961) Housing in England and Wales. Cmnd 1290. HMSO, London

Ministry of Housing & Local Government (1965) Report of the Committee on Housing in Greater London. Cmnd 2605, Milner-Holland Report. HMSO, London

Ministry of Housing & Local Government (1966) Our older homes: a call for action. HMSO, London

Ministry of Housing & Local Government (1967) Report of the Ministry of Housing and Local Government 1965 and 1966. Cmnd 3282. HMSO, London

Ministry of Housing & Local Government (1968a) Old houses into new homes. Cmnd 3602. HMSO, London

Ministry of Housing & Local Government (1968b) Housing condition survey: England and Wales, 1967. Econ Trends 175:87–99

Ministry of Reconstruction (1918a) Housing in England and Wales: Memorandum by the advisory housing panel on the emergency problem. Cd 9087. HMSO, London

Ministry of Reconstruction (1918b) Reconstruction problems 2: housing in England and Wales. HMSO, London

Ministry of Town & Country Planning (1947) Report of the National Parks Committee (England and Wales). Cmd 7121. The Hobhouse report. HMSO, London

Ministry of Works (1945) Temporary housing programme. Cmd 6686. HMSO, London

Ministry of Works & Planning (1942) Report of the Committee on Land Utilisation in Rural Areas. Cmd 6378. Scott report. HMSO, London

Moore-Colyer RJ (1999) From Great Wen to Toad Hall: aspects of the urban-rural divide in inter-war Britain. Rural Hist 10:105–124

Mortimer J (1993) The changing mood of the working people. In: Fyrth J (ed) Labour's high noon: the government and the economy 1945–51. Lawrence & Wishart, London, pp 243–254

Mowat CL (1955) Britain between the wars, 1918–1940. Methuen, London

Murdoch J (1995) Middle class territory? some remarks on the use of class analysis in rural studies. Environ Plan A27:1213–1230

National House Building Committee (1924) Report on the present position in the building industry, with regard to the carrying out of a full housing programme, having particular reference to the means of providing an adequate supply of labour and materials, Cmd 2104. HMSO, London

Newby HE (1972) The low earnings of agricultural workers. J Agric Econ 23:15–24

Newby HE (1975) The deferential dialectic. Comp Stud Soc Hist 17:139–164

Newby HE (1977) The deferential worker: a study of farm workers in East Anglia. Allen Lane, London

Niner P (1989) Homelessness in nine local authorities: case studies of policy and practice. HMSO, London

Nivola PS (1978) Distributing a municipal service: a case study of housing inspection. J Polit 40:59–81

Olechnowicz A (1997) Working class housing in England between the wars. Clarendon, Oxford

Orbach LF (1977) Homes for heroes: a study of the evolution of British public housing 1915–1921. Seeley Service & Co., London

Owen N (2007) MacDonald's parties: the Labour Party and the 'aristocratic embrace', 1922–31. Twent Century Br Hist 18:1–53

Pacione M (1980) Differential quality of life in a metropolitan village. Trans Inst Br Geogr 5:185–206

Parkinson M (1985) Liverpool on the brink: one city's struggle against government cuts. Policy Journals, Hermitage

Pedley WH (1942) Labour on the land: a study of the developments between the two great wars. P.S. King & Staples, London

Penning-Rowsell EC (1997) Who 'betrayed' whom? power and politics in the 1920/21 agricultural crisis. Agric Hist Rev 45:176–194

Perkin H (1989) The rise of professional society: England since 1880. Routledge, London

Perry R, Dean K, Brown B (1986) Counterurbanisation: international case studies of socio-economic change in rural areas. Geo Books, Norwich

Phillips M (2005) Differential productions of rural gentrification: illustrations from north and south Norfolk. Geoforum 36:477–494

Phillips DR, Williams AM (1982) Rural housing and the public sector. Gower, Farnborough

Pieda Consulting DTZ (1998) The nature of demand for housing in rural areas. Report for the Department of the Environment. Transport & the Regions, Edinburgh

Pooley GC, Irish S (1984) The development of corporation housing in Liverpool 1869–1945. University of Lancaster Centre for North West Regional Studies, Lancaster

Popplestone G (1967) Conflict and mediating roles in expanding settlements. Sociol Rev 15:339–355

Powell M (1995) Did politics matter? municipal public health expenditure in the 1930s. Urban Hist 22:360–379

Pressman, J.L. & Wildavsky, A. (1984) Implementation: how great expectations in Washington are dashed in Oakland; or, why It's amazing that federal programs work at all, this being a saga of the Economic Development Administration as told by two sympathetic observers who seek to build morals on a foundation. University of California Press, Berkeley

Pugh M (2008) 'We danced all night': a social history of Britain between the wars. Bodley Head, London

Radford E (1970) The new villagers: urban pressure on rural areas in Worcestershire. Frank Cass, London

Ravetz A (2001) Council housing and culture: the history of a social experiment. Routledge, London

Registrar-General (2002) 1971 census aggregate data. UK Data Service. https://doi.org/10.5257/census/aggregate-1971-1

Rhodes RAW (1981) Control and power in central-local government relations. Gower, Farnborough

Richardson HW (1967) Economic recovery in Britain 1932–39. Weidenfeld & Nicolson, London

Richmond P (1984) Alternative tenures in rural areas: the role of housing associations. In: Clark G, Groenendijk J, Thissen F (eds) The changing countryside. Geo Books, Norwich, pp 339–349

Rose D, Saunders P, Newby HE, Bell C (1976) Ideologies of property. Sociol Rev 24:699–730

Ryder R (1979) Council house building in County Durham 1900–1939: the local implementation of national policy. MPhil thesis University of Durham

Ryder R (1984) Council house building in County Durham 1900–39. In: Daunton MJ (ed) Councillors and tenants. Leicester University Press, Leicester, pp 40–100

Samy L (2012) Extending home ownership before the First World War: the case of the Co-operative Permanent Building Society, 1884–1913. Econ Hist Rev 65: 168-193

Savage WG (1915) Rural housing. T. Fisher Unwin, London

Savage WG (1919) Tuberculosis and housing in rural districts. Br J Tuberc 13:160–162

Scott P (2008a) Marketing mass home ownership and the creation of the modern working-class consumer in inter-war Britain. Bus Hist 50:4–25

Scott P (2008b) Did owner-occupation lead to smaller families for interwar working-class households? Econ Hist Rev 61:99–124

Scott P, Newton LA (2012) Advertising, promotion, and the rise of a national building society movement in interwar Britain. Bus Hist 54:399–423

Seaman LCB (1966) Post-Victorian Britain, 1902–1951. Methuen, London

Self RC (2006) Neville Chamberlain: a biography. Ashgate, Aldershot

Shanks N, Smith SJ (1992) British public policy and the health of homeless people. Policy Polit 20:35–46

Sheail J (1981) Rural conservation in inter-war Britain. Clarendon, Oxford

Shears RT (1936) Housing the agricultural worker. J R Agric Soc Engl 97:1–12

Shucksmith M, Henderson M (1995) A classification of rural housing markets in England. HMSO, London

Simmonds AGV (2002) Raising Rachman: the origins of the Rent Act. Hist J 45:843–868

Skinner D, Langdon J (1974) The story of Clay Cross. Bertrand Russell Peace Foundation, Nottingham

Smith HL (1992) The politics of Conservative reform: the equal pay for equal work issue, 1945–55. Hist J 35:401–415

Spalding R (2018) Narratives of delusion in the political practice of the Labour left 1931–1945. Cambridge Scholars Publishing, Newcastle-upon-Tyne

Swann B (1972) Local initiative and central control: the insulin decision. Policy Polit 1:55–63

Swenarton M (1981) Homes fit for heroes: the politics and architecture of early state housing in Britain. Heinemann, London

Swenarton M, Taylor S (1985) The scale and nature of the growth of owner-occupation in Britain between the wars. Econ Hist Rev 38:373–392

Taylor AJP (1965) English history 1914–1945. Clarendon, Oxford

Thomas CJ (1966) Some geographical aspects of council housing in Nottingham. East Midland Geogr 4:88–98

Thresh JC (1891) The housing of the working classes in the Chelmsford and Maldon rural sanitary districts. Chelmsford & Maldon Rural Sanitary Authorities, Chelmsford

Tilley MF (1947) Housing the country worker. Faber & Faber, London

Townsend P, Davidson N (1982) The Black Report: inequalities in health. Penguin, Harmondsworth

Tylecote AB (1982) German ascent and British decline 1870–1980: the role of upper class structure and values. In: Friedman E (ed) Ascent and decline in the world-system. Sage, Beverly Hills, pp 41–67

Walford NS (2001) Reconstructing the small area geography of mid-Wales for an analysis of population change 1961–1995. Int J Popul Geogr 7:311–338

Ward SV (1988) The geography of interwar Britain: the state and uneven development. Routledge, London

Wellings F (2006) British housebuilders: history and analysis. Blackwell, Oxford

White J (1977) When every room was measured: the overcrowding survey of 1935–36 and its aftermath. Hist Work J 4:86–94

Whitehead CME (1997) Changing needs, changing incentives: trends in the UK housing system. In: Williams P (ed) Directions in housing policy. Paul Chapman, London, pp 7–21

Williams CCP (2012) Gentlemen and players: the death of amateurism in cricket. Weidenfeld & Nicolson, London

Yelling JA (2000) The incidence of slum clearance in England and Wales, 1955–85. Urban Hist 27:234–254

Chapter 3
Rural Exceptionalism? Local Leader Priorities for Country Homes

Abstract Commentary on rural England accuses rural council inaction as a primary cause of poor housing, despite a legal requirement that councils respond to local needs. The accusation of vested interests hangs in the air, with rural districts providing fewer council homes than urban areas. Asking if this was because rural leaders lacked awareness of demand, it is concluded that this interpretation is untenable. Councils received many requests for more dwellings and had applicant lists revealing dissonance between the demand for and the supply of council dwellings, which grew over time. The question of whether councils needed to act, given landed estates provided many homes, is raised. Some estates did assist council-building through land grants and the like but their own contribution to the housing stock declined. Indeed, demand from other employers increased, providing even more need for council supply. Focusing primarily on the inter-war period, how individual councils responded is explored. This reveals diversity, ranging from performances as strong as cities, prioritisation of supply by private-owners, active building of small dwellings within farm-workers' rent capacities and limited activity associated with poor resources and low wages.

Keywords Housing demands · Waiting lists · Landed estates · Key-worker homes · Housing policy diversity

A core premise behind many interpretations of rural housing distress is local leaders' reluctance to support dwelling improvements for the less wealthy. Early in the twentieth-century, rural and urban were arguably little different in this regard, with many city studies finding propertied interests working against state regulation of or direct involvement in working-class housing (e.g. Dale 1980; Finnigan 1980; Smith et al. 1986). Here, as with the countryside, the common cause amongst the propertied classes was opposition to regulatory 'impositions' on private ownership and increased property taxes. In rural areas, such sentiments were reportedly sustained by fears that new working-class homes would diminish worker dependence on tied cottages (Hollis 1987, p.390; Saunders et al. 1978). As the century progressed, the rise of the Labour Party offered the prospect of housing progress for the

© Springer Nature Switzerland AG 2021   95
K. Hoggart, *A Contrived Countryside*, Local and Urban Governance,
https://doi.org/10.1007/978-3-030-62651-8_3

working-classes, especially as the Party's leadership shed nineteenth-century beliefs that life in the countryside was healthy and happy compared with towns (Griffiths 2007, p.233), but in the countryside party politics was weak (Grant 1977), with no-party councillors often holding office for extended, unchallenged periods of time (Lee 1963; Johnson 1972; Axford 1978).[1] Little wonder that many commentators ascribed weak rural housing performance to indifferent, even hostile, local leadership (e.g. Rose et al. 1976). The link between rural leaders and efforts to change housing conditions is the focus of this chapter.

Analysis of this issue requires making allowance for links between intention and feasibility. As shown in Chap. 2, acknowledgement of how many dwellings were deemed unfit could be penetrated by expectations of whether replacement homes would be approved or could be afforded (Parker and Mirrlees 1988, p.368). In such contexts, assessing leadership effects requires attention to intention and hope as much as action. If we assume direct links between (say) new-build completions and leadership commitment, we neglect other influences, like population decline, insufficient resources or national interventions. If each conspired against a council, its leaders might be viewed as under-performing when they had a strong commitment to housing advancement. Likewise, what could seem like strong local housing actions might disguise lethargy or ineptitude hidden underneath external drivers producing change (Niner 1975). In later chapters, attention is given to varied demand conditions, like population change, incomes or household preferences (Chap. 4) as well as to the capacities of councils and builders to produce housing change (Chap. 5). The national priorities (Chap. 6) and mechanisms for achieving change (Chap. 7) imposed on local outcomes are also explored. For this chapter, the focus is on what rural leaders sought to achieve.

Addressing this issue, the chapter comprises three parts. The first concerns how far rural leaders were aware of quantitative or qualitative housing inadequacies. It will be shown they had every opportunity to be mindful of housing distress. The second section explores views on responsibility for addressing deficiencies. This encompasses values disposing leaders towards private or public sector intervention, alongside beliefs about who should have acted. Set within such value dispositions, the final section examines whether there was substance to the claim that rural leaders were reluctant to push for better housing, especially for those of limited means.

---

[1] In the politically charged atmosphere of the 1945 General Election, more than 60% of RDC councillor seats were not contested (Baker 1953, p.185). Increased local political party involvement, alongside local government reorganisation in 1974 (Bristow 1978), lessened this tendency; yet, even in 2019, *The Times* (30 April, p.8) reported that 12 of 39 councillors in Fenland were unopposed, with eight similar posts in each of Rutland, West Suffolk and Wychavon.

3.1 Identifying Housing Distress

Layton (1961) observed that English local government has more opaque statutory duties for services like housing than it does for others, like education. Councils have had responsibilities to inspect and act on deficiencies in local housing since the nineteenth-century (Keith-Lucas and Richards 1978), with the scope of council action reviewed and, for the period under investigation, frequently extended over time (Cullingworth 1966). While 1919 introduced councils to new responsibilities for direct intervention, specification of what constituted 'appropriate' action was left largely to local initiative. This at least is how governments have portrayed the local–national relationship. In reality, this picture was punctured repeatedly when the government had strong preferences. In 1919, a key desire was to secure better knowledge of housing deficiencies:

> Medical Officers of Health were requested to submit a specially full report for the year 1919, and, in particular, to give detailed information in reference to general housing conditions, overcrowding, the fitness or unfitness of houses and the ameliorative measures taken in their respective areas. (MoH 1921, p.75)

Following specific legislation, like the 1935 Act on overcrowding (MoH 1936b), or recommendations from national committees (like Hobhouse Report calls for post-war rural housing surveys; MoH 1944a), governments made further demands on councils for census-like tabulations. Official messages at times bestowed resulting reports with almost a halo of revelation to spur councils into energetic fulfilment of government dreams:

> For over twenty years, the Local Authority have had the duty of inspecting and recording the condition of all working-class property in their area. The records kept in accordance with this duty should now provide a complete picture of the Borough or District. The Local Authority should, therefore, be able to take immediate action. (MoH 1933b, pp.1–2)

Yet, there was substantial variability in both the coverage and the quality of surveys. As one General Inspector cautioned the Ministry:

> You may say, 'but the Sanitary Inspector ought to know all the cases of unfit houses or overcrowded houses'. Perhaps he ought, but in fact I feel convinced that in many cases owing to his numerous duties he cannot have this complete knowledge. The only way he can get it would be by periodically making house-to-house visits to every house in his area, and he has not time to do this.[2]

If deficiency lists were problematical, determining appropriate action was more so. Here, national agencies had more reason to challenge accounts, for councils generally relied on Treasury funding for programme implementation. A 1932 memorandum from the Rural Housing Advisory Committee's Secretary illustrated the point:

> The reports made by the Inspectors show that the applications, as was to be expected, are based on widely different forms of data and in some instances, it would appear, merely on

---

[2]TNA HLG40/19 Letter from A.G. Haywood [Knaresborough] to E.C.H. Salmon, 16 November 1931.

a general impression of the situation. The general effect of the inquiries made is to show that the urgent need for houses is approximately 60 per cent of the number for which applications have been received …[3]

At pinch-points, when support for rapid action was high, staffing problems often contributed to uneven reports, as the 1944 Minister of Health acknowledged:

I have no reason to suppose that, with their limited staffs, local authorities generally are not doing all they can to inform themselves of the housing position in their districts … [however] I should propose when conditions permit to remind local authorities of their duty under Section 5 of the Housing Act, 1936, to carry out periodical inspections of the housing in their districts and to give them advice in the matter.[4]

Such difficulties perhaps weakened national agents' understanding of local conditions. This did not mean there was a lack of local awareness.

Before 1919, councils had a responsibility to identify district housing needs.[5] This did not involve continuous counts or inspections (MHLG 1966, p.5). Systematic inspections were expected no more than once in five years, perhaps then limited to units suspected of defaults.[6] These did not give councils surety over housing distress, as evinced by the number of surveys they instigated, but they offered more security than relying on citizen communications. As the 1927 Walsingham Medical Officer of Health reported: 'Where time allowed a regular house-to-house inspection was the only efficient means to discover grave sanitary defects, as most tenants hesitated to make formal complaints through fears of their landlords'.[7] Offering a more regular short-cut, parish councils were asked to report on housing needs. Even when rural provision was a central national concern, as when agricultural worker dwellings were favoured under the 1938 Housing (Financial Provisions) Act (Martin 1938), councils were keen to identify shortfalls through quick-fire surveys using parish councils.[8] In between national initiatives, rural districts instigated their own reviews. Thus, while the MoH (1944a, p.32) correctly asserted that: '… apart from the survey of overcrowding carried out in 1935–36, which was directed to the size of existing houses and the number of their occupants, and not to their structural

---

[3] TNA HLG40/20 'Rural Housing Advisory Committee Secretary's Memorandum', 1 January 1932.

[4] HCH 2 March 1944, Vol.397, col.1568. Such difficulties were regularly reported locally, as for Ampthill (*WR&WSR* 24 April 1945, p.1) or drew requests for extra staff (e.g. BRO RDBwM1/25 BiRDCM 12 May 1954, p.108).

[5] As noted at a 1914 Hatfield meeting, every quarter the Inspector of Nuisances was supposed to make a systematic inspection of the district and submit the results to Council (HRO RDC7/1/6 HtRDCM 1 January 1914, pp.155–56). The 1930 Housing Act added a further layer of demands by requiring county councils to review housing conditions in RDCs (HCH 5 March 1931, Vol.249, col.579). Slackness over surveys was indicated by periodic reaffirmations that reviews were needed, as with Ampthill resolving that the Housing Manager and Sanitary Inspector commence '… at once, and carry out a regular and periodical examination of all council houses' (BRO RDAM2/22 ARDCHCM 27 November 1950).

[6] For example, BRO RDAR7/5 Ampthill Special and Staffing Committee 12 July 1965.

[7] *FakPost* 20 May 1927, p.5.

[8] See BRO RDAM2/20 ARDCHCM 30 May 1938; HRO RDC3/2/1 BrRDCPHHCM 19 May 1938, p.265; BRO RDBwM1/13 BiRDCM 19 October 1938, pp.395–96.

condition, there has never been a thorough survey of housing conditions in this country on a national basis', in 1943 councils like Braughing and Erpingham had already begun their surveys of post-war needs.[9] Ad hoc surveys additionally supported housing responses;[10] alongside instructions that staff undertake 'regular and periodic' inspections,[11] sometimes with parish council input.[12] Requests from single parishes could prompt a wider review,[13] with councils not averse to advertising to encourage residents to make housing needs known.[14]

3.1.1 Parish Requests for Action

Councils received a barrage of housing requests from women's groups,[15] farmers' organisations,[16] landowners,[17] MPs,[18] Agricultural Executive Committees,[19] trade

---

[9] HRO RDC3/2/2 BrRDCPHHCM 18 February 1943, p.566; *WR&WSR* 30 November 1943, p.1.

[10] This continued to the final years of the old local government system, when in 1974 former rural and urban districts were re-organised into larger authorities (Dearlove 1979). See, for example, NRO DC22/2/30 SmRDCM 25 May 1971, p.100 and BRO RDAR8/54 ARDCMOHar 1973, p.11.

[11] For instance, BRO RDAM2/22 ARDCHCM 27 November 1950.

[12] For example, NRO DC13/5/72 ERDCHCM 18 January 1927, pp.32–33; NRO DC19/6/68 WRDCHCM 30 January 1961.

[13] BRO RDAM2/23 ARDCHCM 20 July 1961.

[14] For example, NRO DC13/5/72 ERDCHCM 27 August 1929, p.290. Walsingham advertised regularly, preferring this to parish waiting lists in the early-1920s (NRO DC19/6/11 WRDCM 31 October 1923, p.72 in binding; TNA HLG40/19 'Applications for Special Assistance Received from RDCs in Norfolk and East Suffolk', undated c1931, p.20; NRO DC19/6/63 WRDCHCM 16 May 1945, p.5).

[15] As in Smallburgh (NRO DC22/2/7 SmRDCM 21 January 1919, p.213), Biggleswade Town (*BC&BG* 22 June 1923, p.1), Ampthill (*W&DR* 23 February 1943, p.2); 27 April 1943, p.3; 31 October 1944, p.1) and Braughing (HRO RDC3/1/2 BrRDCM 7 December 1944, pp.431–32; *H&EO* 7 June 1947, p.8) as well as indirectly in submissions to national agencies (MoH 1937, p.31; TNA HLG37/48 'National Federation of Women's Institutes Evidence', October 1942; TNA HLG37/157 Letter from Norfolk Women's Housing Council Secretary to Sub-Committee on Housing Standards Secretary, 19 October 1959).

[16] On the Beds and Hunts Farmers' Union, BRO RDBwM1/16 BiRDCM 23 May 1945, p.471; BRO UDSM1/3 SaUDCM 25 June 1945, p.238.

[17] NRO DC22/2/11 SmRDCM 1 May 1928, p.110.

[18] For example, A.T. Lennox-Boyd MP on Ampthill, *W&DR* 26 August 1933, p.7.

[19] For example, NRO DC13/5/75 ERDCHCM 3 June 1946, p.54; BRO RDBwM1/18 BiRDCM 8 October 1947, p.502; TNA MAF147/4 Letter from Norfolk Agricultural Executive Committee Assistant Secretary to Erpingham RDC Clerk, 8 February 1951.

unions,[20] public sector units[21] and private companies.[22] These communications often contained straightforward requests but many expressed disappointment or outrage over non-inclusion in council programmes. Table 3.1 provides an indication of the patterning of such requests, in this case from parish councils (the most regular communicators). To interpret this table, a number of points need making. First, entries only tabulate council minute records of parish councils formally requesting new dwellings for their patch. If a single parish requested homes more than once a year, which was common, this counted as one entry. But, if requests were made in four different years in a decade, this counted as four. Second, where it was clear responses were parish returns to a council-initiated survey, they were not counted. Such entries were often self-evident in council minutes, being presented as lists or indicated as responses to a council survey. Of course, there is no certainty over request numbers. There might be over-reporting if a time-lag existed between a council survey and a parish's response or under-reporting if requests did not come from the parish clerk (the most common method) but were made in a council meeting by a councillor representing the parish.[23] Council minutes might also be opaque over parish 'demands'. It follows Table 3.1 is only indicative. Local newspapers reported many occasions when a parish council request was made, yet this was not recorded in council minutes. Most likely, the list underestimates but it still signifies that councils received pungent housing demands.

Even if Table 3.1 under-reports, it sends a strong message. First and foremost, note the scale of approaches made to councils for more dwellings. Recall that this is just one aspect of parish calls for housing improvement; requests to eliminate bad housing, to improve the existing stock and to upgrade household amenities would expand the list. Added to which, parish councils were just one agent drawing attention to the need for housing action. As for patterns, the 1910s were a light period for requests, partly due to the First World War but more significantly owing to the high

---

[20] For example, after the Second World War in Biggleswade, by the National Union of Agricultural Workers (BRO RDBwM1/19 BiRDCM 16 June 1948, p.86) and the Biggleswade and District Joint Trades Council (BRO RDBwM1/21 BiRDCM 25 January 1950, p.32).

[21] Less common requests came from the National Institute of Agricultural Engineering at Silsoe (BRO RDAM2/22 ARDCHCM 10 April 1946), or armed forces (e.g. the RAF at Chicksands, BRO RDBwM1/17 BiRDCM 14 August 1946, p.113, the anti-aircraft camp at Weybourne, *NNN* 17 October 1952, p.1, and the USAF base at Sculthorpe, NRO DC19/6/67 WRDCHCM 11 June 1956, p.77). Requests for houses for nurses or midwives, school teachers, police officers, Forestry Commission workers and county council employees were numerous in every RDC investigated. Statistics on each were not available, although the 1949 Minister of Health indicted that in the immediate post-war years '… more than 1000 houses have already been included in the local authority housing programme for police officers and more are in contemplation' (HCH 20 January 1949, Vol.460, col.311).

[22] For example, in Ampthill there was dialogue across the decades with the Marston Valley Brick Company (e.g. *W&DR* 27 June 1931, p.1; 29 October 1946, p.1; 13 June 1967, p.1).

[23] Such as by Councillor Drane of Erpingham (*NM&PWJ* 22 June 1935, p.5) or Councillor Norris of Ampthill (*W&DR* 28 February 1939, p.3).

Table 3.1 Number of parish council requests for more housing in investigated rural districts, by decade 1900–1969

	Total parishes	Pre-1920	1920s	1930s	1940s	1950s	1960s
	Hertfordshire						
Hatfield	4	0	2	0	3	0	1
Braughing	21	6	0	10	3	13	6
	Bedfordshire						
Ampthill	29	0	30	33	11	8	9
Biggleswade	25	4	27	44	18	15	1
	Norfolk						
Erpingham	44	5	26	8	8	1	1
Smallburgh	35	2	30	50	3	1	1
Walsingham	38	0	13	20	8	12	3

Source: Council minutes and local newspaper reports

Note: The number of parishes in districts changed over time. The total number in this table is for 1951. A major change in parish numbers occurred after the 1929 Local Government Act, when many parishes were merged or transferred from one district to another

cost of new-build under the 1890 legislation.[24] The ineffectiveness of the 1890 Act helped prompt more generous support under the 1919 Housing, Town Planning, Etc. Act (Bowley 1945). As the 1920s' figures show, requests from parishes accelerated, despite severe reservations about high rents under the 1919 Act (Chap. 4). Note that, formal surveys aside, there was no evidence that councils went searching for parish requests. Indeed, in the 1920s and 1930s, it was not uncommon for parishes to complain that they were ignored in housing allocations and receive the reply that the parish had failed to bid for more homes.[25] 'Bid' is appropriate here, rather than request, because councils demonstrated caution over parish calls (despite messages in Whitehall implying not). This was exemplified in instructions to council clerks to ask parishes to report 'genuine' demand for new homes.[26] Records demonstrate a

---

[24] Burnett (1986, p.138) held that the 1890 Housing of the Working Classes Act was more urban than rural in focus, with only eight RDCs building under it by 1919, which is not far from Mingay's claim that, by 1910, only 10 loans to build 180 RDC houses had been sanctioned. The 1909 Housing and Town Planning Act extended 1890 Act provisions and was more successful, as it reduced interest rates for council-building, but only 29 RDCs (out of 655) had applied to borrow under the Act by 1912 (Mingay 1990, p.122).

[25] Two illustrative examples were in Erpingham (*FakPost* 16 January 1925, p.3) and Ampthill (*W&DR* 28 February 1939, p.3).

[26] Messages requesting 'genuine' demand from working-class people were common, as with Erpingham (NRO DC13/5/72 ERDCHCM 18 January 1927, pp.32–33), Hatfield (HRO RDC7/96/2 *HA&SAT* 25 October 1929) and Smallburgh (*NM&PWJ* 5 June 1937, p.9). These examples are pre-1939 but reports continued after 1945.

willingness to turn requests down because others had greater need,[27] because supporting evidence was missing[28] or the parish council's judgement was doubted.[29]

What cannot be ascertained is how far council responses were conditioned by scepticism in Whitehall over RDC bids to build homes. Tension there certainly was over building approvals, which made councils conscious that they had to satisfy the Ministry with evidence,[30] which not unreasonably magnified councillor desires for strong cases. What was apparent was that, just as Whitehall messages were infused with prioritisation of national over local considerations (Chap. 6), so too were parish concerns subsumed by district ones. We see this most evidently in the Norfolk districts, where providing council homes was often discussed as if the intention was to support farmers. Visible in this articulation was a dispute between the Felmingham parish and Smallburgh over dwelling allocations, with the rural council complaining about Felmingham's requests for more dwellings as: 'There are already more houses there than were required for the labourers working on the land there'. Even worse, some erected dwellings had not found tenants amongst farm labourers, leading to homes being allocated to tenants who worked in North Walsham (even if they did live or had lived in Felmingham).[31] Similarly, council minutes show considerable resistance to providing dwellings for employees of (usually non-farm but also many landed) companies. This is a component of rural housing supply that changed over time, at differential paces geographically, but in the more 'traditional' countryside such reluctance was evident pre-1939 especially.[32] In the case of Briston, which housed many workers at the nearby Melton Constable railway workshops, disgruntlement was rife, with parish expressions of disgust over low new-build allocations matched by council assertions that the railway companies should provide homes, all

---

[27] As at Smallburgh (*NWP&ENS* 26 October 1922, p.5; NRO DC22/2/11 SmRDCM 2 October 1928, p.219) and Biggleswade (BRO RDBwM1/11 BiRDCM 6 July 1932).

[28] As in Ampthill (*W&DR* 30 May 1931, p.1).

[29] BRO RDBwM1/11 BiRDCM 6 July 1932. As another example, in Aylsham RDC, doubts were raised over whether a parish council's views were the same as its residents, given the clerk and chair had signed off a statement of need without consulting parishioners (*HMC&WP* 15 January 1926, p.5).

[30] As minuted expressly in HRO RDC7/3/1 Hatfield Joint Housing and Finance Committee Meeting 8 December 1931, p.1, and explicitly in Ministry requests to see applicant details (e.g. NRO DC13/5/73 ERDCHCM 13 January 1932, p.2).

[31] *EDP* 1 November 1928, p.5; *FakPost* 2 November 1928, p.4; *NWP&ENS* 2 November 1928, p.5; *T&WT* 23 March 1929, p.9.

[32] For example, the government noted reluctance on the part of Wiltshire County Council to offer improvement grants for tenanted homes under the 1926 Housing (Rural Workers) Act, with the line separating acceptance and refusal being '… between those who are thought to have means of their own sufficient to carry out improvements and those who have not' (HCH 14 March 1928, Vol.214, col.1914). Governments regularly complained that councils did not see the benefit of home improvement for the tenant but placed weight on the means of the landlord (e.g. MoH 1930, p.80; TNA HLG37/43 'Investigation by General Inspectors 1934', p.12).

made more fraught, until 1935, by the boundary of Erpingham and Walsingham placing Briston and Melton Constable in different districts.[33]

Noting these circumstances, a key point to hold from Table 3.1 is the peak of requests in the 1930s. This peak had built since the late-1920s and extended into the 1940s, although 1940s' figures were lower as house-building on any scale was limited to four years. What is significant is that, after 1933, the government restricted Treasury subsidies for new council homes to the replacement of slum and over-crowded properties. This generated difficulties in 'traditional' rural areas. They had high demand for extra council homes,[34] as articulated in vivid detail by a house-wife's response to a 1935–1936 Northamptonshire rural survey:

> 'It is true that my rent is only 4/6d here,' said Mrs. Y., 'and I should have to pay 6/- for a Council House. But does anyone realise what it costs me – IN WASTE – to live here? I have to fetch every drop of water from the well there' – she pointed down a fairly steep hill across a muddy field. 'Then I have to boil it on that old range for every purpose, cooking, dish-washing, house-cleaning, and the weekly clothes-washing. Every drop of dirty water I have to take across the road and empty down that drain. All refuse, with the contents of the bucket closets, has to be buried in that tiny patch of "garden". You see that floor' – pointing to hills and valleys of rough brick on which her living-room table rocked to and fro – 'every time I try to wash that, we have to keep up a roaring fire, or it won't dry at all. And if I do not keep a regular fire in the parlour, all my furniture gets mouldy … Do you ever think of the expense of having to buy tiny quantities of food, because it goes bad over the weekend? If only I could get a Council House!'. (Mackintosh 1936, p.30)

Demand for general-needs housing like this would have to wait, as made clear in Hatfield's deliberations over housing allocations:

> It is laid down in the Housing Act of 1936 that 'the Authority shall secure that in the selec-tion of their tenants a reasonable preference be given to persons who are occupying insani-tary or overcrowded houses, have large families, or are living under unsatisfactory housing conditions'. This provision of the 1936 Housing Act, with the exception of some compara-tively minor requirements affecting agricultural workers, is the mainspring directing the allocation of houses by local authorities …[35]

It was not that no general-needs homes could be built, just that this had to occur without Treasury subsidies. But, without them, dwellings were beyond the reach of many residents. As a 1955 Cabinet paper made clear: 'There is still a great need for more houses, quite apart from the replacement of slums … We are still well short of

---

[33] NRO DC19/6/16 WRDCM 10 October 1928, p.69; *FakPost* 16 November 1928, p.5.

[34] Two examples from the early-1930s were when advertisements were placed by Erpingham and Walsingham to assess housing demand for the 1931 Act (which was targeted at farm-worker accommodation). They received 155 and 200 applications, respectively (TNA HLG40/19 'Report on Applications for Special Assistance from RDCs in the Counties of Norfolk and East Suffolk', undated c1932, p.12, p.20). While there is little precision in minutes over council stocks at this time, my estimate is that 1931 council dwellings in these districts numbered around 150 and 120, respectively.

[35] HRO RDC7/9/1 HtRDCM 19 October 1943, p.51.

the target of a separate home for every family'.[36] Farm-workers were already unable to meet rents of even moderate quality private rental, with inter-war rents at 25% of wages for most workers but 40% for farm labourers (Benson 1989, p.78). Despite this, parishes pressed for more homes, signalling urgency in requests for dwellings. Unsurprisingly, as the 1930s progressed, and during the Second World War, internal and official reports stressed the need for increasing house-building for the working-classes. The build-up of demand, given low 1930s' council construction and little activity during the War,[37] pushed councils towards more 'professionalised' systems for assessing housing demand after 1945. This saw waiting lists emerge to target home allocations to those in most need.

3.1.2 Waiting Lists

To grasp the importance of waiting lists, we need to acknowledge what came before. As implied by parish councils being asked about local needs, and by parishes being motivated to request district action, localism was a strong component in inter-war dwelling allocations.[38] Complaints were loud if new homes went to non-parish residents,[39] as Harris (1974, p.89) reported for 'Hennage', with tussles over this lasting into the 1950s at least. In most districts, parish councils were part of allocation procedures, either directly by RDCs asking for parish views on applicants or through allocation committees comprising RDC and parish councillors.[40] Tension between these state tiers was not uncommon, with RDC officials commonly emphasising that theirs was the ultimate decision, while parish representatives champi-

---

[36] TNA HLG101/618 'Housing Subsidies', 14 July 1955, p.1. A public statement admitting continuing shortages was made in MHLG (1956, p.9), with both messages containing the common Ministry missive of demand concentrations in industrial centres.

[37] During 1939–1945, the construction for key industries occurred, as for armaments and, to a lesser degree, farm-workers; yet 1940–1945 saw only 51,163 new council dwellings built, compared with 78,952 in the last (partial) pre-war year of 1939 (88,330 in 1938; HCH 11 March 1946, Vol.420, col.161W–62W).

[38] Early under the 1919 Act, for instance, parish councillors selected tenants, even if selections were rubber-stamped by a council official or a councillor (for Erpingham and Biggleswade, NRO DC13/5/82 ERDCHCM 9 January 1920, p.89; BC&BG 15 October 1920, p.3). Council policies commonly stated that parishioners were to be offered tenancies first, with applicants from outside a parish often refused unless no local resident would take a dwelling (HaRDCM 28 October 1920, p.79; NWP&ENS 29 October 1920, p.8; BiRDCM 10 April 1935).

[39] As reported for a North Mymms public meeting in Hatfield (HA&SAT 27 February 1926, p.12; also ERDCHCM 11 October 1927, p.81). Instances of no parish applications did occur, which could result in decisions held over until one was found (as in Walsingham, FakPost 24 August 1923, p.5).

[40] For example, BiRDCM, 5 January 1921, p.78; SMRDCHCM 7 March 1933, p.26; BrRDCM 7 April 1938, p.325. Councils might make all parishioners aware of vacancies and instruct the RDC Clerk to '… refer all applications to the Parish Councils for full particulars and report' (NRO DC13/5/72 ERDCHCM 27 August 1929, p.160).

oned preferred candidates. Moving into the 1930s, councils with active building programmes, like Biggleswade, tended to roll back parish-centred foci, often creating conflict.[41] These interactions moved councils to take more control over applications, as with moving away from parish nominations toward receiving '… the full list of applicants with all necessary particulars [which would] be placed before the Housing Committee'.[42] What underscored these steps was articulated in a 1929 discussion at Walsingham, when it was held that parish nominations were insufficient, as the Council had to assess whether applicants were 'suitable' or not.[43] Before this requirement was introduced, councils had become less convinced by parish inputs, with special boards established to go through all applications, even interviewing some, in order to allocate homes where they were most needed.[44] As another outcome, deeper into the 1930s, consolidated district-wide lists began to emerge, not necessarily for allocations, as parish residence still carried weight, but to quantify the scale of housing demand.[45]

With anticipations of increasing housing need amongst the working-classes following inter-war government prioritisation of middle-class homes (Swenarton and Taylor 1985), and with population growth adding to demand, councils were braced for heavy application volumes after 1945. Handling larger numbers required more systematic allocation mechanisms. The development of points schemes, intended to allocate homes to those in greatest need, became popular. Yet point schemes were problematical. As previous research demonstrates, waiting lists can be inaccurate, given that applicant circumstances change, while the self-referring nature of joining a list means those with the greatest needs can be missed (Gregory 1975).[46] This was not lost on national officials:

---

[41] As occurred between Biggleswade and Stotfold Parish Council (BRO RDBwM1/10 BRDCM 25 November 1931; BRO RDBwM1/13 8 February 1939, p.495).

[42] NRO DC13/5/72 ERDCHCM 15 September 1926, p.15, with another example at HRO RDC4/1/8 BuRDCM 15 August 1929, p.179.

[43] *FakPost* 4 October 1929, p.1.

[44] As in Braughing (*B&NEHG* 4 March 1938, p.4) or Hatfield, where special circumstances were required for a home to be allocated to those earning more than £5 a week (*H&PBG* 1 July 1938, p.4).

[45] For example, BRO RDAM2/22 ARDCHCM 8 June 1939. After 1945, district-wide lists were more common (e.g. BRO RDAM2/22 ARDCHCM 14 November 1946; HRO RDC7/9/1 HtRDCHCM 11 December 1946, p.262), although not everywhere. Braughing and Newport Pagnell RDC both retained parish-based systems in the 1960s, following reviews of the practice (HRO RDC3/2/11 Braughing Tenant Allocation Committee Meeting 3 February 1955, p.2690; *WR&WSR* 2 March 1965, p.2).

[46] Shucksmith (1981, pp.56–62), for example, noted for the Lake District that applications for housing were linked to expectations homes would be available. Shucksmith (1987) found that 78% of Skye caravan dwellers wanted new accommodations but only 28% were on the council list. This pattern was picked up here, with Walsingham reporting 649 houses unfit for habitation in 1950 but only 76 of their occupants had applied for rehousing (NRO DC19/6/64 WRDCHCM 24 March 1950, p.66), while the Ampthill Clerk noted that the waiting list for Shillington '… did not give a complete picture for there were people who did not submit applications until they saw houses being erected' (*WR&WSD* 14 January 1958, p.5).

It is known that some authorities require all applicants to re-register each year and so keep their lists up-to-date, but these are probably a small minority. Before the war many authorities made an occasional check … At the present time the excessive pressure on housing department staffs, which is largely due to the work connected with applications and selection of tenants, has probably made it impossible for most local authorities to attempt any complete screening.[47]

As Larkin (1979) charged, 'arbitrariness' on RDC waiting list procedures excluded many from housing opportunities (for an urban context; Gray 1976). Connell's (1978, pp.117–18) analysis of tenant records at Guildford RDC offered pointed examples, with file references to 'clean', 'dirty' and 'nicely spoken' applicants influencing allocations. Council minutes and newspaper reports raised relatively few such occurrences in this study. That social evaluations could impinge on tenancies was nonetheless suggested by the admonition of a Sandy tenant whose wife had committed an offence, a Smallburgh assessment that an applicant's wife would not be a 'desirable tenant', Ampthill wanting tenants who had moved in from slum properties to be checked because they were 'used to bad housing', a failed attempt to change the Walsingham applicant list after a councillor claimed an applicant had difficulties paying rent, and the councillors of Newport Pagnell RDC still visiting every applicant at home in 1965.[48]

Mainstream tendencies saw increasing demand encourage systematic schemes to allocate tenancies. Thus, soon after 1945, points-based waiting lists came into use in Ampthill, Biggleswade, Hatfield, North Walsham, Sandy, Smallburgh[49] and Walsingham.[50] Some councils never followed this path. No reference to a points scheme was found for Erpingham, while Braughing explicitly refused to have one, claiming: 'The Council had regarded the operation of a points scheme as being too rigid',[51] for '… there were too many difficulties to be overcome'.[52] What lay behind Braughing's decision was partly frustration. Parish lists still existed, although their accuracy was doubted, but more importantly few council homes were being erected: 'Would-be applicants were aware of the slow turnover in tenancies in the respective

---

[47] TNA HLG101/417 'Housing Application Lists', 3 June 1948.

[48] SaUDCM 30 July 1956, p.508; NRO DC22/2/45 SmRDCHCM 9 August 1921; *FakPost* 12 July 1929, p.5; *W&DR* 30 May 1931, p.1. The Newport Pagnell RDC practice was enabled by having only 200 on the waiting list, and justified by Council allocations based mostly on overcrowding and the condition of currently occupied dwellings (*WR&WSR* 2 March 1965, p.2).

[49] In Smallburgh, a proposal to formulate a tenant selection method based on housing need was defeated in 1949 (*NNN* 5 August 1949, p.1). Yet, two months later, the RDC agreed to take account of overcrowding, size of family, agricultural employment, employment in the district, sanitary conditions, applicant lodgers, armed forces service, and living in either requisitioned premises or a converted hut (*NNN* 30 September 1949, p.1).

[50] BRO RDAM1/14 ARDCM 21 November 1946; *NBC&BR* 5 February 1946, p.3; HRO RDC7/9/1 HtRDCM 27 December 1945, pp.145–46; *NNN* 13 January 1950, p.1; BRO UDSM1/3 SaUDCM 26 November 1945, p.270; NRO DC19/6/63 WRDCHCM 15 May 1946, p.44.

[51] HRO RDC3/1/7 BrRDCM 4 December 1958, p.4087.

[52] HRO RDC3/1/9 BrRDCM 5 February 1959, p.4178.

parishes and often concluded that it was futile to approach the Council'.[53] With much lower RDC council-building nationally, this evaluation had wider resonance. Specific examples were easy to find, as when 1955 complaints from Wood Norton over no dwelling allocations met with a Walsingham response 'no applications', which stimulated the charge that villagers would not join lists when they had to wait years for a home. That this response echoed beliefs elsewhere on the Council was affirmed by a vote of 20 to 7 to refer back the decision not to allocate Wood Norton new homes.[54] Potentially, this puts a different gloss on assumptions that, with fewer applications for housing, rural districts had less need for dwellings. For sure, rural districts had shorter lists. In national tabulations in 1949, for example, their applications relative to dwellings under construction fell behind urban centres (Table 3.2). This was so even though rural council construction was then prioritised to support agriculture.[55] On closer examination though, councils like Braughing were not out of line with their neighbours. Thus, compared to its 1951 population, with around 40 applicants per 1,000 inhabitants, Braughing differed little from the larger towns of Hertfordshire, like Watford (40.9), Hitchin (42.1) and Hemel Hempstead (36.5), although Letchworth (50.2) and Welwyn Garden City (58.5) were higher.[56] A similar picture pertained in Bedfordshire, for Biggleswade's score of 29.3 was equivalent to the largest town (30.3 for Luton). Only in Norfolk was there a sharp rural–urban contrast, with Norwich recording 42.8 compared with 17.9 for Erpingham, 26.9 for Smallburgh and 25.3 for Walsingham. These figures might ring memory bells over similarities between urban and rural tenure patterns in parts of England, with wide disparities more characteristic of agricultural and peripheral counties (Table 2.13).

Table 3.2 Applicants for council homes per council dwelling under construction by local government category, September1949

Councils in England	Families without a separate home	Families with a separate home	Total
Cities (CBs)	11.2	5.7	16.8
London (LCC & LMBs)	7.4	5.6	12.9
Boroughs (MBs)	9.5	4.9	14.5
Urban Districts (UDCs)	6.9	4.4	11.3
Rural Districts (RDCs)	4.3	3.7	7.9

Source: TNA HLG101/417 'Review of Local Authority Lists of Housing Applicants. Position at 27 September 1949'

[53] HRO RDC3/1/16 BrRDCECM 6 February 1966, p.6724. By the late-1960s, Braughing had a district-wide priority list. This caused 'great concern in parishes' as tenancies were often allocated to applicants from other parishes (HRO RDC3/1/19 BrRDCM 3 June 1969, p.7626).

[54] *D&FT* 24 June 1955, p.1.

[55] TNA HLG31/14 HI23/47 'Agricultural Housing', undated c1947.

[56] The information in this report did not include St Albans.

Comparability in some counties matched by divergence in others was possible because councils could decide criteria for waiting list inclusion and scoring. This led to dissimilar schemes, as Table 3.3 shows. Such variability was well-known at the national level. Indeed, ministers regularly lauded divergence as a sign of local autonomy.[57] But there is a difference between allowing discretion on dwelling allocation and making decisions across councils on the magnitude of dwelling needs. For sure, when ministers and officials favoured certain outcomes, they were not reluctant to push councils to act in particular ways. This applied to house-building numbers, even though Whitehall lacked information on relative needs, as well as on criteria for allocating homes. One example was the effort to remove or at least diminish residency requirements in home allocations after the Second World War. Initially, this was intended to support those demobbed from the armed forces. Later, helping expanding businesses secure key worker homes carried more weight.[58] But even for priority sectors, like agriculture in the late-1940s, national officials were uncertain about 'real demand', as the MoH articulated in 1948: 'It is not clear whether the waiting lists of local authorities are up-to-date screened lists of agricultural workers adjudged to be in urgent need of homes, or merely lists of agricultural workers who have at one time or another applied to the local authority, or something between these two extremes'.[59] Ministries were not alone in being confused. Councils themselves wanted better guidance on procedures and criteria for handling applicants.[60] Had such direction been given, and followed, if only for core items, the nation might have secured a data base for Whitehall to make better judgements on

---

[57] For example, Harold Macmillan claimed that local discretion with some national guidance was '… the only way in which a thing of this kind could work' (HCH 20 October 1953, Vol.518, col.1786), while the argument put in response to a Parliamentary question in 1959 was that '… local conditions vary. A system of allocation which would be suitable on one area would not be suitable in another' (TNA HLG101/295 'Parliamentary Reply to Graham Page (Conservative MP Crosby)', 21 April 1959).

[58] There were references to residential qualifications for armed forces personnel as an acute problem in official publications (e.g. MHLG 1956, p.19), with Circulars like MHLG 24/55 and MHLG 21/65 asking for favourable attention (BRO RDAM2/22 ARDCHCM 17 March 1955; BRO RDBwM1/36 BiRDCHECM 14 April 1965, p.1011; BRO RDAM1/22 ARDCHPByCM 12 January 1967; HRO RDC7/1/44 HtRDCHTPCM 3 December 1968, p.481). Linking tenancies to local employers was called for soon after 1945; not just for farming or mining (e.g. TNA MAF234/12 'Kent War Agricultural Committee', May 1947) and subject to regular national deliberations (e.g. TNA HLG101/295 'Allocation of Council Houses by Points System', undated c1959). Councils were pressured by other agencies on the same score, such as by the British Legion (BRO RDAM2/22 ARDCHCM 9 January 1947; NBC&BR 24 April 1951, p.7) and Chambers of Commerce (HRO RDC7/9/1 HtRDCM 19 October 1943).

[59] TNA HLG31/15 HI9/48 'Houses for Agricultural Workers', undated c1948.

[60] As an example, TNA HLG101/295 Letter from Guinness Trust Secretary to Ernest Marples, MHLG, 17 October 1952, which held that: '… there is considerable opinion that local authorities generally would welcome some common basis being found on which to build up their own points schemes'.

Table 3.3 Waiting list points schemes in Ampthill, Hatfield and Walsingham RDCs, 1946–1948

Attributes securing points for housing	Ampthill	Hatfield	Walsingham
Insanitary or badly defective house	5		2
Married with no home or in lodgings			5
Two or more families in a house	20	4	
Years married		(2 years) 1, (5 years) 2	
Number in family			Each 1
Number of children		(each to 10 years) 0.25, (each 10–17 years) 0.5	
Overcrowded (moral or legal)	15		Persons/room
Overcrowded persons rehoused	Each 2	[a] (per room) 4	
Expectant mother	5		
Residency years in district	(over 5 years) 5	(maximum 4) 0.5	
Residency in parish over 7 years	3		
Lived in district before 1939			2
Work in district			2
Farm-worker	5		3
Applicant was/is in Armed Forces	5	1	
Years in Armed Forces	(maximum 5) each 1	0.5, (after 1945) 0.25	(each year 1939–1945) 0.5
Years overseas if married before			(each year 1939–1945) 0.5
Disability discharge from Armed Forces			1.5
Special reasons (court order, unable to pay rent)	7		
Medical Officer certifies special case	10	Outside the system	2
Discretionary agreed by Committee	10		
Time on waiting list (per year)		(maximum 2) 0.25	

Source: BRO RDAM2/22 ARDCHCM 14 November 1946; HRO RDC7/1/13 HtRDCM 25 October 1948, pp.344–45; NRO DC19/6/63 WRDCHCM 15 May 1946, p.44

local housing demand. Yet, by not providing this leadership, Whitehall was better placed to declare lists unreliable for assessing local housing needs.[61]

List deficiencies owed much to Whitehall. Internally, Ministry officials admitted: 'There is practically no information in the Department as to the practice of local authorities in screening their application lists'.[62] But MoH Circular 171/48 did instruct councils to review applicants on their waiting lists, using the same form.[63] Potentially, this could have been the first step toward comparable data bases but councils saw the immediate aim as a sifting process to remove those no longer seeking a home.[64] Lists shrank, so far even the Treasury thought they underestimated demand.[65] No doubt, soon after 1945, the need for working-class housing was so high that waiting lists largely functioned to inform local judgements on allocations. Agreement on this 'excessive demand', or at least its electoral significance, saw the 1951–1955 government put aside ideological predilections by supporting council as much as private house-building. At this time, the MHLG was clear that long waiting lists signified real demand for council housing:

> There is no doubt at the present time that there are large numbers of people pestering Local Authorities for houses - and rent arrears are practically non-existent. There is no doubt that for people moving from one district to another or for people getting married their greatest difficulty is to get the tenancy of an unfurnished house on any reasonable terms.[66]

But, in any political party, views vary, with strands within the Conservative Party pressing, even early in the new government's tenure, for a return to the 1930s' favouritism for private-owners (Jones 2010), with documents soon before Cabinet

[61] Thus, Aneurin Bevan spoke of duplication on lists across authorities (HCH 21 February 1946, Vol.419, col.1279), which meant their publication would be 'most misleading' (HCH 9 May 1946, Vol.422, col.115W); a message repeated by Hugh Dalton (HCH 8 May 1951, Vol.487, col.1732). Duncan Sandys declared that '… waiting lists are unreliable as an index of housing need' (HCH 4 December 1956, Vol.561, col.104W), on which Anthony Greenwood concurred (HCH 14 March 1967, Vol.743, col.36W), as did Paul Channon (HCH 29 April 1971, Vol.816, col.191W), while Keith Joseph declared gathering waiting list information a 'waste of time of my Department' (HCH 21 April 1964, Vol.693, col.1066), so repeating Henry Brooke's earlier assessment (HCH 22 July 1958, Vol.592, col.19W). These points were transmitted within ministries and to councils (e.g. TNA HLG31/16 HI26/49 'Housing Applications', undated c1949; TNA HLG118/933 'Memo to Mr. Grimshaw from J.M. Thompson', 2 May 1966).

[62] TNA HLG101/417 'Housing Application Lists', 3 June 1948.

[63] TNA HLG101/417 MoH Circular 171/48. 'Review of Local Authority Waiting Lists', 10 November 1948.

[64] On Circular 171/48: HRO RDC3/2/4 BrRDCPHHCM 18 November 1948, p.1319; BRO UDSM1/3 SaUDCM 29 November 1948, p.520; BRO RDBwM1/19 BiRDCM 1 December 1948, p.250; BRO RDAM2/22 ARDCHCM 2 December 1948; NRO DC19/6/63 WRDCHCM 16 March 1949, p.221.

[65] For example, TNA T229/473 IPC(WP)(50)5 'Investment Review 1951–1952', 12 January 1950.

[66] TNA HLG101/373 'Memo to Mr. Wilkinson from J.C.W.', 16 July 1952.

urging the construction of a 'property-owning democracy'.[67] In this context, irritation over council attention to waiting lists and demands for more council homes grew:

> Local authorities are so obsessed with their waiting lists that they are like a rabbit in front of a snake, paralysed with fear and unable to move from the attitude in which they are set. I have no doubt that most local authorities would welcome the Minister's proposals for doing more slum clearance and keeping the old houses in good repair. In fact local authorities of all sizes are beginning to start slum clearance programmes on their own. But they all hope to build the replacement houses largely as a net addition to their present programme.[68]

This was not what the government wanted at all. Cabinet papers pointed to the distorting effects of rent restrictions and subsidies on housing provision. Rather than asking how unmet housing needs might be met through improved management and production practices, complaints rained down on demand being too high: 'There is no doubt that if people had to pay 'economic rents' – rents which reflected the true cost to the community – a large part of the present demand would disappear'.[69] Of course, to reinvigorate the 1930s' approaches would again narrow the remit for council homes, as well as increasing unmet need. With most of the English population unable to afford home ownership or denied this path by mortgage lenders (Ford 1975; Williams 1978), the majority of households would be renters for decades to come (home ownership crept over 50% in 1971; Table 1.3). Yet, the government was loath to adjust rent controls, so restricting landlords' ability to improve private rental. Standards consequently continued to fall or properties were sold (Holmans 2000, p.448). This bolstered general demand for council homes, for which an effective tool for distributing building permissions across local authorities could have been usable cross-council waiting list data. But such information would hold out the prospect of journalists and others comparing building rates with actual demand. The strengthening mood within the government was not to improve housing prospects in each tenure but to encourage shifts into home ownership. Council-building was to be restricted to slum replacement or old people's homes (MHLG 1961, p.3), wherein: '… entitlement to the slum clearance subsidy shall depend on two things: first, on the number of families rehoused by the local authority from unfit houses after the 3rd November, 1955, and, second, on the building by the local authority, within a reasonable period, of an equivalent number of new houses'.[70] In these circumstances, waiting lists enabling cross-authority comparisons were superfluous.

---

[67] TNA CAB129/53 C(52)207 'A Property Owning Democracy', 20 June 1952; C(52)216 26 June 1952, 30 June 1952. The same message, from the same party, would be prevalent 30–40 years later (Francis 2012).

[68] TNA HLG101/618 'Memo from J.E. Beddoe to S.F. Wilkinson', 4 September 1953.

[69] TNA CAB129/53 'A Property Owning Democracy', 30 June 1952.

[70] HCH 28 February 1956, Vol.549, col.96W.

Faced with limits on new-build, alongside explicit government messages that former slum dwellers should access larger shares of new council homes,[71] councils were pushed to tailor their waiting lists to match expectations for Ministry building allocations. This tendency had existed in the inter-war years and was apparent as early as the late-1940s, when demand outstripped post-war capacities to build. As articulated by the MP for Solihull in 1950:

> ... housing lists include only those families for which the local authority is prepared to accept responsibility, usually those families who lived in the locality at a qualifying date, which is often as far back as 1945. Therefore, these housing lists do not include scores of thousands of families which are just as homeless as the families whose names appear on the housing lists, to say nothing of all those young people who wish to get married but are unable to do so because they have nowhere to live.[72]

Inclusion on a list meant little if councils were denied the capacity to satisfy demand by building more homes. The entrenchment of 'welfare state' principles after 1945 did not sit comfortably alongside 1930s' experiences, such as applicants in Easington, County Durham, waiting for 10–14 years without an offer of a home.[73] Feeling the pinch, councils started purging their lists of applicants before 1939. In Hatfield, for example, 36 of those without a 'local claim' were knocked off in 1931.[74] Sandy removed 43 out of 100 applicants shortly afterwards,[75] while Ampthill reviewed its list just before the Second World War and then declared it out of date in 1944.[76] Regular purges were to follow, with some spectacular falls in numbers.[77] In this regard, rural districts differed little from cities. As an example, a 1970s' review of Kingston-upon-Hull's list led to a reduction from 16,000 to 5793 (Gray 1976). Adjustments of this kind were to be expected if list accuracy was to be maintained, given councils acknowledged that the non-availability of homes meant many left the

---

[71] Statements of intent around the 1956 Housing Subsidies Act were made by Keith Joseph (HCH 14 February 1956, Vol.548, col.2208) and Duncan Sandys (HCH 26 June 1956, Vol.555, col.254–55).

[72] HCH 6 March 1950, Vol.472, col.82.

[73] Thirty years later the WR&WSR (4 April 1967, p.1) reported on an Aspley Guise (Ampthill) resident of 26 years who had been on the waiting list for 16 years, most recently living in a condemned dwelling. Such examples were not uncommon. Another was a resident of Biggleswade Town who had been on the list for 18 years (BC&BG 10 June 1960, p.5).

[74] HA&SAT 27 November 1931, p.12.

[75] NBC 3 March 1933, p.6.

[76] BRO RDAM2/22 ARDCHCM 8 June 1939; WR&WSR 22 August 1944, p.3.

[77] Examples of major waiting list reductions include a drop from 922 to 320 for Braughing (HRO RDC3/2/6 Braughing Tenant Selection Committee Meeting 1 February 1951, p.1770), which had seen a drop from 707 to 412 only two years earlier (HRO RDC3/2/4 BrRDCPHHCM 20 January 1949, p1355), from 804 to 551 for Ampthill in 1953, 735 to 475 in 1956, then from 600 to 445 in 1960 (BRO RDAM2/22 ARDCHCM 19 November 1953; BRO RDAR8/37 ARDCMOHar 1956, p.16; BRO RDAR8/40 ARDCMOHar 1959, p.15), a fall from over 700 to 400 for Hatfield RDC's (1967, p.34) general-needs list, with the 1949 reduction in Walsingham following Circular 171/48 from 992 to 643. Lest it be thought revisions necessarily lowered numbers, as messages from Whitehall implied, Smallburgh's reassessment in 1965 resulted in a minor increase from 247 to 253 (NNN 12 February 1965, p.7).

district or rehoused themselves.[78] Before considering the implications of this, be clear that 1950s' changes in government policy heighten pressure on councils substantially. Local illustrations of this include the 643 applicants on Ampthill's waiting list, of which only 10 were in dwellings associated with slum clearance;[79] the one segment of council-building the government supported. Hardly surprising that, even in Hatfield, which could nominate applicants for new town homes,[80] by 1962 four years were required for a home on the general waiting list. This had fallen to two years by 1967, and by 1968 childless couples were accommodated 6 months after applying (Hatfield RDC 1970, p.36). Table 3.4 indicates the dynamics involved, using a two-year lag to represent gaps between the commissioning and completion of new dwellings. Sharp drops in council completions in the late-1950s occurred across the board, lessening abilities to cater to waiting lists. Note also that very

Table 3.4 Average annual dwelling completions in investigated rural districts for decision years 1952–1969

	For councils			For private-owners		
	1952–1955	1956–1963	1965–1969	1952–1955	1956–1963	1965–1969
Hatfield	169	32	134	186	114	73
Braughing	3	9	17	14	26	159
Ampthill	63	44	64	57	239	199
Biggleswade	112	65	45	48	170	132
Erpingham	32	4	9	42	61	148
Smallburgh	32	4	32	39	84	259
Walsingham	57	24	41	26	40	79

Source: Computed from MHLG (quarterly)
Note: The years selected for comparison were chosen so as to exclude turnover in national governments (1951, 1964 and 1970). To estimate commitments in the time periods shown, a two-year time lag was used. This was a rough estimate of the time between a decision to build and project completion, so dwellings erected in, say, 1957 were on average likely to have been commissioned in 1955. Hence, for these calculations the periods used were 1954–1957, 1959–1965 and 1967–1971. This two-year gap was based on information that dwellings took about a year to build both in 1954 and 1966, although more like 15 months for flats (TNA T229/680 Memo from T.H. Caulcott to J.A.C Robertson, 15 July 1954; HCH 14 June 1966, Vol.729, col.259W–60W). This was construction alone, to which allowance for design and ancillary works needs adding. The year 1955 saw the council-building programme begin to change direction, moving from general needs supply to specialist needs (principally slum clearance and homes for the elderly). Using the two-year lag highlighted shifts in policy direction. In Hatfield, for example, the 143 then 180 new dwellings of 1956 and 1957 were followed by 27 then 43 in 1958 and 1959, while the 83 then 35 new homes of 1965 and 1966 were followed by 116 then 229 in 1967 and 1968

---

[78] As reported in a review by Biggleswade (*WR&WSR* 5 May 1959, p.14).

[79] *WR&WSR* 4 March 1958, p.1.

[80] In the mid-1950s, Hatfield applicants had expectations of long waits, while the Development Corporation had many houses under construction or planned, with few on its waiting list (*H&PBG* 12 October 1956, p.1). In 1960, the Development Corporation accepted 'an agreed number of applicants' from Hatfield's list (Hatfield RDC 1961, p.45), with 103 so housed in 1961 out of 386 Corporation lettings (Hatfield RDC 1962, p.51).

buoyant private sector building in the late-1960s was not matched by increased council construction to anywhere near early-1950s' levels. This would raise the burden on rural councils. For Hatfield, the Development Corporation helped ease these pressures, but councils not endowed with such largesse had fewer prospects of list reductions. Take Biggleswade to illustrate. At the start of 1973, it closed its list to new applicants for 4 months, refused to add new applicants in the middle of the year and rejected even hardship cases a year later '... in view of the very large waiting list and the lack of accommodation in this area'.[81]

The implications of widening gaps between demand and supply for working-class housing were stark. Not for all changes of course, for some waiting list adjustments were tidying-up exercises associated with good management; as in removing duplication between the Hatfield and Development Corporation's lists.[82] More fundamentally, as government policy championed owner-occupiers to the detriment of renters, in a manner not repeated across most of Western Europe (Harloe 1995), waiting times for housing rose significantly. The pattern for Hatfield was representative at one level (Fig. 3.1), although not at another. Where it depicted 'realities' on the ground was in numbers queuing for council housing rising rapidly following reductions in council-building (Table 3.4), and falling in periods when construction was more buoyant. It was less representative in the clarity in which it demonstrated

Source: Mostly Hatfield RDC annual reports of the medical officer of health, supplemented with council minutes and local newspaper reports.

Note: For most years the December figure was used, with November taken in the few years the December value was not found. The gap in the trend arises because no data were found for one year.

Fig. 3.1 Number of applicants on the Hatfield RDC waiting list at end of year, 1945–1973

[81] BRO RDBwM1/44 BiRDCHCM 10 January 1973, p.781; BRO RDBwM1/45 BiRDCHLCM 11 July 1973, pp.115–16; 13 February 1974, p.580.
[82] HRO RDC7/1/16 HtRDCHCM 3 September 1952, p.119.

linkages between council-building and waiting list lengths. Primarily this was because councils responded to their inability to meet demands by shortening their lists. Fig. 3.1 is deliberately based on numbers at the end of each year. Records for the other councils investigated did not give sufficient 'data points' to enable comparisons at one end of the annual cycle in the same way. This is important, for within years there could be wide fluctuations in waiting list numbers. One example is sufficient to illustrate. In 1973, Ampthill undertook a revision of its waiting list in May, which saw entrants drop from 890 pre-May to 780 post-May. By December, the list was back to 879.[83] Ampthill was a regular reviewer of its list, often recording substantial contractions in single years. But if seeking trends in applicant numbers, what figure do you choose in a year? If you select only post-review numbers, you will be disappointed, partly because these are not always reported and secondly because reviews of this kind are not always annual. So, for Ampthill, do you choose the 804 pre-review or the 551 post-review values for 1953 (ignoring a further 91 who lived outside the district post-review), or would you take the Medical Officer of Health's number of 957 at the end of the year?[84] For 1956, would the 735 pre-review be better than the 475 post-review, or should the 600 pre-review in 1959 supplant the 445 post-review?[85] It is tempting to favour the post-review, on the grounds that irrelevant applicants have been sifted out, such as those who left the district or secured other homes.

The problem with this approach is that it ignores criteria alterations during a review. In 1948, for example, Ampthill reported 1650 on its waiting list, which led to discussion about removing those with no local connection from the list. The minutes give no clarity on the outcome of this discussion but by 1949 the list was 798 strong. This was quite a drop without a definitional change.[86] Criteria adjustments were common. In 1954, for instance, Biggleswade divided its list into priority and non-priority applicants, adding that new applicants had to be on the list for at least 12 months and have been resident in the district for two years to qualify.[87] A decade later, a five-year residential qualification was stipulated.[88] Perhaps Braughing saw less demand for its dwellings, for when it introduced a residential qualification this 'only' required two years in the previous seven.[89] Without altering criteria in such ways, councils felt overwhelmed by demand. Ampthill, with more than 1000 on its list in 1970, thought it an impossible task to reconsider its list, noting no revision had occurred for two years by the beginning of 1971, even though council policy

[83] BRO RDAR8/54 ARDCMOHar 1973, p.11. This was not unusual. In 1972, a list of more than 800 was reduced to 690 on review but had risen again to 750 by the end of the year (BRO RDAR8/53 ARDCMOHar 1972, p.16).

[84] BRO RDAM2/22 ARDCHCM 19 November 1953; BRO RDAR8/34 ARDCMOHar 1953, p.16.

[85] BRO RDAR8/37 ARDCMOHar 1956, p.16; BRO RDAR8/40 ARDCMOHar 1959, p.15.

[86] BRO RDAM2/22 ARDCHCM 8 January 1948; 21 July 1948; 9 June 1949. Braughing cut those who lived and worked outside the area from its waiting list in 1950 (*H&EO* 5 January 1951, p.6).

[87] *NB&BC* 27 July 1954, p.7.

[88] BRO RDBwM1/36 BiRDCHLCM 24 February 1965, p.815.

[89] HRO RDC3/1/18 BrRDCECM 9 April 1968, p.7326.

called for checks every 12 months. Yet, confronted with a need to do something, by the end of 1971 a review had cut 25%. The pressure did not ease and, like other councils that contravened government wishes by reintroducing residential qualifications, Ampthill went back to the past by ditching its points scheme, giving parish councillors authority to fill vacancies.[90] Faced with all this, can it be doubted councillors were not fully aware of the scale of local housing demand or of the negative consequences of narrowly specified policies on council-building?

Council waiting lists were adjusted as part of good management practice (removing who had moved on, etc.) and due to incapacity in the face of demand. This inability did not arise solely from government restrictions on new-build, but these certainly heightened them (Table 3.4). Demand had not gone away. But councils were expected to ignore its persistence, given national restraint on council-building. Little wonder that Westminster and Whitehall were dismissive of the notion that waiting lists were valid for assessing housing needs (although in Whitehall critiques centred on applicant duplication not criteria realignment). Conceptually, processes here were no different from council identification of dwellings unfit for habitation (Chap. 2). In both cases, responses were heavily conditioned by what councils considered achievable. National responses were very different. While government commentaries and reports commonly aggregated local counts on unfit dwellings as if this produced a 'true' national picture, no such assumptions surrounded waiting lists. For a brief interlude, national authorities tried to impose uniformity on waiting list compositions, but the effort was short-lived. In effect, there was a similar government attitude towards unfit dwellings and waiting list numbers, one that transgressed political parties. On the surface, this came down to preferring uncertainty over clarity. Yet the dissimilarity of approach towards unfit dwellings and waiting lists suggests a preference towards one form of action (slum removal) over the other (new-build to meet need). These are considerations we return to in later chapters. For now, the point to grasp is that, as possibilities for council action diminished, so did the value of waiting lists. Hence, the attractiveness of points systems declined. Councils complained over government prioritisation of slum clearance, as this meant they had to offer homes for slum rehousing; ignoring many who had been on their lists for years.[91] In a context of declining private rental, falls in council-build

---

[90] BRO RDAR8/51 ARDCMOHar 1970, p.15; BRO RDAM1/26 ARDCHCM 4 January 1971, p.442; BRO RDAR8/52 ARDCMOHar 1971, p.16; RDAR8/53 ARDCMOHar 1972, p.16. Hatfield also abandoned its points system, so applicants were '… housed in date order of registration on the list', in the expectation they spent equal time before being housed, while 'People without housing need were debarred from the list' (HRO RDC7/1/45 HtRDCJMHF 18 June 1969, p.156).

[91] As in Biggleswade (*BC&BG* 14 September 1956, p.1). Councils did not always secure homes to replace those demolished. By 1938, approved replacements covered 94% of demolished units in England and Wales but only 67% had been completed (MoH 1938, p.98). The linkage of demolitions to rehousing was subject to looser fits post-1945, with government ministers claiming '… new houses built to replace unfit houses demolished cannot be separately identified from those built for other purposes' (HCH 3 March 1971, Vol.812, col.448W), which is understandable given the key post-war Act covering dwelling demolitions specified that: '… local authorities are under no statutory obligation to rehouse tenants displaced by demolition orders on unfit houses made

during the late-1950s and early-1960s meant councils offered fewer tenancies,[92] with waiting lists rising faster than accommodation availability as early as 1952 (Biggleswade RDC 1953, p.16). Debate over the utility of point schemes increased, as did their abandonment. From late-1940s and early-1950s council debates on fine-tuning point schemes, to discarding the enterprise in the 1960s and 1970s, signified an important change in policy circumstances.[93] With these changed circumstances, it is worth pondering the temporal juxtaposition of criticisms over rural housing performance in the 1960s and 1970s with the realities that limited enhancements to the rural council stock at that time (e.g. Rose et al. 1976).

3.2   Was Rural Council Action Necessary?

A significant point made long ago by Topham (1970) was that councils could do little to encourage building by the private sector, though they might discourage private investment. To attract private commitments, not only must the general 'economic climate' be right but so too must the local context where funds are spent. With the majority of the twentieth-century marked by long periods of one-party rule or coalition dominance by the Conservative Party, increased social housing provision is not easily explained by 'welfarist' commitments to public sector options. More forceful in their imprint have been 'crises' in housing, most obviously seen in what generated (relatively) vigorous state interventions following two world wars (Orbach 1977; Malpass 2003). That crisis interventions were not short-term in impact, but became grounded within mainstream politics, is evinced in the growth of the public sector. While the idea of a 'property-owning democracy' was an ideological and rhetorical constant in Conservative Party thought from 1923 (Francis 2012), there were only tepid attempts to revive private rental, as in the 1930s (Jackson 1973), and again in 1957 (Merrett 1982, p.137). As revitalisation efforts, they failed. In the 1950s and 1960s, 2.3 million dwellings left private rental for owner-occupation, constituting half the increase in home ownership over the period (Holmans 2000, p. 448). By the early-1970s it was renters, especially in the council sector, who were being encouraged to become home-owners (Harloe 1995, p.290). For much of the century, the allure of home ownership, alongside worries over repercussions if private rents rose, dampened the enthusiasm for reviving the tenure.

---

under Part II of the Housing Act, 1957. There is no right of appeal against the local authority's decision' (HCH 24 January 1972, Vol.829, col.340W).

[92] A point raised variously in Braughing in the late-1960s (e.g. HRO RDC3/1/17 BrRDCECM 13 June 1967, p.7104; HRO RDC3/1/19 BrRDCM 8 July 1969, p.7657).

[93] This trend sheds light on the findings of Bottle and associates (1974) that 19 of the 42 Kent councils they investigated had no points system.

Increasingly the primary housing sectors became owner-occupation and council tenancy. Yet, capacities for home ownership were uneven. For Marshall (1968, p.186), the combination of poorer housing, lower incomes and higher unemployment in the North of England meant a weaker private sector offer. In such regions, councils responded vigorously owing to weak private sector actions (Bowley 1938; Richardson 1967, p.179). This picture also characterised the countryside, especially where agriculture dominated. Despite a short period in the late-1940s when farmworker wages closed in on their manufacturing counterparts (Calder 1969, p.428), the story of the century was low farm labourer wages. Astor and Rowntree (1939, p.213) gave a measure of this, noting that town labourers averaged 50% higher wages in 1936 than farm-workers. Yet, it would be a fallacy to portray 'rurality' as accounting for low wages (Hodge and Monk 2004; Hoggart and Cheng 2006). Today this might seem obvious, with high middle-class inflows into rural locales widening urban shadow effects on rural well-being (e.g. Champion et al. 1987; Henderson and Hoggart 2003). But even when such arrivals were small, income differences persisted in rural areas. In one guise, these were derived from dissimilar industrial compositions. In Hatfield, for example, it arose when the de Havilland Aircraft Company was 'shouldered out' of north London in the 1930s,[94] expanded operations, and in the 1950s was reported to account for 70% of local employment (Hooson 1958, p.202). Such 'imported' jobs came with higher remuneration than offered by many small town manufacturers, which in largely rural regions like Norfolk were commonly dependent on agriculture (Eastwood 1951; Allison 1961). But, even within agriculture there were differences. As the new century dawned, farm-worker wages in Durham and Northumberland were half as much again as they were in Oxfordshire (Rowntree and Kendall 1913, p.24). Summarising trends, Crotch (1901, p.20) identified Cumberland, Durham, Lancashire, Northumberland and Westmorland as a group of higher waged farm-worker counties, with Berkshire, Dorset, Essex, Norfolk, Oxfordshire, Suffolk and Wiltshire at the tail end. Yet Crotch cautioned that comparisons were difficult as farm-workers were paid in different ways (wages or piecework for instance), and were complicated by payments-in-lieu.

3.2.1   Landed Estate Impacts

A compensation for workers was housing at little or no rent coming with employment. According to the Land Enquiry Committee (1913, p.30) 'free cottages' were provided in 23% of English rural parishes, rising to 36% for those tending animals.[95] At the start of the century, this practice was commonly associated with large

---

[94] *HM&CP* 26 January 1934, p.15; Bailey (1978, p.120).

[95] In the Ministry of Labour and National Service (1957, p.197) survey of 1953–1954, 12.7% of the rural sample were living rent-free (the figure for urban centres with less than 100,000 residents was 4.4% and 2.1% for larger centres). Notably by income band, those rural households with incomes

landed estates. These estates had a geography. Captured as the percentage of land in the hands of estates of more than 10,000 acres, Beckett (1986) reported that in the late-nineteenth-century the densest concentrations of estate ownership were in Northumberland and Rutland (holding more than 50% of the land), whereas in the South-East figures below or not much above 10% existed in Cambridgeshire, Essex, Kent, Middlesex, Oxfordshire and Surrey. Moving deeper into the twentieth-century, falling estate profits, death taxes and growing involvement in other sectors pushed estate owners into selling part or all of their holdings (Cannadine 1990; Barnes 1993; Mandler 1997). In the inter-war decades, 130 'great houses' were demolished in England, with more than 1000 taken off Burke's *Landed Gentry* (Beard 1989, p.61). In counties like Norfolk, land sales characterised the very largest and intermediate-sized estates equally (Clemenson 1982, p.154), although those on less productive soils suffered most (Wade-Martins and Williamson 2008, p.79). One outcome was that many tenant farmers became farm-owners, with one-quarter of the land passing from tenant occupation to owner-farmers over 1914–1927 (Beckett and Turner 2007, p.280). For housing, decline in estate fortunes should have been significant, given that cottages were generally larger, better built and with superior maintenance on estates (Mingay 1986, p.129).[96] Many tenants bought their farms to avoid uncertainties of new ownership (Beckett and Turner 2007, p.297) but, with inter-war recession hitting many farm commodity prices (Brassley 2006; Wade-Martin and Williamson 2008), maintaining cottages was a challenge (Howkins 2003, p.65).

How this played out on the ground is instructive, for a substantial stock of employer-provided dwellings fed into beliefs that less public intervention was required. We see this when calls for major housing investment were made. Thus, in 1918 the President of the Board of Agriculture claimed:

> That there is a shortage of cottages for labourers employed in the cultivation of the land is true: that it has been greatly exaggerated is also certain. By far the greater part, if not the whole, of the existing shortage would be satisfactorily met if possession of cottages built by agricultural landlords for agricultural labourers was resumed.[97]

Contributions by landed estates were not limited to estate workers but had a wider remit. Councils were aware of this, as many councillors had landed connections (Table 3.5). As an illustration, in 1936 one Smallburgh councillor reported that his cottages housed more than 70 families with less than 30 his employees.[98] So, when

---

under £3 a week were little different from the overall rural figure, but for those earning £3–£6 a week, the number rose to 15.4% then to 24.5% for those earning £6–£8, dropping below the rural average for higher earners. This was consistent with preserving better quality accommodation for more skilled farm-workers. This group comprised increasing portions of the farm workforce, with attempts to retain these workers signified in a rise from 34.3% of farm-workers living in tied cottages in 1943 to 51.9% in 1969 (Newby 1972).

[96] This message was given to the Cabinet in 1919 (TNA CAB24/73 GT6637 'Housing', 9 January 1919, p.68).

[97] TNA CAB24/43 GT3724 'Rural Housing', 25 February 1918, p.2.

[98] *NM&PWJ* 9 May 1936, p.6.

Table 3.5 Percentage of councillors in investigated rural districts by occupational attributes, 1936–1937

	Hertfordshire		Bedfordshire		Norfolk		
Attribute	Hatfield	Braughing	Ampthill	Biggles wade	Erpingham	Smallburgh	Walsing ham
Farmer-market gardener	0	24	26	23	10	14	9
Principal landholder	21	14	3	8	19	33	23
Own-family business	32	14	11	12	12	12	15
Religious minister	0	5	3	12	14	7	15
Other occupations	26	5	17	8	23	14	17
Private resident	5	0	11	4	6	4	2
No occupation identified	16	38	26	35	16	16	21
(Ex) military officer	0	14	3	0	10	4	7
Justice of the Peace (JP)	16	0	6	0	18	2	4

Source: Council minutes checked against *Kelly's Directories* plus online searches using find-mypast.co.uk, especially of the 1939 Register

Note: These figures are best estimates, as details for many councillors could not be ascertained with confidence. The categories JP and ex-military officer could overlap with listed occupations but other categories did not overlap. To gain a sense of economic background, councillors with no paid work whose spouses' occupations were identified with certainly were listed under their spouse's occupation. This impacted on only four entries, all of which were a farmer's or a principal landholder's spouse. A 'principal landholder' included those listed in *Kelly's Directories* as land agents for a landed estate, principal local landowners or those with at least 150 acres (entries for the last two commonly met both criteria). 'Farmer-market gardener' referred to agricultural producers for which there was no indication of landholding size. For 'own-family business', a cautious approach was taken, so, for example, someone listed as 'baker' or 'plumber' was not included as this was too imprecise. These entries were listed under 'other occupations'. 'Other occupations' included a small number of agricultural labourers. Someone listed with two occupations, even close to one another, like butcher and farmer, were put under 'other occupations'. The 1939 Register was taken just after the Second World War started. It was used to produce identity cards, ration books, for conscription, the placement of labour and mass evacuation. It only collected basic information, such as address, occupant names, ages and occupations. Many farmers found in the 1939 Register were retired, so they could have been large landholders in the past (the 1939 Register gave no indication of farm size). 'Private residents' were listed under their residence in *Kelly's Directory* (suggesting a property of substance) with no occupation, with the 1939 Register adding no clarity, save that some were listed as having private means. Many of those whose occupations could not be identified using the 1939 Register had common names for their local area, so concluding that the right person had been identified was not secure, hence their occupation was 'not identified'

exploring housing needs in 1919, Walsingham's Housing Committee did not inspect Egmere, Holkham and Quarles, '… because it was known that cottages in these parishes were in a superior condition, and Lord Leicester had intimated his intention of building what further cottages are required'.[99] An expectation of landowner contributions was common. These anticipations were not always met. Thus, when Smallburgh asked if three landowners would meet housing needs in 'their parishes' in 1919, negative responses from two meant the Council had to intervene.[100] Similarly, in Ware RDC, landowners expressed willingness to consider building cottages in the future but the high tax and rate charges of 1919 dissuaded them from immediate action.[101] After 1918, estate owners also faced high construction costs, like councils, but lacked Treasury support.[102] Anticipating this problem, a proposal had been put to the Cabinet to offer subsidies for landowner new-build,[103] which the 1919 Housing (Additional Powers) Act later provided. But many estates faced economic difficulties, which limited capacities to respond. However, some had diversified portfolios and defied the demise many experienced, while others had wealth infusions from new owners or marriage (e.g. Adonis 1988; Thompson 2001; Rothery 2007; Macdonald 2017). Here, councils might hope for constructive engagement with estates. This happened in Biggleswade, where council provision in Old Warden was put aside when the Shuttleworth Estate agreed to erect cottages at its own expense.[104] Council gratitude for such actions was encapsulated in an Ampthill resolution when the 11th Duke of Bedford died in 1940:

> DEATH OF HERBRAND 11TH DUKE OF BEDFORD, K.G.- The following resolution was moved from the Chair, seconded by the Vice-Chairman, and carried by a standing vote … In ways too numerous to mention practical help and assistance has been readily given to the Council in connection with its duties in this area. Amongst them - the water supply scheme, established in 1909 to serve the Parishes of Aspley Guise, Aspley Heath and Woburn Sands, and now the means of affording a supply of water to the greater part of the Ampthill Rural District - our Isolation Hospital at Steppingley, made possible by the gift of a large suitable site together with a monetary contribution - the excellent housing scheme

---

[99] NRO DC19/6/8 WRDCM 19 March 1919, p.272. Assumptions about estate provision endured after 1945. In Erpingham, for example, the post-war housing programme did not cover all parishes (TNA MAF147/1 Letter from J. Christie to the MAF Secretary, 16 December 1947), while, in the 1950s, Ampthill redirected an enquiry about housing a nurse in Woburn to the Duke of Bedford's Estate (BRO RDAM2/23 ARDCHCM 23 January 1958).

[100] NRO DC22/2/45 SmRDCHCM 4 November 1919; 17 December 1919.

[101] H&EO 25 January 1919, p.6.

[102] Indicative of price rises, the average cost of a new council home was reported to Parliament as £175/6/7d (excluding land, sewers, water, roads, etc.) for 1911–1913 and £821/13/7d for 1919–1921 (HCH 7 March 1923, Vol.161, col.516W–17W). The figure for 1919–1921 appears to be for all county boroughs, whereas for 1911–1913 it was for 12 cities. These are not strictly comparable but the main difference likely reflects the impact of the 1919 Act, which saw more councils building homes than under the 1890 or 1909 Acts.

[103] TNA CAB24/43 GT3724 'Rural Housing', 25 February 1918, p.2.

[104] BRO RDBwM1/7 BiRDCM 23 July 1919, p.290.

under which houses for the working-classes at low rents were provided by the Woburn Estates in many of the Parishes in the area.[105]

Gauldie (1974, p.53), amongst others, credited the Duke of Bedford's Estate with good quality homes, with reports from other investigated councils bearing witness to similar estate qualities. In 1925, for example, the Walsingham Medical Officer of Health's annual report held that the standard of housing was 'Fair for a rural district, on the large estates a high standard attained'.[106] The equivalent 1930 Ampthill report was more pointed: 'Agricultural labourers on the Woburn Estate are well housed, but in other parts of the district the accommodation should be improved'.[107]

We should not take this observation too far, as it is disputed. For one, so-called closed estate villages only accounted for about one-fifth of rural parishes (Horn 1984, p.24). These often had small populations and only accommodated some estate workers (Linsley 2005, p.23).[108] For another, housing quality varied within estates. Mingay (1986, p.130) exemplified this, noting that: '... the best cottages on Lord Leicester's estates in Norfolk were those by the approach to Holkham Hall, where they would be seen by visitors, the remainder being less well provided'.[109] Bigmore (1979, p.151) offered similar reservations, claiming '... the houses of the Bedford Estate are no more inspiring than the majority of council houses in the Twentieth-Century'; although he praised the Shuttleworth Estate's Old Warden, with its delightful brick and honey-coloured stone cottages with thatched roofs and delicate porches built of uncut timber. Others were more damning. The 1919 MP for Hertford made the point sharply:

> My experience and intimate knowledge of the people of one of the most beautiful parts of England, Hertfordshire, is that the rural property there does not even compare favourably with the slums. I can take the hon. Member to hundreds of houses owned—and I say it advisedly—owned by the lords of the land, standing under the very shadow of some of the most historic castles, in which I would not, and no man who had any respect for anything he bred would, keep pigs.[110]

Even if they were of a quality, there was unevenness. Not all cottages in 'closed' villages belonged to an estate. Reports on decline in estate villages like Great Barrington and Great Tew (Oxfordshire), owing to unresponsive landowners (e.g. Kendall 1963), or Lockinge in Berkshire, which owned virtually all village homes

---

[105] BRO RDAM1/12 ARDCM 5 September 1940.

[106] NRO DC19/6/14 WRDCM 26 May 1926, p.20.

[107] BRO RDAR8/11 ARDCMOHar 1930, p.12.

[108] Estate workers were not just working the land. In the mid-1920s, Hereford RDC had 581 tied cottages, of which 379 were occupied by agricultural labourers, with the others taken up by personal servants, such as grooms, gardeners, chauffeurs, etc. (TNA HLG40/38 'Memo from H.A. Chapman to Tudor Owen on Visits to Hereford and Oxfordshire', undated c1926).

[109] Linsley (2005, p.267) offered a further illustration in recounting the experience of Margery Woodrow, who moved to a Holkham Estate house in 1931 with no water or light, so oil lamps and candles were used and water fetched from a pump 100 yards from the house. Electricity came in 1938 but there was no mains water until 1966.

[110] HCH 7 April 1919, Vol.114, col.1781.

until 1974, after which significant sales for owner-occupation followed (Havinden 1999, pp.210–13), seem to confirm this image. Yet, Wade-Martins (1980, p.190) reported that there was only one parish on the Holkham Estate where the Estate owned as many as half the houses, while Robin (1980, p.217) found about half of Elmdon homes never belonged to the Lofts Estate. Additionally, the circumstances landed estates faced changed substantially over the decades.

Falling agricultural commodity prices damaged many estates from 1870 onwards (Clemenson 1982; Cannadine 1990; Horn 2013). There were differences in timing (Rothery 2007) but examples of estates selling not only land and houses (Bailey 2012, p.418) but also art, books, hunting rights, timber and wine were recorded (Barnes 1993, p.18). The path downwards led to the dismantling of whole estates. As a sign on timing, Godber (1969, p.50) reported that the majority of Bedfordshire estates had been sold by 1939, which point was reiterated by Howkins (2003, p.57) for Derbyshire and Nottinghamshire. Before their demise, less use was made of properties (e.g. Grayson 1992; Houfe 1995, p.281). Then, with political attacks on their 'monopoly' or 'privileged' positions (Cannadine 1990, p.122; Barnes 1993, p.31; Short and Godfrey 2007; Horn 2013, p.72), landowners withdrew from local commitments (Lee 1963; Bealey et al. 1965; Olney 2007). With falling revenues and the payment of death duties,[111] landowners spent less on cottages. For some, the sharp falls were in the nineteenth-century (e.g. Beastall 1966), but for others the decline was a twentieth-century affair, especially after 1918 (Wade-Martins and Williamson 2008, p.157).

Even so, within general commentaries on landed estate decay, observations on estate cottages have been limited. It is a theme that merits more attention, especially given beliefs that estate provision lessened the need for council action. No doubt, around 1919, estate cottages lessened the urgency for council-building in some parishes and many landowners (large and small) offered plots for council-building.[112] The strength of this tendency was revealed when the government reported that RDCs received more than four-fifths of all land gifts for housing in the first year of the 1919 Act (MoH 1920b). Regular offers were also forthcoming of land at low prices.[113] Yet some landowners saw council-building as a potential bonanza. This

---

[111] According to Beard (1989, p.91), after the Second World War, death duties were the primary cause of the break-up of landed estates. Earlier, Barnes (1993, p.57) claimed death duties had drained agriculture of £20 million over 1922–1932, with substantial land sales occurring after a death (Houfe 1995, p.280; Havinden 1999, p.131).

[112] In what became Braughing, for example, two housing sites were offered in 1912 by Mr. Glynn and Robert Balfour (HRO RDC6/1/3 HaRDCM 1 August 1912, p.391; 3 October 1912, p.395), one was given at Sandon in 1915 (HRO RDC4/1/6 BuRDCM 1 April 1915, pp.42–43), and the Chair of Braughing Parish Council offered two acres plus when the 1919 Act came into force (*H&EO* 25 January 1919, p.4). Council minutes list a large number of offers, although entries did not always indicate if payment was expected. That some offers had strings attached was illustrated by John Gowing's offer of a site in Paston provided the resulting homes were let to his workers (NRO DC22/2/45 SmRDCHCM 9 August 1921).

[113] Illustrative of a not uncommon pattern, in early-1919 Hatfield was offered land at prices per acre of £480, £396, £200, £150 and £50; the last from Lord Desborough. The view on Council was

was signified when high prices were demanded for land sales.[114] Thus, the Minister of Health claimed district valuer reductions on over-priced sites saved councils an average of £71 an acre for land under the 1919 Act (£75 if compulsory purchase was used).[115] These figures were for the nation. They indicate a tendency rather than a pattern specific to landed estates. Without access to a list of proposed sale prices, district valuer assessments and selling prices, indications of landowner generosity or profiteering cannot be established with precision. Council minutes were too imprecise to weigh positions with confidence. What can be said is that there was no uniformity in landowner approaches to land sales. This included the attachment of unwelcome conditions on sales. At the curious level, one example of this was the Northaw Estate only agreeing to sell land for council housing if Hatfield built a post office.[116] More commonly, if stipulations were made, they were inclined to follow the Earl of Mexborough's path of donating the land provided he agreed to the housing design.[117] More troubling was Melton Constable, where Walsingham was offered five acres for free by Lord Hastings, who was concerned that, as the preferred site had sewer supply costs, there would be:

> … heavy annual charges which present-day cost of building must cause to fall either on local ratepayers or on the occupiers of the new houses in the form of excessive rents. This has been one of the principal reasons why he has been anxious for the Council to take that site which could be acquired and equipped at the least costs.[118]

The sentiment was appreciated[119] but the site offered was distant from the railway works and was supported by no one save Lord Hastings.[120] Yet, despite such stickiness, in the early years of the 1919 Act, landowner willingness to assist in housing schemes was noteworthy. The tenor of the intervention by the Tempsford Estate (Biggleswade) exemplified a not uncommon spirit of collaboration:

> I am sure you will appreciate that the sale of a site for some eight or nine small houses on the North Road opposite the Hall and Park is most objectionable but he [Colonel Stuart] desires me to say that he will waive his opposition in order to put no difficulty whatever in

these prices were exorbitant, save Lord Desborough's, which was the appropriate agricultural value (*HM&CP* 15 February 1919, p.). Fuelling negativity in the Council's response, the site offered at £396 an acre had been bought for £70 an acre.

[114] Compare, for example, the asking prices for a site at Ludham, for which the owner wanted £240 but the District Valuer assessed it at £115 (NRO DC22/2/45 SmRDCHCM 4 February 1920). Land purchases from the Walsingham Estate regularly had asking prices around twice the District Valuer assessment (e.g. NRO DC13/5/72 ERDCHCM 24 November 1930, p.5; 23 January 1931, p.5; and NRO DC19/6/62 WRDCHCM 23 October 1934, p.56).

[115] HCH 12 July 1920, Vol.131, col.1991W–92W.

[116] HRO RDC7/1/8 HtRDCM 17 April 1924, p.447.

[117] HRO RDC4/1/9 BuRDCM 17 May 1934, p.84.

[118] NRO DC19/6/8 WRDCM 18 February 1920, p.51.

[119] A need for at least 50 houses was reported for Melton Constable owing to the railway company not providing homes for its workers (*NWP&ENS* 21 March 1919, p.1).

[120] *FakPost* 5 March 1920, p.5.

the way of your Authority acquiring what they believe to be the best sites for houses to be built in the future.[121]

Whether caught up with a general mood of gratitude over losses during the First World War or fearful of retribution owing to negativity towards landowners,[122] many landed estates engaged with rural districts to improve housing stocks under the 1919 Act.[123]

But estate decline and high turnover in ownership introduced different owner priorities. Both tended to raise pressure on councils to provide homes. Two examples were new owners for the Walsingham Estate and George Walker's land sale at Dilham (Smallburgh), both of which saw existing cottage tenants ejected, so raising demand for council dwellings.[124] For the time, this was hardly unusual, but these actions hinted at a declining reliability in estate provision. By the early-1930s, government reports were emphasising the point (e.g. MAF and MoH 1932), with the inter-war years in general punctuated by concern over landowner (and farmer) failure to erect or improve cottages. This saw expression in growing concern over the condition of dwellings. By the mid-1930s, for example, Braughing was taking legal action against, and then demolishing, unfit cottages owned by the Earl of Mexborough.[125] With pressure on the Council to replace these lost dwellings, the charitable side of the landed class was demonstrated in the Earl giving land at no cost for housing.[126] Indeed, when needed for his Estate, the Earl even erected a few new dwellings.[127] But the trend was largely in one direction. By 1926, even the National Farmers' Union was arguing that few landowners could meet housing needs on their holdings.[128] Indeed, although the 1926 Housing (Rural Workers) Act

---

[121] BRO WY953 Tempsford Estate Letter on Biggleswade Housing Scheme, 27 April 1920, p.41.

[122] Note, for example, concern in Cabinet over landowner evictions of ex-armed forces tenants of longstanding (TNA CAB24/89 GT8228 'Report on Revolutionary Organisations in the UK', 25 September 1919, p.96–2). There was antagonism toward landlords in Parliament during the First World War when the families of soldiers at the front faced large rent hikes or eviction (e.g. HCH 14 October 1915, Vol.74, col.1566; HCH 30 April 1918, Vol.105, col.1429).

[123] Despite the 1919 Housing (Additional Powers) Act and the 1923 Housing Act explicitly offering subsidies to private-owners, legal difficulties were raised over landowners receiving subsidies under the 1923 Act (TNA HLG48/704 Letter from H.D. Vigor to J.C. Wrigley, 25 June 1925; Reply, 4 July 1925). Whatever these were, under later legislation they did not hold, with the Earl of Leicester taking public subsidies for his Holkham Estate under both the (largely public sector) 1924 Act and the 1926 Housing (Rural Workers) Act; the latter funding dwelling upgrades (NRO DC19/6/14 WRDCM 31 August 1926, p.48; NRO DC19/6/16 WRDCM 12 September 1928, p.56).

[124] HMC&WP 14 March 1924, p.5; FakPost 17 April 1931, p.1.

[125] HRO RDC3/2/1 BrRDCPHHCM 19 June 1935, p.25; HRO RDC3/1/1 BrRDCM 2 July 1936, p.151; HRO RDC3/2/1 BrRDCPHHCM 22 July 1936, p.127.

[126] HRO RDC3/2/1 BrRDCPHHCM 17 December 1936, p.159; HRO RDC3/1/1 BrRDCM 6 May 1937, p.233.

[127] B&NEHG 3 September 1937, p.2.

[128] TNA MAF48/206 'Minutes of Deputations to Ministers of Health and Agriculture', 9 March 1926. This message was repeated a decade later (TNA HLG37/43 'Statement by the NFU', undated c1936).

introduced grants if landowners upgraded properties, its enactment was a failure (when set against government expectations at least, even if 22,840 English dwellings were reconditioned by 1944).[129] A primary cause was the placement of limits on rent rises after improvements. These were supposed to keep upgraded properties within farm-workers' budgets but landowners preferred to keep cottages empty, rent them to weekenders or sell them.[130] This was consistent with general landlord reactions to rent restrictions, which saw council and Parliamentary criticism over increases in unoccupied homes[131] and in dwellings being rented or sold to urban residents.[132] Kingsley Wood, the Minister of Health who introduced the 1926 Act, held that its provisions '... absolutely prevents any possibility of these dwellings being used by the weekender'.[133] But rural councils, like Saffron Walden RDC in 1932, still found farm-worker cottages were lost:

> A large proportion of the cottages were of the lath and plaster type and many of these were now defective, but their thorough repair was difficult and expensive in relation to their value. It was not surprising that many of the owners preferred to sell such property, and, in some cases, the owners got rid of the original tenants, and, having carried out repairs and improvements, let the cottages at a much higher rent to people from other districts.[134]

How extensive this practice was cannot be ascertained with certainty. But, even when farm-worker wages and farm profitability increased after the Second World War, there were ongoing concerns about weekender take-up of farm labourer dwellings, as seen when Braughing investigated requisitioning such dwellings[135] or the North Walsham branch of the Conservative and Liberal Association criticised the impact of holiday homes on the north Norfolk coast.[136] All this occurred long before second homes became a prominent research topic in academic studies.

Of course, weekender cottages were not only secured from large estates, and deteriorating dwellings were not restricted to manorial holdings. Nevertheless, the capacity of landed estates to mitigate council provision was increasingly questioned. More attention was drawn to negative aspects of estates. The quirky

---

[129] HCH 12 December 1944, Vol.406, col.1172.

[130] For example, TNA HLG37/43 'Housing (Rural Workers) Acts', undated c1936; and 'Investigation by General Inspectors 1934', where commentary on Bedford, Berkshire, Buckingham, Northamptonshire, Oxfordshire and Peterborough indicated that: 'The reconditioning of houses for agricultural labourers is discouraged by the opportunities for obtaining high prices for weekend cottages' (p.5), while in Gloucestershire, Warwickshire, Wiltshire and Worcestershire: 'There is tremendous demand for weekend cottages and cottages for persons of the artisan within the reach of Birmingham and Coventry, with the result that owners in these areas object to the restrictions on rent' (p.15).

[131] For example, in Runton (Erpingham), 20 dwellings were identified as unoccupied for 9 months each year (*FakPost* 13 February 1925, p.3).

[132] See the MP for Warwick and Leamington at HCH 7 May 1925, Vol.183, col.1139.

[133] HCH 3 August 1926, Vol.198, col.2910.

[134] *H&EO* 6 August 1932, p.3.

[135] *H&EO* 12 April 1947, p.3.

[136] *NNN* 9 December 1949, p.1.

character of some estate owners might have been longstanding but a decade after universal suffrage was granted to those over 21 years in 1928, it had not disappeared, as when '… the then Lord Stamford used to ride around his estates on a white horse, lashing out with his whip at anyone who did not raise his cap or show suitable deference in other ways – or so it is said – to the great surprise of respectable middle-class retired people' (Harris 1974, p.42). In Rutland, the replacement of landed elites by a new middle-class establishment seemingly offered little better, with the new headmaster of Barrowden in 1972 finding its politics run in an 'almost feudal' manner by a triumvirate of doctor, farmer and rector (Duckers and Davies 1990, p.125). That such 'feudal' attitudes impacted on council housing was evident in the 1930s' accounts of the Duchy of Cornwall opposing new cottages because they might 'spoil the view',[137] with estate strangleholds on land limiting other prospects,[138] just as many tied cottage owners were reluctant to provide piped water to dwellings.[139] Especially after 1945, reports of estates not maintaining their properties increased.[140] By the mid-1950s, even the Duke of Bedford's Estate, which in earlier times was reputed to provide amongst the best cottages in the country (Green 1920, p.156), was in trouble. The ethos of the Estate was laid down in the nineteenth-century, when the then Duke proclaimed: 'I know of no more satisfactory form of philanthropy possible for the owner of a great estate than the provision of good cottages' (Duke of Bedford 1897, p.81). Post-1945, the Estate started selling land again,[141] tenants were evicted,[142] and cottages sold[143] or kept empty or demolished.[144] Such incidents worried council officials, who feared bulging waiting lists.[145] This provoked Ampthill to investigate the Estate's dwellings.[146] The Estate was not on its last legs, for new worker dwellings were still proposed.[147] But a shift

---

[137] TNA HLG37/43 'Report on Local Investigations in Wiltshire, Bedfordshire, Derbyshire and Anglesey', undated c1936, p.13.

[138] Illustrative reports on the Duke of Bedford's holdings include: *W&DR* 28 February 1939, p.3; *WR&WSR* 7 September 1943, p.1.

[139] TNA HLG40/41 Letter from Hugh Molson MP to Henry Willink, MoH, 1 May 1944.

[140] HRO CP35/6/3 Letter from Essendon Parish Council Clerk to Hatfield RDC Clerk, 9 October 1951; BRO RDAM2/22 ARDCHCM 13 December 1951; 20 January 1955. National estimates suggested 127,000 cottages tied to agricultural work in 1945, of which 50% were in need of reconditioning and 10% needed demolishing. Dwellings owned by farmers but not used by their workers were said to have gone by 1945 (TNA HLG40/50 'Tied Cottages', undated c1951). In 1975, the government estimated 70,000 farm-workers lived in tied cottages (HCH 11 December 1975, Vol.902, col.628).

[141] BRO RDAM2/23 ARDCHCM 18 February 1960; 21 September 1961. A previous Duke had caused a sensation by selling nearly half his Estate in 1909 (Thompson 1963, p.322), following this with the sale of Covent Garden holdings in 1913 (Cannadine 1990, p.56, p.122).

[142] *WR&WSR* 13 June 1967, p.3

[143] Such as the 80 reported in the *WR&WSR* 6 June 1961, p.1.

[144] For example, *WR&WSR* 4 December 1962, p.22.

[145] For example, NRO DC19/6/67 WRDCHCM 9 April 1956, p.66.

[146] See BRO RDAM1/15 ARDCM 27 January 1955, p.2; *WR&WSR* 4 October 1955, p.1.

[147] As for three at Woburn in 1969; BRO RDAM1/25 ARDCHPBuCM 13 November 1969.

had occurred, with the Council occupying a central role, not just for housing outside the Estate but also within it. Thus, in what was undoubtedly incomplete coverage given that some entries do not specify numbers (so count as one here), the Bedford Settled Estates started improving its homes with grant aid from the RDC, with applications for six dwellings in 1959, followed by 12 in 1960 and 16 in 1961. By 1970, the Estate's declared intention was '… to provide immediately all houses in their ownership with WCs and hot and cold water supply to the sinks', with applications for 65 improvement grants made for Husborne Crawley and Ridgmont alone (eight later withdrawn).[148] Yet, by the late-1960s, when council homes recorded high levels of housing amenity, evidence had mounted of inadequate dwellings and timid efforts to make improvements, even on large estates.[149]

3.2.2   Homes for Employers

Attention to landed estates is justified because tied cottage accommodation on independent farms often originated in the break-up of estates and because other rural employers generally offered few alternatives to council housing (Beard 1989, p.40; Thompson 2007, p.292).[150] This was recognised as early as 1919, when Cabinet papers suggested public institutions should take responsibility for housing their workers:

> … it is urgently necessary that before the Government seek to compel the erection of working-class houses steps should be taken to make it obligatory on County Councils, District Councils, Railway and Post Office authorities to find houses for their own employees. At present, there is hardly a village of more than 150 or 300 people where it will not be found that from two to even six or seven cottages provided by the local landowners are occupied by men employed by these Authorities.[151]

The veracity of this view was confirmed in a multitude of employer requests for housing, and in parish and RDC discontent over employers' failure to act. Norfolk's Depwade RDC experienced the force of this in 1919 when its housing programme was drawn up following negative local employer responses to enquiries on their building plans (Linsley 2005, p.24). Even large employers were reluctant, as in Walsingham, when the Midland and Great Northern Joint Railway failed to provide

---

[148] BRO RDAM1/25 ARDCHPBuCM 15 January 1970.

[149] As found in Thingoe RDC (TNA HLG118/558 'Improvement Report Eastern Counties', July 1966, p.3).

[150] Inevitably, there are caveats to any 'generalisation'. Here, the qualification is that some industries, like mining, had a tradition of supplying dwellings for workers. Suggesting an ongoing, if declining, importance, the 1961 census reported on homes rented from employers (the 1971 census did not), with the three counties whose RDCs recorded the highest occurrences including a largely agricultural area (Rutland, with 23.4% of all households) and two with a mix of mining and agriculture (Northumberland at 25.0% and Nottinghamshire at 22.6%).

[151] TNA CAB24/73 GT6618 'Housing Memorandum for the War Cabinet', 7 January 1919.

homes at Melton Constable, resulting in demands for 50 new council dwellings.[152] In the investigated districts, other employers who pressed for council homes around 1919 included the London and North Western Railway, the police and the Admiralty.[153] Move forward to the 1930s and demand had not abated, even if the agencies changed, with the Air Ministry and brick companies in Bedfordshire active, alongside the employers of nurses and the police.[154] The volume of requests in these decades was moderate compared with after 1945, when a flood of appeals from public agencies occurred, especially for the fire service, nurses, the police, teachers and the armed forces (for civilian personnel).[155] Private sector applications also grew with company reluctance to offer homes. The de Havilland Company was illustrative. Following its move to Hatfield, the firm initially bused workers from London. Just before and during the Second World War, demand for aircraft workers rose, but the Company was lackadaisical over housing:

> Apparently the problem of housing employees locally, before the designation of the New Towns, never appeared so extremely acute to the de Havillands that they formulated any policy for solving it – except the negative policy of not becoming their employees' landlords. They did not give more than casual support to the idea of siting a new town at Hatfield, though now it has come, and fifty per cent of its houses are reserved for employees of the firm, they find it useful. (Hatfield WEA 1959, Book 12, p.1218)

For varied reasons, after 1945, employer recognition of worker needs rose. Companies pressed for council allocations. What was perhaps unexpected was the increased scale of demand. For instance, compared with 12 houses requested by the Marston Valley Brick Company in 1931, in 1946 the Company sought 400 houses from Ampthill.[156] That the frequency and size of requests distinguished the 1930s from the post-1945 years owed something to a shift away from the laissez-faire economics of the 1930s to a more integrated approach to wealth creation under the 1945–1951 government (Cairncross 1995). One consequence was a dramatic rise in expectations surrounding public services, as expressed in legislation like the 1944 Education Act and the 1946 National Health Service Act (Ashford 1986; Fraser 2009). With concerns over the spatial concentration of industry, given dangers of 'enemy' attack in future wars, plus regional imbalances associated with government inaction in the 1930s (Crafts 1987), job dispersal from London was favoured (e.g. Thirlwall 1967). This necessitated new housing investment, as occurred in World

---

[152] *NWP&ENS* 21 March 1919, p.1.

[153] *Leighton Buzzard Reporter and South Beds Advertiser* 30 August 1919, p.1; NRO DC19/6/9 WRDCM 15 June 1921, p.203; *FakPost* 28 October 1921, p.5.

[154] For example: BRO RDAM1/9 ARDCM 5 March 1931; TNA HLG37/43 'Report on Local Investigations …', undated c1936, p.23; *NBC&BR* 9 June 1937, p.16; *NM&PWJ* 3 July 1937, p.15; *T&WT* 17 December 1938, p.8.

[155] For 1945–1960, recorded requests for nurses alone made to Ampthill and Biggleswade included: *NBC&BR* 17 February 1948, p.8; 14 September 1948, p.5; 8 June 1954, p.2; *WR&WSR* 7 January 1958, p.14; *BC&BG* 22 May 1959, p.1; BRO ARDCHCM 12 December 1946; 19 August 1948; 25 April 1957; 23 January 1958; 23 January 1960.

[156] *W&DR* 7 February 1931, p.1; BRO RDAM2/22 ARDCHCM 21 October 1946.

War Two for armament workers and, less notably, farm-workers.[157] One result was more companies operating beyond previous geographical spheres. With economic trauma in the late-1940s, another consideration was priority for firms securing 'dollar exports'. This led to significant extra allocations for targeted firms (and councils), with the 'dollar export' premium later converted into broader support for 'key worker' homes. The creation of new, expanding and overspill settlements then led to rural districts like Hatfield, Luton, Melford, Seisdon, Sodbury, Thornbury and Tutbury,[158] alongside numerous small market towns, like Huntingdon and Thetford (Moseley 1973), seeing extensive employment and population growth. In combination these initiatives made the post-1945 environment very different from the 1930s. An early sign was the 1950 offer to Hatfield of a special allocation of 60 houses if homes went to dollar-earning workers,[159] with 50 allotted to Biggleswade Town the same year, 12 to Walsingham the year after and the first six in a string of awards to Biggleswade in 1952.[160] These distributions were not made to all RDCs but many, like Smallburgh, as well as numerous market towns, had them. Provision was overwhelmingly public sector. If so 'favoured', localities were supported in expanding housing numbers. Unlike the inter-war years, when the impetus for council expansion was primarily in local hands, post-1945 saw a stronger stamp of national direction.

The imprint of this change should have been visible in non-estate private rental. Here, we find little insight in minutes and council documents, which rarely reported on this tenure, except to identify homes they wanted to close or see improved, while the population census provided no information on tenure until 1961. Before this, commentary on private rental was largely at the national level. Here, in the 1930s, there were regular messages from ministers praising new-build volumes with a low rateable value (under £13 or under £20 in London), which were assumed to provide an '… indication that the extensive activity of private enterprise has been of substantial benefit to members of the working-classes' (MoH 1936a, p.82). The government made pronouncements on the number of new-build private homes that were rented, with 17.5% quoted for 1933,[161] then one-third in 1936.[162] Even if accurate,

---

[157] In all, 3000 new houses were approved early in the War, the bulk for munition workers. For homes built with public subsidy, which most munition worker homes were not, 333 of 704 approved were for farm-workers (HCH 4 March 1940, Vol.358, col.41W).

[158] 'Overspill' arrangements for Birmingham, Bristol, Liverpool, London, Manchester, Newcastle-upon-Tyne, Salford and Wolverhampton can be found at HCH 21 December 1966, Vol.738, col.382W–83W. Some new towns also encompassed parts of RDCs, such as Hatfield, Newton Aycliffe (Darlington and Sedgefield) and Peterlee (Easington).

[159] HRO RDC7/1/14 HtRDCM 3 October 1950, p.114.

[160] NBC&BR 24 October 1950, p.4; D&FT 20 April 1951, p.1; BRO RDBwM1/23 BiRDCM 6 August 1952, p.145.

[161] HCH 8 February 1934, Vol.285, col.1291. This figure was for houses built without subsidy, which included a small number of council-owned dwellings. But, as no-subsidy council construction was low in 1933, their inclusion would have made little impression on the overall percentage (see HCH 11 March 1946, Vol.420, col.161W–62W).

[162] HCH 16 July 1936, Vol.314, col.2286.

the implied responsiveness to working-class housing needs was questioned. Ministry of Labour figures suggested only 17.8% on non-agricultural working-class households owned or were purchasing a dwelling in 1937–1938 (Scott 2008, p.9), which left a large gap in supply at a time when council construction was restricted and older private rental properties were disappearing. This downward slide was noted in 1960, when it was confirmed that: 'There has been virtually no building to let since 1939, except by local authorities and new town development corporations'.[163] The 1957 Rent Act was the Conservatives hoped-for reactivation of private rental, with ministers proclaiming success under its provisions.[164] However, in 1965 the Ministry estimated that 25% of private rental units had been lost since the Act was passed.[165] Movement downwards continued, with generally lower wages amongst rural workers meaning recourse to home ownership was weak. In answer to the question, was council action necessary, the combination of declining availability and worsening standards in private rental, plus cost and lender restrictions on mortgages, all point to the need. Were rural leaders disposed to meet this necessity?

3.3   Rural Values?

Long before 1970s' studies identified farmer-dominated councils' disinclination towards council-building (e.g. Saunders et al. 1978), MPs had reached the same conclusion. A veteran of almost 40 years in Parliament, and the 1945–1951 minister for agriculture, Tom Williams, offered one rendition:

> There are two reasons why rural councils have not built houses in sufficient numbers to enable agricultural labourers to have any sense of freedom. The first is that farmers are afraid of a rise in their rates; and they are the last people in the world to build houses, or do anything else, if it is calculated to increase the rates and, incidentally, increase their expenses. The second reason is that farmers do not wish to lose the powers they have over their workmen which the system of the tied cottage gives.[166]

If this was a general tendency, it helped explain broader critiques of rural councils:

> … the rural district councils who have been the housing authorities have varied to a considerable extent in the enterprise and energy with which they have tackled housing … though there was this great variety, it cannot be claimed on their behalf that it was well done, with energy and with vigour. Comparing them with the urban authorities, the present situation is

---

[163] TNA HLG118/298 'Memo to PM from Henry Brooke', 25 February 1960.

[164] HCH 26 March 1963, Vol.674, col.1109; HCH 18 June 1963, Vol.679, col.26W.

[165] HCH 22 March 1965, Vol.709, col.77.

[166] HCH 4 April 1928, Vol.215, col.2034. Williams made similar charges earlier, claiming: '… there are many rural areas where the water supply could and would have been obtained had it not been for the fact that so many rural property-owners are also members of the rural councils, not for the purpose of making provision for anything, but to see that no money is spent' (HCH 6 December 1926, Vol.200, col.1727). Others referred to 'vested interests' ensuring nothing was done (e.g. HCH 21 February 1930, Vol.235, col.1812).

that in the towns one family in eight is housed in a house provided by the municipal authorities, while in the rural areas one family in 13 is housed in a municipal house.[167]

Farmer self-interest need not have been at the heart of rural sloth. For one, the farming community across the country had dissimilar demands for farm labourers. Illustrating this, for men in rural districts in 1971, out of 45 (non-London) counties only eight had farm-worker shares in the agricultural workforce above 60% (Berkshire the highest at 66.6%), with 10 recording under 40% (Westmorland the lowest at 26.7%). For another, farmers were unevenly spread across districts, with capacities to 'control' councils similarly variable. Thus, while eight 1971 counties had more than 10% of male workers as farm owners-managers in their RDCs (Westmorland the highest at 22.7%), three had shares of under 2% (Berkshire, Hertfordshire and Surrey) and a further two had under 3% (Buckinghamshire and Durham). Note the juxtaposition of highest and lowest counties here, which highlights that some counties had a strong farmer presence without farm labourers, while others had many farm-workers but few farmers. If rural councils experienced an exertion of 'farmer power', this was likely manifest in different ways, with incentives to 'control' employees of little relevance in some areas. Yet, irrespective of whether they employed workers, farmers operated in markets over which they had little control. They were price-takers, compared to the more 'monopolistic' price-makers of pre-1970s' corporations (O'Connor 1973). In this, they had much in common with most small non-farm businesses. In responding to housing problems, the combined strength of this farmer-small business group[168] has led some to portray poor rural reactions as resulting from distinctly rural attitudes. As the RDCA told the Rural Housing Sub-Committee, they '… should realise that the rural mind tends towards liking to persuade the private individual to do his own job'.[169] This interpretation is blind to shared threads across rural and urban settings. These threads expose divisions amongst the middle-classes (Savage 2000), distinguishing those whose roots and self-definition are grounded in organisational affiliation (many in the service-classes) from those grounded in individualism (many in the petit bourgeoisie), with the latter having a strong rural representation for a long time, while the former arrived in force more recently.

As well as these strands, operational cultures were shared across rural and urban governments. In the 1960s attention was paid to the values and behaviour of elected members and non-elected officials partly due to calls for reform. Critical points that emerged were the separation of elected members from the citizenry. This was made apparent in three main ways. First, because local elections were weakly related to council performance (e.g. Green 1972), with councillor candidates increasingly

---

[167] The MP for St Albans at HCH 25 March 1947, Vol.435, col.1144.

[168] In 1971, 15.3% of male workers in English rural districts were farmers or small business owners-managers, compared with 9.1% in MBs-UDCs and 6.3% in county boroughs.

[169] TNA HLG37/51 Rural Housing Sub-Committee Meeting Minutes, 11 April 1946, p.3.

standing uncontested (Harrison and Norton 1967, p.49).[170] Especially in rural districts, where only 43% of councillors became members before the age of 45 (in county boroughs 56%), this led to an elderly, unchanging council membership (Harrison and Norton 1967, p.49; Morris and Newton 1971). Second, councillors reported little constituent interest in or knowledge of local government (MHLG 1967, p.92; Heclo 1969), with local election contests (if party-based) determined more by national considerations than local actions (Green 1972). The outcome was a third consequence, namely, a lack of electoral constraint over councillor actions (e.g. Dearlove 1973). This might appear an ideal breeding ground for vested interests, especially in rural districts lacking the discipline of political party organisation (Grant 1977). Yet local political party impacts were rarely profound. For one, even in cities, the bulk of business was not transacted along party lines (Harrison and Norton 1967, p.100). For another, the dividing line between parties was fluid. Journalistic coverage often points to strong ideologies driving councils, with the implication that the actions of a few characterise the many. Ready examples from the 1980s would be Westminster, Wandsworth, Sheffield, Liverpool and Lambeth (Gyford 1985; Butcher et al. 1990). Yet fleeting expressions of radicalism came and went in local government over the twentieth-century, usually penetrating a minority of councils and rarely staying for long (e.g. Macintyre 1980). Hence, Labour councils with 1980s reputations for Left-wing radicalism, like Islington and Liverpool, were bastions of orthodox tax setting avoidance in the 1960s (Butterworth 1966; Baxter 1972), as were many councils in earlier decades, like inter-war Preston, where Labour had a 'ratepayer's perspective' (Mark-Lawson et al. 1985). Even in cities, council meetings were more like 'club evenings' (Harrison and Norton 1967, p.38), with few councillors revealing political ambition or a desire to achieve policy change. Within active political parties, satisfaction was commonly derived mainly from the status of political office, not policy achievement (Blondel and Hall 1967).[171] What Newton (1976, p.241) reported for Birmingham had wider resonance; viz. '… the mood of the council membership is generally cautious, conservative, and suspicious of change of any kind'.

On rural councils leadership by large landowners declined over the twentieth-century, much as business magnates withdrew from city leadership (Morris and Newton 1970; Harris 1974; Robin 1980; Olney 2007). This withdrawal was uneven, with studies showing longer durations in the 'deeper rural' enclaves of agricultural and peripheral counties (Lee 1963; Johnson 1972; Axford 1978). For the investigated rural districts, Table 3.5 captures one time-slot in this unfolding process.[172] We begin to draw linkage with dissimilar approaches to housing supply in the sec-

---

[170] In 1945, uncontested seats in RDC elections stood at 59.2%, rising to 75.2% in 1964 (MHLG 1967, p. 93). For county boroughs the figures were 7.7% and 18.8%.

[171] This description should not be transposed unchanged onto the post-1974 local government system, which younger councillors dominated (McGrew and Bristow 1984).

[172] The year 1936–1937 was selected as it was flanked by landed estate inputs then farmer ascendancy. On councillor occupations, records lack precision. Rees and Smith (1964) offered one indication, when finding that Barking Council's own records incorrectly identified 21% of councillor

tion below, but to set a context we note the occupational frameworks of the seven councils. The two extremes were Hatfield and Smallburgh. The former had a large non-landed composition, while the latter had the most extensive landed interests. Not that Smallburgh was so far away from Walsingham (or to a lesser extent Erpingham), while Ampthill, Braughing and Biggleswade had substantial agricultural components even if principal landowners were less prominent. Where a differential break-down in agricultural roles emerged was in employment trends. Hatfield always stood apart, with just 31.3% of male workers employed in the sector in 1921, which fell by roughly 10% each census period to reach only 10.7% in 1951. Ampthill and Biggleswade followed suit, declining from 47.3% to 26.1% (Ampthill) and from 46.1% to 22.5% (Biggleswade). Braughing was more like the three Norfolk districts with a fall from the 1921 Buntingford-Hadham figure of around 55% to 41.8% in 1951, adding weight to Bailey's (1978, p.28) observation that the eastern part of Hertfordshire had a traditional rural character. This decline was less than that of Walsingham (50.0% to 23.0%) but came close to Smallburgh (59.5% to 43.9%) and Erpingham (46.1% and 37.5%). In terms of employment trajectories, assuming little change between 1936–1937 and 1951, only Ampthill and Braughing had land-based interests on council similar to their district's workforce. Erpingham had proportionately fewer councillors with a land-based background than its agricultural workforce, although it demonstrated 'traditional establishment' traits as the only district with many councillors from the clergy, the military or justices of the peace. Smallburgh was the sole district where councillors had a knighthood or equivalent (with four), alongside one-third listed by *Kelly's Directory* as local 'principal landowners'. This district perhaps characterised Johnson's (1972) caricature of old-family authority in Norfolk persisting well into the twentieth-century (also Harris 1974; Newby et al. 1978). But it was Hatfield that stood apart. It had more councillors in 'other occupations' or running their own business (Table 3.5) and a greater dispersal of occupations (barrister, brewing, the police). In addition, alongside Ampthill (39.1% in 1951 and 30.6% in 1921), Hatfield had a higher 1951 labour force dependence on external jobs (36.6%, with 20.9% in 1921). This provided sharp contrast with the Norfolk councils, which all had fewer than 20% working outside their district (Walsingham the lowest with 5.5% in 1951). This context for local policy-making highlights a distinct pattern for Braughing. In 1921, 22.9% of employed Hadham residents worked externally (the former district the closest to London) but only 9.7% did in Buntingford. Even within what became a single district, there was divergence, which in some cases fed into council responses.

---

occupations. As a detailed contemporary survey of councillors was not possible, only a general picture can be offered.

3.3.1   Divergent Approaches to Housing Supply

Over the twentieth-century, the character of rural housing options was conditioned by national decline in private rental. As Table 2.2 demonstrates, getting towards 40% of inter-war growth in owner-occupation came not from new-build but the sale of rented properties. From 1938–1960, purchases into owner-occupation even outstripped increments through new-build. Only from the 1960s, with an ever dwindling private rental stock and government exertions to increase house-building did new-build dominate expansion in home ownership. Those in the middle-classes and upper reaches of the working-classes, who had sufficient resources and matched lender criteria, could gain from rental decline by home purchase. For those without such benefits, options revolved around hoping for improvements in private rental, accepting poorer living conditions or securing a council tenancy. Another option was flight, whose impact on rural properties is explored in the next chapter, but about which widespread complaints arose over shortages and disrepair 'forcing' households to leave the countryside.[173] Attention to such shortcomings was perhaps deflected for a long time by repeated messages about rural depopulation (Mitchell 1950; Saville 1957; Bracey 1958; Drudy 1978), the implication being that a bounty of properties were available for those left behind, which burgeoning second home studies in the 1970s fed into (Bielckus et al. 1972; Downing and Dower 1973; Coppock 1977; Coleman 1982). Visions of unwanted rural homes fed politically inspired messages, like the 1960 assertion '… there is no longer a nation-wide shortage of housing accommodation. In many rural areas and small towns there is now no great problem; over a large part of the country the truly urgent needs have been met'.[174] For the middle-classes, this might have been so. Certainly, the roots of concerns about rural housing today focus on channelling and mitigating the impacts of house-building for private-owners (Satsangi et al. 2010), which builds directly onto inter-war 'suburbanisation' trends in rural owner-occupation (Baker 1953, p.186). That these inflows did not bring adequate benefits for the less favoured was demonstrated by the greatest deficiencies in social housing being in the countryside even at the end of the twentieth-century (Bramley and Smart 1995). This was disappointing, given a solid rural performance under the 1919 Act. Thus, RDCs built 4.56 dwellings per 1000 inhabitants under this Act, which was higher than for cities (4.00) or larger towns (4.48), and was only surpassed by smaller towns (UDCs at 5.75; Jennings 1971, p.124). With the exception of the late-1940s, when housing for

---

[173] This was picked up in various districts in the 1930s, as in Ampthill (*W&DR* 3 February 1934, p.6), Smallburgh (*NM&PWJ* 9 May 1936, p.6) and in multi-county investigations (TNA HLG37/43 'Report on Local Investigations …', undated c1936, p.4; MoH 1937, p.7), as well as in academic accounts (e.g. Shears 1936), but it was reported after 1945, as in Newport Pagnell RDC (*WR&WSR* 13 June 1961, p.1; 19 November 1963, p.1) and Ampthill (RDAR8/52 ARDCMOHar 1971, p.16).
[174] TNA CAB129/101 C(60)96 'Housing', 17 June 1960, p.5.

agricultural workers was favoured,[175] commentaries often note weak rural council-building (e.g. Pedley 1942; Marshall 1968; Phillips and Williams 1982). This observation needs treating with caution.

There are three reasons for this. The first was variation across the nation. Let us start with the 1919 Act. There is a sense of congratulation in some accounts of city performances under this Act, as with Finnigan (1980) noting that Leeds built 7.3 dwellings per 1000 inhabitants under the Act, which Jennings (1971) put as the fifth equal city performance. According to Jennings, the highest city output was West Bromwich at 11.0 per 1000. This compares with 26.5 for Biggleswade and 17.1 for Biggleswade Town. Although its population in 1921 was only 23,015, the RDC built 611 Addison homes. Tynemouth, the fifth equal city performer, only managed 490 dwellings for its 63,770 inhabitants (Byrne 1980). The market town of Biggleswade, with just 5395 residents, managed 92 homes. Of course, contrasts using extremes are stretched. Neighbouring Ampthill only achieved a rate of 2.9, while two of the investigated Norfolk councils secured 1.8 (Erpingham) and 1.4 (Walsingham), which placed them in the ballpark of the 10 worst performing cities (Jennings 1971, p.125). Divergence existed, with case studies suggesting limp responses where political dispositions opposed state intervention (e.g. Smith and Whysall 1990), if builders were unwilling to tender (Bedale 1980), if Ministry actions were confused (Dale 1980) or there were difficulties securing materials (Linsley 2005, p.9). Trends in housing output were not simply about rural–urban contrasts. For instance, Jennings (1971, p.125) found that 30% of councils completed no homes under the 1919 Act, but both urban and rural authorities sat in this void. The weak performances at 1971 identified in Chap. 2 for upland-peripheral counties also held for the early-1920s, for '… only in the rural counties of Wales, in Cornwall, in Northumberland, Westmorland and the North Riding of Yorkshire was there a majority of authorities not building' (Jennings 1971, p.125). Elsewhere, rural under-performance was less stark.

By 1961, rural districts in Bedfordshire and Hertfordshire were effectively on par with neighbouring urban authorities as regards council provision. In Norfolk, rural districts fell far behind. Only three rural districts in this county (Depwade, Smallburgh and Swaffham) had proportionately more council tenants than the national average or compared with male manual worker numbers (Table 3.6). There were wide differences between neighbouring councils. In Hertfordshire, images of leafy, middle-class 'suburban' owner-occupied estates appear confirmed by low public sector shares in places like East Barnet (8.9%), Tring (11.0%) or Bushey (14.0%), with another six towns with less than one-fifth of the stock in public ownership. Yet the county also contained a number of 'new towns', like Stevenage (85.9%), Welwyn Garden City (78.2%), Hemel Hempstead (55.4%) and Letchworth (42.1%), where public sector tenancy was high, given a 1961 England average of 23.7%. Some RDCs also had high public sector contributions, as with Elstree

---

[175]TNA CAB129/21 CP(47)284 'Investment Programme Committee. Memorandum by Minister for Economic Affairs', 16 October 1947.

Table 3.6 Percentage of households in Bedfordshire, Hertfordshire and Norfolk with public sector or employer provided accommodation, 1961

	Percent of households as public sector tenants	Percent of households as public sector tenants or in employer-provided homes	Households as public sector tenants per 100 male manual workers	Households as public sector tenants or in employer-provided homes per 100 male manual workers
Hertfordshire urban	33.2	36.6	60.4	66.8
Hertfordshire rural	37.1	45.2	63.5	77.4
Bedfordshire urban	19.4	22.4	27.6	32.0
Bedfordshire rural	21.4	32.1	34.0	51.1
Norfolk urban	34.4	37.7	61.3	67.3
Norfolk rural	19.1	33.3	33.0	57.6
England	23.7	28.6	39.6	47.7

Source: Computed from county reports of the 1961 population census
Note: These figures excluded businesses that come with residential accommodation. 'Urban' refers to all districts that were not RDCs (so county boroughs, boroughs and UDCs combined). In Hertfordshire, occupants of council dwellings included some housed in new town dwellings, as in Hatfield, where nominations to the New Town Development Corporation were made by 1960 (HRO RDC7/1/26 HtRDCHCM 29 March 1960). Manual worker numbers included farm labourers

(60.7%), Watford (48.3%) and Hatfield (42.5%), in part owing to London overspill or new town designations.[176] But a broader message was signified in only one Hertfordshire RDC having less than a fifth of households in public sector homes. At the other extreme, only two authorities in the whole of Bedfordshire and Norfolk had more than 40% in this tenure. These were Biggleswade Town (41.0%), which had programmes for key workers by 1961, although proposed overspill expansion was not mooted until later,[177] and Norwich (40.7%), which demonstrated a strong commitment to public provision up to the 1980s (e.g. Forrest and Murie 1988, p.203). If we look to tie provision levels to political dispositions favouring the public sector, none of the investigated counties were places with traditions in mining or industrial radicalism (e.g. Macintyre 1980), even if there was short-lived farmworker activism in north Norfolk (Howkins 1985). Some link this ephemeral radicalism with robust public sector provision (e.g. Dickens et al. 1985). Yet poor performance in rural Norfolk by 1961 signifies that radical impulses were fleeting. By the time rural councils were abolished in 1974, English rural districts in general had fallen farther behind their urban counterparts. Thus, for 1971 only six counties recorded public sector contributions to RDC stocks over the national average

---

[176] For example, TNA HLG118/933 'Memo to Mr. Douglas from C.T. Jones', 5 April 1966; HCH 10 July 1973, Vol.859, col.332W.
[177] WR&WSR 11 February 1964, p.1; BC&BG 22 October 1965, p.1.

(Durham, Hertfordshire, Lincolnshire-Holland, Northumberland, Warwickshire and the West Riding). In only nine of 45 counties with rural and urban districts (viz. excluding London) were rural shares above urban (Bedfordshire, Berkshire, Derbyshire, Durham, Gloucestershire, Isle of Wight, Lincolnshire-Holland, Surrey and Warwickshire). Commentaries accusing rural councils of weaker public sector performances were valid. However, this picture was not universal, and instances of rural–urban compatibility or even rural ascendancy existed in surprising locations, including counties like Surrey, despite identified rural antagonism towards council provision (e.g. Connell 1978). If urban and rural performed equally in such environments, this suggests deeper forces operated than a peculiar rural disposition.

Adding together public sector and employer-provided accommodation revealed different patterns (Table 3.6). As already indicated, rural councils were aware of landowner housing possibilities. Rural councils operated in an environment where more 1919 employers provided dwellings for workers than in towns. Arguably, RDCs consequently had more scope to fulfil legislative obligations to ensure local populations were appropriately housed. But whether this was the case partly depended upon councils and landlords ensuring dwelling conditions were maintained in tied cottages. That standards in tied dwellings were lower than in council accommodation was true but this extended to owner-occupied dwellings, even towards the end of the century (MHLG 1968). Like the Duke of Bedford's cottages, which were reported to be 'all over 100 years old',[178] studies point to tied dwellings generally being aged (Fletcher 1969); yet they were more likely to have been improved than other private rental units (e.g. Giles and Cowie 1960; Fletcher 1969). Even so, assessing the contribution of employer-provided homes is not straightforward. Public officials repeatedly claimed there was a lack of accurate figures on tied accommodation,[179] although the 1961 census did offer insight. This revealed that council and employer-provided homes gave a rural package of more rental units than urban centres, with 33.2% of English rural households so accommodated, compared with 28.9% for urban.[180] As for specific counties, low rates of council provision still left Norfolk's rural districts under-provided compared with its towns but in Bedfordshire and Hertfordshire this combination gave more housing opportunities relative to housing stock or manual worker numbers (Table 3.6). None of this detracts from concerns, expressed early (Howkins 1985) and much later (Newby 1977), that the tied housing system was exploitative. This concern lies at the heart of assertions that rural councils reluctantly built council homes. As the next section

---

[178] BRO RDAM1/25 ARDCHPBuCM 15 January 1970. This claim gave an exaggerated image of decay, with the Duke of Bedford's Estate erecting new cottages early in the century, as in 1902 (seven), 1903 (six), 1906 (four) and 1912 (eight) (e.g. BRO RDAM1/4 ARDCM 2 May 1912).

[179] For example: Arthur Greenwood (HCH 28 July 1931, Vol.255, col.2116W); Richard Crossman (HCH 24 May 1966, Vol.729, col.264).

[180] The 28.9% figure was computed without London and Middlesex counties. Low provision of council dwellings and employer-provided homes pulled the urban figure down to 27.5% if these were included.

begins to show, there were a variety of reasons for this, as well as unevenness in its accuracy.

3.3.2 Rural Councils as Housing Agents

Views on core aspects of the ethos of rural councils differ. For some, they are the bastions of 'reaction'. As Springall (1936, p.94) held for Norfolk: 'The RDCs became from the first the rural House of Lords, mainly composed of smaller farmers and clergy who were more obstinate and conservative in their outlook than their brethren on the County Council' (cf. Table 3.5). Within official circles, more nuanced evaluations held. Take, for instance, a 1926 Ministry of Health memo:

> … though there is a general feeling that small Urban District Councils and Rural District Councils are slack, there is difficulty in producing any instances. As regards provision of houses, we have not had to default any local authority and as regards the grant of subsidy, correspondence and local inquiry in some cases, has proved that the local authority was probably right in refusing to take action …[181]

Even so, on the surface rural councils generated questions over their performance. Hence, even though the official verdict was that rural council-building compared '… not unreasonably with those for urban areas', by 1931, 113 out of 650 RDCs had no dwellings under a Housing Act (MoH 1931, p.105). This pattern was not one dimensional. In Chap. 4, attention is given to restrictions that lessened rural action. Irrespective of them, a fundamental question was whether rural leaders supported public provision.

Here, the picture was clear-cut in one sense, mixed in another. What is easy to pick out was a preference for private sector endeavours. This is hardly unexpected, given: (a) political dominance by land-based and petit bourgeois interests (Elliott et al. 1988); (b) economic dominance by small enterprises that encourage workers to identify with employers (e.g. Newby 1975); and, (c) an established private sector ascendancy in rural housing supply, with less than 2000 RDC-owned dwellings approved or considered for approval between 1890 and 1914.[182] Yet, in 1918, a common view was that the private sector would not build houses, whether in rural or urban contexts. The Cabinet was clear that subsidising the revitalisation of private building would not be politically astute.[183] Even so, RDC minutes regularly depreciated council action in favour of private operators. Illustrating the sentiment, a 1917 Epsom RDC resolution was antagonistic to the Local Government Board's (LGB) proposed intervention:

---

[181] TNA HLG40/38 'Minute Sheet Addressed to Mr. Forber', 20 February 1926.

[182] HCH 16 March 1914, Vol.59, col.1700W.

[183] See TNA CAB24/72 GT6556 'Housing Scheme. Suggestions by Mr. Chamberlain', 25 December 1918; TNA CAB23/18 7(19) Cabinet Conclusions, 14 November 1919.

... the Council were of opinion that the existing shortage was in the main due to the claims made on builders and others for the land value duties under the Finance (1909–10) Act, 1910, and that, instead of the proposals that houses should be erected by Local Authorities, which would necessarily involve heavy burdens on the tax payers or the ratepayers, the Council respectfully urge the Local Government Board to assist in restoring private enterprise in the building trade by bringing about the repeal of Part 1 of the Finance (1909–10) Act ...[184]

As national pressure for council involvement rose, RDCs like Brixworth wanted to '... shelve the building of cottages, by calling upon large employers to build houses for their workmen in preference to the Council building themselves'.[185] Even where council construction later became noteworthy, as in Smallburgh, there was reluctance initially, preferring '... to first ascertain what houses were likely to be erected by private enterprise'.[186] This emotion was expressed so frequently it comes across as bedrock political orientation. It was not universal, of course, with reports from more industrialised rural districts, as in Durham, signifying a rejection of private sector options, on account of their ongoing failures (e.g. Ryder 1984). No surprise that rural districts covering coalfields undertook significant council-building in the first decade after 1919, with this pattern persisting to 1971 in rural districts with more 'industrial' components (e.g. the low service-class, moderate commuting districts in Table 2.13).[187]

What helped promote complexity in rural responses was diversity in the options afforded by national legislation. Thus, by 1921, the death-knell of the 1919 Act had been rung, with new building approvals terminated (Orbach 1977). As Jennings (1971, p.124) summarised, the funding terms under which councils operated the 1919 Act were generous but procedures were lengthy and inefficient, with sharp rises in building costs following failure to ensure material supplies and regulate prices. Homes under the Act were expected to cost £500, but averaged £1000 or more (Holmans 1987, p.299).[188] Many councils were reluctant builders; especially given government pressure to set rents higher than many rural residents could afford. Middle-class campaigns targeting public spending 'waste' heightened angst, then three Coalition by-election defeats rattled the government (Daunton 1996). When the economic boom after the War ended abruptly, those ideologically opposed to the programme pressed for its closure (Marriner 1976; Smith and Whysall 1990).

---

[184] HRO RDC4/1/6 BuRDCM 25 October 1917, pp.315–16.

[185] HCH 26 March 1919, Vol.114, col.413–14.

[186] NRO DC22/2/8 SmRDCM25 September 1923, p.416.

[187] For a list of building in rural and urban districts on coalfields, see HCH 6 November 1928, Vol.223, col.51W–53W.

[188] Other figures in the text suggest lower costs but this was because most presentations list building costs only, excluding ancillary charges, like land purchase, water and sewer connections, roads, etc. Holmans' figures refer to all-in costs, which were generally not made available in documents. The impact of cost rises for the Treasury were obvious. Late in 1919, the Chancellor of the Exchequer laid down the government's expectation that 600,000 dwellings under the Act would carry a £10 million annual cost (HCH 6 November 1919, Vol.120, col.1662). By July 1921, the estimate was £10 million for just 176,000 homes (HCH 14 July 1921, Vol.144, col.1484). Both figures exclude subsidies for private-owners.

As Bowley (1945, p.26) put it: 'If homes for heroes could only be provided in this way then the heroes would have to go without'. Whatever housing needs existed, the Minister of Health's priorities were clear: 'I consult the local authorities, but mostly I have to consult the national financial position'.[189] Politically, this was a moment of high drama. Christopher Addison, the architect of the 1919 Act, declared that its decimation ' … will widely, and I think rightly, be regarded as a breach of faith on the part of the Government'.[190] The Minister of Health seemingly concurred, given he told Cabinet the termination '… cannot be defended as having any relation to the housing needs of the country but must be defended simply and solely on the ground of financial necessity'.[191] Contextual contributions to the Act's demise included an assumed weakening of working-class 'revolutionary' zeal and government over-commitments elsewhere, amongst which Addison complained about overseas military commitments (Morgan and Morgan 1980, p.143).

But, as Bowley (1945, p.9) pointed out, the 1919 Act let the genie out of the bottle: 'As the Government had once meddled in the housing market, it could not abandon all responsibility for the supply of houses'. With housing shortages worse in 1923 than in 1919 (Bowley 1945, p.23), the government's so-called Chamberlain Act of 1923 benefited from a recession-hit decline in building costs. Subsidies were offered for private building. Rental was permitted but statistics were not kept on numbers.[192] Councils which used the Act had to persuade the Ministry private enterprise left needs unfulfilled (Self 2006, p.91). Shortages persisted. The next year the short-lived Labour government introduced the 1924 Housing (Financial Provisions) Act, known as the Wheatley Act (Clarke 1924). This was limited to providing rental housing, especially by councils. Significantly, given he predicted its abject failure, and his personal antagonism towards the 1924 Act (Self 2000), when a majority Conservative government returned later in 1924, it retained the 1924 Act. In adjusted form, with the slum clearance-centred 1930 Housing Act added, the 1923 and 1924 Acts provided both private and public sector support until they were terminated in 1933. For rural areas, the 1924 Act seemed particularly important, as it gave extra support for building in agricultural parishes for the first time.

Hence, private and public sector solutions were built into national programmes for much of the 1920s. Rural councils had different channels available to address housing needs. A diversity of responses resulted. There was no 'rural response'. Biggleswade RDC (1915, p.18) identified a probable need for 110 new homes as early as 1914, with official reports crediting the Clerk and Medical Officer of Health for their energy in responding positively to housing needs, despite only recently being converted to the cause.[193] By 1919, all parishes, save one that was losing

---

[189] HCH 15 June 1921, Vol.143, col.400.

[190] HCH 14 July 1921, Vol.144, col.1490–91.

[191] TNA CAB24/125 CP3067 'Reduction of Public Expenditure', 22 June 1921, p.5.

[192] HCH 6 March 1924, Vol.170, col.1643W–44W. Even so the Rural Housing Committee concluded that the majority erected by private enterprise were sold (TNA HLG37/42 'Rural Housing Index 1936', undated c1937, p.5).

[193] TNA HLG1/845 'Report of Inquiry by Harry Stewart', 7 July 1913.

people, sought new homes, with the Clerk indicating 500 were needed.[194] This soon rose to 800.[195] There was no need to drive this Council to act. This contrasted with initially slow responses in Biggleswade Town, which led the Ministry to encourage urgency.[196] Yet, difficulties with builders, plus rising costs, stopped the RDC programme at 611 dwellings. Compare this performance with neighbouring Ampthill. At the 1921 census, these districts had notable economic similarities (Table 1.1), with near identical workforce shares in agriculture (47.7% of male workers in Ampthill and 46.1% in Biggleswade), building (7.0% and 6.3%), commerce-finance (5.1% and 4.5%), transport (5.2% and 5.1%), and metal work (4.8% and 4.3%). Only for defence or public administration (1.6% and 11.7%) was there a distinction.[197] These hardly justified output differences of 611 against 56 under the 1919 Act. The disparity looks even greater given the occupations of Biggleswade's tenants. By 1931, for example, when 62 of the 611 had been lost when Sandy was granted UDC status, Biggleswade had 785 council-dwellings (20 pre-1919), with agricultural workers in 393 of them,[198] including 82.3% of all its 1924 Act dwellings.[199] The market gardening focus of mid-Bedfordshire came with relatively high wages (Beavington 1975),[200] which might have favoured Biggleswade somewhat, yet both councils had dwelling applications well above new-build availability by the late-1920s.[201] The explanation for output divergence lay not only in the drive of Biggleswade but also in the guarded approach of Ampthill, which was deeply troubled by high construction costs and, unlike Biggleswade, was reluctant to build homes for well paid brick-workers.[202]

Reticence also pervaded Erpingham and Walsingham. Smallburgh likewise saw little activity, with only 168 dwellings built or under construction over 1918–1924, of which just 48 were council-owned.[203] The Erpingham and Walsingham cases are

---

[194] NBC 21 February 1919, p.3.

[195] NBC 8 August 1919, p.3.

[196] BC&BG 24 October 1919, no page.

[197] These figures altered little if all workers were included, although there was a higher propensity for women to work in Ampthill (24.3% as against 18.1%). Male employment has been used as this was more likely full-time work at this time. The largest sectors for female employment were personal services (42.3% and 42.9%) and makers of textiles-clothes, which accounted for less than 2% of male workers but 26.5% and 14.3% respectively for female.

[198] NBC 19 June 1931, p.7.

[199] TNA HLG40/31 Department Committee on Agricultural Cottages. 'Memorandum to the Minister of Health', April 1931.

[200] In 1913 Biggleswade market garden wages were 18/– to 23/– a week compared with farmworker pay around 14/– in north Norfolk (TNA HLG1/845 'Report of Inquiry by Harry Stewart', 7 July 1913).

[201] For example, in Biggleswade application rates of 2.0 and 3.5 times new house completions were reported for Stotfold and Arlesey, while in Ampthill a rate of more than 4.25 pertained for Westoning (NBC&SN&DN 10 August 1928, p.7; W&DR 10 August 1929, p.1).

[202] BRO RDAR8/1 ARDCMOHar 1920, p.7; TNA HLG37/43 'Report on Local Investigations …', undated c1936, p.23.

[203] NRO DC22/2/9 SmRDCM 6 May 1924, p.80.

instructive, for both carried traces of the radicalism that affected rural Norfolk in the early decades of the century (Howkins 1985). In the case of Erpingham, this was one of the few rural districts in the county (or beyond) to have retained women councillors into the 1910s (it had three, Smallburgh none), as well as Labour Party councillors (Hollis 1987, p.373, p.390).[204] One of its Poor Law Guardians, George Edwards, was an agricultural trade union organiser, a Labour politician, and later a knighted MP.[205] Edwards was a longstanding Walsingham councillor and a Norfolk county councillor (Linsley 2005, p.201). It was Edwards who advised Walsingham to slow 1919 Act building, arguing the government said one thing one day, another the next, with councils in danger of being saddled with heavy fiscal commitments and homes rented at 'ridiculous' levels.[206] Erpingham followed a similar path. Both councils took tentative steps forward before halting work '… until a later date on account of the present inflated prices'.[207] The tone of discussion in both councils reflected a desire to keep costs low to minimise rents for farm labourers. Thus, when the 1924 Act introduced higher subsidies for agricultural parishes, Erpingham adopted a programme of only 20 dwellings, holding that a larger scheme would require the employment of an architect, which would raise costs considerably, while competition for contracts would be less keen for larger schemes.[208] A concern for such councils was securing tender bids from local builders, with outside companies charging higher prices.[209] Note the attention to costs. The 1919 Act limited council contributions to a one penny rate, while for the 1924 Act: 'No subsidy from the rates at all was required' (Bowley 1945, p.36; Clarke 1924); none that is if dwelling costs matched Ministry specified 'appropriate rents' (around pre-1914 levels), otherwise rate contributions could reach £4/10/0d a dwelling. This resulted in Ampthill and Smallburgh focusing on cheaply erected units, so no rate contribution was needed, whereas Biggleswade, Buntingford and Walsingham built 'as before', with local subsidises for 1924 Act homes.[210] Claims rural councils erected few council homes because of rate demands fall flat as a generalisation in this context.

---

[204] Political parties were generally weak in rural England, with 'independents' likely to support the Conservative Party nationally (Grant 1977); yet, in 1925, the Labour Party won 100 of 150 parish council elections, five of 10 county seats and 25 out of 175 district councillors in north Norfolk (Griffiths 2007, p.161).

[205] An account of his life was published in the *NorfChron* 8 December 1933, p.7 (also Edwards 1998).

[206] *FakPost* 12 December 1919, p.5.

[207] NRO DC13/5/82 ERDCHCM 19 April 1921, p.106; NRO DC19/6/9 WRDCHCM 29 June 1921, p.207.

[208] NRO DC13/5/82 ERDCHCM 28 October 1924.

[209] In late-1919, for example, Walsingham only had three tender responses, all from outside the district (NRO DC19/6/8 WRDCM 26 November 1919, p.23).

[210] TNA HLG40/20 'Housing (Rural Authorities) Act 1931. Circular to Members for First Meeting', undated c1931; W&DR 27 February 1926, p.1; 22 August 1931, p.1; 16 August 1938, p.3; NBC&SN&DN 25 March 1927, p.3; NRO DC19/6/15 WRDCM 29 February 1928, p.117; BuRDCM 7 November 1929, p.195; NBC 10 January 1933, p.3; NRO DC19/6/62 WRDCHCM 11 December 1934, after p.65; NRO DC22/2/47 SmRDCHCM 21 July 1936, p.261.

Reticence about tax burdens existed but a wider concern was tenants' ability to pay. This was particularly felt in rural districts, given low wages (Hussey 1997), for, as Jennings (1971, p.129) noted, assuming similar dwellings and building costs, tenants with less resources were asked to pay bigger slices of their wage packets in rent. Of course, building costs were not flat. But variability appeared surprisingly small. For instance, in the first year of the 1919 Act, building costs for rural and urban homes were £773 and £794, respectively (MoH 1920a, p.25).[211] Looking outside this year of inflated prices, little had changed, as for 1936–1937 when the average cost of a three-bedroom non-parlour dwelling was £324 in rural districts and £327 in urban centres, while small one-bedroom dwellings were £231 and £236, respectively (MoH 1938, p.256). One reason for similarity was embedded in one of Neville Chamberlain's criticisms of the 1924 Act, which was that Wheatley subsidies would produce a scramble for labour and materials that would force up prices (Self 2000, p.226). Price increases did occur (Fig. 3.2). For rural councils the effect of rises was especially troubling, since builders were in a strong position to pick and choose urban projects, which offered them larger, single site, lucrative contracts, compared with small, dispersed rural schemes. This discouraged tender responses at

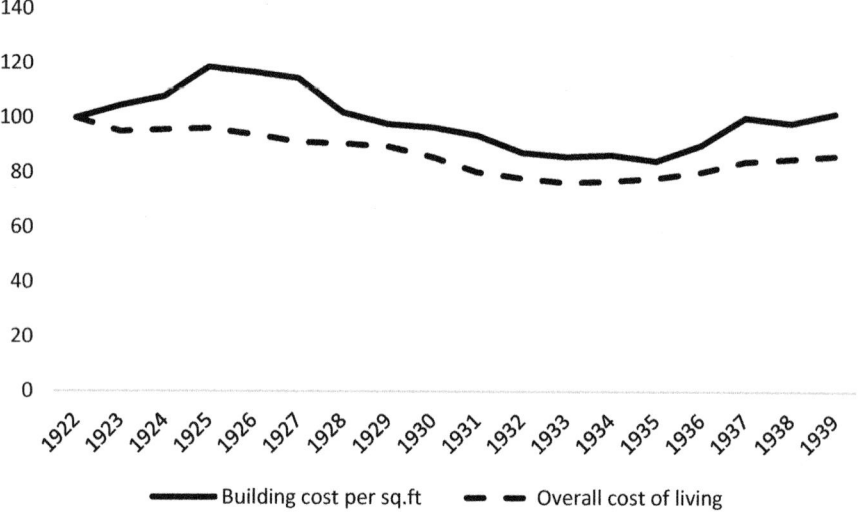

Source: MoH (1944b, p.51).

Fig. 3.2 House-building costs and the cost of living in England and Wales, 1922–1939 (1922 = 100)

---

[211] This difference was affected by an uneven make-up of parlour and non-parlour homes, with the divergence wider under each. Thus, for parlour homes the figures were £808 and £845 and for non-parlour £677 and £728. These costs were for home construction only. Urban charges had higher add-ons for water and sewer systems, road works and similar services that were less common in the countryside.

competitive prices (Chap. 5). With tenants having to pick up extra costs, the pattern of house-building under the 1924 Act was not as expected. RDCs moved forward slowly.

This is despite the availability of extra subsidy for agricultural parishes. When the Act was passed it was expected this higher subsidy would be paid on 7½% of dwellings under the Act (Clarke 1924, p.127). At first this seemed optimistic, as the definition of an agricultural parish was subject to criticism as many counties were poorly covered (like the Home Counties),[212] although the Ministry thought the definition generous, claiming it covered three-quarters of parishes.[213] Yet, by the later 1920s, as building costs fell (Table 3.2), rural interest increased. Even so, rural districts had about one-fifth of the English population (MoH 1944a, p.61), but built fewer homes than this under the 1924 Act (Table 3.7). Private-owners by contrast grasped available subsidies to secure completions well above the rural share of national households. A key problem for rural councils was that, while lower building costs helped, the government cut subsidies under the Act in 1927. What resulted was a drop in rural building rates, which accounted for 9.6% of national completions in 1930–1931 (MoH 1931, p.277), then 3.3% in 1931–1932 (MoH 1932, p.280). After this falling costs produced a revival, with 12.1% in 1932–1933 (MoH 1933a, p.261) and 14.1% for 1933–1934 (MoH 1934, p.302). The imprint of government subsidies on rural action were clear under the Act, with this upsurge coinciding with the government's decision to end general needs subsidies from 1933. Conscious of workers' ability to pay, one feature of the 1924 Act was similarity in council and private sector actions in erecting dwellings in agricultural parishes. This is where 45.2% of all council completions occurred, alongside 41.2% in the private sector (Table 3.8). But even this aspect of the Act signalled a disappointing performance for rural districts, for rather than 7.5% only 5.8% of all dwellings built received the special agricultural subsidy.[214] RDCs were generally disappointed with the Act, as subsidy levels were too low to bring rents within reach of many workers, with exasperation heightened by private builder unwillingness to erect properties

Table 3.7 Percentage of all dwellings under each Housing Act built in the rural districts of England and Wales, 1919 to 1 February 1930

	% for councils	% for private-owners
1919 Housing, Town Planning, Etc. Act	20.2	35.9
1919 Housing (Additional Powers) Act		40.8
1923 Act	11.4	30.4
1924 Act	12.4	22.3

Source: Computed from HCH 19 February 1930, Vol.235, col.1405W–06W

---

[212] HCH 8 April 1925, Vol.182, col.2240W.

[213] TNA HLG29/180 'Rural Housing', 19 February 1931, p.2.

[214] The 5.8% figure was computed by comparing the total erected under the Act for England and Wales (HCH 11 March 1946, Vol.420, col.161W–62W) with figures for private-owners and councils in Table 3.8.

Table 3.8 Dwellings built in rural districts of England and Wales with public subsidies under the 1919, 1923 and 1924 Housing Acts, 1919–1936

	1919 Acts	1923 Act	1924 Act in agricultural parishes	1924 Act in non-agricultural parishes
For rural councils	34,284	8410	28,218	34,152
For private-owners	17,610	109,851	1896	2681

Source: TNA HLG37/43 'Rural Districts. Number of Houses completed since the Armistice', August 1936

suitable for working-class families,[215] or within their rent-paying capacities.[216] Under the 1923 Act, this had led to councils denying subsidies to private-owners, as with Ampthill,[217] or, like Hadham, only granting assistance if rents were within the reach of agricultural labourers, before limiting aid to dwellings of less than £600 value; a tactic also employed by Hatfield, which used a £500 limit.[218] Elsewhere, some rural councils were unperturbed by laying charges on the rates to assist private-owners, many of whom were not from the district and built multiple units.[219] This suggests more than an aversion to raising rate bills was at play.

The performance of rural councils should be set against a backcloth of council disquiet over poor living standards. Consequently, Erpingham, Smallburgh and Walsingham all sought to encourage private building. As well as building under the 1924 Act, they offered enhanced subsidies from the rates under the 1923 Act,[220]

---

[215] There are a many possible citations on this, for the 1924 Act and generally. A selection from across the investigated districts pre-1939 include Biggleswade RDC (1913, p.13; BRO RDBwM1/9 BiRDCM 21 March 1928), Hatfield (*HA&SAT* 26 January 1924, p.8), Cromer (TNA HLG48/73 Letter from Cromer UDC Clerk to MoH Secretary, 6 February 1924), Walsingham (TNA HLG48/868 Letter from Briston Parish Council Clerk to MoH Secretary, 27 March 1935), Ampthill (BRO RDAM2/20 ARDCHCM 5 October 1936) and Braughing (*B&NEHG* 5 May 1939, p.4).

[216] For example, HRO RDC7/3/1 North Mymms Housing Urgency Committee Meeting 29 March 1935, p.239. This rural response extended beyond 1945 (e.g. BRO RDBwM1/44 BiRDCHCM 8 November 1972).

[217] *W&DR* 19 November 1927, p.1.

[218] Respectively, *H&EO* 8 December 1923, p.8; HRO RDC6/1/5 HaRDCM 7 May 1925, p.374; *HA&SAT* 27 September 1924, p.4. Under the 1923 Act, councils made lump sum payments; the money for which was borrowed and paid back over many years (hence interest charges). As Hadham determined private builders would not erect homes at affordable rents, it was not disposed to incur the charges (HRO RDC6/1/5 HaRDCM 6 December 1923, p.294). The Council cited its over-burdened rates, but its reaction suggested a deeper frustration. Interest payments apart, commitments were mostly principal repayments, as maintenance and repair charges were levied on tenants (usually a percentage of rent or per dwelling). The 1923 Act gave councils authority to support dwellings valued up to £1500.

[219] As with the Bedford resident obtaining support for six houses in Mogerhanger (Biggleswade) in 1924 (*NBC* 4 January 1924, p.8).

[220] NRO DC19/6/11 WRDCM 4 September 1923, p.52 in binding; NRO DC19/6/13 WRDCM 1 April 1925, p.3; NRO DC13/5/6 ERDCM 28 July 1924, p.89; *NWP&ENS* 27 August 1926, p.5. The government reported that, of 1769 local authorities, 1436 had schemes under the 1923 Housing Act, of which 375 made additional payments to encourage building (HCH 4 March 1925, Vol.181, col.438–39.). No breakdown by local government category was provided.

although Erpingham scored the Exchequer grant as 'hardly sufficient' to build for 'this class of person' (farm-workers), while stressing that more private dwellings saved public money if providing farm-worker homes.[221] Despite engagement with both Acts, the Norfolk districts saw few dwellings erected in the 1920s. On some projects the construction process was slow,[222] but issuing few tender calls was more significant. Other rural councils behaved the same way. Wycombe RDC (1952, p.3) was an example, with a fear of overloading local builders, and so forcing up prices, leading to little council-building in the 1920s, although 1096 private dwellings were subsidised over 1919–1929. Only when 1923 Act subsidies were withdrawn did Wycombe start building its own dwellings, completing 712 in the less hospitable funding climate of the 1930s (Wycombe RDC 1952, p.11). This might seem counter-intuitive, if you assume councils were driven by a desire to keep the rates low, why build when subsidies were low and not when they were high? Two key reasons were that building costs fell from the late-1920s (Fig. 3.2), especially after the economic crisis of 1931, when Britain came off the gold standard (Seaman 1966; Ham 1981; Ward 1988), and there was an underlying preference for private sector solutions.

Rural districts like Mitford and Launditch, which did not build under the 1919 Act, were enthused by 1923 Act support for private enterprise (Linsley 2005, p.173). That authorities like Hatfield and Walsingham initially found little uptake from the private sector shocked them.[223] But it would not have surprised the Minister of Health, Neville Chamberlain, whose diary entry claimed: 'I should very much doubt if my [1923 Act] subsidy will attract the small builder in rural districts'. Relatively speaking, few made use of the 1923 Act to build council dwellings. Hatfield was one of them. As early as 1924 this Council was proclaiming that, except for a few farm-worker cottages, not many houses were required in the district, save those the private sector would supply.[224] Principally, this was because, even early in the century, rail links meant the district was a convenient place to live for middle-class commuters. With agriculture's share of the occupied male workforce dropping from 31.3% to 22.4% between 1921 and 1931, the Hatfield trend was towards better-paid urban-style jobs. This occupational bias was evident in the composition of the Council (Table 3.5). Disappointing initial builder responses led the Council to commission its own house-building, securing more than 500 under the 1923 Act by early-1930.[225] Jennings (1971, p.126) captured Hatfield's brand of private sector preference in characterising council-building under the 1923 Act as showing little concern with keeping rents down and disliking the 'renting only' stipulation in the Wheatley Act. Hatfield's Council might have been graced by large landowners but its ethos owed more to private sector boosterism aimed at demographic growth than values associ-

---

[221] TNA HLG48/868 Letter from Erpingham RDC Clerk to J.N. Dark, MoH, 7 June 1927.

[222] For example, TNA HLG48/868 Letter from Erpingham RDC Clerk to MoH Secretary, 13 November 1928.

[223] HRO RDC7/1/8 HtRDCM 15 November 1923, p.379; *HA&SAT* 26 January 1924, p.8; NRO DC19/6/11 WRDCM 19 December 1923, p.90.

[224] HRO RDC7/1/9 HtRDCM 25 September 1924, p.29.

[225] TNA HLG48/325 Letter from MoH Secretary to Hatfield RDC Clerk, 7 April 1930.

ated with traditional English rurality.[226] Not that the Council focused on especially wealth incomers, as irritation pervaded reactions to builders, who showed little inclination to erect homes for the better paid working-classes. This led the Council into an extensive 1923 Act programme. This was followed in the 1930s by exasperation over a lack of private builder interest in non-parlour homes, which was all many could afford; again provoking the Council to seek permission to erect 50 non-parlour dwellings.[227] Between 1928 and 1936 (at least) not a single parlour home was built by the Council, which left such properties to the private sector, even though working-class sensibilities were known to be discomforted by their omission (Gardiner 2010, p.261).[228] Utilising the Council as a backstop for private sector shortcomings, rather than as a driver of wider improvements, had its downsides.[229] Requests for Ministry intervention were made by the Hatfield Council Tenants' Association over the RDC not using the 1924 Act, so condemning council tenants to rents in excess of the paying capacity of lower grades on the railways, clerks in London with heavy rail fares or farm-workers.[230] As one councillor described the consequences: 'I know labourers who go half-starved in order to pay the rent of Council houses. We should make an application for thirty [1931 Act dwellings]. We have never done anything for the agricultural labourer'.[231] Put more tactfully, the Medical Officer of Health concluded: 'The problem of housing can no longer be said to be acute, although cottages at a rent which can be paid by the agricultural labourer have yet to be built'.[232] All this was long before a hint of de Havilland leaving London for Hatfield or a potential new town designation. With these events, the future looked very different, with Hatfield becoming a centre for public sector building after 1945 (Table 1.3, Table 3.4). Council minutes are not particularly illuminating on councillor reactions to this shift but built numbers tell their own tale.

---

[226]The large landowners on Hatfield Council in Table 3.5 were all on the Council in 1924, when they comprised a larger share of the chamber, as there were a quarter fewer councillors in 1924 than in 1936.

[227]TNA HLG48/872 Letter from Hatfield RDC Clerk to the MoH, 27 February 1934; *HM&CP* 23 March 1934, p.10; 27 July 1934, p.10.

[228]This point was brought home forcefully in 1939–1945 proposals on how society should be improved once war was over (e.g. TNA HLG40/26 'Note of Interview. War-Time Agricultural Cottages', 25 January 1942; TNA HLG37/50 'Statement by the Rural House Design Panel', undated c1943).

[229]Hatfield was different from the other RDCs investigated, not simply as regards geographical ties to London but also in terms of settlement structure (Chap. 1), with Old Hatfield's 1921 population of 5695 making it larger than all six of the UDCs examined in Bedfordshire and Norfolk. 'Boosterism' (see Molotch 1976 for a general discussion) was played out in slightly different ways in other 'towns'. In Biggleswade Town, for example, it was decided in 1936 that while the UDC could build homes it should step aside to give the private sector the opportunity, while being prepared to purchase land, lay out necessary roads and sewers and sell off plots to speculative builders (TNA HLG49/95 Biggleswade UDC. 'Memo on Interview with the MoH', 26 November 1936).

[230]TNA HLG48/325 Letter from Hatfield Council Tenants' Association to MoH Secretary, 3 December 1930.

[231]*HA&SAT* 28 August 1931, p.7.

[232]*HM&CP* 21 June 1929, p.14.

Thus, for 1932–1939 Hatfield saw 28 council dwellings constructed each year in contrast with 290 homes for private-owners, whereas for 1965–1969 the equivalents were 134 and 73 (Table 3.4).

Few rural councils relied so heavily on private building as Hatfield, largely because unsubsidised construction commonly put dwellings beyond the reach of local workers. Notable for how this fuelled council-building was Smallburgh. This council has been commended for its inter-war housing performance, with unusual volumes of inter-war council construction (Dickens et al. 1985). Smallburgh started slowly as a council-builder and was cautious in approach. Thus, in 1919 the LGB indicated '… that according to information in their possession there was an urgent need for working-class houses in the District, and they did not, therefore, consider there was any justification for deferring'. In 1920 the Housing Commissioner decreed that the Council's proposal to build 20 houses a year was 'not adequate', while Smallburgh sent no delegates to a Norwich conference on the 1923 Act, holding out to see if the private sector would act, then declaring early in 1924 it would build no further dwellings.[233] Pressure from the County Council followed this inaction,[234] which might have lubricated wheels, as Smallburgh started exploring the 1924 Act. In 1925 permission was sought from the Ministry to erect homes under the Act. This created controversy, for the Ministry's preference was for three-bedroom homes (Connor 1936, p.6), whereas Smallburgh considered such dwellings too large for farm labourers. The issue split the Council, as it did many policy-makers. Move forward a few years, for instance, and the government was contemplating ending subsidies for council-building, before preferring smaller dwellings instead (from 950 to 760 sq.ft.; Holmans 1987, p.309; MoH 1932, p.97).[235] The National House Building Committee (1924, p.9) depreciated such shrinkages:

> The attention of the Committee has been called to certain types of unit standard houses, now being constructed under the Housing Act, containing floor areas of 659 and 690 square feet. The Committee takes the strongest possible exception to such types being constructed today. The Committee objects principally to the adverse influences of such limited accommodation upon those living in the houses. The restricted floor area is moreover relatively more costly than the larger floor areas … it is considered that no houses of this construction should be sanctioned unless there are exceptional circumstances.

Smallburgh was well ahead in this game.[236] Its commitment to small dwellings even raised suspicions in the Ministry, which on occasion agreed to the Council building

---

[233] NRO DC22/2/7 SmRDCM 21 January 1919, p.209; NRO DC22/2/45 SmRDCHCM 3 August 1920; NRO DC22/2/8 SmRDCM 25 September 1923, p.416; NRO DC22/2/9 SmRDCM 12 February 1924, p.27.

[234] NRO DC22/2/9 SmRDCM 23 September 1924, p.138.

[235] One of Neville Chamberlain's complaints about the 1924 Act was that house plans were too generous, as larger houses would be let to the better-off and if tenants were poorly-paid they would sub-let, so creating overcrowding (TNA HLG48/16 'Notes of a Conference with the Association of Municipal Corporations and the LCC', 17 June 1926).

[236] T&WT 14 February 1925, p.11; NWP&ENS 5 August 1932, p.1.

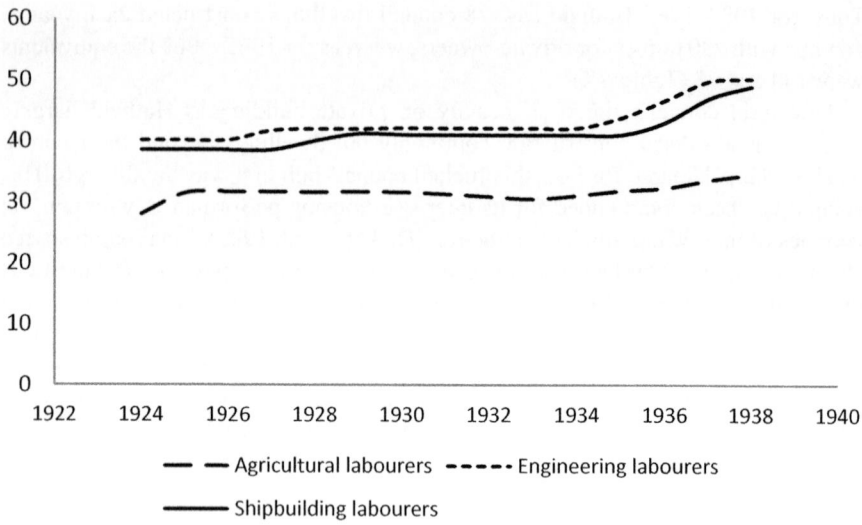

Source: Board of Trade (1940).

Fig. 3.3 Wages per week for labourers in England and Wales (shillings), 1924–1938

bungalows only with assurances they would be let to small families.[237] But smaller homes meant lower rents. At a time when many farmers had mortgages to buy farms (Howkins 2003, p.63), when farm-worker wages were poor (Fig. 3.3) and product prices were low,[238] cheaper homes suited farmer-landowners and farm-workers in substandard accommodation. With a substantial landed interest on the Council (Table 3.5), it is no revelation Smallburgh minutes exposed regular concern over property tax and rent increases. Nor indeed that many 1924 Act dwellings were let to farm-workers. Hence, by 1931, when the Act's implementation was well-grounded, 52.7% of Smallburgh's 1924 Act allocations went to farm-workers.[239]

By 1939, 60.5% of all council homes in Smallburgh had been built under the 1924 Act. This focus on one Act outpaced the 53.2% of the Biggleswade stock coming from the 1919 Act. Per 1000 district residents, Smallburgh built 12.9 homes under the 1924 Act; almost exactly twice the Norfolk average, making it the second highest RDC in the county, and well above other RDCs with high allocations to

---

[237] *NWP&ENS* 2 September 1932, p.4

[238] For instance, Barnes (1993, p.25) noted that a hundredweight of wheat cost 18/10d in 1920, 9/10d in 1923, and reached its nadir in 1934 at 4/10d (also Howkins 2003, p.46, p.83).

[239] Only two Norfolk RDCs did not build under the 1924 Act. Top of the Norfolk pile were the Mitford and Marshland districts, with more than 93% of 1924 Act homes going to farm labourers. The proportion allotted to agricultural labourers was virtually identical in Bedfordshire and Norfolk (at 56.5% and 57.7%, respectively), suggesting similarity in decision criteria (TNA HLG40/31 Department Committee on Agricultural Cottages. 'Memorandum to the Minister of Health', April 1931).

farm-workers (e.g. Biggleswade 3.0, Erpingham 7.0 and Walsingham 4.7). Two significant points need making on this. The first is that these Smallburgh dwellings were rather 'mean' (Table 3.9).[240] Smallburgh prided itself on its low rents. The Council caused a stir in 1931 when its 1924 Act properties were let at weekly rents of 2/3d.[241] How such rents were achieved was reported in the *Buckingham Advertiser and Free Press* (21 November 1931, p.6) as the result of 'exceptionally low building costs'. To explain, the *Press* reported an Exchequer subsidy of £11, no contribution from the rates, with costs kept low because dwellings had no bath or lighting, water was drawn from a well, and the average floor area was only 563 square feet (Table 3.9). Note, no contribution from the rates, for the Act specified an annual council contribution of £3/15/0d per house (if built after September 1927).[242] But this input did not have to come from the rates. It could be taken from other council revenues. Wherever from, at the 1931 Norwich housing conference, Smallburgh was reported as building the smallest non-parlour and parlour homes in Norfolk, as well as the cheapest.[243] Yet, despite their 'poverty', Smallburgh dwellings were not the cheapest for tenants. Even for non-parlour homes, two Norfolk RDCs had lower rents, while the range for parlour houses gave some Smallburgh homes the second highest rents in the county (but the second lowest for others). Explaining this aspect of Smallburgh's response draws us into the Council's attitude towards public spending. Instructive in this regard were reactions to the 1931 Housing (Rural Authorities) Act, which promised more sympathetic funding for farm-workers. Smallburgh's response was miserly. In bids for 1931 Act dwellings, Braughing and Hatfield both proposed council contributions of £3/15/0d a year for 40 years. Biggleswade offered £2 a year and Erpingham £1. Smallburgh, along with Walsingham, offered nothing.[244] This 'offer' was consistent with the Council's general policy, which was to minimise property taxes. From as early as 1932, the rate set by this RDC was zero; the only property tax levied was for the County Council. For some half-years, it was

---

[240] Offering one glimpse of this, despite some modernisation of inter-war dwellings, even by 1960 there were 499 council homes in Smallburgh with no sink and 14 with sinks draining into buckets (NRO DC22/2/27 SmRDCM 17 January 1960, pp.832–33).

[241] Reports on this included the *Taunton Courier and Western Advertiser* (11 November), the *Shepton Mallet Journal* (13 November), the *Cornishman and Cornish Telegraph* (19 November), the *Buckingham Advertiser and Free Press* (21 November) and the *Tamworth Herald* (21 November).

[242] HCH 27 May 1935, Vol.302, col.770W–72W.

[243] NRO DC19/6/19 WRDCM 5 August 1931, p.38. Compared with a reported average of 555 sq. ft. for Smallburgh's non-parlour homes, the district with the next smallest units had 678 sq.ft., while the largest had 800 sq.ft. For parlour homes, Smallburgh's 750 sq.ft. average compared with the second smallest value of 762 and the largest at 940. In two districts, some parlour homes were smaller than in Smallburgh, but they built a range of sizes, with larger units well above the Smallburgh figure and the smallest just below. A few years later, national representatives reported most RDCs found 760 sq.ft. 'unnecessarily restrictive', preferring 800 or even 900 sq.ft. (TNA 37/44 'Evidence of Neville Hobson, RDCA Executive Council Member', undated c1936). For 1946–49, new council dwellings were more than 1000 sq.ft. (MoH 1950, p.32).

[244] TNA HLG40/20 'Secretary's Memorandum', 1 January 1932 Position'.

Table 3.9 Details reported for 1924 Housing Act dwellings built in Biggleswade and Smallburgh, 1927–1931

Rural District	Parish	Bath?	Water supply	Drainage system	Sq.ft.	Weekly rent (s.d.)	Weekly rates (s.d.)	Annual rate subsidy	Cost per house
Biggleswade	Meppershall	Yes	Public	Separate	824	4/00d	1/03d	£3/15/00	£382/07/10d
Smallburgh	Ludham	No	No data	None	872	2/03d	0/11d	£0/15/00	£414/15/06d
Smallburgh	Horning	No	Well	None	750	3/10d	1/04d	£0/15/00	£359/19/05d
Smallburgh	Ingham	No	Well	None	750	3/00d	0/11d	£0/15/00	£346/12/03d
Smallburgh	Ludham	No	Well	None	563	2/03d	0/09d	£0	£239/07/10d

Source: Public Works, Roads and Transport Congress (1931, p.20, pp.84–86)

negative; the budget was so frugal the County charge was effectively reduced.[245] The Council praised its own achievements, not simply for the dwellings it built or reconditioned, but because this was done without rate charges.[246]

To understand what was happening here it is appropriate to draw attention to a 1926 policy proclamation by Aylsham RDC. This captured core elements in the ethos of many Norfolk RDCs.[247] The instigation of the Aylsham articulation was rejection of a Housing Committee report. After this, it was decided not to build houses if there was a charge to the rates. This did not mean no houses were built; whether they were depended on the cost of construction.[248] Here, we capture a peculiarity in some councils. This demonstrated concern for both property-owners and workers, with a bias towards the former. On the one hand, Smallburgh did not push forward with projects that demanded rate tariffs at a time business finances were stretched, and, on the other hand, it built many homes at affordable prices, even if the workers had to wait until conditions favoured property-owners before this happened. How far this policy was deliberate or was stumbled into was difficult to assess. What is clear, if policy is action, not stated aim, then Smallburgh built an impressive number of inter-war council homes; bucking general trends by completing more homes in the 1930s than in the 1920s (Table 3.10). Yet the pattern of a slow start followed by accelerating activity casts Smallburgh in a different mould to other rural councils. In the 1930s councils faced similar economic and political conditions as Smallburgh, but it acted decisively. In doing so, it built cheap, small, poorly equipped dwellings. This differentiated Smallburgh from most districts investigated; not simply over the 1930s but right up to the 1970s. Most evident in this regard was Biggleswade, which examined lower cost building by other councils on various occasions, concluding each time the dwellings were of an unacceptably low standard.[249] The same assessment was made by Biggleswade Town, following visits to Ipswich and Elloe RDC (Lincolnshire) in the 1950s[250] and by Braughing after considering Wellingborough RDC's dwellings.[251] Commitments to quality building

[245] *NWP&ENS* 30 September 1932, p.5; also *NM&PWJ* 17 March 1934, p.6; 16 March 1935, p.7; 28 September 1935, p.7.

[246] *NM&PWJ* 9 May 1936, p.6.

[247] Take Henstead's response to the low cost of Smallburgh's new dwellings, which were described as '… plenty big enough and were admirable for their purpose', clearly preferring them to houses visited in Blofield RDC, which were considered 'too big for Henstead'. Henstead's visiting committee were not perturbed by Smallburgh asking tenants to find their own water, taking on board the Smallburgh argument that '… it is far cheaper to let the tenant find his own water, as he will take more care of it'. Nor was there questioning of Smallburgh not providing paths, nor divisions between gardens. Reservations were directed more at Smallburgh being advantaged by lower railway transport costs and gains from cheaper bricks from local production (*NWP&ENS* 8 February 1929, p.5).

[248] *HMC&WP* 4 June 1926, p.5.

[249] *NBC&SN&DN* 25 March 1927, p.3; BiRDCHCM 13 May 1970, p.1038.

[250] *NBC&BR* 23 October 1951, p.2; *BC&BG* 16 September 1955, p.1; 23 September 1955, p.1; *WR&WSR* 20 September 1955, p.5.

[251] HRO RDC3/1/10 BrRDCM 1 September 1960, p.4859.

Table 3.10 Number of council-owned new dwellings completed in investigated rural districts, 1919–1939

	1919–1930	1931–1939
Hatfield	503	314
Ampthill	228	125
Biggleswade	724	333
Erpingham	216	182
Smallburgh	226	459
Walsingham	162	264

Source: For Ampthill and Biggleswade medical officer of health annual reports. For other districts, numbers come from entries in council minutes and reports

Note: Braughing was omitted as there was insufficient clarity over numbers in 1930 and 1939. In 1943 Braughing reported a total of 380 council homes (HRO RDC3/2/2 BrRDCPHHCM 22 April 1943, p.580). Numbers for Ampthill and Biggleswade excluded Toddington and Sandy, respectively, which were part of these RDCs in 1919 but had left by 1939. Records for Ampthill were unclear on how many council dwellings were built in Toddington before it joined Luton RDC in 1933. By 1928, Toddington had 24 of the 104 council dwellings erected, the largest of any village, but there were no records of 1928–1930 additions for the village. It has been assumed Toddington left with 24 council houses here. When Sandy became a UDC it took 62 council homes from Biggleswade. These were not included in the Biggleswade numbers above. These figures are estimates only. In the 1930s there were many exchanges of parishes across districts, especially in Norfolk, with council minutes generally not providing data on council homes arriving or departing. For instance, while Walsingham recorded 'importing' 26 dwellings after 1930 that had been built under the 1924 Act (NRO DC19/4/1 Register of Houses Provided under Housing (Financial Provisions) Act 1924), comparable information was not available for other Housing Acts. These imports are included in the 1931–1939 total, so the number 264 listed above includes some dwellings not commissioned by Walsingham Council

were also apparent in the 1930s and the 1950s when councils rejected government pressure to erect smaller, less well-provisioned homes; as with Walsingham and Hatfield.[252] Inter-war Smallburgh stood apart in this regard. As we will see later, post-1945, its approach to council-building shared many strands with its inter-war style, although outcomes were different.

Teasing out differences between councils would be strengthened if precise detail on construction volumes could be aligned to explanations for council actions in minutes or reports. But there was little detail on inter-war housing numbers. Two exceptions were Biggleswade and Walsingham. In both cases, caution over the 1924 Act was apparent, even though these councils had divergent housing policies. In Walsingham, excluding transfers following 1930s local government reorganisation, 218 council dwellings were built under the 1923–1924 Housing Acts.[253] Only 120 were completed by 1930, so more than two-fifths were 1930s completions. Biggleswade was no different, except it built more dwellings under the 1924 Act, with 203 completed by the end of 1930 and 168 after. For both councils, the over-whelming majority of these dwellings (even if finished by 1930) were completed after subsidies were reduced in September 1927. A key argument in the December 1926 announcement of subsidy cuts was that building costs would fall.[254] This did happen. Demand was suppressed in the public sector and builders' work dropped off (as did prices). Following the government's announcement, the rush to secure subvention support saw council new-build rise from 61,402 in 1925–1926 to 113,274 in 1926–1927, then fall back to 59,220 in 1927–1928, staying around 50–60 thousand for most of the 1930s (MoH 1944b, p.49). Contract prices had been dropping before the government announcement but fell further. In 1927 prices were 20.5% higher than the 1930 figure, while by 1934 they were nearly 15% below (Bowley 1945, p.277). This drop saw different council responses. In Ampthill, 92 dwellings had been erected under the Act by 1930 but only another 22 were added

---

[252] Opposition to the Ministry's search for more 'economical' building in Walsingham included the claim that the Ministry's plans would see homes become 'nothing more than slums' within two or three years, whereas the Council 'wanted to build houses, not hovels' (*FakPost* 8 July 1932, p.5; NRO DC19/6/20 WRDCM 6 July 1932.p.31). In the 1950s, Hatfield was split, as it recognised more dwellings were needed, which smaller units might help achieve, but the government's so-called 'People's Homes' were considered too small for families. It was made clear to contractors that workmanship, materials, fittings etc. must be to full standard. The Council wanted no jerry-building (HRO RDC7/1/16 HtRDCHCM 10 June 1952, p.18; 3 September 1952; HtRDCM 25 June 1952, p.52; *H&PBG* 19 September 1952, p.2).

[253] The phrase '1923–24 Housing Acts' is used deliberately. Walsingham had 20 dwellings approved under the 1923 Act but transferred them to more generous 1924 Act provisions. These provoked many requests for transfers. Biggleswade records show houses built under the '1923–24 Acts', without clarifying if any were transfers. Searches of minutes suggest they probably were. For councils like Hatfield that considered conditions attached to the 1924 Act onerous (Connor 1936), minutes tended to be explicit if construction was under the 1923 Act. Commentary on the sale of council properties often provided indications of which Act had been used. These were forbidden under the 1924 Act but not under the 1923 Act. The difference was used by Neville Chamberlain to encourage councils not to use the 1924 Act, as with Birmingham (Self 2000, p.237).

[254] HCH 2 December 1926, Vol.200, col.1405.

after. Its Medical Officer of Health informed the Council that most parish populations were stable, so attention should shift to slum removal.[255] Yet, nationally, under
the 1924 Act, 43.7% of dwellings in rural districts were completed after 1930
(almost exactly as in Walsingham).[256] Only 45 rural districts were building under the
1924 Act at this time (MoH 1932, p.280). This constituted a mere 3.3% of all local
authorities building under the Act. Put simply, a small group of RDCs over-
performed. This collection of districts was not undifferentiated, even if they were
united by grasping the opportunity of low building costs. On one side were councils
prepared to commit funds to improve housing conditions, as exemplified in
Biggleswade. On the other, were traditionally risk averse districts, like Smallburgh
and Walsingham. Hence, Smallburgh increased its council stock from 234 to 430 in
the two years 1930 and 1931, reaching 560 by 1935.[257]

Contrasting these numbers with the totals shown in Table 3.10 indicates that the
commentary so far has not covered all 1930s Smallburgh numbers. For one, slum
clearance replacements have not been mentioned. In Walsingham's case, 137 of the
264 added dwellings in the 1930s came this way,[258] with 26 through inter-district
parish transfers, so this was a large slice of the total. But for Smallburgh records
were thin on detail. There were indications the Council condemned fewer dwellings
than others in rural Norfolk, but reconditioned more.[259] In numerical terms, just 26
slum replacement homes were erected by 1935, with a proposal to build 52 more the
following year, at which point 85 old dwellings had been upgraded.[260] More unusual
as a gap-filler were the erection of unsubsidised homes, which were first allowed
under the 1925 Housing Act, then again under the 1936 Act. Reference has already
been made to Felmingham, whose parish council raised the ire of the District
Council by pressing for extra homes. Smallburgh Council was not enamoured with
this request, claiming they were not persuaded demand existed, that homes already
built were unoccupied, that agriculture was in a depressed state and there were '…
already more houses there than were required for the labourers working on the
land'; indeed, that there were twice as many houses as agricultural labourers in the
parish. Encapsulating this antipathy, the Council proclaimed: 'When they built
houses in Felmingham in the past they could not get agricultural labourers to occupy
them because of the rents that had to be charged. The result was that rather than let
some remain empty they had to be let to North Walsham people'.[261] Herein lay a key
to Council policy. It was okay to build council houses for farm labourers, for this

---

[255] BRO RDAR8/11 ARDCMOHar 1930, p.12; BRO RDAR8/13 ARDCMOHar 1932, p.9; BRO RDAR8/15 ARDCMOHar 1934, p.10.

[256] Compare MoH (1930a, p.80) with MoH (1944a, p.64).

[257] FakPost 27 December 1929, p.1; NWP&ENS 22 January 1932, p.5; MoH (1936b, p.92).

[258] NRO DC19/4/2 'Register of New Houses Provided under the 1930 Housing Act'.

[259] EDP 6 June 1935, p.7.

[260] NM&PWJ 8 June 1935, p.6; 9 May 1936, p.6; NRO DC22/2/47 SmRDCHCM 21 July 1936, p.260.

[261] NWP&ENS 11 February 1927, p.3; 2 November 1928, p.5; NRO DC22/2/11 SmRDCM 2 October 1928, p.219; EDP 1 November 1928, p.5; FakPost 2 November 1928, p.4.

supported the agricultural economy, where the roots of most councillors lay. What was less liked was building for those not associated with the land. Yet most farm labourers had to wait until costs were sufficiently low that house-building could be undertaken without adding to the rates.

Hoveton was to be treated this way. Starting in the nineteenth-century, the Norfolk Broads began to develop as a tourist attraction, with Smallburgh villages like Horning, Hoveton and Potter Heigham seeing significant development thanks to their early railway lines (Wade-Martins and Williamson 2008, p.111, p.114). Accompanying this expansion, private building was popular in coastal locations, even as districts reported decline in north Norfolk parishes away from the coast.[262] As with Felmingham, Hoveton's repeated requests for homes bore witness to Smallburgh's inaction; leading one councillor (there were two out of the 57 in 1936–1937 with a boat building background) to express his lack of understanding of why the Council built homes in parishes where they were not wanted; going on to ask why agriculture was favoured when the yachting industry was entitled to consideration. Claims of 100 leaving Hoveton each 1926 night when they wanted a home there were reinforced by 60 firm applications for council homes in 1930.[263] That there was private builder interest in the parish seems to have given councillors justification for assuming housing there was 'fixed'. The Ministry thought so, denying a 1932 application for houses as there were no unfit or overcrowded dwellings in Hoveton.[264] It seems the non-availability of village homes for labourers was not relevant. Hoveton in the 1930s represented what for many was the late-twentieth-century phenomenon of the local working-class not securing homes due to competition from incoming home-buyers and 'gentrifiers' (Clark 1990; Shucksmith 1991).

Two factors prompted the Council to act. One was provocation from a leading councillor (a principal landowner near one of the Broads settlements), who held that tenants could cover all costs in Hoveton.[265] The second was a meeting with Ministry officials to complain about the impact of the 1935 Housing Act on rate levies. These charges had arisen because 24 council homes were transferred into the district following reorganisation under the 1929 Local Government Act, with the Ministry insisting tenants pay the same rents as before. These rents were low as former councils had provided rate subsidies. Smallburgh councillors were alarmed by the charges (which only applied to incoming dwellings, though they feared it might cover all 1924 Act dwellings). More widely, they were disturbed by a lack of subsidies for general needs housing, claiming it was impossible to build without financial assistance. A deputation was sent to the Ministry. During the meeting, the Ministry made clear it was satisfied further dwellings were needed, so construction could

---

[262] This applied post-1945, as reported in the *NNN* 3 April 1964, p.3 (also Wade-Martins 1994, pp.168–69).

[263] *NWP&ENS* 15 January 1926, p.5; 11 February 1927, p.3; 21 March 1930, p.5.

[264] NRO DC22/2/14 SmRDCM 6 July 1932, p.333.

[265] NRO DC22/2/46 SmRDCHCM 2 April 1935, p.272.

occur without Treasury subsidy or rates assistance.[266] This fed into Council thinking.[267] In 1920 Smallburgh had introduced lower rents for farm labourers than
for others, and supported rebates to help low-paid workers.[268] Here, Smallburgh's
practice matched other Norfolk districts; as with Blofield and Flegg RDC having a
'normal rent' at 4/6d a week under the 1924 Act but actually charging tenants
between 4/– and 8/–, or Forehoe RDC proposing to build 50 houses at Costessey
with half let to Norwich people at a rent of 10/– in order to allow rents of 3/– to
4/– for others.[269] With the 1933 Housing (Financial Provisions) Act limiting subsidies for council-building to replacing unfit or overcrowded dwellings, Smallburgh
extended differential rents into building without subsidy for those who could pay.
By 1937 a scheme for 33 non-assisted dwellings was approved by the Ministry, with
24 going to Hoveton.[270] By 1939, 83 no-subsidy dwellings had been completed,
comprising 12.0% of the pre-1939 stock (Smallburgh RDC 1958, p.21).

In this regard, Smallburgh was unusual for a rural district, for nationally only
7.3% of new RDC dwellings over the 1919–1943 period were unsubsidised (MoH
1944a, p.64).[271] Many had none. Where there was a relatively well-paid non-farm
population, the prospect of such homes increased, although council minutes indicate the issue was often not raised or explicitly rejected, as at Ampthill.[272] But for
Biggleswade the scheme was explored, with 121 no-subsidy dwellings erected
between 1935 and 1939. The prompt here was private sector failure. In 1932, the
Council was perturbed by the spending power of RAF personnel at Henlow, who, by
agreeing higher rents, 'took' homes from local people.[273] The next year, a proposal
to build six homes at Wrestlingworth was thwarted by Ministry insistence they

---

[266] NRO DC22/2/47 SmRDCHCM 21 July 1936, p.261.

[267] When discussion began in 1935, councillors held that private-owners would not build homes as
returns were too low, but concern that council-building would compete with the private sector sent
the initial proposal back to the Housing Committee (*NM&PWJ* 20 April 1935, p.6).

[268] NRO DC22/2/45 SmRDCHCM 10 September 1920; NRO DC22/2/8 SmRDCM 6 June 1922,
p.212; *NM&PWJ* 21 April 1945, p.3.

[269] NRO DC22/2/47 SmRDCHCM 18 August 1936, p.281; *T&WT* 29 July 1933, p.9; 23 September
1933, p.5.

[270] NRO DC22/2/47 SmRDCHCM 25 May 1937, p.588.

[271] This was little different from the national figure, for only 7.5% of council-building between
1919 and 1943 was without subsidy in England and Wales (HCH 11 March 1946, Vol.420,
col.161W–62W). Unfortunately information on the geography of no-subsidy rural building could
not be found. The observation that Smallburgh (and Biggleswade) were active in no-subsidy building is based partly on general rural trends. Thus, by 1936, 39,099 council dwellings had been built
since 1919 without state aid in England and Wales (HCH 11 March 1946, Vol.420, col.161W–62W),
with the CHAC noting that only 3685 were in rural districts (TNA HLG37/42 'Rural Housing.
Index: 1936', p. 6). Specific information on other councils suggest many had little no-subsidy
activity, as with a 1936 Bedfordshire RDC list giving unsubsidised numbers as nil for Ampthill,
two for Bedford and 59 for Biggleswade (TNA HLG37/45 'Special Sub-Committee Meeting at
Bedford', 15 September 1936).

[272] BRO RDBwM1/11 BiRDCM 11 April 1934; 26 September 1934; BRO RDAM2/20 ARDCHCM
2 July 1934.

[273] *NBC* 28 October 1932, p.6.

should be provided by private-owners.[274] Despite face-to-face meetings, no local builders were interested.[275] This mirrored Hatfield's experience, when Ministry reluctance to agree no-subsidy council-building was overcome following enquiries '... made of various builders in the locality but they do not seem disposed to proceed with the erection of these smaller type working-class houses'.[276] Like Hatfield, in Biggleswade builder intransigence led to a further application to the Ministry, resulting in approval for a no-subsidy programme.[277] Biggleswade's action was cushioned by recognition that, while largely an agricultural area, five parishes were dormitories of Letchworth or benefited from employment on aerodromes: 'For this reason the Council would welcome a general grant for agricultural housing but they were determined to do their best to meet the need whether they got a subsidy or no'.[278] But this was a limited programme, for even in Biggleswade no-subsidy rents were too steep for farm labourers.[279]

By building properties at higher rents for those not in agriculture, by focusing new-build in the late-1920s and 1930s, when building costs were especially low, and by restricting the size and facilities of new dwellings, Smallburgh had what looked like a vibrant council programme. But this Council's strategy fell a long way short of post-1945 aspirations for quality homes. When Smallburgh provided inter-war homes for farmer-workers, it relieved employers of doing so. The Council did this without troubling wealthier residents for tax contributions to keep rents down. Consequential of this motivation, workers had to put up with inadequate housing until fiscal circumstances favoured no rate contribution building. Self-interest was further evinced in antipathy towards addressing non-agricultural needs. Instances have been recorded of farmer-led councils pursuing vested interests by not building council dwellings (Rose et al. 1976). The Smallburgh case shows how farmer interests could be furthered by building.[280] With farm budgets deemed tight and the future unpredictable, advantages could accrue to farmers if the state under-wrote

---

[274] BRO RDBwM1/11 BiRDCM 25 October 1933. General statements asserting this priority include: TNA HLG52/844 'Deputation from the National Federation of House Builders', press release 26 March 1936; HCH 27 July 1936, Vol.315, col.1085.

[275] BRO RDBwM1/11 BiRDCM 17 January 1934.

[276] TNA HLG48/872 Letter from Hatfield RDC Clerk to MoH, 16 December 1932; RDC Reply, 3 January 1933; MoH Reply, 16 January 1933; RDC response, 7 March 1933, which included the quotation; MoH Reply, 17 Match 1933, which indicated MoH willingness to consider a loan for no-subsidy building.

[277] NBC 28 October 1932, p.6; 7 July 1933, p.3; BRO RDBwM1/11 BRDCM 25 October 1933; 7 January 1934.

[278] TNA HLG37/43 'Report on Local Investigations ...', undated c1936, p.22.

[279] BRO RDBwM1/12 BiRDCM 16 December 1936, p.405; 10 February 1937, p.435.

[280] Another side of this coin was exposed by Erpingham in 1951, when the Council was encouraged by the Agricultural Executive Committee to build in Bessingham and Matlaske only to find that '... when it comes to selecting tenants there appears to be no great demand and no requests were received from farmers for reservation of houses for workers' (TNA MAF147/4 Letter from Erpingham RDC Clerk to Norfolk Agricultural Executive Committee Assistant Secretary, 17 September 1951). The Council, it seems, sought to aid farming by responding to Executive

housing risks. For Smallburgh, as in other districts, councils were told farm production was under threat because workers were leaving due to poor housing.[281] This does not explain why no-subsidy houses could not have been built earlier, save that Smallburgh showed tepid interest in other economic sectors, being drawn into provision when no-subsidy homes could be built without fear of fiscal drain.

But if Smallburgh was so different from Biggleswade, why did the latter only build no-subsidy dwellings two years earlier? After all, the entirety of Biggleswade's no-subsidy stock was erected under the 1925 Housing Act;[282] no new legislation was needed for permission to build. For sure, Biggleswade was as troubled as Smallburgh by difficulties in the agricultural sector. Council discussions emphasised this was an agricultural district, appreciated difficulties for farm-workers meeting council rents and acknowledged rates impacted on farmers.[283] Restricting Biggleswade's field for action was wealth inequality across the parishes. Access to better-paid non-farm work meant residents in some parishes could afford council rents and pressed for more provision. Elsewhere homes were needed but ability to pay was lacking. This dilemma did not confront the Council under the 1919 Act, as the Treasury paid most dwelling costs. After this, Biggleswade wanted to charge RDC subventions to parishes benefiting from new homes rather than meeting costs district-wide, otherwise poorer parishes subsidised richer ones.[284] It was hoped higher subsidies for agricultural parishes under the 1924 Act would offer a solution but subsidies for agricultural parishes were insufficient to address the problem. Plans to erect 104 homes under the 1931 Housing (Rural Authorities) Act kept hopes alive for a bit longer,[285] until this Act was emasculated. Even when prompted by the inaction of private builders, Biggleswade was influenced by concern rents for no-subsidy houses were beyond residents' means.[286] It continued to argue farm labourer houses needed

---

Committee pressure, while the Committee made use of prioritisation for agricultural homes to over-supply.

[281] For example, *FakPost* 11 February 1927, p.3; *NM&PWJ* 9 May 1936, p.6.

[282] BRO RDBwH2/2 'Biggleswade Register of Houses Provided Under 1925 and 1930 Acts'.

[283] For instance, see the description of a council meeting in the *NBC&SN&DN* (25 March 1927, p.3). Note this discussion took place before 1929, when agriculture was effectively de-rated (with cuts also for manufacturing and the railways; Taylor 1965, p.257). This did not mean worries over property rates disappeared, with the Ministry acknowledging '... that many rural districts, as a result largely of the derating of agricultural land, have no longer rateable resources sufficient to carry the ordinary charge for any substantial number of houses' (TNA HLG40/15 'Housing (Rural Authorities) Bill', undated c1931, p.2).

[284] *NBC&SN&DN* 14 August 1925, p.1. Before the 1919 Act, it was often held that levying charges on single parishes, rather than district-wide, froze districts into inaction (Land Enquiry Committee 1913, pp.121–23). The Ministry indicated it was not desirable for parishes to be charged (e.g. HRO RDC7/1/8 HtRDCM 15 February 1923, p.290), which stymied Biggleswade (BRO RDBwM1/9 BiRDCM 17 June 1925).

[285] BRO RDBwM1/10 BiRDCM 2 September 1931.

[286] BRO RDBwM1/11 BiRDCM 3 June 1936, p.290; BRO RDBwM1/12 29 July 1936, p.320; 21 October 1936, p.374; 18 November 1936, p.405; 10 February 1937. p.435.

special Treasury funding, but decided to build without national assistance for those who could afford the rents.

The experiences of the investigated districts show that the same outcome could emerge for different reasons, while similar driving forces could produce divergent outcomes. Hence there was similarity in the midst of divergence between Biggleswade and Smallburgh, while Hatfield and Smallburgh followed quite different housing trajectories, despite their shared commitment to low taxes and reticence over public rather than private solutions. This was demonstrated not only in building council homes but also in disposing of them. Reflecting assumptions that 1919 Act interventions were short-term, the government was soon encouraging councils to sell dwellings to tenants.[287] Hatfield reportedly sold 12 in 1922, regularly reported a willingness to sell more, and was even chastised by the Ministry in 1933 for proposing sales while proclaiming urgent shortages of rental properties for the working-classes.[288] Hatfield apart, there were few inter-war records of council dwelling sales. Smallburgh did explore selling 12 in 1932, but whether this was a one-off or a regular occurrence was unclear. At one level slight evidence of 1919 Act sales is surprising, for national authorities promoted sales, indicating that if councils sold dwellings at half-price they would no longer be liable for their one penny rate contribution, which suggested annual savings to the rates of £21/10/0d per dwelling.[289] If councils were motivated to keep property taxes low, the fact the Treasury would continue paying for properties built, that local residents would still live in them, and that this action was government encouraged, might be expected to have elicited sales. The Ministry was disappointed by uptake (MoH 1923, p.42). Biggleswade rebuffed suggestions there were advantages in disposing of council houses,[290] and Erpingham resisted, noting the possibility but declining action.[291]

In the 1950s and into the 1960s opposition to sales was even stronger, with widespread rejection of 1952 government encouragement. Amongst the six urban districts and seven rural districts explored here, only Sheringham and Smallburgh offered early support for this 1952 policy before Biggleswade Town agreed in 1959.[292] Erpingham contemplated the possibility pre-1952 before coming down against,[293] while Braughing and Walsingham saw no advantage in losing older

---

[287] HCH 22 February 1922, Vol.150, col.1930W.

[288] HRO RDC7/96/1 *HertsMerc* 23 September 1922; HRO RDC7/1/9 HtRDCM 22 October 1925, p.208; HRO RDC7/96/2 *HertsMerc* 29 June 1929; TNA HLG48/872 Letter from MoH to Hatfield RDC Clerk, 12 May 1933. Whether Hatfield did sell 12 houses built under the 1919 Act was uncertain. Years later it was reported nine had been sold (*HM&CP* 20 August 1927, p.8).

[289] *BC&BG* 17 February 1922, p.6.

[290] BRO RDBwM1/9 BiRDCM 20 May 1925.

[291] TNA HLG48/868 Letter from Erpingham RDC Clerk to MoH Secretary, 1 April 1927; NRO DC13/5/73 ERDCHCM 7 November 1932, p.43.

[292] *NNN* 5 September 1952, p.1; NRO DC22/2/27 SmRDCM 4 November 1952, p.45; *BC&BG* 4 December 1959, p.21.

[293] NRO DC13/5/23 ERDCM 7 January 1951; NRO DC13/5/24 ERDCM 5 January 1953, para.182.

properties that generated rent surpluses.[294] More generally, opponents argued that housing needs were greater than provision for the working-classes. This view permeated press reports when the policy was introduced in 1952, with condemnation of private-owner unwillingness to build for rent.[295] Contrary to its pre-1939 stance, Hatfield repeatedly refused to sell homes after 1945. It was enticed to consider the possibility after research suggested benefits for new towns from mixed tenures (Cullingworth and Karn 1968).[296] This led to a review, which fed into policy change after the 1972 Housing Finance Act forced up council rents (Skinner and Langdon 1974; Davies 2013).[297] Even in the face of the 1972 Housing Finance Act, most of the investigated councils continued to oppose sales. Some considered individual requests based on their specific merits but the general message was that waiting lists were too long, there were no guarantees over replacements, and, while sales would be at discounted prices, new properties would be at high cost.[298] In general, irrespective of whether councillors might have preferred private solutions to housing problems, the necessity of state intervention was clear to them. So was the way rural councils took on board their responsibilities. As we have seen, signs of unmet demand for new housing were transparent. While in the 1920s and 1930s governments might have turned a blind-eye when councils paid lip-service to their obligation to review and respond to housing deficiencies, after 1945 housing was an electorally charged policy arena for at least a decade, returned as a politically sensitive topic in the 1960s and was highly controversial in the 1970s (Skinner and Langdon 1974; Eatwell 1979; Fielding 1992; Jones 2000; Simmonds 2002).

3.4   Contributing to Contrivance

The contrast in housing performance between Biggleswade and Smallburgh is instructive. Both had high council-building. Both responded to housing deficiencies, with reactions conditioned by local labour market conditions and council leader values. In both cases, as with most rural councils, private sector solutions were explored but found wanting. This pushed these and other councils into action. That the drive to respond was often muted is suggested by low rates of rural building. The figures are stark. In 1919, 21.9% of all dwellings in England and Wales

---

[294] NRO DC19/6/65 WRDCHCM 15 December 1952, p.173; *D&FT* 30 January 1953, p.1; HRO RDC3/2/8 BrRDCPHHCM 18 September 1952, p.2135; HRO RDC3/1/7 BrRDCFRCM 21 August 1958, p.3958; 18 September 1958, p.3988; 230 November 1958, p.4077.

[295] On the *Municipal Review*'s opposition, see *WR&WSR* 15 January 1952, p.10.

[296] HRO RDC7/1/16 HtRDCHCM 30 September 1952, p.162; HRO RDC7/1/25 HtRDCHCM 3 February 1959, p.545; HRO RDC7/1/26 HtRDCHCM 25 March 1960, p.791; HRO RDC7/1/40 HtRDCHCM 28 February 1967, p.2772; HRO RDC7/1/45 HtRDCJMHF 18 June 1969, p.142.

[297] HRO RDC7/1/47 HtRDCH&TPCM 14 July 1970, p.178; Hatfield RDC (1973, p.41).

[298] For example, BRO RDAM1/23 ARDCHPBuCM 14 September 1967; SaUDCM 20 July 1970; WRDCM 16 December 1970; BRO RDBwM1/44 RiRDCHCM 12 July 1972, p.125.

were in rural districts. This had fallen to 19.0% by 1938 (albeit part of the loss was due to urban encroachment and losses to newly independent urban districts). Yet RDCs accounted for less than 14% of inter-war council-building in England and Wales, compared with more than 23% for private-owners (MoH 1944a, p.61). Rural output was even lower for slum replacement (under 11%) and ameliorating over-crowding (just over 12%). Some mitigation might be claimed, owing to the curtail-ment of the 1931 and 1938 Acts. After all, the 1931 Act only produced 1989 new dwellings, although the scheme was launched as a 40,000 programme before fiscal retrenchment, while the 1938 Act only yielded 3584 dwellings by 1943.[299] What is significant is that when these interventions were made, there was national recogni-tion of a need for focused programmes to increase rural council-building. Yet, dur-ing the 1920s, the rural share of dwellings erected under every Housing Act was smaller for councils than for private-owners (Table 3.7). Across the board, rural councils did not make enough use of 1920s national support, with the prioritisation of the private sector in the 1930s yielding scant gains for the working-classes, espe-cially in rural districts. The 1940s saw some uplift in rural fortunes but these were again deflated during the 1950s (e.g. Table 3.4). Some rural members criticised their own councils for this poor housing performance. On Saffron Walden RDC, for instance, Councillor Dimond attacked the Council in 1962 for its '… dismal failure to maintain a regular high productivity of houses', noting falls in output from 105 a year for 1950–1952 down to 11 a year in 1958–1960.[300] The response he received was that the Council did not have a bottomless pit; the kind of reaction those who tarnish rural leaders with the brush of traditionalism and cost avoidance might find reassuring.

Understanding RDC actions requires a wider perspective than rural leaders' lack of imagination, cautiousness or petit bourgeois inclinations. Rural councils adapted to local circumstances in uneven ways. The next chapters explore this variety in more detail but a core councillor concern over tenant inability to pay rents was com-mon (especially for farm-workers). Without or with thin subsidies, most rural work-ers were unable to take opportunities for better housing, whether via home ownership or council tenancy. If leaders believed new dwellings could be affordable, they acted, as in Biggleswade, Hatfield and Smallburgh. But if building costs were high or subsidies low, councils knew many residents would be reluctant to take council vacancies. This did not mean demand had gone away; as seen in parish requests for houses peaking in the 1930s, with waiting lists rising rapidly in the 1950s and 1960s, despite repeated attempts to slim them down. That rural councils were per-turbed by national failures to promote housing so private and public building was encouraged was evident in reactions at peak times of need. With homes fit for heroes

---

[299] HCH 10 March 1936, Vol.309, col.1960 on 1931 Act numbers. Making a political point, former Labour Minister of Health, Arthur Greenwood, stated that one of the National government's first contributions was '… deliberately to strike a blow against better housing conditions for the agri-cultural workers' by cutting houses under the 1931 Act from 40,000 to 2000 (HCH 30 January 1935, Vol.297, col.385). The figure for the 1938 Act is from MoH (1944a, p.64).

[300] *H&EO* 14 December 1962, p.1.

promises reneged on by 1921, resentment towards national actions became apparent. This was encapsulated in war-time statements by two of the investigated rural councils. The first was a resolution from Ampthill, which highlighted disquiet over the intentions of powerful interests in the nation. These contributed to the 'never again' sentiment that was so influential in the 1945 General Election (Morgan 1990, p.28; Hennessy 1992):

> ... having a lively recollection of the failure to realise a similar programme of re-construction and revival immediately after the Great War of 1914–1918, begs the Minister of Health to make quite sure that on this occasion no financial, or other, vested interests shall interfere to thwart the fervent desire of the people and the declared policy of the present Government to carry through a comprehensive programme of national re-construction based on a prosperous and contented countryside.[301]

Hatfield's resolution the following year drew attention to another 'never again' sentiment, in targeting the socially divisive, even uncaring, as well as top-down strands in 1930s government actions (Calder 1969; Thrift 1986; Ward 1988). Here, the plea was that rural councils:

> ... should be permitted greater freedom of action in existing rural housing schemes, and that if the local authority were prepared to build better types of houses than those recommended by the Ministry they should be allowed to do so as this would not increase any subsidy payable by the Ministry but would enable better built houses to be secured, as distinct from the shoddy erections which have so often been produced in the past at the Ministry's behest.[302]

The tone of these resolutions captures an atmosphere less of rural inhibition that of a desire to break away from national impositions.

Whatever the rural sentiments, hopes for greater rural 'freedoms' would be dashed, aided by short-term shortages of labour and materials and longer term weak national economic performance. For rural housing the nationally inspired decline of private rental continued, leaving rural districts increasingly constrained by a lack of interest amongst private builders or at best enthusiasm biased towards 'suburban' locations, primarily for owner-occupation. For the less well-paid the best prospect for dwelling improvement lay in a council tenancy. But the 1930s were to see the beginning of processes now referred to as the residualisation of the council sector.

---

[301] This resolution was sent to the Ministry and to Bedfordshire MPs. It was supported by Braughing (HRO RDC3/2/2 BrRDCPHHCM 18 November 1943, p.630). The strength of belief that 'combines' in the building industry had forced up prices after 1918, so helping stifle 1919 Act possibilities, received airings in Parliament (e.g. see the MP for Gateshead East at HCH 22 March 1950, Vol.475, col.1725).

[302] This was part of a resolution to a Hertfordshire RDC meeting (HRO RDC3/2/2 BrRDCPHHCM 23 November 1944, p.705). Resolutions '... to nullify the power of the trust and rings which control building materials ...' were common in the early-1920s, as with this passage from Barnet RDC (HA&SAT 17 September 1921, p.5 or the Keighley resolution supported by Ampthill; W&DR 12 May 1923, p.1). In addition to company restrictive practices, in Cabinet some blame for rising costs were laid on labour (Orbach 1977, p.111), with the lead politician on the 1919 Act, Christopher Addison, feeling betrayed by building workers seeking concessions and opposing the employment of unskilled workers.

There might not have been the demonising of council tenancies of the 1950s, 1970s and 1980s (Jacobs et al. 2003; Jones 2010; Davies 2013) but the 1930s still saw transformed expectations for council housing. Before 1933, when housing subsidies were cut for all bar slum rehousing and overcrowding relief, council tenancies were dominated by better-paid workers (Holmans 1987; Lowe 1991; Pooley 1996). Subsidies were sufficiently low that rents were high; so high tenants moving into owner-occupation could afford better homes than council dwellings (O'Carroll 1996). The 1930s could have widened the social composition of council housing, as building costs mostly fell (Fig. 3.2), so making rents affordable for a wider population. But, as prices dropped, the national emphasis was on private ownership (Finnigan 1984; Jones 2010). This led to quantitative restrictions on council-building. Qualitatively it meant building 'down' to the means of the poorest; promoting lower standards so slum dwellers might pay rents. These steps came with tighter specifications for council tenancy, wherein:

> ... it is now a statutory requirement that in the selection of tenants preference is to be given to those living under such conditions [unfit or overcrowded previous homes] and to tenants with large families, an area of choice which should generally concentrate the benefits of subsidised housing upon those most in need of such assistance. (MoH 1939, p.2)

Those outside such bounds were left with a diminishing private rental offer or, for many, unobtainable home ownership.

Such policies have been ascribed to Conservative Party dominance in government (Weiler 2000) but the rationale ran deeper. At the time, adherents in the Conservative and Labour parties supported 'orthodox economic' views that, along with the Treasury, resisted new ideas (Ham 1981, pp.67–68): 'The view that MacDonald, Baldwin, Chamberlain and Runciman could do virtually nothing to cure unemployment because nobody had yet discovered how to do so is a myth' (Seaman 1966, p.246).[303] Visible economic policy failures emphasised social division rather than mitigating distress (Crafts 1987; Ward 1988; Scott 2007), with a fixation on reducing taxes and cutting labour costs providing transparent evidence that pump-priming the already wealthy would not bring trickle-down gains of sufficient magnitude for most in the population. It would require more widely spread investment for rearmament to lift most of the country from its economic gloom (McKibbin 2010). Much has been made of inter-war regional economic disparities and their long-term impacts (Martin 1988; Dunford 1995). These self-imposed harms were equally apparent in rural deprivations. At a time when rural councils were all too aware of demand for more housing (Table 3.1), and when the cost of building was low (Fig. 3.2), they saw shrinkages in output, whereby dwellings were built largely to replace demolished units but not to respond to shortages. Rather than easing housing deficits, increasing reliance had to be placed on a fading private

---

[303] Giving a sense of limitations on thought, Seaman (1966, p.212) described Philip Snowden, the 1929–1931 Labour Chancellor of the Exchequer, as having '... the mentality of a Poor Law Commissioner of the 1830s. It would not be an exaggeration to say that in fiscal matters he was more reactionary than Neville Chamberlain [who followed him as Chancellor], who was almost urbane and humanitarian by comparison'.

rental sector. Given the limited intellectual vision of 1930s orthodox economic policy, perhaps this was to be expected; anticipated if you accept Barnett's (1972) vision of the exaggerated role British politicians had for international engagements and the poverty of British leadership. What might be less easy to understand is why 1950s and 1960s governments, having seen the impact of 1930s policies, slipped so readily into making the same mistakes.[304] As Kynaston (2009, p.416) expressed it, ending general subsidies for council-building in 1955 '… was the start of the long, painful process of "residualisation", by which those living in local authority housing would sink ever further below the average income and status of the population as a whole', while wishful thinking rather than effective policy towards private rental brought electoral repercussions as the early-1960s' government became associated with profiteering and homelessness (Weiler 2000). National action brought home to rural councils the depth of demand for better housing, together with a sharper awareness of supply shortcomings (Fig. 3.1) and quality shortfalls (Chap. 6).

Underscoring these problematic processes, what this chapter begins to point towards is how the English countryside was led towards service-class capture. The rural canvass early in the century was one on which private builders had largely withdrawn, save for supplying the better-off close to larger towns. Private rental was in decline and, as explored in more detail in the following chapters, rural councils were thwarted in their attempts to address housing problems. Yet, rural leaders heard increasingly loud messages about housing inadequacies, set in a context in which most workers were low-paid. That some councils responded to these challenges more effectively than others is clear. Praise them or damn them, over the next chapters, the scope for local action will be shown to have been limited. Freedom of action was constrained within a tight box.

References

Adonis A (1988) Aristocracy, agriculture and liberalism: the politics, finances and estates of the third Lord Carrington. Hist J 31:871–897

Allison KJ (1961) Industrial and agricultural. In: Norwich and its region. British Association for the Advancement of Science Local Executive Committee, Norwich, pp 119–126

Ashford DE (1986) The emergence of the welfare states. Blackwell, Oxford

Astor V, Rowntree BS (1939) British agriculture: the principles of future policy. Penguin, Harmondsworth

Axford B (1978) Charles Selwyn and Mark Woodnutt, political leaders on the Isle of Wight. In: Jones GW, Norton A (eds) Political leadership in local authorities. University of Birmingham Institute of Local Government Studies, Birmingham, pp 81–100

---

[304] Note the November 1967 letter from the Ministry '… drawing the Council's [Ampthill's] attention to the aim, announced in recent Ministerial statements, to relate authorities' house-building programme far more closely than hitherto to their overriding need to rehouse people from the slums and other bad outworn housing, and that all housing schemes submitted will require justification on a strict test of first priorities such as the clearance of slums and other unsatisfactory housing conditions and the housing of old people' (BRO RDAM1/24 ARDCHCM 30 May 1968).

Bailey BJ (1978) Portrait of Hertfordshire. Robert Hale, London

Bailey C (2012) The secret rooms. Penguin, London

Baker WP (1953) The English village. Oxford University Press, London

Barnes P (1993) Norfolk landowners since 1880. University of East Anglia Centre of East Anglian Studies, Norwich

Barnett C (1972) The collapse of British power. Eyre Methuen, London

Baxter R (1972) The working class and Labour politics. Polit Stud 20:97–107

Bealey F, Blondel J, McCann WP (1965) Constituency politics: a study of Newcastle-under-Lyme. Faber & Faber, London

Beard M (1989) English landed society in the twentieth century. Routledge, London

Beastall TW (1966) A south Yorkshire estate in the late nineteenth century. Agric Hist Rev 14:40–44

Beavington F (1975) The development of market gardening in Bedfordshire 1799–1939. Agric Hist Rev 23:23–47

Beckett JV (1986) The aristocracy in England 1660–1914. Blackwell, Oxford

Beckett JV, Turner ME (2007) End of the old order? F.M.L. Thompson, the land question, and the burden of ownership in England, c1880–c1925. Agric Hist Rev 55:269–288

Bedale J (1980) Property relations and housing policy: Oldham in the late nineteenth century and early twentieth century. In: Melling J (ed) Housing, social policy and the state. Croom Helm, London, pp 37–72

Benson J (1989) The working class in Britain, 1850–1939. Longman, Harlow

Bielckus CL, Rogers AW, Wibberley GP (1972) Second homes in England and Wales. Wye College studies in rural land use 11. Ashford

Biggleswade Rural District Council (1913) Annual report of the medical officer of health and sanitary inspector 1912. Biggleswade

Biggleswade Rural District Council (1915) Annual report of the medical officer of health and sanitary inspector 1914. Biggleswade

Biggleswade Rural District Council (1953) Annual report of the medical officer of health and sanitary inspector 1952. Biggleswade

Bigmore P (1979) The Bedfordshire and Huntingdonshire landscape. Hodder & Stoughton, London

Blondel J, Hall R (1967) Conflict, decision-making and the perceptions of local councilors. Polit Stud 15:322–350

Board of Trade (1940) Statistical abstract for the United Kingdom for each of the fifteen years 1924 to 1938. HMSO, London

Bowley M (1938) Some regional aspects of the building boom, 1924–36. Rev Econ Stud 5:172–186

Bowley M (1945) Housing and the state 1919–1944. Allen & Unwin, London

Bracey HE (1958) A note on rural depopulation and social provision. Sociol Rev 6:67–74

Bramley G, Smart G (1995) Rural incomes and housing affordability. Rural Development Commission, Salisbury

Brassley P (2006) British farming between the wars. In: Brassley P, Burchardt J, Thompson L (eds) The English countryside between the wars: regeneration or decline? Boydell, Woodbridge, pp 187–199

Bristow SL (1978) Local politics after reorganisation – the homogenisation of local government in England and Wales. Public Admin Bull 28:17–33

Burnett J (1986) A social history of housing 1815–1985, 2nd edn. Methuen, London

Butcher H, Law IG, Leach R, Mullard M (1990) Local government and Thatcherism. Routledge, London

Butterworth R (1966) Islington borough council: some characteristics of single-party rule. Politics 1(1):21–31

Byrne DS (1980) The standard of council housing in inter-war North Shields – a case study on the politics of reproduction. In: Melling J (ed) Housing, social policy and the state. Croom Helm, London, pp 168–193

Cairncross A (1995) The British economy since 1945, 2nd edn. Blackwell, Oxford

Calder A (1969) The people's war: Britain 1939–1945. Pimlico, London

Cannadine D (1990) The decline and fall of the British aristocracy. Yale University Press, New Haven

Champion AG, Green AE, Owen DW, Ellin DJ, Coombes MG (1987) Changing places: Britain's demographic, economic and social complexion. Edward Arnold, London

Clark DM (1990) Affordable rural housing: challenge for the nineties. Rural Development Commission, Salisbury

Clarke JJ (1924) The new Housing Act, 1924. Town Plan Rev 11(2):119–127

Clemenson HA (1982) English country houses and landed estates. Croom Helm, London

Coleman R (1982) Second homes in north Norfolk. In: Moseley MJ (ed) Power, planning and people in rural East Anglia. University of East Anglia Centre for East Anglian Studies, Norwich, pp 97–117

Connell J (1978) The end of tradition: country life in central Surrey. Routledge & Kegan Paul, London

Connor LR (1936) Urban housing in England and Wales. J R Stat Soc 94:1–65

Coppock JT (1977) Second homes: curse or blessing? Pergamon, Oxford

Crafts NFR (1987) Long-term unemployment in Britain in the 1930s. Econ Hist Rev 40:418–432

Crotch WW (1901) The cottage homes of England: the case against the housing system in rural districts, 2nd edn. P.S. King & Son, London

Cullingworth JB (1966) Housing and local government in England and Wales. Allen & Unwin, London

Cullingworth JB, Karn VA (1968) The ownership and management of housing in new towns. HMSO, London

Dale J (1980) Class struggle, social policy and state structure: central-local relations and housing policy, 1919–1939. In: Melling J (ed) Housing, social policy and the state. Croom Helm, London, pp 194–223

Daunton MJ (1996) How to pay for the war: state, society and taxation in Britain, 1917–24. Engl Hist Rev 111:882–919

Davies A (2013) 'Right to buy': the development of a Conservative housing policy, 1945–1980. Contemp Br Hist 27:421–444

Dearlove J (1973) The politics of policy in local government. Cambridge University Press, Cambridge

Dearlove J (1979) The reorganisation of British local government. Cambridge University Press, Cambridge

Dickens P, Duncan SS, Goodwin M, Gray F (1985) Housing, states and localities. Methuen, London

Downing P, Dower M (1973) Second homes in England and Wales. Countryside Commission CCP 65. Countryside Commission, London

Drudy PJ (1978) Depopulation in a prosperous agricultural region. Reg Stud 12:49–60

Duckers N, Davies H (1990) A place in the country. Michael Joseph, London

Duke of Bedford (1897) A great agricultural estate: being the story of the origin and administration of Woburn and Thorney. John Murray, London

Dunford M (1995) Metropolitan polarization, the north-south divide and socio-spatial inequality in Britain: a long-term perspective. Eur Urban Reg Stud 2:145–170

Eastwood T (1951) Industry in the country towns of Norfolk and Suffolk. Oxford University Press, London

Eatwell R (1979) The 1945–1951 Labour government. Batsford, London

Edwards N (1998) Ploughboy's progress: the life of Sir George Edwards. University of East Anglia Centre for East Anglian Studies, Norwich

Elliott B, McCrone D, Bechhofer F (1988) Anxieties and ambitions: the *petit bourgeoisie* and the new right in Britain. In: Rose D (ed) Social stratification and economic change. Hutchinson, London, pp 263–278

Fielding S (1992) What did 'the people' want? the meaning of the 1945 General Election. Hist J 35:623–639

Finnigan R (1980) Housing policy in Leeds between the wars. In: Melling J (ed) Housing, social policy and the state. Croom Helm, London, pp 113–138

Finnigan R (1984) Council housing in Leeds 1919–1939: social policy and urban change. In: Daunton MJ (ed) Councillors and tenants. Leicester University Press, Leicester, pp 102–153

Fletcher P (1969) The agricultural housing problem. Soc Econ Adm 3:155–166

Ford J (1975) The role of the building society manager in the urban stratification system: autonomy versus constraint. Urban Stud 12:295–302

Forrest R, Murie A (1988) Selling the welfare state: the privatisation of public housing. Routledge, London

Francis M (2012) 'A crusade to enfranchise the many': Thatcherism and the 'property-owning democracy. Twent Century Br Hist 23:275–297

Fraser D (2009) The evolution of the British welfare state, 4th edn. Palgrave, Basingstoke

Gardiner J (2010) The thirties: an intimate history. Harper Press, London

Gauldie E (1974) Cruel habitations: a history of working-class housing 1780–1918. Allen & Unwin, London

Giles AK, Cowie WJG (1960) Some social and economic aspects of agricultural workers' accommodation. J Agric Econ 14(2):147–169

Godber J (1969) History of Bedfordshire 1066–1888. Bedfordshire County Council, Bedford

Grant W (1977) Independent local politics in England and Wales. Saxon House, Farnborough

Gray F (1976) Selection and allocation in council housing. Trans Inst Br Geogr 1:34–46

Grayson WC (1992) Chicksands: a millenium history. Shefford Press, Shefford

Green FE (1920) A history of the English agricultural Labourer 1870–1920. P.S. King & Co., London

Green G (1972) National, city and ward components of local voting. Policy Polit 1:45–54

Gregory P (1975) Waiting lists and the demand for public housing. Policy Polit 3(4):71–87

Griffiths CVJ (2007) Labour and the countryside: the politics of rural Britain 1918–1939. Oxford University Press, Oxford

Gyford J (1985) The politicisation of local government. In: Loughlin M, Gelfand MD, Young K (eds) Half a century of municipal decline. Allen & Unwin, London, pp 77–97

Ham A (1981) Treasury rules: recurrent themes in British economic policy. Quartet, London

Harloe M (1995) The people's home? social rented housing in Europe and America. Blackwell, Oxford

Harris C (1974) Hennage: a social system in miniature. Holt, Rinehart & Winston, New York

Harrison M, Norton A (1967) Local government administration in England and Wales. Maud Committee report on the management of local government volume five. HMSO, London

Hatfield Rural District Council (1961) Annual report of the medical officer of health and public health inspector 1960. Hatfield

Hatfield Rural District Council (1962) Annual report of the medical officer of health and public health inspector 1961. Hatfield

Hatfield Rural District Council (1967) Annual report of the medical officer of health and public health inspector 1966. Hatfield

Hatfield Rural District Council (1970) Annual report of the medical officer of health and public health inspector 1969. Hatfield

Hatfield Rural District Council (1973) Annual report of the medical officer of health and public health inspector 1972. Hatfield

Hatfield WEA (1959) Hatfield and its people, 12 vols. Workers' Educational Association Hatfield Branch, Hatfield

Havinden MA (1999) Estate villages revisited. University of Reading Rural History Centre, Reading

Heclo HH (1969) The councillor's job. Public Adm 47:185–202

Henderson SR, Hoggart K (2003) Ruralities and gender divisions of labour in Eastern England. Sociol Rural 43:349–378

Hennessy P (1992) Never again: Britain 1945–1951. Vintage Books, London

Hodge I, Monk S (2004) The economic diversity of rural England: stylised fallacies and uncertain evidence. J Rural Stud 20:263–272

Hoggart K, Cheng S (2006) Women's pay in English rural districts. Geoforum 37:287–306

Hollis P (1987) Ladies elect: women in English local government 1865–1914. Clarendon Press, Oxford

Holmans AE (1987) Housing policy in Britain: a history. Croom Helm, London

Holmans AE (2000) Housing. In: Halsey AH, Webb J (eds) Twentieth-century British social trends. Macmillan, Basingstoke, pp 469–510

Hooson DJM (1958) The recent growth of population and industry in Hertfordshire. Trans Inst Br Geogr 25:197–208

Horn P (1984) The changing countryside in Victorian and Edwardian England and Wales. Athlone, London

Horn P (2013) Country house society: the private lives of England's upper class after the First World War. Amberley Publishing, Stroud

Houfe S (1995) Bedfordshire. Pimlico, London

Howkins A (1985) Poor labouring men: rural radicalism in Norfolk 1870–1923. Routledge, London

Howkins A (2003) The death of rural England: a social history of the countryside since 1900. Routledge, London

Hussey S (1997) Low pay, underemployment and multiple occupations: Men's work in the inter-war countryside. Rural Hist 8:217–235

Jackson AA (1973) Semi-detached London: suburban development, life and transport, 1900–39. Allen & Unwin, London

Jacobs K, Kemeny J, Manzi T (2003) Privileged or exploited council tenants? the discursive change in Conservative housing policy from 1972 to 1980. Policy Polit 31:307–320

Jennings JH (1971) Geographical implications of the municipal housing programme in England and Wales 1919-39. Urban Stud 8:121–138

Johnson RW (1972) The nationalisation of English rural politics: Norfolk South West, 1945-1970. Parliam Aff 26:8–55

Jones B (2010) Slum clearance, privatization and residualization: the practices and politics of council housing in mid-twentieth-century England. Twent Century Br Hist 21:510–539

Jones H (2000) 'This is magnificent!': 300,000 houses a year and the Tory revival after 1945. Contemp Br Hist 14:99–121

Keith-Lucas B, Richards PG (1978) A history of local government in the twentieth century. Allen & Unwin, London

Kendall D (1963) Portrait of a disappearing English village. Sociol Rural 3:157–165

Kynaston D (2009) Family Britain 1951–57. Bloomsbury, London

Land Enquiry Committee (1913) The land – volume one: rural, 3rd edn. Hodder & Stoughton, London

Larkin A (1979) Rural housing and housing needs. In: Shaw JM (ed) Rural deprivation and planning. Geo Books, Norwich, pp 71–80

Layton E (1961) Building by local authorities. Allen & Unwin, London

Lee JM (1963) Social leaders and public persons: a study of county government in Cheshire since 1888. Clarendon, Oxford

Linsley B (2005) Homes for heroes: housing legislation and its effects on housing in rural Norfolk 1918–1939. PhD thesis University of East Anglia

Lowe S (1991) One hundred years of social housing. In: Lowe S, Hughes D (eds) A new century of social housing. Leicester University Press, Leicester, pp 1–12

Macdonald P (2017) Rural settlement change in East Suffolk, 1850–1939. PhD thesis University of East Anglia

McGrew T, Bristow S (1984) Candidate to councillor: a study of political recruitment. In: Bristow SL, Kermode D, Mannin M (eds) The redundant counties? G.W. & A. Hesketh, Ormskirk, pp 69–100

Macintyre S (1980) Little moscows: communism and working-class militancy in inter-war Britain. Croom Helm, London

McKibbin R (2010) Parties and people: England 1914–1951. Oxford University Press, Oxford

Mackintosh JM (1936) Rural housing. Northamptonshire County Council, Northampton

Malpass P (2003) Private enterprise in eclipse? a reassessment of British housing policy in the 1940s. Hous Stud 18:645–659

Mandler P (1997) The fall and rise of the stately home. Yale University Press, New Haven

Mark-Lawson J, Savage M, Warde A (1985) Gender and local politics: struggles over welfare politics 1918–39. In: Lancaster Regionalism Group, Localities, class and gender. Pion, London, pp 195–215

Marriner S (1976) Liquidity problems in the mass-production of 'homes for heroes'. Bus Hist 18:152–189

Marshall JL (1968) The pattern of housebuilding in the inter-war period in England and Wales. Scott J Polit Econ 15:184–205

Martin JG (1938) Memorandum upon the Housing (Financial Provisions) Act, 1938 (revised November 1938). National Housing & Town Planning Council, London

Martin RL (1988) The political economy of Britain's north-south divide. Trans Inst Br Geogr 13:389–418

Merrett S (1982) Owner-occupation in Britain. Routledge & Kegan Paul, London

Mingay GE (1986) The transformation of Britain 1830–1939. Routledge & Kegan Paul, London

Mingay GE (1990) The rural slum. In: Gaskell SM (ed) Slums. Leicester University Press, Leicester, pp 92–143

Ministry of Agriculture & Fisheries and Ministry of Health (1932) Report of the Inter-Departmental Committee on Agricultural Tied Cottages. Cmd 4148. HMSO, London

Ministry of Health (1920a) First annual report, 1919–1920: part II – housing and town planning. Cmd 917. HMSO, London

Ministry of Health (1920b) Gifts of land for housing purposes: statement showing the names of donors of sites which have been approved by the Ministry of Health for the erection of houses for the working classes. Cmd 559. HMSO, London

Ministry of Health (1921) Second annual report, 1920–1921. Cmd 1446. HMSO, London

Ministry of Health (1923) Fourth annual report, 1922–1923. Cmd 1944. HMSO, London

Ministry of Health (1930) Eleventh annual report, 1929–1930. Cmd 3667. HMSO, London

Ministry of Health (1931) Twelfth annual report, 1930–1931. Cmd 3937. HMSO, London

Ministry of Health (1932) Thirteenth annual report, 1931–1932. Cmd 4113. HMSO, London

Ministry of Health (1933a) Fourteenth annual report, 1932–1933. Cmd 4372. HMSO, London

Ministry of Health (1933b) Housing Act, 1930: part I. Circular 1331. HMSO, London

Ministry of Health (1934) Fifteenth annual report, 1933–1934. Cmd 4664. HMSO, London

Ministry of Health (1936a) Seventeenth annual report, 1935–1936. Cmd 5287. HMSO, London

Ministry of Health (1936b) Housing Act, 1935: report on the overcrowding survey in England and Wales 1936. HMSO, London

Ministry of Health (1937) Rural housing: second report of the Rural Housing Sub-Committee of the Central Housing Advisory Committee. HMSO, London

Ministry of Health (1938) Nineteenth annual report, 1937–1938. Cmd 5801. HMSO, London

Ministry of Health (1939) Report on the management of municipal housing estates. Circular 1740. HMSO, London

Ministry of Health (1944a) Rural housing: third report of the Rural Housing Sub-Committee of the Central Housing Advisory Committee. HMSO, London

Ministry of Health (1944b) Private enterprise housing: report of the Private Enterprise Sub-Committee of the Central Housing Advisory Committee of the Ministry of Health. HMSO, London

Ministry of Health (1950) The cost of house-building: second report of the committee of inquiry appointed by the Minister of Health. HMSO, London

Ministry of Housing & Local Government (1956) Report of the Ministry of Housing and Local Government for the year 1955. Cmd 9876. HMSO, London

Ministry of Housing & Local Government (1961) Housing in England and Wales. Cmnd 1290. HMSO, London

Ministry of Housing & Local Government (1966) Our older homes: a call for action. HMSO, London

Ministry of Housing & Local Government (1967) Management of local government. Maud Committee report. HMSO, London

Ministry of Housing & Local Government (1968) Housing condition survey: England and Wales, 1967. Econ Trends 175:87–99

Ministry of Housing & Local Government (quarterly) Housing return for England and Wales [Before 1951 Ministry of Health]. HMSO, London

Ministry of Labour & National Service (1957) Enquiry into household expenditure 1953–54. HMSO, London

Mitchell GD (1950) Depopulation and rural social structure. Sociol Rev 42:69–85

Molotch H (1976) The city as a growth machine. Am J Sociol 82:309–332

Morgan KO (1990) The people's peace: British history 1945–1989. Oxford University Press, Oxford

Morgan KO, Morgan J (1980) Portrait of a progressive: the political career of Christopher, Viscount Addison. Clarendon, Oxford

Morris DS, Newton K (1970) Profile of a local political elite: businessmen as community decision-makers in Birmingham 1838-1966. New Atlantis 1(2):111–123

Morris DS, Newton K (1971) The social composition of a city council: Birmingham 1925–1966. Soc Econ Adm 5(1):29–33

Moseley MJ (1973) The impact of growth centres in rural regions: an analysis of spatial flows in East Anglia. Reg Stud 7:77–94

National House Building Committee (1924) Report on the present position in the building industry, with regard to the carrying out of a full housing programme, having particular reference to the means of providing an adequate supply of labour and materials, Cmd 2104. HMSO, London

Newby HE (1972) The low earnings of agricultural workers. J Agric Econ 23:15–24

Newby HE (1975) The deferential dialectic. Comp Stud Soc Hist 17:139–164

Newby HE (1977) The deferential worker: a study of farm workers in East Anglia. Allen Lane, London

Newby HE, Bell C, Rose D, Saunders P (1978) Property, paternalism and power. Hutchinson, London

Newton K (1976) Second city politics: democratic processes and decision-making in Birmingham. Oxford University Press, Oxford

Niner P (1975) Local authority housing policy and practice – a case study approach. Occasional Paper 31. University of Birmingham Centre for Urban & Regional Studies, Birmingham

O'Carroll A (1996) The sale of council housing in the inter-war period. Hous Stud 11:527–541

O'Connor J (1973) The fiscal crisis of the state. St Martin's, New York

Olney R (2007) Squire and community: T.G. Dixon at Holton-le-Moor, 1906–1937. Rural Hist 18:201–216

Orbach LF (1977) Homes for heroes: a study of the evolution of British public housing 1915–1921. Seeley Service & Co., London

Parker J, Mirrlees C (1988) Housing. In: Halsey AH (ed) British social trends since 1900, 2nd edn. Macmillan, Basingstoke, pp 357–397

Pedley WH (1942) Labour on the land: a study of the developments between the two great wars. P.S. King & Staples, London

Phillips DR, Williams AM (1982) Rural housing and the public sector. Gower, Farnborough

Pooley GC (1996) Local authority housing: origins and development. The Historical Association, London

Public Works, Roads & Transport Congress (1931) Rural housing: a selection from the exhibition of photographs of rural housing schemes and of the houses reconditioned under the Housing (Rural Workers) Act, 1926; with relevant statistics. Congress Organising Committee, London

Rees AM, Smith T (1964) Town councillors: a study of Barking. Acton Society Trust, London

Richardson HW (1967) Economic recovery in Britain 1932–39. Weidenfeld & Nicolson, London

Robin J (1980) Elmdon: continuity and change in a north-west Essex village 1861–1964. Cambridge University Press, Cambridge

Rose D, Saunders P, Newby HE, Bell C (1976) Ideologies of property. Sociol Rev 24:699–730

Rothery M (2007) The wealth of the English landed gentry, 1870-1935. Agric Hist Rev 55:251–268

Rowntree S, Kendall M (1913) How the labourer lives: a study of the rural labour problem. Thomas Nelson & Sons, London

Ryder R (1984) Council house building in County Durham 1900–39. In: Daunton MJ (ed) Councillors and tenants. Leicester University Press, Leicester, pp 40–100

Satsangi M, Gallent N, Bevan M (2010) The rural housing question. Policy Press, Bristol

Saunders P, Newby HE, Bell C, Rose D (1978) Rural community and rural community power. In: Newby HE (ed) International perspectives in rural sociology. Wiley, Chichester, pp 55–85

Savage M (2000) Class analysis and social transformation. Open University Press, Buckingham

Saville J (1957) Rural depopulation in England and Wales 1851–1951. Routledge & Kegan Paul, London

Scott P (2007) Triumph of the south: a regional economic history of early twentieth century Britain. Ashgate, Aldershot

Scott P (2008) Marketing mass home ownership and the creation of the modern working-class consumer in inter-war Britain. Bus Hist 50:4–25

Seaman LCB (1966) Post-Victorian Britain, 1902–1951. Methuen, London

Self RC (2000) The Neville Chamberlain diary letters: volume two, the reform years, 1921–27. Ashgate, Aldershot

Self RC (2006) Neville Chamberlain: a biography. Ashgate, Aldershot

Shears RT (1936) Housing the agricultural worker. J R Agric Soc Engl 97:1–12

Short BM, Godfrey J (2007) 'The Outhwaite controversy': a micro-history of the Edwardian land campaign. J Hist Geogr 33:45–71

Shucksmith M (1981) No homes for locals? Gower, Farnborough

Shucksmith M (1987) Rural housing in Scotland: the policy context. In: MacGregor BD, Robertson DS, Shucksmith M (eds) Rural housing in Scotland. Aberdeen University Press, Aberdeen, pp 17–27

Shucksmith M (1991) Still no homes for locals? affordable housing and planning controls in rural areas. In: Champion AG, Watkins C (eds) People in the countryside. Paul Chapman, London, pp 53–66

Simmonds AGV (2002) Raising Rachman: the origins of the Rent Act. Hist J 45:843–868

Skinner D, Langdon J (1974) The story of clay cross. Bertrand Russell Peace Foundation, Nottingham

Smallburgh Rural District Council (1958) Smallburgh RDC medical officer of health annual report 1957. Stalham

Smith R, Whysall P (1990) The Addison Act and the local authority response: housing policy formulation and implementation in Nottingham 1917-1922. Town Plan Rev 61:185–206

Smith R, Whysall P, Beuvrin C (1986) Local authority inertia in housing improvement 1890-1914: a Nottingham study. Town Plan Rev 57:404–424

Springall LM (1936) Labouring life in Norfolk villages 1834–1914. Allen & Unwin, London

Swenarton M, Taylor S (1985) The scale and nature of the growth of owner-occupation in Britain between the wars. Econ Hist Rev 38:373–392

Taylor AJP (1965) English history 1914–1945. Clarendon, Oxford

Thirlwall AP (1967) A measure of the 'proper distribution of industry'. Oxf Econ Pap 19:46–58

Thompson FML (1963) English landed society in the nineteenth century. Routledge & Kegan Paul, London

Thompson FML (2001) Gentrification and the enterprise culture: Britain 1780–1980. Oxford University Press, Oxford

Thompson M (2007) The land market, 1880–1925: a reappraisal reappraised. Agric Hist Rev 55:289–300

Thrift NJ (1986) Little games and big stories: accounting for the practice of personality and politics in the 1945 General Election. In: Hoggart K, Kofman E (eds) Politics, geography and social stratification. Croom Helm, London, pp 86–143

Topham N (1970) Housing authorities and the investment decision. Manchester School Econ Soc Stud 38:285–302

Wade-Martins P (1994) An historical atlas of Norfolk, 2nd edn. Norfolk Museums Service, Norwich

Wade-Martins S (1980) A great estate at work: the Holkham estate and its inhabitants in the nineteenth century. Cambridge University Press, Cambridge

Wade-Martins S, Williamson T (2008) The countryside of East Anglia: changing landscapes 1870–1950. Boydell, Woodbridge

Ward SV (1988) The geography of interwar Britain: the state and uneven development. Routledge, London

Weiler P (2000) The rise and fall of the Conservatives' 'grand design for housing', 1951–64. Contemp Br Hist 14:122–150

Williams P (1978) Building societies and the inner city. Trans Inst Br Geogr 3:23–34

Wycombe Rural District Council (1952) Housing progress: one thousand houses in six years. High Wycombe

Chapter 4
Uneven Demand: Depopulation, Repopulation and Housing Pressure

Abstract Common portrayals of rural England up to the last quarter of the twentieth-century paint a picture of rural decline; of job losses, depopulation and outmigration. In this context, it was arguably unreasonable to expect rural councils to be active builders of new homes. This chapter shows this argument is false. Rural districts in general saw increases in population and, more especially, in households throughout the decades. Relatively few saw no increased demand for dwellings, both at district and parish levels. Weaker pressure did exist in places distant from cities but the general pattern was clear. Moreover, rural areas increasingly received urban interest from those seeking recreational bolt-holes, which further squeezed the availability of homes for local residents. Exploring efforts to enhance accommodation supply, this chapter shows how rural districts were badly served by national slum clearance drives, which proceeded with stipulations detrimental to rural action; resulting in depressed rural building, as in the 1930s. Added to which, under most Housing Acts, a serious problem for rural areas was low wages, which commonly put new dwellings outside the reach of rural workers' pockets.

Keywords Demographic sustainability · Urban incomers · 1930s slum clearance · Rural wages · Housing non-affordability

Irrespective of the predilections, preferences and priorities rural leaders want to act on, they must operate within constraining structures. By way of analogy, if you want to know who is the faster driver, organise a race with near-equal vehicles rather than a new Jaguar against a decrepit Citroen 2CV. Throughout the twentieth-century, rural leaders were subject to criticism over housing failures (Larkin 1979; Shucksmith 1990; Satsangi et al. 2010), but so were British politicians in cities and nationally (Berry 1974; Malpass 1986). Any assumption that inadequate rural homes were somehow unique is quickly disabused by photos of city housing, right up to the 1970s (e.g. McCullin 2007), or films of the time, like *Cathy Come Home*.[1]

---

[1] A 1966 BBC television play directed by Ken Loach about a homeless young family, which has regularly been heralded as one of the best television dramas made.

© Springer Nature Switzerland AG 2021   175
K. Hoggart, *A Contrived Countryside*, Local and Urban Governance,
https://doi.org/10.1007/978-3-030-62651-8_4

The chronic nature of Britain's housing performance was symbolised in words like 'crisis' and 'failure' that punctuated book and article titles over the century. It is hardly fruitful to condemn rural leaders when the nation as a whole, or at least its corporate and political leaders, deserve equal or more censure. To put a critical spotlight appropriately on the countryside requires asking about the demand and supply conditions that incited local responses. Within these structures, how effective was rural performance? This constitutes the key question for the next four chapters. Here, we assess the scale of demographic, economic and social forces that provoked demand for housing advancement.

4.1   The Demographic Imperative

Mainstream messages on rural England over most of the twentieth-century draw attention to demographic decline. Early in the century, Mackinder (1907, p.334) charged that: 'A decrease of population appears to be in progress in nearly all the purely rural portions of Britain'. This theme dominated accounts of the countryside (e.g. Astor and Rowntree 1939; Saville 1957; Parr 1966), particularly over the loss of young people to higher pay and better working conditions in towns (Land Enquiry Committee 1913; Mitchell 1950). Much of this decline was associated with falling labour demand in traditional rural industries like agriculture (Drudy and Wallace 1971), resulting in a countryside distinguished by its inability to attract compensatory in-migration (Johnston 1967; Grafton 1982; Weekley 1988). Around cities, such impulses were depressed, eliminated and reversed as the century progressed, as urban commuter fields spread outwards (Champion et al. 1987; Boyle et al. 2001). Yet there was a dynamism to rural demography (Williams 1963; Goodwin-Hawkins 2015), with later analysts drawing attention to the longstanding roots of a vibrant rural population geography, in which even'remoter' areas played a part (Cross 1990; Pooley and Turnbull 1998; Burchardt 2012). Despite these changes, in the popular imagination, in official accounts and in political commentaries, the messages of the first three-quarters of the century emphasised falling or in better circumstances stable rural numbers, whose imprint was overturned under the impress of expanding urban shadowlands. In this context, an expectation of rising housing demand close to cities was not unreasonable, nor was declining calls for housing investment in the wider countryside. Thus, Tilley (1947, p.39) noted small demand for new rural homes, for: 'In walking through many of our older villages, one usually finds gaps in the street picture, open spaces where once a cottage stood. Derelict and tumbledown cottages and fire-scarred ruins are also not difficult to find'. Perhaps rural council sloth over housing was a rational response to weak demand?

This view permeated official documents and council minutes. These commonly offer little reason to press for more rural dwellings. In the report on an official 1924 Erpingham deputation to Bessingham, in Ampthill's 1930 Medical Officer of Health's annual report, and in its equivalent report for Walsingham in 1935, entries like this were evident.[2] But to accept the proposition that population decline lessened the need for housing improvement requires agreement that depopulation and falling demand were occurring. Looking back from today, this view is difficult to sustain. For Moseley (1980), depopulation was never the norm for rural Britain. More than 20 years later, Hodge and Monk (2004) formalised the argument by depicting commentaries on rural England as influenced by 'stylised fallacies'. One was the claim rural depopulation was persistent. According to Hodge and Monk, over the previous 40 years, rural growth was higher than urban in all regions except the South-East, where urban was slightly ahead. Howkins (2006) provided earlier evidence of rural vibrancy. He reported that if we use standard boundaries for areas, then even for 1911–1921, rural districts on average grew, with upsurges intensifying inter-war.[3] Using standardised boundaries is critical when evaluating population change. Of course, in some cases, this requires significant computational expertise due to boundary changes, as evinced in local reconstructions (e.g. Walford 2001, 2005, 2010). In other cases, comparisons are straightforward. In Biggleswade, for example, the parish of Sandy became an independent Urban District Council in 1927, with no other boundary changes in the district. Population totals for Biggleswade in 1921 and 1931 suggest a fall from 23,015 to 20,962 residents. But the 1931 figure excluded Sandy, unlike that for 1921. Within the 1931 boundaries of Biggleswade, the 19,606 inhabitants of 1921 had risen to 20,962 in 1931 (Sandy had 3409 inhabitants in 1921).[4] As Walford (2001) showed, comparisons for small areas can be complex. This is not so for district comparisons across the nation, as county census reports give population totals (albeit not much else) for the same geographic area at proximate censuses.

Table 4.1 was generated from these county reports, comparing populations by local government category for the same areas across censuses. This presentation uses boundaries at the last census date. Hence, in the case of Biggleswade, this table records a rise in inhabitants from 19,606 to 20,962 for 1921–1931. In this way, the practice of depressing rural population changes because territory was lost through annexation or new urban designations is removed. Eliminating inflation in urban totals, and accompanying depressions of rural numbers, gives insight on how far urban and rural districts at the later census date experienced population change. Viewed in this light, Howkins, Hodge, Monk and Moseley correctly identified that

---

[2] *HMC&WP* 18 January 1924, p.5; BRO RDAR8/11 ARDCMOHar 1930; *EDP* 6 June 1935, p.6. Around the same time, national politicians were proclaiming falling demand for rural housing, commonly citing reduced agricultural employment in their orchestrations (e.g. HCH 10 July 1931, Vol.254, col.2508; HCH 15 March 1933, Vol.275, col.2059).

[3] Further back, Armstrong (1981, p.74) found only three English counties (Cornwall, Huntingdon, Rutland), plus three Welsh counties (Cardigan, Montgomery, Radnor) had absolute 1841–1911 population losses.

[4] Between 1889 and 1927, 270 UDCs were carved out of RDCs, while around 400 UDCs and boroughs had their boundaries extended. Between 1929 and 1938, 159 UDCs were abolished, as were 169 RDCs, with 1300 boundaries altered (Keith-Lucas and Richards 1978, p.200). For RDCs, the 644 rural districts in 1919 had fallen to 475 in 1939 (MoH 1944a, p.61), then to 412 in 1966 (HCH 24 October 1966, Vol.734, col.113W).

Table 4.1 Percent population change by English local government category, 1921–1971

	1921–1931	1931–1951	1951–1961	1961–1971
Rural District councils	4.0	17.5	7.6	15.7
Boroughs-Urban District councils (towns)	7.8	21.1	11.7	14.8
County boroughs (cities)	3.8	1.4	- 0.7	- 3.0

Source: Computed from county reports of the population censuses
Note: These computations used boundaries at the end of each census period, so numbers were for the same geographical areas across census periods. For 1971, the calculations excluded Greater London and for earlier censuses London and Middlesex counties

Table 4.2 Percentage of English and Welsh counties with population growth in rural districts, 1921–1971

	1921–1931	1931–1951	1951–1961	1961–1971
% English counties with rural growth	74.5	97.9	89.4	95.6
% Welsh counties with rural growth	38.5	38.5	30.8	46.2

Source: Computed from county reports of the censuses
Note: These computations used boundaries at the end of each census period, so numbers were for the same geographical areas across census periods. For 1971, the calculations excluded Greater London and for earlier censuses, London and Middlesex counties

rural districts in general saw continuous population growth between 1921 and 1971. This was not simply in growth regions like South-East England. The dominant trend for English counties was positive, with no county experiencing rural losses in each of the four census 'decades'. Only one did so in three census periods (Westmorland) and only three for two of them (Cumberland, Herefordshire and Shropshire). One factor that contributed to doom and gloom commentaries on rural population was bundling England and Wales together. If you include Wales in this analysis, images of rural buoyancy are deflated, although not eliminated (Table 4.2).

To illustrate patterns at finer resolution, Table 4.3 shows population shifts in the three investigated counties. As might be expected, being closer to London, growth impulses came earlier in Hertfordshire, as Howkins (2006) suggested, with this effect extending around a decade later to more distant Bedfordshire. The pattern in both counties differed little between rural and urban districts. Based on population growth, pressure for housing expansion was no less in rural than in urban zones. Norfolk saw more muted expansionary urges, although demographic uplifts were stronger in rural districts than in towns. This rural dynamism was apparent across a substantial proportion of rural districts in each county (Table 4.4), although Norfolk's rural districts performed relatively poorly in the 1950s. To nuance this, we must dig a little deeper.

Table 4.5 takes us to the parish level. Here, Hatfield needs to be distinguished from the other districts, owing to the size of its component parishes. There were only four parishes in the district at every census. Two had more than 2000 residents in 1921 (rising to three by 1951), with none under 500. Elsewhere, small parishes abounded. In the case of Walsingham, for example, 73.7% had fewer than 500

Table 4.3 Percent population change for districts in Bedfordshire, Hertfordshire and Norfolk, 1921–1971

	1921–1931	1931–1951	1951–1961	1961–1971
Hertfordshire rural	22.1	67.1	39.0	14.9
Hertfordshire urban	21.8	46.5	41.0	20.6
Bedfordshire rural	7.5	35.0	23.9	27.3
Bedfordshire urban	6.9	45.4	21.3	18.8
Norfolk rural	1.4	19.6	2.2	12.8
Norfolk urban	- 1.2	- 1.5	2.7	6.8

Source: Computed from county reports of the population censuses
Note: These computations used boundaries at the end of each census period, so numbers were for the same geographical areas across census periods. 'Rural' refers to rural district councils and 'urban' to county boroughs, boroughs and urban districts councils combined

Table 4.4 Percentage of rural districts in Bedfordshire, Hertfordshire and Norfolk with population growth, 1921–1971

	1921–1931	1931–1951	1951–1961	1961–1971
Hertfordshire	76.9	100.0	90.9	100.0
Bedfordshire	83.3	100.0	100.0	100.0
Norfolk	50.0	100.0	40.0	86.7

Source: Computed from county reports of the population censuses
Note: These computations used boundaries at the end of each census period, so numbers were for the same geographical areas across census periods

Table 4.5 Percentage of parishes in investigated rural districts with population growth between census periods, 1921–1971

	1921–1931	1931–1951	1951–1961	1961–1971
Hatfield	75.0	100.0	100.0	75.0
Braughing	26.3	84.2	31.6	63.2
Ampthill	46.7	65.5	62.1	62.1
Biggleswade	44.0	80.0	60.0	72.0
Erpingham	40.9	52.3	31.8	27.3
Smallburgh	41.5	60.0	25.7	62.9
Walsingham	31.6	34.2	15.8	15.8

Source: Computed from county reports of the population censuses
Note: The parishes used in computations were those at the 1971 census. The procedure followed and the handling of boundary changes are described in Table 1.2

residents in 1921.[5] In the other Norfolk districts, more than 65% of parishes had less than 500 residents in 1921, with Erpingham at 75% for both 1921 and 1971. Braughing in Hertfordshire was close to these values (57.9% under 500 in 1921, rising to 63.2% by 1971), with the two Bedfordshire districts around the 50% mark

---

[5] For 1921 parishes, rather than the 1971 parishes used in Table 4.5, 18.6% had fewer than 100 residents.

Table 4.6 Percent change in population and households for selected Walsingham parishes 1931–1971

	% population change			% change in households				
	1931–1951	1951–1961	1961–1971	1931–1951	1951–1961	1961–1971	1951 population	Military role
Sculthorpe	472.5	6.5	−78.4	22.2	14.5	1.8	3040	RAF/USAF base 1942–1962
Stiffkey	181.2	−66.2	−14.2	19.6	0.0	−5.7	1001	Anti-aircraft base 1939–1950s
Raynham	297.4	−24.5	−52.0	0.8	157.4	−34.7	1848	RAF/FAA base 1939–1964
Langham	245.2	−76.3	3.3	15.3	−1.2	−2.4	908	RAF base 1940–1961
Little snoring	163.3	−46.0	−9.7	186.2	−42.8	5.3	632	RAF base 1943–1958

Source: Computed from the Norfolk County report of the population censuses
Note: This list does not include all parishes within Walsingham impacted by military bases. It also does not pick out Walsingham particularly, in that many parishes across Norfolk were so affected, as were some in Bedfordshire. As an illustration, in Smallburgh, Scottow (1951 population 1376) experienced the effects of Coltishall airfield (RAF/USAAF 1940–2006), with the parish seeing population percentage changes of 328.7%, 0.9% and − 11.2%, respectively, for the three inter-census periods listed above

in 1921 and 40% or less in 1971. Seeing most change in this smallest category was Ampthill, for which the proportion with fewer than 500 inhabitants fell from 56.0% to 34.5% over the 50 years. But assuming population change proxies housing demand is problematical. Take, for example, the relatively small population increases recorded for the 1950s, especially in Norfolk (Table 4.3). Walsingham illustrates the issue, with five parishes expanding, then contracting demographically with the opening and closing of military bases.[6] Thus, using consistent boundaries across census periods, Walsingham grew by 4889 inhabitants between 1931 and 1951, yet there was growth by 5574 in five parishes with military bases (Table 4.6). Following the run-down and closure of bases in the 1950s, the same parishes had population losses of 1387 out of a 1951–1961 district loss of 1975. Changes in household numbers over these periods were weakly related to demographic change (Table 4.6).[7] Reflecting the national position closely, the average size of households

---

[6] These effects were more general, with 800 of a 1000 1951–1961 population loss in Erpingham linked to the Weybourne Army Base closure (*NNN* 25 October 1963, p.12). Similarly, Biggleswade's 1936 population growth of 3190 largely came from expansion at the Henlow RAF Depot, with a fall of 1170 the following year primarily due to fewer personnel at the base (Biggleswade RDC 1937, 1938).

[7] The 1921 and 1931 censuses presented 'family' numbers, whereas from 1951, 'households' were reported. After 1951, there have been adjustments in how households were defined, as in 1981 (Parker and Mirrlees 1988, p.358). However, as Thomas (1957, p.131) reported, the term 'family',

Table 4.7 Percent change in population and households in investigated rural districts between census periods, 1921–1971

	Population number changes				Household number changes			
	1921–1931	1931–1951	1951–1961	1961–1971	1921–1931	1931–1951	1951–1961	1961–1971
Hatfield	21.3	112.1	70.1	13.7	41.0	130.6	78.5	20.3
Braughing	−4.2	10.6	−1.7	24.3	4.7	25.5	5.3	23.5
Ampthill	0.9	31.3	13.3	29.7	9.1	39.4	20.9	32.5
Biggleswade	6.9	26.1	3.2	30.7	14.6	28.2	21.6	36.2
Erpingham	−5.3	10.7	−5.3	1.2	8.0	20.5	12.1	7.3
Smallburgh	0.0	17.5	−5.7	11.6	9.8	24.4	5.1	16.1
Walsingham	−2.1	32.7	−8.6	−16.3	5.1	19.4	11.1	0.4
English RDCs	4.0	17.5	7.6	15.7	16.7	28.9	11.9	12.8

Source: Computed from county reports of the population censuses
Note: The districts used in computations were based on parishes in each district at the 1971 census. The procedure followed and the handling of boundary changes are described in Table 1.2

over the period dropped in the investigated rural districts from between 3.9 and 4.1 in 1921 to between 2.8 and 3.0 in 1971 (the mean averages from England at these dates were 4.1 and 2.8).[8] Even where demographic decline occurred, demand for extra housing could persist.

This was exemplified by comparing household and population changes (Table 4.7). Overall, there was a consistent pattern; where population numbers swelled, household totals rose more rapidly, while demographic decline might come with household increases (e.g. Walsingham after 1951). Demand for more homes was driven by more than population numbers. Failure to provide more housing could encourage population loss. In Rural Housing Sub-Committee surveys, dwelling shortfalls, especially for young couples, were recorded in four of the nine rural districts visited in the mid-1930s; as found for Depwade in Norfolk.[9] This tendency

which covered all persons boarding together, was used unchanged from 1801 to 1931. Then, in 1951, the term 'household' replaced 'family' without a change of meaning. In this book, reference is generally made to 'households', taking 'families' as equivalent to them in early censuses.

[8] There was little to separate rural from urban in this regard. In Hertfordshire, rural and urban districts had the same number of persons per household in both 1921 and 1971 (computed to one decimal point, 4.1 then 3.0). In Bedfordshire, urban households were always marginally larger than rural (4.1 and 3.9 in 1921, then 3.1 and 3.0 in 1971), while in Norfolk towns were larger in 1921 (3.9 to 4.0) but smaller in 1971 (2.8 to 2.7).

[9] TNA HLG37/43 'Report on Local Investigations in Wiltshire, Bedfordshire, Derbyshire and Anglesey', undated c1936; TNA HLG37/44 'NUAW Memorandum on Rural Housing', October 1936. Such sentiments were repeated regularly in Whitehall memos and letters (e.g. TNA HLG37/50 Letter from NFU Deputy Secretary to Rural Housing Sub-Committee Secretary, 6 August 1943), as well as finding local expression, as in Ampthill (*W&DR* 3 February 1934, p.6) and Walsingham (TNA MAF147/3 'Housing for Agricultural Workers. Walsingham RDC', 3 March 1948). Appeals from parish councils on this point were common, in Bedfordshire (e.g. BRO RDBwM1/20 BiRDCM 23 March 1949, p.49; *WR&WSR* 27 February 1962, p.2), Hertfordshire

raised concern at district and parish levels, as exemplified by calls for additional houses to stop families leaving.[10] As the Ministry of Health (1939, p.94) accepted: 'The lack of cottages supplied with modern amenities is one of the main factors which accounts for the desertion of the land, especially by the younger generation, for industrial employment in towns' (also Ministry of Works and Planning 1942, p.18). Hence, in calling for more rural homes, in 1938, the Hertfordshire branch of the National Farmers' Union argued that: 'The drift from the land continues and we feel that indifferent or inefficient housing accommodation is partly responsible for this very regrettable state of affairs'.[11] Shortage was not the sole issue, as dwelling quality was also problematical. As the Rural Housing Sub-Committee found in Mere and Tilsbury RDC, population was stagnant because lack of housing investment created accommodation losses, since: 'Houses frequently fell down and disappeared'.[12] Almost 20 years later, Braughing, along with Mitford and Launditch RDC, found farm-workers driven from the land owing to poor housing amenities,[13] which can be put alongside Bracey's (1958) Somerset conclusion that depopulating rural parishes were more likely to lack mains water, gas or electricity (also Humphrys 1968). This parallels Turner's (1953, p.75) charge that it was:

> ... because too many of our villages and country towns have been starved of new investment over the last 75 years that the life they offer is not attractive to the rising generation either materially or in scope of opportunities. They are not 'woman worthy', to use a graphic phrase employed by Lord Hungarton, and parents think their children will suffer educationally and in prospects generally.

Even in the 1960s, Walsingham councillors blamed weak demographic trends on slight housing investment, with the Clerk of Mitford and Launditch RDC pointing to '... a gradual but almost certain disappearance of many small communities in mid-Norfolk'.[14] All this when rural populations were growing nationally (Table 4.1), as they were in the three investigated counties (Table 4.3), if not in every district (Table 4.7) or parish (Table 4.5).

According to Saville (1957), the causes of rural depopulation had not changed notably for more than 150 years. Falling economic opportunities and the centralisation of economic life were at the heart of rural decline. Alternatives to agriculture were limited across much of the countryside, with low wages, coupled with falling demand for farm labour, weakening rural economies (Pedley 1942; Hodge and Whitby 1981; Hussey 1997). Even when jobs were available, living conditions were

---

(e.g. *H&EO* 9 March 1935, p.10; 3 April 1937, p.10) and Norfolk (e.g. NRO DC19/6/66 WRDCHCM 22 November 1954, p.96; *NorfChron* 24 June 1955, p.1; NRO DC19/6/67 WRDCHCM 8 April 1957, p.128; *NNN* 12 February 1966, p.7).

[10] An early reference to this was TNA RECO1/592 'Notes on Rural Housing', undated c1918.

[11] HRO RDC3/2/1 BrRDCPHHCM 22 December 1938, p.311.

[12] TNA HLG37/43 'Report on Local Investigations ...', undated c1936, p.12.

[13] *H&EO* 8 May 1948, p.5; *D&FT* 16 January 1953, p.10.

[14] On Walsingham, *D&FT* 29 November 1963, p.1; on Mitford and Launditch, *D&FT* 6 March 1964, p.1. Similar worries of village disintegration unless more council homes were built were expressed by St Faith's and Aylsham RDC (*NNN* 16 December 1949, p.7).

often poor, not simply in the workplace but also for community and household amenities. The former was captured in the wry comment of Jim, a Cambridgeshire farm-
worker: 'Those who refer to "the good old days", he says, obviously haven't spent
days walking behind a horse and plough in the cold and wet' (Page 1974, p.167).
This view was expressed particularly by young adults, who characterised country
living as 'too humdrum' and isolated (on Okehampton, see Martin 1965). However,
irrespective of images of decline, rural areas held onto residential numbers more
effectively than contemporary commentators led us to believe. Dwelling numbers
were often sustained in villages despite outmigration (e.g. Robin 1980, p.204),
although supply was often poor quality or too expensive for local residents (Savage
1915; Mackintosh 1936; Penfold 1974). Nevertheless, even in the often difficult
operating conditions of the inter-war years (Ward 1988), official investigations
found only around 10% of rural districts were uncertain of a need for more
dwellings.[15]

4.2 Countervailing Tendencies

Significantly, while the 1920s saw encouragement for councils and private owners
to build more homes, in the 1930s, governments dampened and restricted council
action. Barring support for slum clearance and the relief of overcrowding, council-
building subsidies were eschewed, with the private sector expected to drive responses
to housing shortage (Bowley 1945; Marshall 1968). For the government of the time,
private sector actions were highly effective. As early as 1933, for instance, the
Cabinet was told that: '… in many districts the shortage must have been overtaken
or at least largely reduced, and the problem is now more of a local character. On the
other hand, only the surface of the slum problem has been scratched'.[16] A decade
later, Conservative politicians held that even the slum problem would have been
addressed, but for the inconvenience of the Second World War: 'If one honestly
looks at the figures, one will find that the Conservative slum clearance scheme
before the war was making considerable progress, and it is not unfair to say that, if
the war had not come, the whole of that problem would now be solved'.[17] As Gay
(1987, p.419) observed, by 1939, the Ministry of Health thought the housing crisis
was well on the way to a solution, with Churchill's war-time coalition seeing post-
war housing intervention as short-term, requiring 300,000 new dwellings in
two years, rather than a long-term campaign. For rural districts, such assumptions
rested on a warped vision of reality. A troubling issue was the partial manner in
which the private sector assisted rural populations. First, if homes for sale were

---

[15] TNA HLG37/44 'Evidence of Neville Hobson, RDCA Executive Council Member', undated
c1936, p.1.

[16] TNA CAB24/234 CP386(32) 'Housing Policy', 27 January 1933, p.3.

[17] Robert Conant MP (Bewdley) at HCH 17 October 1945, vol.414, col.1272.

beyond the purse of most rural residents, with few new-build private homes for rent, then the fact that more than 81% of 1919–1943 rural new-build was privately owned would do little to alleviate rural housing distress (MoH 1944a, p.61).[18] Those in policy circles knew council-building offered little compensation. Thus, Rural Housing Sub-Committee reports claimed that, while 159,000 inter-war dwellings were constructed in rural districts:

> A great many RDC areas, of course, are adjacent to towns and many of their housing estates border these towns, with the result that they are almost completely occupied by town workers, thus giving a false picture of rural housing ... [such that] It is doubtful whether one in every thousand is occupied by an agricultural worker.[19]

Parliament regularly heard the same message, as from former Minister of Health, Arthur Greenwood:

> The figures given for building in rural district council areas tell us nothing whatever, as hon. Members know, about the real problem of rural housing, because so many of these houses built in rural district council areas are in fact on the edge of urban district areas. Everyone knows that the amount of house-building that has been carried out in the rural areas is relatively less than in the urban and semi-urbanised areas.[20]

Despite this 'knowledge', systematic evidence was sparse, owing to inadequate rural construction statistics. As the 1924 Minister of Health reported: 'Accurate statistics on this point are not available and would only be prepared with some difficulty; it is estimated, however, that of the 1053 houses completed under the Housing Act, 1923, in rural districts some 800 are in rural districts which are contiguous to towns of over 20,000 population'.[21] Outside national censuses, which lacked tenure codes, assessing housing change required detailed local investigation or relied on bundling all rural districts together as if they were subject to the same change forces.

Stripping out this effect required local detail. One offering was the third report of the Rural Housing Sub-Committee (MoH 1944a), which identified six rural districts in England and Wales amongst the highest and lowest for population size, property tax potential and acreage, alongside six in the middle ground. Table 4.8 lists the percentage of new inter-war council-owned dwellings in two categories. Note the dominance of council-building. In all, for 21 of the 27 named districts, council supply outstripped the private sector over these 20 years.[22] Predictably, the strongest private showing was in the wealthiest districts, where only 38.0% of new

---

[18] The same point was made in Whitehall 30 years later, in noting that '... it is quite likely that much of the new [rural] housing is out of reach of the pocket of the average worker. The majority of these houses are for the people working in the cities who are faced by shortage of land and higher prices to find accommodation away from the built-up urban areas' (TNA HLG118/767 'Note to Mr. Williams from T.A. Doughty', attached note 'Thoughts on the Hobhouse Report of 1947 on Rural Housing', 27 September 1967, p.2).

[19] TNA HLG37/52 'Memorandum from Mr. Monks', undated c1946.

[20] HCH 4 April 1928, vol.215, col.2021.

[21] HCH 28 February 1924, Vol.170, col.735W.

[22] Figures for districts by acreage are little different, with 73.1% of rural districts in the report (excluding double-counts) recording higher public sector new-build totals.

Table 4.8 Percent of all new dwellings that were council-owned in selected English rural districts, 1919–1939

Rural district	County	% council	Rural district	County	% council
Districts with the largest populations			*Districts with the highest penny rate product*		
Easington	Durham	57.6	Eton	Buckinghamshire	27.8
Chesterfield	Derbyshire	68.3	Guildford	Surrey	48.1
Shardlow	Derbyshire	35.4	Godstone	Surrey	64.4
Doncaster	West Yorkshire	13.4	Amersham	Buckinghamshire	34.5
Hemsworth	West Yorkshire	60.8	Uckfield	Sussex	34.7
Districts with medium size populations			*Districts with medium sized penny rate products*		
Hereford	Herefordshire	82.4	Faringdon	Berkshire	82.0
Pershore	Worcestershire	78.7	Erpingham	Norfolk	74.1
Ely	Isle of Ely	85.2	Smallburgh	Norfolk	80.2
Isle of Axholme	Lincolnshire Lindsey	68.0	North Westmorland	Westmorland	58.0
Banbury	Oxfordshire	89.9	Wadebridge	Cornwall	100.0
Towcester	Northamptonshire	98.1	Oswestry	Shropshire	57.5
Districts with the smallest populations			*Districts with the lowest penny rate products*		
Croft	North Yorkshire	55.6	Thorney	Isle of Ely	70.8
Masham	North Yorkshire	60.9	Broadwoodwidger	Devon	100.0
Tintwistle	Cheshire	83.3			

Source: MoH (1944a, p.67)
Note: The publication lists six RDCs in each category in England and Wales. Only those for England are shown. Two districts were reported under two headings but are only listed once. One was Shardlow (largest population and highest penny rate product), the other was Broadwoodwidger (smallest population and lowest penny rate product). The product of a penny rate reflects the local revenue capacity of a rural district council

dwellings were council-owned, which contrasted with 72.7% in the six districts with mid-ranked property wealth (about the same for the poorest councils). Note the location of these rural districts. Listed Buckinghamshire and Surrey councils had the lowest rates of council-building and by the 1930s were part of London's commuter belt (Connell 1978; Horn 1984; Howkins 2003). Even so, the figures in Table 4.8 suggest a more vibrant council sector than expected. That is, until built numbers are noted. So, the two councils with the lowest penny rate product only built 36 houses between them over 20 years, while the three smallest by population only built 54. Private sector numbers were worse, at 14 and 29, respectively. Context was critical. None of the 'poorer' or 'smaller' councils had a combined private–public building rate equivalent to more than 10% of their 1919 housing stock (few were over 5%, some under 1%), whereas every council with the largest population saw additions over 10% with three at more than 30%, while the wealthiest councils saw growth of 8.3–22.0%. These figures give a glimpse of the uneven geography of house-building but largely exclude rural councils experiencing intense urban spill-over. Here, insight was offered in Mackintosh's (1936, p.18) description of rural

Northamptonshire, where 185 of 458 new private dwellings erected over 1921–1925 and 403 of 802 during 1926–1929 were located in two of the county's 16 RDCs (Brixworth and Northampton), both essentially 'suburban'. Leicestershire figures for 1918–1926 offer more detail. Here, across all rural districts, 19.0% of new-build was council-owned (43.2% subsidised private and 37.8% unsubsidised private). In the four rural districts closest to Leicester (Barrow on Soar, Billesdon, Blaby and Hinckley), the figures were 15.2%, 42.3% and 42.5%, respectively. There were 13 RDCs in the county. These four accounted for 63.3% of total RDC council-building, 80.2% of subsidised private and 91.1% of unsubsidised private new-build.[23] By 1929–1930, intra-rural distinctions had sharpened. These four councils had 16.2% of their new-build as council-owned, so little change there. However, the four districts now accounted for three-quarters of new council dwellings in rural Leicestershire. Subsidised private building had faded significantly, accounting for 2.2% of rural construction, but these four pocketed 88.2% of them, alongside 81.5% of unsubsidised private building.[24]

Two connected messages should be carried forward. The first is that districts close to cities attracted particularly high levels of private investment. The second is the prospect this extended to council-building; that urban spillover created general pressure on rural districts close to towns. This might have been the case in some areas but local outcomes embedded social overtones. In Leicestershire, for example, over 1929–1930, council dwellings were only built in two of the four urban shadow districts, the same two accounting for all subsidised private homes. This matches official observations that some councils bordering large towns built no inter-war council dwellings (MoH 1944a, p.25). Thus, while the two districts with new council homes accounted for 37.8% of unsubsidised private building, 47.4% occurred in the other two districts. Signalling the extremes, Hinckley saw increases of 186 council dwellings and 405 private over 1918–1926, with 58 council and 65 private additions in 1929–1930, whereas Blaby recorded values of 2 and 580, then 0 and 139. Some rural spillover councils saw building largely restricted to private owners, whereas others had more mixed tenures. The hand of vested interest should not be excluded from explanations for such patterns. Note, for example, the 1930 views of the Eton-educated, landowning MP for Essex South-Eastern, whose experience of that rapidly growing county led him to bewail rural councils that built no council homes, charging that:

> … often on account of the vested interest of the council, you are going to get nothing done. The curse of these rapidly-developing districts is, surely, that the most important people are the people who are interested in the preliminary speculation of the land, and they are the people who first get on the rural district councils in these small places, and play into each other's hand.[25]

---

[23] Data from HCH 20 April 1926, Vol.194, col.1043W–44W.

[24] Calculated from HCH 23 February 1931, Vol.248, col.1783W–84W.

[25] HCH 21 February 1930, Vol.235, col.1812–13.

Table 4.9 Percent change in households for rural districts in Bedfordshire, Hertfordshire and Norfolk, 1921–1971

	1921–1931	1931–1951	1951–1961	1961–1971
Hertfordshire	27.9	64.7	46.6	17.9
Bedfordshire rural commuter	9.9	67.9	56.4	9.1
Bedfordshire other rural	4.3	5.8	21.2	34.5
Norfolk rural commuter	20.4	31.4	27.4	33.8
Norfolk other rural	5.9	20.1	10.1	12.5

Source: Computed from county reports of the population censuses
Note: 'Rural commuter' districts were those immediately adjacent to the largest towns in the county (Bedford, Great Yarmouth, Luton and Norwich), with all RDCs in Hertfordshire taken to be in commuter territory, given London's proximity and the county's numerous urban centres

Parts of inter-war Essex became notorious for the development of sprawling 'plot-lands' of substandard shacks for townies and weekenders (Gayler 1970). This represented a different private enterprise world from the well-healed detached abodes of the better endowed. But the promotion of sectional interest can take a variety of forms, sometimes promoting development (Molotch 1976), other times resisting it (Saunders et al. 1978).

Growth impulses certainly created rural 'dormitories' near towns. Their expansion in Bedfordshire, Hertfordshire and Norfolk was apparent in growing household numbers. Comparing rural districts adjacent to larger urban centres from others, Table 4.9 shows that growth in neighbouring rural districts was higher than elsewhere before 1931, and outpaced other districts by substantial margins up to 1961. The 1960s saw change, with the pull of major towns declining in the more London-centred counties of Hertfordshire and Bedfordshire, while 'remoter' areas continued to lag in Norfolk. The attractions of urbanising zones for the private sector lay in higher town wages, which could transition into rural districts if householders would commute. Signifying that the rural–urban divide extended even to those with modest incomes, 1937–1938 Ministry of Labour figures for insured workers found 17.8% of urban dwellers with wages below £250 a year were owner-occupiers against only 4.4% in rural districts (Francis 1997, p.177). But potential buyer power was not alone in encouraging urban spillover, for town proximity also lessened builder costs.

A key component in the search to minimise building and infrastructure costs was urban sprawl, with private construction hugging the curb-side of transport arteries between towns. The principle of a 'free market', that penetrated much 1930s' government orthodoxy, weighed against restricting builders' actions, especially when unfettered building was the backbone of 1930s' British economic recovery (disregarding long-term costs from enhanced social deprivation and inefficient public services; Richardson 1967; Humphries 1987; McKibbin 2010). As in Suffolk, builders were reluctant to move away from public investment in roads, water and sewer systems, with ribbon development resulting, embracing roadsides and leisure and seaside vistas (Macdonald 2017). Antagonism towards such straggling settlements provoked the 1935 Restriction of Ribbon Development Act (Clarke 1936; Sheail

1981), followed by the 1938 London Green Belt Act (Munton 1983), alongside general pressure for more controlled development (Lowerson 1980; Booth 1999). Even so, urban spillover persisted as public services farther from towns were deficient:

> With the rising standard of comfort and convenience, piped water supplies have become one of the amenities commonly sought, and accordingly there is a marked disposition to build houses in the more progressive districts possessing such supplies, rather than elsewhere. This, it is true, illustrates the urban trend of the population and the development of the rural areas in the neighbourhood of the towns and near the coast, at a time when the population of the purely country districts generally remains stationary, even when it does not decline. (MoH 1929c, p.21)

A reason for such tendencies was the growing incidence of urban-centred comprehensive supply schemes. Examples were the extension of Nottingham's water network into parishes in Basford and Bingham RDCs (MoH 1932a, p.13) and the 1935 approval for Exeter's network growth into 13 nearby parishes (Minchinton 1987, p.61). These comprehensive schemes were not restricted to urban-focused networks but could be forged across rural parishes, as when more urbanised Essex RDCs sought loans for sewerage schemes in the late-1920s (MoH 1930a, p.109). However: 'The [funding] system at present applicable in the case of Rural Districts does not always work out altogether equitably in practice and gives rise to friction between parish and parish' (MoH 1925, p.39). Following changes to regulations, and the arrival of grant support, under the 1929 Local Government Act (MoH 1929b), an increasing number of RDCs promoted rural schemes (MoH 1932a, p.13), although districts distant from larger towns lagged far behind (Chap. 5). As the Parliamentary Secretary to the Ministry of Local Government and Planning expressed it in 1951:

> … with the power of county council supervision and contributions provided under the 1929 Act, water supply was provided to a quarter of the parishes of this country up to 1939 … naturally the sequence of events was that provision was first made to the parishes which it was easiest to supply. Most of them, or a very large proportion, were very much more urban in character than rural and the reason for the sequence of events was the question of the ability to carry the rate charge …[26]

Irrespective of the rationale for councils, private estate link-ups to electricity, gas, water and sewerage reduced builder costs and raised sales prospects (Jackson 1973). Places more distant from towns lost out, partly due to no-supply and partly because: 'In some rural areas the water supply was seriously depleted in the interests of urban water undertakings'.[27]

Following the Second World War, with war-time encouragement for a more interventionist state (e.g. Gay 1987), plans were drawn up for stronger short- and long-term involvement in housing (Malpass 2003). A shift in the geography of housing supply might have been expected. Yet, at least for two decades after 1945, the rural picture did not match this presumption. Thus, despite builder and middle-class complaints about restrictions on private construction (Short et al. 1986; Sturzaker 2010),

---

[26] HCH 25 June 1951, Vol.489, col.1022.

[27] TNA HLG50/1879 'Notes on Deputation to the Minister of Health, from the Parliamentary Agricultural Committee', 21 December 1933.

Table 4.10 Council and private owner house-building in Norfolk's rural districts, 1945–1964

	Cumulative from 1945 to		
	1948	1956	1964
% council-built in rural commuter districts	55.7	38.9	21.3
% council-built in other rural districts	76.5	75.3	51.2
Council-built per thousand residents in rural commuter districts	5.6	24.7	28.3
Council-built per thousand residents in other rural districts	7.7	33.3	40.8
Privately built per thousand residents in rural commuter districts	4.4	38.8	104.7
Privately built per thousand residents in other rural districts	2.4	10.9	38.9

Source: NRO DC19/6/63 WRDCHCM 16 February 1949, p.218; NRO DC19/6/67 WRDCHCM 11 February 1957, p.121; NRO DC19/6/69 WRDCHCM 8 March 1965, p.221
Note: 'Rural commuter districts' were adjacent to Great Yarmouth or Norwich, so they were comprised of Blofield and Flegg, Forehoe and Henstead and St Faith's and Aylsham

private builders had a freer hand than was commonly acknowledged. In the case of Norfolk, close to cities, around 35% of all dwellings built up to 1948 were private homes (Table 4.10). Only in more distant districts was the share closer to 20%. During 1946–1951, ministers tussled with councils that issued larger numbers of private building licences than local capacities could fulfil, were perturbed when private demands left insufficient materials for council-building, as in Kettering RDC, and were concerned that labour usage on private homes was one-third higher than for council dwellings.[28] By the end of 1946, councils that had issued so many private licences they were not permitted to grant more included five county boroughs, 16 boroughs, 48 UDCs and 31 RDCs (including Hatfield).[29] Offering insight on urban spillover, by 1947, Norwich's neighbour, St Faith's and Aylsham RDC, had 28 council completions, 88 private licence completions and a further 31 private rebuilds. To the south of Norwich, Forehoe and Henstead RDC went further, with 72 new private homes and three rebuilt compared to just six council completions.[30] The government had previously expressed a desire to see around three-quarters of new-build as council-owned in order to house those in greatest need, so it was little surprise action came to block generous private licence awards. Quotas on private building were introduced, although ministers were regularly drawn to inform Parliament that rural districts issued above their quota.[31] Minutes of the seven investigated rural districts featured regular calls for increased private building, which owed something to

---

[28] TNA HLG36/30 CHAC Minute Book, 12 April 1946, p.300; 19 July 1946, p.310; HCH 9 May 1946, Vol.422, col.1212–13.

[29] TNA HLG31/13 HI24/46:' Houses Under Licence, 1946'.

[30] T&WT 12 April 1947, p.8.

[31] Even as late as 1950, as with Leek RDC (HCH 18 May 1947, Vol.475, col.179W–80W) and Sherborne RDC (HCH 29 June 1950, Vol.476, col.242W). There was also considerable lobbying for more private building licences, as with Dartford RDC (HCH 29 June 1950, Vol.476, col.2438) and Newbury RDC (HCH 9 November 1950, Vol.480, col.74W). As reports in Parliament made clear, ministers increased allocations where they believed the case deserving, as with 15 councils granted increases in May 1951 (HCH 10 May 1951, Vol.487, col.255W).

unwelcome calls on the rates for council-build but also stemmed from a desire to see the private sector functioning effectively. Going one step further, Norfolk's urban spillover districts consistently built less council homes per capita than more distant places, which continued to be (relatively at any rate) starved of private housing investment. Rather than those much-criticised rural districts, namely peripheral ones, failing to supply council homes, they constructed them faster than commuter belt districts, even when national prioritisation for farm-worker supply evaporated and, from 1956 to 1964, national policy effectively receded to slum clearance (Table 4.10). This pattern will be explored beyond Norfolk in later chapters. For now, note how increased government overview of residential growth immediately after 1945 led to a narrowing in private sector building between districts adjacent to large towns and farther away. Following the loosening of controls in the 1950s, construction firm preferences for proximity to towns returned. Explaining this changing pattern, former Minister of Health, Aneurin Bevan, held that:

> Almost every rural area is bordered by belts of speculative building, where the speculative builders made fortunes before the war by building the ugliest houses ever seen ... The only way in which I could drive them to build houses in the rural areas, and the only way in which they have been driven, was by refusing licences in the urban belts, so that if they wanted to continue to make a living building houses, they would have to build them in the deep rural areas ... one of the reasons why rural housing is now declining is because the speculative builder now deserts the deep rural areas and is operating once more in the urban belts.[32]

4.2.1   Outbidding Local Residents

All that noted, housing availability was affected by more than new-build, as retaining and improving the stock had an impact. With improvements in transport, inter-war villages close to towns became more attractive to artisans, whose wages were above the rural norm.[33] But rural councils reacted negatively to 'outsiders' applying for council homes. They resisted attempts by urban councils to build in their territory,[34] and complained to urban councils when their feeble council-building raised demand for rural dwellings. Two inter-war Norfolk examples were Smallburgh's protests to North Walsham and Erpingham's to Cromer.[35] Council discomfort was furthered by landowners selling or renting to urbanites from far away,

---

[32] HCH 21 November 1955, Vol.546, col.1065–66.

[33] MAF and MoH (1932, pp.6–7); TNA HLG37/43 'Replies to Questionnaire to Local Authorities', undated c1936, p.2; MoH (1937b, p.24).

[34] As with Ware RDC's rejection of Leyton and Walthamstow in 1923 (*H&EO* 24 November 1923, p.8) or Stotfold Parish's reaction to a Letchworth proposal three decades later (*BC&BG* 12 July 1957, p.1).

[35] *NWP&ENS* 24 January 1919, p.4; 4 November 1927, p.1; *FakPost* 22 February 1929, p.3. These complaints persisted after 1945, as in Erpingham's Clerk writing to Cromer asking the Town to 'make some effort' housing its own people (*NNN* 6 April 1950, p.1).

who used properties seasonally and deprived local workers of homes.[36] This was known in policy circles, as Lloyd George amongst others made clear in Parliament as early as 1926:

> In the areas there ought to be an investigation into this subject, and especially in the neighbourhood of the great towns, because the housing conditions are getting worse from the fact that people in the towns are going into the country and buying those old cottages, snapping them up without taking the slightest care to find out whether there is a room or a cottage to which the dispossessed labourer can go. There is a very strong feeling on this subject among agricultural labourers within 30 or 40 miles of London, and, I think, of all the great cities. There is very strong resentment against the kind of weekender who comes and takes up those cottages and turns the labourer out.[37]

The enduring force of this demand was captured 20 years later, when the RDCA reported that landlords were repaying grants for cottage improvements under the Housing (Rural Workers) Act in order to avoid rent and sales restrictions.[38] The significance of such occurrences goes beyond reduced stock availability into lower living standards for local residents. Thus, while acknowledging they occupied a thin wedge of rural dwellings, Tilley (1947, p.46) observed that footloose intellectuals, artists, writers and other weekenders who bought old cottages took the best properties. This foretold one of the first nation-wide reviews of second-homes, which reported that they had only recently come to be viewed as a problem (Downing and Dower 1973). Perhaps, but the stamp of urban influence had grown sufficiently in South-East England for a 1950 Whitehall official to proclaim: 'We are not sure that we have in the S.E. Region any areas where the problems are strictly rural as most of the difficulties, though found in rural areas, are non-rural in nature, such as accommodating London dormitory population and holiday development'.[39] Localised impacts could be intense and arrived earlier. Thus, in 1920, the Minister of Health reported 50 cottages in Middleton-in-Teesdale were weekend cottages only,[40] while, almost 20 years later, in Braughing's Furneux Pelham '… more and more houses were being taken by people who came for only weekends, and who offered to pay higher rents than agricultural workers could afford'.[41] This problem was officially recognised in the Scott Report (Ministry of Works and Planning 1942, p.18). Later academic research highlighted second home concentrations, as in the Lake District (Clark 1982) or the seven parishes in north Norfolk with more than

---

[36] Early perturbations of this kind were reported in Erpingham (*NWP&ENS* 24 January 1919, p.4; *FakPost* 13 February 1925, p.3).

[37] HCH 24 June 1926, Vol.197, col.624.

[38] TNA HLG37/43 'Housing (Rural Workers) Acts', undated c1936, p.4; 'Investigation by General Inspectors 1934', p.5, p.15; TNA HLG37/51 'Rural Housing Sub-Committee Meeting Minutes', 11 April 1946, p.3. As Martin (1938, p.2) outlined, under the Act, after improvement, rents should not exceed normal agricultural rents plus 3% of owner's expenditure (4% if the tenant was not an employee; Shears 1936, p.6). Parliamentary debates suggested rent restrictions reduced the sale value of reconditioned properties (e.g. HCH 9 May 1938, Vol.335, col.1255–322).

[39] TNA HLG125/10 Letter from M.C. Halliday, MTCP to Mr. Kiff, 13 March 1950.

[40] HCH 5 August 1920, Vol.132, col.2675.

[41] *B&NEHG* 6 January 1939, p.4.

25% of dwellings as second properties (Coleman 1982).[42] Most attention has focused on these high-demand places, with impacts on housing availability exposed (e.g. Penfold 1974; Shucksmith 1981) and potential alleviations for resulting housing shortages drawn (Shucksmith 1991; Gallent and Tewdwr-Jones 2000).

One dimension that has received less attention is weekenders securing dwellings when there were no local takers. As for Hatfield in the 1920s, former agricultural cottages went to weekenders because of declining demand from farm-workers.[43] By the 1960s and 1970s, this was more common, with derelict farm dwellings regularly turned into second homes (Bollom 1978; Gallent 1997). Less commonly identified were urbanites taking council properties because no local tenant was forthcoming. Remember the government pressed councils to build under the 1919 Act (with 1795 eligible authorities submitting schemes by 1920–1921; MoH 1921a, p.57). Accept also, for the time being, that the government wanted rents on these dwellings rural councils thought unaffordable (Ravetz 2001). Given all this, was it a surprise that rural councils, like Ware RDC in Hertfordshire, wondered whether high rents meant they '… might let the houses for weekenders from town; though they were not built for them'.[44] Ministry messages hint that this practice was more common than is realised. The MoH Parliamentary Secretary suggested this, when contrasting the provisions of the 1926 Housing (Rural Workers) Act with the 1924 Wheatley Act; asserting that '… this scheme absolutely prevents any possibility of these dwellings being used by the weekender. There is no provision of that kind in the Wheatley Act'.[45] Parliamentarians had drawn attention to negative weekender impacts before 1914,[46] with expansion seemingly unabated after 1919.[47] By 1927, there were calls in Buntingford for a review of rents because farm-workers could not pay them, so houses were let to Londoners and others.[48] By 1929, the practice was so common Stansted RDC decided no more council homes should be let to weekenders '… as there were so many [local] people requiring the cottages as permanent residences'.[49]

Weekender, or more broadly service-class, interest in rural living would strengthen over the decades. Late-twentieth-century analysts ascribed further constraints on working-class housing to such inflows, namely middle-class antagonism towards 'social mixing'. This was a specific manifestation of broader middle-class

---

[42] Nationally, the government assumed second homes constituted perhaps 150,000 dwellings at the 1961 census (TNA HLG118/413 'The Housing Programme in the 1970s', undated c1966).

[43] HM&CP 28 June 1929, p.14.

[44] H&EO 19 February 1921, p.5.

[45] HCH 3 August 1926, Vol.198, col.2910.

[46] For example, HCH 18 April 1913, Vol.51, col.2238.

[47] Three interventions from different political parties within a few 1926 months make the point (HCH 8 June 1926, Vol.196, col.1284; HCH 24 June 1926, Vol.197, col.624, HCH 3 August 1926, Vol.198, col.2840).

[48] HM&CP 27 August 1927, p.2.

[49] H&EO 14 September 1929, p.5.

tendencies, viz. traits of fear and resentment towards the working classes and using social networks to exclude others (Mottram 1940).[50] For Seaman (1966, p.119), the inter-war middle-classes had a quasi-theological detestation of welfare services, including council-provided accommodation:

> Like the dole, council houses were greatly resented by the classes who did not need them but were compelled to help pay for them through increased local rates and through Government taxation: two recurrent axioms about the working-class in the small talk of the more well-to-do were than many of the unemployed were unemployable, and that if bath-rooms were put in council houses the tenants would use them to keep the coals in.

As Bayliss (2001, p.193) noted, and tenant occupations confirm, council estates were far from one-class territory, although they were often projected as solely (low-paid) working-class, which raised alarm because in the inter-war period the '... working-class – in many contexts seen as urban, unionised, "communist", uncultured, and destructive – was suspect'. The war years enlightened some middle-class misconceptions (Thrift 1986), but inter-war anxieties fostered quests for social separation. Finnigan (1984, p.144) illustrated this in Leeds, when middle-class Hollin Park residents objected to new neighbouring higher income working-class homes on the grounds of amenity loss and property value impacts, leading the government to reduce the size of the estate by over 20%, so increasing dwelling costs. More notoriously, middle-class residents in Oxford's Cuttleslowe district built a wall across a communicating road to keep the working-classes out (Collison 1963). While not relying on such extreme steps, the social geography of rural England carried many hallmarks of social division. In larger villages, social differentiation commonly resulted from building estates in segregated blocks (Crichton 1964; Ambrose 1974; Connell 1978), while in smaller villages, a regular complaint was that council houses were grouped on the periphery, so '... contributing to a feeling of being excluded from the main part of the village' (Tilley 1947, p.45; Henson 1957, p.106; Strathern 1981; p.114).[51] Sentiments favouring social segregation did not arise in a political vacuum. The scapegoating of the working-classes and more generally of council tenants has roots in Conservative convictions that those in private accommodation were more inclined to vote Tory, with populist campaigns to undermine council tenancies characterising the 1950s, 1970s and 1980s as well as inter-war (e.g. Forrest and Murie 1988; Francis 2012; Davies 2013). The success of these strategies did not speak to their brilliance, for the sentiments expressed drilled deep into societal biases.

Long before these campaigns, there was opposition to council-building. In the 1920s, council minutes were often silent on the nature of English social antagonism, merely noting objections to this tenure (as at Biggleswade and Sandy).[52] Reports in

---

[50] Garfield's (2004) collection from the diaries of 'everyday' folk provides an exposition of the sentiments.

[51] Peripheral locations were not necessarily deliberately chosen (Chap. 7). Search processes often brought numerous disappointments over acquisition, cost or suitability before a usable site was found. In some cases, it never was.

[52] BRO RDBwM1/9 BiRDCM 5 October 1927; BRO UDSM1/1 SaUDCM 25 March 1929, p.170.

the 1930s were more insightful on opponents and their angst, detailing objectors as property owners, who also campaigned in the 1950s fearing property price falls, the introduction of less salubrious neighbouring houses or occupants paying less than them for homes.[53] As with most interventions, delays to council-building resulted. These could lower building volumes if government regulations or timetables changed. But in the districts investigated, there was little evidence campaigning made major direct impressions on council-building, although, as time progressed, amenity societies became more vocal, arguing towns should take development and the countryside little change.[54] Opposition to council-building continued into the 1970s, although again seemingly with little obvious success.[55] More commonly, the wrath of villagers turned against private owners who sought personal gain from village development.[56] But such instances were not common. This, however, only relates to visible opposition, when more potent impacts are made by structuring operational frameworks (Buller and Hoggart 1986; Gilg and Kelly 1997; Sturzaker 2010). As regards restoring the housing lot of the rural working-classes, such structuring effects were very evident in 1930s' national policies.

4.2.2 1930s Failures to Re-Provision

For the inter-war rural working-classes, housing prospects might be caricatured as deprived of ownership by poor pay and lender conditions, condemned to private rental disintegration by lack of investment and starved of council-house salvation by weak supply. This exaggerates somewhat, as rural councils did 'hold their own' under 1919 Act building, but by the late-1920s, the zenith had been reached. In October of 1927, subsidies under both the 1923 and the 1924 Housing Acts were reduced. A short-lived rise in housing output followed, as builders and councils rushed to complete dwellings before the chop (Fig. 4.1). After this, new-build numbers declined, until subventions ended in 1929 (for the 1923 Act) or 1933 (for 1924 Act). For most of the 1930s, especially after 1933, council-building was largely

---

[53] One example was opposition to the Drove Road estate in Biggleswade Town (TNA HLG49/952 Letter from J.H. Sapsford to MoH Secretary, 11 November 1933). This file starts with a 3 November letter to Sapsford asking for objections to be outlined. A second example was an attempt to block council-building in Cuffley and Brookmans Park in Hatfield (*H&PBG* 13 February 1953, p.1; 20 February 1953, p.1; 27 February 1952, p.1).

[54] As with the Norfolk Association of Amenities Societies (*NNN* 26 May 1967, p.13).

[55] As with protests over Braughing building homes in Westmill (HRO RDC3/1/21 BrRDCHCM 29 February 1972, pp.8583–85; 9 May 1972, p.8661).

[56] Longstanding opposition arose in leafy residential places like Aspley Guise, which resisted private building in the 1950s, fearing reductions in woodland and grassland spaces between homes (BRO RDAM2/23 ARDCHCM 23 July 1959). In the 1960s, the target was those with large gardens, who reportedly sold plots for £2000–£3000, for homes within easy reach of the M1 motorway. This village's opposition to developers was referred to as 'the war of the roses' (*WR&WSR* 18 May 1965, p.1; 22 August 1967, p.10).

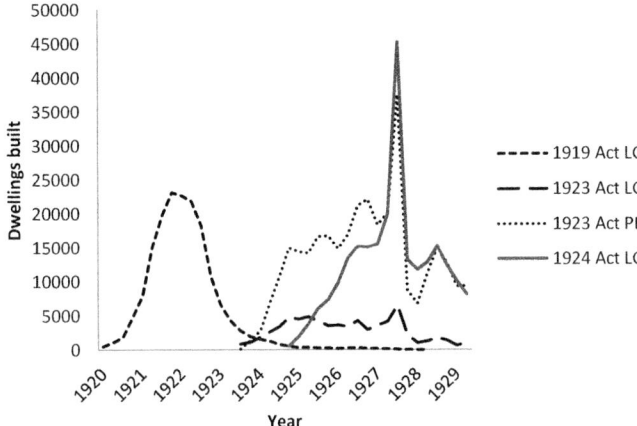

Source: HCH 9 July 1929, Vol.229, col.709W–10W.

Note: LG refers to council-built, PE to building for private owners. The 1923 Act accounted for 87.2% of private sector houses built with public subsidy between the fourth quarter of 1919 and May 1929. Some 85.5% of dwellings for councils came through the 1919 and 1924 Acts. Private building with public subsidies also occurred under the 1924 Act, in a minor way under the 1919 Housing, Town Planning, Etc. Act and with higher volumes under the 1919 Housing (Additional Powers) Act. The last of these was a private sector focused companion to the Housing, Town Planning, Etc. Act.

Fig. 4.1 Number of dwellings built in England and Wales per quarter under Housing Acts, 1919–1929

restricted to slum clearance (1930 Housing Act) and the relief of overcrowding (the 1935 Act, with the two Acts consolidated in the 1936 Act), alongside a few homes for the elderly. The year 1933 marked a new phase in council housing, as the government shifted its priority for council tenancies onto poorer households. The aim was spelt out in official publications: 'The Minister has found it necessary to remind several Local Authorities that the primary object of the Housing Acts is to provide houses at rents within the capacity of the more poorly paid wage earners, and the achievement of this object is not facilitated by the building of houses of an expensive kind' (MoH 1931, p.101). Such statements were re-writing previous communications, as the view that it was '… good policy that houses should be made available for the class for whom they were intended',[57] neglected messages in 1919 and 1924 legislation that dwellings were for the 'working-classes' (then the majority of the rural population, as signalled in Table 1.1). As the Local Government Board (1919, p.2) spelt out:

> The shortage has affected the houses of all classes of working people and is not confined to those of the poorer classes … the most serious shortage is of good houses, adequate in size, equipment and amenity to afford satisfactory dwellings for a working man's family; and that the building of this class of house should be energetically undertaken.

---

[57] HCH 2 June 1932, Vol.266, col.1311.

After 1933, 'working-class' was re-fashioned as the poorest of the working-classes. Hence, under the 1930 Act, the aim was to '... secure the provision of small houses at the very least possible cost to meet the needs of the poorer-paid workers' (MoH 1932a, p.99), so '... the heavy subsidisation of the new houses should not be placed at the disposal of any but the poorest inhabitants' (MoH 1933a, p.88). The needs of those outside this group were left aside.

Under this regime, many low-paid rural households failed to secure council properties owing to the organisation of the anti-slum campaign. A primary difficulty was the subsidy regime. On the surface, rural districts were favoured by subvention rates, with payments of £2/10/0d per displaced person compared with £2/5/0d for towns (although additional payments for flats and expensive sites benefited cities; Clarke 1931; Martin 1934). In reality, this regime meant lower rural payments. This was brought home forcefully in Depwade RDC's presentation to the Rural Housing Sub-Committee: 'Grants in replacement are made on the basis of persons rehoused, and whereas in towns the average is taken as five persons to a house, yielding a grant of £12.10.0, the actual figure for this part of the country is 3.1 persons or only £7.15.0 per house'.[58] The official 1944 report on rural housing agreed:

> The bulk of the unfit houses in the rural slum clearance programmes were however individual cottages which had not been replaced by new houses to the same extent as in urban areas. One of the reasons for this is probably to be found in the form of the subsidy available for replacement ... In the rural areas it was common for individual unfit cottages to be occupied by old people, married couples and even single people ... where such cottages were demolished the amount of subsidy payable in respect of a single person or even a couple was not sufficient to enable a new house to be let at a very low rent. (MoH 1944a, pp.11–12)

Hardly surprisingly, rural districts built fewer slum replacements, with just 50.8% of unfit dwellings replaced rather than 65.8% in towns (MoH 1944a, p.61). Local manifestations were evident in RDC reports, like Amesbury's, where 20 replacements were built for 100 cleared former agricultural workers' cottages, with companion values of 4 for 128 in Barnard Castle, 34 for 143 in Salisbury and Wilton and 14 for 75 in Weardale.[59] Owing to mergers, dissolutions and widespread parish transfers consequent on county reviews under the 1929 Local Government Act, there was a slow start for rural slum clearance.[60] But when pondering how rural councils were criticised for poor inter-war council-building,[61] note that 18.9% of all rural new-build over 1919–1939 was council-owned, which was better than dismal 1930s' slum clearance efforts (Table 4.11). Rural councils even performed better when erecting no-subsidy homes for general needs than they did for slum clearance.

---

[58] TNA HLG37/43 'Memorandum by Depwade RDC Housing Committee', undated c1936, p.1. This point was made earlier by Forehoe RDC (*T&WT* 6 May 1933, p.9).

[59] TNA HLG37/43 'Report on Local Investigations ...', undated c1936, p.10; HCH 3 March 1938, Vol.332, col.1278.

[60] TNA HLG37/45 'Rural District Councils' Association Submission', c1936.

[61] Examples noting criticisms include: TNA HLG40/38 'Minute Sheet addressed to Mr. Forber', 20 February 1926; TNA HLG37/48 'Work of Rural District Councils on Housing', undated c1943; MoH (1944a, p.14); HCH 25 March 1947, Vol.435, col.1144–45.

Table 4.11 Percent of council new-build in England and Wales for RDCs by purpose, 1933–1934 to 1938–1939

	1933–1934	1934–1935	1935–1936	1936–1937	1937–1938	1938–1939
For general needs	14.1	4.0	17.4	19.8	15.5	16.5
To replace slums	1.9	3.6	12.1	10.5	10.8	14.3
To ameliorate overcrowding				10.7	23.7	27.3

Source: Computed from MoH annual reports
Note: For 1933–1934 and 1934–1935 the general needs figures refer to late completions under the 1924 Act. After this, numbers refer to no-subsidy constructions under the 1925 (then 1925 and 1936) Housing Acts. Figures for no-subsidy building prior to October 1935 were not tabulated separately. Slum replacements were generally funded under the 1930 Act, with the amelioration of overcrowding generally coming under the 1935 Act (both consolidated into the 1936 Act)

On this, it is difficult not to see the provisions of the 1930 Act as a significant contributor.

Additional to difficult subsidy arrangements, the geography of dwelling unfitness and the administration of the 1930 Act was problematical. As a Rural Housing Sub-Committee submission explained:

> In a rural area slum clearance means nothing but the replacement of ancient houses which through past neglect have been allowed to fall into a state of decay. As often as not the rural slum house is a detached dwelling standing in its own ground and garden, and if put into a proper state of repair would be far more desirable than the semi-detached council house of the standard pattern. In almost all cases the only obstacle to repair is cost, which is either beyond the means of the owner, or else in the opinion of the local authority is 'unreasonable' …[62]

Unlike concentrations of 'slums' in cities, low-quality rural dwellings were often dispersed. This devalued their 'unfitness' in Whitehall's eyes (as in the 1950s and 1960s; Chap. 6), for the government only requested plans for slum removal from urban centres with at least 20,000 inhabitants (English et al. 1976, p.21). Attention centred on clearance areas, which disadvantaged rural districts as only 43.5% of declared unfit dwellings were in such zones, compared with 78.9% in towns (MoH 1944a, p.61). Yet, within clearance areas, RDCs performed well, with 83.3% of unfit dwellings having demolition orders confirmed, against 75.9% in towns (MoH 1944a, p.61). Noteworthy in this regard, Linsley's (2005, p.261) Norfolk research found rural districts close to Norwich made best use of the 1930 Act, since urban spillover created 'closely populated' zones which suited clearance area designation. Outside these zones, unfit dwellings received less Ministry overview. This generated criticism from the RDCA, which held that rural councils had exhausted their authority to address unfitness under the Housing Acts. The Ministry response was, use the Public Health Acts. The RDCA did not think this feasible:

---

[62] TNA HLG37/43 'Memorandum by Depwade RDC Housing Committee', undated c1936, p.1.

> The larger urban authorities are sometimes faced with the same problem but it is not so difficult in their case because they usually have large housing estates and can deal with the problem by gradually moving tenants of condemned houses into existing Council houses which become vacant.[63]

The scale of housing change in rural districts after 1918 had not transformed rural accommodation sufficiently to remove previous handicaps. More limited habitable stocks lessened capacities for decisive action. In this regard, the stricture of the Ministry of Reconstruction (1918, p.4) still held good: 'It must be borne in mind that were it not that cottages are so scarce throughout the district, a much larger number would be condemned and really required to be closed'. Rural areas did not have acceptable dwellings into which occupants of deteriorated properties could be transferred. The option that remained was upgrading existing hovels to make them habitable. But many landlords preferred properties to decline further than spend with no anticipation of a substantial return. In this context, the RDCA rightly questioned the legality of using Public Health Acts to force expensive repairs on property owners, believing '… that local Benches of Magistrates, especially in farming areas, would refuse orders under the Acts'.[64]

Hopes that the second Housing Act to dominate the 1930s might offer rural succour were unfounded, for 1935 Housing Act specifications again conspired against rural districts. For one, relieving overcrowding was not the most fundamental housing deficit. Indeed, the overcrowding survey for the Act concluded that rural districts had just 2.8% of privately owned and 3.7% of council-owned dwellings overcrowded. This contrasted with county borough values of 4.0% and 5.4%, with 6.8% and 10.5% in London (MoH 1936, p.xxi). That part of this divergence was probably definitional was reflected in rural assessments, with officials, like the Walsingham Sanitary Inspector, not impressed:

> In my opinion the above figures do not give an accurate indication of the overcrowding prevalent in many of the villages, as the standards laid down in the Housing Act allow for too much elasticity in determining whether or not a house is overcrowded, in as much as the living rooms are also taken into consideration and allowed for in the computation. Thus a family may be badly overcrowded as regards sleeping accommodation yet under the system laid down the house proves to be sufficient. From the health point of view this seems fantastic to say the least.[65]

The same point was made to the Rural Housing Sub-Committee:

> In the country too the object of the Act has been defeated by the inclusion of rooms which are never used as bedrooms in estimating the accommodation of a dwelling, by ignoring the question of the separation of the sexes save in houses of a single room, such dwellings being non-existent in rural areas. As a result it is impossible to deal with known cases of scandal-

---

[63] TNA HLG101/258A 'Note to John Maude', 7 March 1940.

[64] TNA HLG101/258A 'Note of Interview', 27 March 1940.

[65] NRO DC19/6/34, WRDCM 4 January 1937. Citation from Linsley (2005, p.274).

ous overcrowding at all, and the addition to the number of houses under the Act of 1935 has been very small.[66]

When they were added, many overcrowded families turned down new homes owing to an inability to pay more rent.[67] Not surprisingly, rural districts favoured low-cost solutions. Ten years before the Act, Ampthill had lessened density pressures by recommending parents board their children with relatives.[68] Medical officer of health annual reports show that, even after 1935, such recommendations continued. Alleviation occurred, but new incidences emerged every year.[69] Reports were rarely forthcoming on council actions, but a 1938 figure that stood out was 70% of Ampthill overcrowding being settled without a new dwelling.

This would have been welcomed in Whitehall, given ongoing searches to cut public expenditure (Committee on National Expenditure 1931; MoH 1932b). Indeed, with restraint urged, 1930 Act provisions were portrayed as overly generous:

> For many areas the present rate of subsidy under the Act of 1930 is both unnecessarily and embarrassingly high. The rents resulting from its application are lower than it is reasonable to charge the tenants, or many of them, and the comparison between the rents of the 1930 Act houses and similar Act houses is awkward for the local authority.[70]

Perhaps, but not in the countryside, as subsidies were insufficient for rural circumstances. Yet visions of bountiful funding pervaded the corridors of Whitehall, with officials even reporting that '... most local authorities who have applied for subsidy under the 1935 Act are engaged in building under the 1930 Act and that the surplus of 1930 Act subsidy compensates for any inadequacy in the 1935 Act grant'.[71] Where to go if there was no surplus and 1930 Act funding discouraged building was left unanswered.

Rather than addressing the 'realities' of rural districts, Westminster politicians and Whitehall officials promoted policies that internal ministry evaluations concluded did not work. In 1933, for example, a Ministry housing report proclaimed:

> An important difference between reconditioning in rural districts and similar work undertaken in urban districts is that in rural districts it is practicable and not uncommon to increase the existing accommodation by the addition of extra bedrooms as part of the work of reconditioning. Our recommendation, therefore, in regard to new building to abate overcrowding in the acquired houses in urban areas need not be extended to rural areas, where the same result can be achieved by an enlargement of the reconditioned house for which subsidy under the Housing (Rural Workers) Acts is available. (MoH 1933c, p.44)

The same tone characterised the Ministry's annual report, which held that '... in the present state of agricultural industry of the country the need in most rural districts is

---

[66] TNA HLG37/43 'Memorandum by Depwade RDC Housing Committee', undated c1936, p.2.
[67] NBC 19 June 1931, p.7; BRO RDAR8/11 ARDCMOHar 1930, p.13.
[68] BRO RDAR8/6 ARDCMOHar 1925, p.8.
[69] For example, BRO RDAR8/17 ARDCMOHar 1936, p.14; Biggleswade RDC (1937, p.14).
[70] TNA HLG101/30 'Memo to the Solicitor', 15 March 1933.
[71] TNA HLG48/685 Document 23 'Housing Subsidies', undated c1937, p.6.

for improving existing accommodation rather than for the provision of new houses'
(MoH 1933a, p.98). The sting in the tail was widespread awareness that few landlords or councils were enticed into reconditioning homes under the Housing (Rural
Workers) Act.[72] The mantra 'reconditioning not new homes' was nonetheless rife, as
in the Minister's speech of 15 December 1932.[73] The misplaced notion that rural
areas had minor new-build needs was embedded in the 1935 Housing Act:

> The core of the overcrowding problem is in the centres of the larger towns, where badly
> developed and congested areas are crowded with people who must be near their work, who
> can afford only low rents and who have never been helped by all the post-war subsidised
> efforts to rehouse them further afield in new housing estates.[74]

Whatever the national mood, rural councils responded by building the equivalent of
19.3% of identified overcrowded dwellings by 1939. The figure for urban England
was 9.9%, although the rural effort was less impressive than at first glance, as the
overall rate of overcrowding in rural districts was half that of urban centres (MoH
1944a, p.61). Put against this, extra funding for rural new-build to relieve overcrowding was restricted to the agricultural population. Only 8098 dwellings were
built to relieve rural overcrowding (MoH 1944a, p.61), yet rural councils secured
higher building rates under the 1935 Act than the 1919–1939 rural norm (Table 4.11),
despite unfavourable legislative stipulations (MoH 1935, p.160). Overall, given
national attention was directed at towns, alongside rural councils having less prospect of cross-subsidisation from 1930 Act subventions, this was a creditable effort.

One nuance on this interpretation is the prospect that rural districts were more
active on the 1935 Act because its funding was targeted at farm-workers. Chapter 3
indicated how Smallburgh had built many 1924 Act homes for agricultural labourers, while not responding vigorously to non-farm needs. This policy was by all
appearances subsidisation for the farm sector. As this continued in the 1930s, it
prompts asking whether Smallburgh used the 1935 Act in the same way. The answer
appears to be yes. In the Smallburgh overcrowding survey, just 69 dwellings needed
attention. With the English RDC rate of new-build to help eliminate overcrowding
running at 19.3%, Smallburgh should have built 14 dwellings by 1939 to match the
national norm. Data on building by individual councils were sparse, but indications
of early activity were found. These revealed that Smallburgh planned to build 52
dwellings for overcrowded families in 1936. Progress had been made by 1937 erecting 16 in some villages with overcrowded families.[75] After this, no relevant information was found in council documents. Quick action after the overcrowding survey
and the scale of building proposed was nonetheless consistent with Smallburgh
utilising Treasury subsidies and low building costs to spark council-building.

---

[72] See Hilton Young, Minister of Health, at HCH 2 June 1932, Vol.266, col.1311; HCH 28 February
1933, Vol.275, col.213; also Martin (1938).

[73] HCH 15 December 1932, Vol.273, col.561–62.

[74] TNA HLG52/828 'The New Housing Bill. Overcrowding and Redevelopment', undated
c1934, p.3.

[75] NRO DC22/2/47 SmRDCHCM 21 July 1936, p.260; 25 May 1937, p.588.

Table 4.12 Cumulative percentage of all state-assisted dwellings built since 1919 in England and Wales that were located in rural districts, 1928–1929 to 1938–1939

	1928–1929	1929–1930	1930–1931	1931–1932	1932–1933	1933–1934	1934–1935	1935–1936	1936–1937	1937–1938	1938–1939
For councils	15.0	15.0	14.3	14.4	14.1	14.0	13.4	13.0	13.0	12.9	13.2
For private owners	31.2	30.4	30.5	30.5	30.5	31.4	31.3	31.3	31.2	31.1	30.9

Source: Computed from MoH annual reports

Across much of England, the 1930s saw rural housing slipping compared to urban. By August 1936, only 6.7% of rural council completions since 1919 came under 1930s Housing Acts.[76] Despite friendly provisions for farm-workers in the 1931 Housing (Rural Authorities) and the 1938 Housing (Financial Provisions) Acts, the cumulative rural share of council new-build fell during the 1930s (Table 4.12). This at a time when private rental was deteriorating, physically and numerically, while urban interest in acquiring rural homes was rising, even around smaller towns (e.g. MAF and MoH 1932, p.6). Faced with declining availability, the majority of rural councils wanted to build more dwellings.[77] This was even in the 'deep' countryside, like much of Norfolk. Here housing shortages were accompanied by little private building for the working-classes.[78] The constraints on effective council responses were articulated by the MP for Norfolk Eastern:

> Three main facts come out of the present position: first, that very little can be done, however willing a local authority is to help; secondly, that no cottage of good construction can be built at an inclusive rent of less than 8s.6d. per week; and, thirdly, that local authorities can only build for workers who are displaced from unfit cottages and for agricultural workers who are living in overcrowded conditions. The large majority of people who are on the waiting list of local authorities today form only a small proportion of these. Rural district councils, therefore, have deferred their building schemes, because they know that many of the applicants on their list really cannot afford to pay a rent of 8s.6d …[79]

A key contributing handicap was that the 1930, 1935 and 1936 Acts only offered replacement of one building with another (or with fewer), not addressing shortages. Illustrating one consequence, in 1936, Depwade RDC had 300 on its housing list, of which: '… about 70 per cent are from persons who have no hope of obtaining relief under the Acts of 1930 and 1935 … [as] action in rural areas must be confined to further replacement of decayed dwellings by raising the standard gradually, without any alleviation of the real needs'.[80] While not directly comparable, Smallburgh

---

[76] HLG37/43 'Houses Completed Since the Armistice', August 1936.

[77] HLG37/44 'Evidence of Neville Hobson, RDCA Executive Council Member', undated c1936.

[78] For example: *NM&PWJ* 1 September 1934, p.7; *EDP* 9 May 1935, p.5; *T&WT* 21 December 1935, p.8.

[79] HCH 8 June 1937, Vol.324, col.1677.

[80] TNA HLG37/43 'Memorandum by Depwade RDC Housing Committee', undated c1936, p.2.

similarly had 550 (mainly agricultural) applicants on its 1936 list,[81] compared with an occupied 1931 housing stock of 3914. Providing such numbers for other districts was complicated as most inter-war councils recorded applicants by parish. Hence, council minutes mainly reported applicants for vacant properties, as with 13 applying for one house on Braughing's Bridgewater site in 1939.[82] Yet rising demand was clear, with councils reporting they were overwhelmed by their lists, leading to applicant reviews and new criteria for inclusion, to reduce pressure. This took place at Hatfield in 1938 and Ampthill in 1939.[83] After 1945, the process was more continuous (Chap. 3).

4.3   Restricted Housing Access

Compromises often had to be made between supplying and equipping dwellings and making homes available to those requiring better, more suitable or even a first home. Chapter 3 showed that Smallburgh built many small, relatively poorly equipped inter-war council homes. This occurred under the 1924 Housing Act, which Neville Chamberlain poured scorn on, because he believed rents would be too high (Self 2000, pp.222–26, pp.233–36). In some regards, Chamberlain was right; even if higher subsidies for agricultural parishes attracted enthusiasm from councils like Smallburgh. Thus, by 1926, Ministry documents noted: 'The Rural District Councils have not shown any keenness to build under the 1924 Act. Only 206 are building under that Act, and about 4,000 out of 8,000 houses are in agricultural parishes'.[84] Even politicians from the political Left had reservations about the Act. The MP Ernest Simon (1933, p.26) saw the Wheatley Act as a failure, for its rents were beyond low-paid workers, so subsidies went to those who did not need them (as some local leaders concluded; e.g. Finnigan 1980, p.109). The issue of quality versus cost posed a conundrum. When criticising the 1924 Act, Chamberlain held that its subsidies would produce a scramble for labour and materials, which would inflate costs. He believed extra charges would fall on tenants, forcing rents to rise above capacities to pay, causing house-building to cease. 'This certainly is not socialism', he proclaimed (Self 2000, p.222). We capture here Chamberlain's worldview. Rents could have been lower with greater subsidies or lower building costs with a more efficient construction industry. Neither drew legislation from Chamberlain; on the one hand, because it meant higher taxes and more demand for house-building; on the other, because it would 'interfere' with an industry that had

---

[81] NRO DC22/2/47 SmRDCHCM 31 March 1936, Item 172.

[82] *B&NEHG* 5 May 1939, p.4.

[83] *H&PBG* 25 March 1938, p.7; BRO RDAM2/22 ARDCHCM 8 June 1939.

[84] TNA 40/38 'Minute Sheet Addressed to Mr. Forber', 20 February 1926.

done little to improve itself.[85] This 'leave it as it is' attitude contrasted with Bevan's 1947 view on what the country needed from its housing:

> … comparisons between output in 1935–36–37 and the present day are entirely unfair. They are unfair to the building industry; and to building operatives. In the first place, the houses that are being built today are much bigger and much better than the houses which were built before the War. One has only to take a motor ride out of London to see the brick boxes which were described as houses by their speculative builders. But they all count as houses, whereas the houses being built today are, superficially, one-third or one-fourth more than the area of those houses. We do this deliberately. We know that we shall not get as many houses that way, but we are building houses for a long time and we do not want to build bad houses.[86]

His reaction to 1951 Conservative plans for more new dwellings than under his government was blunt:

> I have always been of the opinion that it was possible for the Conservative administration to build more houses than we built—always. We have never been in any doubt at all about that. If we reduce the size of the houses to rabbit hutches, of course we can build more. There has never been any doubt about that. Is it a recent discovery on the part of the right hon. Gentleman [Harold Macmillan] that by reducing the accommodation, by taking out certain amenities and by reducing the superficial area of the house we can build more houses? Of course we can.[87]

Bevan's interpretation of a good housing programme differentiated him from Chamberlain. Both might have agreed a 'socialist' programme involved more engagement with construction companies and more homes for the less fortunate. Where they would have disagreed was in Chamberlain's association of socialism with building council houses. Bevan's priority was building quality homes.

But quality cost. Recall that low costs helped many Smallburgh farm-workers secure new homes. There were certainly those who saw farmer inputs on wage boards as responsible for poor inter-war farm-worker wages (e.g. Addison 1939). Although farmers spent most inter-war years festering grievance over government cuts to farm commodity prices in 1921 (Pugh 2008, p.267), viz. the 'Great Betrayal'

---

[85] As the Departmental Committee on the High Cost of Building Working Class Dwellings reported: 'The previous experience of the Building Trade in regard to Government Housing Schemes has not been of a nature to inspire confidence in the industry' (MoH 1921b, p.8). Wheatley was withering in his criticism, holding that: 'Private enterprise is something which should be ashamed to ask for a subsidy, because private enterprise subsidised is a confession of the failure of private enterprise … [yet] practically all the houses being erected by private enterprise, are being helped by the state and getting the subsidy …' (HCH 20 February 1924, Vol.169, col.1853). Rather than leaving private companies alone, Wheatley wanted to work with them, so they would help ease the nation's housing crisis. This distinguished him sharply from Chamberlain. Wheatley's 1924 Act was surrounded by discussions with the construction industry, leading to a '… programme extending over a period of 15 years, and aiming at a production, at a gradually increasing rate, of approximately 2,500,000 houses in Great Britain' (MoH 1924b, p.1). This programme was intended to raise confidence in the industry to augment its depleted resources, promote apprenticeships and ensure stability in house-building (National House Building Committee 1924, p.8).

[86] HCH 28 July 1947, Vol.441, col.87.

[87] HCH 4 December 1951, Vol.494, col.2255.

(Whetham 1974), many farmers saw significant income gains over these decades (Howkins 2003; Wade-Martins and Williamson 2008). The war-years treated them even more favourably, with 1938–1942 wages bills rising by 61% compared with 207% for net farmer income (100% acknowledging 1938–1939 was a bad year for farmers). Just as farmers gained significantly after the 'Great Betrayal' (Penning-Rowsell 1997), they were the only unequivocal beneficiaries of the new post-war settlement, as embodied in the 1947 Agriculture Act (Self and Storing 1962; Chase 1993). Farm labourers by contrast saw sharp wage falls in the early-1920s, with county boards maintaining low inter-war wages (Fig. 3.3).[88] The brunt of economic discomfort over the decades fell on farm-workers, whose employment was relatively intermittent (Hussey 1997), often included periods of unemployment, with no national wage bargaining mechanism until 1948 (Howkins and Verdon 2009). Even if councils wanted to address low wages, they were not well-placed to do so. Their resources were limited (Chap. 5), and if they ignored government expenditure constraints, this did not go unpunished, as seen when councils sought to ease local hardships through programme enhancements (e.g. Branson 1979; Ward 1984). Councils had hard choices between inaction and building 'meanly', given insufficiency of Treasury subsidies put rents beyond many residents. This applied especially in rural districts, but also in cities (see: Dresser 1984, on Bristol; Pooley and Irish 1984, on Liverpool; Jones 2010, on Brighton).

For sure, many politicians did not believe councils should erect homes, holding that better paid workers should occupy private accommodation. But low subsidies (in a national context of low wages for the working-classes) or, from another angle, high building costs, resulted in the better paid taking council tenancies. Even though much 1930s council-building was driven by price minimisation imperatives (Ryder 1984; McKenna 1991; Linsley 2005), by 1953–1954, household incomes for council tenants were above the national average, even with income overlaps across

---

[88] Howkins (1991, p.283) cited a fall in weekly wages from 45/– to 25/– for 1921–1923; a sharper drop than the cost of living. County committees fixed minimum wages from 1924 to 1948, at around 30/– a week during the 1920s (Mowat 1955, p.251), with price collapses in 1931–1932 returning wages to 1923 levels (Howkins 2003, p.83). By the late-1930s, wages were only 35/– on average (Pugh 2008, p.271). Comparisons with urban wages vary with comparator and over time but a sense of stability in disparities was indicated in Astor and Rowntree's (1939, p.213) message that farm-worker wages were half of town labourers in the nineteenth-century and in 1936. Comparable figures come from Horn (1984, p.90), who reported 1884–1896 general agricultural wages as 55% of industrial, although working hours were longer, while Mackintosh (1936, p.21) recorded 1930s' values closer to 60%. Wages rose during 1939–1945 and immediately after, trebling from 1938 to 1950 (Calder 1969, p.428). They reached a peak of 75% of industrial wages in 1949 (Chase 1993, p.83) and were at 72% in 1961 and 70% in 1971 (Drudy 1978). As an illustration of low-wage effects, a 1936 survey of Cuckfield RDC found that, despite almost no unemployment, farm-workers were the worst-fed, with 99 of their 304 children having subnormal nutrition (Pugh 2008, p.270). Hardly surprising Newby and associates' (1978, p.231) surveys found more than 70% of farm-workers believed their wages unjustifiably low, attaching blame on government cheap food policies. Lobbying by farm organisations raised returns for farmers (Self and Storing 1962; Wilson 1977; Bowers 1985), but rural workers had to accept lower rewards to secure cheap food for a largely urban electorate (Davey et al. 1976; Bowers and Cheshire 1983; Hill and Ray 1987).

all tenures (Bentham 1986, p.159). 'A fair generalisation would seem to be that "general needs" council house-building [viz. excluding slum clearance and the like] in the inter-war years provided primarily for better-paid manual workers plus some clerks, and only in a small way for retired people and others not in the labour force' (Holmans 1987, p.178). This pattern was diluted under 1930s' slum clearance and overcrowding relief measures, with further shifts after 1951, as the government pushed for smaller, less well-equipped houses (Holmans 1987, p.119). This 1950s' transition from quality to quantity created what Byrne (1976, p.26) claimed were probably the worst council homes built. Council tenancies became less attractive for the better paid, aided by fiscal and other measures to lubricate home-ownership (Merrett 1982; Parker and Mirrlees 1988). By 1973, just 22% of council households had annual incomes over £3000 compared with 32% nationally.[89]

Following investigation of a rural Cornish council estate, Forrest and Murie (1992, p.63) concluded that: '… it is not clear that [rural] council housing ever provided for the privileged, skilled elite of the working-class as it did in urban areas. It provided housing for lower paid families'. This does not match the experience of the seven investigated rural districts. More pointedly, wages in the countryside were generally low, although this alone did not account for many workers' inability to afford council rents. Compared to urban workers, if paid the same, rural workers were still disadvantaged. The first post-1945 national survey of household expenditure illustrated this (Table 4.13). For households with roughly the same income, expenditure on housing was if anything lower in rural districts. Spend on housing was not high, nor on food, nor even transport and vehicles. Of course, it might be argued that rural districts were poorly supplied with public transport, and this 1953–1954 survey was before car usage was widespread; in effect, there were fewer opportunities to spend on transport. This might be true if the eye does not move away from the bus, car or train, but what about shoe leather? Divergent spending across settlement types in clothing and footwear were almost wholly accounted for by footwear. Rural households on average spent five and a half times as much a week on shoes as those in larger towns and more than thrice the amount spent in smaller urban centres (Ministry of Labour and National Service 1957). Similarly, for fuel, light and power, rural expenditure was around a shilling a week more than urban. Whether this arose from costs of delivery or costs associated with more isolated, detached dwellings cannot be ascertained from the data. What is clear is that various household expenditure items combined to push total spend in rural areas above urban figures. Rural wages were generally lower but paucity was intensified by higher spending demands. Hence, housing affordability in rural areas was double-edged. It was not just a matter of lower incomes, for, as brought to light almost a half-century later by Monk and associates (1999), securing work in rural areas also carried significant participatory costs.

For the 1920s in particular, tenants tended to be drawn from working-class upper reaches and the lower middle-classes. Councils often had difficulty securing tenants

---

[89] HCH 17 March 1975, Vol.888, col.293W.

Table 4.13 Weekly expenditure by household income and settlement category, 1953–1954

District type and urban population	£20	£14 but under £20	£10 but under £14	£8 but under £10	£6 but under £8	£3 but under £6	Under £3
	Weekly household income at least						
	Housing spend (£)						
Rural districts	1.57	1.07	0.87	0.73	0.55	0.57	0.47
Urban areas under 100,000	1.81	1.29	1.10	0.98	0.89	0.81	0.62
London and urban over 100,000	1.79	1.34	1.10	0.97	0.84	0.70	0.61
	Food spend (£)						
Rural districts	6.54	5.01	4.13	3.66	3.14	2.23	1.30
Urban areas under 100,000	6.24	4.93	4.13	3.57	3.00	2.16	1.29
London and urban over 100,000	6.43	5.06	4.18	3.66	3.01	2.13	1.25
	Transport and vehicle spend (£)						
Rural districts	2.11	1.51	0.90	0.52	0.49	0.25	0.10
Urban areas under 100,000	2.26	1.14	0.75	0.63	0.38	0.18	0.12
London and urban over 100,000	1.88	1.06	0.85	0.46	0.38	0.20	0.08
	Fuel, light and power spend (£)						
Rural districts	0.98	0.73	0.63	0.61	0.58	0.53	0.45
Urban areas under 100,000	0.84	0.67	0.61	0.58	0.53	0.49	0.41
London and urban over 100,000	0.84	0.66	0.60	0.58	0.52	0.46	0.37
	Clothing and footwear spend (£)						
Rural districts	5.46	1.85	1.45	1.18	0.97	0.64	0.29
Urban areas under 100,000	2.93	1.86	1.30	0.91	0.77	0.45	0.23
London and urban over 100,000	2.96	1.90	1.27	0.90	0.66	0.42	0.18
	Total spend (£)						
Rural districts	26.92	15.43	11.83	9.89	8.15	5.90	3.51
Urban areas under 100,000	22.94	15.40	11.72	9.73	8.07	5.53	3.51
London and urban over 100,000	22.53	15.50	12.06	9.77	7.79	5.49	3.18

Source: Ministry of Labour and National Service (1957, pp.187–201)

Note: The original presentations of these numbers as pounds, shillings and pence have been converted to whole and decimal portions of pounds to ease comparison

for their dwellings. Minutes are nowhere near secure enough in coverage for quantitative measures of this, but there were sufficient pointers to convince of its occurrence. From the start of the 1919 Act, dwelling take-up revealed a pattern that persisted over the inter-war years and even after. In 1919, Erpingham had no applicants for two homes at Sidestrand.[90] In 1920, Ampthill Town would not build houses approved by the Ministry due to lack of demand.[91] Walsingham had only 12 applicants for 12 houses under erection in Fakenham,[92] while Smallburgh reported just one 1921 applicant for four houses at Hickling.[93] Accounts of meagre applicant numbers for 1919 Act homes were rife. In Walsingham, only four sought six houses at Wiveton (only two deemed 'suitable'), with just six applying for four houses at Sculthorpe.[94] Reports of withdrawn applications were common, as with seven of the 18 seeking homes on Ampthill Town's Saunders Piece site and all but two for Walsingham's four Ryburgh homes.[95] Councils complained dwellings were left unoccupied as the Ministry demanded high rents, with councils carrying unmet costs.[96] For farm-workers, the 1919 Act was widely seen as a failure. For Stansted RDC, for instance, just one in eight houses at Birchanger was occupied by a household from the parish, with several tenanted by people from Bishop's Stortford, leading to the view that the housing scheme had failed as '… the subsidy was intended to relieve the shortage among agricultural labourers, but it had barely touched them'.[97] Little wonder, councils did not discourage tenants from taking lodgers. Evidence on this was ephemeral but telling, as with Erpingham and Walsingham allowing tenants to take paying summer visitors so rents could be covered.[98]

This was occurring when, fuelled by fears of political unrest (Swenarton 1981), national authorities expected councils to build homes. For councils, this was a reasonable request financially, as the bulk of 1919 Act costs fell on the Exchequer. But early enthusiasm for rewarding veterans, creating jobs for demobilising troops,

---

[90] *FakPost* 9 May 1919, p.8.

[91] BRO UDA6/1 AUDCHBCM 8 October 1920.

[92] *FakPost* 14 May 1920, p.8.

[93] NRO DC22/2/45 SmRDCHCM 3 March 1921.

[94] *FakPost* 15 October 1920, p.5; NRO DC19/6/9 WRDCM 24 November 1920, p.141.

[95] NRO DC19/6/9 WRDCM 24 November 1920, p.141; *FakPost* 15 October 1920, p.5; BRO UDA20/1 AUDCMOHar 1920; NRO DC22/2/45 SmRDCHCM 23 March 1921; NRO DC19/6/9 WRDCM 1 June 1921, p.196.

[96] As with Hadham (*H&EO* 7 January 1922, p.8) and Saffron Walden RDC (*H&EO* 26 August 1922, p.2).

[97] *H&EO* 14 July 1923, p.8.

[98] As the Walsingham Medical Office of Health put it:' The rent problem is being solved by either the taking in of lodgers or sharing the house with another family' (NRO DC19/6/12 WRDCM 14 May 1924 p.19, in binding). That problems of rent affordability troubled councillors was evinced in districts like Erpingham reversing previous objections to this practice (*NWP&ENS* 29 July 1927, p.5). This was taken-up to such an extent that, when overcrowding became a policy concern, Erpingham banned taking summer visitors (NRO DC13/5/72 ERDCHCM 3 June 1930, p.19). This was not an issue for coastal areas alone, for Biggleswade minutes had most references to lodgers in the 1920s, although it did have the largest stock of high-rent 1919 Act dwellings.

promoting the building industry and boosting local economies,[99] soon dissipated under accusations that material prices were too high, while building companies and their workers were believed to have reached tacit agreements producing excessive wages and a refusal to accept unskilled workers, so lessening labour availability.[100] The government was seemingly oblivious to its own contribution to this state of affairs. This was a self-serving blindness. As Perkin (1989, pp.188–92) noted, 'total war' was a widely accepted 1914–1918 concept, with businesses brought into government in collaborative ventures to achieve national goals. The need for urgent action did not dissolve with the end of hostilities. There had been a massive increase in the suffrage, with social unrest signalling the country had entered a new era. Pre-1914 practices could not be revived. The nation's leaders needed to act. Their efforts were hampered by not ensuring mechanisms for goal achievement. Rather than building frameworks to support policy, almost as soon as the war ended, a bonfire was lit on war-time controls (Perkin 1989, p.192; Arnold 1999, p.47). Any hope the private sector would fill vacated spaces was lost in the face of demands on the public purse to repay war debt (Daunton 1996), labour discord (Beavan 2006), disquiet over a continuance of war-time profiteering (leading to a swath of investigations; e.g. Standing Committee on Prices and Trusts 1920a, 1920b, 1920c, 1921a, 1921b, 1921c)[101] and weak attention to low productivity (Dowie 1975). War-time organisational requirements might have taught the government the need for coordinated action, especially as the uncertainties of the time meant the economic environment was not conducive to private investment. The government's response was characteristic of what was to become a long line of failures to acknowledge, and then act in a coordinated manner towards, the scale of problems facing the nation (Barnett 1972; Allen 1976). The people would have to wait as unprecedented demand for housing investment was quashed when the state's gears shifted towards retrenchment as early as 1920 (Branson 1975; Morgan and Morgan 1980). The possibility of suspending the housing programme was mooted by June that year.[102] Calls for 'economy' became strident.[103]

To mitigate impacts on the Exchequer, the Ministry of Health asked rural districts to levy rents councils thought so disproportionate homes were out of most

---

[99] A sense of the points made to councils can be found in TNA HLG1/999 Letter from LGB President to Walsingham RDC Chair, 27 June 1919.

[100] For example, TNA CAB23/18 7(19) Cabinet Conclusions, 14 November 1919, p.1.

[101] Disquiet over inflated building costs punctuated inter-war House of Commons debates right up to the Second World War. Debates on the issue included: HCH 28 March 1923, Vol.162, col.673–94; HCH 15 May 1925, Vol.183, col.2203–94; HCH 19 March 1926, Vol.193, col.757–841; HCH 4 October 1939, Vol.351, col.1969 W–70 W. Parliamentary questions on the issue were numerous.

[102] TNA HLG68/29 'Housing Liabilities', 2 June 1920.

[103] TNA HLG68/29 Letter M.P.A. Hankey, Cabinet Office, to Minister of Health, 30 November 1920; TNA HLG68/29 'Housing', 25 January 1921; TNA CAB24/125 CP3067 'Reduction of Public Expenditure', 22 June 1921.

residents' reach. Repeated protests over Ministry rent demands resulted.[104] Even in Biggleswade, where workers in Sandy were paid 55/– to £3 a week, the Ministry's suggested 12/6d a week rent (excluding rates) was deemed 'excessive and prohibitive'.[105] Complaints rained in from tenants, women's guilds and workers' organisations.[106] Public meetings to attract tenants to 1919 Act dwellings, such as those organised by Aylsham RDC, attracting few attendees and, in some cases, not a single house let.[107] One consequence was caution amongst rural councils over building more homes. As Ampthill's Medical Officer of Health explained in 1920:

> In regard to building houses, my Council have adopted a cautious attitude, and in my opin-
> ion quite rightly. In 1919, and during 1920, wages and the cost of material stood at a very
> high level. Under these circumstances, they decided, for the present, to only build a com-
> paratively few houses in parishes where there was an urgent need. By thus doing, they were
> able to attend to any pressing want, and at the same time wait for the coming fall in the cost
> of materials and the drop in wages.[108]

The hoped-for shrinkage in construction costs would come too late for the 1919 Act, for by July 1921 the government had announced it would '… limit construction to the number built or being built',[109] even if existing approvals produced completions up to the late-1920s (Fig. 4.1). But Ministry pressure to retain elevated 1919 Act rents continued until the 1935 Housing Act allowed the pooling of rents across all Housing Acts. Pooling was permitted earlier but excluded 1919 Act dwellings, which weakened incentives to introduce schemes. Local requests for lower 1919 Act rents continued into the 1930s.[110] They were accompanied by complaints that inadequate subsidies unduly raised rents under later Acts. As a Cabinet paper stated in 1926, even with higher subsidies in agricultural parishes, under the 1924 Act, the lowest rent charged was 4/6d a week, yet 3/– a week was generally seen as afford-able for farm-workers.[111] Depressed wages meant that a decade later the Central Landowners' Association proclaimed that '… a rural worker can hardly afford to pay more than 3/- a week',[112] although this national figure hid regional variation and more pay for specialists (Crotch 1901; Howkins 2003). Non-farm wages were often

---

[104] Even with London's higher wages, by 1924, 50 of 107 councils in the Metropolitan Police area had applied for rent reductions under the 1919 Act (HCH 6 March 1924, Vol.170, col.1641W).

[105] *BC&BG* 17 September 1920, p.6; BRO UDSM2/3 Sandy Parish Council Meeting 29 October 1920, p.37.

[106] For example, *NWP&ENS* 24 January 1919, p.4; BRO RDBwM1/8 BiRDCM 10 November 1920, p.60; 2 February 1921, p.83; BRO RDBwM1/8 BiRDCM 23 May 1923, p.350; *BC&BG* 22 June 1923, p.1.

[107] For descriptions of a Cawston meeting, see *FakPost* 20 May 1921, p.3; *NWP&ENS* 20 May 1921, p.3.

[108] BRO RDAR8/1 ARDCMOHar 1920, p.7.

[109] HCH 14 July 1921, Vol.144, col.1484.

[110] For example, NRO DC22/2/14 SmRDCM 19 January 1932, p.153; BRO RDAM2/20 ARDCHCM 11 July 1933.

[111] TNA CAB27/309 RH(26) Meeting 26 January 1926, p.4.

[112] TNA HLG37/45 'Central Landowners' Association Submission', undated c1936–37.

as low as agricultural pay, as farm wages depressed other rural stipends. This was noted regularly in council meetings, as with Erpingham's 1920 charge that labourers in Holt received lower wages than farm-workers, in a 1921 Walsingham councillor's request 'in the cause of common humanity' to place roadmen's wages on par with farm labourers and in Braughing laments over the '… hardship caused to non-agricultural workers (whose wages are, in many cases, below the agricultural minimum wage)'.[113] This placed question marks against Ministry assertions that: 'The root of the housing problem in rural areas is to be found in the comparatively low rent-paying capacity of the agricultural population' (MoH 1937a, p.117). This might have captured contrasts between urban manufacturing jobs and rural farm-workers, but it ignored low-pay in many rural occupations that lacked access to agricultural subsidies.[114] Not surprisingly, slight take-up of council homes continued, in both rural and urban settings. Hence, in 1928, Sheringham found 39 petitioners for council homes could only afford half the rent the Town charged, Walsingham failed to secure a single applicant for its six houses at Blakeney in 1929 and Erpingham had no tenants for two 1933 homes in West Beckham.[115] Meanwhile, in Biggleswade, Potton Parish Council ripostes to an RDC survey on housing demand identified urgent need but no ability to pay required rents.[116] The RDC did not proceed.

If tenancies were obtained, rent arrears might not be far away. Inter-war, this could be hastened by cuts in wages and rising unemployment. For instance, in a 1928 report on mine-workers, arrears under the 1919 Act were reported to be 56% in Northumberland, 49% in Durham and 39% in Yorkshire. This was explained more by unemployment than low wages.[117] The pay of other rural workers was commonly below that of miners, as was unemployment insurance cover,[118] which placed

---

[113] *FakPost* 3 September 1920, p.7; NRO DC19/6/9 WRDCM 30 November 1921, p.249; HRO RDC3/1/4 BrRDCM 4 May 1950, p.236.

[114] Care is needed interpreting this point, as conditions under Acts of Parliament for extra agricultural labourer support were not uniform. The 1924 Act, for example, had higher subsidies for new dwellings in agricultural parishes (Clarke 1924). The 1931 Housing (Rural Authorities) Act focused on farm-workers, whether inside or outside such parishes (TNA CAB23/67 34(31), 17 June 1930), alongside '… provision of houses for agricultural workers and others of a similarly low rent paying capacity in agricultural parishes' (MoH 1932a, p.109). This led to difficulties down the line, as in the Second World War when councils had 1931 Act homes with no farm-workers wanting them (e.g. TNA HLG48/868 Letter from Erpingham RDC Clerk to MoH Secretary, 24 April 1941). Under the 1946 Act, extra subsidy was for the agricultural population only, wherever they lived, with a top-up if the rateable value of the district was particularly low (TNA HLG101/227 'MoH Circular 118/46', 12 July 1946, pp.1–2).

[115] *FakPost* 14 September 1928, p.5; 4 January 1929, p.8; NRO DC13/5/73 ERDCHCM 14 August 1933, p.86.

[116] BRO RDBwM1/12 BiRDCM 29 July 1936, p.320; *NBC* 27 November 1936, p.3.

[117] TNA HLG101/18 'Housing Act 1919. Rents and Arrears of Rents in Mining Areas', undated c1928, p.2, p.7.

[118] Farm-workers were outside the national insurance scheme until 1936 (Gardiner 2010, p.242).

Table 4.14 Weekly rents for September after public subsidy inputs compared to the equivalent no-subsidy rent under the 1924 Housing Act

	1924	1925	1926	1927	1928	1929	1930	1931	1932	1933	1934
Subsidised rent	6/10d	7/8d	7/9d	7/5d	7/1d	6/6d	6/5d	6/8d	4/11d	8/3d	8/2d
No-subsidy rent	11/6d	12/4d	12/5d	12/1d	11/0d	10/5d	10/4d	10/7d	8/6d	8/3d	8/2d
Difference	4/8d	4/8d	4/8d	4/8d	3/11d	3/11d	3/11d	3/11d	3/9d	0	0

Source: Connor (1936, p.39)
Note: All these figures exclude rate charges. The figures are in shillings and pennies

many closer to the economic edge.[119] While not naming the authority concerned, the Ministry signalled awareness of difficulties by noting a district with 90% of tenants in arrears, but suggested a 'solution' from another district, which was to appoint a full-time rent collector and bailiff (MoH 1930a, p.82). Evictions from council tenancies became an ongoing concern. Ampthill served notices to quit on all tenants with arrears over 10/− in 1932, raising this in 1936 to require that '... all arrears of rent are discharged before the expiry of the notices'.[120] In this context, many councils were reluctant to push forward with house-building. After all, Exchequer subsidies for new 1924 Act homes were terminated in 1933, although council authority to guarantee building society mortgages for private owners was extended (MoH 1933b). With 1924 Act support withdrawn, subsidised house-building had to rely on the 1930, 1935 or 1936 Acts, which only funded special needs housing or stock additions for the elderly (MoH 1930b, p.19). Councils addressing shortfalls in working-class housing were restricted to erecting no-subsidy homes with 'economic rents'. Many considered this option but, as the *Eastern Daily Press* signalled, were wary due to high rent charges.[121] Some, like Ampthill, which circulated parish councils for views, drew back once responses arrived.[122] No surprise as councils already had arrears issues for lower rent homes built with subsidies (Table 4.14). That building costs had fallen since the 1920s, even if they began rising in 1935 (Fig. 3.2), did not make council dwellings affordable to most residents.

Official estimates were that council rents took more from earnings in 1936 than at any time up to 1973–1974, with average 1936 rents not surpassed in real terms until the 1960s (DoE 1974, p.43). The pattern of the 1930s was reproduced in the late-1950s into the 1960s. Early in the 1960s, the government pushed councils to

---

[119] Eastwood (1951, p.11), for example, reported that wages for male farm-workers were 35/− a week in 1939 and 80/− a week in 1946. This was a substantial rise, brought on by fears over possible worker shortages into agriculture. These compare with wage rates of 47/6d and 95/− in the food and drink industry, which was the lowest for a Norfolk industrial sector in 1939 and 1946. Eastwood noted that 45% of the workforce in Norfolk was employed in agriculture in 1931.

[120] BRO RDAM1/10 ARDCM 13 October 1932; BRO RDAM1/11 ARDCM 10 September 1936.

[121] *EDP* 3 July 1935, p.8.

[122] BRO RDAM2/20 ARDCHCM 26 February 1934; 2 July 1934. Even in districts that built no-subsidy homes, in agricultural parishes rents were above capacities to pay (e.g. BRO RDBwM1/12 BiRDCM 18 November 1936, p.389; 10 February 1937, p.435). In some cases, councils pre-empted the issue by informing parishes that without subsidy it would not build or had no leeway save for slum clearance (e.g. NRO DC13/5/73 ERDCHCM 25 March 1935, p.179).

charge 'economic' rents, offering rebates for those of lesser means.[123] Rent arrears expanded again. In Braughing, they reached 30% of total weekly revenue in 1960 (£1079 was owed). Four years later, 183 tenants were affected (around 22%) when arrears were about 20% of the money to be collected. By 1971, just 74 were in arrears and £579 owed.[124] These figures were high compared to the other investigated districts. The most detailed record on arrears was for inter-war Ampthill, where arrears were generally low. The highest inter-war figure for a quarter was £23/0/3d. The triviality of this value was shown by just £15/1/3d being unpaid in 1938 out of an annual rental income of £4475/5/0d.[125] The wide disparity in the situations of 1930s' Ampthill and 1960s' Braughing was apparent in council minutes. These revealed sharp differences in management practices, with Ampthill assiduous in tackling non-payment early and vigorously. This strategy was linked to low rates of inter-war house-building, with Ampthill erecting less dwellings than any investigated rural district (Table 3.10). With considerable attention given to keeping arrears down, could widening the pool from which tenants were drawn be risked? In reality, non-payment, rent demands and tenancy take-up were all linked to building standards and subsidy payments. Hence, when the government sought improved living conditions by applying Parker Morris standards to council-building in the late-1960s, this dampened interest in council tenancies. As a 1968 Biggleswade minute noted: 'The Clerk informed the Committee that 50 offers of tenancy were made for the Council's present stock of 38 Parker Morris houses before these were let and it was known that five of the 38 tenants were having difficulty with payment of rent'.[126] This was occurring at a time of long waiting lists (Chap. 3).

Ignore for the moment ideological or other reservations councillors had about house-building under the Housing Acts. Focus on what determined rents. This involved three components: subsidies from the Treasury; subsides from the council; and building costs (including allowances for dwelling repairs and maintenance). Under most Housing Acts, two of the three were fixed. For the 1919 Act, the most rigid was the council subvention, which was set at a one penny rate (viz. one penny for every pound sterling of a property's hypothetical annual rental). Rents were also fixed through agreement, even if there was much too-ing and fro-ing between national and local officials over what was a 'fair' rent. Walsingham had an early engagement with the process, referring its case to a Rent Tribunal in October 1920. The decision 10 months later was that the RDC's rents of 7/9d, 6/7d and 5/5d (in contrast with the Ministry's preferred 11/–, 9/– and 8/– for non-parlour dwellings)

[123] HCH 12 March 1957, Vol.566, col.958; TNA CAB129/101 C(60)96 'Housing', 17 June 1960, pp.6–7; HCH 25 October 1962, Vol.664, col.100W-01W; HCH 22 February 1963, Vol.672, col.104W.

[124] H&EO 12 February 1960, p.13; 15 May 1964, p.9; 11 September 1964, p.1; HRO RDC3/1/21 BrRDCHCM 21 December 1971, p.8488.

[125] W&DR 16 August 1938, p.3. Likewise, Biggleswade, despite a stock dominated by expensive 1919 Act dwellings, had only £100 arrears from an expected income of £11,000 in 1923 (BC&BG 20 July 1923, p.5).

[126] BRO RDBwM1/39 BiRDCHLCM 27 March 1968, p.900.

were sufficient.[127] Many others came to an arrangement with Whitehall, with around 1100 councils reaching rent agreements by 1921–1922 and just 56 failing to do so; this latter number rose by 46 in 1922–1923, by 24 in 1933–1924 and by six in 1924–1925 (MoH 1922, p.44; 1923, p.42; 1924a, p.51; 1925, p.53). Once rents were agreed, the variable element in the equation was the cost of dwellings. Under the 1919 Act, the Treasury took the hit on uncertainty and price fluctuation. By contrast, Acts that followed, both before and after the Second World War, removed the Treasury's open-ended commitment. This did not remove uncertainty, for there were various mechanisms, such as extra aid for high-rise buildings or building on high-cost sites (perhaps due to potential subsidence), as well as extra assistance for farm-worker homes, the precise incidence of which might not be assessed until applications for homes were made or homes completed. But as applications to the Ministry had to be made, national officials could estimate Treasury costs.[128]

Mostly council contributions were fixed by each Act, although they might contribute above the legislated minimum. When tenders were approved, rents could be estimated, as dwelling prices were approved, which, taking subsidies away, left a cost remant for which there was a well-trodden path for fixing covering rent levels. Unfortunately, final costs were less assured (Chap. 5). For one, builders commonly failed to complete houses at the price quoted. For another, it became increasingly obvious that maintenance allowances were too low, both because of building deficiencies and through better awareness (and rising expectations) of maintenance needs. Added to this, councils were borrowing money to erect new homes, paying these back over 20, 40 or 60 years, which meant charges varied as interest rates fluctuated. In the 1950s, the British economy was overloaded by the government playing a global role beyond the nation's means, by ambitious military spending, alongside low investment and poor productivity, which folded into balance of payments crises (Brittan 1964; Cairncross 1995; Barnett 2001). A roller-coaster ride of boom and bust followed with regular deflationary interventions. These heralded rising interest rates, the main element in dwelling costs subject to ongoing variability (Table 4.15). This generated anguish amongst councils. Many refused to construct dwellings owing to rising repayment costs.[129] Higher rents meant more turned down council tenancies.[130] As early as 1952, councils like Braughing began to complain

---

[127] *FakPost* 15 October 1920, p.5, with descriptions of the ongoing process at NRO DC19/6/9 WRDCM 5 January 1921, p.153; *FakPost* 15 April 1921, p.1; and the decision noted at NRO DC19/6/9 WRDCM 1 June 1921, p.196 in binding.

[128] 1930 Housing Act subsidies were on a per capita basis for those moved into new properties. How many people were removed was estimated, with numbers moved potentially not matching those assumed at the time of subsidy application.

[129] Henry Brooke, the Minister of Housing, reported that 39 English councils (including Biggleswade) had '… decided to reduce or stop their housing programmes in consequence of the latest rise in interest rates' (HCH 26 November 1957, Vol.578, col.95W–96W).

[130] As in Salford (TNA HLG101/748 'Press Cuttings'. *Manchester Evening News* 5 December 1956), Biggleswade (*BC&BG* 11 October 1957, p.12) and Mitford and Launditch RDC (where five of eight offered homes in Fransham refused them; *D&FT* 16 January 1953, p.10). Tenants in old properties turned down moves to new homes with higher rents (BRO RDBwM1/29 BiRDCM 15

Table 4.15 Annual
repayment cost for new loans
of £100,000 over 60 years
using Public Works Loan
Board interest rates at 31
March 1951–1961

Year	% interest	Annual cost to nearest £
1951	3.00	3604
1952	4.25	4621
1953	4.25	4621
1954	4.00	4410
1955	4.00	4410
1956	5.50	5721
1957	5.50	5721
1958	6.25	6410
1959	5.75	5948
1960	5.75	6063
1961	6.25	6294

Source: HCH 1 May 1962, Vol.658, col.807–08

they '… were finding it increasingly difficult to build houses to be let at a rent which would meet the needs of the tenants without throwing a burden on other ratepayers'.[131] The MP for Norfolk South-West explained the setting:

> … councils in Norfolk and in the Eastern Counties have already taken the decision to build no new houses in rural areas. We have, therefore, arrived at the position when rural districts—largely with Conservative majorities—have taken a decision not to build new houses because of the increasing cost of the houses, the cost of the loans, and the lowering of the subsidies.[132]

For rural districts, the 1950s saw a re-run of inter-war tenant difficulties paying rents.

When reducing housing subsidies for the 1923 Act, the government argued that falling building costs made them unnecessary (MoH 1929a, p.66). Following the Great Depression, there was a shift of weight in this argument. As expressed by the Committee on National Expenditure (1931, p.181), housing costs should be covered by wages; subsidised rents were anathema:

> There is serious danger of the nation, gradually and without forethought, finding itself committed to the principle that a man's wages are not normally intended to enable him to pay fully for his housing. In our view such a development would be a grave mistake from every point of view, and we can see no ground of principle why it should stop at housing.

Given the 'orthodox economics' (or fiscal conservativism) that pervaded national policy circles, it is little surprise scant weight was given to improving wages or

---

January 1958, p.9). The modernisation of old council dwellings was also hit, as tenants feared improvements would inflate rents (HRO RDC3/1/12 BrRDCFCM 16 January 1962, p.5388).

[131] *H&EO* 12 September 1952, p.1.

[132] HCH 25 January 1956, Vol.548, col.312. Illustrating the point, the building of eight houses in Mundesley (Erpingham) was curtailed, as it would increase the deficit on the HRA, even with a rent rise of 2½d or 3d a week (*NNN* 8 November 1957, p.1). Biggleswade similarly recommended slum clearance ceased owing to high interest rates (*BC&BG* 15 August 1958, p.11).

raising productivity to address the issue. The Exchequer was seen to be overly burdened, so cuts in subsidies were deemed essential. The argument of the time rather conveniently held that subsidies sustained high building costs. Without them, it was claimed, not only was there '… strong evidence that private enterprise in the building trade is ready to undertake the construction of smaller houses' (MoH 1933a, p.90) but it was also expected that '… reduction in the cost of building and the lowering of rates of interest enabled local authorities to build without subsidy small houses which could be let at rents within a few pence of 7s.9d weekly'.[133] Those removed from inappropriate accommodation as their homes were slums or overcrowded were exceptions, as rehoused families had low incomes, for which the Ministry was keen to remind councils to build cheaply (e.g. MoH 1932a, p.103). But, if most farm-workers could not afford more than about 3/– a week, 7/9d rents were unlikely to benefit them. By the mid-1930s at least, although it is hard to believe not before, the Ministry's own investigations showed this (Table 4.16). Dwellings built without Exchequer subsidy exceeded farm-worker affordability (Table 4.14). Hardly surprisingly, rural councils protested that without subsidies they could not build for needy families. Walsingham was particularly active in sending resolutions to the Ministry regretting subsidy withdrawal, noting a continuing shortage of working-class dwellings at reasonable rents and judging that private builders would not act.[134] This view was not shared in Smallburgh, which refused to

Table 4.16 Rent scenarios for selected RDCs under the 1936 Housing Act

Rural district	County	No-subsidy rent	Rent with maximum subsidy	Normal rent for farm-workers	RDC estimate of affordable rent
Braughing	Hertfordshire	7/09d	4/06d	2/06d	3/00d
Depwade	Norfolk	7/10d	4/07d	2/06d	3/00d
Ely	Isle of Ely	8/10d	5/06d	3/00d	4/02d
Erpingham	Norfolk	7/04d	4/06d	2/06d	3/00d
Smallburgh	Norfolk	7/07d	4/03d	2/06d	3/06d
Ware	Hertfordshire	7/09d	4/05d	3/00d	5/08d*

Source: TNA HLG40/3 'Applications Under Sec.108, Housing Act 1936. Notes on Financial Recommendations Made', undated c1937
Note: *For Ware this was the average rent at letting, but the RDC indicated farm-workers could not afford more than 3/6d a week. The expression an 'economic rent' refers to the required rent if there were no public subsidies. These values were reported for specific housing schemes for each council, so disparities across RDCs owe something to varied dwelling sizes. The Ware scheme, for example, included no four-bedroom dwellings, whereas Ely had 13 of its 17 dwellings in this category. The figures are in shillings and pennies

---

[133] TNA CAB24/247 CP12(34) 'Housing Policy', 1 February 1934, p.1.

[134] For example, NRO DC19/6/20 WRDCM 21 December 1932, p.80; *NM&PWJ* 11 May 1935, p.7. Its 1935 protest was supported by, amongst others, Depwade, Erpingham and St Faith's and Aylsham (*Diss Express* 24 May 1935, p.9; *T&WT* 25 May 1935, p.12; 22 June 1935, p.9).

support a similar appeal from Wisbech RDC.[135] By this time, of course, Smallburgh was well along the path of providing small, poorly equipped homes, as well as turning to non-subsidised dwellings for its non-farm population.

Restraint on house-building and rent non-affordability sit uncomfortably alongside messages from Evelyn Sharp (1956, p.295), the MHLG Permanent Secretary in the 1950s–1960s, who contended that: 'Traditionally authorities had built only for the poorer families; they had been limited by statute to building for the working-class'. This misconstrued housing policies significantly. In the 1930s and from the late-1950s, governments prioritised council-building for the lowest paid, with lower quality dwellings accompanying this emphasis, leading to accusations that governments created 'ghettos of the poor' (Bayliss 2001; Jones 2010). But this approach contrasted with Sharp's political overlords of a few years before her statement. The Attlee government favoured 'engineering' a social mix on council estates, stipulating that council-building could be for any social group (Adonis and Pollard 1997, p.202). This 1945–1951 emphasis paralleled earlier Ministry messages, which acknowledged that care of homes was better in neighbourhoods with mixed owner-occupied and tenanted populations, rather than segregating classes (MoH 1930a, p.77). Not that dwellings built prior to the 1930s favoured the lowest paid. As Bowley (1945, p.169) highlighted: 'On the whole the local authorities had provided their houses for the upper part of the working-class market only; they had failed to solve the problem of how to provide houses for the semi-skilled and unskilled workers' (also Lowe 1991). Benson (1989, p.78) clarified, claiming the 1930s emphasis on slum clearance and relief of overcrowding introduced a 'rough' element in council tenancy (Holmans 1987, p.178). As the 1919 Act gave no definition of the 'working-class',[136] this gave officials flexibility, if they needed it. That they did was seen in difficulties letting properties, not just under the 1919 Act but also for its 1924 equivalent. Hardly surprisingly, even in cities (e.g. Pooley and Irish 1984, p.89), councils kept an eye on the rent-paying capacity of tenants, being '… most unwilling to accommodate in their new houses persons who they suspect will prove bad tenants or be unable to pay the full rent'.[137] As the Biggleswade Clerk put it decades later, '… a 'clean' rent book sometimes seemed to be essential qualifications for eligibility – at least for new houses'.[138] Access for the low-paid was more difficult, with lower middle-class, clerical and skilled workers favoured as tenants (e.g. Smyth and Robertson 2013). Thus, in 1929, Walsingham reported 31 different professions amongst its roughly 100 tenants, of which the four largest occupational groups were railwaymen (25 tenants), farm labourers (12), motor mechanics (9) and clerks (6), some distance off 46.7% of 1931 male workers being agricultural labourers.[139] Nationally, by the 1940s, the word in the Ministry was that council houses in

---

[135] NRO DC22/2/46 SmRDCHCM 4 April 1933, p.39.

[136] HCH 25 June 1919, Vol.117, col.165–66.

[137] TNA HLG37/43 'Report on Local Investigations …', undated c1936, p.5.

[138] BRO RDBwM1/41 BiRDCHCM 14 January 1970, p.667.

[139] *FakPost* 17 May 1929, p.5.

remoter rural villages were occupied mainly by miners, railwaymen, postmen, teachers and other professional people.[140]

Systematic evidence on tenant attributes in the early years of council housing is thin. As Holmans (1987, p.176) noted, the 1931 Census offered information on tenants in London's Becontree Estate, but we wait until 1961 for wider census reporting by tenure. Information on the 1939 rateable values of dwellings did have tenure codes, but statistics combined rural and urban county districts (MoH 1944c). Council documents provided little comfort, with detail on new inter-war tenants more likely to list parish of residence than occupation. Nonetheless, there were messages in the records. Capturing an early flavour, Linsley (2005, p.234) found the first tenants in Docking RDC's 1919 Act dwellings were a builder, a minister, a school master (retired), a dentist, a storekeeper, a grocer, an insurance agent, a bricklayer, a grocer's assistant, a clerk, a plumber, a carpenter, a policeman (retired), a motor mechanic, an engine driver, a builder's foreman and a sergeant major in the Territorial Army. The Conservative MP for Wells went further, reciting tenants in 230 of the 1919 Act dwellings in an unnamed RDC as including '... 40 people of no occupation with private means, 37 railway employeés — I will not trouble the House with a long list — 9 farmers, 7 school teachers, 6 rural postmen, 7 motor drivers, 4 grooms, 3 gardeners, 4 butchers, and a Congregational minister'.[141] Not many low-paid working-class occupants were in these lists. If rural councils favoured agriculture, where were the farm-workers?[142] Part of the answer was apparent in support Erpingham gave to a 1924 Grimsby RDC resolution, which charged that: 'Under the present arrangement houses could not be let to the class needing them most – the agricultural labourers – because the rents were too high'.[143] Hence, we find Smallburgh advertising six houses in Hoveton and six in Horning in 1921, with all 12 going to non-agricultural workers after the withdrawal of the sole agricultural applicant.[144] Reports on farm labourer attempts to become tenants come with sad tinges, as in Walsingham, which in 1922 had only three farm-worker tenants (out of 36), all of whom needed other family members to meet rent payments.[145]

If rural councils were bastions of farmers seeking workforce servitude, we might not expect loud calls for rent reductions, nor the introduction of differential rent schemes long before this idea was widespread. Yet, this happened. Ampthill had farm-worker reductions for parlour homes of 2/– on a 10/– base in 1920, while

---

[140] TNA HLG37/52 'Memorandum from Mr. Monks', undated c1946.

[141] HCH 2 August 1926, Vol.198, col.2861.

[142] This was the MP for Wells's point, with the quotation referenced in the previous footnote continuing that houses were let at '... a rent very few agricultural labourers can pay'.

[143] HMC&WP 14 March 1924, p.3. Revealing how later lower subsidies adjusted perspectives, in the mid-1930s, the NFU claimed that: 'With the exception of the Act of 1924 the subsidy granted did not enable local authorities to build cottages which could be let at a rent within the means of agricultural workers' (TNA HLG37/43 'Statement by the National Farmers' Union', undated c1936, p.1).

[144] NRO DC22/2/45 SmRDCHCM 3 March 1921; 23 March 1921.

[145] FakPost 19 May 1922, p.5; 9 March 1923, p.5.

Smallburgh agreed weekly rents of 5/− for farm-workers and 6/6d for others.[146] With extra funds for agricultural parishes under the 1924 Act,[147] Biggleswade charged 5/3d a week in non-agricultural parishes and 3/5d in agricultural.[148] Walsingham's rents at the time were between 2/6d and 4/6d in agricultural parishes, while elsewhere they were 7/0d (8/3d for dwellings begun under the 1923 Act but completed under the 1924 Act).[149] For new-build under 1930s Acts, Ampthill similarly set rents at 3/− or 4/− a week,[150] while as early as 1930, Erpingham determined rents by ability to pay, not cost to the RDC.[151] That most of these figures were over the 3/− a week many claimed farm-workers could afford, suggests why districts like Amesbury RDC had no farm-worker council tenants as late as 1936.[152] It matched what Whitehall knew:

> It is illuminating to find for example that out of 102,000 houses owned by rural district councils at 30th June, 1936, only 4,600 are let at rents not exceeding 3/- per week *exclusive* of rates, while only a little over 13,000 (including the 4,600 mentioned above) are let at rents not exceeding 4/- per week *exclusive* of rates - this in spite of the fact that 30,000 houses were erected in agricultural parishes with the aid of extra subsidy under the Act of 1924.[153]

---

[146] For Ampthill, BRO RDAR8/1 ARDCMOHar 1920, p.7; *W&DR* 10 May 1924, p.1. There were comparable reductions for non-parlour dwellings in Smallburgh (SmRDCHCM 10 September 1920). Other examples include Erpingham noting its ability to fix rents itself under the 1924 Act and agreeing a rent of 3/6d for farm-workers (*HMC&WP* 29 August 1924, p.4). Buntingford also sought lower rents for farm-workers in 1927 (HRO RDC4/1/8 BuRDCM 20 June 1927).

[147] Rather than £9 a year for 40 years, in agricultural parishes the Exchequer grant was £12/10/0d for the same period.

[148] *NBC* 20 January 1933, p.3. Rising to 5/8½d and 4/4d in 1936 (BRO RDBwM1/12 BiRDCM 15 January 1936, p.198).

[149] NRO DC19/4/1 'Walsingham Register of Houses Provided under Housing (Financial Provisions) Act 1924'.

[150] BRO RDAM2/20 ARDCHCM 8 April 1936.

[151] TNA HLG48/868 Letter from Erpingham RDC Clerk to MoH Secretary, 10 May 1930. Another way of describing the scheme was that 'as far as possible a uniform standard of rents' was applied, with those who could afford it paying a near economic rent (NRO DC13/5/74 ERDCHCM 18 May 1937, p.17).

[152] TNA 37/43 'Report on Local Investigations ...', undated c1936, p.9. In 1936, the RDCA suggested 5/− inclusive could be met by agricultural workers (TNA HLG37/44 'Evidence of Neville Hobson, RDCA Executive Council Member', undated c1936, p.6). The key word was 'inclusive', for most assessments of rent capacities referred to 'exclusive' rents (excluding property taxes, water charges and the like). In 1924 the gap between inclusive and exclusive was 1/− for non-metropolitan areas (MoH 1924a, p.51), which had risen across all councils to 1/6d – 2/6d by the early-1940s (MoH 1944a, p.10). Hence, the RDCA figure was little different from the 3/− others quoted.

[153] TNA HLG37/43 Paper M13 'Supplement to Second Report of the Rural Housing Sub-Committee', undated c1936, p.3.

Extra subsidies for agricultural parishes under the 1924 Act were too limp to fit farm-worker pockets. Organised differently, the 1930 and 1935 Acts continued making higher awards for farm-worker homes, with national officials hoping the latter Act would yield rents of 3/– to 5/–.[154] After all, 1930s' legislation was intended to cater for tenants of lesser means, with low building costs adding to the prospect that the poor achieved council tenancies (Fig. 4.2).

Assessing how far this prospect was achieved is made difficult by weak reporting. Nuanced figures, using equivalent measurement units for separate geographical and/or functional categories, are especially difficult to find. On rents, as the government agreed levels, data on the 1919 Act are available. After that, finding national figures is hit and miss, as: 'It is not necessary for local authorities to submit to the Minister of Health the actual rents which they propose to charge for their houses. Therefore, we do not get a succession of statistics on the subject, from which information would be available'.[155] This remained largely unchanged for decades, save for incomplete information collected by the Institute of Municipal Treasurers and Accountants (later the Chartered Institute of Public Finance and Accountancy), as confirmed by various ministers, such as James MacColl's statement of 1969 that reliance was placed on '… the small sample covered by the Family Expenditure Survey' for information on average rents and family incomes.[156] Some figures were available. Accepting the usual caveats about weak coverage for rural districts, or that those near large towns were substantially 'suburban', does not detract from the few surveys that exist. Whether looking at the 1919 Act (Table 4.17) or figures that agglomerate dwellings from a number of Acts (like Table 4.18 for 1936), patterns were the same. Tenants in rural districts generally paid lower rents, not simply across the nation but also in comparison with nearby urban centres (Table 4.19). The main change in this pattern occurred early after 1945, when farm-worker wages rose significantly to attract more into agriculture, with house-building for farm-workers prioritised for the same reason (Chap. 7). Then, as Table 4.20 shows for 1948, rural rents outstripped urban charges. Yet this perturbation did nothing to disturb the essential message that rural councils charged higher rents than many in the working-classes could afford. This started with the 1919 Act but stretched well beyond it. As Keith Joseph informed Cabinet in 1962:

> Municipal rents vary a great deal. Some, particularly in rural areas, are already pretty well as high as the tenants can afford. But in the larger towns, although rents have been rising slowly under the pressure of mounting costs not matched by subsidy increases, the rent of a new 3 bedroom house is still often less than 30s. a week, sometimes much less.[157]

---

[154] TNA HLG40/2 'Memo to Mr. George', 12 February 1936.

[155] Neville Chamberlain at HCH 2 December 1926, Vol.200, col.1402–1403.

[156] HCH 18 April 1969, Vol.781, col.306W.

[157] TNA CAB129/110 C(62)145 'Housing', 2 October 1962, p.2.

Table 4.17 Percentage of three-bedroom dwellings by agreed exclusive weekly rent under the 1919 Housing, Town Planning, Etc. Act in rural and urban districts, 1923

	Rent level									
	13/– or more	12/– to 12/11d	11/– to 11/11d	10/– to 10s/11d	9/– to 9/11d	8/– to 8/11d	7/– to 7/11d	6/– to 6/11d	5/– to 5/11d	4/– to 4/11d
	Dwellings comprising a living-room, scullery and three bedrooms (non-parlour dwelling)									
RDCs	0.2	1.0	0.8	7.6	6.4	19.7	27.0	22.7	11.3	3.4
Urban	3.9	3.8	4.2	11.4	19.6	27.7	23.9	5.4	0.7	0.0
	Dwellings comprising a parlour, living room, scullery and three bedrooms (parlour dwelling)									
RDCs	3.7	6.1	7.1	19.4	13.0	17.9	19.9	8.6	3.5	1.1
Urban	18.7	11.1	14.9	25.4	17.6	10.9	3.6	0.8	0.1	0.0

Source: Computed from HCH 22 February 1923, Vol.160, col.1051W–52W
Note: 'Urban' refers to boroughs and urban district councils. The data source did not specify if 'boroughs' included 'county boroughs' but this was likely as the information was provided in response to a general question about rents under the Act, with no indication county boroughs should not be included. 'Exclusive rents' means without charges for property taxes, water and sewerage charges, etc.

Table 4.18 Percentage of council-owned dwellings by exclusive weekly rent by local government category, 30 June 1936

	Percent of tenants within local government category paying			
	over 10/–	8/1d – 10/0d	5/1d – 8/–	Up to 5/–
Rural districts	1.9	11.1	58.0	28.9
Urban districts	10.0	21.5	56.5	12.0
Non-county boroughs	14.8	20.7	51.9	12.2
County boroughs	6.8	23.4	57.8	12.0
London county council	58.3	27.7	12.9	1.1
England & Wales	13.3	21.5	52.2	13.0

Source: Computed from MoH (1937c, p.3)
Note: 'Exclusive rents' means without charges for property taxes, water and sewerage charges, etc.

Table 4.19 Percentage of council-owned dwellings in rural and urban districts by exclusive weekly rents in Bedfordshire, Hertfordshire and Norfolk, 30 June 1936

	Bedfordshire		Hertfordshire		Norfolk	
	'Urban'	Rural	'Urban'	Rural	'Urban'	Rural
Under 3/–	1.6	3.3	0.4	3.0	13.3	31.0
Under 5/–	9.9	31.8	5.6	17.3	33.5	81.1
Under 7/–	35.4	85.3	24.1	50.7	79.5	97.0
Under 9/–	75.8	98.3	57.1	78.8	98.4	100.0
Under 11/–	98.1	100.0	85.2	95.3	100.0	100.0

Source: Computed from MoH (1937c, pp.10–15)
Note: For information at the county level, the source excluded county boroughs under the 'urban' heading. This had no effect on Bedfordshire and Hertfordshire, which had no county boroughs at the time, but Norfolk's 'urban' values excluded Great Yarmouth and Norwich. 'Exclusive rents' means without charges for property taxes, water and sewerage charges, etc.

Table 4.20 Weighted average rents for pre-war and post-war council dwellings by local government category, 1948

	Pre-war dwellings rents for			Post-1945 dwellings rents
	1938	1948	1938–1948 increase	in 1948
Rural district councils	6/04d	9/00d	2/08d	14/10d
Urban district councils	4/04d	9/01d	1/09d	13/07d
Boroughs	8/03d	9/11d	1/08d	14/01d
County boroughs	7/06d	8/11d	1/05d	13/04d

Source: TNA HLG101/26 'Minute to Mr. Hutchinson from A.G. Rayner', 26 August 1948

4.4 Contributing to Contrivance

This chapter has focused largely on the inter-war years, as this was the era when depopulation was considered rife in the countryside, in which agriculture was the dominant economic venture, when, except close to towns, external housing demand was in its infancy, and when the private sector was given its head to 'solve' housing problems. Nationally, the view persisted that rural areas were in decline, with their housing problems treated as low priority. What should have been evident even then, had officials taken note of internal reports or examined census accounts rigorously, was that rural populations were generally growing. The agricultural labour force was falling but housing demand was sustained and magnified through demographic and household expansion. Yet, with national policies discriminating against private landlords, and with economic deterioration amongst landed estates, rural accommodation standards and availability fell, with building for private owners largely limited to urban spillover and, if elsewhere, beyond the budgets of most rural families. This left the council sector as the rural working-classes best hope for good accommodation (Mowat 1955, p.460). Weak coordination of state actions following the First World War,[158] coupled with wishful thinking that housing problems were short-term, limited capacities to make inroads into rural housing distress for at least a decade after 1918. By then, building costs had fallen, raising the prospect that new housing would come within rural rent-paying capacities. However, even before the Great Depression, cuts in public spending were prioritised over the betterment of citizens' living conditions. The Depression and its aftermath ensured low building costs would persist for years but governments were predisposed to private sector solutions without troubling private providers with expectations of improved productivity or performance. Low 1930s' construction costs were wasted as governments shunned addressing housing stock and dwelling quality problems effectively. With

---

[158] As an illustrative example, the Minister of Health, when rebuffing the charge that no steps had been taken to secure building materials in advance, pointed out that 2000 million bricks had been ordered in 1919 (HCH 17 February 1920, Vol.125, col.854) but had to agree the next day that '… the brickyards at Peterborough and Durham are congested with millions of bricks owing to lack of transport to remove them' (HCH 18 February 1920, Vol.125, col.920W).

national wage bargaining for agriculture enforcing low wages on most of the rural population, the state had to intervene to improve conditions. With a more interventionist government, perhaps rural wages could have been higher. Little was done inter-war to improve productivity in the countryside (Moore-Colyer 1999), yet the Second World War and its aftermath showed that even unskilled prisoners of war could be managed without compulsion into high productivity (Custodis 2012). Yet post-1945 saw continuing government appeasement of urban interests, with farmers favoured over farm-workers, so perpetuating low farm labourer wages (Self and Storing 1962; Chase 1993). Although wages after 1945 were higher relative to their manufacturing equivalent than inter-war (Drudy 1978), most rural workers were not in a position to pay the high rents state-imposed schemes for rent calculation produced. In this framework, to bring new homes within the reach of rural workers required state subventions. For much of the 1930s, subsidy eligibility criteria limited council action to substituting dilapidated and overcrowded properties with mean-spirited dwellings. Even here, rural districts received timid support, resulting in swaths of decrepit habitations lingering on owing to the insufficiency of alternative accommodation. Little wonder, housing shortages increased.

Yet many rural districts saw substantial building investment. Largely, this was from private owners, with 81.2% of all 1919–1943 new rural dwellings privately built (MoH 1944a, p.64). But away from the immediate proximity of towns, councils consistently complained builders offered little or nothing for the working-classes. This prompted councils to build without subsidy, provided they found potential tenants to pay the rent. The conundrum for national politicians was the way such activity highlighted policy failure and emphasised the need for public investment. If councils built without subsidies, this was an admission that housing shortages were not met by the private sector. Moreover, despite the absence of subsidy, such dwellings needed Whitehall approval, so knowledge of policy lapses could hardly be avoided nationally. Indeed, it was the duty of councils to draw attention to policy gaps, since they had a legal obligation to respond to local housing needs. If their residents were unable to buy homes or, with rents rising faster than living standards (Fig. 4.2), were unable to afford private rents or find accommodation of an acceptable standard, councils were pushed towards no-subsidy construction. That most held back from activating this option owes much to associated rent levels. But even in considering this option, messages to the Ministry were clear: either the private sector was not working or council-building was cheaper. The quandary was not lost on councillors. In Smallburgh, for example, acceptance of no-subsidy building led to worries that the Council would be portrayed as a speculative builder. The decision to take action was supported by a long list of people wanting village homes, who had no expectation of positive private sector action. This still generated fears that the Council would be in 'competition with private interests'.[159] Uncomfortably for national authorities, when allowing no-subsidy

---

[159] *NM&PWJ* 20 April 1935, p.6.

Source: MoH 1944b, p.51.

Fig. 4.2 House-building costs, rents and the cost of living in England and Wales, 1919–1939 (1919 = 100)

construction, they accepted council accommodation was to be occupied by better-paid workers, by those who could afford higher rents, which national politicians had decreed should be supplied by the private sector. This must have provoked further contortions in ministers' minds, since such occupants contradicted post-1933 policy that council property was for the poorly paid.

As often, the inter-war years had parallels with the 1950s and with the 1970s, 1980s and 2010s, albeit not always in identical ways or with the same outcomes (Weiler 2000; Jones 2010; Francis 2012). It is nonetheless worth noting how council responses to limp national commitments to improving working-class housing in the 1930s were manifest in new guises in the 1950s–1960s and early-1970s. In the late-1950s, the Ministry again diminished public sector contributions in favour of advancing private interests: 'The Government stated in the White Paper their view that the householder must be prepared to meet the cost of his house where he is able to do so; otherwise he can expect little freedom of choice' (MHLG 1964, p.16). Councils again found little private sector building for the working-classes, even for sale, or charges were too high.[160] As in the 1930s, councils responded by exploring construction for direct sale to local residents. Some decided to do so, as with Hatfield and Biggleswade in 1963–1964 and 1970,[161] while others decided against, as with

---

[160] On Oxfordshire's Bullingdon RDC, see TNA HLG117/171 'Report by K.F. Munn to Mr. Stone', August 1963; TNA HLG117/172 Letter to R.C. Wort from K.F. Munn, December1963.

[161] HRO RDC7/1/34 HtRDCM 18 December 1963, p.437; HtRDCHCM 23 April 1964, pp.711–12; HRO RDC7/1/36 Hatfield Houses for Sale Sub-Committee Meeting 11 November 1964, p.415; HRO RDC7/1/47 HtRDCH&TPCM 14 July 1970, p.179; *BC&BG* 20 November 1964, p.11.

Walsingham in 1960, Hatfield in 1965, Sandy in 1969 and Biggleswade in 1972–1973.[162] In most cases, interventions were short-lived. For instance, a 1960–1967 list of councils that had built more than 20 dwellings for sale in a year found that 61.8% of the 89 only sold homes in one year. Just three built in four of the eight years covered, with average annual completions across the 89 of only 902 dwellings.[163] Council records for the 1930s, and again for the 1960s and 1970s, reveal a sense of desperation over involvement with such processes. Action was needed as there were housing shortages, so councils tried something new. Significantly, when national policy failure was stark, as in 1973–1974, the government diluted ideological shackles, encouraging councils to build for direct sale, as few private builder homes were erected at affordable prices.[164]

This chapter has demonstrated no shortage of demand for extra rural homes. Rural populations were growing (Tables 4.1, 4.3 and 4.7), across much of the countryside (Tables 4.2, 4.4 and 4.5), with household numbers increasing (Tables 4.7 and 4.9). With most inter-war governments prioritising private building, the missing ingredients were concentrations of incomes sufficient to afford home-ownership. With government constraints on actions to increase the stock for those unable to buy, the weight of housing options lay with private rental. But this was not an undifferentiated sector. Thus, the Walsingham Clerk '… emphasised the poverty of both owners and tenants' in a submission to the Rural Housing Advisory Committee.[165] This applied especially to small-scale landlords, but many landed estates were in financial difficulties, often on the road to dispersal through auction (Barnes 1993; Houfe 1995; Beckett and Turner 2007). Those estate owners that rode the turmoil of the late-nineteenth-century and early-twentieth-century often diversified away from the land (Rothery 2007), or had wider investments when buying an estate (Crook 1999; Macdonald 2017). These individuals behaved more like industrialists or financiers than landed grandees (Perkin 1989, p.254). Estate dependence on immediate localities fell, accompanied by a reduced engagement in local affairs (Harris 1974; Robin 1980). With low rent-paying capacities in the rural working-classes,

---

[162] *D&FT* 21 October 1960, p.1; NRO DC19/6/68 WRDCHCM 7 November 1960, p.263; HRO RDC7/1/36 HtRDCHCM 6 April 1965, p.772; BRO UDSM1/10 SaUDCM 20 January 1969; BRO RDBwM1/44 BiRDCHCM 8 November 1972; BRO RDBwM1/45 BiRDCHCM 13 June 1973; 11 July 1973; 25 July 1973.

[163] HCH 26 October 1967, Vol.751, col.543W–46W. RDCs built 10.6% of homes built by councils for sale over these years.

[164] HCH 30 April 1973, Vol.855, col.243W–44W; BRO RDBwM1/45 BiRDCHCM 14 November 1973; HCH 14 November 1973, Vol.864, col.504–05; HCH 8 February 1974, Vol.868, col.448W–49W. This call for council action followed government statements a year before that council-building for sale would be refused unless private builders were unable or unwilling to satisfy demand for home ownership (HCH 27 April 1972, Vol.835, col.356W).

[165] TNA HLG40/19 'Applications for Special Assistance Received from RDCs in Norfolk and East Suffolk', undated c1931, p.6.

there were sales to weekenders, reluctance to take grant-aid to improve cottages lest this hampered sale or rental returns and dwelling disintegration as repairs lapsed.

Unfortunately for landlords, waiting for the bounty of a sale to an external buyer often carried overtones of *Waiting for Godot*.[166] The image Mackinder (1907, p.258) presented of all south-eastern England as part of a wider London by 1900 was only one of the accounts suggesting strong urban influences on the countryside early in the century. Beard (1989, p.44) offered a similar perspective on Sussex, with Horn (1984, p.234) reporting: 'By the early twentieth-century complaints were heard of the "great run on cottages for weekend purposes for golfers" in the Chiltern district of Buckinghamshire, and of the demands of "riverside" weekenders in the vicinity of the Thames'. But we can place too much weight on inter-war weekenders flocking to country pads (Lowerson 1980) or country dives (Gayler 1970; Hardy and Ward 1984). As Moore-Colyer (1999) explained, these 'new ruralites' were drawn to visit not stay: 'What those from industry, the professions or the "purple of commerce" wanted was country life not agriculture' (Howkins 2003, p.62). As detailed investigations of village evolution reveal, urban commuters became a driving force in social dynamics after, sometimes well after, 1945 (Robin 1980; Bell 1994). As Duckers and Davies (1990, p.94) illustrated for Rutland:

> Ross Johnson founded his building company, Wolds, in 1959, when Rutland was still a backwater and the villages were in decline. 'When I started off with the first planning application … they thought new housing was a jolly good thing. Housing was seen as progressive but it was also seen as tolerated amusement. People said, "Where the hell are the folks going to come from?". 'Ross Johnson had to create the market for new housing. 'You ask me what was going on in the early 60s? Nothing'.

Although Johnson's advertising worked, like other places distant from the capital (or other metropolitan centres), the weight of urban interest came later than in the Home Counties (Harris 1974). Yet, away from London, closer to towns, urban spill-over was important, even if property ownership by urbanites covered a small portion of rural dwellings at mid-century (Tilley 1947, p.46). Yet interest in the countryside intensified inter-war, both in the values it was believed to embody and in its preservation (e.g. Sheail 1981; Jeans 1990; Lowe et al. 1995).

It seems Whitehall officials and Westminster politicians missed the significance of this growing interest and affection. Regional offices sought to educate London officials that the countryside was not in decline. In 1950, for example, the MCTP's South-West Office asserted that '… any enquiry into causes of depopulation has significance only in so far as it seeks to prevent any recurrence of the bad old days', suggested an analysis of '… the reasons for the present comparative prosperity of the countryside', while signifying that 1939–1947 RDC population increases were 5% in Cornwall, 7% in Devon and Somerset, 9% in Wiltshire and 12% in

---

[166] A play by Samuel Beckett first performed in 1955 focusing on the musings of two characters while waiting for someone called Godot to arrive, who never does.

Gloucestershire, with noteworthy in-migration into the region.[167] Given the seeming bewilderment almost 20 years later over countryside demographic expansion, such messages clearly did not disrupt mainstream visions of decline. In 1967, Whitehall officials noted that agricultural workers were leaving the countryside, so rural homes should be vacant: 'Yet the building rate for new houses implies that at least five per cent of the population is moving back'.[168] The MHLG perhaps thought no one wanted country living unless born or bred there, suggesting lack of land near cities might be forcing people further out. In the same year, the MHLG (1967, p.3) published *Settlement in the Countryside*, which admitted to urban movement to the countryside, but thought explanations for it had not been investigated systematically. This document at least acknowledged some rural places saw demographic pressures beyond urban spillover. Locally, of course, decline characterised swaths of parishes in some districts (Table 4.5). In Norfolk, there were laments in the 1960s over villages being 'virtually dead',[169] with even Hatfield, where growth pressures were high, suggesting the availability of new houses would lessen demand for old cottages, so: 'It is likely therefore that the sentimental value attached to old property will depreciate, and that properties which have outlived their useful life will have to be demolished'.[170] Yet signs of vitality were there, even as rural and national leaders promoted gloom. Hence, well away from London, when the USAF base at Sculthorpe (Walsingham) was run-down in the early-1960s, fears of massed unoccupied homes were soon assuaged '… by "big demand" for weekender boltholes, for which trade was "as sharp as ever" '.[171] The impetus for urbanite interest might not have been equally intense across time and space, but it is difficult to absolve governments from failure to appreciate rural dynamics.

There is in England a peculiarity relative to most nations, which is the 'aura' surrounding owner-occupation as a housing goal. Throughout Europe, and even in the United States (Harloe 1985), tenures tend to be treated more equitably and are less differentiated by social status (Harloe 1995). These divisions draw on a preoccupation with class politics within the Conservative Party stretching back to the mid-nineteenth-century (Jarvis 1996). Having regular reminders of the political damage associations with the landlord class could bring (Daunton 1984; Simmonds 2002), the Party has long promoted 'a property-owning democracy' (Jones 2000; Francis 2012), fuelled in this passion as '… the owner occupier was seen as a natural Conservative voter' (Finnigan 1984, p.109; Williams et al. 1987).[172] In many

---

[167] TNA HLG125/10 Letter from R.S. Taylor, MTCP South-West Region, to D.G. Stewart-Smith, MTCP London, 13 March 1950.

[168] TNA HLG118/767 'Note to Mr. Williams from T.A. Doughty', 27 September 1967: Appendix II.

[169] For instance, *NNN* 26 October 1962, p.1; 3 April 1964, p.3.

[170] HRO RDC7/1/21 'Hatfield Report of Senior Sanitary Inspector 1955', p.121.

[171] *D&FT* 20 July 1962, p.8.

[172] Perhaps with justification, noting Saunders' (1990, p.229) observation that 59% of those who bought their council homes voted Conservative at the next election. Of course, there is no indication this figure applied to earlier decades. Probably it did not, given the 1980s was a time of par-

regards, this was clever politics, as it enabled the Party to draw on the defensiveness of working-class culture, at least in its deferential tones (Newby 1975), in themes of adoration for celebrity and status (Owen 2007), and amongst the many who believed the well-to-do had the right to govern (McKibbin 2010). The downside of this orientation was that it was divisive. This was demonstrated by a failure to address inter-war working-class housing issues due to an aversion to utilising council energies and knowledge. Viewed from this perspective, Larkin's (1978) view that middle-class willingness to buy rural homes in almost any condition encouraged landlord neglect must be questioned. There might have been truth in this claim for some 1970s landlords, but by then private rental was wilting. It would be a stretch of the imagination to hold that landlords held onto increasingly decrepit properties in anticipation of the arrival of wealthy urban buyers. Time spans from properties reaching a ruinous state to urban buyer interest would often have been long, weakening the reliability of such a strategy. Indeed, council reports indicate that many rented properties collapsed or received a hefty council push without finding urban buyers. Besides this, landlords were reluctant to evict longstanding tenants, preferring to wait until properties became vacant.[173] After this, some were converted into storage facilities or animal shelters. These elongations increased the life-span of buildings while external interest grew. Recall that rural councils were conscious of small landlord income dependence and local people's residential dependence on crumbling buildings, which encouraged light-touch action in enforcing maintenance, upgrade or demolition (Chap. 2). Added to this 1930s' (and 1950s') policies for replacing unfit buildings left numerous inadequate rural dwellings untouched (MoH 1944a, p.61), or, put another way, enabled poor-quality dwellings to linger on. The recipe you are left with cooks concentrations of old, occupied unfit dwellings, which characterised rural districts more than conurbations by the late-1960s (MHLG 1968). While it might not have been a deliberate landlord strategy to prolong the life of disintegrating cottages until service-class buyers arrived,

---

ticularly poor elections for the Labour Party (Johnston et al. 1988). In addition, as Saunders himself noted, working-class home owners in general were not especially drawn to the Conservatives. Thus, Heath et al. (1985) reported on a 1983 MORI poll showing council tenants voted 49% Labour and 29% Conservative, with three-quarters of Labour supporting council home purchasers not changing how they voted in 1983. This hardly pointed to a secure assumption that tenure determined party support. Note, though, that in the 1980s, tenant-purchased properties should have had higher rents, being disproportionately detached or semi-detached, with larger gardens, garages, in cul-de-sacs and more likely in smaller villages or villages rather than towns (e.g. Beazley et al. 1980; Phillips and Williams 1982; Constable et al. 1987; Forrest and Murie 1988). To pay the required rents, residents were likely from economically secure social strata (Sewell et al. 1984). Given how voting behaviour had bifurcated into Conservative gains in economically buoyant areas and losses in areas left behind (Warde 1986), this might have affected electoral behaviour but it might also be that home purchasers were more predisposed to vote Conservative.

[173] This is not to suggest landlords did not seek a quick eviction of tenants if buyers were knocking on their door, as examples in this book identify.

government restrictions on rural councils' ability to build new, or upgrade and enforce standards, created the same outcome.

A stock of dilapidated buildings existed when heightened urban interest brought funds to rejuvenate older properties into desirable bolt-holes (Phillips 2005). Giving one indication of magnitude, in 1955, Braughing estimated that without improvement to the existing stock, the number of seriously unfit dwellings would rise to half the stock over the next five to 10 years. The potential availability of these properties for rehabilitation was suggested by the district's substandard houses often being occupied by retired people 'many from the metropolitan areas'.[174] Of course, upgrades would have occurred for many of these properties, so half the housing stock would not have been unfit 10 or 15 years later. Yet, the enduring presence of older, run-down dwellings that beckoned urban gentrifiers was real. Many of these properties were occupied, but this might have merely delayed sales to outsiders. Take three examples from 1972 to illustrate the potential for the more well-to-do to acquire a rural wreck. Ampthill and Biggleswade revealed similar conditions at the time. Amongst owner-occupied and private rental dwellings, some 1118 out of 6860 in Ampthill were unfit for human habitation but capable of being raised to acceptable living standards (16.3%), with companion figures of 1084 and 6820 in Biggleswade (15.9%).[175] The situation for a narrower sliver of the housing stock, that of unoccupied dwellings, was captured in the same year in Smallburgh, where a survey of 300 empty homes found 60% unfit for habitation, 30% empty due to rent restrictions and only 10% suitable for immediate occupation.[176] Urbanites unconcerned about significant building renovation might have to wait for their ideal property to be available but they were hardly faced with a shortage of prospects. Magnifying the attractiveness of such acquisitions were land-use planning and other pressures that directed new-build to larger villages (Cloke 1979). With council homes in smaller villages sold disproportionately to sitting tenants (Beazley et al. 1980; Phillips and Williams 1982), followed by later re-sales to service-class in-migrants (Chaney and Sherwood 2000), the combined effect of neglecting private rental while offering few council tenancies fuelled social segregation across villages. Policy neglect set up the countryside in such a way that housing offered too little to retain workers and low wages helped to drive them away (Pedley 1942; Drudy 1978). Once white-collar workers lost their geographical shackles as transport and communication improved and new work practices were introduced, those with the resources could exploit lower prices, stunted village stocks and promises of development restraint, to secure their own 'rural idyll'.

---

[174] HRO RDC3/2/11 BrRDCHCM 17 July 1955, p.2831.

[175] BRO RDAM1/28 ARDCHPBuCM 14 September 1972, p.260; BRO RDBwM1/44 Biggleswade Chief Public Health Inspector's Report to Public Health Committee Meeting 11 October 1972, p.393.

[176] NRO DC22/2/30 SmRDCM 21 March 1972, p.166.

References

Addison C (1939) A policy for British agriculture. Victor Gollancz, London

Adonis A, Pollard S (1997) A class act: the myth of Britain's classless society. Hamish Hamilton, London

Allen GC (1976) The British disease: a short essay on the nature and causes of the nation's lagging wealth, Hobart Paper 67. Institute of Economic Affairs, London

Ambrose PJ (1974) The quiet revolution: social change in a Sussex Village 1871–1971. Chatto & Windus, London

Armstrong WA (1981) The influence of demographic factors on the position of the agricultural labourer in England and Wales, c1750-1914. Agric His Rev 29:71–82

Arnold AJ (1999) Profitability and capital accumulation in British industry during the transwar period, 1913-1924. Econ His Rev 52:45–68

Astor V, Rowntree BS (1939) British agriculture: the principles of future policy. Penguin, Harmondsworth

Barnes P (1993) Norfolk landowners since 1880. University of East Anglia Centre of East Anglian Studies, Norwich

Barnett C (1972) The collapse of British power. Eyre Methuen, London

Barnett C (2001) The verdict of peace: Britain between her yesterday and the future. Macmillan, London

Bayliss D (2001) Revisiting the cottage council estates: England, 1919-39. Plan Perspect 16:169–200

Beard M (1989) English landed society in the twentieth century. Routledge, London

Beavan B (2006) Challenges to civic governance in post-war England: the peace day disturbances of 1919. Urban His 33:369–392

Beazley M, Gavin D, Gillon S, Raine C, Staunton M (1980) The sale of council houses in rural areas: a case study of South Oxfordshire. Working Paper 44. Oxford Polytechnic Department of Town Planning, Oxford

Beckett JV, Turner ME (2007) End of the old order? F.M.L. Thompson, the land question, and the burden of ownership in England, c1880-c1925. Agric His Rev 55:269–288

Bell MM (1994) Childerley: nature and morality in a country village. University of Chicago Press, Chicago

Benson J (1989) The working class in Britain, 1850–1939. Longman, Harlow

Bentham GC (1986) Socio-tenurial polarization in the United Kingdom, 1953-83: the income evidence. Urban Stud 23:157–162

Berry F (1974) Housing: the great British failure. Charles Knight, London

Biggleswade Rural District Council (1937) Annual report of the medical officer of health and sanitary inspector 1936. Biggleswade

Biggleswade Rural District Council (1938) Annual report of the medical officer of health and sanitary inspector 1937. Biggleswade

Bollom C (1978) Attitudes and second homes in rural Wales. University of Wales Press, Cardiff

Booth P (1999) From regulation to discretion: the evolution of development control in the British planning system 1909-1947. Plan Perspect 14:277–289

Bowers JK (1985) British agricultural policy since the Second World War. Agric His Rev 33:66–76

Bowers JK, Cheshire P (1983) Agriculture, the countryside and land use: an economic critique. Methuen, London

Bowley M (1945) Housing and the state 1919–1944. Allen & Unwin, London

Boyle PJ, Cassidy S, Duke-Williams O, Rees PH, Stokes G, Turner A (2001) Commuting patterns in rural areas. Countryside Agency Publications CAX 58, Wetherby

Bracey HE (1958) A note on rural depopulation and social provision. Sociol Rev 6:67–74

Branson N (1975) Britain in the nineteen twenties. Weidenfeld & Nicolson, London

Branson N (1979) Poplarism 1919–25: George Lansbury and the councillors' revolt. Lawrence & Wishart, London

Brittan S (1964) The Treasury under the Tories 1951–1964. Penguin, Harmondsworth

Buller HJ, Hoggart K (1986) Nondecision-making and community power: the case of residential development control in rural areas. Prog Plan 25:133–203

Burchardt J (2012) Historicizing counterurbanization: in-migration and the construction of rural space in Berkshire (UK), 1901–51. J Hist Geogr 38:155–166

Byrne DS (1976) Allocation, the council ghetto and the political economy of housing. Antipode 8(1):24–29

Cairncross A (1995) The British economy since 1945, 2nd edn. Blackwell, Oxford

Calder A (1969) The people's war: Britain 1939–1945. Pimlico, London

Champion AG, Green AE, Owen DW, Ellin DJ, Coombes MG (1987) Changing places: Britain's demographic, economic and social complexion. Edward Arnold, London

Chaney P, Sherwood K (2000) The resale of right to buy dwellings: a case study of migration and social change in rural England. J Rural Stud 16:79–94

Chase M (1993) 'Nothing less than a revolution?': Labour's agricultural policy. In: Fyrth J (ed) Labour's high noon: the government and the economy 1945–51. Lawrence & Wishart, London, pp 78–95

Clark G (1982) Housing and planning in the countryside. Wiley, Chichester

Clarke JJ (1924) The new Housing Act, 1924. Town Plan Rev 11(2):119–127

Clarke JJ (1931) Slums and the Housing Act, 1930. Town Plan Rev 14(3):163–193

Clarke JJ (1936) Restriction of Ribbon Development Act, 1935. Town Plan Rev 17(1):11–32

Cloke PJ (1979) Key settlements in rural areas. Methuen, London

Coleman R (1982) Second homes in north Norfolk. In: Moseley MJ (ed) Power, planning and people in rural East Anglia. University of East Anglia Centre for East Anglian Studies, Norwich, pp 97–117

Collison P (1963) The Cutteslowe Wall: a study in social class. Faber & Faber, London

Committee on National Expenditure (1931) Report. Cmd 3920. HMSO, London

Connell J (1978) The end of tradition: country life in central Surrey. Routledge & Kegan Paul, London

Connor LR (1936) Urban housing in England and Wales. J R Stat Soc 94:1–65

Constable M, Lawes G, Bacon N (1987) Village homes for village people. NAC Rural Trust, London

Crichton RM (1964) Commuters' village: a study of community and commuters in the Berkshire village of Stratford Mortimer. David & Charles, Dawlish

Crook MJ (1999) The rise of the nouveaux riches: style and status in Victorian and Edwardian architecture. John Murray, London

Cross DFW (1990) Counterurbanization in England and Wales. Avebury, Aldershot

Crotch WW (1901) The cottage homes of England: the case against the housing system in rural districts, 2nd edn. P.S. King & Son, London

Custodis J (2012) Employing the enemy: the contribution of German and Italian prisoners of war to British agriculture during and after the Second World War. Agric His Rev 60:243–265

Daunton MJ (1984) Introduction. In: Daunton MJ (ed) Councillors and tenants. Leicester University Press, Leicester, pp 1–38

Daunton MJ (1996) How to pay for the war: state, society and taxation in Britain, 1917-24. Engl Hist Rev 111:882–919

Davey B, Josling TE, McFarquhar A (1976, eds) Agriculture and the state: British policy in a world context. Macmillan, London

Davies A (2013) 'Right to buy': the development of a Conservative housing policy, 1945-1980. Contemp Br Hist 27:421–444

Department of the Environment (1974) Rates and rateable values in England and Wales 1973–74. HMSO, London

Dowie JA (1975) 1919-20 is in need of attention. Econ His Rev 28:429–450

Downing P, Dower M (1973) Second homes in England and Wales. Countryside Commission CCP 65. Countryside Commission, London

Dresser M (1984) Housing policy in Bristol 1919-30. In: Daunton MJ (ed) Councillors and tenants. Leicester University Press, Leicester, pp 156–216

Drudy PJ (1978) Depopulation in a prosperous agricultural region. Reg Stud 12:49–60

Drudy PJ, Wallace DB (1971) Towards a development programme for remote rural areas: a case study in north Norfolk. Reg Stud 5:281–288

Duckers N, Davies H (1990) A place in the country. Michael Joseph, London

Eastwood T (1951) Industry in the country towns of Norfolk and Suffolk. Oxford University Press, London

English J, Madigan R, Norman P (1976) Slum clearance: the social and administrative context in England and Wales. Croom Helm, London

Finnigan R (1980) Housing policy in Leeds between the wars. In: Melling J (ed) Housing, social policy and the state. Croom Helm, London, pp 113–138

Finnigan R (1984) Council housing in Leeds 1919-1939: social policy and urban change. In: Daunton MJ (ed) Councillors and tenants. Leicester University Press, Leicester, pp 102–153

Forrest R, Murie A (1988) Selling the welfare state: the privatisation of public housing. Routledge, London

Forrest R, Murie A (1992) Change on a rural council estate: an analysis of dwelling histories. J Rural Stud 8:53–65

Francis M (1997) Ideas and policies under Labour 1945–1951: building a new Britain. Manchester University Press, Manchester

Francis M (2012) 'A crusade to enfranchise the many': Thatcherism and the 'property-owning democracy. Twent Century Br Hist 23:275–297

Gallent N (1997) Improvement grants, second homes and planning control in England and Wales: a policy review. Plan Pract Res 12:401–410

Gallent N, Tewdwr-Jones M (2000) Rural second homes in Europe: examining housing supply and planning control. Ashgate, Aldershot

Gardiner J (2010) The thirties: an intimate history. Harper Press, London

Garfield S (2004) Our hidden lives: the everyday diaries of a forgotten Britain 1945–1948. Edbury Press, London

Gay O (1987) Pre-fabs: a study in policy-making. Public Adm 65:407–422

Gayler HJ (1970) Land speculation and urban development: contrasts in south-east Essex, 1880-1940. Urban Stud 7:21–36

Gilg AW, Kelly M (1997) Rural planning in practice: the case of agricultural dwellings. Prog Plan 47:75–157

Goodwin-Hawkins B (2015) Mobilities and the English village: moving beyond fixity in rural West Yorkshire. Sociol Rural 55:167–181

Grafton DJ (1982) Net migration, outmigration and remote rural areas: a cautionary note. Area 14:313–318

Hardy D, Ward C (1984) Arcadia for all: the legacy of a makeshift landscape. Mansell, London

Harloe M (1985) Private rented housing in the United States and Europe. Routledge, London

Harloe M (1995) The people's home? social rented housing in Europe and America. Blackwell, Oxford

Harris C (1974) Hennage: a social system in miniature. Holt, Rinehart & Winston, New York

Heath A, Jowell R, Curtice J (1985) How Britain votes. Pergamon, Oxford

Henson AE (1957) Rural housing. In: British housing and planning yearbook 1957. National Housing and Town Planning Council, London, pp 103–110

Hill BE, Ray D (1987) Economics for agriculture: food, farming and rural economics. Macmillan, Basingstoke

Hodge I, Monk S (2004) The economic diversity of rural England: stylised fallacies and uncertain evidence. J Rural Stud 20:263–272

Hodge I, Whitby MC (1981) Rural employment: trends, options, choices. Methuen, London

Holmans AE (1987) Housing policy in Britain: a history. Croom Helm, London

Horn P (1984) The changing countryside in Victorian and Edwardian England and Wales. Athlone, London

Houfe S (1995) Bedfordshire. Pimlico, London

Howkins A (1991) Reshaping rural England: a social history 1850–1925. Harper Collins Academic, London

Howkins A (2003) The death of rural England: a social history of the countryside since 1900. Routledge, London

Howkins A (2006) Death or rebirth? English rural society, 1920-1940. In: Brassey P, Burchardt J, Thompson L (eds) The English countryside between the wars: regeneration or decline? Boydell, Woodbridge, pp 10–25

Howkins A, Verdon N (2009) The state and the farm worker: the evolution of the minimum wage in agriculture in England and Wales, 1909-24. Agric His Rev 57:257–274

Humphries J (1987) Inter-war house building, cheap money and building societies: the housing boom revisited. Bus Hist 29:325–345

Humphrys G (1968) A map of housing quality in the United Kingdom. Trans Inst Br Geogr 43:31–36

Hussey S (1997) Low pay, underemployment and multiple occupations: Men's work in the inter-war countryside. Rural Hist 8:217–235

Jackson AA (1973) Semi-detached London: suburban development, life and transport, 1900–39. Allen & Unwin, London

Jarvis D (1996) British Conservatism and class politics in the 1920s. Engl Hist Rev 111:59–84

Jeans DN (1990) Planning and the myth of the English countryside in the interwar period. Rural Hist 1:249–264

Johnston RJ (1967) A reconnaissance study of population change in Nidderdale, 1951-61. Trans Inst Br Geogr 41:113–123

Johnston RJ, Pattie CJ, Allsopp JG (1988) A nation dividing? The electoral map of Great Britain 1979–87. Longman, Harlow

Jones H (2000) 'This is magnificent!': 300,000 houses a year and the Tory revival after 1945. Contemp Br Hist 14:99–121

Jones B (2010) Slum clearance, privatization and residualization: the practices and politics of council housing in mid-twentieth-century England. Twent Century Br Hist 21:510–539

Keith-Lucas B, Richards PG (1978) A history of local government in the twentieth century. Allen & Unwin, London

Land Enquiry Committee (1913) The land - volume one: rural, 3rd edn. Hodder & Stoughton, London

Larkin A (1978) Rural housing - too dear, too few and too far. Roof 3:15–17

Larkin A (1979) Rural housing and housing needs. In: Shaw JM (ed) Rural deprivation and planning. Geo Books, Norwich, pp 71–80

Linsley, B. (2005) Homes for heroes: housing legislation and its effects on housing in rural Norfolk 1918–1939. PhD thesis University of East Anglia

Local Government Board (1919) Manual on the preparation of state-aided housing schemes. HMSO, London

Lowe S (1991) One hundred years of social housing. In: Lowe S, Hughes D (eds) A new century of social housing. Leicester University Press, Leicester, pp 1–12

Lowe PD, Murdoch J, Cox G (1995) A civilised retreat? anti-urbanism, rurality and the making of an anglo-centric culture. In: Healey P, Cameron S, Davoudi S, Graham S, Madani-Pour A (eds) Managing cities. Wiley, Chichester, pp 63–82

Lowerson J (1980) Battles for the countryside. In: Gloversmith F (ed) Class, culture and social change: a new view of the 1930s. Harvester, Brighton, pp 258–280

Macdonald, P. (2017) Rural settlement change in East Suffolk, 1850–1939. PhD thesis University of East Anglia

Mackinder HJ (1907) Britain and the British seas, 2nd edn. Clarendon, Oxford

Mackintosh JM (1936) Rural housing. Northamptonshire County Council, Northampton

Malpass P (1986) The housing crisis. Croom Helm, London

Malpass P (2003) Private enterprise in eclipse? a reassessment of British housing policy in the 1940s. Hous Stud 18:645–659

Marshall JL (1968) The pattern of housebuilding in the inter-war period in England and Wales. Scottish J Pol Econ 15:184–205

Martin JG (1934) Memorandum upon the provisions of the Housing Act, 1930. National Housing & Town Planning Council, London

Martin JG (1938) Memorandum upon the Housing (Rural Workers) Acts 1926 to 1938. National Housing & Town Planning Council, London

Martin EW (1965) The shearers and the shorn: a study of life in a Devon community. Routledge & Kegan Paul, London

McCullin D (2007) In England. Jonathan Cape, London

McKenna M (1991) The suburbanization of the working-class population of Liverpool between the wars. Soc Hist 16:173–189

McKibbin R (2010) Parties and people: England 1914–1951. Oxford University Press, Oxford

Meinistry of Health (1937) Rents of houses and flats owned by local authorities (England and Wales). Cmd 5527. HMSO, London

Merrett S (1982) Owner-occupation in Britain. Routledge & Kegan Paul, London

Minchinton W (1987) Life to the city: an illustrated history of Exeter's water supply from the Romans to the present day. Devon Books, Exeter

Ministry of Agriculture & Fisheries and Ministry of Health (1932) Report of the Inter-Departmental Committee on Agricultural Tied Cottages. Cmd 4148. HMSO, London

Ministry of Health (1921a) Second annual report, 1920–1921. Cmd 1446. HMSO, London

Ministry of Health (1921b) Report of the departmental committee on the high cost of building working class dwellings, Cmd 1447. HMSO, London

Ministry of Health (1922) Third annual report, 1921–1922. Cmd 1713. HMSO, London

Ministry of Health (1923) Fourth annual report, 1922–1923. Cmd 1944. HMSO, London

Ministry of Health (1924a) Fifth annual report, 1923–1924. Cmd 2218. HMSO, London

Ministry of Health (1924b) Circular to local authorities on the Housing (Financial Provisions) Act, 1924. Circular 520. HMSO, London

Ministry of Health (1925) Sixth annual report, 1924–1925. Cmd 2450. HMSO, London

Ministry of Health (1929a) Tenth annual report, 1928–1929. Cmd 3662. HMSO, London

Ministry of Health (1929b) General circular on the Local Government Act, 1929. Circular 1000. HMSO, London

Ministry of Health (1929c) Advisory Committee on Water report on rural water supplies. HMSO, London

Ministry of Health (1930a) Eleventh annual report, 1929–1930. Cmd 3667. HMSO, London

Ministry of Health (1930b) Housing Act, 1930. Circular 1138. HMSO, London

Ministry of Health (1931) Twelfth annual report, 1930–1931. Cmd 3937. HMSO, London

Ministry of Health (1932a) Thirteenth annual report, 1931–1932. Cmd 4113. HMSO, London

Ministry of Health (1932b) Report of the Committee on Local Expenditure (England and Wales). Cmd 4200. HMSO, London

Ministry of Health (1933a) Fourteenth annual report, 1932–1933. Cmd 4372. HMSO, London

Ministry of Health (1933b) Housing (Financial Provisions) Act, 1933. Circular 1334. HMSO, London

Ministry of Health (1933c) Report of the departmental committee on housing. Cmd 4397. HMSO, London

Ministry of Health (1935) Sixteenth annual report, 1934–1935. Cmd 4978. HMSO, London

Ministry of Health (1936) Housing Act, 1935: report on the overcrowding survey in England and Wales 1936. HMSO, London

Ministry of Health (1937a) Eighteenth annual report, 1936–1937. Cmd 5516. HMSO, London

Ministry of Health (1937b) Rural housing: second report of the Rural Housing Sub-Committee of the Central Housing Advisory Committee. HMSO, London

Ministry of Health (1937c) Rents of houses and flats owned by local authorities (England and Wales). Cmd 5527. HMSO, London

Ministry of Health (1939) Twentieth annual report, 1938–1939. Cmd 6089. HMSO, London

Ministry of Health (1944a) Rural housing: third report of the Rural Housing Sub-Committee of the Central Housing Advisory Committee. HMSO, London

Ministry of Health (1944b) Private enterprise housing: report of the Private Enterprise Sub-Committee of the Central Housing Advisory Committee of the Ministry of Health. HMSO, London

Ministry of Health (1944c) Valuation for rates 1939. HMSO, London

Ministry of Housing & Local Government (1964) Report of the Ministry of Housing and Local Government 1963. Cmnd 2338. HMSO, London

Ministry of Housing & Local Government (1967) Settlement in the countryside: a planning method. HMSO, London

Ministry of Housing & Local Government (1968) Housing condition survey: England and Wales, 1967. Econ Trends, 175:87–99

Ministry of Labour & National Service (1957) Enquiry into household expenditure 1953–54. HMSO, London

Ministry of Reconstruction (1918) Reconstruction problems 2: housing in England and Wales. HMSO, London

Ministry of Works & Planning (1942) Report of the Committee on Land Utilisation in Rural Areas. Cmd 6378. Scott Report. HMSO, London

Mitchell GD (1950) Depopulativon and rural social structure. Sociol Rev 42:69–85

Molotch H (1976) The city as a growth machine. Am J Sociol 82:309–332

Monk S, Dunn J, Fitzgerald M, Hodge I (1999) Finding work in rural areas. Joseph Rowntree Foundation, York

Moore-Colyer RJ (1999) From Great Wen to Toad Hall: aspects of the urban-rural divide in inter-war Britain. Rural Hist 10:105–124

Morgan KO, Morgan J (1980) Portrait of a progressive: the political career of Christopher, Viscount Addison. Clarendon, Oxford

Moseley MJ (1980) Rural development and its relevance to the inner city debate. Inner City in Context Report 7, Social Science Research Council, London

Mottram RH (1940) Bowler hat: a last glance at the old country banking. Hutchinson, London

Mowat CL (1955) Britain between the wars, 1918–1940. Methuen, London

Munton RJC (1983) London's green nelt: containment in practice. Allen & Unwin, London

National House Building Committee (1924) Report on the present position in the building industry, with regard to the carrying out of a full housing programme, having particular reference to the means of providing an adequate supply of labour and materials, Cmd 2104. HMSO, London

Newby HE (1975) The deferential dialectic. Comp Stud Soc Hist 17:139–164

Newby HE, Bell C, Rose D, Saunders P (1978) Property, paternalism and power. Hutchinson, London

Owen N (2007) MacDonald's parties: the Labour Party and the 'aristocratic embrace', 1922–31. Twent Century Br Hist 18:1–53

Page R (1974) The decline of an English village. Davis-Poynter, London

Parker J, Mirrlees C (1988) Housing. In: Halsey AH (ed) British social trends since 1900, 2nd edn. Macmillan, Basingstoke, pp 357–397

Parr JB (1966) Outmigration and the depressed rural area problem. Land Econ 42:149–159

Pedley WH (1942) Labour on the land: a study of the developments between the two great wars. P.S. King & Staples, London

Penfold SF (1974) Housing problems of local people in rural pressure areas: the Peak District experience. Report TRP 7. University of Sheffield Department of Town & Regional Planning, Sheffield

Penning-Rowsell EC (1997) Who 'betrayed' whom? power and politics in the 1920/21 agricultural crisis. Agric His Rev 45:176–194

Perkin H (1989) The rise of professional society: England since 1880. Routledge, London

Phillips M (2005) Differential productions of rural gentrification: illustrations from north and south Norfolk. Geoforum 36:477–494

Phillips DR, Williams AM (1982) Rural housing and the public sector. Gower, Farnborough

Pooley GC, Irish S (1984) The development of corporation housing in Liverpool 1869–1945. University of Lancaster Centre for North West Regional Studies, Lancaster

Pooley CG, Turnbull J (1998) Migration and mobility in Britain since the eighteenth century. UCL Press, London

Pugh M (2008) 'We danced all night': a social history of Britain between the wars. Bodley Head, London

Ravetz A (2001) Council housing and culture: the history of a social experiment. Routledge, London

Richardson HW (1967) Economic recovery in Britain 1932–39. Weidenfeld & Nicolson, London

Robin J (1980) Elmdon: continuity and change in a north-west Essex Village 1861–1964. Cambridge University Press, Cambridge

Rothery M (2007) The wealth of the English landed gentry, 1870-1935. Agric His Rev 55:251–268

Ryder R (1984) Council house building in county Durham 1900-39. In: Daunton MJ (ed) Councillors and tenants. Leicester University Press, Leicester, pp 40–100

Satsangi M, Gallent N, Bevan M (2010) The rural housing question. Policy Press, Bristol

Saunders P (1990) A nation of home owners. Unwin Hyman, London

Saunders P, Newby HE, Bell C, Rose D (1978) Rural community and rural community power. In: Newby HE (ed) International perspectives in rural sociology. Wiley, Chichester, pp 55–85

Savage WG (1915) Rural housing. T. Fisher Unwin, London

Saville J (1957) Rural depopulation in England and Wales 1851–1951. Routledge & Kegan Paul, London

Seaman LCB (1966) Post-Victorian Britain, 1902–1951. Methuen, London

Self RC (2000, ed) The Neville Chamberlain diary letters: volume two, the reform years, 1921–27. Ashgate, Aldershot

Self P, Storing HJ (1962) The state and the farmer. Allen & Unwin, London

Sewel J, Twine F, Williams NJ (1984) The sale of council houses: some empirical evidence. Urban Stud 21:439–450

Sharp E (1956) Housing: the past ten years. Chartered Survey 89:291–296

Sheail J (1981) Rural conservation in inter-war Britain. Clarendon, Oxford

Shears RT (1936) Housing the agricultural worker. J R Agric Soc Engl 97:1–12

Short JR, Fleming S, Witt SJG (1986) Housebuilding, planning and community action: the production and negotiation of the built environment. Routledge & Kegan Paul, London

Shucksmith M (1981) No homes for locals? Gower, Farnborough

Shucksmith M (1990) Housebuilding in Britain's countryside. Routledge, London

Shucksmith M (1991) Still no homes for locals? affordable housing and planning controls in rural areas. In: Champion AG, Watkins C (eds) People in the countryside. Paul Chapman, London, pp 53–66

Simmonds AGV (2002) Raising Rachman: the origins of the Rent Act. Hist J 45:843–868

Simon ED (1933) The anti-slum campaign. Longmans, Green & Co., London

Smyth J, Robertson D (2013) Local elites and social control: building council houses in Stirling between the wars. Urban His 40:336–354

Standing Committee on Prices and Trusts (1920a) Profiteering Acts, 1919 and 1920: interim report on the prices, costs and profits of the brick trade. Cmd 959. HMSO, London

Standing Committee on Prices and Trusts (1920b) Profiteering Acts, 1919 and 1920: findings and decisions of a sectional committee appointed by the Building Materials Sub-Committee of the Standing Committee on Prices and Trusts to investigate the prices, costs and profits at all stages of timber. Cmd 985. HMSO, London

Standing Committee on Prices and Trusts (1920c) Profiteering Acts, 1919 and 1920: interim report on cement and mortar. Cmd 1091. HMSO, London

Standing Committee on Prices and Trusts (1921a) Profiteering Acts, 1919 and 1920: report on light castings. Cmd 1200. HMSO, London

Standing Committee on Prices and Trusts (1921b) Profiteering Acts, 1919 and 1920: final report on stone, brick and clayware trades. Cmd 1209. HMSO, London

Standing Committee on Prices and Trusts (1921c) Profiteering Acts, 1919 and 1920: report on pipes and castings. Cmd 1217. HMSO, London

Strathern M (1981) Kinship at the core: an anthropology of Elmdon, a village in north-west Essex in the nineteen-sixties. Cambridge University Press, Cambridge

Sturzaker J (2010) The exercise of power to limit the development of new housing in the English countryside. Environ Plan A42:1001–1016

Swenarton M (1981) Homes fit for heroes: the politics and architecture of early state housing in Britain. Heinemann, London

Thomas CJ (1957) The census: and the estimation of housing need and housing progress. Town Plan Rev 28(2):131–144

Thrift NJ (1986) Little games and big stories: accounting for the practice of personality and politics in the 1945 General Election. In: Hoggart K, Kofman E (eds) Politics, geography and social stratification. Croom Helm, London, pp 86–143

Tilley MF (1947) Housing the country worker. Faber & Faber, London

Turner J (1953) Rural housing and planning: a statement on the use of agricultural land for housing. In: British housing and planning yearbook 1957. National Housing and Town Planning Council, London, pp 73–78

Wade-Martins S, Williamson T (2008) The countryside of East Anglia: changing landscapes 1870–1950. Boydell, Woodbridge

Walford NS (2001) Reconstructing the small area geography of mid-Wales for an analysis of population change 1961-1995. Int J Popul Geogr 7:311–338

Walford NS (2005) Connecting historical and contemporary small-area geography in Britain: the creation of digital boundary data for 1971 and 1981 census. Int J Geogr Inf Sci 19:749–767

Walford NS (2010) An analysis of the changing dependency ratios for small areas in 1981, 1991 and 2001: a Norfolk case study. J Maps 6:370–381

Ward SV (1984) List Q: a missing link in inter-war public investment. Public Adm 62:348–358

Ward SV (1988) The geography of interwar Britain: the state and uneven development. Routledge, London

Warde A (1986) Space, class and voting in Britain. In: Hoggart K, Kofman E (eds) Politics, geography and social stratification. Croom Helm, London, pp 33–61

Weekley IG (1988) Rural depopulation and counterurbanisation: a paradox. Area 20:127–134

Weiler P (2000) The rise and fall of the Conservatives' 'grand design for housing', 1951–64. Contemp Br Hist 14:122–150

Whetham EH (1974) The Agriculture Act, 1920 and its repeal - the 'great betrayal'. Agric His Rev 22:36–49

Williams WM (1963) A West Country village, Ashworthy: family, kinship and land. Routledge & Kegan Paul, London

Williams NJ, Sewel J, Twine F (1987) Council house sales and the electorate: voting behaviour and ideological implications. Hous Stud 2:274–282

Wilson GK (1977) Special interests in policy-making: agricultural policies and politics in Britain and the United States. Wiley, Chichester

Chapter 5
The English Disease: Capacity and Capability for Housing Improvement

Abstract The core question in this chapter is whether the operating environment of rural councils gave a firm base for active housing interventions. Examining the resource base of councils shows that even national assessments deemed rural authorities had insufficient capacity to fund new-build effectively, with weak funding streams carrying into inadequate staff numbers and skills. Adding to the discomfort, countryside builders were of questionable reliability in housing provision. Their existence was unstable, their skills limited and their willingness to engage with council work low; commonly resulting in few applications to build council dwellings, alongside inflated prices for the standard of building specified. Rural homes were often built to a lower standard than urban, in part due to the non-availability of water and sewer systems. This was cast in positive light early in the century, as rents were kept down and large gardens enabled crop growth to supplement wages. Later, lack of supply was a handicap, as new-build began to be refused where services were not available. Yet, in the 1950s, the government cut funds for their provision, proclaiming cities should have priority as their water and sewer systems paid their own way.

Keywords Rural government resources · Rural builders · Water-sewer supply · House-building constraints · Poor productivity

In earlier chapters, basic tenets in mainstream accounts of poor rural housing performance have been questioned. Explanations based on employers limiting housing options and lack of demand amongst the rural populace are over-simplified, while damage to housing prospects was well advanced before egocentric service-class in-migrants helped thwart working-class housing gains. This chapter explores another possibility; namely, that institutions in rural England were not equipped to address housing problems effectively. So far, chapters have examined the role of local leaders and demands put on them. Put another way, the book so far has explored actors and pressures to act, but not the capability to act. This is the focus here. In effect, the question raised is, even if rural leaders had the will-power to respond to housing problems, did they lack the tools to alleviate them?

© Springer Nature Switzerland AG 2021
K. Hoggart, *A Contrived Countryside*, Local and Urban Governance,
https://doi.org/10.1007/978-3-030-62651-8_5

This query is tied to a wider issue, which centres on the (relative) economic and political decline of Britain.[1] The causes of this decay are subject to controversy. Ostriches of political commentary excuse trends over the last 150 years as if no decline has occurred. Or, like Johnson (1985, pp.viii–ix), explain it away as somehow inevitable:

> In large part Britain's failings now are the result of past success. Her early industrial strength, the enormous benefits of Empire and her freedom from dislocation by war or revolution all helped create uniquely powerful relations of social domination. The British bourgeoisie fused with the older ruling class and thus took over many of the attitudes and prerogatives while the British working-class – the world's oldest – learnt to internalise its own subordination. Thus while the British class structure is statistically similar to that found in other developed capitalist states, it still has a unique rigidity of manner and attitude, the ossified clarity of an ideal type.

More convincing analyses, whether from the political Left (e.g. Gamble 1981) or Right (e.g. Allen 1976), offer multi-faceted accounts. Commonly within these interpretations weight is given to the peculiarity of international finance within the British economy and expensive commitments to overseas entanglements (e.g. Tylecote 1982; Ingham 1984). Our interest focuses on internal aspects of British society. These have been examined intensively and, given their sweep across the decades, extensively in four volumes by Correlli Barnett (1972, 1986, 1995, 2001); the first on the inter-war years, the next the Second World War, the third the immediate aftermath of the War and, finally, the 1950s and beyond. In a nutshell, Barnett's thesis posits that the internal dynamism of decline emerged from an adherence to outdated practices, a lack of effective investment, poor productivity, failure to innovate, prioritising generalist over technical knowledge, insufficient job training, weak dialogue between business and government, poor labour relations, short-term planning horizons and the below-average quality of British management. That these conditions are inter-related, in themselves and in an exaggerated vision of the nation's role in the world, has been exposed in other accounts reaching similar conclusions (Kynaston 2014; Brown 2017). Summarising the situation, Allen (1976) placed most blame on inappropriate institutions and attitudes. The last relates to leadership, the former, the centre of our attention in this chapter, the context in which leaders acted. The focus is the framework within which local housing policy was made. Hence, we start with the framework for rural government, asking whether this provided a base for positive housing responses. The construction industry is investigated next, asking if the sector helped or hindered addressing rural needs. Finally, attention is directed at ancillary services, the presence or absence of which encouraged or depressed housing provision, asking how investment geared towards societal improvement impacted on rural living conditions.

---

[1] Readers might complain about the reference to Britain, when the chapter title refers to the English disease. There is no wish to absolve Irish, Scottish and Welsh contributions. However, the core of economic and political power in Britain lies in the Conservative-dominated heartland of England (Hechter 1975; Bulpitt 1983).

5.1   Rural Governance Capacities

Writing on the eve of local government reorganisation in England and Wales, Sharpe (1973, p.3) proclaimed that '… in many ways rural local government never quite seems like local government in the classical sense'. The 1974 local government structure introduced bigger, largely urban-centred councils, changing the local government scene profoundly. Resources for councils were more evenly (albeit not equitably) distributed, staffing and facilities generally improved, and councillors and policy became more heavily politicised (Bristow 1978; Dearlove 1979; Gyford 1985). For rural areas the contrast was stark. After 1974 the average size of lower-tier local government units was over 122,000 inhabitants. By contrast, early in the 1920s, out of 663 Rural Districts, 11 had populations of less than 1000, 117 had between 1000 and 5000, another 209 were below 10,000, and just 93 had over 20,000 residents, with only five over 50,000 (Royal Commission on Local Government 1925, pp.135–36). Criticism that councils were too small persisted into the 1960s (Royal Commission on Local Government in England 1969). Despite ongoing readjustments to boundaries, functions and even rural–urban status (Keith-Lucas and Richards 1978), rural government was dominated by small, poorly resourced councils. Small incursions into inequalities arrived under the 1929 Local Government Act (Dunbabin 1977), with more substantial change from its 1948 equivalent (Foster et al. 1980, p.186).[2] The ill-health of local resources was acknowledged, with increased Treasury grants resulting, even if their extraction came slowly and grudgingly (Rhodes 1976). Increased complexity in allocation criteria raised questions of distributional bias (Newton 1980), but Treasury contributions to local expenditure did rise from 15% in 1913 to 34% in 1945 and then 45% in 1973–1974 (Committee of Inquiry into Local Government Finance 1976, p.17). By the early-1970s, less than 30% of local spending was covered by property taxes (the rates). For rural districts this had important if complex ramifications, as governments tinkered with local revenue and spending frameworks regularly (Loughlin et al. 1985). Thus, the 1929 Act de-rated agricultural land and buildings and significantly reduced taxes on industrial property. Public transport was down-graded in 1948, along with electricity. Then 1957 saw reductions for commercial property. All of these, save agriculture, were revoked in 1964. From 1929, shifts in responsibility for local services were enforced (Dunbabin 1977).[3] Yet, despite minor intrusions by county councils, core housing responsibilities stayed with rural districts up to 1974. That apart, as many commentators have asserted, if local government can be so readily adjusted to meet national priorities, it should be seen as integral to the

---

[2] One stimulus for 1948 Local Government Act changes was Bevan's dislike of the 1930s system of Treasury grants to support local authority revenue, which left those with the smallest property tax bases bearing the heaviest burdens; the poor were kept poor by Chamberlain's 1929 system (Foot 1973, p.99).

[3] The list of changes in functional responsibilities is extensive, including poor relief in 1935, trunk roads in 1936, supplementary benefits in 1940, hospitals in 1946, electricity in 1947, gas in 1948, then water and sewerage treatment and community health in the 1970s (Saunders 1983, 1985).

national state rather than a manifestation of local democracy (e.g. Sharpe 1978; Saunders 1981; Ashford 1982). Despite the camouflage of political rhetoric, understanding local policies requires a firm eye on national agencies. This is especially so for housing, as control over capital spending is more problematic for governments (Layton 1961; Ball 1980). As Sharpe (1982) reminded us, with ongoing national economic problems, government efforts to control local spending have never been far away.

Set within changes to local government, politics counted. It is notable, for example, that following the loss of so many rural (and urban) districts after the 1929 Local Government Act, numerically little changed from 1935 to 1974. In 1940 there were 478 RDCs, with 1971 seeing a drop of only nine (Wood 1988, p.353). For Freeman (1968), such tinkering can be traced to government reluctance to embark on what was really required, namely fundamental change. Whitehall officials were as guilty as Westminster politicians in their reticence. That local government reform in 1974 was initiated by one politician, following fumbling government efforts over the previous 50 years (e.g. Young and Garside 1982), with its announcement made when the Ministry's Permanent Secretary was on holiday (Keith-Lucas and Richards 1978, p.211; Ashford 1981, p.175), signalled the intellectual sludge that permeated governments. Rather than seeking improved performance throughout the state apparatus, the driver was 'business as usual', that is 'weak, temporising government' (Johnson 1985, p.ix). The 'practical' nature of the British state, which encouraged inaction, was the same 'pragmatism' others criticise as a root cause of economic and political decline (e.g. Barnett 2001; Brown 2017). Vision, strategy and purpose have been shunned in favour of 'muddling through' (Lindblom 1959; Hennessy 1996). Yet, when national politicians felt challenged by local authorities, they acted vigorously. While the 1929 Local Government Act barely inched towards the major transformation local government required, the process did see the abolition of councils like Poplar that had challenged national policies (Taylor 1965, p.256; Dunbabin 1977; Branson 1979).[4] The pattern was repeated in the 1980s, when the government failed to take the positive steps its own commissioned investigation recommended, instead abolishing the Greater London Council and metropolitan authorities, which had caused embarrassment by pursuing alternative policies to those the government favoured (Flynn et al. 1985; Wheen 1985; O'Leary 1987). Governments have the capacity to enthuse and enable lower state tiers. Unfortunately for rural councils, this potential failed to be energised; drift and tinkering have been the norm.

---

[4]The 1929 Act introduced disqualification for councillors deemed by a district auditor to have incurred costs (or lost revenue) that was 'unreasonable'. As with Clay Cross in the 1970s, this could lead to financial penalties for councillors who contravened government wishes (Minns 1973; Skinner and Langdon 1974). Note, first, that such penalties for 'waste' could be imposed even if local politicians were supported by their electorate; national policy had priority over local. Note, second, that such penalties did not apply to national politicians. Had they done so, many a case might have been brought against them. Take Harold Macmillan as an example. To encourage electoral support, he intervened to push the British steel industry to open two, rather than the preferred one, new strip mill, so saddling the industry with two operations that lacked the economies of scale of competitors (Willetts 1992, p.41; Scott 1996, p.54).

5.1.1   District Council Resources

One element in this failure was lethargy over inadequate resources. That national politicians and officials were long aware of deficiencies in funding mechanisms for rural councils was evinced in internal ministry documents. Early examples include a 1931 report to the MoH Deputy Secretary, which noted that: 'The principal obstacle in the way of housing in rural districts (as in many small urban districts) has been (and will continue to be) the acceptance of a charge, however small, upon the rates'.[5] More bluntly, within the MAF, a 'notorious apathy' amongst rural councils towards spending was observed.[6] Similarly, in preparatory meetings over the 1931 Housing (Rural Authorities) Act, it was charged that local authorities: '… were in general reactionary and in many cases very hard hit financially, and it might therefore be expected that their attitude generally would be obstructive'.[7] If such attitudes existed, their impetus was fuelled by a British peculiarity. This is that the UK (and Ireland, as part of the same polity when local revenue systems started) has been unique in not allowing councils to tax directly (Rhodes 1976; Karran 1988). Whereas other nations gave local access to buoyant revenue streams, like income tax, sales tax or value-added tax (occasionally even corporate tax), taxation for English councils was property-based.[8] This originated in compromises in the nineteenth-century, when landed elites opposed more public spending, whereas business leaders wanted higher commitments to raise city competitiveness (Ashford 1980). To lessen tension, national assistance was introduced based on local expenditure; more spending brought more compensation. Placing weight on property taxes favoured the rich, as taxes could be levied on a wide population, unlike more elastic sources like income tax or death duties, whose payment early in the century was largely confined to the very wealthy. But property taxes had a major drawback; their inelasticity. Whereas national revenues increased as incomes and wealth grew, raising funds through property taxes required notifying the public of increases. This fostered caution over spending, whether urban or rural. As Jennings (1977, p.87) explained: '… the first

---

[5] TNA HLG40/30 'Untitled Report', 20 April 1931, p.6. This orientation did not come solely from rural councillors. In the investigated districts, there was little evidence of ratepayer pressure on councils, although occasionally ratepayer and tenant associations asserted rate demands were too high (e.g. HRO RDC7/1/12 HtRDCM 27 April 1939, p.34). But most rate payments went to county councils not rural districts. For instance, in Biggleswade the County levy was 4/- in 1927, with a further 1/4½d going to the Poor Law Guardians and just 9½d to the RDC (BRO RDBwM1/9 BiRDCM 6 April 1927). Forty years later the RDC rate was 2/2d compared to the County's 9/- (BRO RDBwM1/38 Biggleswade RDC Rates Estimates 1967–68 Meeting 22 February 1967, p.717). Similar figures held elsewhere, as with Smallburgh in 1966 with 2/- for the RDC and 9/2d for the County (*NNN* 11 March 1966, p.9).

[6] TNA MAF48/207 'Tied Cottages', 18 November 1929, p.3.

[7] TNA HLG29/180 'Notes on Rural Housing from 15 April 1931 Meeting on Tudor Walters' Scheme'.

[8] The peculiarity was noted by Ashford (1982, p.255): 'Despite the fact that Britain has one of the most heavily burdened local government systems in the world, the British fiscal system provides less flexibility and fewer alternatives at the local level than any other major country'.

concern of every council is the rates. Many people judge how well or how poorly the council is doing by the rates it sets. The actual rate seems to be less important than the increases'. After decades of criticism, a major enquiry recommended local income taxes (Committee of Inquiry into Local Government Finance 1976). Few will be amazed that over four decades later, little has changed in council revenues.[9] For councils, the funding regime inhibited action. With a farm cost-price squeeze (Hill and Ray 1987), with much of rural England struggling to attract employment outside agriculture and associated industries (Hodge and Whitby 1981), the rural policy environment was structured to limit revenue and repress spending (e.g. Green 1920, p.125; Rose et al. 1976).

What casts doubt on unwillingness to spend as an explanation for poor rural housing performance was the low net cost of housing. In Bowley's (1945, p.100) words: 'When the local authorities fail to carry out any scheme with enthusiasm, it is usually argued that this is because to do so would place too heavy a burden on the rates. In the case of housing schemes this argument breaks down'. Thus, for 1923–1933 just 0.8% of net spending from the rates went to housing. The housing rate burden was not high. This was the national picture. Locally, pressure might still exist to keep spending low. Even in relatively wealthy districts, like Newport Pagnell RDC, stresses were evident:

> Some councillors were down-right hostile to any improvement which cost additional money so, up to 1927, the Council had pressure from central government for improvements and strong pressure from the parishes to hold down the rate, particularly as parish councils were usually elected by a show of hands up to 1948 and in small parishes a good many inhabitants were locally employed. (Eley 1973, no page numbers)

But was housing critical to rate poundage pressures? The Ministry of Health believed so when housing programmes were in their infancy, but thought improved subsidies 'removed this difficulty' by 1939.[10] Perhaps, but the de-rating of agriculture in 1929 led to heavier relative householder contributions in RDCs (Table 5.1). Wealthier non-farm small-business owners were thereby incentivised to watch council spending closely, as their two contributions – one for their home and the other via a family business – made deeper impression on their costs and on council revenue than for urban corporate leaders. As Molotch (1976) spelt out, for economic sectors dependent on locally grounded profits, business leaders can take keen interest in council activities, whether to boost local economic activity or restrain 'extravagance'. Around such considerations, rural districts followed similar leadership

---

[9] Some might quibble over this message, as the basis on which property taxes were raised changed over the 40 years. Even after the assessment of property was handed to the Inland Revenue in 1948, so as to provide more equitable evaluations, property assessments favoured more expensive dwellings (Ford and Brown 1978). In effect, property taxes were regressive (Hepworth 1971), leading in 1967 to rate rebates to mitigate effects (Committee of Inquiry into Local Government Finance 1976). National politicians were reluctant to update property valuations. This meant local wealth components in allocation formulae gave economically buoyant places higher grant receipts, and areas in relative decline lower, than real property values merited (Audit Commission 1984).

[10] TNA HLG37/48 'Work of Rural District Councils on Housing', undated c1943.

Table 5.1 Property tax indicators for England and Wales by local government category, 1938–1939 and 1973–1974

	London	CBs	MBs-UDCs	RDCs
	1938–1939			
Rateable value per inhabitant (£)	15.20	7.35	7.15	4.60
Average rate poundage (£)	0.60	0.71	0.64	0.62
	1973–1974			
Penny rate product per inhabitant (£)	2.39	1.17	1.15	1.00
Average rate poundage (£)	0.39	0.45	0.40	0.35
% rateable value from domestic hereditaments	38.2	43.2	54.5	63.8

Source: MoH (1939b, p.4); DoE (1974, pp.10–48)
Note: Values for 1973–1974 are for England but for England and Wales for 1938–1939. Rate poundage information was not included in the source for 1938–1939. In 1973–1974 rateable value and penny rate product are very close, with penny rate product preferred as it indicates resource available to councils (some property was exempt from local rate charges). Because the value of property underwent revaluations, comparison across decades did not indicate change in resource availability. However, within the same year, penny rate products and rateable values did indicate relative resources. The rate poundage refers to the charge levied on each £1 in property a rate-payer owns (or rents if they pay the property taxes rather than the owner)

patterns as urban centres, with receding economic dependence on landed aristocrats as they withdrew from local affairs (Lee 1963; Harris 1974; Olney 2007), just as company expansion drew urban business leaders away from city towards national and international networks (Birch 1959; Morris and Newton 1970; Garrard 1977).

Being petit bourgeois dominated, it is perhaps no surprise that rural councillors preferred private solutions, not public sector intervention, as in Blyth RDC in Suffolk:

> The Housing Committee of Blyth Rural District Council view with concern the mounting burden of subsidies and the ever-increasing cost of administrative expenses in the erection of council houses. They therefore appeal the Minister of Housing and Local Government to promote legislation under which private individuals may be encouraged to build and own their own houses …[11]

Such attitudes gathered support from the local press, itself an element in the local business 'establishment'. Illustrative of the tone of this backing were commentaries on the 1922 election in Biggleswade Town. Under the headline 'Vote for the Business Twelve', the *Biggleswade Chronicle and Bedfordshire Gazette* (24 March 1922, p.1) made no apology for supporting local businessmen (all men), arguing the Council needed their perspective:

> We believe that by far the greater majority of the ratepayers are properly dissatisfied with the conduct of the affairs of the Town which has obtained in recent years. In the retiring Council men of sound business capacity who are again standing for election and have abundantly shown that they had the best interests of the Town uppermost in their minds, such as F.C. Kitchiner and H.C. Gee, have had their efforts frustrated by an opposition consisting

---

[11] TNA HLG101/724 'Blyth RDC Memorandum on the Provision of Houses by Way of Grant to Private Individuals', undated c1953.

partly of men who are not directly ratepayers, augmented by men of more or less cranky ideas who have wasted the time of the Council, and the money of the ratepayers in the advancement of schemes which were not really needed and which have entailed unnecessary burdens on the rates.

With maintaining a low tax rate perceived as integral to 'business attitudes', rural councils regularly complained about 'unnecessarily' county council taxes.[12] Of course, county councils were the major spenders in rural local government. The mid-1930s illustrate, with the rate poundage levied by the county council 2.4 times that of the RDC in Hatfield, 5.1 times greater in Braughing and 7.8 times more in Walsingham.[13] Closer to 1974 reorganisation, divergence increased, as with the Biggleswade ratio rising from 6.9 in 1959–1960 to 9.1 in 1973–1974.[14] Yet, by the 1960s, the fiscal environment had changed. For one, there was more reluctance to criticise county council spending, as with Braughing not condoning Ware UDC's complaints over high rates, instead acknowledging demand for education, burdens from population growth and health service needs.[15] Attitudinal shift also occurred in Biggleswade Town, which moved in four years from proclaiming the lowest Bedfordshire tax rate to embracing one of the highest as councillors came to believe the Town had to grow or die, with the prospect of London overspill encouraging community improvements like sewage works.[16] Business sentiments that prioritised low taxes when growth prospects were weak now pressed for public investment to enhance business fortunes (Molotch 1976).[17]

As with this temporal shift, there was RDC resource variability. As a 1930 Cabinet paper noted: '… there are some Rural District Councils whose rate resources have been so restricted under the Local Government Act of 1929 that they are unable to bear a further rate charge for housing'.[18] Similarly, in 1951, referring to slow progress on extending rural water supplies, the minister for local government

---

[12] Looking across the decades, examples include Hatfield's support for a resolution by Ware RDC (*HA&SAT* 26 October 1928, p.16), Biggleswade Town's resolution to Bedfordshire County Council (BRO UDBwM1/10 BiUDCM 17 May 1938, p.193), Braughing's support for a Hertford RDC resolution (HRO RDC3/2/3 BrRDCPH&HCM 22 May 1947, pp.1046–47), and Smallburgh's letter to the Minister about property taxes reaching a level 'the average individual cannot afford' owing to 'the avariciousness of the County Council' (*NNN* 9 August 1957, p.4).

[13] *H&PBG* 27 March 1936, p.6; *H&EO* 4 April 1936, p.5; *NM&PWJ* 28 September 1935, p.6.

[14] BRO RDBwM1/31 Biggleswade Finance and General Purposes Committee Meeting 24 February 1960, p.329; BRO RDBwM1/44 Biggleswade 1973–74 Rates Estimates Meeting 28 February 1973, p.1051.

[15] HRO RDC3/1/11 BrRDCFCM 21 March 1961, p.5096.

[16] *BC&BG* 1 April 1960, p.12; 20 March 1964, p.1; 19 March 1965, p.1; 16 April 1965, p.8; 10 March 1967, p.13.

[17] In what held out the promise of a profit bonanza for local businesses, regional planning statements of the time suggested Biggleswade Town should grow from 8000 to 16,000 by 1981, and eventually to 52,000 (*WR&WSR* 11 February 1964, p.1). The projected growth did not materialise, with Biggleswade only reaching 15,383 inhabitants in 2001, although there was a 19.3% population rise in 1961–1971 compared with 8.3% in 1951–1961.

[18] TNA CAB24/221 CP104(31) 'Rural Housing', 23 April 1931, p.5.

argued: 'The real problem has not been the wicked rural district council, because no rural district council in a really rural area has ever had the resources in rateable value behind it to enable it to provide a water supply'.[19] Put another way, revenue-raising potentialities made it unreasonable to fund demands made on them. But some were more deprived than others, as the 1931 Minister of Health highlighted:

> Godstone, in Surrey, has a general rate of 7s.6d in the £, and is obviously not overburdened. The produce of a penny rate approaches £900, and they could build 100 houses at a cost of less than one half penny on the rates. If you go to Swaffham in Norfolk the general district rate is 13s.6d, a heavy burden, and the produce of a penny rate instead of being £870 is £87, and it would mean an additional 4d on the rates to build 100 houses … In the Isle of Thanet the general rate is 8s.6d and a penny rate yields £459. They could build 100 houses for less than a penny rate, but in the Isle of Axholme the general rate is 11s.3d in the £, and a penny rate brings in only £48. For them to produce 100 houses would mean an additional 7½d in the £ on the rates.[20]

Diversity was startling given these councils had the same responsibilities. Across all English RDCs, for 1935–1936, a penny rate product varied from £1183 in Eton RDC to £17 for Broadwoodwidger RDC, with the general rate levied ranging from 18/3d in West Auckland RDC to 4/11d for the Isle of Wight RDC.[21] Fortunately, at the extremes, numbers were small. Out of 487 rural districts in England and Wales in 1936, 18 had penny rate products under £50, with a further 65 at £50–£100, while only 90 had products over £400.[22] To contextualise the investigated rural districts, Hatfield had the highest penny product at a shade over £400 (with a 1931 population of 11,001), Ampthill and Biggleswade straddled £300 (populations close to 20,000), while the districts at the core of Braughing (Buntingford and Hadham) and the Norfolk districts ranged from around £150–£250, which given their lower populations (ranging from about 10,000 to 17,000) per capita placed them close to Ampthill and Biggleswade.[23] Hatfield apart, then, these were 'average' rural districts, although most were slightly below the rural 'norm'.[24]

---

[19] HCH 25 June 1951, Vol.489, col.1121–22.

[20] HCH 10 July 1931, Vol.254, col.2440.

[21] TNA HLG40/9 'Advantages and Disadvantages of a Sliding Subsidy', undated (for meeting of 9 September 1936).

[22] TNA HLG37/45 'Particulars as to the Product of a Penny Rate in the Rural Districts of England and Wales', undated c1936.

[23] TNA HLG32/2161 'Accounts of Rural District Councils Bedfordshire to Buckinghamshire, 1934–1935'; Hatfield RDC (1936, pp.4–5); TNA HLG40/3 'Rural Housing Committee. Applications Under Sec. 108, Housing Act 1936. Notes on Financial Recommendations Made', undated c1937. Compared with post-1945, data were not readily available for rural councils; reporting was intermittent and available figures were often not for the same year.

[24] Note that both Erpingham and Smallburgh were defined as 'middling' in Table 4.8. According to MoH (1939b), the average rateable value per capital for RDCs in England and Wales was £4.60 in 1938–1939 (£4.75 for Wales), compared with values for the investigated districts ranging from the highest at £8.60 (Hatfield) down to £4.45 (Braughing), £4.15 (Ampthill), £3.75 (Erpingham), £3.60 (Biggleswade), £3.10 (Smallburgh) and £3.00 (Walsingham). Only within year comparisons are valid over time, owing to property revaluations. For 1973–1974, the DoE (1974) reported an average RDC penny rate product of £1.00 (£1.17 for CBs and £1.15 for MBs-UDCs), with values

What were the implications for housing? The literature implies that a general aversion to public spending should translate into subdued investment. This impression is over-blown. An early indication was tax-shy Biggleswade Town, which made its required one penny contribution towards its 92 council dwellings under the 1919 Act, yet saw a net fiscal benefit in 1923 of almost £284 a year from these houses, as their occupiers paid more in rates than the subsidy cost. This £284 compared with a total net UDC spend of £6116 that year.[25] Rather than draining tax resources, council dwellings could enhance them. Similar inter-war assessments of minor or no calls on the rates were common.[26] Hence, a positive balance on the housing revenue account (HRA) was reported for Ampthill in 1925.[27] Except its subsidy for 1919 Act homes, 1931 Hatfield reported it built at practically no cost to the ratepayer.[28] By 1930, Smallburgh had lost practically nothing under its housing scheme,[29] while Sandy's housing liability worked out at less than a half-penny rate.[30] For most, housing was a minor fiscal item. Walsingham illustrated this, for its 1928 half-year 'loss' of £320 on housing compared with a highways spend of £4685, with similar proportionality in 1949–1950 Biggleswade, when a housing contribution of £2075 compared with total spending of £31,565.[31] By the mid-1930s, both Ampthill and Biggleswade had HRA surpluses sufficient to subsidise the general rates; so council tenants (assisted by national grants) 'bankrolled' property-owners.[32] HRA surpluses were not exceptional at the time. Norfolk's Depwade had

---

for the investigated RDCs at £1.56 (Hatfield), £1.24 (Smallburgh), £1.11 (Braughing), £1.05 (Ampthill), £0.88 (Biggleswade), £0.87 (Walsingham) and £0.81 (Erpingham). Little had changed over the decades, save for the improved position of Smallburgh, which owed much to gains from tourism on the Norfolk Broads and the north Norfolk coast plus retirement migration (Yaxley 1977; Coleman 1982; Coles 1982).

[25] BRO UDBwM1/7 BiUDCM 20 March 1923, p.163; *NBC* 23 March 1923, p.7. In Biggleswade Town, the message council dwellings brought 'profit' to the UDC's budget was stated regularly inter-war (e.g. *NBC&SN&DN* 5 March 1926, p.1; *NBC* 28 September 1937, p.7).

[26] The Rural Housing Sub-Committee concluded that housing contributions from the rates varied, but the burden was low (TNA HLG37/47 'Notes on Visits to East Anglia and South Midlands', undated c1943).

[27] BRO RDAM1/7 ARDCM 18 June 1925.

[28] HRO RDC7/96/1 *Welwyn Garden City Pilot* 4 November 1927.

[29] *NWP&ENS* 21 February 1930, p.5.

[30] *NBC* 3 April 1936, p.7. Thirty years later, Erpingham reached the same conclusion (NRO DC13/5/34 ERDCM 27 December 1967, para.105), while Sandy, like Biggleswade Town, was making no rates contribution to housing (BRO UDSM1/5 SaUDCM 28 March 1960, p.221; BRO UDSM1/8 County Review for Sandy and Biggleswade UDCs), with Newport Pagnell RDC offering no rate support for housing over much of the 1950s and 1960s (*WR&WSR* 13 March 1956, p.1; 15 November 1960, p.1; 5 March 1963, p.1; 14 March 1967, p.1).

[31] NRO DC19/6/15 WRDCM 29 February 1928, p.117; BRO RDBwM1/21 BiRDCM 22 February 1950, p.70.

[32] Ampthill requested Ministry permission to subsidise the rates by £8 per council house in 1936 (BRO RDAM2/20 ARDCHCM 5 October 1936). Despite a 1938 surplus in Biggleswade, the previous year the HRA was in deficit (*NBC&BR* 6 July 1937, p.11; BRO RDBwM1/13 BiRDCM 16 November 1938, p.416).

one, while Smallburgh asked ratepayers for no contribution for district services in the mid-1930s (Chap. 3), and was refused subsidy for new houses in 1939 due to its HRA 'profits'.[33] Indeed, by 1940, the Ministry was worried by the size of HRA surpluses.[34]

The situation changed after the Second World War. Attitudes shifted during the War, with awareness growing of deprivation amongst the less advantaged (e.g. Calder 1969; Thrift 1986). Within this reassessment, public support for better housing rose; as analytical studies (e.g. Eastwell 1979; Hinton 1988) and archival evidence shows.[35] In this regard, government priorities were in line with public sentiment, with political parties acknowledging the electoral significance of housing. For Barnett (1995, pp.153–54) adjusted Conservative thinking drew on the calamitous consequences of the Lloyd George government's failure to provide 'homes fit for heroes' after 1918, which '… ruthlessly made of housing a bludgeon with which to thump an administration stumbling through the aftermath of war'. No surprise the Girdwood Committee reported in 1948 that more than one-quarter of the higher cost of post-war houses (compared to pre-war) was due to their greater size and superior amenities (MoH 1950a, p.322). But, as we saw in Chap. 4, when housing costs rise, rents generally follow, unless mitigated by subsidies. Here, the 1946 Housing (Financial and Miscellaneous Provisions) Act offered succour to rural districts, with a Treasury subsidy of £16/10/0d a year raised to £25/10/0d for the agricultural population (both for 60 years).[36] There were additional subsidies for districts with low penny products and, with Ministerial approval, exceptionally high property taxes (MoH 1946). Council contributions for farm-workers likewise generated lower demands on councils; with the standard rate contribution of £5/10/0d a year reduced to £1/10/0d, with county councils adding the same.[37] The figures vouch for a national priority in the late-1940s for building for farm-workers. The Ministry of Health even turned down applications for new dwellings that included insufficient farm-worker homes, emphasising in 1947 that it expected more units in this category, with regular reminders to councils that farm-worker homes were the priority.[38]

---

[33] TNA HLG37/43 'Memorandum by Depwade RDC Housing Committee', undated c1936; *NM&PWJ* 16 March 1935, p.7; NRO DC22/2/47 SmRDCHCM 3 January 1939, p.991. It was later estimated that Smallburgh made a surplus of £950 a year on council houses built in 1939–1940 (NRO DC22/2/48 SmRDCHCM 23 November 1948, p.3656).

[34] TNA HLG101/243 'MoH Circular 2008', 26 April 1940.

[35] MOA TC1366 31.7.42 'Post-War Questionnaire. Fabian Society Public Opinion Survey'; MOA TC1607 February 1943 'Topics of the Day. Housing' [Part of the Bulletin]; TNA RG23/113 'Knowledge and Opinion about the Housing Situation. Fieldwork September 1950'.

[36] Raised to £26/14/0d and £35/14/0d in 1952, then lowered to £22/1/0d and £31/1/0d in 1955 (HCH 9 March 1962, Vol.655, col.95W-96W).

[37] There were enhanced national subsidies for flats, sites of potential subsidence and for non-traditional construction that promised an early and substantial additional housing output. Privately owned homes could be supported for farm-workers, with a £15 subsidy for 40 years.

[38] Amongst other messages, for Biggleswade, see *NBC&BR* 11 November 1947, p.6; BRO RDBwM1/18 BiRDCM 5 November 1947, p.532; 28 January 1948, p.613.

This prioritisation lasted a short time. Thus, in the Ministry's review of housing waiting lists for September 1949, the number of families with no separate home was 15.3 times greater for non-farm workers in Hertfordshire RDCs than for farm labourers, with ratios of 7.5 and 3.0 for Bedfordshire and Norfolk.[39] Amongst those on waiting lists who had a home, with applications usually due to dwelling inadequacies, space needs, etc., the ratios were 6.0, 3.2 and 1.8, respectively.[40] Hardly surprisingly, while provision leaned towards farm-workers, over time most new homes went to non-farm residents. So, for 1945–1951, out of 129,664 new RDC dwellings, 27,466 went to farm-workers.[41] Despite favourable funding for farm-worker dwellings, post-1945, most rural districts made substantial rate contributions to their HRA, partly because they built so many houses. In the seven investigated RDCs, all bar two increased the council stock by more in the 10 years after 1945 than inter-war (Table 5.2).[42] The exceptions, significantly, were Biggleswade, which built disproportionately under the 1919 Act, and Smallburgh, which erected low-cost 1930s dwellings when prices were subdued, largely without making rate fund contributions.[43]

The Smallburgh pattern offers a hint on underlying policy. After 1933, Treasury support for council-building was largely restricted to ameliorating overcrowding and slum clearance (Chap. 4). Outside this support, councils built without subsidy by charging an 'economic rent'. Smallburgh used this capacity at meagre or no cost to the Council. But 1946 Act rate contributions were comparatively high.[44] In the Act's early years, Smallburgh was not perturbed, as surpluses on pre-war homes covered rate contributions.[45] However, fewer dwellings than anticipated ended up

[39] TNA HLG101/417 'Review of Local Authority Lists of Housing Applicants at 27 September 1949 (Provisional). Applications Region 4'.

[40] Urban districts contributed to farm-worker housing demand, with 19.0% of all farm-worker families lacking a home coming from urban centres in Bedfordshire (14.9% for those with an existing home), as compared with 47.9% (18.9%) in Hertfordshire and 12.6% (3.8%) in Norfolk.

[41] TNA MAF234/18 'NFU Memo on Rural Housing', 7 February 1952, p.2.

[42] Technically, post-war completions cover eight not 10 years, since the annual *Housing Return for England and Wales* listed no completions in these districts until March 1947, at which point only 130 were finished across the seven councils.

[43] This was something Smallburgh sought to avoid inter-war. Why the Ministry of Health took so long to catch up with the Council was unclear. Nevertheless, when the Ministry informed Smallburgh in 1936 that it had to contribute £3/15/0d a year for each of the 388 houses built under the 1924 Housing Act, this caused alarm (*NM&PWJ* 9 May 1936, p.6). After meetings with the Ministry, it was agreed to meet losses from HRA surpluses (NRO DC22/2/47 SmRDCHCM 21 July 1936, p.261; *NM&PWJ* 1 August 1936, p.11).

[44] For instance, Hatfield reported total rate fund subsidies for 1949–1950 as £730 under the 1919 Act, £264 under the post-1945 temporary accommodation scheme, and £1724 under 1946 scheme. The only other contribution for housing was £27 under the Housing (Rural Workers) Act (HRO RDC7/1/15 'Hatfield Rate Estimates. Year Ending 31 March 1952'). For 1950–1951 these figures were £745, £110, £2159 and £35 (HRO RDC7/1/15 'Hatfield Rate Estimates 1952–1953').

[45] NRO DC22/2/48 SmRDCHCM 23 November 1948, p.3656; NRO DC22/2/49 SmRDCHCM 6 November 1951, p.51. By 1963 'profits' on pre-war dwellings were still giving Smallburgh a HRA surplus (*NNN* 7 June 1963, p.3).

Table 5.2 Pre-war and post-war council dwellings built in investigated rural districts up to 1955

	To 1939–1941	1945–1955
Hatfield	817	997
Braughing	380	396
Ampthill	353	1102
Biggleswade	1057	855
Erpingham	398	552
Smallburgh	685	520
Walsingham	426	456

Source: For 1945–1955 MoH-MHLG (quarterly) for the financial year April–March, for 1939–1941 from council minutes and medical officer of health annual reports

Note: These numbers have inconsistencies in reporting, partly because they were not available every year. Most figures for 1939–1941 were for 1939 but for Braughing it was 1941. The numbers recorded above approximated those in the *Municipal Yearbook 1945* (giving minor leeway for war-time additions or losses), except for Walsingham, for which the *Municipal Yearbook* added 331 to the number shown here. The *Municipal Yearbook* figure was clearly incorrect, given Walsingham minutes long after 1939 gave 426 as the pre-war council stock (e.g. NRO DC19/6/66 WRDCHCM 22 November 1954, pp.99–100) and, had it been correct, the number of Walsingham households in council homes should have been c1,500 in 1961, when it was 1268. In this table, 1955 is the cut-off for the post-war period because this was the year the government's 1951 General Election commitment to build more council dwellings diminished, with the council share of total house-building falling thereafter

rented to farm-workers, so less than expected Treasury support arrived. By the mid-1950s surpluses were used up and interest rises added to costs (Table 4.15), which for Smallburgh was at '… a level which can truly be described as a hardship to the ratepayers'.[46] The Council's capital programme was stopped. The Ministry was approached for additional assistance '… without imposing a penal rate on the ratepayers of the district'. This led to criticism from Swaffham RDC, with accusations Smallburgh was admitting it could not run its own district. But support for Smallburgh came from the Erpingham Chair, who suggested it was ahead of other

---

[46] *NNN* 17 May 1957, p.5.

councils in recognising the fiscal toll of investment.[47] Although Smallburgh effectively avoided making rate contributions to housing up to the 1970s,[48] sympathy was aroused as the Ministry sought to include within housing schemes '… expensive water supply and sewage disposal arrangements which were not contemplated'. Faced with this demand, Smallburgh abolished its rent rebate scheme.[49] Compulsory charges were levied on anyone lodging with council tenants. This 25% levy signified that fiscal strain was a general problem, with councils like Biggleswade also introducing a flat-rate lodger charge.[50] Councils were seeing demand for improved services increase, with minutes revealing reluctance to spend beyond legal necessities. For instance, after meeting parish councillors in June 1948, Hatfield decided that due '… to the new and very high burden provided by the 1946 legislation' it would cease contributing additional rate funds to housing.[51] Although Treasury subsidies were increased in 1948,[52] rate contributions were often blamed for pushing districts into the red; as with Walsingham, which expected HRA deficits of £629 in 1953 rising to £2350 by 1955.[53] By 1955, even Smallburgh had a deficit of £3054.[54] Higher rents resulted. Smallburgh started raising them before building commenced in the mid-1940s but in the early-1950s others, like Erpingham, followed, while in 1955 Biggleswade started requiring council estates to be self-funded.[55] Such actions signalled less concern over rent non-affordability for farm-workers. Whitehall contributed to weakening the potency of this consideration. On the one hand, this was because farm-worker wages had risen, with Ministry claims of near parity with

---

[47] NNN 14 June 1957, p.9.

[48] By the late-1950s, Smallburgh was making a surplus on its HRA again (NRO DC22/2/27 SmRDCM 18 February 1958, p.565). Losses on 1963 bungalows were covered by HRA surpluses (NNN 7 June 1963, p.3) and, when rate contributions seemed inevitable, Smallburgh decided not to allow them (NRO DC22/2/29 SmRDCM 25 June 1968, p.596).

[49] NRO DC22/2/48 SmRDCHCM 23 November 1948, p.3656.

[50] NNN 7 July 1950, p.1; NBC&BR 8 November 1949, p.4. The Biggleswade levy was short-lived, being rescinded in 1950 (BRO RDBwM1/21 BiRDCM 25 January 1950, p.28), then reintroduced in 1953 (BRO RDBwM1/24 BiRDCM 18 March 1953, p.31). The Biggleswade lodger levy raised £900, equivalent to 2d on all rents for the first half-year of 1954 (NBC&BR 15 June 1954, p.2).

[51] HRO CP35/6/2 'Essendon Parish Council Correspondence on Housing and Rating'.

[52] TNA HLG101/582 'Agricultural Housing Subsidies and Improvement Grants. Note for Discussion Between Ministers on 17 January 1952'; 'Suggested Amendments', 12 January 1952; TNA MAF255/112 'Agricultural Housing Subsidies and Improvement Grants. Note for Discussion Between Ministers on 17 January 1952'.

[53] D&FT 6 March 1953, p.5; 28 January 1955, p.1.

[54] NorfChron 4 November 1955, p.1.

[55] NRO DC22/2/47 SmRDCHCM 6 February 1945, p.2226; NRO DC13/5/24 ERDCM 15 September 1952, para.79; WR&WSR 11 October 1955, p.7. Braughing also looked to make estates self-funding, reporting in 1962 that, other than its post-1945 houses, they were 'self-supporting' (HRO RDC3/1/12 BrRDCFCM 16 January 1962, p.5389).

non-farm levels,[56] which provoked asking if extra subsidies were justified.[57] On the other hand, it was claimed falling farm-worker numbers reduced the need for council-building.[58] As a substantial literature shows, the former of these tendencies was short-lived (Newby 1977; Bowers and Cheshire 1983), while analysts continued to find low-quality farm-worker homes decades later (Giles and Cowie 1960; Fletcher 1969; Gasson 1975).

On a broader canvass, these currents captured a groundswell of disquiet in Whitehall over housing costs. In part, the alarm had ideological impetus, for, after the 1951 Election, there was tension in the ruling Conservatives between supporters of a 'property owning democracy' campaign and those wanting election pledges met first.[59] Adding friction, housing took resources wanted for national economic recovery,[60] anticipating analytical critiques of later decades (e.g. Barnett 1995, 2001). This tension provided a backcloth to what became the 1956 Housing Subsidies Act, which reduced and then eliminated subsidies for general needs housing, with consequent rent rises of 5.4% a year in real terms from 1955–1956 to 1960–1961 (Murie et al. 1976, p.97; Holmans 1987, p.331). This shift reignited 1930s policy emphases, with subsidies concentrated on slum clearance (plus urban overspill), with home ownership preferred (rhetorically even over private rental). Protests from councils quickly arose, with widespread reductions in building following and even, as in Maldon in Essex, the abolition of council housing committees.[61] The arguments to justify the change are instructive. Leaving aside ideological commitment to the private sector, support was grounded in the technicalities of housing budgets. As concluded at a meeting of Treasury and MHLG officials:

> … big local authorities now have huge blocks of council housing, mostly built with generous subsidies related to low notional rents. Now that they are beginning to get their rents moving upwards they will be in a position to make very large surpluses on their Housing Revenue Accounts. The need for subsidy has to be looked at not in relation to present costs and present rents of a new building, but in relation to the prospects of the Housing Revenue Accounts - on which already a lot of authorities are showing sizeable surpluses. As private

---

[56] TNA HLG101/582 'Draft Paper from John Wrigley to J.E. Beddoe', 17 June 1949; TNA MAF255/112 'Agricultural Housing Subsidies and Improvement Grants. Note for Discussion Between Ministers on 17 January 1952'; TNA MAF255/112 AWB4752 'Agricultural Wages Board. Memorandum by MAF', undated c1952.

[57] TNA MAF255/112 'Special Subsidy for Rural Houses', undated c1952.

[58] For example, TNA MAF234/18 'NFU Memo on Rural Housing', 7 February 1952, p.2.

[59] TNA T229/475 C(52)207 and C(52)216 'A Property Owning Democracy', 30 June 1952; TNA T229/476 C(52)241 'Housing 1953', 16 July 1952; Letter from J.C. Wrigley, MHLG, to F.F. Turnbull, The Treasury, 25 August 1952; TNA T227/805 Memo from E.N. Plowden to Chancellor of the Exchequer, 23 October 1952; TNA HLG101/433 Letter to the PM from R.A.B., 28 May 1953.

[60] TNA CAB129/48 C(51)45 'Civil Investment in 1952', 17 December 1951; TNA HLG101/505 GEN.411/3 'Investment in 1953', 28 June 1952.

[61] TNA HLG101/748 'Press Cuttings'. *Daily Telegraph* 26 November 1956.

rents become unfrozen, clearing the way for further increases in rents of council houses, this becomes tremendously important.[62]

Thus, Institute of Municipal Treasurers and Accountants' 1952–1953 figures showed that 33.7% of cities, 34.8% of Non-County Boroughs, 48.4% of UDCs and 43.1% of RDCs had increased HRA surpluses.[63] The point, made a decade later, was that councils benefited if they had large building programmes in the late-1920s and 1930s when construction costs and loan charges were low.[64] Councils that responded late to housing inadequacies faced greater costs even with more national subsidies. Early builders could charge rents well above the day-to-day running costs for dwellings, while rents for new homes did not meet costs.[65] Although councils pooled Treasury and rate subsidies across Housing Acts after 1935,[66] ministers like Harold Macmillan complained of 'extraordinary variations' in rent '… between houses of exactly the same type, the same rateable value, the same amenities, and in the same street; variations from one tenant paying 17/6d down to another paying 7/6d'.[67] Added to which, there was growing resentment over reports of wealthy council tenants. As Lord Balfour expressed it in 1951: '… there must be thousands of quite well-off families who are being educated to believe that they have a right to decent housing accommodation, largely at the public expense or at the expense of a private-owner, at a weekly cost to themselves of less than they spend on cigarettes'.[68] This sentiment was alive on council floors, as in Braughing, where the claim was made '… that some of the Council's tenants were better off financially that many ratepayers', for '… owners lived in poorer circumstances in private accommodation than many of the Council's tenants'.[69]

In response, the 1956 Housing Subsidies Act enabled the equalisation of rents and associate charges, sought to bring private and public rents closer, and ended requiring rate fund contributions to the HRA. Rural councils often used these HRA freedoms to water down rate commitments. In the three counties investigated, early action came from urban districts, with Sandy ending rate contributions and raising rents in 1956, although Biggleswade Town retained rate inputs at £4390.[70] Newport Pagnell

---

[62] TNA T227/808 'Housing Memo from R.W.B.C. to Edward Bridges', 25 August 1955.

[63] TNA HLG101/739 'The Housing (Review of Contributions) Order, 1954', undated c1954–55. Computed surpluses did include statutory council and Treasury contributions.

[64] For example, TNA HLG118/293 'Housing Finance. Meeting in Minister's Room on 6th May 1965'.

[65] As one example, Walsingham's Chief Financial Officer reported the 760 council homes built from 1945–1964 had weekly rents of £1/6/11d on average but the all-inclusive cost was £1/18/11d. In total, 8/9d was received in national subsidies which left the Council with 3/3d a week to find for each home (NRO DC19/6/69 WRDCHCM 7 December 1964, p.203).

[66] TNA HLG37/42 'Index 1936' p.7.

[67] HCH 4 November 1953, Vol.520, col.180.

[68] TNA T227/1088 Letter from Lord Balfour of Burleigh, Lloyds Bank, to Hugh Gaitskell, Chancellor of the Exchequer, 11 May 1951.

[69] HRO RDC3/1/9 BrRDCFCM 22 January 1959, p.4152.

[70] BRO UDSM1/4 SaUDCM 31 January 1956, p.456; *BC&BG* 9 March 1956, p.1.

RDC, by contrast, looked for a HRA surplus of £10,781 in 1956–1957, while Smallburgh councillors congratulated themselves on only having raised rents by 40% (rather than a proposed 75%) given an expected HRA surplus.[71] Elsewhere revenue rose at the margins. Thus, Erpingham introduced levies on all lodgers of 5/- a week for those aged over 18, including tenants' daughters or sons aged over 21, while Smallburgh adjusted lodger 'taxes' to a sliding scale of 1/- a week if wages were near £1 to 9/- for those earning over £4.[72] There were also impacts through terminating council-building or restricting it to slum clearance. Mitford and Launditch RDC justified this by noting that even with a rent of 17/6d a week the Council had to find £38/12/5d per house per year for slum replacement compared with £60 for general needs housing.[73] Here, we see parallels with themes in Chap. 2, in the interaction of acknowledging slums and covering the expense of acting on them.

For this chapter, whether rural councils prioritised low taxes is central. We have already seen that housing made a minor impression on rural budgets until after the Second World War, when compulsory rate fund contributions rose substantially as the nation committed to building more homes. The crunch came with the 1956 Housing Subsidies Act, after which councils received no Treasury subsidy for general needs housing. Even for completions, which lagged behind intentions given the months it took to finish projects, the Act quickly depressed building (Table 5.3). By 1966, the rural portion of new-build was only 14%, well below its population share.[74] This fall came alongside a belief in Whitehall that 16% of all slums were in rural districts.[75] Indeed, for 1955–1966, rural districts accounted for 16% of national slum removals.[76] When subsidies were available, rural districts performed on par, when they were not they under-performed. It merits recalling the early-1930s, the previous occasion when a slimming of focus was enforced. Then, as in the 1950s, the rural stake in the national house-building programme fell (Table 5.4). But the early-1930s was a time of global economic stress following the Great Crash of 1929 (Stevenson and Cook 1977), when the government pressed for lower public spending (Committee on National Expenditure 1931; MoH 1932b). Reflecting the mood of that time, although perhaps with close votes, 1930s motions to condemn cuts in Treasury subsidies were rejected at Walsingham, Smallburgh, Buntingford and Ampthill.[77] Embedded within these responses was support for private sector

---

[71] *WR&WSR* 13 March 1956, p.1; *NNN* 7 September 1956, p.1.

[72] *NorfChron* 16 September 1955, p.1; *NNN* 27 January 1956, p.5.

[73] *D&FT* 15 February 1957, p.1.

[74] TNA HLG118/767 'RDCs New Houses in 1966. Appendix II', 27 September 1967.

[75] TNA HLG101/748 'Notes for Parliamentary Secretary on Slum Clearance, Prepared for the Institute of Housing's 25th Annual Conference at Scarborough, undated c1956–57'.

[76] TNA HLG118/767 'House Building. RDCs New Houses in 1966. Appendix I', 27 September 1967. This represented a higher response than for 1930–1945, when rural districts accounted for 10.9% of replacement homes under the slum clearance programme; viz. 34,495 out of the England and Wales total of 315,258 (TNA HLG40/56 'Memo to Mr. Ryan', 22 March 1947).

[77] NRO DC19/6/20 WRDCM 21 December 1932, p.20; NRO DC22/2/46 SmRDCHCM 7 February 1933, p.22; 4 April 1933, p.39; 6 March 1934, pp.140–41; HRO RDC4/1/9 BuRDCM 22 February 1934, p.61; *W&DR* 3 March 1934, p.9.

Table 5.3 Council dwellings built in England and Wales, with percentages for rural districts, 1948–1959

Year	1948	1949	1950	1951	1952	1953	1954	1955	1956	1957	1958	1959
# built	170,823	141,766	139,356	141,587	165,637	202,891	199,642	162,525	139,977	137,584	113,146	99,456
% RDC	19.1	21.3	23.1	14.4	20.6	21.6	22.4	20.2	19.4	18.2	16.1	14.7

Source: TNA MAF186/86 'Brief by R.J.E. Taylor for the Parliamentary Secretary: Appendix IV', 14 September 1960
Note: The source does not specify if the data were for England or for England and Wales, but the numbers match those of Mitchell and Jones (1971, p.118) for England and Wales

Table 5.4 Council dwellings built in England and Wales, with percentages for rural districts, 1919–1939

Year	1919– 1926	1926– 1928	1928– 1930	1930– 1932	1932– 1934	1934– 1936	1936– 1938	1938– 1939
# built	281,899	121,079	117,518	120,090	108,439	80,631	148,537	100,967
% RDC	17.0	14.1	10.2	12.9	11.6	7.8	12.6	16.2

Source: Computed from HCH 15 December 1926, Vol.200, col.2957W-58W; HCH 17 February 1928, Vol.213, col.1095W-96W; MoH (1930, p.247); MoH (1932a, p.280); MoH (1934, p.302); MoH (1936, p.251), MoH (1938a, p.257); MoH (1939a, p.251)

Note: Figures for 1926, 1928 and 1930 were from reports listing the number of completions since 1919, so 1928 and 1930 values were taken as differences in cumulative totals. These 1920s numbers do not match fiscal years, as the 1926 value, though not stated in *Hansard*, appears to be from 1919 to 1 December 1926, whereas both 1928 and 1930 figures were from 1919 to 1 February. As the fiscal year was from April to March, this means 1928–1930 numbers lack February and March completions. No months were missing for 1919–1928, nor after 1930. As was the norm at this time, public utility society numbers were excluded from the public sector total. The value for 1934–1936 requires comment, as this covers 1934–1935 when many RDCs were reorganised under the 1929 Local Government Act, which resulted in many losing territory to other local authorities. Indicating the importance of urban encroachment into rural districts at the time, MoH (1935, p.295) reports that over 1934–1935 RDC dwelling numbers erected under the 1924 Act fell by 485 (viz. net losses due to territorial losses). Slum clearance replacements under the 1930 Act rose by 837 in that year, adding 352 in total to the RDC stock. This compared with gains of 6473 for 1933–1934 and 8801 for 1935–1936. From figures available, it was not possible to ascertain how many council-owned homes were lost in 1934–1935 from reorganisation as only net figures were available but it was clear many general needs homes (1924 Act) and some slum rehousing units (1930 Act) went to urban districts, so the 1934–1936 RDC value in this table will be lower than the sum of new-build commissioned by RDCs

solutions, as with a 1934 debate at Smallburgh.[78] Even so, both rural and urban councils pressed for a return of subsidised general needs building, with support for such motions increasing as the decade progressed. This was especially so amongst Norfolk councils, where the non-affordability of no-subsidy rents saw even Smallburgh reverse its unwillingness to support subsidy rises.[79] Critically, while visions of the 1930s as an era of fiscal restraint might be over-blown, given its detrimental effects by-passed much of southern England (Stevenson and Cook 1977; Ward 1988), places like Norfolk were economically depressed at the time. By

---

[78] *NM&PWJ* 17 March 1934, p.6.

[79] As for Wayland RDC (*T&WT* 18 February 1933, p.4), Erpingham (*H&FP* 3 March 1933, p.4), Hadham (*H&EO* 3 March 1934, p.5), the Norfolk Housing Conference (*NM&PWJ* 31 March 1934, p.9), Depwade RDC (*Diss Express* 24 May 1935, p.9), St Faith's and Aylsham RDC (*T&WT* 22 June 1935, p.9), Blofield and Flegg RDC (*T&WT* 22 February 1936, p.13), then Smallburgh (NRO DC22/2/47 SmRDCHCM 31 March 1936, item 172). In some cases, responses to formal resolutions were not found, but, as for Biggleswade and Walsingham, appeals were made to the Ministry for general needs subsidies (BRO RDBwM1/12 BiRDCM 23 September 1936, p.357; *EDP* 9 May 1935, p.5). Walsingham reversed its unwillingness to call for a return of subsidies and passed its own resolution for a return, which other councils were asked to support (e.g. *T&WT* 22 June 1935, p.9).

contrast, in the 1950s, according to Harold Macmillan, Britain had 'never had it so good' (Sandbrook 2005; Hennessy 2006). Both were times when national support for housing contracted but in different economic circumstances. This offers a context for delayed opposition to cuts amongst 1950s rural councils, as many felt that some of their tenants could afford higher rents. But others could not. For them, to meet legal obligations to respond to housing needs, councils required national subsidies for new-build.

Real concern existed over rent affordability (Chap. 4). There were councils that avoided elements, even major parts, of required rate commitments to housing. Most took responsibilities seriously when faced with weak private sector activity. An aversion to higher property taxes existed but its impact can be over-played. Note the conclusion of the Rural Housing Sub-Committee:

> There remains a small number of Rural District Councils whose resources seem to us to be so inadequate for the proper discharge of their responsibilities that we do not think it feasible or desirable to attempt to bridge the gap with yet larger Exchequer subsidies. These districts are often very small and we feel that the right solution is that they should be amalgamated ... (MoH 1944a, p.15)

Despite their generally small size, few rural councils were so handicapped this placed major restrictions on their actions.[80] Otherwise, capacity was constrained but not absent. Hence, as in urban centres, inaction came from lack of demand (due to high rents), a national disinclination to support local initiatives, insufficient urgency[81] or local political unwillingness. One indication the last of these was not as pervasive as rural commentators can imply was the readiness of councils to subsidise rents for the elderly. An early example was Smallburgh's 1941 rent increases, which were approved subject to them not applying to widows and pensioners.[82] Committing rate funds to help the elderly was common. Thus, in 1957 Hatfield pledged rates cover for differences between actual rentals on old people's homes and the 'normal' rent for such properties. This was irrespective of a HRA deficit or surplus from 1960, resulting in a transfer of £12,000 into the HRA by 1969.[83]

---

[80] This point was made more than a decade earlier with the observation: 'There is no doubt that there are some rural district councils in most counties and several urban district councils in the coalfields and elsewhere whose rate resources are so strained that they are unable, without further assistance, to make the housing provision which is needed in their areas' (TNA CAB24/221 CP127(31) 'Rural Housing', 15 May 1931).

[81] In Walsingham, for example, Councillor Carter complained that not providing replacement houses for unfit dwellings was '... not so much the fault of the Government as it was that of the Rural District Councils in not taking advantage of the subsidies when they were in existence' (NM&PWJ 11 May 1935, p.7). This point was repeated by Smallburgh's the Medical Officer of Health: '... there are many Councils who wish now that they had taken advantage of the generous terms offered under the various Acts, and who now find that they have a serious shortage of working-class houses' (EDP 6 June 1935, p.7).

[82] NRO DC22/2/47 SmRDCHCM 15 July 1941.

[83] HRO RDC7/1/23 HtRDCM 30 April 1957, p.775; HRO RDC7/1/25 HtRDCM 18 March 1959, p.656; HRO RDC7/1/29 HtRDCM 5 December 1961, p.362; HRO RDC7/1/46 HtRDCJMHF 11 November 1969, p.610.

Elsewhere, voluntary contributions were thinner but often regular. In Braughing, as early as 1950, a statutory rates obligation of £1666/10/8d into the HRA was topped-up with an additional £984/5/11d.[84] At this time, Walsingham's rent rebate scheme cost the Council £567 compared with a rates input to the HRA of £167/12/7½d.[85] After 1956, when councils had no obligation to subsidise the HRA, they continued to do so, with 1959–1960 figures of £1270 for Erpingham and £3385 for Walsingham, both of which had relatively few council houses compared with Biggleswade (Table 5.2), which had a £7500 subsidy.[86] All these numbers were small on a per dwelling basis, working out at around £1 each in Erpingham or closer to £3/10/0d for Biggleswade and Walsingham. But not every household received them; rent alleviation was targeted. This matched national policy emphases, which encouraged full rents for those who could afford them.

This commitment to housing the elderly is by way of example. The real point is that councils were conscious they had tenants who could afford higher rents and rate subsidised those who could not. As the Chair of Flegg RDC put it in 1925, when noting ratepayers would be charged £4/10/0d per dwelling per year for new council homes: 'Even if the houses did cost them something they were justified in going on to meet the housing needs of the district'.[87] The general impression from council documents was not of a single-minded drive to keep rates down, but acceptance of a 'social' purpose in council action. For sure, opponents of rent subsidies commonly declared that existing rents were affordable, with the sentiment that those who could pay should do so extending to a reluctance to subsidise private house-building[88] or home improvements.[89] There was an obvious preference, certainly more so after 1945 than before, for targeting support (viz. on poorer residents). This nuanced appreciation distinguished councils from exaggerated attacks by national politicians on council tenants as the feather-bedded wealthy (Jarvis 1996; Weiler 2000; Jacobs et al. 2003; Davies 2013). Inter-war few of the lowest waged secured council dwellings. Failure to meet housing shortages in the 1920s and 1930s created such a backlog that policy was drawn to favour the most needy in the late-1940s and

---

[84] HRO RDC3/2/5 BrRDCFCM 24 January 1950, p.1545.

[85] NRO DC19/6/65 WRDCHCM 29 August 1951, p.24.

[86] *Norfolk News* 1 January 1960, p.1; *D&FT* 8 July 1960, p.1; BRO RDBwM1/31 BiRDCHECM 14 October 1959, p.177.

[87] *Yarmouth Mercury, Gorleston Herald and East Norfolk Advertiser* 18 April 1925, p.3.

[88] For instance, HRO RDC6/1/5 HaRDCM 6 December 1925, p.294; or for Biggleswade *BC&BG* 15 August 1958, p.11.

[89] For example, at Erpingham (*NWP&ENS* 16 September 1932, p.4), Peninstone UDC (TNA HLG118/576 Memo L. Whitaker to Mr. Cowley, Mr. Blackshaw and Mr. Niven 'Discretionary Grants', 3 July 1962), Sawbridgeworth (TNA HLG118/576 'Memo from H.A.M. Cruickshank to Miss Williams, 6 July 1962), or more generally (TNA HLG37/43 'Housing (Rural Workers) Acts', undated c1936, p.3; 'Investigation by General Inspectors 1934', undated c1936, pp.11–12).

early-1950s.[90] This era contrasted with the 1930s (e.g. MoH 1932b, p.65; MoH 1935, p.156) and the late-1950s and early-1960s (MHLG 1961, p.3), as the aim was to provide all tenants with quality homes rather than erecting inferior dwellings the low-paid might afford. This residual role for the public sector sought to appease middle-class antagonism towards council housing. Despite value shifts in war-time, it did not take many peace-time years before egalitarian sentiments lost momentum. Reports from the 1940s into the 1950s signified a middle-class sense of deprivation brought on by austerity (Kynaston 2007, pp.260–62).[91] Commentaries note how the middle-classes viewed the inter-war years with nostalgia, as a time of domestic servants, creature comforts, elegant, available private housing and greater shopping opportunities. These feelings were accompanied by mournful newspaper reports on the plight of the middle-classes (Morgan 1990, p.82). As Saville (1993, p.xxxi) explained:

> It has never been difficult to bring out the anti-trade union prejudices of the British middle-classes, because these are built into their traditional ways of thinking, and the continued reiteration by the political Right of the wildest and most absurd stories of the power of 'our new masters' found an easy and vigorous response. At the centre of this propaganda was the widespread conviction that egalitarianism was being pushed forward at the expense of the middle ranks of society.

That this was a return to the past was captured in Seaman's (1966, p.177) observation that: 'Rarely have wealthy people pleaded poverty with such monotonous and unjustifiable regularity as the well-to-do classes in England between the wars' (also James 2006, p.451). With generally low district wages and a middle-class council with petit bourgeois tones, most RDCs not surprisingly favoured low tax regimes; questioning subsidising council tenants. That these sentiments were not innately rural was evinced in similar views in Labour-controlled cities, as in 1960s Islington (Butterworth 1966) and Liverpool (Baxter 1972). For sure, some RDCs, in counties like Durham, were committed politically to council-building (e.g. Ryder 1984), while some in leafier surrounds subsidised private house-building with enthusiasm (Wycombe RDC 1952; Eley 1973). That political disposition alone was not predictive of this divide was apparent in a lack of discernible differences in redistributive policy commitments in 1945–1974 Conservative and Labour authorities, except for dwelling completions (Hoggart 1987). Even then, all 1950s and 1960s governments favoured council-building in areas that happened to be Labour-controlled (Chap. 6).

---

[90] For Bevan: 'The wrong sort of people ... are those who get a house merely because they can afford to buy it ... Local authorities have been instructed ... in selecting the tenants for the houses, they should have no regard whatsoever to the social class from which the applicant comes, but that the applicant should be judged solely on the ground of his need for a house' (HCH 21 October 1946, Vol.427, col.1341).

[91] As Morgan (1984, pp.326–27) expressed it: 'The general picture of the mood after 1945, then, is of a social structure still sharply divided, and under pressure from middle-class aspirations and from a culture still traditional in values. There was a veering away from the classless ethos that the wartime years had suggested'. For Kynaston (2007, p.174): '... society at large remained riddled by petty snobbery and infinite gradations of class'.

Political party control is short-hand for political leader orientations. That it is an imprecise predictor of action is well-known. This was evinced in fluctuating political persuasions within the same party over time; as in the lethargy of Liverpool in the 1960s compared with its assertiveness in the 1980s (Baxter 1972; Parkinson 1985). Within this pattern, differences might have less to do with political parties than with divergent leadership styles. Too often it has been assumed leaders have been dynamic, forceful characters; akin to Birmingham's Harry Watton, who claimed '… I made the decisions and I sought the authority afterwards' (Sutcliffe 1976, p.15), or Newcastle-upon-Tyne's T. Dan Smith, whose assessment of his fellow councillors was: 'If 95% of them never went near the council chamber it would make no difference' (Green 1981, p.65). Such forceful characters were not the norm. As Norton (1978) noted, there could be a cyclical element in styles, with 'monarchic' and 'diffuse' approaches alternating. Moreover, for rural councils, which saw few political party councillor affiliations before 1974 (Grant 1977), 'controls' over councillors were weak. Councils were more akin to 'gentleman's clubs' than ideological battlegrounds, with professional officers complaining elected members were reluctant to go home (e.g. Harrison and Norton 1967; Dyer 1978). Evidence finds councillors entering local politics to contribute to the community, not due to political conviction. As Blondel and Hall (1967, p.331) concluded for Colchester and Maldon:

> Councillors are not in political life locally in order to put their personal mark on the present and future development of the town. They are modest – both in their ambitions and their capabilities. Though they are not at all unwilling to spare their time and efforts, it is more in order to achieve political status than to modify policies crucially important to the community.[92]

With councillors having different personality and interests, the ethos of councils varied (Corina 1974; Grant 1977). This did not mean leadership was unimportant. It was not a peculiarity of local social structures but charismatic local leaders that led to inter-war communist control of rural and small town councils (Macintyre 1980). Less politically charged in temperament, Read (2003, p.75) reported on how Arthur Letts, one of the first Henley RDC councillors not from a privileged background, pushed through additions of 214 council and 267 private dwellings as Chair of the Housing Committee, despite vociferous objections from other councillors. In the investigated rural councils, no such dynamism was evident. Even if the leader of the council was clearly respected, they did not appear to carry council policies in the face of opposition. Within newspaper reports, a sense of focused coverage came across for only one councillor, a Dr. Campbell of Sandy, whose distinction was largely in regular complaints about 'waste' and the non-affordability of decisions, alongside grumbles other councillors did not support him.[93] Overall, the impression

---

[92] Even for a city like Birmingham, Newton (1976, p.241) concluded that '… the mood of the council membership is generally cautious, conservative and suspicious of change of any kind'.

[93] For example, *NBC&SN&DN* 3 June 1927, p.7; *NBC* 4 January 1929, p.2; 31 January 1930, p.7; 4 July 1930, pp.6–7; 2 January 1931, p.7; 1 July 1932, p.6; 2 September 1932, p.7; 3 March 1933, p.6; 4 August 1933, p.3.

was of little dissension over housing. Disagreements existed but councils were not riven by them.

5.1.2   Council Professional Officers

In these circumstances, it might be expected professional officers had considerable latitude over policy, especially when senior officers stayed with the same council for long periods.[94] As one council Clerk reported to the Maud Committee on local government management: 'I can come to no other conclusion but that, in the main, policy springs from the official side', although this applied unevenly across policy fields (Harrison and Norton 1967, p.196, pp.368–69). Much evidence supports this view. Specific examples include the central role of the Clerk in Swindon's adoption of London overspill (Harloe 1975). Offering a different perspective on officer roles, Lee (1963) found councillor advancement on Cheshire County Council was determined by receptiveness to administrator advice and demonstrating a county rather than a ward-based perspective. Such insights are only suggestive, as officer roles varied with council size and complexity,[95] party control,[96] and the professionalisation of the bureaucracy. On the last of these, for Alderson (1962, p.104): 'That local authorities became more autonomous [from Whitehall] during the 1950s was due less to the relaxation of the housing drive than to the growing number of surveyors, architects, and accountants on local authorities' staffs'; a telling point, given many rural councils felt they were unable to afford architects (Layton 1961). Viewed differently, for the MHLG, housing proposals were more likely approved if prepared by qualified people.[97] In this context, Whitehall's view of rural administration was often dismissive, as a Downing Street memo revealed in 1931:

> In rural areas there was often a lack of leadership; rural administrators were alarmed by the procedure necessary to carry through small schemes and their officials were often incapable of proper supervision. It was for these reasons as well as owing to inertia that there had been little housing in the country areas.[98]

---

[94] To offer a few examples, the Biggleswade Housing Manager retired in 1947 after joining the Council in 1912 (*NBC&BR* 29 April 1947, p.1), Erpingham lost its Clerk in 1955 after 41 years' service (*NorfChron* 18 March 1955, p.9) and its Surveyor in 1963 after 32 years (*NNN* 28 June 1963, p.1).

[95] Hartley (1980), for instance, found that under a political regime that encouraged professional officers to take initiatives, housing in Leeds produced at least four housing policies, each supported by a departmental head (the Architect, the Health Inspector, the Housing Manager and the Medical Officer of Health).

[96] Adamson (1974) is one of many to conclude Conservative politicians have been more willing to delegate authority over council decisions to officers than their Labour counterparts.

[97] TNA HLG31/24 'Discussions with Local Authorities on Layouts, Tenders, etc. Note on a Meeting on 1 January 1957'.

[98] TNA HLG29/180 'Downing Street Conference Notes on Rural Housing', 10 February 1931, p.4.

On leadership and professionalism grounds, it seems, rural councils fell on the wrong side of whatever divide existed between more or less autonomy.

This expectation was put to Cabinet in the run-up to the 1919 Act: 'Many if not most Rural District Councils have not amongst their members or their salaried staff the business experience or capacity to carry out a large scheme. To entrust the work to these Councils will lead to certain failure'.[99] The Minister of Health made the same point more than a decade later, observing that many RDCs '… have not the resources, the technical knowledge, the skill, or the experience to deal with the [housing] problem'.[100] Signifying the magnitude of deficits, in 1938 only 42 of 416 respondent RDCs employed a housing manager; and they largely collected rents and organised repairs, but offered little welfare support (MoH 1938b, p.15, p.17). Hardly surprisingly, Ministry reports identified insufficient professional capacity, effectiveness and time availability for RDC staff to perform housing functions (MoH 1944a, p.26). Offering a different perspective, although when fighting amalgamation of rural councils into urban-centred authorities, the RDCA (1966, p.11), rather disingenuously, held that: 'Many of the duties which fall to local authorities are so close to other statutory duties discharged by a [rural] district council that no great staffing difficulty exists'. Thirty years earlier, when RDCs were similarly small in scale and limited in resources, Lewis Silkin, the Minister of Town and Country Planning from 1945–1950, was equally convinced that it was '… quite hopeless to expect them to carry out housing on an extensive scale when they cannot possibly afford to employ the necessary staff to carry it out'.[101] Note the emphasis on an inability to afford, not an unwillingness to appoint.

The weight of records for the investigated rural districts comes down more on Silkin's side than the RDCA's. Two early gauges of sparse staffing came in 1924. One was for Cromer, where the house-building programme went into abeyance when the Town Clerk died. The other was Erpingham's decision to restrict its building programme to 20 dwellings because an architect was necessary for more.[102] Cost limited the appointment of housing specialists, as in Walsingham.[103] Often districts shared appointees, as with the Clerk of Cromer and Erpingham,[104] with this practice common for medical officers of health and architects. For example, the Biggleswades, RDC and UDC, shared a medical officer from before the First World War until the 1960s. Even Hatfield, with its relatively large housing programme (Table 5.2), had

---

[99] TNA CAB24/72 GT6556 'Housing Scheme. Suggestions by Mr. Chamberlain', 25 December 1918, p.266.

[100] HCH 7 July 1931, Vol.254, col.2000.

[101] HCH 8 June 1937, Vol.324, col.1657.

[102] TNA HLG48/73 Letter to the MoH Secretary, 22 May 1924; NRO DC13/5/82 ERDCHCM 28 October 1924.

[103] NRO DC19/6/11 WRDCM 23 January 1924, p.99.

[104] FakPost 18 March 1927, p.3. In 1948 Norfolk County Council pushed for full-time medical officers of health in every RDC, which Blofield and Flegg and Smallburgh resisted (T&WT 17 April 1948, p.5).

no full-time architect until after 1945.[105] The cost of appointments troubled councils, as with Blofield and Flegg RDC's 1937 decision not to share a full-time medical officer of health with two other RDCs.[106] Lack of effective support did not go unnoticed in Whitehall, as seen in Ministry discussions with Warwickshire's Southam RDC: '... as the result of which the Council was pressed, because [dwelling] layouts they had submitted were of poor quality, to employ an architect in preference to making use of the services of their Sanitary Inspector'.[107] That fiscal constraint played a part in such scenarios was suggested when Biggleswade's Clerk of Works left for double-pay, while Ampthill's Clerk had no travel expenses at all to supervise Council work in a dispersed district.[108] Widespread geographically and temporally were complaints that officers had such heavy workloads they were unable to meet statutory obligations.[109] Accompanying, and partly accounting for such reports, were recruitment difficulties, with no applications for posts, ongoing efforts to fill posts and delays to projects due to a lack of required skills.[110] Staff shortfalls frequently limited task completions.[111]

To round-off this point note that deficiencies were not restricted to council staff. Also significant was unreliability amongst private contractors, on whom rural councils depended for most housing work. Despite recruitment problems, this prompted

---

[105] HRO RDC7/1/14 HtRDCM 12 May 1949, p.2.

[106] *YarmInd* 20 February 1937, p.13.

[107] TNA HLG31/24 'Discussions with Local Authorities on Layouts, Tenders, Etc. Note on Meeting', 1 January 1957. Comparable messages can be found in TNA HLG47/11 'Memo to Arthur Lowry', 2 March 1933; TNA HLG52/759 'Minute Sheet to Mr. Rucker', 7 May 1935; MoH (1944a).

[108] *BC&BG* 6 January 1922, p.3; *WR&WSR* 7 September 1943, p.1.

[109] A flavour is found in early reports (e.g. HRO RDC4/1/8 BuRDCM 23 March 1933, p.480; or, for Walsingham, *H&FP* 1 September 1933, p.8). The lead-up to and immediate years after 1945 were particularly difficult (HRO RDC7/9/1 HtRDCM 11 July 1944; HRO RDC3/1/2 BrRDCM 25 July 1944; MoH 1944c, pp.2–3; *WR&WSR* 24 April 1945, p.1; TNA 40/50 'Memo for House of Commons Agricultural and Food Group Meeting', 28 November (no year c1945)). Evidence of strains persisted until the eventual abolition of RDCs, as for Braughing (HRO RDC3/1/17 BrRDCFGPCM 19 December 1967; HRO RDC3/1/22 BrRDCFGPCM 1 August 1972, pp.8788–89).

[110] For instance, for Braughing (HRO RDC3/2/3 BrRDCPHHCM 19 July 1945, p.776; HRO RDC3/1/15 BrRDCECM 14 January 1965, p.6415), for Erpingham (*NM&PWJ* 15 February 1947, p.6), for Biggleswade (*NBC&BR* 8 August 1950, p.4), and for Smallburgh (NRO DC22/2/29 SmRDCM 19 October 1965, p.347). Even when appointments were made, they were not always filled, as with Reginald Nowell of Blaby RDC, who turned down the post of Smallburgh Clerk owing to housing difficulties in the Norfolk district (*Leicester Daily Mercury* 22 November 1950, p.5).

[111] As recorded for the inter-war era for Biggleswade (BRO RDBwM1/8 30 March 1921, p.97), Blofield RDC (*NWP&ENS* 1 January 1926, p.1), Hatfield (HRO RDC7/1/10 HtRDCM 11 October 1928, p.149), Walsingham (*EDP* 24 October 1935, p.1) and Braughing (*H&EO* 6 February 1937, p.10) and after 1945 for Braughing (*H&EO* 15 September 1945, p.3), Ampthill (*WR&WSR* 16 October 1945, p.1; 9 April 1946, p.1) and Biggleswade Town (*BC&BG* 17 September 1965, p.17).

some councils to appoint their own housing technicians (viz. direct labour units). In some cases these appointments were for smaller jobs, like maintenance and repair, as with Hatfield engaging painters in 1946 (although they were soon redirected to other work by the Ministry of Labour).[112] Ampthill and Biggleswade sought to appoint carpenters and joiners a few years later, owing to the high cost of small repairs and difficulties getting work done; although Biggleswade's investigation of direct labour for house-building was put on hold given '… considerable expenditure would be involved in providing plant, materials and additional accommodation and clerical staff if this method was adopted'.[113] Surveying council minutes produced no discussions on direct labour in Erpingham or Smallburgh, but in Walsingham dissatisfaction with private providers led to its consideration over many years, and houses were built by direct labour in Norfolk RDCs like St Faith's and Aylsham.[114] The debate over direct labour was heated at times, with opposition and support often associated with ideological stances. Support on Left-leaning city councils has often been reported (e.g. Finnigan 1984, p.115), suggesting pro-private sector rural councils would shun the possibility. Yet even 'traditional' rural councils were drawn to direct labour. In general, the prompt was not cost but reliability, alongside a desire to improve accommodation prospects.[115]

---

[112] HRO CP35/6/2 'Essendon Parish Council Correspondence on Housing and Rating'. Letter to Mr. S.G. Gee, 17 July 1946.

[113] BRO RDAM2/22 ARDCHCM 17 May 1951; BRO RDBwM1/23 BiRDCM 11 June 1952, p.96; 9 July 1952, p.122. The same conclusion was reached by Biggleswade almost 30 years earlier (*NBC&SN&DN* 24 July 1925, p.2).

[114] On Walsingham, see NRO DC19/6/63 WRDCHCM 20 February 1946, p.34; NRO DC19/6/68 9 June 1958, p.67; and, on St Faith's and Aylsham, *NNN* 3 October 1958, p.5.

[115] Arguments about cost can be fraught. Up to 1927, even Neville Chamberlain reported direct labour costs for dwellings not much different from private producers, although unit prices were generally higher by the late-1920s (HCH 2 June 1927, Vol.207, col.565W-66W). In the 1960s, some rural councils reported building homes cheaper than private constructors, as with Bullingdon RDC (TNA HLG117/171 'Report by K.F. Munn to Mr. Stone', August 1963). The difficulty with comparisons is evident from Marriner's (1979) investigation of the Office of Works, which highlighted dissimilar conditions for building by the Office, including only taking larger projects and more difficult schemes. Dissimilar specifications for finished houses were common (TNA HLG101/708 'Note from D.K. Mason to Mr. Bilbey', 7 August 1953). Additionally, direct labour was sometimes used to lower local unemployment (Ryder 1984), with less skilled labour employed. This practice was commonplace inter-war, with national financial support enabling councils to hire the unemployed, as on the roads and in sanitary works (e.g. TNA CAB24/140 CP4319 'Unemployment Committee. Note by the Minister of Health', 22 November 1922; TNA HLG29/180 'Notes on Rural Housing from 15 April 1931 Meeting on Tudor Walters' Scheme'; MoH (1925, p.169); Eley (1973)). A huge number of examples of this existed in the investigated districts.

5.2   Countryside Builders

To understand the draw of direct labour possibilities, problematic construction options need appreciating. On this, rural councils faced an intense articulation of British construction sector shortcomings. Summarising the position at the end of the twentieth-century, the Construction Task Force to the Deputy Prime Minister on the Scope for Improving the Quality and Efficiency of UK Construction (1998) spelt out that the sector had low and unreliable profitability, with profit margins too narrow to sustain healthy development, resulting in slight investment in research and development, innovation or technology. Training for workers was poor. There was growing dissatisfaction amongst clients. Fragmentation of the industry inhibited performance improvement. None of this had recent origins (Smyth 1985; Wellings 2006). Almost 40 years earlier general agreement was expected that in the construction industry:

(a) Too many small firms were ignorant or complacent
(b) Site supervision in firms of all sizes was inadequate
(c) There were haphazard systems of employing labour
(d) The system of apprenticeships was too tight
(e) The set-up for different crafts resulted in demarcation disputes
(f) Education at all workforce stages was accepted reluctantly
(g) There was reluctance to pay for advisory services[116]

This is not to place all discredit on the industry, for it operated with national policies that countered effective action. As Marriner (1976) pointed out, this started as early as the 1919 Act, when the government laid bare the poverty of its strategic thinking by responding to capital shortages for construction and building materials by refusing to support the industry.[117] Governments then failed to build on the collaborative framework established with the industry under the 1924 Act, which was unique in

---

[116] TNA WORK45/263 Management Enquiry into Improved Efficiency in the Construction Industry. 'Note for File', 5 May 1961 (also TNA WORK45/283 Review of Problems Before the Construction Industries. 'Paper by National Federation of Building Trades Employers Working Party', undated c1961).

[117] There were public sector equivalents to this. One was the refusal of the Local Government Board to appoint people who could help local authorities develop and implement housing schemes, which Addison (1934, p.495) suspected was mainly to avoid accusations the LGB was appointing more officials. A second was insisting councils had to raise funds through local housing bonds rather than via the PWLB (TNA CAB24/93 CP153 'Housing Policy', 19 November 1919; TNA HLG48/873 Letter from MoH Assistant Secretary to Hatfield RDC Clerk, 13 May 1920). This caused significant delay as councils chased potential funding, with small RDCs having particular difficulties securing funding, so the government ultimately had to step in. This happened in Hatfield (*HM&CP* 8 May 1920, p.10), while the two Biggleswade councils worked together to secure funding and, given the scale of their joint programme, expected success (BRO RDBwM1/8 BiRDCM 23 June 1920, p.25; *NBC* 25 June 1920, p.3) but found little interest and ended up drawing on the PWLB (*BC&BG* 10 December 1920, p.2; 17 December 1920, p.6).

contemplating a minimum house-building programme over many years.[118] Striking agreement with the industry, Wheatley impressed many Conservative politicians (Lyman 1957, pp.116–17). In intent, his Act marked a break from the past, for, as Ravetz (2001, p.78) noted, little thought had been given to how the building industry would respond to the 1919 Act, while Chamberlain's 1923 Act failed to address capacity issues (Bowley 1945, p.37). Reportedly stemming from Wheatley's own vision for what was needed, rather than Labour Party conviction (Taylor 1965, p.210), the 1924 Act has been seen as the most successful inter-war housing measure (Burnett 1986, p.233). Yet it exposed weaknesses in the sector. As former MP and Manchester councillor, Ernest Simon (1933, p.22) reported, the 'price' paid for securing the industry's agreement was higher dwelling prices. Expansion was met first by higher bills and only later by capacity gains (Ball 1983, p.44).

Given the industry was dominated by small producers, this was a reminder of the inelastic nature of operations, as well as the ease with which new firms entered the sector. The latter was further visible after 1945, with 22,187 additional firms registering as building and civil engineering contractors from July 1946 to June 1947 alone.[119] This signalled easy entry (and departure), alongside uncertain links between building and general economic performance. With inter-war minimalist government, plus prioritisation of finance and commerce over manufacturing (Scott 2007), strategies for improving economic performance or responding to citizen needs were weak. Cuts to housing subsidies helped engineer boom-bust conditions for the industry (Fig. 4.1), even before the Great Depression struck.[120] The deflationary policies pursued in the early-1920s were designed for the (1925) return to the gold standard, which over-valued sterling and stagnated the economy (Ham 1981; Booth 1987). Coming off the gold standard in 1931 allowed interest rates to fall (Marshall 1968), which, with much of the rest of the economy disrupted (Stevenson and Cook 1977), left early-1930s investors with few options but housing. Funds flowed into mortgages (Holmans 1990, p.127; Gardiner 2010, p.303). Construction soon took-off, aided by measures to encourage mortgage uptake, with low building costs encouraging slum clearance (Connor 1936, p.6; Bowley 1945, pp.139–40). Turmoil returned in the first decade after 1945, with material and labour shortages restricting a return to 'normality'. The 1950s (and 1960s) saw cut-backs in output as economic weakness sucked in imports, which created balance of payments crises, to which governments responded with 'stop-go' policies that often dampened capital

---

[118] TNA HLG40/15 'Housing and Slum Clearance Since the War', undated c1931, p.3.

[119] HCH 4 August 1947, Vol.441, col.109 W. This feature of the industry might have diminished but it has not gone away. Thus, Wellings (2006, p.137) recorded 16,000 registered builders in 2004 (down from 29,000 in 1990), 10,600 of whom built no dwelling, with 4600 erecting one to 10 units a year.

[120] TNA HLG52/850 'Deputation from the NFBTO', undated c1931. Fears over boom-bust in the industry, even in the late-1930s, were discussed in Cabinet (TNA CAB24/274 CP6(38) 'Public Capital Expenditure', 20 January 1938, pp.2–3), with legislation like the 1938 Act surrounded by overtones of bailing private builders out of saturated supplies created by market forces (Berry 1974, p.111).

spending (Ball 1980; Smyth 1985). This made '… difficulties not only for the Consulting Engineers and for the Contractors, but also for the suppliers of materials and for industry generally'.[121] Despite operating under a business-friendly regime over most of these decades, the lessons the CHAC gleaned on inter-war private house-building had not been learnt:

> It is axiomatic that the conditions in which the builder who is engaged in building in antici-pation of sale or letting can most effectively operate, in the sense of building to his fullest capacity, are those in which his risks are least and his prospects of making a profit are great-est. He will operate if he is sufficiently sure that there will be ready demand for his houses when they are complete, at a price which will return him a profit, and the more certainty there is of this demand, the more he be disposed to extend his activities to the full extent to which capital, materials and labour are to be had. (MoH 1944b, p.23)

Builders preferred working in the private sector, not just because public contracts came with a 'grilling' to ensure tax-payers' money was not 'wasted' but also because governments created instability by using local capital projects to enforce stop-go policies to bail-out economic under-performance (Ball 1980).

Disappointing levels of rural private-owner house-building have been noted for early decades in the twentieth-century (Chap. 3). The core problem was national. A longstanding peculiarity of the British house-building industry has been its specula-tive orientation, unlike much of continental Europe, where construction is to con-tract (Dickens et al. 1985; Wellings 2006, p.111). One consequence was the disinclination of major firms to build for the public sector. Thus, moving from the buoyant inter-war private market into a more controlled environment post-1945, only Wimpey and Laing amongst the largest builders made notable public sector contributors. Rather than work under the new regime, large firms looked outside house-building (Smyth 1985, p.111; Wellings 2006, p.63). As the 1950s progressed, close ties between senior Conservative politicians and large builders eased the path towards industrialised building, which led to a small band of firms dominating council provision; as seen when seven firms built three-quarters of high-rise blocks between 1963 and 1973 (Dunleavy 1981, pp.20–22, pp.66–67). Yet, the 1960s was a particular era for the industry, as exemplified by the 1960–1970 production share of the 10 largest companies rising from 20% to 50% (Smyth 1985, p.166). This change came largely through mergers, which built on resource concentrations developed during the Second World War, when the government forged closer ties with favoured firms in the early war-years, followed by reduced building later, which hit smaller, regional companies hardest (Smyth 1985, pp.81–106; Gay 1987). The transition towards larger firms did not improve the sector. For one, over-provision, as under speculative building for inter-war owner-occupation (Berry 1974; Pugh 2008, p.68), did not disappear despite huge contracts for high-rises in the 1950s and 1960s (Dunleavy 1981, p.22). Higher Treasury subsidies for flats

---

[121] TNA WORK45/284 Letter from Institution of Civil Engineers Secretary to Harold Emmerson, Ministry of Works, 2 November 1961.

encouraged their construction,[122] but did not protect against over-production. Excess factory capacity for components resulted, which was particularly problematic after the 1968 collapse of Ronan Point, an industrialised East London tower block, which helped turn public opinion further against high-rises (Smyth 1985, p.176, p.190; Darke 1991).

The sector has been characterised by low productivity and lack of innovation, as seen today in the sluggish manner in which environmental enhancements have been introduced (Congreve 2013). UK investment in housing has been one of the smallest in Europe as a share of gross national savings (Feddes and Dieleman 1996). Slight research and development investment has long been a weakness; as the Cabinet was informed in 1950: '… the main problem was to get the industry itself to adopt the improvements in building practices, which resulted from scientific research'.[123] This was only part of the story. While costs in Britain have been close to the European average, house prices have risen more rapidly (Ball and Grilli 1997).[124] Perhaps sector under-performance might be 'forgiven' for the turmoil post-1919 and after 1945 (MoH 1944b, p.11; 1950b, 1952; Reiner and Broughton 1953), but the sector has generally performed badly. For 1937–1951, for example, it saw a 2.5% fall in productivity when other sectors improved (Powell 1996, p.167), with the industry only regaining pre-war productivity levels in the 1960s. In this, companies were handicapped by changes in government policies, which left them with massive stocks of unused bricks as council programmes collapsed faster than private building expanded in the mid-1950s.[125] Recurring stop-go policies did not impress construction firms:

> The tap has been turned on and off so often – and in so disconcerting a way (my memory goes back to the most ridiculous example of all, the Geddes axe [of 1921] – paralysing the industry for many years) that the characteristic adjective now about the industry would be uncertainty.[126]

The Ministry itself recognised how changing government policies impacted negatively on the sector: (a) by militating against efficiency; (b) by not encouraging

---

[122] Powell (1996, p.155) indicated that the average cost per square foot was more than 67% higher for flats than for houses. Dunleavy (1981) has an extensive commentary on higher costs and subsidies for high-rise flats.

[123] TNA CAB132/11 'Recent Activities Designed to Improve Building Practice', 13 May 1949, p.5; TNA T229/471 IPC(WP)(49)61 'Productivity in the Building Industry', 18 March 1949; MoH (1950b, 1952).

[124] One indication of this, although publication started after the period investigated here, is in Eurostat (annual). This *Eurostat Yearbook* has regular figures on the relative cost of living. To give one example, compared to Belgium, the general cost of living in the UK was 15% higher according to the 1997 Yearbook (p.252), which placed the nation as the equal fifth most expensive country. But for housing costs, the UK was 116% higher than Belgium, putting it massively out in front (the next highest was France at 55% higher). The disparity by 1999 was even greater (Hoggart 2003, p.154).

[125] TNA T227/1154 'Memo HOP8/292/01: Mr. Ross from Miss J. Keeley', 20 January 1960.

[126] TNA WORK45/284 Letter from Robert Matthew of Robert Matthew, Johnson-Marshall and Partners, Edinburgh, to W.V. Wastie, Ministry of Works, 6 November 1961.

apprentices; and (c) by affecting material supplies so demand was not always met.[127] As a consequence, when increased output was desperately needed, there were '[s]hortages of land and labour and the overload on the building industry' (MHLG 1963, p.12). No doubt government policies contributed to a lack of investment that inhibited performance. But this applied to other sectors as well. More needed to be done about shortages of skilled workers and weak material supply chains,[128] but this applied elsewhere. Troubles were aplenty but relatively speaking the construction industry performed worse than other sectors and fellow travellers in other nations (Smyth 1985; Barlow and Duncan 1994; Golland 1998). If Britain had never had it so good in the 1950s (Sandbrook 2005), the construction sector had made faltering contributions.

Perhaps it is unfair to point fingers at the construction industry. Adam Smith's (1776) famous dictum decrying meetings between those of the same trade soon turning to price-fixing carries the roots of many criticisms of the English political economy, especially over prioritising status and networking over entrepreneurship, innovation and investment. What characterised the sector was less a sense of growth dynamics than a search for stability. By the 1950s, this quest was transparent across British industry. As Kynaston (2007, p.464) articulated, collusion seemed to be everywhere, with the cartel arrangements that affected 25–30% of British manufacturing output in the mid-1930s looking puny compared with 50–60% in the mid-1950s (also Broadberry and Crafts 1996, p.77). The construction sector was instrumental in this movement. We see glimpses soon after 1919, when there was a '… decided slowness on the part of the contractors in nearly all parts of the country in taking up tenders. This seems to be largely due to the fact that builders have been very generally engaged on repairs, which they find more remunerative than the construction of new houses' (MoH 1920, p.22).[129] This was expressed locally by builder unwillingness to seek council work unless tenders were restricted to local applicants.[130] More generally, the industry worked to reduce council-building. Locally, this was expressed as grumbles councils built at all:

> We understand from our Federation, the National Federation of House Builders that if private enterprise was prepared to build houses under the above [1933] Act the Ministry of

---

[127] TNA WORK45/295 'Memo from Mrs. F.E. Lea to Mr. Digney', January 1962.

[128] TNA T227/1154 'The Load on the Building Industry in 1960', 17 December 1959; TNA WORK45/284 Letter from Robert Matthew of Robert Matthew, Johnson-Marshall and Partners, Edinburgh, to W.V. Wastie, Ministry of Works, 6 November 1961; TNA WORK45/295 'Efficiency of Construction Industries', January 1962; TNA WORK45/295 'Survey of Problems Before the Construction Industries', undated c1962; TNA T224/711 'Memo from Keith Joseph to PM', 13 January 1964.

[129] Internal Ministry communications reveal the same preference for repairs and repairing war-damage rather than new-build in discussions on Battle RDC in 1949 (TNA HLG101/213 'Memo to Mr. Bilbey from Terry Powell, Regional Architect', 30 September 1949).

[130] For example, BRO UDA6/1 AUDCHBCM 17 February 1920.

Health would not give the local Council approval to build in that district. We understand that it was an undertaking given to our Federation before the Act was passed into Law …[131]

As remarked within the Ministry:

The Federation always pressed the need for the removal of subsidies and they were much to the fore at the time of the Act of 1933. They used to agree that Local Authorities could properly build houses for the replacement of slums, which admittedly was not a paying business. They are now apprehensive because Local Authorities are building and are likely to build so many houses for the abatement of slums and overcrowding.[132]

The Federation's view was: '… local authorities should not commence to build until it had been shown that private enterprise was incapable of meeting demand'.[133] Councils were building relatively few homes, the private sector was beginning to boom (Bowley 1945), and yet there were complaints over possible competition, even for projects deemed not profitable. Post-1945, Whitehall was conscious that not controlling prices, materials and labour supplies after 1918 had unsettled the industry (MoH 1944b, p.11) and emphasised '… the Government's long-term policy to maintain stability in the building industry'.[134] The building programme after 1945 offered opportunities for revitalisation, although difficulties with labour, materials, exports and even the weather (Robertson 1987), made the transition less smooth than wished. Approaches to lessen competition soon emerged, with Ampthill agreeing in 1947 to take proposals from a builder to ensure the company had work to do,[135] Walsingham deciding to extend contracts rather than advertising new tenders,[136] and Biggleswade negotiating contracts with a local firm in return for selling land to the council.[137] These early glimpses of an emerging trend were to see 29% of contracts with private firms coming through negotiation rather than tender by 1966 (37.5% by value),[138] with claims that by mid-1969 only 12.7% of dwelling contracts were awarded through open competition.[139] The growing influence of corporate builders in directing the high-rise construction programme can be credited with part of the impetus behind this, with Dunleavy (1981, p.130) noting that where local authorities gave contracts to only one firm, this very likely led to high-rise proposals from the firm. But rural areas saw little high-rise construction. How did their builders fare?

---

[131] TNA HLG52/844 Letter from D. Preston, for Watford Garden Estates Ltd., to MoH, 5 February 1936.

[132] TNA HLG52/844 'Memo to Mr. Wilkinson', 26 February 1936.

[133] TNA HLG52/844 'Deputation from the National Federation of House Builders', press release 26 March 1936.

[134] HCH 6 April 1944, Vol.398, col.2180W.

[135] BRO RDAM2/22 ARDCHCM 25 August 1947.

[136] NRO DC19/6/65 WRDCHCM 12 March 1952, p.82.

[137] BRO RDBwM1/26 BiRDCM 23 November 1955, p.266.

[138] HCH 19 July 1966, Vol.732, col.46W.

[139] HCH 3 March 1970, Vol.797, col.237.

5.2.1   Rural Construction Company Attributes

In what is a somewhat rambling account of a single company, Jennings (1969, pp.109–10) reported on a builder in Cornwall, which shines lights on rural building firms:

> In 1930 Donald Oliver took over the business of carpenter and wheelwright from Mr Arthur Coad, who had carried on for fifty years in what was once Mr Solomon's poultry-picking and egg-packing shed ... The business was carried on under the name of F.D. Oliver, Wheelwright, Carpenter and Undertaker until 1964, when a young man of the village, Anthony Mannell, was made a partner, and the business became Oliver and Mannell Ltd., with offices at Miranda. They carry on the business of builders and undertakers etc. with some casual labour but no permanent employees. They are the village 'factotums' and do everything from clearing drains to building bungalows, and whether you give their status a 'shove-up' by calling them Builders, or merely Country Codgers, they are typical of the few remaining village craftsmen ...

Offering a broader perspective, in 1924 the MP for East Norfolk explained that: 'The village builders in most parts of Norfolk are very small men and it is more or less useless to rely on them for any considerable progress'.[140] This might be harsh, for the minister for housing in the early-1950s envisaged significant contributions by small builders to the housing drive: 'No one seemed to pay any regard to the possibility of rapidly attracting the small builders and filling up small vacant plots in a village or town not suitable for large-scale development' (Macmillan 1969, p.405); an assessment that received considerable praise from later commentators on 1950s housing expansion (e.g. Turner 1994, p.81). Of course, the 1930s' and 1950s' construction industries were different; with small firms more prevalent earlier (Wellings 2006). But within this generality, rural builders stood apart, as the MP for Hitchin indicated in 1948:

> I do not suggest that small firms of builders of this kind are necessarily peculiar to rural areas, although, as I shall show, they are in the nature of things found very much more frequently in villages than in towns. Very many of them are small-scale family businesses consisting of three or four members. They have little transport and, therefore, they are confined in their activities to their immediate neighbourhood. That makes them, of course, willing to take on contracts for people in the immediate neighbourhood. They have no clerks or quantity surveyors and, therefore, they are unable to enter into the somewhat detailed specifications and bills of quantities which are clearly necessary in a local authority contract. They have no elaborate equipment and their financial resources are not normally sufficient to warrant the entry into a bond. On the other hand, they are remarkably versatile—one man may be able to do quite a number of jobs—and they do not have the same difficulty with regard to finding specialist labour as do sometimes larger businesses.[141]

These attributes made deep impressions on rural council-building. In 1949, for instance, 36.6% of new-build contracts for rural councils were for 10 or less dwellings, compared with 14.3% in towns with fewer than 25,000 residents, and 3.9% in

---

[140] LInsley (2005, p. 186), citing TNA HLG48/859 Letter from R.J. Neville to Neville Chamberlain, 9 December 1924.

[141] HCH 13 December 1948, Vol.459, col.980.

towns with more than 75,000 inhabitants. Around 94% of rural contracts were for less than 50 dwellings (MoH 1950b, p.16). Yet, even inter-war, large sites were critical for builder profits, with Jackson (1973, p.65) holding that a reasonable return required a company to own land already or build in batches of least 100 dwellings, while the Ministry identified savings of £53–£68 per house if contracts were let for 40 dwellings rather than 20 (MoH 1950b, p.16). While small country builders were praised for their cheapness, local knowledge and willingness to accept low profit margins (MoH 1944a), they raised difficulties for councils.

One of these was a council desire to employ local people. This was evinced in debates on contract awarding, as in Walsingham in 1929, when employment for local workers was a key issue,[142] while Biggleswade wanted those awarded contracts '… to employ local labour as far as possible'.[143] Contracts for external companies, even for maintenance or re-decorating, could generate criticism on the council floor.[144] Councils wanted to support local firms, although discrimination in their favour regularly brought Ministry insistence the lowest quote be accepted.[145] However, local builders were not always attracted to house-building.[146] As inter-war Ministry investigations found, rural transport difficulties often meant firms would not bid for 'distant' sites.[147] As an example, W.J. Bushby Ltd., which secured at least 10 contracts with Biggleswade between 1950 and 1960, indicated in 1955 a willingness to tender for contracts at Caldecote, Clifford and Shefford (12–15 miles from its base at Kempston) but not at Stotfold (nearly 18 miles away), which was deemed too far from its depot.[148] In addition, local builders had limited experience of house-building. Even under the 1919 Act, this encouraged councils to advertise widely for

---

[142] *FakPost* 6 September 1929, p.5.

[143] BRO RBDwM1/11 BiRDCM 11 May 1932.

[144] This applied into the 1960s, as in Walsingham, when a Norwich firm secured a large painting contract (*D&FT* 19 February 1960, p.1) and at Sandy, where those to be invited to tender was extended to ensure local firm inclusion (BRO UDSM1/11 SaUDCM 9 June 1969).

[145] Councils would argue a case with the Ministry nonetheless, as in Walsingham during the Great Depression, when the local firm Fisher & Sons was preferred to a Hunstanton company on two separate occasions because it would employ local people and the Hunstanton bid was only £20 less (NRO DC19/6/20 WRDCM 31 August 1931, p.43; *H&FP* 2 September 1932, p.5). More commonly the Ministry would not budge over accepting the lowest offer, as with Buntingford (HRO RDC4/1/8 BuRDCM 3 November 1932, p.449; 1 December 1932, p.455; 29 December 1932, p.462).

[146] When subsidies for privately-owned homes were available under the 1923 Housing Act, Swaffham attempted to encourage local builders on several occasions but there was no interest (Linsley 2005, p.173). For council homes, examples include Walsingham's initial inability to get local builders to tender for 1919 Act homes (NRO DC19/6/8 WRDCM 26 November 1919, p.23), with similar responses at North Walsham (*NWP&ENS* 11 June 1920, p.1), Ware RDC (*H&EO* 16 April 1921, p.3) and, for later Acts, for North Mymms in Hatfield in both 1924 and 1932 (*HA&SAT* 26 January 1924, p.8; TNA HLG48/872 Letter from Hatfield RDC Clerk to MoH, 16 December 1932).

[147] For example, HLG40/19 'The Possibility of Cooperative Action by Local Authorities in the Norfolk and East Suffolk Areas', undated c1931.

[148] BRO RDBwM1/26 BiRDCM 26 October 1955, p.240.

tenders. Thus, Walsingham used the *Contractors' Journal* and the *Eastern Daily Press* to promote its Fakenham site, securing just three bids, from Fakenham, Norwich and Birmingham,[149] with tender calls often securing no applications from the district.[150] Having a bigger building programme, which called for more homes on larger sites, as with 32 at Clifton, 42 at Langford, 44 at Arlesey and 61 at Stotfold,[151] Biggleswade advertised widely, in *The Builder*, *The Beds Times*, *The Beds Express* and two local papers.[152] Inter-war publicity often produced no applications beyond the county or the borders of neighbouring counties. Given added costs working at a distance, 'external' bids were often expensive, although some were competitive. In the Walsingham example cited above, the Birmingham company only cited £12 more per dwelling than the Fakenham firm, while both Ampthill and Biggleswade awarded contracts to different Barnet companies against local opposition in the mid-1930s.[153] However, with most contracts for a few dwellings in a single place, the attraction of bidding for work from a distance was usually low.

This worried the Ministry as 1945 approached, since a step-change was needed in builder behaviour post-war: 'Many small builders in country districts are at present relegated to the jobbing repairs which they can carry out single-handed. We consider it vital that the small builder should be able to start business again on a wider scale by the time general building can be resumed' (MoH 1944a, p.42).[154] There would be repair and upgrading work in rural districts, which little interested large firms,[155] but as Jennings' (1969) description captured, many rural builders were not equipped to gear-up to house-building beyond a minimal level. The situation in Wales was little different from England:

> … apart from shortage of labour and materials, the main difficulty in securing building operations in rural areas is the scarcity indeed often the absence of local building contractors … There is no doubt that the small local contractor is nervous of tendering in today's conditions even for orthodox houses and there is little reason for hoping that he can be induced to tender for building with prefabricated units of construction. He will feel all at sea in the matter.[156]

---

[149] *NWP&ENS* 27 June 1919, p.5; 8 August 1919, p.5.

[150] NRO DC19/6/8 WRDCM 26 November 1919, p.23.

[151] *NBC* 14 November 1919, p.1.

[152] *NBC* 19 September 1919, p.3; 19 March 1920, p.2.

[153] *W&DR* 23 November 1935, p.1; BRO RDAM1/11 ARDCM 2 January 1936; BRO RDBwM1/12 BiRDCM 31 July 1935, pp.83–84.

[154] See also TNA HLG37/54 Letter from NUAW General Secretary to Aneurin Bevan, MoH, 17 December 1945; Letter from Kent Joint Advisory Rural Housing Committee Clerk to Rural Housing Sub-Committee Secretary, 15 November 1945.

[155] By 1949, 85.7% of operatives in firms of 1–5 employees were working on repairs and maintenance (14.3% on new work). This figure declined steadily as firm size grew, to 71.0% for 6–19 employees, 53.8% for 20–99 and 38.2% for 100–499, and down to 11.9% for firms with more than 5000 workers (TNA WORK45/283 'Measurement of Productivity', undated c1961, Table 4).

[156] TNA HLG101/59 Teleprint Message to E.A. Sharp, MoH, from J.D. Morris, Welsh Board of Health, 16 February 1946.

When demand for new-build was high, with economic strain ever-present, pressure to build cheaply was intense. Consequently, the government's investigation on the cost of building concluded:

> … the fact that the building industry includes very many small firms able to undertake only small contracts, results in many contracts let for the erection of small numbers of houses. Since however the evidence suggests that a saving in cost per house can be secured by building houses in larger contracts, we consider that, where circumstances permit, local authorities should plan their housing programme accordingly. (MoH 1950b, p.17)

The difficulty for rural councils after 1945 was that larger companies were primed to build on bigger sites (MoH 1944a, p.42) and had to be drawn away from usual spheres of operation. This happened somewhat in the late-1930s when the London market ran out of steam as securing sites became difficult, inducing builders to look farther afield (Wellings 2006, p.50). But horizons rarely stretched far from towns. Moreover, there was a great deal of maintenance work for companies adapted to it (Table 5.5). One outcome was few local firms bid for rural new-build. For instance, in Hitchin RDC, five contractors from outside the district were erecting all homes in 1948.[157] The problem even extended to some towns, like St Albans, where nearly half the 1945–1948 building allocation went '… to outside contractors because the local firms were unable or unwilling to compete'.[158] Reminiscent of the 1919 Act, tender calls might induce one or no responses.[159] Meagre uptake was not restricted to early post-war turmoil. Intensity varied over time, but extended to the 1970s. Some councils responded by grouping projects across multiple villages in a single package, hoping to encourage builder interest. This was prompted by fears local builders would not take contracts, so councils would have to look farther

Table 5.5 Percentage distribution of output in the construction industry by type of work, 1935–1960

	1935	1947	1948	1960
New housing	48	34	31	26
New industrial building	5	10	10	13
New shops, offices, hotels, etc.	6	1	1	10
Other new building (mainly for public authorities)	8	9	9	8
New civil engineering works	7	10	11	12
Repair and maintenance	26	36	38	31
Total	100	100	100	100

Source: TNA WORK45/283 'Measurement of Productivity', undated c1961

---

[157] HCH 13 December 1948, Vol.459, col.984–85.

[158] HCH 16 December 1948, Vol.459, col.1371.

[159] This applied even in Biggleswade, which had smaller projects on offer than in 1919, with its building programme now circumscribed by Whitehall, rather than selecting its own targets (BRO RDBwM1/20 BiRDCM 10 August 1949, p.174; BRO RDBwM1/23 BiRDCM 9 July 1952, p.123).

afield.[160] The practice copied South Cambridgeshire RDC, but when Biggleswade tried it in 1972 there was slight builder reaction.[161] Concern over builders not tendering persisted, with the Engineer and Surveyor explaining that the builders were over-committed and unwilling to bid for fixed price contracts.[162] Hatfield faced similar problems in 1971 when: 'A great deal of difficulty has been encountered in establishing a list of suitable firms for building contractors willing to submit a tender', with 21 firms approached before five showed interest.[163]

New ways had to be found to secure builder cooperation. This was visible in 'tendering' shifting from open calls to selective invitations. Either only a few firms were asked to bid or ad hoc arrangements with single builders were negotiated (Table 5.6). Companies were now placed on, and approached councils to be added to, approved bidder lists.[164] It was still difficult to attract suitable firms, even for large projects. As Dunleavy (1981) found for high-rise building, an over-heated

Table 5.6 Method of tendering for new council and new town dwellings in England and Wales, 1964–1970

	Competitive tenders		Negotiated	Package deals	Total
	Open	Selective			
	Percentage of schemes approved				
1964	50	18	25	7	100
1965	43	20	29	8	100
1966	36	23	26	15	100
1967	36	27	28	9	100
1968	30	37	23	10	100
1969†	26	47	18	9	100
1970† January–September	27	49	14	10	100
	Percentage of dwellings in schemes				
1964	32	22	31	15	100
1965	28	21	38	13	100
1966	21	24	40	15	100
1967	19	28	39	14	100
1968	14	40	33	13	100
1969†	16	47	24	13	100
1970† January–September	14	55	19	12	100

Source: HCH 22 March 1971, Vol.814, col.37W-38W
Note: *The figures exclude tenders for the London County Council and Greater London Council.
† Provisional

[160] As Braughing concluded in 1965 (HRO RDC3/1/15 BrRDCECM 11 February 1965, p.6446).

[161] BRO RDBwM1/43 BiRDCHCM 9 February 1972, p.767. Although this option continued to be explored (BRO RDBwM1/44 BiRDCHCM 10 January 1973, p.781).

[162] BRO RDBwM1/45 BiRDCHCM 13 June 1973.

[163] HRO RDC7/1/49 HtRDCHTPCM 7 September 1971, p.308.

[164] BRO RDAM1/24 ARDCHCM 10 April 1969, p.766; BRO UDSM1/11 Sandy UDC Housing Committee Meeting 9 June 1969; BRO RDAM1/27 ARDCHCM 7 September 1971, p.201.

market and low productivity (Reiner and Broughton 1953; Wellings 2006) gave construction companies the upper hand. Moreover, larger firms were gaining a stronger hold on the industry, with output concentration into fewer corporations. These firms pressured for bigger contracts and the security of package deals, with many smaller councils only working with one firm (Dunleavy 1981, p.23, p.131). This disadvantaged rural councils. Council minutes and newspaper reports revealed that 1969 was the first year one of the nation's largest builders worked with one of the investigated rural districts.[165] This did not become the norm. Rural contracts were still small, even if larger than in earlier decades (Table 5.7). Securing evidence on trends was not straightforward as council minutes were uneven in naming builder applicants for contracts, firms awarded contracts, site locations and dwellings to be erected; perhaps only enumerating the cost of the project. Easily the most comprehensive records were for Ampthill and Biggleswade. Biggleswade raised issues over representativeness, as the Council was more active than many cities under the 1919 Act. Seeking to build in large numbers, Biggleswade attracted firms from far away. Trends in the average size of contract in Ampthill consequently summarise mainstream rural patterns better. For Ampthill there was a steady rise in the average size of contract over time, accompanied by a fall in projects of five or less dwellings, which previews messages in Chap. 6 about councils being pushed to build on fewer, larger sites:

> … many Rural District Councils, faced with the problem of building on a number of small and scattered sites, found that among other advantages lower tenders could be obtained if the advertisement of contracts was postponed until proposals covering a number of parishes could be dealt with together. This procedure necessarily slowed down the rate of progress at the outset of the [1930 Housing Act] campaign, but has resulted in rapid expansion at a later stage. (MoH 1936, p.86)

Biggleswade, by contrast, started its house-building campaign with a series of larger projects, favouring smaller schemes after 1945. Given difficulties securing local builders, cost pressures, sector production concentration and both government and large builder preference for larger sites, as expected both councils saw reduced reliance on companies from their own district over time (Table 5.7).

---

[165] The first link between a large builder and an investigated rural district was when a Laing tender was accepted (BRO RDBwM1/41 BiRDCHCM 3 December 1969, p.555). Laing then built 85 homes in Clifton in 1970–1971 (BRO RDBwH2/8 'Biggleswade Register of New Dwellings Under Part I of the Housing Subsidies Act 1967'). Perhaps its late-1960s slow-down limited Hatfield's engagement with large firms (Table 4.7), but by 1971 it was approaching Wimpey, Laing, Wates and various others over a new estate (HRO RDC7/1/49 HtRDCHTPCM 8 June 1971, p.41). This effort was not successful, with no tender below the Ministry cost yardstick (HRO RDC7/1/49 HtRDCHTPCM 19 October 1971, p.496).

Table 5.7 Attributes of house-building contracts awarded by Ampthill and Biggleswade RDCs, 1919–1974

	1919–1929	1930–1939	1945–1955	1956–1964	1965–1974
	Ampthill				
Companies awarded contracts in period	9	16	18	9	13
Average dwellings awarded per company	6.0	5.8	15.6	25.0	18.4
Average dwellings awarded per contract	4.9	3.2	7.4	12.5	14.1
Per cent contracts for 1–5 dwellings	72.7	89.7	31.6	22.2	17.6
Per cent contracts for more than 20 dwellings	0.0	0.0	5.3	16.7	17.6
Tenders awarded to firms within the district	75.0	53.3	53.8	16.7	8.3
Tenders awarded to firms elsewhere in Bedfordshire	25.0	33.3	23.1	66.7	66.7
Tenders awarded to firms outside Bedfordshire	0.0	13.3	23.1	16.7	25.0
	Biggleswade				
Companies awarded contracts in period	11	15	15	34	18
Average dwellings awarded per company	72.2	27.6	16.5	19.7	37.2
Average dwellings awarded per contract	35.6	10.9	6.0	4.3	7.8
Per cent contracts for 1–5 dwellings	0.0	31.6	54.3	77.2	35.3
Per cent contracts for more than 20 dwellings	28.6	13.2	0.0	1.3	21.6
Tenders awarded to firms within the district	72.7	58.3	61.5	37.5	40.0
Tenders awarded to firms elsewhere in Bedfordshire	0.0	16.7	15.4	37.5	20.0
Tenders awarded to firms outside Bedfordshire	27.3	25.0	23.1	25.0	40.0

Source: Computed from council minutes and newspaper reports
Note: The figures for Biggleswade cover the whole period shown but for Ampthill data entries started in 1926 and finished in 1969. For 1920–1929, if Biggleswade's largest 1919 Act contract to one firm – 405 dwellings – was excluded, the average for all other contracts was 38.9 dwellings per company and 19.5 per contract. Calculations for the geographical distribution of contracts only included firms whose office could be clearly identified. Council minutes often failed to give this information, so this was sought using *Kelly's Directories*, the National House Builders' Registration Council (1968, and later years) and online searches (e.g. telephone directories). For both districts, around one-fifth of company offices were not found. In a few cases, a company's office was recorded but not the company itself, as when minutes indicated a firm from 'X' had been awarded the contract without naming it. Examining companies whose office could not be identified, these were mostly awarded contracts of 1–5 dwellings

5.2.2   Builder Reliability

An expected characteristic for a sluggish industry like construction is company closure. Figures on this over time are not readily available for rural districts. Even
nationally they need handling with care, as statistics on the sector include retail
units like timber merchants. By the 1960s more data were reported, with an annual
average of 6229 construction firms removed from the DoE's register during
1961–1970.[166] To put this in context, 10,000 companies had signed with the National
House Builders' Registration Council by the end of 1968 (MHLG 1969, p.7). With
their generally small size, rural builders were particularly prone to closure. In some
cases, for reasons less critical to larger firms, such as the death of an owner.[167]
Otherwise, with easy entry into the sector, lack of experience came into play. Take
the case with R.W. Linnell & W.E. Payen, a West Runton firm, whose owners were
a clerk and a joiner looking for employment after leaving the army at the end of the
First World War. They found houses took longer to build than anticipated, resulting
in them taking less out of the business than they put in.[168] Insufficient longevity or
naivety were not the only factors at play, for low profit margins, difficulties securing
skilled workers or materials, or unexpected costs, could see longstanding firms
close. In the case of Biggleswade, this included Alban Richards & Co., which
received the biggest contract awarded by the Council (405 dwellings under the 1919
Act), it applied to Wilstead's Philip Mann, a builder of almost 20 years, who also
entered the trade after the First World War, it extended to Ampthill's E. & R.J. Sharpe,
a company with 140 workers at closure, to the Cromer firm Girling & Smith, established in 1894 and closed in 1957 due to deterioration in trade following government austerity measures, and to Tooley & Youngs, which had built for Smallburgh
from 1920 but closed in 1971 with an unfinished £120,000 contract for Erpingham.[169]
Even in buoyant house-building periods, like the late-1940s, failures were common,
as were delays, as the 1950 MP for Lichfield and Tamworth explained:

> Experience over the last three or four years is that the present system tends to result in
> contracts being approved, work being started and then, after a long interval of time, either
> the contractor goes bankrupt in some cases or his rate of completion slows up very seriously
> indeed. And may I say that, as far as the local authority is concerned, a quick bankruptcy is

---

[166] HCH 17 November 1971, Vol.826, col.136W. Data on firm terminations were available for 1969
and 1970, when 5558 a year closed, which was 83% of those removed from the register (others
leaving due to amalgamation, moving to other industries or could not be traced). Reporting on
1969, 6750 firms were said to have ceased trading, of which 6400 had less than 25 workers and
2900 were one-person businesses (HCH 14 April 1970, Vol.799, col.1199).

[167] Owners who died holding contracts created difficulties for council programmes, as in Ampthill
and Biggleswade (W&DR 15 October 1927, p.1; BRO RDBwM1/24 BiRDCM 15 April 1953, p.60).

[168] NWP&ENS 16 September 1921, p.5.

[169] BRO CD957 1–49 'Biggleswade RDC and Messrs. Alban Richards & Co. Ltd'; W&DR 17
October 1936, p.2; 16 February 1937, p.13; NNN 22 February 1957, p.1; NRO DC13/5/35 ERDCM
23 March 1971, para.126.

the lesser evil. Sometimes, after a long period of time, one has a contractor either going bankrupt or having to own up to the local authority that he cannot complete the work for some reason. There was a case in my constituency where only after four years was quite a small contract being completed, and there must have been some reason other than availability of supplies for its slow rate of completion.[170]

As Ampthill experienced in 1934, when a builder failed to complete four contracts, with his company then closing, terminations elongated project times, requiring new negotiations with Whitehall, potentially followed by new tender calls.[171] The absence of systematically collected data means it is difficult to assess how widespread and troublesome this was. Even scanning council minutes was not that helpful, as there was often silence over actions consequential on closures (and consequent timetabling), partly because whatever followed was not tied-back to the closure in written records.

Less uncertainty accompanied builder tenders, since these were regularly reported. Here poor professionalism was apparent, which owed something to the small scale of rural operations, to a scarcity of specialised staff and to pressure to cost minimise for government contracts. Council minutes were replete with examples of company contractual failings. Take, for instance, mistakes in bids for contracts (and post-award). Builders regularly came back to councils indicating mistakes in tenders. This happened across the decades, with the local press highlighting the practice. In one report a 'high proportion' of tenders with arithmetical errors were noted with at least one councillor becoming very outspoken after the third tender of the afternoon had 'large-scale mistakes'.[172] Such errors were not only regular before decisions were made, but after (Table 5.8)[173] and even once dwellings were erected.[174] On other occasions, companies raised prices the day decisions were

---

[170] HCH 10 November 1950, Vol.480, col.1321.

[171] BRO RDAM2/20 ARDCHCM 13 June 1934. A similar experience was recounted to the House of Commons for Lincolnshire's Spilsby RDC in 1947 (HCH 24 November 1947, Vol.444, col.237W).

[172] *NBC&BR* 22 January 1952, p.9. Often precise figures were not indicated but an early sign was provided in H.J. Jackson's 1920 bid to Biggleswade Town, which was initially for £5932 but raised to £8667 when an error was discovered. The Jackson submission, along with that of the second lowest bid (£13,851), was sent to the Surveyor before a decision was made. At the same meeting, tenders for 188 houses were considered in five lots. All five were won by Messrs. C. Wright & Son, a company that erected many dwellings for various councils up to the 1950s. Even here, the company failed to include items in its bid, asking for quoted prices to be raised.

[173] This applied across the decades and not only for house-building but also for water and sewer systems, as with Biggleswade having to tell Clifton and Shefford their sewerage scheme would be delayed '… because the contractor had made an error of £30,000 in his tender and had had to withdraw it' (*BC&BG* 11 February 1955, p.7).

[174] BRO RDAM2/20 ARDCHCM 20 June 1935. This also occurred when large firms built for investigated districts, as with Wimpey's final bill for its Biggleswade Town estate coming in at nearly £20,000 over the tender price (*BC&BG* 16 February 1968, p.24).

Table 5.8 Illustrative examples of builders wanting higher payments after tender acceptance

Year	District	Per cent rise requested
1919	Welwyn RDC	15.6
1920	Hatfield RDC	19.0
1930	Ampthill RDC	3.8
1937	Biggleswade RDC	17.1
1948	Biggleswade RDC	20.7
1948	Biggleswade RDC	5.7
1952	Biggleswade RDC	0.7
1952	Biggleswade RDC	5.6

Source: HRO RDC7/96/1 *HertsMerc* 20 December 1919; *HM&CP* 28 August 1920, p.4; *W&DR* 9 August 1930, p.1; BRO RDBwM1/13 BiRDCM 15 December 1937, p.191; BRO RDBwM1/18 BiRDCM 25 February 1948, p.650; BRO RDBwM1/22 BiRDCM 23 January 1952, pp.343–44

to be made,[175] withdrew applications[176] or occasionally admitting a mistake and stood by the tendered price.[177] Sometimes, councils insisted the bid be honoured[178] or withdrew contracts because work had not started by the fixed date.[179] Requests for extensions on the length of contracts were very common,[180] as were complaints made by and to councils (e.g. from parish councils) over unsatisfactory progress.[181] Little surprise national organisations were critical of rural builders. For instance, in 1931 the National Federation of Building Trades Operatives argued that: 'Our previous experience has been that contracts have been let, particularly in rural parts of

---

[175] With early experience of this in Biggleswade, when two companies raised bids by 5% and 10% on the morning of the meeting (*NBC* 14 November 1919, p.1).

[176] As in Ampthill (*W&DR* 13 October 1934, p.2; BRO RDAM1/25 ARDCHPBuCM 1 January 1970), Biggleswade (*NBC* 14 November 1919, p.1; BRO RDBwM1/20 BiRDCM 20 June 1949, p.137; BRO RDBwM1/27 BiRDCM 15 February 1956, p.25), Erpingham (NRO DC13/5/72 ERDCHCM 25 February 1928, p.96), Sandy (BRO UDSM1/1 SaUDCM 20 June 1932, p.477) and Walsingham (*D&FT* 23 October 1959, p.1).

[177] BRO RDBwM1/20 BiRDCM 10 August 1949, p.177.

[178] BRO RDBwM1/22 BiRDCM 27 December 1950, p.11.

[179] *BC&BG* 9 April 1920, p.1; BRO RDAM2/22 ARDCHCM 20 April 1950; BRO RDBwM1/24 BiRDCM 8 July 1953, p.131.

[180] Examples include: BRO RDBwM1/9 BiRDCM 30 December 1925; NRO DC13/5/72 ERDCHCM 11 May 1927, p.54; BRO UDA6/1 AUDCHBCM 13 August 1931; BRO RDAM2/22 ARDCHCM 18 November 1954.

[181] For post-war house-building examples in Biggleswade alone, see: *NBC&BR* 5 March 1946, p.4; 15 April 1952, p.2; BRO RDBwM1/24 BiRDCM 8 July 1953, p.131; *BC&BG* 21 October 1955, p.1; 21 February 1958, p.15; 26 May 1961, p.12. Complaints were also voiced over home improvements (BRO RDBwM1/39 BiRDCHCM 12 July 1967, p.160).

the country, to builders who are in the main irresponsible'.[182] When housing investment expanded rapidly, as after the 1919 Act, official reports had similar reservations. On the one hand, companies slowed progress by poor preparation and fitful action: 'The slowness of contractors to tender and, in some cases, even after tenders have been accepted, to enter into contracts, has seriously checked schemes which were otherwise in a position to go forward to completion' (MoH 1920, p.6). On the other hand, councils were pushed to depend on unreliable, costly options: 'Impelled to undertake this work and urged to the utmost acceleration, the local authorities were forced to enter into contracts with a class of builder who had had but little experience of this class of building, who did not desire to undertake it and who could command his own price … ' (MoH 1921, p.8).

What did you get for the money? Generally, assessments of rural builders were concerning. From the first completions under the 1919 Act, shoddy work was identified. In Biggleswade, for example:

> Mr Fenn, the Clerk of Works, said he wished the Council to have confidence in him to get them the best they could possibly get for their money. They were in great difficulty with regard to building. Work that he passed now, ten years ago he should not have passed. He was bound to pass it, otherwise they would not get their buildings up. He explained that he had condemned the defective work and said that there was much material on the sites which had been condemned.[183]

For certain there were problems over supplies, with builders given permission to substitute one material for another to ease progress.[184] This did not excuse shoddy work. Reports of this were plentiful for 1919 Act dwellings: in North Walsham, the gable ends of houses were 'completed' with several blocks missing and bitumen was omitted from damp courses;[185] the builder of 1920 Stotfold dwellings accepted their door frames were of uneven depth, joints were unevenly spaced and concrete foundations had crumbled;[186] and, in 1924, a Wells tenant complained that his bedroom ceiling had fallen down for the sixth time.[187] Characteristic grievances were Walsingham tenants finding a lack of drains, dampness, uninhabitable bedrooms and faulty roof construction, or rain coming through roofs as in Hadham and Erpingham.[188] But when construction quality was at fault, some builders became aggressive, as with a Biggleswade contractor threatening legal action after criticism of its dwellings.[189] Concern over building standards led councils to refuse to work

---

[182] TNA HLG52/850 Letter from National Federation of Building Trades Operatives General Secretary to Arthur Greenwood, MoH, 4 June 1931.

[183] *BC&BG* 23 July 1920, p.5.

[184] *BC&BG* 12 November 1920, p.5.

[185] *FakPost* 29 October 1920, p.8.

[186] *BC&BG* 23 July 1920, p.5.

[187] *YarmInd* 12 July 1924, p.2.

[188] NRO DC19/6/9 WRDCM 11 January 1922; *H&EO* 6 May 1922, p.5; *FakPost* 8 April 1927, p.3.

[189] *BC&BG* 20 August 1920, p.5. This occurrence was not limited to 1919 Act dwellings, as noted when the builder of Stiffkey homes wanted a public apology after remarks by Walsingham councillors and the Housing Officer (*NM&PWJ* 28 September 1935, p.6).

with some builders.[190] In other cases, parishes would not accept more dwellings; as with Sandy refusing Biggleswade's offer of 20 more council homes, stating: 'That more cottages in this Parish are undoubtedly needed, but they regret they are so dissatisfied with the price and workmanship of the cottages recently built that they will not ask for any more built by the same contractor or at the same exorbitant price'.[191] Similar responses were found in Erpingham, where Holt Parish Council complained about the condition of new houses, while the Council resisted efforts by the Ministry to raise rents on council dwellings until '… houses had been put in a habitable state of repair', with reproaches made that dwellings had no fences, so tenants were put to inconvenience from pigs, sheep and cattle grazing in their gardens, had to put up with unsatisfactory chimneys and had doors requiring more than gentle persuasion to open and close.[192] Walsingham added that houses a long way from town had approach-roads in pitiable condition, with poor lighting, while brickwork was so bad the mortar could be pulled out with fingers and windows were so draughty houses were cold.[193] With such provocations, why did councils not respond vigorously?

What should not be discounted is the possible impact of friendship and connections, for builders with contracts were largely small business owners, like many councillors, although few councillors were in the building trade (the 1936–1937 councillor occupations revealed none, one or two per council; Table 3.5). Connections through business organisations there might have been or simply regular contact after numerous contracts with the same council but neither council minutes nor newspapers hinted at specific relationships. Perhaps councillors were simply keen to help local firms, and appreciated the difficulties of small companies operating in a rural environment (Chap. 3). Against this positive gloss, councillors had restricted choice. They tried to encourage better standards but found companies resistant. Early attempts to impose rigour included Biggleswade Town's failed efforts to have contracts include a time limit or penalty clause.[194] This 'set-back' troubled both Biggleswade councils, which explored introducing such stipulations up to the 1950s.[195] With or without such conditions, substandard finishes were common. In Biggleswade, for example, poor 'workmanship' in the installation of roof-

---

[190] For example, NRO DC19/6/18 WRDCM 11 June 1930, p.27.

[191] BRO UDSM2/3 Sandy Parish Council Meeting 29 July 1921, p.79.

[192] NRO DC13/5/15 ERDCM 13 February 1922, p.418; *FakPost* 19 January 1923, p.3; NRO DC13/5/82 ERDCHCM 14 July 1925, p.202; 11 May 1926, p.250. The animal incursion issue was also problematical in Hadham (*H&EO* 6 May 1922, p.5).

[193] *FakPost* 4 May 1923, p.5.

[194] *BC&BG* 19 November 1920, p.3.

[195] *BC&BG* 21 October 1955, p.1; 18 January 1957, p.1. Why they failed over such a long time period was unclear, for some councils managed to secure such commitments, like Hatfield (HRO RDC7/96/2 *HertsMerc* 24 March 1928), Braughing (HRO RDC3/1/1 BrRDCM 7 November 1935, p.86), Erpingham (NRO DC13/5/25 ERDCM 9 November 1953, para.170) and Mitford and Launditch RDC (*D&FT* 16 September 1960, p.1). Councils were not always limited by few builders bidding for contracts.

ing was reported in the 1960s,[196] Hatfield Residents' Association complained in the 1950s of 'legalised jerry-building', which led to one house style being nicknamed 'The Barracks', with broader concerns provoking an appeal to the Ministry over rotten woodwork and condensation.[197] Grievances over badly fitting doors and windows letting in the rain persisted long after 1945.[198]

By 1960, the County Councils' Association believed lapses extended to houses for sale:

> In recent years, in most counties, and noticeably in recent months standards of private building have tended to fall. This lowering of standards is evident in the reduction in floor space, and in the size and depth of plots, the lower quality of design both internal and external and a lack of variety in the type and character of dwellings.[199]

The point was well made, for governments had long recognised the state should promote better building in the private sector. You did not have to digest *The Ragged Trousered Philanthropists* (Tressell 1955)[200] to know the building trade had deep-seated flaws. In the mid-1960s, 91% of a sample of new home occupiers found them faulty, with government admissions that much private building was below public sector standards.[201] Early government acknowledgement came in the building manual for the 1919 Act, which '... should serve as a model or standard for building by private enterprise in the future' (LGB 1919, p.3). Such wishes punctuated official statements thereafter, as in expectations that new-build for private-owners with state aid should not fall below the standard of council homes (MoH 1944b, p.36), with concern over variable quality in new private homes leading to a national registration scheme for house builders in 1936 (NHBC Foundation 2015). But it had to wait until the mid-1960s for effective government action over this initiative. In 1965, local authorities were told to move towards Parker Morris building standards, which had been first accepted in 1961.[202] Accompanying this step, firms building for sale were expected to sign-up and adhere to standards of the National Housebuilders' Registration Council, whose quality guarantees to home-buyers were expected to improve over time.[203] Only 1772 companies had registered with the Council in March 1964. This rose to 4500 by late-1966, to 5800 a year later and by March 1969 there were 11,805 members covering an estimated at 95% of new private homes

---

[196] BRO RDBwM1/38 BiRDCHCM 8 February 1967, p.646, p.650.

[197] *H&PBG* 17 February 1956, p.3; 6 March 1956, p.1; 23 March 1956, p.1.

[198] See the Housing Manager report in the *BC&BG* 15 November 1957, p.1.

[199] TNA HLG37/186 'HS Evidence Paper 73', July 1960, p.2.

[200] Tressell died in 1911. An incomplete version of his manuscript on practices and exploitative relationships in house-building was first released in 1914. The full manuscript was published in 1955.

[201] HCH 9 February 1965, Vol.706, col.59W; HCH 16 December 1970, Vol.808, col.1343.

[202] TNA HLG118/591 Circular 21/65 'Housing', 1 April 1965.

[203] HCH 25 June 1965, Vol.714, col.285W-86W.

built.[204] Despite this initiative, for the decades investigated here, private firms often built to lower standards. Even today, widespread claims of inferior quality and excessive profits dog the industry.[205] This poses the question, how far did private practices filter into council contracts, given most council homes were erected by private firms?[206] Like home-buyers, there was disgruntlement over quality lapses in the council sector. This was poignantly captured when Councillor Burrows of Biggleswade Town refused to accept a council house in 1965 due to faults with its damp course, a leaking roof, plaster needing replacing throughout and skirting boards appearing to have dry-rot.[207]

Yet there was some praise for the quality of council homes. What we were promised on returning from fighting, as one Ampthill tenant put it in 1924[208] or a mother '… referring to the joy and happiness of her daughter at being housed under such nice conditions', as a letter to Hatfield Council stated.[209] Moreover, although rarely appearing in council minutes (perhaps as they were not 'noteworthy'), some builders remedied defects with grace.[210] The impact of government intervention on builders' actions should also be acknowledged. In Ware RDC, for instance, the collapse of ceilings was ascribed to Ministry insistence on only two plaster coats to save money.[211] Often, however, apportioning 'blame' between builders, councils and the Ministry could not be determined; as with weaknesses in the design or installation of roofs leading to snow drifting into lofts (and then bedrooms), which happened across the decades.[212]

---

[204] HCH 12 July 1966, Vol.731, col.175W; HCH 1 November 1966, Vol.735, col.239; HCH 20 June 1967, Vol.748, col.1399; HCH 2 April 1969, Vol.781, col.119W. Parker Morris standards were not compulsory for councils, with many rural tenants finding associated rents too rich, although councils were encouraged to adopt them, with council-building to full standards rising from 14% in 1964 to 70% in 1968 (HCH 2 April 1969, Vol.781, col.119 W).

[205] Recent examples from the *Times* and *Sunday Times* include: 'Help-to-buy homeowners pay £33,000 more than others' (5 April 2017, p.4); 'Greedy house developers face losing right to build' (31 January 2018, p.1); 'Snagging list reveals housing market's shaky foundations' (1 February 2018, pp.14–15); 'Builders told home truths on failings' (27 March 2019, p.39); 'Easy money turns builders into bodgers' (6 September 2019, p.7); 'Building companies face ban on "exploitative" leasehold contracts' (21 July 2020, p.4); and, 'Grenfell exposes culture of bad building: Inquiry into tragedy has revealed a trade in which too many costs and corners are cut' (4 August 2020,p.14).

[206] For example, in 1966, it was reported that '… 91 per cent of everything built by local authorities is built by private enterprise' (HCH 15 December 1966, Vol.738, col.791). The rest largely used council workers (HCH 29 April 1968, Vol.763, col.774).

[207] *BC&BG* 18 June 1965, p.13. The Town's Surveyor challenged this assessment but the controversy sparked consideration of appointing a Housing Manager for the Town's dwellings.

[208] *W&DR* 19 July 1924, p.1.

[209] HRO RDC7/1/18 HtRDCHCM 6 April 1954, p.393.

[210] For example, BRO RDBwM1/10 BiRDCM 8 July 1931; 25 November 1931.

[211] *H&EO* 19 January 1924, p.8. A more general consideration of national impacts on building standards is provided in Chap. 6.

[212] As reported in Stansted RDC (*H&EO* 14 January 1928, p.5), Biggleswade (*NBC&BR* 1 April 1947, p.6; 15 April 1952, p.2), and Braughing (*H&EO* 9 April 1954, p.8).

It was nonetheless clear that rural councils were generally dealt a poor hand by the construction sector. The industry as a whole was under-capitalised (Dickens et al. 1985; Feddes and Dieleman 1996), which allowed many 'suspect' companies to operate. With a primary focus on speculative building for private-owners, the countryside was at the tail-end of builder interest, especially early in the twentieth-century, when there were few opportunities for speculation (Ministry of Reconstruction 1918). In this context, the small jobbing rural builder felt few feathers ruffled by outside competition (see Ampthill in Table 5.7). Prior to 1945, this effect was enhanced because both rural and urban house-builders 'were almost entirely local businesses' (Wellings 2006, p.48). At times these circumstances left rural councils devoid of bidders for contracts. Yet, the 'poverty' of potential council tenants meant building firms were pressured to minimise costs.[213] In this, they were advantaged, as rural labour costs were low and contracts for rural homes often came with lower building and layout anticipations. Yet building costs were equivalent in rural and urban areas, at least up to the 1950s when national authorities pushed costlier high-rise options onto urban councils. These circumstances point to rural homes being relatively expensive, given lower costs and reduced design expectations, although the lack of cost divergence also indicates large urban builders secured few economies of scale (Powell 1996; Wellings 2006). In this regard, rural firms merit praise, as they were confronted with far from straightforward building contracts, amongst which dispersal created issues which complicated expanding the housing stock. Most evident in this regard was poor infrastructure.

5.3   Amenity Deficiencies

As well as projecting a bold vision for housing improvement after the 1914–1918 War, the Coalition Government stressed basic services should improve. Upgrading meant more than better quality, for often minimal provision was lacking. As presentations to the Cabinet on water supply made clear, significant advances were a priority:

> There are, however, other questions connected with the building of houses which require the immediate attention of the Government if the problem is to be solved satisfactorily in country districts. First and foremost of these is the question of water supply. It is very hard upon the agricultural owner if he is to be called upon at his own cost to provide water supply for cottages in parts of the country where water is very difficult to get and has frequently to be brought very long distances. In some areas, largely owing to the action of the owners themselves, water supplies have been provided by the locality. This and a proper system of drainage ought to be universal, and the cost should not be borne solely by the locality, as it is in the interests of the public health of the nation that this work should be properly done …[214]

---

[213] For a flavour of this from the 1930s, see Arthur Greenwood's speech on the impoverishment of rural councils (HCH 28 February 1933, Vol.275, col.205).

[214] TNA CAB24/73 GT6618 'Housing. Memorandum for the War Cabinet', 7 January 1919, p.68.

To turn this sentiment into physical fabric, huge investment was needed. In 1913, out of 12,860 rural parishes in England and Wales, around 9000 had piped water for less than one-third of inhabitants. Excluding extremely small or demographically scattered parishes still left 2097 'unsupplied'. Inhabitant numbers in the 1901–1921 censuses revealed that only 20% of these parishes experienced demographic decline; 59% were more or less stationary and 21% had grown (MoH 1929, pp.7–8). The picture for other services was similar. So, while Germany had 90% of farms electricity connected in 1928, only 2700 British farms were so linked, with just 7% on the national grid by 1938 (Moore-Colyer 1999, p.120). House of Commons debates pointed to the national origins of poor performance:

> A very fair way of judging the progress made is to see how many units per head of the population we produce. In Great Britain it is 356 units per head; in the United States 844, in Germany 402, in Canada 1,600, and in Switzerland 1,175 ... Why is it that this country lags behind? The reason is that because other countries, particularly Germany and the United States, have done so much in industrial electrification. For instance, in Germany and the United States it is 78 per cent, Canada 90 per cent, and France 85 per cent, whilst Great Britain has only 51 per cent ...[215]

Even in the 1960s, the UK was well behind other European nations. Thus, in 1963, connecting farms to supply networks was either completed or nearing completion, with only very remote farms missed, in Austria, Belgium, Czechoslovakia, Denmark, East Germany, Luxembourg, the Netherlands, Sweden, Switzerland and West Germany, whereas only 83.2% of farms were connected in England and Wales, with total rural connections at only 88.6% (UN Economic Commission for Europe 1964, p.11, p.24). This hints at the lack of vision, innovation, investment and organisation critics see in the nation's leadership (Barnett 1972; Allen 1976; Brown 2017). At the very least, it points to a disregard for improving agricultural performance and an indifference to rural well-being. Throw into the mix the paucity of water and sewerage services and the message extends to neglect of rural health. Hence, in 1944, one-quarter of rural parishes still lacked piped water, and, if provided to a parish, one-half of inhabitants might be without (MoH 1944a, p.50). By the early-1950s the picture had improved with around 80% of dwellings having piped water, which was not out of line with the Netherlands, Sweden and West Germany, although France had over 90% coverage (Economic Commission for Europe Geneva 1958, 1962). Herein lies another tale. This, alongside the causes and consequences of changing household amenity provision, is the central issue for this section.

Thresh (1891, pp.4–5) gave a sense of the health problems resulting from poor infrastructure at the turn of the twentieth-century, in a report on rural Chelmsford and Maldon:

> Very many privies are without receptacle of any kind, being merely placed over a ditch. During the winter and in rainy seasons no nuisance arises from this arrangement, but during the summer and in dry weather a most abominable nuisance results. At the present time we have a group of four cottages, in which seven cases of typhoid fever have occurred during

---

[215] Daniel Hopkin, MP for Carmarthen, HCH 11 December 1929, Vol.233, col.491–92.

the last three months. Each has a privy over the ditch which runs a few feet from the houses, and about which the children are constantly playing.

It might seem a long time from the late-nineteenth-century to 1974 but health issues associated with water and sewerage provision were ever present. Of course as infrastructure improved, concerns lessened (albeit expectations rose). Health implications were prominent in amenity deficiencies but they were not the only concern. Also important was fire risk. Arthur Greenwood pointed to this, following a 1938 fire close to the Bedford and District Mental Home, where: '... it was nearly 25 minutes before the water supply was properly available', with the continuance of this risk reported in 1950s Braughing when water tests at High Wych saw water supply fail after 14 min.[216] Capturing national sentiments on shortfalls, the 1933 Minister of Health charged that:

> Of all the things that can be done to help country people to a better and healthier life, there is nothing in which you can get so big a return of health, happiness and profit at a reasonable cost as in an improvement of the supply of water to village and to cottage. We have lagged behind what can and ought to be done in improvement there ...[217]

Water supply was far from satisfactory. Illustrating common problems, the 1925 Walsingham Medical Officer of Health reported:

> The water supply of the district (with the exception of the artesian wells at Melton Constable and Fakenham Council Housing Scheme) is exclusively derived from surface wells of varying depths. These wells are in many cases defective in structure and are very liable to pollution from their immediate surroundings.[218]

Council minutes were peppered with reports on rural parishes where water supply was '... grossly polluted with a more or less semi-filtered product of sewage'.[219] Pollution was especially high near highly manured soil, with streams polluted enough to kill fish.[220] Water tests regularly found unsatisfactory supplies; as with Walsingham in the mid-1920s, when 25 of 53 wells were polluted.[221] The Ministry's own 1929 report on rural water supplies drew attention to unsatisfactory private wells (MoH 1929, pp.17–18). The private well issue had not disappeared by the 1970s. For example, Smallburgh's Medical Officer of Health reported that, of the 2761 bacteriological tests undertaken on public wells from 1957 to 1970, 5.4% had unacceptable water purity, but 58.2% of 552 tests on private wells were similarly

---

[216] HCH 28 July 1938, Vol.338, col.3356–57; *H&EO* 14 September 1951, p.4; 14 March 1952, p.6.

[217] TNA HLG50/1879 'Minister of Health's Speech at the Annual Dinner of Kent County Officers Guild, Maidstone, 12 December 1933'.

[218] NRO DC19/6/14 WRDCM 26 May 1926, p.20.

[219] Also for Walsingham, see *FakPost* 26 October 1923, p.5.

[220] This was for Ampthill (*W&DR* 5 June 1926, p.1).

[221] *FakPost* 15 May 1925, p. 5; 20 May 1927, p.5. This figure was not particularly high. For example, former Housing Inspector Sayle (1924, p.57) reported a parish near Banbury with 92% of inspected wells having water unfit for human consumption, while, as late as 1954, 61.5% of wells in Smallburgh were 'bad' (*NNN* 5 November 1954, p.1).

graded.[222] Not surprisingly, there was pressure to improve supplies. In Ampthill, the Council adopted a 1936 Housing Committee recommendation to provide mains water to all council houses, given the link between good water and health, plus a desire to help the district's poorer people.[223] What changed the policy atmosphere around water in the mid-1930s were two Acts of Parliament. The first was the 1929 Local Government Act, which facilitated rural schemes '… by the removal of the obligation imposed by the Public Health Acts of meeting the cost of rural water schemes on a strictly parochial [parish] basis', so easing the path to comprehensive or joint (cross-parish) schemes. The second was the 1934 Rural Water Supplies Act, which added Treasury funds to district and county council contributions (MoH 1934, p.13).

What prompted the latter Act was a recurring rural theme; namely, water shortage. In 1930 drought was '… very severely felt in rural areas, many of which are dependent for their supply on surface water and shallow wells, with no margin for contingencies …' (MoH 1930, p.13). Areas like Marston in Ampthill reported many wells had dried up.[224] Indicative of the hazards that could result, the 1929–1930 drought was followed by outbreaks of typhoid in Yorkshire villages (Pedley 1942, p.94). While steps to improve supplies were made, there was a long way to go before conditions were satisfactory, let alone good (MoH 1930, p.13). Just three years later, the lack of rain was described as unparalleled for 50 years, with the crisis met '… in 31 districts by the use of alternative supplies relatively near, in 48 districts by the carrying and carting of water from more distant sources, in 17 districts by deepening wells and in 56 districts by obtaining water supplies from neighbouring private wells and similar measures' (MoH 1934, p.11, p.13). In Hatfield the

---

[222] The source for these figures was Smallburgh RDC (1958) and the equivalent following annual reports. Establishing the geographical spread of private wells was not straightforward, as data were not available. Suggesting they were relatively restricted, in 1944 the Minister of Health identified 1203 parishes in England with private supplies (HCH 6 April 1944, Vol.398, col.2182W-83W). However, this list omits some counties, including Bedfordshire, and holds that there were only 12 private wells in Norfolk, when five years later the County Sanitary Officer charged that individual sources of water covered a considerable portion of the county (TNA HLG50/2317 'Observations Relating to the MoH Publication. Norfolk Water Survey', 1 December 1949). The likelihood was there were many private wells. Take the case of Meppershall. In 1920 it was reported that, at the Biggleswade end of the village: 'There were only two wells, one was in the Vicarage garden. This was a shallow one and the Rector allowed the inhabitants of cottages nearby to use it, but was loth to allow anyone else the use of it in case it should run out' (*BC&BG* 20 August 1920, p.5). Yet, by 1924, across the whole village, 41 shallow wells and one deep one were counted (Biggleswade RDC 1925, p.7). This pattern was common, with Walsingham having most dwellings supplied by wells at two houses per well (TNA HLG50/1830 Letter from Walsingham RDC Clerk to MoH Secretary, 27 February 1934). As for Meppershall, after 20 plus years of lobbying, mains water had not been extended to the village, with a further postponement recommended owing to high material prices post-1945 (*NBC&BR* 5 March 1946, p.1). For sewerage, not until 1964 was a scheme for the village funded (BRO RDBwM1/36 Biggleswade Sewerage Committee Meeting 28 October 1964, pp.426–27).

[223] *W&DR* 10 October 1936, p.7.

[224] *W&DR* 26 April 1930, p.1.

water supply of Northaw village failed (Hatfield RDC 1934, p.8), while Ampthill had water in eight villages surrounded by scarcity nearby on isolated farms and houses plus definite shortage in six villages.[225] Little wonder the Ministry received demands to improved supplies, from councils, industries and landowners. One of these was Magdalen College, which owned the greater part of various villages in six counties, which drew particular attention to 11 villages suffering from drought.[226] If the mood in Whitehall was sombre, this at least came with recognition that improvement was needed, as a 1933 Cabinet note made clear:

> The conditions in some villages are deplorable. There are grave risks to health and decent cleanliness cannot be maintained. The rising standards of life have rendered intolerable conditions which have been endured in the past, and during recent years there has been a marked increase of discontent and an agitation which is growing. During the last year Members representing rural areas have frequently raised the subject in the House and not without cause. The dry summer brought serious hardship to a large number of villages, and though the drought was exceptional, it but brought to a head conditions which are chronic in many of them.[227]

However, 1930s' governments were reluctant to take responsibility for public well-being. The 1934 Rural Water Supplies Act was a first step but it demonstrated timidity and lack of ambition. Even for the time, the £1 million in funding the Act made available was derisory, given the scale of the problem. Desperate times soon returned, as when Biggleswade made urgent 1938 appeals to save water and cut supplies, when emergency measures were introduced in Plympton St Mary in the 1944 drought, and when the majority of wells in parts of Smallburgh dried-up in 1957.[228]

5.3.1   Difficulties Extending Amenity

As so often when exploring what underpins social life, answers are more complex than assigning credit or deficit to simple explanations. The role national agencies played in the rural drama of housing and amenity supplies have certainly been profound (Chap. 6), perhaps in ways not given due accord in the literature. The contribution of national agencies has been more diverse and intrusive than often acknowledged. Concerning national inaction, the 1929 Minister of Transport exemplified the issues for electricity using the Post Office for comparison:

---

[225] TNA HLG50/1694 Letter from Ampthill RDC Clerk to MoH Secretary, 2 March 1934.

[226] TNA HLG50/1879 Letters from Magdalen College Estates Bursar to MoH Secretary, 29 December 1933; 3 January 1934.

[227] TNA CAB24/244 CP275(33) 'Water Supply in Rural Areas', 16 November 1933, p.1.

[228] W&DR 28 June 1938, p.8; TNA HLG50/1880 'Water Supply. RDCA Deputation to Minister', 7 June 1944. In Smallburgh, 10 of the 15 wells near Station Road in Worstead dried up (NNN 9 August 1957, p.5).

The demand for electricity in the rural areas is lower than in the industrial areas and in the towns; and the supply undertakings, being locally organised, have to consider the price which they can fix for electricity as justified by the load which their undertaking carries. The Post Office is an admirable institution in this way ... It obviously costs the Post Office much more to deliver a letter in a far distant rural area than in the County of London, but, nevertheless, they charge exactly the same price in the rural area as they do in the County of London. The reason is that the Post Office is nationally organised, and strikes an average of its costs. But the electricity undertaking, whether company or municipal, is organised locally, and must have regard to costs in the district in which it is working ... the rural areas are to some extent the victims of the local and restricted organisation of the electricity supply industry.[229]

That governments chose not to organise basic amenities on a national or even a regional basis was characteristic of regimes slow to adapt to the economic and social 'realities' of people's lives and industrial operations. The drawn-out journey to the reform of local government testified to lethargy in the national polity (Royal Commission on Local Government in England 1969; Dunbabin 1977; Dearlove 1979). Yet, confronted with seeming immobility nationally, local agents had scope to make improvements. That they were slow to do so needs accounting for.

Soon after 1919, funding mechanisms demanding payment at parish level delayed amenity improvements (Baker 1953, p.183; MoH 1932a, p.13). There was little scope for positive action when small parishes were charged full costs, as with house-building before the 1919 Act. But moving levies up from parish to district did not produce step-change, as many rural councils were themselves fiscally strained.[230] This was well known in Whitehall.[231] Only slow progress could be expected without significant national intervention. Up to the Second World War (and later under 1950s stop-go policies), Waddington's (2012, p.198) description of the Victorian era rings true; namely, that rural amenity enhancement was problematical as many ratepayers were on the verge of pauperism, while topography, climate and connecting isolated communities made improvements costly and difficult.[232] On inability to pay, extensions to public services were often refused because householders could

---

[229] HCH 11 December 1929, Vol.233, col.525–26.

[230] Rural Housing Sub-Committee visits to various RDCs found water and sewer costs were referred to as a rate burden, rather than housing (TNA HLG37/47 'Notes on Visits to East Anglia and South Midlands', undated c1943).

[231] On water supply, see TNA CAB24/244 CP275(33) 'Water Supply in Rural Areas', 16 November 1933; TNA CAB24/254 CP51(35) 'Water Policy', 8 March 1935; HCH 25 June 1951, Vol.489, col.1121–24. Sewage disposal was more difficult, as central facilities were generally considered uneconomical except for 20 dwelling groupings (TNA HLG50/2060 MoH Circular 87/47 'Rural Water Supplies and Sewerage Act 1944', 12 May 1947).

[232] Take the case of Udimore in Battle RDC. Twelve houses were to be built here but water would not be available until Hastings completed a distant reservoir and was able to bring water four miles from their waterworks. The houses had to be built on a hill above a spring with water pumped to a tower built into one house. The MoH Tunbridge Wells approved a costing at £2050 a house, of which only £1425 related to the cost of a normal house, with £337 for water and sewerage and for having to locate houses on a slope. Roads and sites also needed to be cut out of the slope (TNA HLG101/213 Letter from Battle RDC Clerk to MoH Secretary, 7 September 1949). A more common added cost was reported earlier for Hoxne RDC, which had to provide a deep artesian well to

Table 5.9 Per cent of dwellings in the rural districts of five counties with water and sewer supply, 1940

	Per cent dwellings with piped water			Per cent all dwellings without piped water with			
	Overall	Worst RDC in county	Best RDC in county	Mains supply within 100 yards	Mains supply within 100–440 yards	Mains supply over 440 yards away	Per cent dwellings without a sewer supply but in a group of at least 20 dwellings
Bedfordshire	63.0	47.5	96.5	26.6	2.1	8.3	60.4
Cambridgeshire	48.2	32.8	55.4	22.5	17.2	12.1	80.4
Hertfordshire	78.2	62.2	99.7	10.8	0.8	10.2	22.2
Isle of Ely	68.4	34.4	92.3	3.3	6.7	21.6	46.7
Norfolk	23.4	0.0	64.8	9.5	27.8	39.3	51.2

Source: TNA HLG50/2152 Rural Water Supplies and Sewerage: Circular 2815. 'Rural Districts. Showing the Number as at 1.1.40'
Note: The figures for sewers were for houses without a connection that were part of a proximate group of at least 20 dwellings, which was the concentration for which providing a supply was regarded as essential. Other forms of supply to smaller groups of dwellings were considered problematical at the time (see TNA HLG71/582 Letter to Miss Fox, MTCP, from MoH, 28 April 1949)

not afford associated charges.[233] On the physicality of this claim, Table 5.9 gives a sense of the varied circumstances confronting funders of main line supplies in five counties. As regards fiscal incapacity, the case of Fakenham in the 1920s is pertinent. Here, the Ministry of Health praised Walsingham for its successful provision of water, encouraging the Council '… to provide a proper supply of wholesome water for the [whole] district'. The reaction of the Walsingham Clerk reflected contemporary sentiments: '… it would be disastrous for the town at the present time to incur such an increase on the rates, as would be necessitated by such a scheme'.[234] The problem was not just raising taxes but the ability to raise the capital, '… due to the limit laid down in the Public Health Act, 1875, for borrowing by Local Authorities for all purposes of the Act, viz., twice the assessable value of the District' (MoH 1926, p.51). Hardly surprisingly, even those RDCs prepared to fund schemes had to look for contributions from property-owners.

As with 1927 proposals to extend water pipes to Sheeptie End, Shillington, the process could stretch across years, with estimates for work received, contributions sought from parish councils and property-owners, insufficiency of resources determined, tenders adjusted, new cost estimates obtained and the cycle repeated. In such

---

service 12 houses on six sites, at a cost of £60 a house (TNA HLG40/16 Housing (Rural Authorities) Act 1931. 'Advisory Committee Report', undated c1931, pp.11–12).

[233] This applied in Hatfield prior to the de Havilland factory (*HA&SAT* 29 June 1928, p.16; *HM&CP* 31 May 1929, p.10), in Braughing (*B&NEHG* 8 September 1939, p.4; HRO RDC3/2/2 BrRDCPH&HCM 17 April 1941), in Biggleswade (*NBC&BR* 13 July 1948, p.1), in Walsingham (*NNN* 3 November 1950, p.1) and in Henley RDC (Read 2003, p.59).

[234] *FakPost* 5 January 1923, p.5.

processes parish councils were often reluctant to contribute, as demand was commonly associated with 'newcomers' who had not been paying rates for 'any time'.[235] Acknowledging the designation 'newcomer' might be nuanced to justify inaction (Harris 1974; Strathern 1982; Rapport 1993), even 40 years later councils reported demand for service improvements was particularly high amongst new residents from towns.[236] Longstanding village residents were more prone to be horrified over improvement costs. Take the case of Hadham, which had water problems at Stocking Pelham in 1933:

> [Councillor] Rev S. Leigh-Lye said there had been a shortage on account of the drought. Those needing water could all have come to him: he allowed everybody to take a couple of pails every day. He could not supply water for baths ... [but] There would be great indignation if the people of the village were called upon for water rates.[237]

Two years after this drought, a multi-parish scheme with strong public support was agreed for Buntingford but councillors were resistant. Thus, for Major Barclay:

> ... most of us landlords hardly know how to scrap round as it is. Where we are paying the rates we are to have this extra rate put on. We cannot put up the rents. In this one village we pay all the rates and employ all the labour. There is no one else to help pay the rates. I really do not know what is the best thing to do.[238]

The decision was initially deferred, then agreed. This was despite a resolution from Much Hadham Parish Council fearing the scheme would be financially detrimental, while Albury Parish Council held that its scattered settlement would make costs disproportionate to gains.[239] Under the new Braughing Council, dispute continued, with Councillor Pigg complaining: '... thousands were being spent on this scheme where hundreds would have sufficed. [So that] In years to come many ratepayers would think it was very foolish'. The Chair gave no weight to this argument, asserting '... the ratepayers would eventually say the scheme was one of the best things undertaken by the Council'.[240] Changes in public attitudes accompanying the Second World War saw views closer to the Chair's. Official reports made plain public support for improved rural water and sewerage (MoH 1944a, p.8, p.28), to which the 1944 Rural Water Supplies and Sewerage Act gave legislative and financial muscle.

Hence, shortly after 1945, a spate of commitments began to extend public services. Following the Scott Committee's call for electricity to be available throughout the country,[241] the 1940s saw installation in all council dwellings in some

---

[235] *W&DR* 10 September 1927, p.1; 15 October 1927, p.1; 20 October 1928, p.1.

[236] As reported, for example, for Ampthill (*WR&WSR* 2 March 1965, p.12).

[237] *H&EO* 10 February 1934, p.8.

[238] *H&EO* 9 March 1935, p.10.

[239] *H&EO* 23 March 1935, p.5. At a public inquiry two years later, Much Hadham was still protesting over the financial implications (*H&EO* 30 January 1937, p.9).

[240] *B&NEHG* 8 May 1936, p.4.

[241] TNA HLG37/48 'Summary of Report to the Lord Justice Scott Committee', undated c1942; Ministry of Works and Planning (1942).

districts, as with Biggleswade.[242] This was accompanied by assurances that piped water would extend throughout districts, as with Ampthill, Swaffham and Walsingham,[243] alongside rebukes for counties like Norfolk, which were reported to be the poorest providers in the nation, with 383 out of 523 parishes lacking piped water.[244] Yet, despite a 40% rise over three years in Norfolk farm hook-ups to the electricity grid,[245] costs slowed advancement. An example was when the Ministry of Health insisted piped (not mains) sewer and water systems were required for pre-fabricated temporary dwellings, which resulted in Smallburgh not applying for such homes.[246] Then Biggleswade backtracked on a commitment to provide piped water for all when council tenants refused to pay more rent to cover costs.[247] There were also qualms over service quality, as in Erpingham, where the electricity supplied was only suitable for lighting. The Council still agreed to support extensions.[248] This was occurring when there was agreement that improvement was needed; but delays occurred as the economy shifted from a war-time to a peace-time footing, with attendant problems with labour and material supplies, inflation and organisational immaturity (Morgan 1984; Cairncross 1995; Kynaston 2007). By 1947: 'Because of the shortages of labour and materials, very little has yet been done to give effect to the policy of improving rural water supplies and sewerage for which financial assistance was provided by legislation passed in 1944'.[249] Resulting frustrations found expression in Erpingham's complaint it was one of the first councils with a rural water scheme but due to endless delays could be one of the last to get a scheme; a situation not helped by complications arising from proposals to supply Weybourne RAF Camp within the district.[250] Shortages of steel were the government's explanation,[251] while delay in acquiring poles, cables and transformers was behind delayed electricity extensions in Erpingham and Smallburgh.[252]

Worse was to follow, for at least during the late-1940s the government saw better rural conditions and improved food production as priorities (Barnett 1995, p.156). But weak construction industry productivity raised Whitehall fears of overload from rural water and sewerage extensions,[253] with similar worries lowering housing specifications in the last days of the 1945–1951 government (Francis 1997, p.129; Jones

---

[242] *NBC&BR* 4 March 1947, p.4.

[243] *T&WT* 4 November 1944, p.4; *WR&WSR* 20 March 1945, p.1.

[244] *T&WT* 25 October 1947, p.4.

[245] *NNN* 19 October 1951, p.9.

[246] NRO DC22/2/47 SmRDCHCM 20 March 1945, p.2245.

[247] *NBC&BR* 13 July 1948, p.1.

[248] *NNN* 29 July 1949, p.1.

[249] TNA T229/473 IPC(WP)(47) 'Review of Investment Programme', 23 August 1947.

[250] *NNN* 26 August 1949, p.1.

[251] HCH 25 March 1948, Vol.448, col.3328.

[252] *NM&PWJ* 4 January 1947, p.3; 15 February 1947, p.6.

[253] For example, TNA HLG50/2060 'Memorandum Relating to the Need for a Revision of Costs in 1951', June 1951; TNA CAB129/48 C(51)55 'Rural Electrification', 19 December 1951.

2000, p.111). But the new government from October 1951 reduced commitments quickly. Conceivably, as Horne (1988, p.333) implied, a quick shift was encouraged by the new government finding economic conditions worse than anticipated; although one might go far to find a politician not claiming things were worse than expected on gaining a majority (e.g. on housing problems faced by the 1964 Labour government, see Crossman 1975, p.332). Certainly, the expansion of council-building owed much to electoral considerations (Jones 2000). But with an election promise of 300,000 new homes a year, the cards favoured deep housing investment (Eatwell 1979, p.152). No equivalent electoral undertaking applied to infrastructure. Almost immediately the new government informed rural councils of programme deferrals, as with Biggleswade's four-parish sewer scheme in December 1951.[254] Rural schemes were particularly open to question, with Whitehall documents repeatedly asserting that urban schemes largely paid for themselves through charges, whereas capital spending in the countryside did not.[255] The intent was spelt out in a December 1953 Treasury document on water and sewerage:

> After six years of war (during which annual expenditure dropped to less than a fifth of the pre-War amount) and eight years of post-War restriction (during which the annual volume of work was always less than two-thirds of pre-War), we are proposing to try, in 1954–55, to keep local authorities down to a volume of work very considerably less than that allowed in 1938–39.[256]

Visions of rural improvement in war-time pronouncements were side-lined (Ministry of Works and Planning 1942; MoH 1944a), but quietly so as not to ruffle the feathers of those committed to the goal:

> The Ministry does not put this very high on its own agenda (the real problem is that of *urban* water and sewerage, which is formidable, but financially self-sufficient). But it is very difficult for any Minister (egged on by Welsh interest) to let the backlog of schemes grow and grow, while going on paying lip-service to an advanced rural social policy.[257]

Despite the appearance of a commitment, spend on rural water-sewerage schemes in England and Wales dropped, from £10 million in 1950–1951, to £7.6 million in 1951–1952, then £6.9 million in 1952–1953 and £6.8 million in 1953–1954. As the MHLG Deputy Secretary wrote internally about 1954 investment: 'The fact is that with the expanding housing programme on the one hand, and our capital investment limits on the other, we have had to concentrate on schemes which will benefit the greatest number of people – mainly water and sewerage for urban housing schemes'.[258] Despite actual and expected improvement in the national economy,

---

[254] BRO RDBwM1/22 BiRDCM 19 December 1951, p.321.

[255] For instance, T229/680 'Memo on Meeting at The Treasury', 2 December 1953, p.4.

[256] TNA T227/1162 'Memo to G.B. Blaker, The Treasury, from J.D. Jones, MHLG', 17 December 1953, p.1.

[257] TNA T227/1162 'Rural Water and Sewerage', 30 December 1953.

[258] TNA T227/1162 'Investment Proposals Water and Sewerage. England and Wales', 1 December 1953, p.3.

government priorities favoured limited spending and urban projects, such that, when proposing investment from 1954–1955 to 1956–1967, officials admitted that:

> Expenditure in this sector has for years been kept to a relatively low level only by a restrictive policy increasingly difficult to apply. Thousands of sizeable communities and farms still lack proper water supplies. In few rural districts are there more than one or two parishes – if any – with decent drainage facilities. In many places the conditions are downright scandalous and a real danger to public health. The present rate of spending to remedy these conditions is absurdly small in relation to the needs.[259]

The same file acknowledged that spending on rural sewers and water schemes was wholly inadequate, with projects valued at £70 million waiting to be started, and more schemes submitted all the time. Even by 1957, the capital authorised for rural schemes in England and Wales was only £5.4 million for water and £7.2 million for sewerage.[260] Underspending was more than a rural issue, for it had important national bearing:

> The law against pollution, the efforts to end insanitary living conditions, and the national policy of encouraging agricultural development through better rural housing and better farming techniques, are all being frustrated by lack of piped water supplies in some areas and lack of proper drainage in others.[261]

But while progress was slower than expected, by 1957, only 10% of rural residents in England and Wales did not have piped water.[262] Sewerage was a long way behind, although by 1965 some £157 million had been spent on rural subsidies since 1945. Yet the continuing under-performance of the British economy, along with sluggish productivity gains (Brittan 1964; Cairncross 1995), led to further cuts in the mid-1960s when schemes were refused if not '… urgently needed for housing, industry, public health, or to end gross pollution of beaches'.[263] Note that despite the UK's relative under-performance, the economy still grew by 28% in the 1950s and then by 38% in the 1960s (Cairncross 1996, p.262). More funds could have been made available. Indeed, impediments to enriching rural districts had been lessened. For one, the 1958 Local Government Act increased RDC resources, recognising the heavy burden water and sewerage projects placed on them.[264] Unfortunately, this Act also strengthened urban opposition to rural schemes. This antagonism had been noted in Whitehall in the 1940s,[265] as boroughs and UDCs contributed a significant

---

[259] TNA T227/1162 'Water Supply and Sewerage Investment 1954–55 to 1956–57', undated c1954.

[260] HCH 29 April 1958, Vol.587, col.24W.

[261] TNA T227/1162 'Water Supply and Sewerage Investment 1954–55 to 1956–57', undated c1954.

[262] HCH 22 May 1957, Vol.570, col.1228.

[263] HCH 6 December 1966, Vol.737, col.248 W.

[264] The additional funding only brought rural districts up to the average, which was insufficient for many given capital demands to meet needed water and sewer investment (see TNA HLG127/115).

[265] TNA HLG50/1880 'Note on RDCA Executive Council Meeting with Minister and John Wrigley on 7 June 1944'.

part of county council contributions to schemes.[266] Foretelling change that would engulf local government (outside London) in the 1970s, since the early-1950s the Ministry had pushed to eliminate small rural works and create 'regional' water and sewerage authorities (RDCA 1966, p.16). These changes brought benefits but exposed rural districts to being 'outvoted' by urban interests prioritising their own schemes. This was the national scene writ small. Hence, in the early-1960s, when the Treasury was drawing attention to the most important water and sewerage projects, the focus for rural projects was largely to provide reservoirs for towns.[267] Then, with fiscal retrenchment in 1967, rural water and sewerage schemes took 'very stiff cuts'.[268] To indicate that delay caused by such decisions caused distress in rural districts would be an exercise in understatement. Examples of councils expressing disappointment, disgust and alarm over refusals or delays are too numerous to capture convincingly.

A sketch that should leave the reader with a sense of the disquiet is the experience of Potton in Biggleswade. A sewerage scheme for the village was first mooted when it was sent to the engineers for consideration in 1930. A scheme for west of the railway started in 1931 and finished in March 1932 with 80 homes connected (Biggleswade RDC 1931, p.10; 1932, p.11; 1933, p.25). By 1944 a scheme for the parish and two neighbouring parishes was deemed '… a necessity which has long been recognised and one which should have post-war priority' (Biggleswade RDC 1945, p.7). It took until 1965 before the RDC was able to put forward what became a £200,000 project for the parish, a decision whose importance was indicated by the RDC telling the County Council that all new building in the village should cease until an adequate sewage disposal system was operational.[269] Yet it was not until late-1970 that the Ministry accepted the need for improved sewerage and sewage disposal and engineers were instructed to begin detailed drawings for sewage disposal.[270] In this regard, Potton exemplified what lay behind the Ministry's suggestion, nearly half a century earlier, that (at least) a 20-year time-span was needed for water schemes: 'Experience shows that even a comparatively small scheme may involve many years of work from its first inception to its completion, and that planning well ahead of requirements is therefore but common prudence' (MoH 1926, p.46). That the Potton scheme took more like 40 years is a testament to the low priority afforded to rural schemes in government circles.

---

[266] TNA HLG127/116 'Memo from J.H. Waddell for The Secretary', 8 May 1959; TNA HLG127/116 'Memo from F.L. Edwards for The Secretary and J.H. Waddell', 5 June 1959; TNA HLG127/115 'Grants for Rural Water, Sewerage and Sewage Disposal. Revising of Basis of Grants', July 1959.

[267] TNA CAB129/107 C(61)151 'Civil Public Investment. White Paper, 1961', 6 October 1961, p.26; TNA CAB129/111 C(62)159 'Civil Public Investment. White Paper 1962', 17 October 1962, p.50–25.

[268] TNA CAB129/126 C(66)109 'The Economic Situation', 18 July 1966, p.1. Water and sewerage was the third largest itemised reduction, after roads in England and swimming baths.

[269] BC&BG 25 June 1965, p.1; 1 July 1966, p.19.

[270] BC&BG 27 November 1970, p.36.

5.3.2   Geographical Diversity

Examples like Potton might be a peculiarity or misfortune of timing but system-rigging forces produced a geography of their own. One element was highlighted in the 1957 Merioneth MP's reaction to the claim only 10% of rural residents in England and Wales lacked piped water:

> It is very interesting to make a comparison between the position prevailing in Wales and the position in Cumberland, Northumberland and Westmorland. The percentage of piped water supplies in the rural district of Wales as a whole is 72 per cent, but included in that percentage are the three densely populated counties of Denbigh, Flint and Glamorganshire. If those three counties are omitted the percentage falls to about 56 per cent. In Cumberland, the percentage is 82 per cent; in Northumberland, 83 per cent; and in Westmorland, 86 per cent.[271]

Calder (1969, pp.419–20) expressed the position somewhat differently, when observing that the Home Counties in the early-1940s were relatively well provided but Wales and South-West England '... lived and worked in conditions which were coming to seem unbelievably primitive'.[272] Significantly, of course, these were two regions in which access from country districts to towns was problematic (Chap. 2). Urban access was central to the expansion of rural services.

Pronouncing on the merits of this approach, the Ministry of Health (1937, p.69) cast light on Whitehall's view that improved services came from closer rural–urban ties:

> Comprehensive scheme[s] [of water supply and sewage disposal] ... often benefit rural areas, particularly the parts adjoining large towns. There has also been a steady increasing demand in rural areas generally for better sanitary services. Improved transport facilities have enabled the town worker to live further out in the country, and to the urban mind the village or cottage well, the cesspool and the earth-closet are relics of a barbarous age. Further, the higher standard of education, the newspapers, the wireless set and readier means of visiting neighbouring towns have all contributed to a gradual change in the outlook of the rural inhabitants themselves and consequent dissatisfaction with the arrangements which seemed sufficient and unobjectionable to the rural population of former days.

As seen in early schemes to extend electricity networks, national authorities used largely urban-centred programmes to reach country residences:

> There are in this country at the present time three [electricity] supply experiments. One is in Bedfordshire, another in Lincolnshire and the third in Cheshire. The plan in Bedfordshire covers three rural districts and 101 square miles, and in that area there are about 15,000 people with 4,000 houses. The cost of the scheme is estimated at £116,500 and the Treasury have agreed to make advances not exceeding 10 years and not exceeding £8,000 to meet 75 per cent of the annual deficit. The scheme depends on taking a bulk supply from Bedford, then to run a cable out into the villages and hamlets and often to individual farmhouses, and after they have run out a cable to do as they do in America, send out a canvasser to see that the people take the supply.[273]

---

[271] HCH 22 May 1957, Vol.570, col.1247–48.

[272] Calder cited the 1941–43 National Farm Survey (MAF 1946).

[273] HCH 11 December 1929, Vol.233, col.493.

Hence, rural advances were mainly in urban shadows, as the 1951 MHLG's Parliamentary Secretary accepted:

> … water supply was provided to a quarter of the parishes of this country up to 1939. What hon. Gentlemen opposite have not so far admitted is that naturally the sequence of events was that provision was first made to the parishes which it was easiest to supply. Most of them, or a very large proportion, were very much more urban in character than rural and the reason for the sequence of events was the question of the ability to carry the rate charge and the problem which the county council had to face in that respect.[274]

The economics of service provision, in-migrant impacts on revenue bases, service delivery costs and a lack of technical capacities in small councils, all favoured this solution. Market principles favoured population concentrations and wealthier geographical zones; the hope, exemplified in the diffusion of many innovations, was that the geographical and social 'periphery' benefited down the line (e.g. Berry 1970).

If so, this occurred with frustrating delays. Take the extension of Bedford's electricity supply into Ampthill. In 1923, Bedford Corporation proposed extending its supply into the district.[275] Six months later, the decision was reversed.[276] Nearly two years later the Corporation returned, renewing its proposal, adding Ampthill Town.[277] In 1926, the programme was delayed, as the scheme needed the approval of Biggleswade, which withheld consent unless three of its villages were supplied.[278] This was something of a Biggleswade pattern, for this RDC's approval also threatened Letchworth supplying Biggleswade Town.[279] By 1929, when Parliamentary speeches were lauding the Bedford initiative, the Electricity Commissioners were pressing the Corporation to reach all rural parts of the demonstration area.[280] Progress was made, with only four villages not connected by 1932. Since residents could not be forced to connect, a key question was economic viability. By 1935, the Bedford Electricity Undertaking had an annual loss of £16,638, of which £5956/10/0d was attributable to the Rural Demonstration Scheme. The capital cost for the Rural Scheme was £235,789, against an original estimate of £129,385; where '… the great increase was due to the very considerable, but relatively scattered, development which had taken place in the area since the adoption of the Scheme'. Thus, the 2712 rural subscribers of 1932 rose to 4496 in 1935 (71.8% of premises, compared with 57.5% in 1932). However, at the outset, the Demonstration area had only 4600 dwellings.[281] The electricity scheme was certainly demonstrating, by revealing demand for services. Provision was easier in Hatfield with its

---

[274] HCH 25 June 1951, Vol.489, col.1122.

[275] W&DR 6 January 1923, p.1.

[276] W&DR 14 July 1923, p.1.

[277] W&DR 23 May 1925, p.1.

[278] W&DR 23 January 1926, p.1.

[279] NBC&SN&DN 14 March 1924, p.1; 20 June 1924, p.3.

[280] W&DR 16 March 1929, p.1.

[281] W&DR 1 October 1932, p.1; 28 September 1935, p.1.

city-focused transport links and proximity to London's urban edge. As early as 1929, Hatfield was able to insist inadequate water wells either be closed or dwellings be connected to supplies from the Barnet Gas and Water Company.[282] The 1933 drought hastened connections, with the villages of Cuffley, Northaw and new housing developments like Brookmans Park joining (Hatfield RDC 1934, p.8; 1935, p.8). The Council's policy was to extend the Company's supply to all settlements by 1935.[283] The elongation of networks into the countryside was not spurred by charity. As Jackson (1973, p.84) spelt out, water authorities wanted a deposit equivalent to their outlay on mains supply or would only lay mains with a guaranteed 10% return on capital invested. Even London electricity companies of the 1920s and 1930s imposed conditions before laying mains, with gas companies usually requiring a specified number of rooms be 'carcassed' before installation. The result, as Neville Chamberlain reported for Risley in Lancashire, was that urban suppliers, who were under no obligation to make extensions since estimated revenue generally fell short of statutory entitlements, required rural councils to guarantee statutory returns.[284] Outside the reach of urban-centred operations, dwelling owners made hefty contributions to costs and council tenants saw rents rise when supply lines were extended.[285]

Ampthill's electricity supply faced buffeting from two fronts on account of such arrangements. To the north, they had their experience with Bedford. To the south, Luton's grudging behaviour confronted them. Hopeful in 1924, when dialogue started, deflated in 1926, when Luton's revenue demands became clear, uplifted again in 1927, when Luton indicated it would supply any part of the district Bedford did not cover, by 1929 there no indication of when work would start.[286] The reason given was landowner opposition, which also caused delays in Hatfield, although in Ampthill there were additional problems securing Ministry of Transport approval.[287] Progress was nonetheless made, although Luton was accused of supplying the 'plums', while leaving small and 'outside' parishes without supply. Cutting a long story short, after claiming delays were 'entirely' out of their control, by 1947 Luton Corporation had still not supplied smaller villages. The blame was now apportioned to material shortages.[288] The story was mainstream, not just for electricity. In the case of Smallburgh, for example, collaboration with Norwich began 1939 when the

---

[282] *HM&CP* 21 June 1929, p.14.

[283] *H&PBG* 5 July 1935, p.2.

[284] HCH 15 July 1926, Vol.198, col.607.

[285] Examples were found across the investigated districts. Their regularity is suggested by instances from the late inter-war period in Braughing (*H&EO* 16 March 1929, p.1; 9 March 1935, p.10; HRO RDC3/2/1 BrRDCPHHCM 23 September 1937, p.215; *Hertford Mercury and Reformer* 12 May 1939, p.14; *B&NEHG* 8 September 1939, p.4; HRO RDC3/1/2 BrRDCM 5 October 1939, p.43).

[286] *W&DR* 23 May 1925, p.1; 16 January 1926, p.1; 19 June 1926, p.1; 7 May 1927, p.1; 9 February 1929, p.1.

[287] *HM&CP* 31 May 1929, p.10; *W&DR* 19 October 1929, p.1.

[288] Commentaries on the Luton electricity supply saga include: *W&DR* 6 February 1932, p.1; 11 November 1933, p.7; *WR&WSR* 21 January 1947, p.1.

City applied to supply water to seven parishes.[289] Hoveton was connected in that year but it was not until 1955 that the other settlements joined; indeed by 1961 just 145 miles of water mains had been laid (Smallburgh RDC 1970, p.15). All this should not be taken to indicate complete reliance on towns. In Norfolk, for example, starting from 1947, Wells-next-the-Sea increased the water volumes it bought from Walsingham, while Erpingham, which had relied on Cromer to supply electricity from the 1920s and water from the 1940s to some parishes, had wells supplying Smallburgh, whose own supply system was developed in the mid-1950s and covered two-thirds of the district's population by the mid-1960s.[290]

The complexity of multiple providers and a multitude of collaborative arrangements did not bode well for efficiency or effectiveness. An amalgam of private companies and public agencies acting as profit-making enterprises led to confusion, uncertainty and incompatible systems. The merits of government intervention to organise the growing 'mess' were recognised early:

> The generation and main transmission of electricity have now been fully organised as a result of the Act of 1926 and the establishment of the Central Electricity Board. The numerous frequencies of supply have been replaced by a uniform frequency of 50 cycles per second — a necessary preliminary to the complete functioning of the Board ... Just as different frequencies of supply prevented the economic interconnection of generating stations, so today numerous voltages of supply hamper distribution. There are 19 principal voltages, whereas it is desirable to reach a minimum of two, namely, 230 volts for lighting and domestic purposes and 400 volts for power and industrial purposes ... Although, at the end of 1934–35, as many as 407 undertakings were supplying consumers at the standard voltages, namely, 230 and 400 volts, various undertakings were still giving supplies at 19 different voltages, varying between 100 and 250 volts, thus involving an unnecessarily high cost in the manufacture of lamps and apparatus at a variety of miscellaneous voltages. There are no less than 625 separate authorised undertakers operating 635 undertakings.[291]

Fears of inefficiency in manufacturing were critical to rationalising the electricity industry, just as the 1933 drought prompted change in the water industry:

> The experience of the drought has emphasised the need, which has long been felt, of better organisation of water resources, by the rationalisation of administrative areas so as to bring them into closer correspondence with natural areas, and by better control of access to sources of supply; of more effective planning of future schemes of water supply between undertakers with common interests in sources of supply; of the more equitable distribution of water in streams and rivers between water undertakers and riparian interests; and of the modernisation of the Waterworks Clauses Act.[292]

---

[289] *T&WT* 22 July 1939, p.11.

[290] *FakPost* 6 May 1927, p.3; *NM&PWJ* 9 June 1945, p.8; *T&WT* 25 October 1947, p.4; *NNN* 25 February 1955, p.9; 2 November 1956, p.9; *D&FT* 29 July 1966, p.11; Smallburgh RDC (1967, p.17). To offer a non-Norfolk example, in what became Braughing, by 1936 part of Hadham's water was to come from Ware RDC, while Buntingford had a joint scheme with Hitchin RDC (*H&EO* 5 September 1936, p.10).

[291] TNA CAB24/268 CP64(37) 'Committee on Electricity Distribution: Second Report', February 1937, p.157–2.

[292] TNA CAB24/251 CP242(34) 'Water Services', 2 November 1934, p.1.

Hence, inter-war, steps to bring coherence to the supply of collective services started. Rationalising the administrative structures that controlled production and distribution was accepted.[293] After 1945, the lessons of 1939–1945 strengthened calls for coherence in supply chains (Kynaston 2007, p.23). Into and beyond the 1940s, new operational milieu emerged, in which inadequacies of resources and staffing became less influential in rural electrification. Significantly, however, the backlog of inaction or thwarted action meant households in many hamlets, villages and small towns waited decades for services. Despite opposition from some quarters, at least in terms of wanting expensive underground lines rather than overhead cables,[294] near universal coverage for electricity was proclaimed in the 1960s, with supplies even to isolated Forestry Commission dwellings.[295] For water, 96% of rural properties were said to be mains connected by 1964.[296] The UN Economic Commission for Europe (1964, p.17) acknowledged improvement covered isolated hill areas. Water supply improved more slowly but came a long way ahead of sewerage. This was despite many rural districts shifting priorities onto this service in the mid-1950s as water needs came closer to being met. Even so, while Erpingham had 20 sewerage schemes completed by 1971, there were still nine in preparation or under construction.[297] Ampthill fared better, with just six out of 29 parishes without a mains sewer by 1973,[298] while, as might be expected by its more urbanised rurality, Hatfield had almost complete coverage, save in outposts too distant from sewerage systems for cost effect connections (Hatfield RDC 1973, p.48). Herein, of course, lies the rub. For out of these collective services, it was sewers and water that impacted most on rural housing improvement.

5.3.3   Amenity and Housing Numbers

In the first decades of the twentieth-century, the link between housing and these services was not considered critical. Applications for dwelling approvals (viz. loan sanction) before 1919 made this clear. For instance, when Smallburgh applied for council dwellings under the 1890–1909 Acts, the proposals for Happisburgh, Horning (1911) and Potter Heigham (1913) called for ample gardens around

---

[293] TNA CAB24/254 CP51(35) 'Water Policy', 8 March 1935, p.1.

[294] As seen early in Hatfield (*HM&CP* 31 May 1929, p.10) and Erpingham (*FakPost* 26 June 1931, p.5; 24 July 1931, p.4), although by 1936 Erpingham supported overhead cables (*YarmInd* 1 February 1936, p.1; *T&WT* 28 August 1937, p.10), albeit calls for underground lines were still made in the 1960s (HCH 25 March 1968, Vol.761, col.219W).

[295] HCH 20 July 1964, Vol.699, col.22W; 28 July 1964, Vol.699, col.273W.

[296] HCH 22 December 1964, Vol.704, col.225W.

[297] NRO DC13/5/35 ERDCM 29 June 1971, para.24.

[298] BRO RDAR8/54 ARDCMOHar 1973, p.4. This figure contrasts with 1955, when only six parishes had a supply.

dwellings so 'waste' could be dispersed, with wells for water.[299] Gains from large gardens were viewed as multiple, as they gave a capacity to grow food, which Biggleswade equated with weekly earnings of 1/-; a compensation for the high rents of new dwellings.[300] Indeed, RDCs approved tenant applications to keep pigs or poultry in their gardens, including building pigstys and other relevant buildings approved by sanitary inspectors.[301] Councils emphasised such advantages when seeking tenants, as with Aylsham RDC's 1919 Act homes.[302] Given the cost of servicing early council-homes, the Ministry supported excluding baths on sites with insufficient drainage or water supply.[303] Attitudes changed. For instance, in 1925 dispute arose with the Agent for Eustace Gurney over new dwellings for Great Walsingham. The Agent claimed '… a drainage system for labourer's cottages [was] probably dangerous and quite unnecessary', arguing that distributing waste onto gardens was '… the sensible way of disposing of the sewage in County districts'. The local press was forthcoming on councillors' responses. Noting that a large number of cottages had been erected in nearby St Faith's, Blofield and Aylsham RDCs, the *Fakenham Post* recorded Councillor Rev. Tatham's charge that: 'The suggestion that refuse should be put on the garden was the filthiest idea he had ever heard. They did not want to go back to the system of 100 years ago. They tried to educate the people to live decently'. The Council rejected Eustace Gurney's fears that draining into rivers would cause problems for cows, prioritising drainage for human health.[304] Possibly this decision emerged from previous Walsingham experience, for dwellings built over 1912–1914 had a quarter acre of land, which had proved insufficient '… to enable the tenants to dispose of excreta in an efficient manner'.[305]

Many rural dwellings had poor amenities. Even in the more urbanised environment of Henley RDC, by 1952 only 200 out of 5000 houses were connected to a public sewer, with 1500 households still using a pail closet (Read 2003, p.110). Such arrangements increasingly attracted criticism. This negativity was captured in legislation like the 1925 Housing Act, which laid down instructions over items like

---

[299] TNA HLG1/972 'Loan Sanctions. Smallburgh RDC', file covers 1909–1915.

[300] See TNA HLG1/845 'Report of Inquiry by Harry Stewart', 7 July 1913. A further advantage, according to Biggleswade Councillor Rev Ewbank, was that large gardens '… would keep them [tenants] at home and out of the public house' (*NBC* 1 August 1919, p.6).

[301] As in Biggleswade (*NBC* 1 April 1921, p.8; *BC&BG* 2 February 1923, p.3) and Walsingham (*FakPost* 4 September 1931, p.1).

[302] *NWP&ENS* 20 May 1921, p.3.

[303] BRO RDAM1/7 ARDCM 27 September 1923; TNA HLG48/297 Letter from Clutton RDC Clerk to MoH Secretary, 9 January 1924; Reply, 17 January 1924. By 1939 the Ministry was requesting baths be fitted in council houses if there was piped water, as in Ampthill (*W&DR* 31 January 1939, p.2).

[304] This debate started at the Council meeting of 27 May 1925 (NRO DC19/6/13, p.23) and was reported in the *FakPost* (29 May 1925, p.5; 12 June 1925, p.5).

[305] NRO DC19/6/16 WRDCM 10 October 1928, p.69.

water supply, closet accommodation, drainage and lighting for dwellings (MoH 1931), and verbally in speeches like that of the 1937 Normanton MP:

> This is from the local secretary of the Agricultural Workers Union: 'I am writing to you with regard to the sanitation of the council houses which some of our members and myself live in. We have buckets just outside the door, where we have to have our own meals, and we have to empty these buckets twice a week on our gardens. There are no cesspits provided, which, to my mind, I think is a standing disgrace'. It is an absolutely rotten position to have earth closets just outside the back doors of council houses, with pantries close to the closets.[306]

For councils, the implications of building to lower specifications became obvious. In Biggleswade, pressure to wire council dwellings for electricity was exerted as early as 1925.[307] In larger settlements across the investigated districts, the supply of electricity and gas was very much on the agenda at that time.[308] By 1930 Biggleswade was surveying council tenants in all villages on their preference for electricity or gas supply.[309] Activity around these two services intensified during the 1930s, but it was not until 1939 that council minutes reported the modernisation of council homes to add baths.[310] More provoking and irritating for councils were Ministry refusals to countenance house-building if sites lacked water or sewerage facilities.

This was less of an issue for private house-building. Builders concentrating on homes for sale were more reluctant to move into areas not already equipped with these services. This applied even during London's dynamic inter-war growth, when new housing numbers accelerated once drainage schemes were completed (Jackson 1973, p.84). As the Ministry of Health acknowledged: 'A piped water supply tends to attract the builder and the progress in extending water piped supplies more than keeps pace with the progress of building, even in rural areas' (MoH 1929, p.6). No-supply impacted negatively on selling price. Hence, builders would terminate schemes if councils failed to build water or sewerage networks, although a few built facilities themselves, as with the Brookmans Park Estate in Hatfield.[311] Of course, if the latter solution was the only option, as when Messrs Fisher & Sons proposed 25 homes in Sculthorpe (Walsingham), but were refused a £700 grant for a sewer, the outcome might be problematic. After this rejection, the builder proposed a sewer,

---

[306] HCH 18 June 1937, Vol.325, col.744.

[307] BRO RDBwM1/9 BiRDCM 15 July 1925; 12 August 1925.

[308] As for Fakenham homes (*FakPost* 1 April 1927, p.5) and especially in Hatfield (*HM&CP* 20 August 1927, p.8; HRO RDC7/96/2 *HM&CP* 24 March 1928). Concerns over charges on tenants and difficulties constructing networks were reported for more agricultural parts of Hatfield (*HA&SAT* 29 June 1928, p.16; *HM&CP* 31 May 1929, p.10).

[309] BRO RDBwM1/10 BiRDCM 9 July 1930. It is unclear how many tenants were surveyed but if all, the responses represent about 53% of homes, out of which 64.7% favoured electricity, 27.9% gas and 7.5% neither.

[310] *W&DR* 31 January 1939, p.2.

[311] For instance: HCH 14 April 1931, Vol.251, col.73; *W&DR* 22 April 1933, p.1; and, for Brookmans Park, TNA HLG48/324 Letter from Hatfield RDC Clerk to MoH, 26 January 1924.

which was reviewed by the Council, and accepted subject to conditions on effluent content. Fisher & Sons rejected the conditions. With an urgent need for dwellings, the Council waived its opposition; provoking the Surveyor to seek absolution from the decision.[312] As with building council homes to poorer standards, down the line there would be a bill to pay. Costs would be higher the more isolated the development. Yet councils were pressured to build in such locales. As Chap. 3 showed, lobbying came from 'below' to provide homes in parishes. Then, in the 1940s, in order to increase farm output, governments lessened opposition to building on isolated plots near farms (albeit for a limited time).

Urges for housing in smaller places came from other sources, with implications for amenity provision. As seen for electricity supply under Bedford's Rural Demonstration project, service extensions often attracted more building than anticipated. Take Biggleswade to explore this phenomenon. From the 1930s to 1950, by which time water supply covered most of the district, notable household growth occurred in large and small parishes (Table 5.10). The Council was committed to service improvements, as evinced by its major commitment to the 1919 Act, and the district offered relatively highly paid employment in brick-making and market gardening, plus commuting prospects to urban centres in Hertfordshire,[313] alongside opportunities like the RAF base at Henlow. Overall, these prospects gave comfortable household budgets compared with mainly agricultural districts.[314] No shock to find relatively high levels of water supplied to householders, with all parishes having mains connections by 1935 (Biggleswade RDC 1936, p.9). Predictably, the largest parishes had the best supply (Table 5.10), although provision improved across the board over time. Yet, even in 1950, a significant tranche of dwellings in small- and medium-sized parishes only had standpipes. Offering comparators, Braughing reported 20.4% of dwellings accessed water from standpipes in 1949, while Ampthill did better for larger parishes, with no dwellings standpipe supplied in 1951, with just below 6% in both medium and small parishes.[315] Although figures were more difficult to find, Norfolk districts were less well-covered. Smallburgh's mains supply only covered 39.7% of dwellings in Horning, Hoveton and Stalham in 1949, with just 7.0% more accessing standpipes.[316] Even by 1957, mains supply

---

[312] NRO DC19/6/12 WRDCM 18 February 1925, p.102; 4 March 1925, p.106; 18 March 1925, p.111. This was not a problem for the early decades of the century alone. In 1950, for example, the Ministry rejected the sewerage treatment proposed for new houses at Mogerhanger (Biggleswade) but house-building was allowed to proceed with '… the drainage system to be agreed with the Ministry later' (BRO RDBwM1/21 BiRDCM 4 January 1950, p.9).

[313] By 1950 some parishes in Ampthill, like Flitwick, were considered dormitories for urban centres (BRO RDAR8/32 ARDCMOHar 1951, p.3). Likewise, by 1965 64% of newcomers to Biggleswade's Arlesey worked in Hertfordshire and 12% in London (*BC&BG* 6 November 1959, p.1; 16 July 1965, p.1).

[314] TNA HLG37/43 'Report on Local Investigations in Wiltshire, Bedfordshire, Derbyshire and Anglesey', undated c1936; *BC&BG* 16 July 1965, p.1.

[315] HRO RDC3/28/11 Annual Report for the East Hertfordshire Combined Districts Medical Officer of Health 1949, p.84; BRO RDAR8/32 ARDCMOHar 1951, p.10.

[316] *NNN* 27 October 1950, p.8.

Table 5.10 Water supply coverage in Biggleswade parishes, 1912–1950

	Largest parishes	Middle parishes	Smallest parishes
	Per cent of dwellings with water supplied		
1912	68.7	43.5	11.2
1922	98.9	76.9	60.4
1932	97.0	77.6	74.8
1950 by mains supply	89.3	73.6	60.7
1950 by standpipe	10.7	24.7	19.8
1950 by mains or standpipe	100.0	98.2	80.5
	Per cent of all dwellings in RDC		
1912	72.3	22.3	5.4
1922	72.3	22.4	5.4
1932	73.1	21.4	5.5
1950	77.4	18.2	4.4
	Per cent change in dwelling numbers		
1912–1922	6.0	6.6	5.6
1922–1932	11.8	5.9	13.5
1932–1950	37.9	10.3	24.4

Source: Biggleswade RDC (1913, p.9; 1923, p.6; 1933, p.10; 1951, p.25)
Note: The largest category had more than 300 dwellings in 1950 and the smallest less than 100.
Parishes in the three categories were unchanged over the period shown, with eight or nine parishes
in each category. Up to 1950 data were reported as 'dwellings supplied', whereas for 1950 they
were broken down into mains or standpipe supply

across the district only stood at 70.2% for large parishes, 59.0% for medium-sized,
and 30.6% for the smallest (Smallburgh RDC 1958, p.17). Even in Biggleswade, as
late as 1939 standpipes were installed on the Tempsford Estate to improve neighbourhood water supply.[317] What contributed to so late a use of standpipes and wells?

With standpipe numbers not available before 1950, we can offer only cautious
interpretation. Even so, trends in rural housing raise questions worth exploring. In
the 1930s the nation failed to provide housing for the less well-paid, with limited
construction during the Second World War following. This created severe shortages
by 1945. Former Minister of Health, Arthur Greenwood, made a valid point on this
in 1944, noting that estimates of the shortfall depended on assumptions about the
quality of the existing stock. For some, around 5,500,000 additional dwellings were
needed, whereas others talked about 3–4 million.[318] Whatever the number favoured,
deficits were large. This applied as much to rural areas as to urban, for, despite the
countryside seeing less war-damage (MoH 1944a, p.13), there were notable inter-
war deficiencies in the supply of rural homes (Ministry of Works and Planning
1942). Public impatience over shortages soon led to a squatter movement.
Commentaries on squatting often focus on unoccupied properties in cities (Hinton
1988), but incidences were also occasioned by the decommissioning of rural

---

[317] BRO WY928 'Tempsford Estate Correspondence on Cottages, 1920–1943'.
[318] HCH 15 March 1944, Vol.398, col.282.

military bases. Some bases even became integral to rural councils' post-war housing programmes, for substandard though the accommodation was, even after improvement, camps still provided roofs over heads when these were in short supply. In Biggleswade, squatters occupied hutments at Potton, Shefford and the former Everton WAAF Camp, with further huts at Southill and Tempsford offered to the Council as temporary accommodation (both turned down). The arrangement was not ideal, as indicated by a 1951 survey, which reported tenants found the Everton huts 'horrible'.[319] Many camp occupations, whether later officially sanctioned or not, were accompanied by poor conditions. Getting a handle on numbers is not easy, as commentary is muted in council minutes; or, like the Everton Camp, offers insight then goes silent. From Hatfield Medical Officer of Health annual reports, we can say that occupant volumes shifted substantially and quickly. Thus, there were 28 families in Hatfield huts in 1948, which rose to 173 in 1951, before dropping to none in 1955 (Hatfield RDC 1950, p.37; 1951, p.47; 1955, p.36). This falling off in the 1950s was common. By 1956, for example, the Ministry recorded just 12 families in camps in Biggleswade (all at Everton), with 20 at Braughing, none at Erpingham or Smallburgh, and 71 in Walsingham.[320] These figures suggest temporary camps might have contributed to, but were insufficient to account for, the extent of standpipe usage in 1950. Nonetheless, rural council reliance on former military bases should not be forgotten. Even by 1954, Norfolk reported 26 temporary camps housing 357 families, and a further 16 were converted into semi-permanent residences for 645 families.[321]

Well before the War, another rural dynamic increased pressure for standpipe or well provision. As part of an inter-war flood of largely uncontrolled expansion into the countryside, many 'shanty-towns' appeared like blots on the landscape, with locations often distant from towns or villages (Gayler 1970; Lowerson 1980; Hardy and Ward 1984). Built on small, irregular plots, which cash-strapped landowners were keen to sell (Gayler 1970), such unprincipled speculations were promoted by urban authorities, as with the LCC, which advertised trams for sale as holiday homes throughout the 1920s (Moore-Colyer 1999, p.117). 'Converted railway carriages, redundant trams and pink-roofed asbestos shacks (the most hated of all by aesthetes) popped up like excrescences, their cheap incongruity masking hundreds of individual hopes and patiently saved-for ambitions that made them possible' (Lowerson 1980, p.258). These landscape intrusions were present in the investigated districts. Ten railway carriages were used as homes in Walsingham in 1926,

---

[319] BRO RDBwM1/17 BiRDCM 11 September 1946, p.138; *NBC&BR* 27 April 1948, p.2; *WR&WSR* 23 January 1951, p.7.

[320] TNA HLG31/22-23 HI14/56 'The Administration of Housing Subsidies Under the Housing Subsidies Act, 1956. Appendix F'. Walsingham reported 98 families in 1957 (*D&FT* 5 July 1957, p.9). Complaints that replacements were not built for hutments stretched into the 1960s (e.g. *D&FT* 16 June 1961, p.12; 19 April 1963, p.3). Nationally, at the end of 1959, when the last camp was closed in Braughing (HRO RDC3/1/10 BrRDCM 4 February 1960, p.4614; *H&EO* 13 May 1960, p.6), 69 camps were still used for accommodation (1210 families; MHLG 1960, p.66).

[321] *T&WT* 13 August 1954, p.8.

Erpingham supported Rotherham RDC's call for legislation discouraging the use of caravans as dwellings in 1929 and Smallburgh was discomforted over the continuous occupation of Bacton beach huts for 12–18 months in 1932.[322] Coastal areas like north Norfolk attracted incursions, with accommodation often flimsy, as well as geographically concentrated (Gardiner 2010, pp.236–37). This worked against these 'dwellings' in the longer term, with many destroyed during the Second World War, as the land they occupied was taken for the war effort (Hardy and Ward 1984). This should not distract from the continuance of such structures in the post-war era. In both Ampthill and Hatfield, for example, buses were used for accommodation post-war, while Braughing reported workshop, garage and timber poultry house 'conversions' for human occupation.[323] Admittedly, after 1945, these 'dwellings' often graced minutes because councils sought to eliminate them; as with the small, converted bus a family with three children was occupying in Hatfield, which had no lavatory or drains.[324] Of course, councils could impose conditions on such dwellings through their inspection regimes; although, as Chap. 2 indicated, there was reluctance to follow this route. Housing shortages often resulted in substandard homes being 'conveniently' ignored.[325] Rural councils were working to improve housing amenities, but accommodation shortfalls gave impetus to countervailing forces, which ensured amenity and quality deficits required close attention down the line.

The link between water and sewer availability and house-building was troublesome, as previous studies have shown. Difficulties finding suitable water supplies restricted site options for the earliest projects under the 1919 Act (Sayle 1924, p.57), with new-build concentrations at times focused on villages with water mains as a result (e.g. Sherwood 1996, p.53). By the late-1930s, development delays or lower-quality completions were linked to water shortage,[326] with land-use planning schemes gearing up to tackle this problem, as in Norfolk North-East, by looking to restrict development to areas served by sewers or where economically viable schemes enabled drainage by extensions.[327] Such impacts continued after 1945.[328] In 1949, for example, the Ministry limited action by Newport Pagnell RDC due to

---

[322] NRO DC19/6/14 WRDCM 26 May 1926, p.11; *FakPost* 13 December 1929, p.3; *NWP&ENS* 10 June 1932, p.1.

[323] Ampthill decided to demolish the lived-in double-decker bus (BRO RDAM1/15 ARDCM 27 March 1952, p.17). For Braughing and Hatfield, see HRO RDC3/1/2 BrRDCM 3 December 1942, p.266; *H&PBG* 24 July 1953, p.1.

[324] *H&PBG* 24 July 1953, p.1. The Smallburgh Medical Officer of Health similarly sought action over 'shacks' on the coast and near the Broads (*NNN* 5 November 1954, p.1).

[325] Noting a difference in approach, in 1932 Smallburgh did not proceed against buildings erected in contravention of bye-laws but said it would exercise its relevant powers in the future (*NWP&ENS* 30 September 1932, p.5).

[326] For three examples, see BRO RDBwM1/11 BiRDCM 13 February 1935; BRO RDAM2/20 ARDCHCM 8 April 1936; *W&DR* 31 January 1939, p.2.

[327] *YarmInd* 9 May 1936, p.15.

[328] For a description of how a plan to build in four villages in Kington RDC, that started with site selection in April 1943, was still held up by water considerations mid-1949, see HCH 30 June 1949, Vol.466, col.1650.

water insufficiency, restricting development to pre-1939 levels until the 1961 Great Ouse Water Act removed water curbs (Eley 1973). Inadequate water and sewer systems restrained rural house-building in many places, including Beckham and Northrepps in Erpingham, Meppershall in Biggleswade, Lidlington in Ampthill, Briston in Walsingham and in Hereford RDC.[329] Encased within a kaleidoscope of deferments were regular visitors to water supply delays. As in Braughing's Thorley, there were frustrations over network extensions from nearby towns.[330] Commonly, interplay occurred between requirements for water or sewer systems and house-building volumes. For Erpingham this was manifest in fears the Ministry would insist on water and sewerage services for larger housing sites.[331] It was anticipated that the Ministry might accept small additions to hamlets or villages but, if 20 or more dwellings were proposed, a sewerage scheme was expected, so driving up costs.[332]

   This led to more building deferments as the 1950s progressed and the government sought lower public spending. Commonly, this led to deferrals, even for large multi-parish schemes, as with the four-parish sewer for Clifton, Henlow, Langford and Shefford (four of the largest parishes in Biggleswade, with a combined population over 8000 in 1951). A deputation to the Ministry in 1939 reported that financial difficulties were barring the scheme's progress. The Council continued to seek approval but was put off in 1951 and 1953, when a proposal was made to divide the project into two in the hope of advancement. Eventually, a start date in early-1955 was approved. By late-1955 work at Clifton and Shefford was only at the planning stage, although progress had been made at Henlow and Langford. That this was far from sufficient was revealed in late-1956 when Langford's frustration over progress led to requests for cesspool drainage to circumvent delay in meeting housing shortages. While recognising the merits of the mains scheme, the Ministry again deemed the project low priority. This time the national economic situation was blamed, whereas in 1951 it was material and labour shortages. Only in mid-1957 did the Council receive approval for Henlow and Langford, but progress was slow. In 1960 the expectation was that the project would end in 1961. As 1962 closed, all council homes were sewer connected in the four parishes, compared with just 61.2% for privately owned homes.[333] This cameo of one project, which took more than 20 years

---

[329] HCH 24 October 1947, Vol.443, col.8W; NRO DC13/5/20 ERDCM 13 December 1948, p.4; TNA HLG50/2317 'Observations Relating to the MoH Publication Norfolk Water Survey', 1 December 1949; BRO RDBwM1/21 BiRDCM 17 May 1950, p.130; NRO DC13/5/24 ERDCM 15 September 1952, para.79; BRO RDAM2/22 ARDCHCM 20 November 1952; NRO DC19/6/66 WRDCHCM 31 August 1953, p.13; 26 October 1953, p.23.

[330] HRO RDC3/1/3 BrRDCM 6 May 1948, p.418.

[331] NRO DC13/5/20 ERDCM 4 April 1949, p.4.

[332] TNA HLG71/582 'Memorandum on Rural Planning to the Minister from J.W.S.', 26 April 1949, p.2; Letter to Miss Fox, MTCP, from MoH, 28 April 1949.

[333] W&DR 6 June 1939, p.15; BRO RDBwM1/22 BiRDCM 19 December 1951, p.321; BRO RDBwM1/24 BiRDCM 18 March 1953, p.31; 28 October 1953, p.228; BRO RDBwM1/25 BiRDCM 24 November 1954, p.301; BRO RDBwM1/26 BiRDCM 26 October 1955; BC&BG 28

of frustration to reach resolution, was characteristic not simply of Biggleswade but well beyond this district.

Often, the thread outlining the development of these schemes disappeared in written reports, so making identification of project termination (or even origin) difficult to establish. Nevertheless, there were clear indications of significant hold-ups in housing development owing to laggardly supply of amenities. Take sewerage to illustrate. Two examples from Ampthill are Aspley Guise, where 32 new homes were approved in 1947 with the proviso that improvement in sewerage was needed, which was approved in 1954, but where new-build was still restricted in 1960 owing to drainage problems, and Cranfield where a 1958 Parish Council meeting concluded the sewerage problem was no nearer solution after 10 years.[334] On Braughing Council, calls to fund drainage systems were made as early as 1938, with a scheme proposed for the whole district in 1947. By 1950, the situation in the village of Braughing was deemed urgent, with a proposal to move forward with a scheme in 1955, which was approved in 1957, although construction was not expected to start until late-1958. In 1961, nightsoil collections were terminated to push landlords to connect with the system. Yet, by 1969, only 11 out of 19 parishes were partly or completely linked to mains sewers.[335] For the three Norfolk districts progress was similarly slow, as expected with more dispersed populations (Chap. 1).[336] There was early awareness of the merits of sewer systems, with proposals for Fakenham (which had a larger population than two of the four adjacent UDCs), and Melton Constable, with its railway repair works (Wrottesley 1970; Yaxley 1977, p.118), put forward as early as 1919. By 1951, however, no appreciable progress was reported for cross-district sewerage schemes. This was despite expectations as early as 1948 that the Ministry would insist new housing sites had sewage disposal plants. An indicative expression of council concerns came from Smallburgh RDC (1965, p.19):

> The necessity for more sewerage in the district increasingly gives cause for concern by reason of the more possible danger to health that could arise in the more closely built up parts of the district where the drainage from new and improved properties cannot adequately be treated by the various types of individual disposal units.

Despite such fears, fiscal constraints were notable; as with high interest rates shelving many capital plans in 1957 (Smallburgh RDC 1958, p.16). Remember, all three

September 1956, p.1; 19 October 1956, p.1; BRO RDBwM1/28 BiRDCM 5 June 1957, p.122; BRO RDBwM1/30 BiRDCM 14 January 1959, p.14; Biggleswade RDC (1961, p.22; 1963, p.13).

[334] WR&WSR 21 January 1947, p.1; 25 March 1958, p.1; BRO RDAM2/22 ARDCHCM 21 January 1954; BRO RDAM2/23 ARDCHCM 20 January 1960.

[335] H&EO 10 December 1938, p.7; 8 November 1947, p.5; 15 September 1950, p.5; 11 January 1957, p.6; 9 May 1958, p.6; 14 April 1961, p.12; HRO RDC3/2/11 BrRDCJFHCM 13 December 1955, p.2958; HRO RDC3/28/28 Braughing Annual Report 1969, p.30.

[336] That dispersal had cost implications was acknowledged in Whitehall, with the cost guidance for sewers laid out in MoH Circular 87/47 as £50 a dwelling for a compact village in semi-urban conditions, £100 for scattered villages and £120 if similar to a scattered village but involving difficult subsoil and works (TNA HLG50/2060 'Rural Sewerage and Sewerage Disposal: Circular 87/47 and Costs per House. The Need for a Revision of Costs in 1951', June 1951, p.1).

of the investigated Norfolk districts lost population over 1951–1961, although 1961–1971 was more uneven with continued loss, stability and, for Smallburgh, growth. No surprise there were worries over paying for capital schemes, as expressed volubly in Erpingham in 1960.[337] With national pressure to limit capital spending recurring, securing a head of steam behind investment programmes was not easy. By the late-1960s, the Norfolk districts had a long way to go with their programmes. Smallburgh reported mains sewers only in the built-up parts of three parishes, alongside zones in five more, with calls to plan for an additional eight plus extensions in two more with partial coverage (Smallburgh RDC 1970, p.20).[338] Delays in improving amenities generated anxiety, as with Smallburgh writing to Norwich Corporation in 1947 asking it to speed up extending the electricity network, since lack of electricity was a factor in people leaving villages.[339] Decades later, attempts to improve housing conditions were held back as initiatives were put aside behind the halo of higher national priorities. Such side-stepping had a repeated geographical tread, which discriminated against rural locations (Chap. 6).

Note that the Biggleswade example above captured the experience of larger settlements in the district. When we look at smaller places, the effect was more marked; for what had to be overcome were both discriminations against rural districts and within districts. Although mains water supplies became nearly universal as the 1950s shuffled into the 1960s, schemes for drainage continued to hold-up housing schemes, especially in smaller places. This arose not simply owing to Ministry refusal to sanction schemes without mains drainage, as at Lemsford in Hatfield and Tempsford in Biggleswade, but also because the modernisation of old properties was denied for the same reason, as happened for nine parishes in Biggleswade in 1964, as well as in Braughing and Erpingham in the same year.[340] Seeing the writing on the wall, councils began to exclude villages from new development owing to amenity deficiencies, often with no indication of when or if a decision might be adjusted. Examples include Husborne Crawley and Salford in Ampthill, Potton and Upper Caldecote in Biggleswade and even an extension to Fakenham in Walsingham.[341] The consequences were evident to councils, which, like Ampthill,

---

[337] NNN 26 February 1960, p.1.

[338] TNA HLG1/999 Letter from LGB President to Walsingham RDC Chair, 27 June 1919; FakPost 5 March 1920, p.5; T&WT 30 March 1951, p.8; NRO DC22/2/48 SmRDCHCM 22 June 1948, p.3486; NNN 18 April 1957, p.5; 26 February 1960, p.1; Smallburgh RDC (1970, p.20); NRO DC13/5/35 ERDCM 29 June 1971, para.24.

[339] NM&PWJ 4 January 1947, p.3.

[340] HRO RDC7/1/22 HtRDCM 6 November 1956, p.239; BRO RDBwM1/34 BiRDCHECM 11 July 1962, p.81; BC&BG 17 January 1964, p.17; HRO RDC3/1/14 BrRDCFCM 18 February 1964, p.6104; NRO DC13/5/32 ERDCM 28 July 1964, para.41. Braughing even debated whether to modernise council dwellings without installing baths and WCs in 1962 (HRO RDC3/1/12 BrRDCFCM 16 January 1962, p.5388).

[341] D&FT 4 January 1957, p.5; BRO RDBwM1/31 BiRDCHECM 9 March 1960, p.354; BC&BG 1 July 1966, p.19; WR&WSR 1 August 1967, p.1; B&BR 31 October 1967, p.1.

reported to the Ministry increased planning applications for new dwellings after mains drainage was installed.[342]

5.4 Contributing to Contrivance

The context for this chapter is the changing place of rural areas in England's evolving socio-demographic geography. The academic literature was relatively slow to wake up to the 'suburbanisation' of the middle-classes into 'metropolitan villages', on which Pahl (1965) particularly raised the profile. Almost two decades later 'counterurbanisation' secured currency as migration from towns to 'remoter' areas was identified as something more than movement by 'drop-outs' and quirky individuals (Fielding 1982; Perry et al. 1986). Historical analysis and contemporary accounts showed these tendencies existed decades before the literature acknowledged (Bourne 1912; Hardy and Ward 1984; Pooley and Turnbull 1998; Howkins 2003; Burchardt 2012). But what were trickles in earlier decades became an avalanche with changes to transport, communications and workplace patterns (Champion et al. 1987; Cross 1990; Boyle et al. 2001). Significantly, this upward trajectory came at the same time as many rural areas experienced out-migration. The literature rightly highlighted employment prospects as a significant factor in this trend (e.g. Pedley 1942; Saville 1957; Drudy and Wallace 1971) but for local residents limited housing opportunities and inadequate dwelling standards also encouraged departure, especially as exhaustion could result from waiting for improvement.[343] Implicated in these deficiencies was the blocking, delaying or diminishing of rural opportunities as rural councils lacked the resources to pay for upgrades, had difficulty securing builder cooperation to deliver them, and were thwarted by inadequate amenity provision to underpin them. Deliberate intervention by vested interests was not necessary to produce these endings. While it might be inappropriate to read-off specific outcomes from deep-seated structural relationships in society, it is relevant to trace how dominant economic, political and social practices, which differentially enabled opportunities and imposed constraints, drew action towards end-products reflecting dominant power relationships. As regards the capacity of rural councils to respond to housing deficiencies, this chapter has sought to demonstrate three main points: first, rural councils were restricted by

---

[342] TNA HLG118/558 'Improvement Report Eastern Counties', July 1966, p.4.

[343] Illustrative reports from across the decades can be found for Ampthill (BRO RDAR8/11 ARDCMOHar 1930, p.12), Biggleswade (BRO RDBwM1/20 BiRDCM 23 March 1949, p.49), Braughing (H&EO 9 March 1935, p.10; 3 April 1937, p.10), Hatfield (HRO RDC7/1/22 HtRDCM 6 November 1956, p.238), Smallburgh (NM&PWJ 9 May 1936, p.6), Walsingham (NRO DC19/6/67 WRDCHCM 8 April 1957, p.128), and was widely acknowledged in government circles (TNA HLG37/43 'Report on Local Investigations ...', undated c1936, p.2; Ministry of Works and Planning (1942, p.18); TNA MAF147/1 Letter to J. Christie, Norfolk War Agricultural Executive Committee, from F.W.C. Chartres, MAF Rural Land Utilisation Office Woodbridge, 3 December 1946; TNA CAB129/110 C(62)145 'Housing', 2 October 1962).

imposed operational structures that did not equip them to mount an effective campaign to challenge rural housing weaknesses; second, emerging from the same essential causes, rural councils lacked the capacity to 'fix' amenities such that improvements to the rural housing stock were more easily achieved, with this 'failure' giving national authorities convenient excuses for delay, suspension or termination of programmes to enhance the housing stock; and, third, that, in combination, an industry oriented towards speculative building, of comparatively low productivity, worked against the private sector contributing effectively to rural housing advancement for the lower paid. With construction companies largely limiting their rural excursions to arenas subsidised by the extension of public infrastructure, councils with inadequate resources were the principal hope for housing advancement in the 'deep' countryside.

There is within the British literature on local–central government relations a commonly expressed view that national authorities have the capability to impose their wishes on local authorities but choose not to (e.g. Jackman 1978). But irrespective of how far you believe governments constrain council activity, there is a deeper issue of how far they enable it. Enabling has tended to be muted. Reforming local government, so as to improve responsiveness to the needs of local citizens, has been repeatedly put to one side by national authorities. The drift has been towards bigger, better equipped organisations, but the channels taken to achieve service improvements have regularly reduced democratic accountability by taking functions from elected councils and giving them to non-elected 'regional' authorities (Saunders 1983, 1985). When the practices and procedures of local government have themselves been targeted for reform, recommendations that could produce real change have been ignored (e.g. Committee of Inquiry into Local Government Finance 1976), with solutions usurped to foster political party advantage (Young 1975; Sharpe 1978), while the handicaps of the past, especially as regards inflexible fiscal regimes, have lingered to retain national control (Self 2006, p.133; Foley 1972; Dearlove 1979). National governments had multiple opportunities to address questions of inadequate resources, fiscal and human, amongst rural councils but failed to act. Rather than addressing funding difficulties at grassroots level, adjustments to funding shortfalls were grudgingly addressed by raising central funding, so increasing dependence on the centre. This pattern was very different from many other nations (Page and Goldsmith 1987; Karran 1988). Whether in government circles or more widely there was a tendency to dismiss rural councils as inactive because they did not spend. But, as we have seen, net housing costs were low, at times even providing income to ameliorate property tax bills. If rural councils put too little into housing construction, at core this can hardly be laid at the door of a reluctance to spend.

A caveat needs raising against this point, for a precursor to housing investment was a large spending item. When rural councils at first erected council homes they were encouraged by national authorities and local landowners to minimise amenity provision. What lay behind this was a desire to keep costs down, alongside views that such facilities were unnecessary (even extravagant). But as the decades rolled forward, demand from the public, changing views on acceptable living standards, and growing acknowledgement of health and other problems, pushed governments towards expecting such facilities. What resulted was a tale of national neglect. The costs of mains water and sewerage were beyond the capacity of rural councils to provide given their low tax bases; yet it was not until 1944 that a system of funding for rural provision was even remotely close to addressing needs. During the 1950s, when economic conditions were more favourable, investment in the rural realm was deliberately stifled, despite national politicians extolling the virtues of these services. Indeed, they were so virtuous Whitehall was soon blocking councils from building homes in places without mains supplies; the very hypothetical supplies that had been denied to the countryside through a lack of vision and funding from the centre. Note that in 1947 both electricity and gas supplies were removed from municipal government to enhance provision quality and consistency but water and sewage systems were left in under-funded council hands. There was opportunity to act but the challenge was not taken up by governments.

A similar tussle was played out with private builders. Delays, missed targets, general under-provision, cost over-runs and deficient quality in house-building owed much to the building industry. Providing close to all council homes, the common focus on speculative building meant many companies were drawn away from the 'deep' countryside, with weak competition reinforcing low-productivity, resulting in relatively expensive homes, especially in low-wage local economies. Until later in the century, the companies rural contracts attracted tended to be smaller, unstable commercially and characterised by slow dwelling completions. Regularly, councils had to rely on firms lacking the capacity to build to required standards. Neither rural councils nor rural builders had the ability to break free from the structural constraints in which they operated. Councils had restricted resources and limited autonomy (Ashford 1982), while builders encapsulated inner drives within their industry, with the added intensified twists of small operator restraints in an under-performing sector (Barlow and Duncan 1994; Powell 1996; Wellings 2006).

A good part of the problem for both was the failure of the state to show leadership. Elsewhere in the world the emergence of once-called newly industrialising countries, like South Korea, had seen private and public collaboration to raise productivity, mitigate economic instability and foster socio-economic advancement (Harris 1986; Chowdhury and Islam 1993; Schwartz 1994). Perhaps timid by South Korean standards, such collaboration was sought by Wheatley with the 1924 Housing Act, in offering builders assurances on volumes and requiring commitments, like apprenticeships, in return.[344] As explained in 1932 debates in Parliament, the 1924 Act:

> … was the first real attempt to reorganise the industry with something like a guarantee. It was a guarantee for 15 years. No wonder that people say that they cannot trust Governments, for the proposal today is at the end of eight years definitely to abandon the promise that was given publicly for a 15 years' guarantee.[345]

---

[344] HCH 16 April 1924, Vol.172, col.1367–70; MoH (1925, p.47).
[345] HCH 15 December 1932, Vol.273, col.645–46.

The agreement was reneged on by subsidy cuts then their abolition, leaving housing policy primarily focused on the well-to-do, without nurturing improvement in the industry. After 1945 there were further opportunities for advancement but 1945–1951 efforts were dissipated by overload. For Malpass (2003, p.657), fragmentation in responsibility for construction, housing and land-use planning were well known before 1945, yet, knowing there were massive accommodation shortages and severe quality deficits, Prime Minister Attlee gave Bevan the massive tasks of housing and setting up the NHS. Placing health with housing under one ministry proved too much, especially when economic turmoil required considerable effort to preserve the NHS (Campbell 1987, p.162): '… to leave one Minister, whoever he was, responsible for both health and housing at a time when both were going to be in the forefront of the political battle was a serious mistake' (also Morgan 1984, pp.163–66; Malpass 2003, p.656).[346] Bevan let too many schemes start when resources were not available (Bowley 1949). Even so, the 1945–1951 house-building programme gave demand stability and an environment encouraging new ideas.

This offered a base for productivity rises, especially as economic problems eased in the 1950s (Malpass 2003, p.657). Perhaps experiments in prefabrication had made a stumbling start after 1918, following their introduction by Addison to alleviate skills shortages (Ravetz 2001, p.78), but this was at least followed by Chamberlain's establishment of the Building Research Station to improve practices (Swenarton 2007). During and after 1945 a massive exercise in experimentation occurred, with great emphasis on standardisation and prefabrication (Gay 1987). In Scandinavia, France and Germany this led to successful industrialised building programmes that enabled high production at reasonable prices (Smyth 1985; Golland 1998). In Britain, like the inter-war years, the industry did not capitalise on these initiatives. When more industrialised methods were adopted under the high-rise programme, the industry did not use even its own resources effectively (Smyth 1985, pp.174–75). As Harold Macmillan grasped in the early-1950s, restrictive practices by management and workers characterised the sector (Catterall 2003, p.197). Not tackling these obstructions had long-term costs. The Treasury was damning in assessments of the industry's performance: 'For an industry which has such an assured programme of work extending over several years ahead it is little short of scandalous that progress in these fields has been so slow' (viz. improving productivity and reducing costs).[347] Where Macmillan did score was in attracting Percy Mills, an industrialist who knew Whitehall, as his 'housing czar'. Mills worked with the industry and established 10 regional production boards for better local coordination (Macmillan 1969, pp.395–96, pp.459–60). Some questioned Macmillan's contribution to housing expansion, believing he had been '… handed

---

[346] For Macmillan (1969, p.66): 'Bevan was in many ways much the most exciting of all the Labour team. Unexpectedly he proved to be a good administrator and a good Minister. He failed over his housing policy for the simple reason that the Ministry over which he presided was too wide in its responsibilities'.

[347] TNA T229/471 PC(49)37 'The Cost of Building', 7 April 1949.

success on a plate'; yet, there was little doubt his housing programme left an impression the Conservatives got things done (Horne 1988, p.332, p.340). Electoral gains aside, the fundamental critique of Macmillan was that he changed little. The working relationship developed by Mills between the industry and the state quickly dissipated. The inflexibility of the industry again generated palpitations in the Treasury, where officials fretted they had little scope for action if the industry became overloaded.[348] Macmillan gained promotion to higher office, but accolades for his work were not based on improved industrial performance, nor a new vision for state-business operations. Instead, after 1955, policies returned to the 1930s model. Conservative actions depreciating state involvement, returning housing largely to private builders, leaving a residualised council segment (Jones 2000, 2010). Governments neither pushed the industry towards higher productivity nor provided an environment conducive to long-term investment, while the industry did too little to improve performance compared with its continental counterparts. In combination, both government and industry failed to address mainstream housing demand, as the Conservatives began to realise as they smelled electoral 'disaster' emerging from housing failures in the early-1960s (Chap. 6).

References

Adamson S (1974) The politics of improvement grants: a survey of local authority procedures for implementing housing improvement grants. Town Plan Rev 45:375–386

Addison C (1934) Four and a half years: a personal diary from June 1914 to January 1919. Hutchinson & Co., London

Alderson S (1962) Britain in the sixties: housing. Penguin, Harmondsworth

Allen GC (1976) The British disease: a short essay on the nature and causes of the nation's lagging wealth. Hobart Paper 67. Institute of Economic Affairs, London

Ashford DE (1980) A Victorian drama: the fiscal subordination of British local government. In: Ashford DE (ed) Financing urban government in the welfare state. St. Martin's, New York, pp 71–96

Ashford DE (1981) Policy and politics in Britain: the limits of consensus. Blackwell, Oxford

Ashford DE (1982) British dogmatism and French pragmatism: central-local policy-making in the welfare state. Allen & Unwin, London

Audit Commission (1984) The impact on local authorities' economy, efficiency and effectiveness of the block grant distribution system. HMSO, London

Baker WP (1953) The English village. Oxford University Press, London

Ball ID (1980) Urban investment controls in Britain. In: Ashford DE (ed) National resources and urban policy. Croom Helm, London, pp 115–142

Ball M (1983) Housing policy and economic power: the political economy of owner occupation. Methuen, London

Ball M, Grilli M (1997) Housing markets and economic convergence in the European Union. Royal Institution of Chartered Surveyors, London

Barlow J, Duncan SS (1994) Success and failure in housing provision: European systems compared. Pergamon, Oxford

---

[348] TNA T229/680 'Memo from T.H. Caulcott to Mr. Jarrett and Mr. Blaker', 10 August 1954, p.2.

Barnett C (1972) The collapse of British power. Eyre Methuen, London

Barnett C (1986) The audit of war: the illusion and reality of Britain as a great nation. Macmillan, London

Barnett C (1995) The lost victory: British dreams, British realities 1945–1950. Macmillan, London

Barnett C (2001) The verdict of peace: Britain between her yesterday and the future. Macmillan, London

Baxter R (1972) The working class and Labour politics. Polit Stud 20:97–107

Berry BJL (1970) Commuting patterns: labour market participation and regional potential. Growth Chang 1(4):3–10

Berry F (1974) Housing: the great British failure. Charles Knight, London

Biggleswade Rural District Council (1913) Annual report of the medical officer of health and sanitary inspector 1912. Biggleswade

Biggleswade Rural District Council (1923) Annual report of the medical officer of health and sanitary inspector 1922. Biggleswade

Biggleswade Rural District Council (1925) Annual report of the medical officer of health and sanitary inspector 1924. Biggleswade

Biggleswade Rural District Council (1931) Annual report of the medical officer of health and sanitary inspector 1930. Biggleswade

Biggleswade Rural District Council (1932) Annual report of the medical officer of health and sanitary inspector 1931. Biggleswade

Biggleswade Rural District Council (1933) Annual report of the medical officer of health and sanitary inspector 1932. Biggleswade

Biggleswade Rural District Council (1936) Annual report of the medical officer of health and sanitary inspector 1935. Biggleswade

Biggleswade Rural District Council (1945) Annual report of the medical officer of health and sanitary inspector 1944. Biggleswade

Biggleswade Rural District Council (1951) Annual report of the medical officer of health and sanitary inspector 1950. Biggleswade

Biggleswade Rural District Council (1961) Annual report of the medical officer of health and sanitary inspector 1960. Biggleswade

Biggleswade Rural District Council (1963) Annual report of the medical officer of health and sanitary inspector 1963. Biggleswade

Birch AH (1959) Small-town politics: a study of political life in Glossop. Oxford University Press, London

Blondel J, Hall R (1967) Conflict, decision-making and the perceptions of local councillors. Polit Stud 15:322–350

Booth A (1987) A managed economy? Econ Hist Rev 40:499–522

Bourne G [pseudonym for Sturt G] (1912) Change in the village, 1955 edn. Duckworth, London

Bowers JK, Cheshire P (1983) Agriculture, the countryside and land use: an economic critique. Methuen, London

Bowley M (1945) Housing and the state 1919–1944. Allen & Unwin, London

Bowley M (1949) Housing and the economic crisis in Great Britain. Int Labour Rev 59:127–153

Boyle PJ, Cassidy S, Duke-Williams O, Rees PH, Stokes G, Turner A (2001) Commuting patterns in rural areas. Countryside Agency Publications, Wetherby

Branson N (1979) Poplarism 1919–25: George Lansbury and the councillors' revolt. Lawrence & Wishart, London

Bristow SL (1978) Local politics after reorganisation – the homogenisation of local government in England and Wales. Publ Admin Bull 28:17–33

Brittan S (1964) The Treasury under the Tories 1951–1964. Penguin, Harmondsworth

Broadberry SN, Crafts NFR (1996) British economic policy and industrial performance in the early post-war period. Bus Hist 38:65–91

Brown T (2017) Tragedy and challenge: an inside view of UK engineering's decline and the challenges of the Brexit economy. Matador, Kibworth Beauchamp

Bulpitt JG (1983) Territory and power in the United Kingdom. Manchester University Press, Manchester

Burchardt J (2012) Historicizing counterurbanization: in-migration and the construction of rural space in Berkshire (UK), 1901–51. J Hist Geogr 38:155–166

Burnett J (1986) A social history of housing 1815–1985, 2nd edn. Methuen, London

Butterworth R (1966) Islington Borough Council: some characteristics of single-party rule. Politics 1(1):21–31

Cairncross A (1995) The British economy since 1945, 2nd edn. Blackwell, Oxford

Cairncross A (1996) Managing the British economy in the 1960s. Macmillan, Basingstoke

Calder A (1969) The people's war: Britain 1939–1945. Pimlico, London

Campbell J (1987) Nye Bevan: a biography. Hodder & Stoughton, London

Catterall P (2003, ed) The Macmillan diaries: the Cabinet years, 1950–1957. Macmillan, London

Champion AG, Green AE, Owen DW, Ellin DJ, Coombes MG (1987) Changing places: Britain's demographic, economic and social complexion. Edward Arnold, London

Chowdhury A, Islam I (1993) The newly industrialised economies of East Asia. Routledge, London

Coleman R (1982) Second homes in north Norfolk. In: Moseley MJ (ed) Power, planning and people in rural East Anglia. University of East Anglia Centre for East Anglian Studies, Norwich, pp 97–117

Coles R (1982) Retirement in rural north Norfolk. In: Moseley MJ (ed) Power, planning and people in rural East Anglia. University of East Anglia Centre for East Anglian Studies, Norwich, pp 119–136

Committee of Inquiry into Local Government Finance (1976) Report. Cmnd 6453. The Layfield Committee. HMSO, London

Committee on National Expenditure (1931) Report. Cmd 3920. HMSO, London

Congreve A (2013) Sustainability in new housing development. Routledge, London

Connor LR (1936) Urban housing in England and Wales. J R Stat Soc 94:1–65

Construction Task Force to the Deputy Prime Minister on the Scope for Improving the Quality & Efficiency of UK Construction (1998) Rethinking construction. Department of the Environment, Transport & the Regions, London

Corina L (1974) Elected representatives in a party system: a typology. Policy Polit 3:69–87

Cross DFW (1990) Counterurbanization in England and Wales. Avebury, Aldershot

Crossman R (1975) The diaries of a Cabinet Minister: volume one – Minister of Housing 1964–66. Hamish Hamilton and Jonathan Cape, London

Darke J (1991) Local political attitudes and council housing. In: Lowe S, Hughes D (eds) A new century of social housing. Leicester University Press, Leicester, pp 159–174

Davies A (2013) 'Right to buy': the development of a Conservative housing policy, 1945–1980. Contemp Br Hist 27:421–444

Dearlove J (1979) The reorganisation of British local government. Cambridge University Press, Cambridge

Department of the Environment (1974) Rates and rateable values in England and Wales 1973–74. HMSO, London

Dickens P, Duncan SS, Goodwin M, Gray F (1985) Housing, states and localities. Methuen, London

Drudy PJ, Wallace DB (1971) Towards a development programme for remote rural areas: a case study in north Norfolk. Reg Stud 5:281–288

Dunbabin JPD (1977) British local government reform: the nineteenth century and after. Engl Hist Rev 92:777–805

Dunleavy PJ (1981) The politics of mass housing in Britain 1945–75. Clarendon, Oxford

Dyer MC (1978) Leadership in a rural Scottish county. In: Jones GW, Norton A (eds) Political leadership in local government. University of Birmingham Institute of Local Government Studies, Birmingham, pp 30–50

Eastwell R (1979) The 1945–1951 Labour government. Batsford, London

Economic Commission for Europe, Geneva (1958, 1962) Annual bulletin of housing and building statistics for Europe. United Nations, New York

Eley AW (1973) The passing of independence: the story of a rural district council. Occasional Paper 1. Bradwell Abbey Field Centre for the Study of Archaeology, Natural History & Environmental Studies, Milton Keynes

Eurostat. (annual) Eurostat yearbook. Office for Official Publications of the European Communities, Luxembourg

Feddes A, Dieleman FM (1996) Investment in housing in ten northwest European countries 1950–1985. Tijdschr Econ Soc Geogr 87:73–79

Fielding AJ (1982) Counterurbanization in Western Europe. Prog Plan 17:1–52

Finnigan R (1984) Council housing in Leeds 1919–1939: social policy and urban change. In: Daunton MJ (ed) Councillors and tenants. Leicester University Press, Leicester, pp 102–153

Fletcher P (1969) The agricultural housing problem. Soc Econ Adm 3:155–166

Flynn N, Leach S, Vielba C (1985) Abolition or reform? the GLC and the metropolitan county councils. Allen & Unwin, London

Foley DL (1972) Governing the London region. University of California Press, Berkeley

Foot M (1973) Aneurin Bevan: a biography – volume II 1945–1960. David-Poynter, London

Ford RG, Brown CJ (1978) Rating reform and urban structure. Area 10:8–14

Foster CD, Jackman RA, Perlman M (1980) Local government finance in a unitary state. Allen & Unwin, London

Francis M (1997) Ideas and policies under Labour 1945–1951: building a new Britain. Manchester University Press, Manchester

Freeman TW (1968) Geography and regional administration: England and Wales 1830–1968. Hutchinson, London

Gamble AM (1981) Britain in decline: economic policy, political strategy and the British state. Macmillan, Basingstoke

Gardiner J (2010) The thirties: an intimate history. Harper Press, London

Garrard JA (1977) The history of local political power. Polit Stud 25:252–269

Gasson RM (1975) The provision of tied cottages. Occasional Paper 4. University of Cambridge Department of Land Economy, Cambridge

Gay O (1987) Pre-fabs: a study in policy-making. Public Adm 65:407–422

Gayler HJ (1970) Land speculation and urban development: contrasts in south-east Essex, 1880–1940. Urban Stud 7:21–36

Giles AK, Cowie WJG (1960) Some social and economic aspects of agricultural workers' accommodation. J Agric Econ 14(2):147–169

Golland A (1998) Systems of housing supply and housing production in Europe: a comparison of the United Kingdom, The Netherlands and Germany. Ashgate, Aldershot

Grant W (1977) Independent local politics in England and Wales. Saxon House, Farnborough

Green FE (1920) A history of the English agricultural labourer 1870–1920. P.S. King & Co., London

Green DG (1981) Power and party in an English city: an account of single-party rule. Allen & Unwin, London

Gyford J (1985) The politicisation of local government. In: Loughlin M, Gelfand MD, Young K (eds) Half a century of municipal decline. Allen & Unwin, London, pp 77–97

Ham A (1981) Treasury rules: recurrent themes in British economic policy. Quartet, London

Hardy D, Ward C (1984) Arcadia for all: the legacy of a makeshift landscape. Mansell, London

Harloe M (1975) Swindon: a town in transition: a study in urban development and overspill policy. Heinemann, London

Harris C (1974) Hennage: a social system in miniature. Holt, Rinehart & Winston, New York

Harris N (1986) The end of the third world: newly industrializing countries and the decline of an ideology. Penguin, Harmondsworth

Harrison M, Norton A (1967) Local government administration in England and Wales. Maud Committee report on the management of local government volume five. HMSO, London

Hartley OA (1980) The Second World War and after. In: Fraser D (ed) A history of modern Leeds. Manchester University Press, Manchester, pp 437–461

Hatfield Rural District Council (1934) Report of the medical officer of health 1933. Hatfield

Hatfield Rural District Council (1935) Report of the medical officer of health 1934. Hatfield

Hatfield Rural District Council (1936) Report of the medical officer of health 1935. Hatfield

Hatfield Rural District Council (1950) Report of the medical officer of health and public health inspector 1949. Hatfield

Hatfield Rural District Council (1951) Report of the medical officer of health and public health inspector 1950. Hatfield

Hatfield Rural District Council (1955) Annual report of the medical officer of health and public health inspector 1954. Hatfield

Hatfield Rural District Council (1973) Annual report of the medical officer of health and public health inspector 1972. Hatfield

Hechter M (1975) Internal colonialism. Routledge & Kegan Paul, London

Hennessy P (1996) Muddling through: power, politics and the quality of government in postwar Britain. Victor Gollancz, London

Hennessy P (2006) Having it so good: Britain in the fifties. Allen Lane, London

Hepworth NP (1971) The finance of local government. Allen & Unwin, London

Hill BE, Ray D (1987) Economics for agriculture: food, farming and rural economics. Macmillan, Basingstoke

Hinton J (1988) Self-help and socialism: the squatters' movement of 1946. Hist Work J 25:100–126

Hodge I, Whitby MC (1981) Rural employment: trends, options, choices. Methuen, London

Hoggart K (1987) Does politics matter? redistributive policies in English cities 1949–74. Br J Polit Sci 17:359–371

Hoggart K (2003) England. In: Gallent N, Shucksmith DM, Tewdwr-Jones M (eds) Housing in the European countryside: rural pressure and policy in Western Europe. Routledge, London, pp 153–167

Holmans AE (1987) Housing policy in Britain: a history. Croom Helm, London

Holmans AE (1990) House prices: changes through time at national and subnational level. Working Paper 110. Department of the Environment Government Economic Service, London

Horne A (1988) Macmillan 1894–1956: volume one of the official biography. Macmillan, Basingstoke

Howkins A (2003) The death of rural England: a social history of the countryside since 1900. Routledge, London

Ingham G (1984) Capitalism divided? the city and industry in British social development. Macmillan, Basingstoke

Jackman R (1978) Issues in financial allocation. In: Davies RL, Hall PG (eds) Issues in urban society. Penguin, Harmondsworth, pp 268–299

Jackson AA (1973) Semi-detached London: suburban development, life and transport, 1900–39. Allen & Unwin, London

Jacobs K, Kemeny J, Manzi T (2003) Privileged or exploited council tenants? the discursive change in Conservative housing policy from 1972 to 1980. Policy Polit 31:307–320

James L (2006) The middle class: a history. Little Brown, London

Jarvis D (1996) British Conservatism and class politics in the 1920s. Engl Hist Rev 111:59–84

Jennings P (1969) The living village: a report on rural life in England and Wales based on actual village scrapbooks. Country Book Club, London

Jennings RE (1977) Education and politics: policy-making in local education authorities. Batsford, London

Johnson RW (1985) The politics of recession. Macmillan, Basingstoke

Jones H (2000) 'This is magnificent!': 300,000 houses a year and the Tory revival after 1945. Contemp Br Hist 14:99–121

Jones B (2010) Slum clearance, privatization and residualisation: the practices and politics of council housing in mid-twentieth-century England. Twentieth Cent Br Hist 21:510–539

Karran TJ (1988) Local taxing and local spending: international comparisons. In: Paddison R, Bailey S (eds) Local government finance: international perspectives. Routledge, London, pp 53–84

Keith-Lucas B, Richards PG (1978) A history of local government in the twentieth century. Allen & Unwin, London

Kynaston D (2007) Austerity Britain 1945–51. Bloomsbury, London

Kynaston D (2014) Modernity Britain: a shake of the dice, 1959–62. Bloomsbury, London

Layton E (1961) Building by local authorities. Allen & Unwin, London

Lee JM (1963) Social leaders and public persons: a study of county government in Cheshire since 1888. Clarendon, Oxford

Lindblom CE (1959) The science of 'muddling through'. Public Adm Rev 19(2):79–88

Linsley B (2005) Homes for heroes: housing legislation and its effects on housing in rural Norfolk 1918–1939. PhD thesis University of East Anglia

Local Government Board (1919) Manual on the preparation of state-aided housing schemes. HMSO, London

Loughlin M, Gelfand MD, Young K (1985, eds) Half a century of municipal decline. Allen & Unwin, London

Lowerson J (1980) Battles for the countryside. In: Gloversmith F (ed) Class, culture and social change: a new view of the 1930s. Harvester, Brighton, pp 258–280

Lyman RW (1957) The first Labour government 1924. Chapman & Hall, London

Macintyre S (1980) Little moscows: communism and working-class militancy in inter-war Britain. Croom Helm, London

Macmillan H (1969) Tides of fortune 1945–1955. Macmillan, London

Malpass P (2003) Private enterprise in eclipse? a reassessment of British housing policy in the 1940s. Hous Stud 18:645–659

Marriner S (1976) Liquidity problems in the mass-production of 'homes for heroes'. Bus Hist 18:152–189

Marriner S (1979) Sir Alfred Mond's octopus: a nationalised house-building business. Bus Hist 21:23–44

Marshall JL (1968) The pattern of housebuilding in the inter-war period in England and Wales. Scottish J Polit Econ 15:184–205

Ministry of Agriculture & Fisheries (1946) National farm survey of England and Wales (1941–43). HMSO, London

Ministry of Health (1920) First annual report, 1919–1920: part II – housing and town planning. Cmd 917. HMSO, London

Ministry of Health (1921) Report of the departmental committee on the high cost of building working class dwellings, Cmd 1447. HMSO, London

Ministry of Health (1925) Sixth annual report, 1924–1925. Cmd 2450. HMSO, London

Ministry of Health (1926) Seventh annual report, 1925–1926. Cmd 2724. HMSO, London

Ministry of Health (1929) Advisory Committee on Water report on rural water supplies. HMSO, London

Ministry of Health (1930) Eleventh annual report, 1929–1930. Cmd 3667. HMSO, London

Ministry of Health (1931) Model byelaws issued from the Ministry of Health: XIIIc improvement areas. HMSO, London

Ministry of Health (1932a) Thirteenth annual report, 1931–1932. Cmd 4113. HMSO, London

Ministry of Health (1932b) Report of the Committee on Local Expenditure (England and Wales). Cmd 4200. HMSO, London

Ministry of Health (1934) Fifteenth annual report, 1933–1934. Cmd 4664. HMSO, London

Ministry of Health (1935) Sixteenth annual report, 1934–1935. Cmd 4978. HMSO, London

Ministry of Health (1936) Seventeenth annual report, 1935–1936. Cmd 5287. HMSO, London

Ministry of Health (1937) Eighteenth annual report, 1936–1937. Cmd 5516. HMSO, London

Ministry of Health (1938a) Nineteenth annual report, 1937–1938. Cmd 5801. HMSO, London

Ministry of Health (1938b) The management of municipal housing estates. HMSO, London

Ministry of Health (1939a) Twentieth annual report, 1938–1939. Cmd 6089. HMSO, London

Ministry of Health (1939b) Rates and rateable values in England and Wales 1938–39. HMSO, London

Ministry of Health (1944a) Rural housing: third report of the Rural Housing Sub-Committee of the Central Housing Advisory Committee. HMSO, London

Ministry of Health (1944b) Private enterprise housing: report of the Private Enterprise Sub-Committee of the Central Housing Advisory Committee of the Ministry of Health. HMSO, London

Ministry of Health (1944c) Rural housing. Circular 64/44. HMSO, London

Ministry of Health (1946) Housing (Financial and Miscellaneous Provisions) Act, 1946. Circular 118/46. HMSO, London

Ministry of Health (1950a) Report of the Ministry of Health for the year ended 31st March 1949. Cmd 7910. HMSO, London

Ministry of Health (1950b) The cost of house-building: second report of the committee of inquiry appointed by the Minister of Health. HMSO, London

Ministry of Health (1952) The cost of house-building: third report of the committee of inquiry. HMSO, London

Ministry of Health. (quarterly) Housing return for England and Wales. [From 1951 Ministry of Housing & Local Government.] HMSO, London

Ministry of Housing & Local Government (1960) Report of the Ministry of Housing and Local Government 1959. Cmnd 1027. HMSO, London

Ministry of Housing & Local Government (1961) Housing in England and Wales. Cmnd 1290. HMSO, London

Ministry of Housing & Local Government (1963) Report of the Ministry of Housing and Local Government 1962. Cmnd 1976. HMSO, London

Ministry of Housing & Local Government (1969) Report of the Ministry of Housing and Local Government 1967 and 1968. Cmnd 4009. HMSO, London

Ministry of Housing & Local Government. (quarterly) Housing return for England and Wales. [Before 1951 Ministry of Health.] HMSO, London

Ministry of Reconstruction (1918) Housing in England and Wales: memorandum by the advisory housing panel on the emergency problem. Cd 9087. HMSO, London

Ministry of Works & Planning (1942) Report of the Committee on Land Utilisation in Rural Areas. Cmd 6378. Scott Report. HMSO, London

Minns R (1973) The significance of Clay Cross: another look at district audit. Policy Polit 2:309–329

Mitchell BR, Jones HG (1971) Second abstract of British historical statistics. Cambridge University Press, Cambridge

Molotch H (1976) The city as a growth machine. Am J Sociol 82:309–332

Moore-Colyer RJ (1999) From Great Wen to Toad Hall: aspects of the urban-rural divide in inter-war Britain. Rural Hist 10:105–124

Morgan KO (1984) Labour in power, 1945–1951. Clarendon, Oxford

Morgan KO (1990) The people's peace: British history 1945–1989. Oxford University Press, Oxford

Morris DS, Newton K (1970) Profile of a local political elite: businessmen as community decision-makers in Birmingham 1838–1966. New Atlantis 1(2):111–123

Murie A, Niner P, Watson CJ (1976) Housing policy and the housing system. Allen & Unwin, London

National House Builders' Registration Council (1968) The national register of house-builders, first edition. London

Newby HE (1977) The deferential worker: a study of farm workers in East Anglia. Allen Lane, London

Newton K (1976) Second city politics: democratic processes and decision-making in Birmingham. Oxford University Press, Oxford

Newton K (1980) Central government grants, territorial justice and local democracy in post-war Britain. In: Ashford DE (ed) Financing urban government in the welfare state. Croom Helm, London, pp 97–118

NHBC Foundation (2015) Homes through the decades: the making of modern housing. Milton Keynes

Norton A (1978) The evidence considered. In: Jones GW, Norton A (eds) Political leadership in local authorities. University of Birmingham Institute of Local Government Studies, Birmingham, pp 206–231

O'Leary B (1987) Why was the GLC abolished? Int J Urban Reg Res 11:193–217

Olney R (2007) Squire and community: T.G. Dixon at Holton-le-Moor, 1906–1937. Rural Hist 18:201–216

Page EC, Goldsmith M (1987) Centre and locality: explaining crossnational variation. In: Page EC, Goldsmith M (eds) Central and local government relations. Sage, London, pp 156–168

Pahl RE (1965) Urbs in rure: the metropolitan fringe in Hertfordshire. Geographical Paper 2. London School of Economics, London

Parkinson M (1985) Liverpool on the brink: one city's struggle against government cuts. Policy Journals, Hermitage

Pedley WH (1942) Labour on the land: a study of the developments between the two great wars. P.S. King & Staples, London

Perry R, Dean K, Brown B (1986) Counterurbanization: international case studies of socio-economic change in rural areas. Geo Books, Norwich

Pooley CG, Turnbull J (1998) Migration and mobility in Britain since the eighteenth century. UCL Press, London

Powell C (1996) The British building industry since 1800: an economic history, 2nd edn. Spon, London

Pugh M (2008) 'We danced all night': a social history of Britain between the wars. Bodley Head, London

Rapport N (1993) Diverse world-views in an English village. Edinburgh University Press, Edinburgh

Ravetz A (2001) Council housing and culture: the history of a social experiment. Routledge, London

Read B (2003) Henley rural: the history of a rural district council in Oxfordshire 1894–1932. ELSP, Bradford-on-Avon

Reiner WJ, Broughton HF (1953) Productivity in house-building: second report. Department of Scientific & Industrial Research, Building Research Station, National Building Studies 21. HMSO, London

Rhodes G (1976) Local government finance 1918–1966. In: Committee of Inquiry into Local Government Finance, Local government finance: appendix six. HMSO, London, pp 102–173

Robertson AJ (1987) The bleak midwinter 1947. Manchester University Press, Manchester

Rose D, Saunders P, Newby HE, Bell C (1976) Ideologies of property. Sociol Rev 24:699–730

Royal Commission on Local Government (1925) First report: constitution and extension of county boroughs. Cmd 2506. HMSO, London

Royal Commission on Local Government in England (1969) Report. Cmnd 4040, Redcliffe-Maud report. HMSO, London

Rural District Councils' Association (1966) Evidence of the Rural District Councils' Association to the Royal Commission on Local Government in England. HMSO, London

Ryder R (1984) Council house building in County Durham 1900–39. In: Daunton MJ (ed) Councillors and tenants. Leicester University Press, Leicester, pp 40–100

Sandbrook D (2005) Never had it so good: a history of Britain from Suez to the Beatles. Little, Brown, London

Saunders P (1981) Community power, urban managerialism and the local state. In: Harloe M (ed) New perspectives in urban change and conflict. Heinemann, London, pp 27–49

Saunders P (1983) The 'regional state': a review of the literature and agenda for research. Working Paper 35. University of Sussex Urban and Regional Studies, Falmer

Saunders P (1985) The forgotten dimension of central-local relations: theorising the 'regional state'. Environ Plann C: Govern Policy 3:149–162

Saville J (1957) Rural depopulation in England and Wales 1851–1951. Routledge & Kegan Paul, London

Saville J (1993) Introduction. In: Fyrth J (ed) Labour's high noon: the government and the economy 1945–51. Lawrence & Wishart, London, pp xv–xxxviii

Sayle A (1924) The houses of the workers. T Fisher Unwin, London

Schwartz HM (1994) States versus markets. St Martin's Press, New York

Scott P (1996) The worst of both worlds: British regional policy, 1951–64. Bus Hist 38:41–64

Scott P (2007) Triumph of the south: a regional economic history of early twentieth century Britain. Ashgate, Aldershot

Seaman LCB (1966) Post-Victorian Britain, 1902–1951. Methuen, London

Self RC (2006) Neville Chamberlain: a biography. Ashgate, Aldershot

Sharpe LJ (1960) The politics of local government in Greater London. Public Adm 38:157–172

Sharpe LJ (1973) American democracy reconsidered: part one. Br J Polit Sci 3:1–28

Sharpe LJ (1978) Reforming the grass roots: an alternative analysis. In: Halsey AH, Butler DE (eds) Policy and politics. Macmillan, London, pp 82–110

Sharpe LJ (1982) The Labour Party and the geography of inequality: a puzzle. In: Kavanagh D (ed) The politics of the Labour Party. Allen & Unwin, London, pp 135–170

Sherwood KB (1996) Housing provision and population change in the countryside 1919–1939: some evidence from Northamptonshire. East Midland Geogr 19(2):43–58

Simon ED (1933) The anti-slum campaign. Longmans, Green & Co., London

Skinner D, Langdon J (1974) The story of Clay Cross. Bertrand Russell Peace Foundation, Nottingham

Smallburgh Rural District Council (1958) Smallburgh RDC medical officer of health annual report 1957. Stalham

Smallburgh Rural District Council (1965) Smallburgh RDC medical officer of health annual report 1964. Stalham

Smallburgh Rural District Council (1967) Smallburgh RDC medical officer of health annual report 1966. Stalham

Smallburgh Rural District Council (1970) Smallburgh RDC medical officer of health annual report 1969. Stalham

Smith A (1776) An inquiry into the nature and causes of the wealth of nations. W. Strahan & T. Cadell, London

Smyth H (1985) Property companies and the construction industry in Britain. Cambridge University Press, Cambridge

Stevenson J, Cook C (1977) The slump: society and politics during the depression. Jonathan Cape, London

Strathern M (1982) The village as an idea: constructs of village-ness in Elmdon, Essex. In: Cohen AP (ed) Belonging: identity and social organization in British rural cultures. Manchester University Press, Manchester, pp 247–277

Sutcliffe AS (1976) Political leadership in Labour-controlled Birmingham: the contrasting styles of Harry Watton (1959–66) and Stanley Yapp (1972–74). Local Gov Stud 2(1):15–32

Swenarton M (2007) Houses of paper and brown cardboard: Neville Chamberlain and the establishment of the Building Research Station at Garston in 1925. Plan Perspect 22:257–281

Taylor AJP (1965) English history 1914–1945. Clarendon, Oxford

Thresh JC (1891) The housing of the working classes in the Chelmsford and Maldon rural sanitary districts. Chelmsford & Maldon Rural Sanitary Authorities, Chelmsford

Thrift NJ (1986) Little games and big stories: accounting for the practice of personality and politics in the 1945 General Election. In: Hoggart K, Kofman E (eds) Politics, geography and social stratification. Croom Helm, London, pp 86–143

Tressell R [pseudonym for Noonan, R.] (1955) The ragged trousered philanthropists. Lawrence & Wishart, London

Turner J (1994) Macmillan. Longman, Harlow

Tylecote AB (1982) German ascent and British decline 1870–1980: the role of upper class structure and values. In: Friedman E (ed) Ascent and decline in the world-system. Sage, Beverly Hills, pp 41–67

UN Economic Commission for Europe (1964) The state of rural electrification in Europe during the three-year period from 1 January 1960 to 1 January 1963. United Nations, New York

Waddington K (2012) 'It might not be a nuisance in a country cottage': sanitary conditions and images of health in Victorian rural Wales. Rural Hist 23:185–204

Ward SV (1988) The geography of interwar Britain: the state and uneven development. Routledge, London

Weiler P (2000) The rise and fall of the Conservatives' 'grand design for housing', 1951–64. Contemp Br Hist 14:122–150

Wellings F (2006) British housebuilders: history and analysis. Blackwell, Oxford

Wheen F (1985) The battle for London. Pluto Press, London

Willetts D (1992) Modern Conservativism. Penguin, Harmondsworth

Wood B (1988) Urbanisation and local government. In: Halsey AH (ed) British social trends since 1900: a guide to the changing social structure of Britain, 2nd edn. Macmillan, Basingstoke, pp 322–356

Wrottesley AJ (1970) The Midland and Great Northern Joint Railway. David & Charles, Newton Abbot

Wycombe Rural District Council (1952) Housing progress: one thousand houses in six years. Wycombe Rural District Council, High Wycombe

Yaxley D (1977) Portrait of Norfolk. Robert Hale, London

Young K (1975) The Conservative strategy for London, 1855–1975. London J 1(1):56–81

Young K, Garside PL (1982) Metropolitan London: politics and urban change 1837–1981. Edward Arnold, London

Chapter 6
A Subservient Countryside: National Priorities and Housing

Abstract Focusing primarily on the decades after 1945, this chapter investigates emphases in national policy, drawing out their rural implications. After 1945 and for electoral reasons stretching until around 1955, the principal national aim was to increase new-build numbers to address the deficits left by inter-war policies. Labour and Conservative governments pursued virtually the same numerical policies, except for higher output under the Conservatives, who adjusted housing specifications downwards. After 1955, a return to the slum clearance emphasis of the 1930s pertained. Rural areas, which benefited in the late-1940s from recognition of their appalling housing conditions, alongside a prioritisation of farm-worker homes to enhance agricultural production, again saw weak new-build numbers, even to below demolition volumes. Councils responded by being more flexible in their approach, switching attention to homes for the elderly and sometimes to no-subsidy dwellings. The urban bias in late-1950s' allocations continued into the 1960s, with the character and basis of this bias investigated. In 1967, the national housing condition survey showed rural areas had worse housing conditions than urban, which leads to an examination of data shortcomings that contributed to governments continuously proclaiming the ascendancy of urban deprivations.

Keywords National housing priorities · Old people's housing · Reconditioning · Urban bias · Information deficits

Attention in this chapter is directed at national policy affecting rural housing. In essence, the chapter examines not what politicians and government statements declared, but how actions and commitments revealed priorities. Then, in Chap. 7, the focus is on how local institutions interacted with national direction, tracing local footprints on the rural housing scene. Some might quibble over this focus, pointing out this framework suggests 'the state' determined housing outcomes, thereby downplaying market forces. It is not intended to diminish this contribution to the evolution of rural housing. But there are good reasons for examining change through the lens of the state. As already shown, early in the twentieth-century, the countryside was near abandoned by private house-builders (Chap. 2). As the decades rolled forward, there was increased interest in building for rural home-owners, but the geographical focus was largely where the state eased pathways with infrastructure

© Springer Nature Switzerland AG 2021
K. Hoggart, *A Contrived Countryside*, Local and Urban Governance,
https://doi.org/10.1007/978-3-030-62651-8_6

like roads, sewers and water systems (Chaps. 4 and 5). If these systems had not arrived, private builder interest waned; 'suburbanisation' into the countryside occurred aplenty but not much beyond. Then, post-1945, public sector new-build was dominant in the first decade; private completions did not top them until 1958.[1] Accompanying these trends, akin to the inter-war pattern, the post-1945 decades saw limited rural action for those of lesser means. With few alternatives available, the rural housing stock had little to pull it out of stagnation or deterioration. A pool of dwellings unwanted by inhabitants or landlords resulted. As the service-classes sought to move beyond 'suburbanisation' to embrace an imagined 'rurality' (Bolton and Chalkley 1990; Halliday and Coombes 1995), a stock of properties existed, which local residents found less attractive or could not afford. With house-building policies increasingly favouring larger settlements, a bifurcation in the rural landscape distinguished places seeing larger housing estate expansion and villages with restricted growth (Henson 1957; Hertfordshire County Council 1961; Cloke 1979; Phillips and Williams 1982). In this and the next chapter, these trends are explored through the prism of state policies.

Quality accounts of national housing policies already exist (e.g. Merrett 1979, 1982; Ball 1983; Burnett 1986; Harloe 1995). It is not intended to repeat them, nor to cover the breadth they encompassed. Rather, the focus is on key features in housing programmes, asking how rural areas fared under them. Most obviously, when accommodation shortages exist, gains can be made through building more. However, living experiences can also be enhanced by better design, estate planning or building standards. Assessments of new-build should not be just about numbers but construction quality, amenity inclusion and cost. Pointedly after the collapse of the Ronan Point tower block in 1968 (Dunleavy 1977), greater resistance arose to urban redevelopment based on high-rise flats.[2] This 'solution' to housing problems was promoted by governments (Dunleavy 1981) but was a failure financially and socially (NHBC Foundation 2015, pp.19–24). Embedded in criticism of the programme were questions about tenant selection (e.g. families with children). This highlighted a further aspect of housing quality, namely occupant–dwelling interaction. The 1935 Housing Act drew attention to this issue in acknowledging that well-built homes were inadequate if overcrowded (Frazer 1935; MoH 1936). On the reverse side, questions can be raised over 'under-occupation'. For much of the twentieth-century, debate on this issue focused on building homes of different sizes. Family-sized dwellings were in short supply early in the century, but later many singles or couples were unable to downsize owing to a shortage of smaller dwellings, leading to criticism that under-occupation deprived families with children.[3] This leads to asking how far those leaving dwellings create opportunities for others to fulfil

---

[1] HCH 16 November 1965, Vol.720, col.924.

[2] TNA HLG118/1044 'Housing Programme 1969'.

[3] This was linked to calls for smaller dwellings to free up larger ones (e.g. HCH 11 May 1950, Vol.475, col.555; BRO RDBwM1/29 BiRDCM 15 January 1958, p.9; BRO RDAR8/39 ARDCMOHar 1958, p.15; BRO RDAH4/4 'Ampthill Correspondence on Housing'). There were even proposals to eject elderly residents who would not move to smaller dwellings (as in

accommodation ambitions (Harris 2012). Such hopes can be satisfied without moving, as in upgrading the physical fabric and plant of a home (MHLG 1954). Given such options, where was the locus of state action? Was it towards new-build, the replacement of inadequate stock or its upgrading, and how did physical fabric relate to occupancy? In exploring these options, a key question is how their articulation impacted on rural districts.

6.1   Construction Volumes

Faced with major shortages, with private builder returns on home construction unattractive, the 1919 Housing, Town Planning, Etc. Act introduced the first major public ownership incursion into the English housing market. Ministry documents of the time vary in their estimate of how many dwellings were needed, but the number cited was at least 500,000, with 800,000 mentioned by some.[4] In the end, just 174,635 council dwellings were completed, alongside 39,186 for private-owners, for the latter largely under the accompanying 1919 Housing (Additional Powers) Act (MoH 1939, p.253). As early as 1920, the termination of the 1919 programme was under discussion. By 1921, ministers were sounding its demise publicly.[5] Accounting for its termination has generated disagreement. Daunton (1984), for instance, suggested that Swenarton's (1981) emphasis on a weakening of working-class political clout, given economic turmoil after the First World War, misses the point that post-war price distortions provoked state intervention. The case has regularly been made that national leaders saw private sector withdrawal from residential building as temporary, requiring minor surgery before a return to normality (Bowley 1945, p.15; Ravetz 2001, p.77). Builder disengagement with the sector intensified in the War, with the introduction of rent controls under the 1915 Rent and Mortgage Interest (War Restrictions) Act fuelling builder disquiet, although 'imbalance' existed before 1914, as declining completions show.[6] But the 1919 Act was high cost.[7] For the Committee on building costs, no community of interest existed to secure economy (MoH 1921b, p.8). As Dresser (1984) articulated for Bristol, builders preferred more lucrative non-residential work, so they were reluctant to tender

---

Biggleswade, *BC&BG* 3 March 1967, p.10), although I found no evidence this was acted on (e.g. BRO RDBwM1/40 BiRDCHCM 9 October 1968, p.384).

[4] TNA CAB23/18 7(19) Cabinet Conclusions, 14 November 1919, p.2; TNA HLG68/29 'Closing Down of Addison Scheme. Minute Sheet', 13 December 1920.

[5] HCH 15 June 1921, Vol.143, col.400; HCH 14 July 1921, Vol.144, col.1488–92.

[6] For example, total dwelling completions in England and Wales over five-years were 581,848 for 1900–1904, 513,529 for 1905–1909 and 303,238 for 1910–1914 (HCH 3 July 1922, Vol.156, col.50W).

[7] TNA HLG68/29 'Housing Liabilities', 2 June 1920; 'Minute to the Secretary', 6 July 1920; Letter M.P.A. Hankey, Cabinet Office, to Dr. Addison, MoH, 30 November 1920; 'Housing', 25 January 1921.

for council dwellings and, when they did, they reinvigorated combines to limit competition, hiked prices above tendered quotations and erected low-quality dwellings. With councils having little direct experience of construction, the absence of financial auditing for projects meant cost overruns were common. Both councils and the Ministry were criticised for lacking the armoury and political will to economise (Morgan and Morgan 1980, p.142). The 1914–1918 War had seen state direction shift into 'total war' mode, but a bonfire of controls followed afterward (Perkin 1989, p.188, p.192). With no effective government preparation for housing expansion (Addison 1934, p.495; Council for Research on Housing Construction 1934, p.14; Ravetz 2001, p.77), weak regulation of the building industry was a recipe for failure. But political leaders, the economic establishment and the middle-classes were traumatised by the taxation burden of the recent war (Daunton 1996; James 2006). They sought the comfort of pre-war minimalist government. The necessity of Chamberlain's 1923 Housing Act testified that the private sector would not bring enough housing improvement if left alone. Supporting state-aid for private building, Chamberlain proclaimed that '… every consideration of humanity, of patriotism, and even of prudent care for the future must impel us to the conclusion that there is no question more urgent, and none that cries more loudly for immediate attention than this question of housing'.[8] The housing crisis was not over. The state needed to pump-prime private action.

More was needed. The 1919 Act was weakened by material supply deficiencies (MoH 1921a, p.57) and a failure to demobilise troops quickly enough to secure a return to peace-time production (Addison 1924, p.219). Lack of coordinated action was transparent:

> Instances frequently occurred, where an adequate supply of labour was available, but no progress could be made owing to the non-delivery of essential material, and per contra, there have been numerous cases where a large stock of materials has been kept lying idle, either because there was no labour to make use of it, or because the contractor was obliged to accumulate stocks, wherever the opportunity offered, in excess of his immediate requirements owing to the uncertainty of obtaining supplies at a later date as and when required. (MoH 1921b, p.20)

One Chamberlain response was to create the Building Research Station to promote new methods of construction (Swenarton 2007), but: 'Always anxious to avoid any unnecessary interference with private enterprise, Chamberlain was reluctant to intervene directly to tackle the problems of labour and material shortages which had driven up building costs since the Armistice' (Self 2006, p.110). Labour and material shortages regularly held up construction (e.g. MoH 1920a, p.6, 1922, p.39, 1924, p.54, 1926, p.59). Rural areas had particular difficulties:

> The Minister is fully alive to the importance of the Housing problem in agricultural districts, and has been giving the matter his very close attention. He realises that the question of housing the agricultural worker is a problem which has special features distinguishing it from the urban problem and in many respects making it more difficult. But the provision of houses whether in urban or rural districts has hitherto been conditioned by the shortage of

---

[8] HCH 24 April 1923, Vol.163, col.304.

skilled building labour, and until there is an increase in the number of skilled operatives the
output of houses by the ordinary methods of building is necessarily limited.[9]

Wheatley's 15-year agreement with the construction industry sought such improvements (Simon 1933, p.18), but cuts to subsidies from 1927 and the Great Crash of
1929 dampened markets and council activity (Stevenson and Cook 1977). It was not
until 1932–1933 that house-building began to take-off (Fig. 6.1), but council-
building was deliberately restrained. Limited mostly to slum rehousing and relieving overcrowding, rural districts contributed declining shares to the council stock
(Table 4.12).

This 1930s' under-performance did not apply to all inter-war legislation. Notably,
whereas the 1919 Act accounted for 14.6% of all 1919–1943 additions to the council stock, the RDC figure was 20.9% (Table 6.1).[10] Given high costs slowed

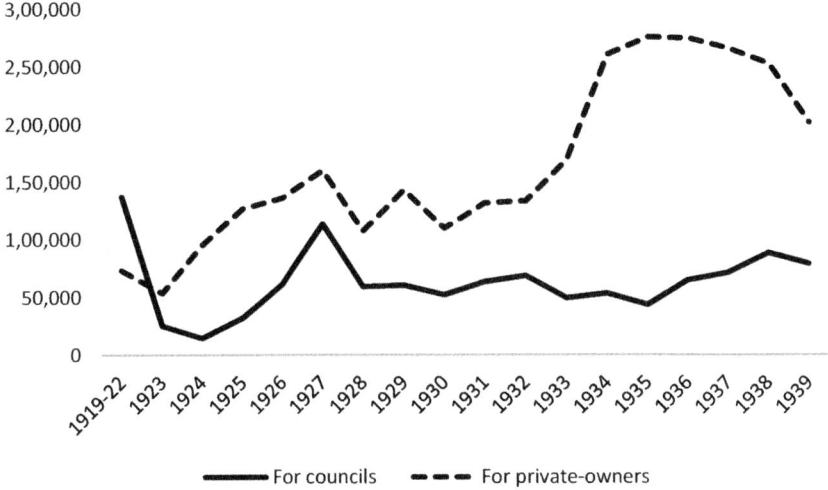

Source: HCH 11 February 1948 Vol.447, col.93W–94W.

Note: Accurate information for the private sector was not available before 1922, so the government
estimated numbers for 1919–22. The same periods were used for both sectors here.

Fig. 6.1 Annual new-build completions for councils and private-owners in England and Wales,
1919–1939

---

[9] TNA HLG40/38 'Housing of Agricultural Workers', 13 May 1925.

[10] The figures for England and Wales are from MoH (1944b, p.49), which provided completion
rates by Act of Parliament, excluding the 1931 Act, which was added to the computations. The data
for 1943 were for up to 31 March 1943, but MoH (1944b) only reported to 31 March 1940. For the
1919, 1923 and 1924 Acts, this had no impact, as no dwellings under these Acts were completed
after 1940. For other Acts this was not the case, although completions between 1940 and 1943
were few. Some 105,434 dwellings were built by councils between October 1938 and the end of
March 1940 in England and Wales (MoH 1944b), yet only 149,875 had been built between 1
August 1939 and 31 March 1943 (HCH 23 March 1944, Vol.398, col.1026), with just 10,505 under
construction at the latter date. This suggests a minor adjustment is merited to figures in Table 6.1.

Table 6.1 Per cent new-build completions in rural districts of England and Wales by Housing Act, 1919–1943

| Acts | Per cent of new-build 1919–1943 under Act | | Per cent RDC-owned by Act |
	For rural councils	For private-owners	
Housing, Town Planning, Etc. Act 1919 (general needs)	3.9	0.2	20.9
Housing (Additional Powers) Act 1919 (general needs)	0.0	1.8	0.0
Housing Act 1923 (general needs)	1.0	12.6	5.1
Housing (Financial Provisions) 1924 (general needs)	7.2	0.5	38.0
Housing Acts 1930, 1936, 1938 (slum clearance)	3.6	0.1	19.3
Housing (Rural Authorities) Act 1931 (agricultural population)	0.2	0.0	1.2
Housing Acts 1935, 1936, 1938 (abating overcrowding)	0.8	0.0	4.4
Housing Acts 1925, 1936 (general needs, no subsidy)	1.3	0.1	7.0
Housing (Financial Provisions) Act 1938 (agricultural population)	0.4	0.1	2.2
Outside Housing Acts (no subsidy)	0.6	65.6	3.0
Total completions all Acts	18.8	81.2	100.0

Source: MoH (1944a, p.64)

construction under the Act, this rural output was impressive. Other than the 1919 Act, above-average rural shares only occurred in two circumstances: the explicitly countryside Acts of 1931 and 1938 and to alleviate overcrowding under the 1935 and 1936 Acts (although officially overcrowding was lower in RDCs; MoH 1936). Rural under-performance was marked for the 1924 Act, which accounted for 43.3% of national inter-war council stock additions (MoH 1944b, p.49) but only 38.5% in RDCs (MoH 1944a, p.64).[11] This shortfall was starker than these percentages suggest, as total inter-war rural council-build was only 13.9% of the England and Wales total, compared with a rural population share of 17.5% in 1939 (20.1% in 1919; MoH 1944a, p.61). An even larger gap arose for slum clearance. Here, for urban councils, 27.6% of council new-build replaced unfit inter-war dwellings, but only 21.0% did in rural districts. Hence, only 50.8% of RDC dwellings designated as unfit were replaced by new homes over 1919–1939 compared with an urban figure of 68.3%. Expressed differently, 4.0% of all new private or public 1919–1943

[11] Both percentages excluded 1931 Act totals, as the source did not include them.

dwellings in rural districts were built to replace unfit dwellings, whereas 8.3% were in urban districts (MoH 1944a, p.61). This divergence existed despite Minister of Health acknowledgement that 'There is almost as big a slum problem in the rural areas as sometimes there is in the towns'.[12] The slum clearance pattern was poignant, especially as it repeated in later decades. This arose with little ministerial overview. As the Minister of Health acknowledged in 1938, 'I regret that I have no complete information in regard to the number of houses demolished since 1918, as the figures of demolitions furnished to my Department relate only to slum clearance operations'.[13] Policymaking without basic information continued for decades, with the relevant 1971 Minister admitting 'I have no information about unfit houses dealt with singly [viz. outside designated clearance zones] since these are not referred to the Department'.[14] Yet unfit rural dwellings were mostly found outside clearance areas (MoH 1944a, p.61), with slum clearance programmes effectively by-passing much of rural England.

6.1.1   The Push for Numbers, 1946–1955

The immediate post-1945 decade saw substantial change. As Morgan (1990, p.17) summarised,

> Britain in the 1930s had been governed in terms of social division, with the thriving middle-class suburbs and shopping precincts in the Midlands and southern England, on which the Conservative ascendancy was based, carefully segregated from the working-class 'tribe apart' in Labour-run South Wales, the North of England and industrial Scotland.

Recognising the implications, Prime Minister Attlee believed: 'It was essential that housing should be regarded as having the same sort of urgency as military operations in the war' (Campbell 1987, p.159). The new government had good reason to seek rapid progress, for even official memos referred to 1918–1921 housing efforts as disastrous (Gay 1987), with Mass Observation making clear that the Lloyd George government's failure at the time had significant bearing on the 1945 General Election (Eatwell 1979, p.37, p.128), as had socially divisive inter-war housing programmes (Hinton 1988; Francis 2012). There was also the unedifying spectacle of Parliamentary controversy over 1914–1918 war and post-war profiteering in the supply and sale of materials,[15] which led to a series of investigations into specific industries.[16] Fears of a repetition generated inter-war debate, which did not favour control of prices and profits but sought better cooperation between business and

---

[12] HCH 8 June 1937, Vol.324, col.1614.

[13] HCH 3 March 1938, Vol.332, col.1278.

[14] HCH 5 May 1971, Vol.816, col.372 W.

[15] HCH 11 August 1919, Vol.119, col.923–1027; HCH 15 March 1920, Vol.126, col.1869–1983.

[16] Housing-related examples included Standing Committee on Prices and Trusts (1920a, b, c, 1921a, b, c).

labour (Rollings 2001). With Churchill's vague ideas on social policy (Perkin 1989; Jones 1991), the war-time coalition was able to propose dramatic post-war change (as under the Beveridge Report and the Butler Act). Here: 'The Labour Party … came forward with most of the petrol to fill up the tank of reconstruction, but strange to say played only a negligible part in the design and development of the engine' (Addison 1994, p.166). A heavy defeat in the 1945 Election lessened Conservative resistance to this 'new world'; indeed, the importance of housing in the General Election soon saw the Party attacking the new government for not building enough council homes (Barnett 1995, pp.153–54). Despite this, housing output was markedly better than after 1918 (Table 6.2). A key difference resulted from continued government overview and parking voices calling for policy change.

A shift in the government from Labour to Conservative in 1951 occurred when housing was still a hot political issue,[17] yet:

> The slimness of the margin [17 over all parties] was to bedevil Conservative policy-making, curbing its audacity for many years to come. The experience of the cataclysm of 1945, followed by those six frustrating wilderness years, was to set a limit on the political risks Tory leaders would be prepared to take henceforth. (Horne 1988, p.322)

Housing played a key role in the revival of the Conservatives, with the promise of higher new-build volumes playing a major part in this success. As the Party was perturbed by public fears it would dismantle the welfare state (Jones 2000), the new government effectively took on Labour's social plans up to 1953, with sensitivity over public opinion leading to vote-catching social measures right up to 1955 (e.g. Smith 1992). For housing, friction within the Party intensified. This owed something to dogma, given public sector building was prioritised, but also to concerns over housing's balance of payments impacts.[18] The housing minister, Harold Macmillan (1969, pp.434–35), rejected the criticism, leading to tussles over building volumes with the Chancellor of the Exchequer, Rab Butler. Macmillan asserted it would be 'political folly' to build fewer public sector homes than Labour

Table 6.2 New-build completions in England and Wales for the six years after the First and Second World Wars

	1918–1924	1945–1951
For councils	176,914	590,406
For private-owners	221,552	124,054
Total	398,466	714,460

Source: HCH 26 November 1951, Vol.494, col.114W

[17] As the Minister of Works put it late in 1950: 'Politically, housing is dynamite: anything we can do with the existing housing labour force to increase the number of houses produced should in my view be done' (TNA T229/471 Letter from R.R. Stokes to Hugh Gaitskell, 6 September 1950).

[18] In the Treasury, it was argued that £8–£10 million in foreign exchange could be earned or saved with materials used to erect 30,000 extra houses (TNA T229/475 'Memo to Mr. Strath from F.F. Turnbull', 24 March 1952). As Jones (2000, pp.107–08) noted, the timber needed to build an additional 100,000 houses cost nearly 4% of all imports from dollar areas.

managed in its last year. Butler's retort was that housing diverted resources from economic growth.[19] As Macmillan (1969, p.429, p.498) acknowledged, Churchill's abhorrence of the unfair treatment of 'humble folk' helped his cause, as he could rely on his backing (Horne 1988, pp.332–40; Turner 1994). 'Macmillan's new homes, weatherproofed by the great human political roof that was Winston Churchill, surged ahead' (Hennessy 2006, p.217). Macmillan single-mindedly pushed house-building numbers, resisting cuts and chaffing over funds spent on other commitments, as captured in his question: 'Will there ever come an end to pouring cement into the ground for American bombers?' (Campbell 1987, pp.252–53). But away from the War, demands for a return to 'normality' increased, with a Conservative-styled housing policy ready for launch once electoral fears subsided (Jones 1991, p.34). Reductions in council-building were planned for after the next (1955) General Election, although this was not made immediately public.[20]

Early after 1945, rural districts were praised publicly and internally for their 'excellent start' on new housing (MoH 1947a, p.169; 1947b, p.8).[21] Between 1945 and 1951, some 129,664 dwellings were erected in rural districts.[22] By comparison, although there were more RDCs in 1918 than in 1945, from 1918 until early-1925 just 67,733 dwellings were built.[23] Of course, soon after 1945, housing for agricultural workers was a national priority.[24] The rural new-build share was generally above its population quota at least up to 1956 (Table 5.3), and much higher than in the 1930s (Table 5.4). Table 6.3 gives more details. The Table is limited to 1946–1955 because the Ministry's *Housing Return for England and Wales* changed after this

---

[19] TNA CAB129/53 C(52)239 'The Investment Programme', 15 July 1952; TNA T227/805 'Memo from E.N. Plowden to the Chancellor of the Exchequer', 23 October 1952; TNA HLG101/433 Letter to the PM from R.A.B., 28 May 1953; TNA HLG101/433 Letter from R.A. Butler to Harold Macmillan, 16 November 1953; TNA T227/1162 'Investment. Housing England and Wales', 25 November 1953; TNA HLG101/433 'Memo from J.E. Beddoe to S.F. Wilkinson', 26 November 1953, plus 15 December 1953 note. The poignancy of foreign earnings in place of 30,000 added homes should not be lost, as Macmillan assumed Labour built 170,00 dwellings in its last year, when only 140,000 were built. This 'error' only came to light in 1954 (TNA HLG101/433 Letter from J. Rogers to L. Petch, The Treasury, 1 January 1954; TNA T227/808 'Housing Memo to Bernard Gilbert from R.W.B. Clarke', 5 August 1955).

[20] TNA CAB129/71 CP(54)344 'Investment and Housing', 12 November 1954; TNA T227/808 'Housing Memo to Strath, Herbert Brittain and Bernard Gilbert from R.W.B. Clarke', 16 February 1955; TNA T227/808 'Housing Memo from R.W.B. Clarke', 23 February 1955.

[21] In May 1947 Aneurin Bevan indicated that 93% of RDCs had started building new homes and 60% had completions, which placed this local government category second only to county boroughs (*NBC&BR* 20 May 1947, p.5). This did not stop MPs like Cyril Dumpleton (St Albans) complaining rural council provision was too low (HCH 25 March 1947, Vol.435, col.1144), although his evidence was largely based on poor inter-war totals, whereas government praise was for the previous two years (TNA HLG40/56 'Housing for Rural Workers', prepared for Parliamentary debate on 25 March 1947).

[22] TNA MAF234/18 'Rural Housing', 7 February 1952, p.2.

[23] HCH 12 March 1925, Vol.181, col.1549W–50W.

[24] TNA CAB129/21 CP(47)284 'Investment Programme Committee. Minister for Economic Affairs', 16 October 1947.

year, with a diminution of information, including the categories in the Table (MoH-MHLG quarterly). Instructive nonetheless is the patterning under both Labour and Conservative governments. As in the inter-war decades, RDCs saw under-performance for 'virgin' council completions but over-achievement for private-owners. However, this separation can be drawn too rigidly, for if new homes were added to rebuilt war-damaged volumes, the rural private sector portion was 22.6%, compared with 24.6% for the largest towns (excluding the LCC and Metropolitan Boroughs) and 23.9% for intermediate towns. Moreover, while the rural council slice was relatively low, one reason was government departments, as they built extensively in the countryside, albeit often for the military rather than the general population.[25] Over the decade, rural performance was not out of line with urban, with homes added comparable with most towns on a per capita basis (Table 6.4).[26] This is despite labour and material supplies handicapping rural output:

> … one of the difficulties in getting enough houses put up in rural areas quickly is that the normal building labour is not there in sufficient quantities. We desire to use building labour where it exists, and normally the building force distributes itself in accordance with local needs. But there are two exceptions, rural areas and blitzed areas. In the rural areas we want all the building forces to be used by the rural authorities to build traditional houses, but I

Table 6.3 Per cent of permanent new-build completions in England and Wales by settlement category, 1946–1955

	LCC and LMBs	Towns over 75,000	Towns of 25,000–75,000	Towns under 25,000	Rural districts
For councils	85.7	74.7	74.1	76.8	70.6
For private-owners	3.2	17.2	19.5	18.7	22.1
For housing associations	0.9	0.4	1.1	1.8	1.8
For government departments	0.8	1.0	1.4	2.0	5.1
Rebuilt war-damaged for councils	6.8	1.4	0.6	0.2	0.1
Rebuilt war-damaged privately	5.7	7.4	4.5	0.8	0.5
Per cent of all permanent dwellings	6.7	27.8	24.2	19.1	22.2

Source: MoH-MHLG (quarterly)
Note: Data for the rebuilding of war-damaged dwellings were available for 1949–1954 only. At the time, the London County Council (LCC) and London's Metropolitan Boroughs (LMBs) did not encompass the whole of what is now Greater London. Other urban districts in Greater London came under relevant settlement size categories

---

[25] TNA CAB134/776 B(51)2 Building Committee, 28 November 1951, indicated building by government departments was largely for the military.

[26] The LCC and the metropolitan boroughs had larger gains, but disproportionately from repairing war-damaged properties and requisitioned dwellings. By June 1955, 89,539 requisitioned units existed in England and Wales, with 51,465 in London's metropolitan boroughs. By 30 September 1959 the national total had fallen to 17,786 with 12,713 in the metropolitan boroughs (HCH 18 November 1959, Vol.613, col.142W).

Table 6.4 Per cent of additional units by dwelling type and settlement category in England and Wales, 1946–1955

	LCC and LMBs	Towns over 75,000	Towns 25,000–75,000	Towns under 25,000	Rural districts
% new permanent	48.5	78.7	84.6	88.8	90.2
% temporary prefabricated dwellings	6.3	9.1	5.5	4.1	2.2
% conversions and adaptations	12.6	5.2	6.4	5.8	7.1
% repaired as unoccupied war-damaged	32.6	7.0	3.6	1.3	0.5
Additional dwellings per thousand inhabitants	73.0	39.3	50.9	57.0	52.4

Source: MoH-MHLG (quarterly)
Note: Dwelling types not listed above included requisitioned properties, plus former military camps and huts. At the time, the London County Council (LCC) and London's Metropolitan Boroughs (LMBs) did not encompass the whole of what is now Greater London. Other urban districts in Greater London came under relevant settlement size categories

want to tell the House with perfect frankness that it will not be possible to solve the rural housing problem unless we can find ways of reinforcing building labour in the rural areas.[27]

Using labour 'where it lies' continued as a policy goal, as demand for housing was widespread (MoH 1947a, p.160). Shortages of skilled labour encouraged prefabricated designs, which '… made little demand on bricklayers and plasterers, which were the types of labour in shortest supply, [so] authorities who build Airey houses would get more houses than their labour resources would ordinarily allow'. The shell of an Airey house could be erected in 70 hours with only six workers, with the rest of the house 'a straightforward traditional job'.[28] Moreover, rural builders bidding for such dwellings would not compete with large builders, since the Ministry was '… very reluctant to involve the big contractors in this scheme which will only put up the cost and freeze out the local builder for whom the scheme is specially designed'.[29] Rural builders were unconvinced.[30] The Ministry became concerned the novelty of prefabrication was problematical.[31] One consequence was a refusal to agree Airey contracts until councils identified builders and workers willing to undertake the work, after which councils had to wait until Ministry officials investigated the prospect.[32] Discussion with local builders resulted, after which some councils

---

[27] Aneurin Bevan at HCH 26 November 1945, Vol.416, col.997.

[28] *NBC&BR* 20 May 1947, p.5.

[29] TNA HLG101/59 Teleprint Message to J.D. Morris, Welsh Board of Health, from E.A. Sharp, MoH, 18 February 1946.

[30] TNA HLG40/56 'Debate on Rural Housing 25 March 1947'.

[31] TNA MAF234/9 Letter from Bevan, MoH, to Chair of Housing Committee, 15 August 1947.

[32] As with Biggleswade (*NBC&BR* 11 November 1947, p.6).

concluded labour was better employed on traditional building.[33] When they were made, tender bids for prefabricated dwelling were high, given '... the natural hesitation of the small rural builder confronted with a type of construction entirely new to him'.[34] Concrete prefabrications also challenged aesthetic views,[35] with questions about their lifespan-limiting adoption.[36] Set against this, councils like Ampthill and Erpingham saw the potential of non-traditional designs.[37] These two authorities saw great improvement on inter-war housing output over 1946–1955; Erpingham's percentage increase was almost twice that of Hatfield, despite the boost of Hatfield's New Town designation,[38] while Ampthill's completions in less than 10 years were more than three times its pre-1939 total (Table 5.2). Despite such enthusiasts, nationally progress on 20,000 planned Airey homes saw only 3600 contract approvals by August 1947,[39] with 11,059 completed by 31 March 1949 (MoH 1950, p.322) and 18,831 by 31 March 1950 (MoH 1951, p.124). Note two contexts for this. First, the prefabricated programme was designed for over 150,000 dwellings, so the rural share was well below its population and new-build shares (Ministry of Works 1948). Second, progress in rural districts was especially slow. All but 396 of 31,048 urban-located British Iron and Steel Federation houses had been completed by 31 March 1949 (MoH 1950, p.322). One reason was the Ministry did not invite RDCs to bid for prefabs until after urban authorities had applied for more than 150,000.[40] Put in this context, and compared to the 1930s, rural additions over 1945–1955 were

---

[33] As at Braughing (*H&EO* 19 July 1947, p.2).

[34] TNA HLG40/56 'Debate on Rural Housing. Points from Speeches', 25 Match 1947. See also TNA HLG101/59 Teleprint Message to E.A. Sharp, MoH, from J.D. Morris, Welsh Board of Health, 16 February 1946.

[35] As with Biggleswade (*NBC&BR* 9 December 1947, p.6) and Braughing (*H&EO* 10 March 1945, p.3). Even Ministry officials had reservations about dwelling aesthetics (e.g. TNA HLG40/50 'Memo for House of Commons Agricultural and Food Group Meeting', 28 November (no year c1945)).

[36] As for St Faith's and Aylsham (*NNN* 16 December 1949, p.7).

[37] NRO DC13/5/75 ERDCHCM 28 May 1946; BRO RDAM2/22 ARDCHCM 30 May 1946; 25 August 1947; *NNN* 22 August 1952, p.3.

[38] Hatfield RDC did not receive New Town allocations. The New Town Development Corporation received them. However, having completed its first homes in 1951, as early as 1953 the Corporation was accused of not keeping to its remit of housing Londoners, as it offered homes to local people (*H&PBG* 17 April 1953, p.1). An arrangement allowing RDC applicants to access Corporation homes was formalised in 1959 (HRO RDC7/1/31 HtRDCM 11 September 1962, p.214), with reverse flows to meet particular needs in the package (Hatfield RDC 1964, p.39). The initial agreement gave the RDC access to 300 Corporation dwellings (HRO RDC7/1/32 HtRDCHCM 4 December 1962, p.376), with RDC residents accepted as tenants at a ratio of one-in-five. The Council sought increases in the quota (HRO RDC7/1/32 HtRDCHCM 26 February 1963, p.522; HRO RDC7/1/48 HtRDCH&TPCM 23 February 1971, p.943). Yet the primary effect of the New Town was on jobs not housing, with 11 vacancies for every unemployed local person in the mid-1950s (*H&PBG* 13 July 1956, p.1), and acute labour shortages in the 1960s (HRO RDC7/1/45 HtRDCJMHF 18 June 1969, p.131).

[39] TNA MAF234/9 Letter from Aneurin Bevan to Chair of Housing Committee, 15 August 1947.

[40] HCH 1 February 1945, Vol.407, col.1624.

impressive. One indication was the Ministry's 1952 list of leading authorities as regards additions to the housing stock, in which the five named English RDCs averaged 27.7 new council homes per 1000 residents post-1945, compared with 15.5 for highlighted UDCs, 17.4 for boroughs and 15.1 for county boroughs.[41] Larger towns were understandably more active in rebuilding war-damaged dwellings, but city building was limited by a lack of undeveloped land (e.g. Muchnick 1970; Sutcliffe and Smith 1974).[42] This helped narrow the city–rural divide for temporary prefabricated homes.[43]

6.1.2 Policy Emphases and Diminished Rural Action, 1955–1964

After 1955, the situation changed. The Conservative government's commitment to council-building had been confirmed by raising subsidies in 1952, but a 1955 shift in gear saw their reduction (Table 6.5). The 1956 Housing Subsidies Act followed, which removed support for general needs building, leaving subsidies available only for specific schemes, like slum clearance and old people's accommodation. Encouragement for home-buying was heightened by council rent rises of 30% in real terms from 1955–1956 to 1960–1961, twice as fast as earnings increased (Holmans 1987, p.331). Not surprisingly, public sector volumes dropped from nearly 200,000 additions in 1953 and 1954 to around 100,000 each year between 1959 and 1963 (Fig. 6.2). Initial mid-1950s' reductions were 25–30% in many regions, which raised political concerns that insufficient numbers were left for cities. The London County Council's special status meant it did not require loan sanction from Whitehall, so the only way to reduce London building was to refuse Treasury subsidies, but '… when they [MHLG Housing Division] begin to refuse London, they expect trouble'. Despite proposed cuts, officials believed they had not reduced allocations to '… the non-urban areas enough to give them enough elbow-room to avoid a dusty encounter with the urban local authorities'.[44] Moreover, justifying cutbacks was problematical:

> It had been difficult for the authorities to dispute the physical limitations of the past, and the allocation of 'rations' had been defensible. The difficulty now would be to explain why, when private investment of a less urgent character was going ahead, when labour and mate-

---

[41] TNA HLG68/82 'Leading Housing Authorities in September', undated file covers 1952.

[42] TNA HLG52/828 'The Housing Problem in Large Cities', undated c1934.

[43] New temporary dwellings per 1000 residents by local government category were 3.1 (RDCs), 3.0 (UDCs), 3.4 (Boroughs) and 4.9 (CBs) (TNA HLG68/82 'Leading Housing Authorities in September', undated file covers 1952).

[44] TNA T227/808 'Housing Memo to James Crombie, Herbert Brittain, Bernard Gilbert, Mr. Couzens and Mr. Petch from R.W.B. Clarke', 5 March 1955. This follows on from TNA T227/808 'Note of Meeting in Mr. Clarke's Room on 3 March', undated c1955, which cited cuts up to 50% for East Anglia and the South-East, warning of pressure to raise allocations from these regions and large cities.

Table 6.5 Annual Exchequer subsidies for new-build houses under Housing Acts, 1919–1972

Act	Payment
Housing, Town Planning, Etc. Act 1919	Annual deficiency payment (all costs minus rent payments and the yield of a penny rate product). The government decided to terminate the programme in 1921 at 176,000 dwellings, although the last 14 approved dwellings were not finished until 1929–1930
Housing (Additional Powers) Act 1919	The subsidy was for private building. Councils applied for funds to give to builders. In aggregate, paid subventions were not to exceed £15 million, with lump sum payments per dwelling of £130–£160. This was raised to £230–£260 in May 1920. The subsidy was withdrawn for completions after 23 June 1922
Housing Act 1923	£6 a dwelling, falling to £4 on 1 October 1927, then the subsidy was withdrawn if dwellings were completed after 1 October 1929
Housing (Financial Provisions) Act 1924	£12/10/0d a year for a house in an agricultural parish (for 40 years), which was reduced to £11 for dwellings completed after 30 September 1927. The same applied for the drop from £9 to £7/10/0d for dwellings in non-agricultural parishes. A subsidy of £5 was available for homes for aged persons (£7/6/8d in agricultural parishes). A local subsidy from nothing up to £4/10/0d per house per annum for 40 years was made for houses completed by 30 September, 1927, so rents did not exceed pre-1914 levels. This was reduced to £3/10/0d after that date. The Act ceased operating when the 1933 Housing (Financial Provisions) Act became operational
Housing Act 1930	£2/5/0d a year for each displaced person rehoused payable for 40 years (£2/10/0d in agricultural parishes), with £3/10/0d for flats over three storeys if the new accommodation was erected in slum clearance areas or on land valued at more than £3000 an acre. A council contribution of £3/15/0d was expected each year (MoH 1933a, p.3). For dwellings in agricultural parishes, there was an additional annual contribution of £1 from the relevant county council. 'The subsidy under the 1930 Act was intentionally made more generous having regard to the class of persons living in slums'. (TNA HLG48/685 Document 25 'Housing Subsidies', 5 May 1937)
Housing (Rural Authorities) Act 1931	For houses in agricultural parishes £11 per annum and £7/10/0d for those in nonagricultural parishes (assumed three-quarters of dwellings built would be in agricultural parishes)
Housing Act 1935	This act did not interfere with the operation of 1930 Act payments for new dwellings to replace slum dwellings but added the condition that subsidy required councils making appropriate contributions. The act also repealed public utility society and housing trust provisions in the 1930 act, so councils might (with ministerial consent) arrange for provision of working-class housing through third parties. For flats of three or more storeys on sites costing more than £1500 (and less than £4000) an acre, a payment was made of £6 per flat, which increased by £1 a flat for each £1000 in site value up to £6000, thence by £1 for every £2000. For cottages for agricultural workers, a discretionary subsidy was available. This varied from £2 to £8, as recommended by the Rural Housing Sub-Committee

(continued)

Table 6.5 (continued)

Act	Payment
Housing Act 1936	Under Section 105, for slum clearance, £2/5/0d a year for each displaced person (£2/10/0d in agricultural parishes, with £3/10/0d if the new accommodation is on expensive land). Under sections 106–108, £6 and up each year for a flat based on site cost, with not more than £5 a year per house for relief of overcrowding, and £2–£8 a year for dwellings for agricultural workers
Housing (Financial Provisions) Act 1938	£5/10/0d or £6/10/0d for a house each year, with £10 or £12 for agricultural dwellings. Not over £10 if provided by private enterprise (increased to £15 by the 1946 act)
Housing (Financial and Miscellaneous Provisions) Act 1946	Under Sections 1 and 11, £16/10/0d for a house each year, with £25/10/0d for agricultural dwellings and in poorer areas, with £2 extra for protection from subsidence. The general subsidies were raised to £26/14/0d and £35/14/0d, respectively, from 29 February 1952, then lowered to £22/01/0d and £31/01/0d after 1 April 1955. Under Section 17, the capital contribution for the extra costs of non-traditional building methods was from £55 to £70 per dwelling
Housing Subsidies Act 1956	For slum clearance £22/01/0d per dwelling, with £24 for overspill and the urgent needs for housing of industry, £10 for one-bedroom houses and £10 for other approved needs. From 1 November 1956, the payment for other approved needs was removed
Housing Act 1961	This Act reintroduced a general needs subsidy for housing, weakening the previous limits on council supply to specific needs. Normally, £8 or £24 was paid for each dwelling. Councils with particularly limited resources received the higher rate, which could range up to £40. For overspill, the rate was £28, with £24 for dwellings for the urgent needs of industry
Housing Subsidies Act 1967	The Sct introduced a formal system of cost yardsticks, against which new-build proposals had to comply to qualify for subsidy. This Act changed the basis of Exchequer grants from the equivalent of a lump sum (paid over 20, 40 or 60 years) to low-interest loans for councils for housing-building (effectively at 4%)
Housing Finance Act 1972	The Act terminated subsidies from previous Acts. It introduced into subsidy computations the concepts of 'fair rent' and HRA 'reckonable expenditure'. A key aim of the Act was to force rents up to private rental levels. As rents rose to reckonable levels, subsidy was withdrawn

Source: MoH (1920b), MoH (1930a, pp.76–77), TNA AO30/47 'Housing Act 1930', 6 January 1937; TNA HLG48/685 'Housing Subsidies', 5 May 1937; TNA HLG52/182 'Housing Finance', undated, file covers 1932–1937; TNA HLG101/247 Letter from MHLG Minister to A.C. Bossom MP, 19 February 1952; HCH 9 March 1962, Vol.655, col.95W–96W; HCH 1 July 1969, Vol.786, col.63W. Commentary on these provisions can be found in Burnett (1986) and Merrett (1979)

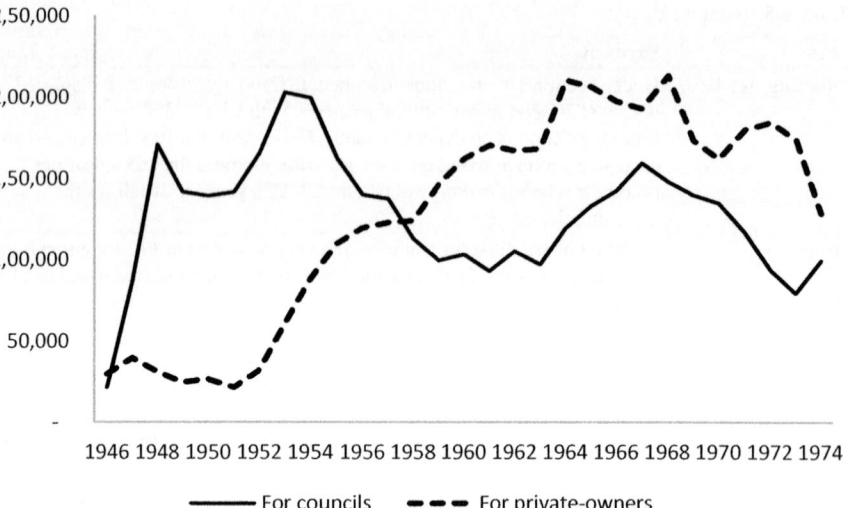

2,50,000

2,00,000

1,50,000

1,00,000

50,000

-

1946 1948 1950 1952 1954 1956 1958 1960 1962 1964 1966 1968 1970 1972 1974

———— For councils   ▬ ▬ ▬ For private-owners

Source: ONS (annual).

Fig. 6.2 Number of permanent dwellings built for councils and private-owners in England and Wales, 1946–1974

rials were available and the money, so far as the local authority was concerned, was obtainable, public investment which they regarded as urgent should not proceed.[45]

These concerns were well founded. Some councils were chaffing over inconsistencies, as with Hatfield's 1952 questioning on being told to build smaller, less well-equipped dwellings due to material shortages alongside instructions to offer larger loans so those with high incomes could build bigger private dwellings.[46] Conservative supporters were fearful over electoral consequences.[47] Ministers were pressed to provide a 'strategic reserve' of allocations for difficult councils.[48] These were awarded flexibly, as '… largely matters of judgement, and are heavily dependent upon what they can get away with', which would be essential given

---

[45] TNA T229/680 'Memo J.A. Jukes to Mr. Robertson', 25 November 1953, p.1.

[46] *H&PBG* 1 August 1952, p.4.

[47] For instance, TNA HLG101/812 Private letter (on Royal Insurance Company, Plymouth, headed paper), to S.F. Wilkinson, MHLG, 27 July 1953; TNA HLG101/812 Letter from Warrington RDC, 8 January 1954; TNA HLG101/812 Letter from Conservative Research Department to Ernest Marples, MHLG, 28 January 1954; TNA HLG101/812 Letter from H. Brabin, Conservative and Unionist Central Office, to Ernest Marples, MHLG, 10 February 1954; TNA HLG101/812 Letter from Woking Conservative Association, 28 June 1954; TNA HLG101/812 Letter from the Earl of Woolton to Henry Brooke, 10 September 1957.

[48] TNA T227/808 'Housing Memo to James Crombie, Herbert Brittain, Bernard Gilbert, Mr. Couzens and Mr. Petch from R.W.B. Clarke', 5 March 1955.

> ... there is a considerable volume of complaints and it is believed that very ferocious rows may blow up with Manchester, Leeds, London, and some other important and politically critical areas ... Nevertheless they [the Housing Division] feel that if they could have authority to hand out another 10–15,000 authorisations in the course of the summer, they might be able to prevent a major political controversy.[49]

Given their electoral clout, cities were expected to gain most from 'strategic reserves'. In the next decade, the problem was different but the response similar. By 1968, larger towns were favoured in building approvals but were not meeting their targets, leading to officials pondering allocation cuts, with a reallocation of unused permissions wherever possible.[50] However, 'Birmingham gives an illustration of a case where the surest way of starting a controversy would be to tell them they can have their 1968 allocation as fixed in 1966'.[51] London was similarly protected from 1968 cuts.[52] Favouritism in the treatment of councils did not only benefit cities, for special pleading brought some rural gains. At Hatfield, for example, higher subsidies for flats were secured, raising payments per dwelling from £26/14/0d to £52/16/0d, with the change seen to be '... a direct result of the Treasurer's tenacity in securing the higher subsidy'. This produced a reduction in 1955–1963 flat rents to the level of new three-bedroomed and two-bedroomed houses.[53]

The government hoped rising stocks of private-owner homes would consume slack in house-building volumes. Increases there were, from around 120,000 (1956–1958) to 170,000 (1961–1963), but housing needs were not met. Politically, the government faced a backlash against its 1957 Rent Act, which decontrolled rents on many properties to encourage private rental provision. This policy failed. Despite multiple claims by ministers that landlords had stopped selling their properties,[54] sales continued at pace (Merrett 1982). Moreover, the government was

---

[49] TNA T227/808 'Memo from D.M.B. Butt to Mr. Strath on Local Authority Housing', 4 March 1955.

[50] HCH 14 October 1969, Vol.788, col.53W.

[51] TNA HLG118/934 'Memo to Mr. R.C. Jones from Mr. Brain', 9 February 1968.

[52] TNA HLG118/875 'Memo on London Housing Programme 1968', undated c1967.

[53] HRO RDC7/1/32 HtRDCM 9 April 1963, p.672. Other examples of extra RDC subsidies included those '... specially designed to help rural authorities in the more remote parts of the country, such as Central Wales', to ensure rates and rents were not too high, plus additional aid of £2 for mining subsidence, £5 for houses built of stone, such as '... in the Cotswold areas, to preserve the amenities of the district' and £9 for isolated agricultural workers' houses (TNA T227/809 Letter from S.W.C. Phillips, MHLG, to F.F. Turnbull, The Treasury, 28 September 1956).

[54] HCH 29 July 1958, Vol.592, col.1125; HCH 30 June 1959, Vol.608, col.26W; HCH 6 December 1962, Vol.668, col.1487; HCH 26 March 1963, Vol.674, col.1109; HCH 18 June 1963, Vol.679, col.26W. At times the claims contradicted other messages, like: 'The Donnison report published in 1961 estimated that in 1958 five million dwellings in England were let by private landlords, that 100,000 were being sold each year for owner-occupation and about 60,000 were being demolished for slum clearance' (HCH 17 June 1963, Vol.679, col.32). No surprise the Labour Party made political hay over this. Labour criticism of Conservative rent policy was rife, as in Richard Crossman's speech on the Milner Holland Report (MHLG 1965): 'There is something desperately wrong with private landlordism today. Sir Milner shows that misery, vile conditions, overcrowding and persecution by landlords are virtually limited to private rented property. There are no complaints about owner-occupation and council estates. It is only in this realm of private landlordism

blamed for failing to regulate the sector, as 'rouge' landlords like Peter Rachman harassed tenants to leave rent-controlled properties (Simmonds 2002). But alternatives were thin on the ground for the less wealthy, as council-building had declined and many council additions merely replaced slums. By 1960, the shortcomings of government policy were clear. The Cabinet was told the '… housing effort needs to be increased, if we are really to throw off the reproach of the "Two Nations"'. As the minister for housing put the case in 1960:

> … in a number of cities and large towns there are a great many families on the waiting lists still without a separate home of their own. Some double up with other members of the family, a potent cause of friction, especially when newly marrieds have to live with in-laws. Others have rooms in multi-occupied houses, a family on each floor with inadequate sanitary arrangements, and are often living under conditions worse than if they had a slum house to themselves. Then there are people who urgently need rehousing on health grounds, or because of some other disability. These are types of 'general housing' need which cannot be met by private building (because the families cannot afford to buy), yet for which little is being done as yet by the local authorities because of the priority which existing subsidy arrangements give to slum clearance and other specified purposes.[55]

Fuelling this position was awareness that financial arrangements favoured (predominantly Labour supporting urban) councils that had built extensively under earlier Housing Acts:

> … the Government are now satisfied that Exchequer assistance is being distributed among housing authorities without regard to their present or future need for financial assistance. For instance, a small authority owning a few pre-war houses may be at a serious disadvantage in their ability to continue building houses at rents which their tenants can afford to that of a big authority with relatively many pre-war houses …[56]

For a long time, there had been grumblings in Westminster over high inter-war subsidies giving cities advantages, as surpluses on the housing revenue account (HRA) enabled them to charge low rents. By 1952–1953, 60% of councils were reported to have HRA surpluses.[57] This was seen to justify keeping subsidies down into the early-1960s.

At this point, adverse rural impacts were noted: 'An anomalous effect of the present position is that, by and large rents of council houses are higher in the rural areas than in the big towns, though the incomes of the tenants are almost certainly lower' (e.g. MHLG 1961b, p.6).[58] When subsidy cuts were being proposed, no concessions were made. Indeed, housing minister Enoch Powell stretched the argument to claim

---

that all these evils occur … In the nation as a whole, my Ministry reckons that since the introduction of the Rent Act — that great measure for conserving property — the figure for private rented housing has sunk from just over 5 million to about 3¾ million. That is a 25% decrease in the total stock of rented housing' (HCH 22 March 1965, Vol.709, col.72, col.77).

[55] TNA CAB129/101 C(60)96 'Housing', 17 June 1960. The first citation is from p.5, the longer one from p.6.

[56] HRO RDC7/1/28 HtRDCM 28 March 1961, pp.813–14.

[57] TNA T227/808 'Surpluses on the Housing Revenue Account', 29 March 1955.

[58] TNA HLG101/618 'Housing Costs and the Subsidy', undated c1954.

there were '… many rural councils which have a large reservoir of pre-war and post-war houses', so they could manoeuvre funds to reduce rents or subsidise building.[59] Powell provided three examples, all urban spillover districts whose inhabitants had access to higher town wages (Blofield and Flegg, Chelmsford and Hitchin). More generally, council stocks were thin in rural districts (Chap. 2), with the particularly 'over-subsidised' 1930 Act offering few bounties, while 1940s' and early-1950s' new-builds were expensive for local residents (Chap. 4). Both rural and urban areas saw housing programmes that fell short of requirements, with attempts to catch up thwarted by a lack of support for general needs building.

When this was acknowledged, the 1961 Housing Act reintroduced general subsidies (Table 6.5), targeting aid to poorer authorities, which received £24 per dwelling compared with £8 for those not 'resource deficient' (MHLG 1962, pp.10–11). The changes took time to feed into completions, for 1961 was another year of public sector retrenchment.[60] Approvals for council-building slowed.[61] When Keith Joseph became minister for housing in 1962, the situation was dire:

> We need a new impetus in housing. The four million post-war houses – three million of them under Conservative administration – have been largely absorbed by the rise in the number of households, caused by changing habits and prosperity. And for various reasons building in and for the great cities has not kept pace with the need. So that, in spite of all we have done, housing is still desperately short in many places; hundreds of thousands of families are living in slums; many more in houses grossly ill-equipped. For young people wanting to set up home, and for people who want or need to move, the problem of getting a

---

[59] HCH 25 January 1956, Vol.548, col.318.

[60] Economic troubles triggered regular 1950s council-building cuts. The government wanted to reorient building towards private buyers (HRO RDC7/1/20 HtRDCM 5 April 1955, p.388; NRO DC19/6/66 WRDCHCM 14 March 1955, p.128; NRO DC19/6/67 13 February 1956, p.57; HRO RDC3/2/11 BrRDCHCM 17 July 1955, p.2832). Demands for cuts due to 'economic necessity' were frequent (e.g. TNA CAB195/13 C80(54) 'Parliamentary Debate on the Address', 29 November 1954; TNA T227/808 'Housing Memo from R.W.B.C. to Edward Bridges', 25 August 1955), and fed down to councils (e.g. HRO RDC3/2/11 BrRDCJFHCM 13 December 1955, p.2958; D&FT 20 April 1956, p.3; MHLG 1959, p.58). Such messaging occurred right up to 1960 (e.g. TNA HLG118/298 'Memo to PM from Henry Brooke', 25 February 1960), although in late-1958 councils were asked to bring forward capital investments (e.g. NRO DC19/6/68 WRDCHCM 8 December 1958, p.110). For Willetts (1992, p.41), this marked a turning point in Conservative policy, which moved to plan and coordinate economic activity. This did not address core failings. Economic trauma recurred in 1961, although in 1962 the purse-strings were loosened again (TNA CAB129/111 C(62)159 'Civil Public Investment. White Paper 1962', 17 October 1962, pp.41–47). In 1964, the government pushed councils to build more but found it difficult to convince them given 'penal interest rates', 'low subsidies' and a conviction the housing drive was a pre-election manoeuvre (TNA HLG117/172 Letter to W.A. Wood, HMLG, from J. Davey, Welsh Office, 3 September 1964).

[61] For example, HCH 1 August 1961, Vol.645, col.1133. The impact of the message was signified by minutes on the need for cuts (HRO RDC3/1/11 BrRDCFCM 22 August 1961, p.5259; HRO RDC7/1/29 HtRDCM 12 September 1961, p.151; BRO RDBwM1/33 BiRDCHECM 13 September 1961, p.144; NRO DC19/6/69 WRDCHCM 18 September 1961, p.15). The media picked up on the cuts, as with NNN reports on Erpingham (21 July 1961, p.9) and Smallburgh (29 September 1961, p.5).

house is still often insoluble. Accommodation suitable for the ever-increasing numbers of old people is still hopelessly inadequate.[62]

But it was not until 1964 that a serious rise in building volumes occurred, with government failure to improve construction coordination and productivity seeing output rises hampered by labour and material shortages.[63] By 1964, completions were still under 120,000 (Fig. 6.2).[64]

Post-1945, temporary prefabricated houses marked a change in housing construction (Gay 1987), although the search for improved production practices had been on the agenda since at least the 1919 Act, under which 50 different methods using 'non-traditional' materials and processes were approved.[65] After 1945, homes of aluminium, concrete, steel and wood were tried, alongside encouragement to modularise production processes and fittings.[66] Permanent prefabricated dwellings were explored,[67] while building flats came on the agenda even in rural areas,[68] although '… there is a great deal of room for argument about flat costs. The cost of building a flat can vary very widely according to the design of the block of flats in which it is put. There is not the same wide variation in the cost of building a cottage'.[69] But flats offered prospects for cities facing site difficulties (Muchnick 1970; Newton 1976) and brought possibilities of improved construction practices. Initially, numbers were small, as steel shortages brought an early-1950s' ban on-

---

[62] TNA CAB129/110 C(62)145 'Housing', 2 October 1962, p.1.

[63] BC&BG 4 May 1962, p.20; BRO RDAM1/19 ARDCHPByCM 10 October 1963, p.243; NRO DC22/2/29 SmRDCM 10 March 1964, p.182; TNA WORK45/290 'Complaints from Individual Firms 1962–64'; Hatfield RDC (1965, p.55).

[64] Housing policy change in the early-1960s owed much to electoral fears (Simmonds 2002). For Keith Joseph, a target of 400,000 new (private and public sector) homes '… is essential as evidence of our determination to overtake with all possible speed, the present absolute shortage of houses which is the underlying cause of most if not all of the remaining black spots in our housing record' (TNA T224/710 'Minute from Keith Joseph to PM', October 1963). I found no Conservative advertising for General Elections in local newspapers prior to 1964 but there was a great deal that year, with housing prominent. For instance, the WR&WSR (28 January 1964, p.21) included the messages: 'We are impatient to end the remaining housing shortage and bad housing' and 'Nearly half our householders are now owner-occupiers. For those who can't quite afford to own a new house there will be our new Housing Societies, building without profit or subsidy. We're well on the way to our target of 400,000 new houses a year and 200,000 older ones modernised every year. Half a million slums are down'.

[65] HCH 7 May 1924, Vol.173, col.422. Official references to these methods include: HCH 28 October 1919, Vol.120, col.493W; HCH 23 July 1925, Vol.186, col.2426W; MoH (1925, pp.49–50); HCH 11 February 1926, Vol.191, col.1223–24; HCH 24 February 1927, Vol.202, col.1911.

[66] TNA CAB129/3 CP(45)224 'Housing', 13 October 1945.

[67] HCH 6 March 1946, Vol.420, col.347.

[68] For rural districts, this was for one- or two-bedroom units, as with the Biggleswades (NBC&BR 5 February 1946, p.3; 22 April 1947, p.6), Smallburgh (NNN 30 September 1949, p.1) and Sandy (BRO UDSM1/4 SaUDCM 26 June 1950, p.18). Biggleswade's programme accounted for 23.3% of its 206 completions in 1950–1951 (Biggleswade RDC 1952, p.15).

[69] TNA HLG71/2377 'Memo from J.E. Beddoe to A.G.', 10 September 1955.

blocks unless using load-bearing bricks.[70] Hence, only 16.7% of new 1945–1954 council dwellings in England and Wales were flats. This reached 25% in 1955, rose to 35% in 1958 and was a sliver short of 50% in 1963 (MHLG annual reports). During this period, there was intense lobbying by firms for council contracts, with strong ties between Cabinet members and the seven firms dominating flat construction (Dunleavy 1981). The combination of possible productivity improvement and replacing city slums saw ministers extolling industrialised methods,[71] with councils pushed towards larger contracts with long production runs to raise productivity.[72] Local authorities were told consortia of councils were needed for larger building volumes, although conferences organised to impress this message were only open to councils building more than 50 dwellings a year,[73] so eliminating many RDCs.[74] Not surprisingly, flats played little part in council-building in the investigated districts. Erpingham signified early that it did not think they were suited to the rural environment,[75] with other councils giving the possibility scant attention or only tentative exploration. One exception was Braughing, which built 24 two-storey flatlets in Much Hadham, as high land prices and roadwork costs made it uneconomical to construct 12 bungalows on the site,[76] while Smallburgh contemplated speeding up new-build by erecting flats at Stalham or on the coast at Sea Palling, the former generating disquiet on Council and the latter with the County planners.[77] Hatfield's more urbanised character saw it build flats early, with 24 of its 817 pre-1939 dwellings of this kind. It had added 73 flats-maisonettes by the mid-1960s (Hatfield RDC 1966, p.36) and used redevelopment opportunities to increase numbers later (like 68 above a new Woolco store).[78] Yet council minutes rarely mentioned flats (save for warden-serviced accommodation for the elderly).[79] Biggleswade offered a similar

---

[70] TNA HLG31/19 HI8/52 CON 'Multi-Storey Flats (Six Storeys and Above) in Big Provincial Cities', undated c1952.

[71] For example, HCH 17 December 1963, Vol.686, col.178W.

[72] TNA T224/711 'Memo from Keith Joseph to the PM', 13 January 1964; HCH 18 March 1964, Vol.691, col.1423; TNA HLG117/86 Letter from Keith Joseph to Geoffrey Rippon, 20 May 1964. Illustrative of the impact, Sheringham UDC was told it would take two years to secure the bricks required for old people's dwellings, with prefabricated dwellings suggested instead (NNN 1 January 1965, p.1).

[73] One response was Biggleswade, which concluded the RDC could gain little from the change (BRO RDBwM1/35 BiRDCHECM 8 April 1964, p.754), even though the Council had built 74 dwellings in 1964 (Biggleswade RDC 1965, p.17).

[74] Even by the end of 1964, only Forehoe and Henstead of Norfolk's 15 RDCs had 50 dwellings under construction (NRO DC19/6/69 WRDCHCM 8 March 1965, p.221). Hatfield only erected 21 dwellings in the year to 31 March 1964 (HRO RDC7/1/35 'Hatfield Financial Accounts for the Year Ending 31 March 1964', p.247).

[75] NNN 2 May 1952, p.1.

[76] HRO RDC3/1/11 BrRDCECM 11 May 1961, p.5151; 8 June 1961, p.5176; BrRDCM 5 April 1962, p.5452.

[77] NNN 7 July 1950, p.1; 7 April 1967, p.11.

[78] HRO RDC7/1/51 HtRDCH&TPCM 6 June 1972, p.64.

[79] HRO RDC7/1/37 'Hatfield Financial Accounts for the Year Ending 31 March 1965', p.1110.

picture, with 72 flats out of 1473 post-war dwellings in late-1959 (48 were up by 1951; Biggleswade RDC 1952, p.15). After this, they were rarely mentioned, save for rejecting one possibility, until the early-1970s when Bedfordshire planners objected to flats in the countryside.[80] Before then Ampthill had erected 31 from a post-war total of 1722 by 1968.[81] This gives a fitting message about the minor direct impact of rural flat construction, although indirectly flat-building drew policy attention away from the countryside.

6.1.3   Shortfalls Raise Rural Discomfort, 1964–1970

As Table 6.6 suggests, rural districts had similar or worse housing problems as towns, although 'leafier' counties like Hertfordshire and Bedfordshire had planned demolitions below the national average. More broadly, in internal 1956 reports, cities (including London) recorded the highest levels of unfit homes, followed by small urban centres (under 5000 dwellings), rural districts and medium-sized towns, with larger towns having the least (over 15,000 dwellings). Amongst the 12 authorities with more than 25% of their dwellings deemed unfit, city and countryside were again not far apart, with three county boroughs and two rural districts on the list.[82] Publicly, this was not the image ministers projected. Thus, the 1960 schedule of priority councils with long-term slum clearance problems had 47 English entries, of which only three were rural districts, but 20 were cities (excluding London).[83] The 1961, 1962 and 1963 lists were similar, although RDCs slipped to two while cities rose to 25 (excluding London).[84] The rationale for this rural myopia was signalled in the mid-1950s' message: 'Most of the rural district councils will clear their slums

Table 6.6 Slum clearance proposals in Bedfordshire, Hertfordshire and Norfolk, 1955

	Per cent of dwellings to be demolished		Per cent in clearance areas	
	Urban authorities	Rural districts	Urban authorities	Rural districts
Hertfordshire	1.4	2.3	62.9	39.6
Bedfordshire	1.9	2.2	70.0	1.2
Norfolk	4.6	4.3	73.8	32.9

Source: Computed from data in MHLG (1955)
Note: 'Urban authorities' includes county boroughs, boroughs and urban district councils

---

[80] BRO RDBwM1/31 BiRECHECM 14 October 1959, p.176; *BC&BG* 18 September 1964, p.15; BRO RDBwM1/42 BiRDCHCM 13 January 1971, p.615; 12 May 1971, p.1022.

[81] BRO RDAM1/24 'Ampthill Abstract of Accounts for the Year Ending 31 March 1968', p.323.

[82] TNA HLG125/42 Memo SRT56/28 'Slum Clearance', January 1956.

[83] HCH 22 November 1960, Vol.630, col.95W.

[84] HCH 9 May 1961, Vol.640, col.20W; HCH 6 November 1962, Vol.666, col.45W–46W; HCH 31 July 1964, Vol.682, col.105W.

by 1960'.[85] Nothing even remotely approaching this happened, with rural frustration over being left behind typified by Biggleswade's response to a Ministry enquiry on the pace of demolitions: '… on the basis of the present allocation and until some indication is given as to future allocations it is impossible to state precisely in terms of years as to the period in which the houses could be demolished'.[86] With priority on slum replacement, we might expect council-building closely matched demolitions. Data giving secure insight on this was difficult to find except for Norfolk. Here 1956–1964 demolitions outpaced new-build in RDCs (Table 6.7). Only in five of the 15 Norfolk RDCs did new council dwellings outnumber demolitions, and then barely. The largest net surplus was 48. Seven of the 10 losers had larger net deficits, with the largest at minus 465. Two points should be made here. The first is that council-building was not the only tenure that could replace demolitions. That said, councils had a duty to respond to housing needs and were encouraged by government to replace inadequate dwellings. The most practical vehicle for doing so was council-build. The second is that not all demolished dwellings would have been occupied, so replacements were not necessarily needed. At the start of the slum clearance campaign, for example, Ampthill had 201 dwellings targeted for removal, with 39 unoccupied.[87] Biggleswade Town originally scheduled 79 for demolition, of

Table 6.7   Council new-build and demolition numbers in Norfolk RDCs, 1956–1964

Rural district	New-build council	Demolitions all tenures	Net difference
Blofield and Flegg	281	233	48
Depwade	26	271	−245
Docking	111	171	−60
Downham	226	691	−465
Erpingham	32	76	−44
Forehoe and Henstead	237	213	24
Freebridge Lynn	126	95	31
Loddon	90	160	−70
Marshland	202	228	−26
Mitford and Launditch	207	200	7
St Faiths and Aylsham	309	484	−175
Smallburgh	63	228	−165
Swaffham	162	218	−56
Walsingham	175	216	−41
Wayland	60	27	33
All Norfolk RDCs	2307	3511	−1204

Source: Computed from NRO DC19/6/67 WRDCHCM 11 February 1957, p.121, NRO DC19/6/69 WRDCHCM 8 March 1965, p.221

---

[85] TNA HLG101/748 'Notes for Parliamentary Secretary on Slum Clearance, Prepared for the Institute of Housing's 25th Annual Conference at Scarborough, undated c1956–57'.

[86] BRO RDBwM1/26 BiRDCM 3 August 1955, p.177.

[87] BRO RDAM2/22 ARDCHCM 'Confidential Slum Clearance Programme', January 1956.

which 22 were empty by early-1956,[88] Smallburgh (RDC 1957, p.21) issued 63 closing orders and 100 demolition orders in 1956 of which 96 were occupied and the next year had 89 demolition orders covering 80 occupied dwellings (Smallburgh RDC 1958, p.24), while, somewhat later, Biggleswade was shocked to discover 74 properties with demolition orders against them, some made as long ago as 1939, of which 48 still had residents.[89] The picture was uneven, but demolitions did encompass some unoccupied properties. For the urbanites looking for a shell to reinvigorate, the countryside of the 1950s and 1960s had much to offer. For those living in soon-to-be demolished dwellings, council-building might have covered losses, but with limited scope for other needs.

The new Labour government of 1964 held out little prospect of change. Under new criteria, 130 priority authorities were declared in 1966.[90] They were charged with 'building the most houses', with four-year rolling programmes in London and three-year elsewhere.[91] A more 'select' 54, which had '… 10 per cent or more excess of households over dwellings according to the 1961 census, and who had 100 or more houses or flats approved but not started, or under construction, at the end of November, 1965' received backdated subsidy concessions.[92] This 54 did not reflect a tightening of the programme, for the original 130 were 'limited only by the authority's capacity to build', while a further 177 authorities were allowed forward programmes because their '… needs, though less pressing, required sizable programmes of house-building' (MHLG 1967, p.62). Revisions to these lists were presented periodically but whatever changes were made they included no rural districts.[93] Instead, RDCs saw their building programmes elongated.[94] Thus, 1967 Ministry papers acknowledged that '… policies for dealing with rural slums do not fit happily into the main stream of our current legislative review, and there is a good deal to be said for making them the subject of a special inquiry'. The continuation of this sentence signified that rural action should be 'with not quite the same urgency'.[95] A message to Braughing exemplified the rationale:

> Because a much greater part of the housing programme now had to be allocated to authorities with slum clearance problems, allocations even for secondary priority needs such as the housing of old people were having to be given on the basis that not all the schemes involved could be started as soon as local authorities would like.[96]

---

[88] *WR&WSR* 14 February 1956, p.4.

[89] *BC&BG* 24 May 1963, p.9.

[90] HCH 11 May 1966, Vol.728, col.96W–97W.

[91] HCH 15 December 1966, Vol.738, col.790.

[92] Listed at HCH 20 December 1966, Vol.738, col.262W–63W.

[93] For example, HCH 30 January 1967, Vol.740, col.27W–28W.

[94] This even applied to Hatfield, which was informally instructed that its four-year programme needed to be stretched to six years (HRO RDC7/1/41 HtRDCHCM 24 October 1967, p.436).

[95] TNA HLG118/767 'Note to Mr. Summers from J.E. Hannigan', 18 October 1967.

[96] HRO RDC3/1/18 BrRDCECM 12 March 1968, p.7306. Put another way: 'The concentration on the areas of greatest need meant that authorities elsewhere could not always be allowed to build as many houses as they would have liked. Such areas have had to be limited too meeting urgent need

The Ministry would not agree firm commitments, leading rural councils to contemplate a temporary discontinuance of programmes.[97] The allocation and assistance regime was targeted largely towards cities, with proposals from others not considered justified even if 100 new dwellings a year were proposed.[98] This was despite priority authorities regularly building below Westminster wishes. Thus, when priority and non-priority areas were compared for 1967, this showed completions of 75,801 and 66,544, respectively, with the narrow disparity not discomforting officials: 'Most of the 66,000 houses completed by non-priority authorities in England will have been for the priority needs of overspill, slum clearance and housing for the elderly'.[99] This might have offered some comfort as regards housing for the elderly, but there were still constraints on councils wanting to tackle unfitness levels. The 1967 national housing condition survey showed that dwelling unfitness was higher in RDCs than in conurbations or other urban centres (MHLG 1968b).[100] Ministry officials began to realise that attention to rural deficits was so retarded it would take 54 years to clear slums.[101] This revelation came three years after ministers had proclaimed most slums would be eradicated by 1973.[102] Following the housing condition survey, estimates for clearing rural slums moved closer to 60 years.[103] The national framework underpinning the geography of council-building in the 1950s–1960s was reigniting 1930s' rural neglect.

The 1930s' patterns were also repeated through substantial building for private-owners. The early-1960s saw the greatest opportunities for private buyers since 1939, while 1964–1968 saw homes for sale at levels not surpassed to this day (albeit below the second half of the 1930s; Bowley 1945; ONS annual). Alongside 100% guarantees for builders, new mortgage schemes – like option mortgages – were introduced to help low-income borrowers (Merrett 1982). This one scheme was to account for more than 20% of all mortgages by 1972.[104] Numerous entries in Crossman's (1975) diaries bear testament to the 1964–1970 government's eagerness to secure building society cooperation.[105] Collaboration was essential, as mortgage

---

such as slum clearance and the housing of old people' (MHLG 1969, p.2). As a consequence, Smallburgh revised its scheme (NRO DC22/2/29 SmRDCM 22 April 1968, p.573) and Hatfield had casualties (HRO RDC7/1/45 HtRDCJMHF 18 June 1969, p.128).

[97] As with Biggleswade (*BC&BG* 29 November 1968, p.1; BRO RDBwM1/40 BiRDCHCM 4 December 1968, p.529), which decided to continue trying to build given a waiting list of over 800 (*BC&BG* 27 December 1968, p.1).

[98] TNA HLG118/933 'Memo to Mr. Milefanti and Mr. Grant from Miss H.M. Gooding', 15 April 1966.

[99] TNA HLG118/934 'Memo to Mr. Girling from MHLG Assistant Secretary', 18 March 1968.

[100] TNA HLG118/767 'National Housing Condition Survey 1967', May 1967.

[101] TNA HLG118/767 'Note to Mr. Williams from T.A. Doughty, Appendix I', 27 September 1967.

[102] HCH 18 March 1964, Vol.691, col.1418.

[103] TNA HLG118/1392 'Unfit Houses in Rural Districts', undated c1970, p.1.

[104] HCH 10 November 1975, Vol.899, col.415W.

[105] One building society executive reportedly claimed the government was the first to have '… ever called the building societies in to consult about a major issue of housing policy' (Crossman 1975, p.325).

Table 6.8 Weekly cost of accommodation by tenure, 1969

Total cost of dwelling	Weekly tenant rent			Owner-occupier payment after tax relief
	Local authority	Housing association	Private landlord	
	£.s.d	£.s.d	£.s.d	£.s.d
£7600	4/16/6d	14/03/3d	17/07/9d	10/05/9d
£5200	3/10/6d	9/17/6d	12/01/6d	7/01/0d

Source: HCH 22 May 1969, Vol.784, col.141W–42W

demand outstripped supply,[106] which lessened the impact of initiatives like option mortgages until the early-1970s.[107] Home ownership was spurred by mortgage tax relief. Its cost rose from £80–£100 million in 1964 to £135 million in 1967, then to £215 million in 1969–1970.[108] By this date, Treasury relief covered 4.5 million home-owners, in comparison with subsidies of £163 million for 5.4 million council tenants. This helped make home ownership attractive, although the sharpest distinctions financially were with tenants of private landlords or housing associations, who saw no rent-reducing contributions, unlike in many European nations (Harloe 1995; Doling 1997). Apart from benefits from capital gains, everyday costs made home ownership attractive (Table 6.8). In rural districts, this did not help alleviate housing discomforts amongst the low-paid, with housing affordability problematical to this day (Clark 1990; Bramley and Smart 1995; Satsangi et al. 2010). However, as in the 1930s, favourable terms for home ownership encouraged owner-occupied expansion, with rural areas seeing sharper rises than elsewhere. One difference from earlier decades was a less marked disparity in growth rates between districts close to larger urban centres and farther afield (Table 6.9). This was associated with outward waves of population growth from metropolitan centres (Warnes 1991), with a notable emerging trend of moves by the elderly (Grundy 1987), helped by local builders erecting bungalows for sale (e.g. Lemon 1973).

6.1.4   Housing the Elderly Eases Rural Discomfort

A number of differences in building style distinguished private from public sector dwellings post-1945. One was the minor role played by flats in the private sector. Figures from the 1960s illustrate the point. When units erected by councils hovered

---

[106] HCH 24 June 1969, Vol.785, col.237W.

[107] Although some existing borrowers switched to option mortgages, the take-up rate for new borrowers in the late-1960s was around 10% (e.g. HCH 7 May 1968, Vol.764, col.200–01).

[108] HCH 21 July 1964, Vol.699, col.45W; HCH 11 April 1967, Vol.744, col.155W–56W; HCH 22 July 1970, Vol.804, col.147W. Taking the mid-year of 1967, average benefits per dwelling were reported to be £36/0/0d for mortgage interest relief and £20/11/0d for subsidies to council rents (HCH 7 July 1967, Vol.749, col.305W).

Table 6.9 Household tenure in Bedfordshire, Hertfordshire and Norfolk, 1961–1971

	% change in household numbers 1961–1971				% households by tenure in 1971		
	All tenures	Owner-occupied	Public sector	Private rental	Owner-occupied	Public sector	Private rental
Hertfordshire urban	10.5	17.7	29.3	−29.0	48.3	38.4	13.3
Hertfordshire rural commuter	17.9	41.6	19.8	−20.3	47.5	37.2	15.3
Bedfordshire urban	26.4	41.5	48.7	−16.4	60.0	22.6	17.4
Bedfordshire rural commuter	9.1	24.1	34.1	−28.5	59.5	21.8	18,7
Bedfordshire other rural	34.5	97.3	29.2	−16.6	52.0	24.7	23.3
Norfolk urban	11.5	30.9	32.3	−27.3	40.4	40.0	19.5
Norfolk rural commuter	33.8	71.3	21.0	−24.7	69.8	14.3	15.9
Norfolk other rural	12.5	63.6	18.6	−26.5	50.4	21.5	28.1
English RDCs	23.9	57.0	30.2	−23.4	56.7	22.1	21.3
England	10.9	34.1	32.9	−28.0	50.1	28.0	21.9

Source: Computed from county reports of the population censuses
Note: 'Commuter rural' refers to rural districts adjacent to the largest towns in the county (Bedford, Great Yarmouth, Luton and Norwich), except for Hertfordshire where all rural districts were taken to be commuter territory, given London's proximity and the county's numerous urban centres. For consistency, the computation for 'all tenures' was based on household numbers in census tables on household tenure. These figures differ slightly from those used in Table 4.10, as the latter included the small percentage of census returns for which tenure was not recorded

close to 50%, flats for private-owners were just creeping above 10% (MHLG 1962, p.15; 1963, p.12; 1964, p.18). Similarly, with the share of council-building edging towards 30% for one-bedroom units, completions in the private sector stuck at around 2% (MHLG 1962, p.14; 1964, p.17; 1967, p.65). In building styles, the two tenures existed in different spheres, adding grounds for Dudley Committee complaints about the geographical segregation of these 'tribes' (MoH 1944c, p.11). Yet, for rural areas, housing the elderly provided a counter-weight to the urban drift of public sector building. This was not always so. While around 60% of 1930–1936 one-bedroomed non-parlour dwellings were erected to rehouse those displaced from unfit dwellings,[109] only 13.2% of RDCs saw these units, compared with 22.1% of UDCs and 45.5% of cities.[110] Three-bedroomed homes had been the rural 'norm' since the 1919 Act, as they were considered the most under-supplied dwelling

[109] HCH 6 May 1937, Vol.323, col.1232.
[110] HCH 8 December 1936, Vol.318, col.1845W.

type.[111] Even when cost reductions were favoured, as under 1930s' slum clearance, the Ministry was suspicious when councils proposed smaller dwellings. For Whitehall, three-bedroom homes were needed.[112] The elderly and the young looking for small homes faced slim prospects. Change was nonetheless in the air. By the mid-1930s, the government had accepted old people's homes were needed in villages,[113] even if progress bringing them was slow. For 1924–1939, only 44,800 one-bedroom council dwellings were approved for all England and Wales.[114] There seemed little prospect of major change after 1945, as the Dudley Committee recommended prioritising three bedrooms (MoH 1944c).[115] Some councils nevertheless pressed forward, with bungalows for the elderly built even in 1946.[116] Yet the list of councils allowed to build one-bedroom dwellings in October 1946 named only 41 RDCs out of 281 English councils.[117] Rural districts proposing one-bedroom units, as with Erpingham,[118] found proposals decreed too costly. Thus, Hatfield's exploration found even two-bedroom dwellings saved little compared with three-bedroomed (Hatfield RDC 1952, p.41),[119] while Braughing, with Ministry support for a 1945 application, found the lowest tender for old people's cottages was 34/9d per square foot compared with 23/4d for houses.[120] Despite their relative expense, requests for

[111] HCH 20 April 1920, Vol.140, col.1857. Local reports on this include Biggleswade (*NBC* 8 August 1919, p.3) and Hadham (HRO RDC6/1/4 HaRDCM 5 December 1918, p.369). The Ministry limited two-bedroom dwellings to 5% of new-build under the 1919 Act (MoH 1920b, p.4).

[112] NRO DC22/2/14 SmRDCM 2 August 1932, p.359. A common rural response was that councils '… prefer to erect houses which are of a size suitable for the needs of a man and his wife and family rather than erect houses for a smaller type' (NRO DC19/6/62 WRDCHCM 11 December 1934, p.67). This was where the Ministry placed most weight (e.g. HCH 23 December 1937, Vol.330, col.2165W), with opposition to one- and two-bedroom units in the early-1930s (e.g. TNA HLG40/30 'Untitled Report for Ernest Strohmenger', 20 April 1931).

[113] HCH 4 December 1935, Vol.307, col.282.

[114] HCH 5 July 1939, Vol.349, col.1309W. Although by early-1938 23% of RDCs had approvals for one-bedroom dwellings (HCH 16 February 1938, Vol.331, col.1896W).

[115] Hence, the Ministry responded negatively to high applications for two-bedroom homes in allocations, as with Chelmsford RDC, which sought 600 out of 1700 new dwellings (TNA HLG101/417 'Memo Mr. Blackshaw to Mr. Kerwood', 31 July 1947).

[116] NRO DC13/5/75 ERDCHCM 28 May 1946, p.51; NRO DC22/2/48 SmRDCHCM 23 July 1946, p.2723; BRO RDBwM1/17 BiRDCM 11 September 1946, p.142.

[117] HCH 21 October 1946, Vol.428, col.131W–36W. They were dispersed across regions. The most obvious pattern was only three in the North (defined as Lancashire-Yorkshire northwards).

[118] *NM&PWJ* 17 January 1948, p.6.

[119] The same conclusion was reached comparing one-bedroom with three-bedroom dwellings elsewhere (e.g. BRO RDAM2/22 ARDCHCM 13 July 1949).

[120] HRO RDC3/2/3 BrRDCPHHCM 22 November 1945, p.815; HRO RDC3/1/3 BrRDCM 1 August 1946, p.196. Fifteen years later, Walsingham reached a similar conclusion, when the Chief Finance Officer costed a new bungalow at £1450 compared with £1650 for a three-bedroom house (*D&FT* 22 January 1960, p.1).

one-bedroom units rose.[121] Whitehall acknowledged the proposals,[122] hoping moves into bungalows would free up family homes.[123] Numbers were still small but, with tenders for 29,490 one-bedroom and 92,414 two-bedroom dwellings approved over 1945–1949, volumes were healthier than inter-war.[124] Moreover, the trend was upwards. Only 5% of new council completions over 1945–1951 were one-bedroom (16% two-bedroom), but 8% (and 34%) were in March 1951.[125]

Lesser demands on materials, building smaller units and achieving 300,000 annual completions sustained support from the new 1951 government, which drew attention to the need for coordinating construction with welfare services (e.g. MHLG Circulars 36/51 and 21/52).[126] Despite concern on councils like Hatfield that the real need was for family homes,[127] demand for smaller dwellings was unabated.[128] The Ministry's research showed demand was higher for one- and two-bedroom dwellings than contracts supplied,[129] although this information was treated cautiously when minor price distinctions were found between two- and three-bedroom dwellings.[130] Even so, the proportion of one-bedroomed completions rose from 3.4% in 1948 to 7.5% in 1952, with companion rises of 13.2% and 35.1% for two-bedroomed.[131] One-bedroom completions were close to 10% in 1955 and continued to rise, reaching almost 18% in 1958, then 26.2% in 1960 (MHLG 1956, p.11; 1959, p.164; 1961a, p.154). This was despite threatened 1955–1956 public spending restraints,[132] when subsidy removal was contemplated. A combination of low subsidy payments for one-bedroom dwellings (Table 6.5), plus transfers possibly emptying larger homes encouraged retention.[133] Covering roughly the same building period as the 44,800 approvals for one-bedroom units over 1924–1939,

---

[121] HRO RDC3/2/4 BrRDCPHHCM 17 June 1948, p.1243; NRO DC13/5/20 ERDCM 20 September 1948, p.4; BRO RDBwM1/19 BiRDCM 1 December 1948, p.251; *Potters Bar, Brookmans Park and Hatfield Observer* 31 December 1948, p.1; BRO RDAM2/22 ARDCHCM 14 April 1949.

[122] TNA HLG31/16 HI31/49 'Housing Programme 1950', 1 July 1949. Many submissions from national organisations pushed for homes for single people, the aged and young families (for 1950–59 see TNA HLG101/424).

[123] HCH 11 May 1950, Vol.475, col.555. By the end of 1949, 603 councils had had one-bedroom dwellings approved, while 983 had secured agreement for two-bedroom units.

[124] HCH 23 March 1950, Vol.472, col.125W.

[125] HCH 19 June 1951, Vol.489, col.35W.

[126] TNA HLG72/1 Circular 36 'Housing for Special Purposes'; TNA HLG72/2 Circular 21/52 'Houses to be Built Under Licence', 12 February 1952.

[127] *H&PBG* 26 September 1952, p.8.

[128] Such as BRO RDBwM1/23 BiRDCM 11 June 1952, p.92; NRO DC19/6/65 WRDCHCM 3 September 1952, p.137; HRO RDC3/1/5 BrRDCM 4 December 1952, p.71.

[129] TNA HLG101/373 'How Many Two-Bedroomed Houses?', 28 January 1953.

[130] TNA HLG101/373 'Memo to Mr. Blackshaw', 16 March 1953.

[131] HCH 31 March 1953, Vol.513, col.139W–40W.

[132] TNA T227/1018 Letter to Chancellor of the Exchequer from Minister of Health, 20 July 1956.

[133] TNA T227/809 Letter from K.G.H. Binning, Private Secretary to Financial Secretary, to W.R. Cox, 29 October 1956.

1945–1962 saw nearly 256,000 new one-bedroom public sector dwellings (MHLG 1963, p.13). Helped by the 1964 government's push to raise output, the trend continued upward. 'Between 1964 and 1969 local and new town authorities in England and Wales built 224,000 one-bedroom dwellings, suitable for elderly people … Over the five-year period from 1960 to 1964 the total was only 140,000'.[134]

How far smaller dwellings allowed larger homes to be let to families is unclear. Council minutes offered ephemeral indications. Ampthill had 87 tenancy transfers over 1955–58, 22 of which involved leaving three-bedroom units for one- or two-bedroom units,[135] while Walsingham's 34 newly built old people's homes at Fakenham took six tenants from council houses, five from condemned buildings, five from converted hutments and 18 from the general waiting list.[136] Otherwise, records did not specify numbers with sufficient clarity (nor regularity) for general conclusions, added to which, when three-bedroom units became available, they often went to households who were not on the waiting list. For instance, alongside the 87 tenant transfers in Ampthill, the Council made 36 new allocations to privately housed families with Notices to Quit and 13 with Court Orders to Quit. Explicit statements that families on such Orders were prioritised were rare,[137] although minutes reveal commitments to placing families in council dwellings to avoid homelessness.[138] With these additional demands on councils, smaller dwellings were a mechanism for freeing family homes, so councils encouraged 'downsizing'.[139] It was not clear whether smaller dwellings had appropriate facilities for elderly residents despite tangential references to their desirability.[140] With their smaller stocks, rural councils might have had difficulty providing specialised dwelling facilities, as demand for smaller homes came from the young as well as the elderly.[141] This did

---

[134] HCH 5 May 1970, Vol.801, col.178–79.

[135] BRO RDAM2/23 ARDCHCM 23 April 1959.

[136] NRO DC19/6/68 WRDCHCM 21 July 1959, p.158.

[137] Exceptions were Biggleswade Town (*WR&WSR* 13 July 1954, p.7) and Ampthill (BRO RDAR8/41 ARDCMOHar 1960, p.15).

[138] As with various examples in Biggleswade (BRO RDBwM1/20 BiRDCM 13 July 1949, p.164; *BC&BG* 14 August 1959, p.9; 16 October 1964, p.15).

[139] As with St Faith's and Aylsham (*NNN* 7 November 1958, p.5), Erpingham (NRO DC13/5/33 ERDCM 28 September 1965, para.56), Ampthill (BRO RDAM1/18 ARDCHPByCM 23 October 1962, p.287; BRO RDAH4/4 'Ampthill Correspondence on Housing') and Biggleswade (*BC&BG* 26 December 1969, p.1), although Biggleswade had reservations, as elderly residents might find a relocation upsetting, while shifts into flats were considered socially questionable (BRO RDBwM1/40 BiRDCHCM 9 October 1968, p.384; *BC&BG* 18 January 1963, p.14; 3 March 1967, p.10; 26 December 1969, p.1).

[140] HRO RDC7/1/23 HtRDCM 2 April 1957, p.702; HRO RDC3/1/11 BrRDCFCM 24 January 1961, p.5026; BRO RDBwM1/42 BiRDCHCM 10 June 1970, p.22.

[141] This was most often expressed in Ampthill, which was explicit in wanting bungalows suitable for young and old alike to avoid 'old people's colonies' (BRO RDAM2/23 ARDCHCM 21 March 1957; 22 January 1959; BRO RDAR8/38 ARDCMOHar 1957, p.15; *Bedfordshire Magazine* 6 (1957) 13). Even so, 80% of bungalows were occupied by pensioners (BRO RDAM1/24 ARDCHCM 13 February 1969, pp.550–51).

not apply to warden-serviced facilities. Here, specialised building and welfare-support from county councils were expected. The difficulty for rural districts, given residents' localism,[142] was securing economically viable warden schemes, even in larger villages.[143] Yet, from the late-1950s, warden schemes were explored in many districts.[144] Multiple schemes resulted, as with Ampthill's 1971 programme for Clophill, Flitwick, Harlington and Shillington.[145]

6.1.5 Flexible in Rural Responses

In the second half of the 1950s up to the late-1960s, priorities for council-building were restricted, with slum clearance prioritised and accommodation for the elderly treated favourably. Special programmes, like city overspill, expanding towns and new towns were also favoured (Cullingworth 1959; Clapson 1998) but, outside priority councils, general needs building was seemingly less welcome. The change in government in 1964 made little difference. Like the 1951 Conservatives, the 1964 Labour government accepted the main thrust of existing programmes (Crossman 1975, p.267), while instilling more urgency, given the depth of under-supply. There was a widening of the net for priority status, but it was not until the 1967 Housing Subsidies Act that defining Labour legislation appeared, although this was largely noteworthy for introducing cost yardsticks and removing subsidies for flats over six storeys (Diacon 1991, p.198). Outside the main strands of policy, diversity in response was occurring, both due to national action and local initiative. One symbol of a changed atmosphere was the ratio of demolitions to new-build. Focus on the three investigated Norfolk districts in Table 6.10, as these provide comparison for 1966–1974 with 1956–1964 (Table 6.7). The two-year gap between 1964 and 1966 arises in these Tables because the data sources did not cover these years. Comparing 1956–1964 and 1966–1974 reveals that Erpingham erected 32 new council dwellings in the first period but 77 in the latter, with comparable figures for Smallburgh of 63 and 227 and for Walsingham 175 and 238. Further changes in stock size came from a fall in demolitions, with Erpingham figures for the two periods running at 76 and 33, Smallburgh's at 228 and 99 and Walsingham's at 216 and 101 (Table 6.10).

---

[142] Investigation into flatlets in Cambridge by Braughing concluded that 'The scheme was an excellent one but would be impracticable in a scattered rural district' (HRO RDC3/1/10 BrRDCM 1 December 1960, p.4962). The draw of localism embedded in this statement was captured nationally by the Royal Commission on Local Government in England (1969), which found 85% of rural dwellers thought of a parish or smaller as their 'home area', with only 2% equating it with a RDC.

[143] For example, for Braughing, HRO RDC3/1/7 BrRDCHCM 2 October 1958, p.4008.

[144] As well as Braughing, possibilities were explored in Erpingham (NorfChron 4 February 1955, p.7), Walsingham (NRO DC19/6/67 WRDCHCM 18 July 1955, pp.14–15), Ampthill (BRO RDAM2/23 ARDCHCM 22 January 1959), Biggleswade (BRO RDBwM1/33 BiRDCHECM 14 March 1962, p.520) and Hatfield (HRO RDC7/1/3 Hatfield Financial Accounts for the Year Ending 31 March 1965, p.1110).

[145] BRO RDAM1/27 ARDCHCM 7 September 1971, p.195.

Table 6.10 Council new-build and demolition numbers in the investigated rural districts, 1966–1974

Cities involved	1966–1970		1971–1974	
	New-build council	Demolitions all tenures	New-build council	Demolitions all tenures
Hatfield	659	25	339	6
Braughing	38	30	39	3
Ampthill	403	107	168	70
Biggleswade	250	135	101	140
Erpingham	38	30	39	3
Smallburgh	132	59	95	40
Walsingham	93	63	145	38

Source: MoH-MHLG (quarterly)
Note: The period 1971–1974 only covers the first quarter of 1974, after which these local government units were disbanded

There was a shift in government policy at this time, as economic turmoil in 1967–1968 led to the 1969 Housing Act, which promoted upgrading rather than demolition. This did not account for falls in demolition numbers. Across the seven RDCs, apart from a dip in 1972 and the part year of 1974, the two smallest years for demolitions were before the 1969 Act (1966 and 1967). Indeed, demolitions in 1966 were less than half those for the peak year of 1971, suggesting different forces at play under the 1964–1970 government.

Examining across government eras provides a different perspective from explorations across decades. The 1950s, for example, bundles together two periods of Conservative government that were very different in content: the early-1950s characterised by strenuous efforts to increase public sector building, while the second half of the decade saw pressure to restrict it. Then in the 1960s we see the reverse, with lethargic commitments in early years followed by stronger performances later. The combined effect was that 1950s' growth in public sector building was greater than in the 1960s (Table 6.11). However, in so far as the investigated rural districts represent national trends, increases in rural contributions over the 1950s were proportionately lower than the national rise, even with Hatfield's new town spin-offs. Even for private-owner homes, 1950s' increases in these rural areas fell below the national average, save for Ampthill. In the 1960s, the same pattern held, with Biggleswade being alone in matching the national average for public sector increases, although only Hatfield fell below the national rate for private-owner dwellings. The key highlight is that rural districts saw proportionately less increase in public sector numbers than the nation, which fits policy emphases favouring urban locales. This applied across the decades, whereas for private-owners there was a shift from rural areas lagging behind to running ahead of the nation from the 1950s into the 1960s. Significantly, the districts investigated were not those in closest proximity to larger county towns (Fig. 1.1). Indeed, although it was relatively close to London, Braughing had the weakest private-owner growth across both decades, while Smallburgh in north Norfolk had one of the strongest.

Table 6.11 New-build dwelling numbers in investigated rural districts 1951–1971

	Number built		% change in number built		
	1951–1961	1961–1971	1951–1961	1961–1971	1951–1961 to 1961–1971
	For councils				
Hatfield	1035	807	242.4	55.2	−22.0
Braughing	127	116	41.6	26.9	−8.7
Ampthill	666	646	99.1	48.3	−3.0
Biggleswade	753	678	204.1	60.4	−10.0
Erpingham	385	72	173.9	11.8	−81.3
Smallburgh	380	195	169.6	31.5	−50.0
Walsingham	470	274	179.4	37.4	−41.7
England and Wales	1,463,550	1,221,226	250.4	59.6	−16.6
	For private-owners				
Hatfield	1333	949	701.6	62.3	−28.8
Braughing	156	895	229.4	339.6	473.7
Ampthill	900	2402	1084.3	244.4	166.9
Biggleswade	493	1654	566.7	285.2	235.5
Erpingham	330	1129	417.7	276.0	242.1
Smallburgh	373	1886	556.7	428.6	405.6
Walsingham	249	617	469.8	204.3	147.8
England and Wales	1,054,310	1,849,642	849.9	157.0	75.4

Source: MoH-MHLG (quarterly)
Note: The figures were computed for financial years April–March, so 1951 refers to April 1950 to March 1951 and so on. The percentage change figures for 1951–1961 and 1961–1971 are for dwellings built after 1945. The percentage change from 1951 to 1961 is a percentage completed in 1951 compared with the number in 1961, etc.

These patterns confirm growth numbers by tenure (Table 6.9). Compared with urban centres in the same county, public sector tenures grew less rapidly in rural districts, although disparities between districts abutting larger urban centres and others were small, while owner-occupation volumes generally rose more in rural than urban zones. The key point in Table 6.9 is the performance of rural districts across the nation. Far from falling behind, for England as a whole, rural growth in public sector tenures was close to the national average. This was not because of high rates of rural expansion in areas with a manufacturing or mining base. Rural districts in counties like Derbyshire, Durham and the West Riding saw increases well below the national average. The rural places with the highest public sector increases were in Lancashire, Shropshire and Warwickshire (the latter two having expansion rates over 100%). One reason was national direction, as with the development of expanding and new towns.[146] In the case of Shropshire, this was seen in the creation

---

[146] 'Planned' redistributions to help the economy had been self-evident for a long time, for 'The effect of lack of housing in hampering the development and redistribution of industry is only too well known' (TNA T229/473 'Investment Review 1951–1952. Memo for Cabinet IPC(WP)(50)5', 12 January 1950, p.2).

of Dawley New Town (now Telford), which covered Shifnal and Wellington RDCs. Rural Lancashire figures expanded through places like Preston and Chorley RDCs growing as elements of the Central Lancashire New Town, while substantial growth associated with unofficial new town expansion in places like Tamworth brought knock-on rural impacts in Warwickshire. Similar tendencies, on a smaller scale, were seen in Hertfordshire, where planned expansion saw 1971 rural tenure distributions between owner-occupation and the public sector at times favour the latter, as in Elstree (28.4% and 61.4%) and Hatfield (42.1% and 47.9%). These patterns highlight an important tendency in 1960s' settlement planning, which included devolving employment and population from London and other major cities. New Towns, expanding towns and overspill zones were often based on urban districts (or separate development corporations), but they also brought expansion – private and public – to rural districts. For overspill, rural districts received many dwellings built by cities, with formal arrangements near various metropolitan centres. Table 6.12 actually underplays rural contributions. This was apparent when Ministry memos exposed increased housing allocations for London overspill in South Cambridgeshire, Elstree and Luton RDCs, of which only Luton was an overspill destination in the *Hansard* list.[147] Rural towns like Sandy similarly saw London overspill,[148] added to which, less formal programmes, like homes for key workers in companies relocating from cities or attracted from overseas, scattered provision compared with the past.[149] Put simply, as planned developments took a stronger hold on the settlement system, the geography of house-building and tenure shifted, in ways that could confound prior expectations.

This helps explain why the national picture differs from single counties (Table 6.9). The real question of interest, given national priorities, is why rural districts did as well as they did? A good part of the answer was that they adapted, taking on board what options they could to secure Ministry approval. Take Ampthill as

Table 6.12 Number of councils involved in city overspill schemes by local government category, 1966

Cities involved	Local government category of receiving council			
	CBs	MBs	UDCs	RDCs
London	1	11	8	3
West Midlands		6	5	4
Greater Manchester		2	2	
Bristol			2	2
Liverpool		1	1	
Tyneside			2	

Source: HCH 21 December 1966, Vol.738, col.382W–83W

---

[147]TNA HLG118/933 'Memo to Mr. Douglas from C.T. Jones', 5 April 1966.

[148]*BC&BG* 27 January 1967, p.1; BRO UDSM1/9 SaUDCM 19 September 1967.

[149]As for Biggleswade Town (*WR&WSR* 11 February 1964, p.1; *BC&BG* 22 October 1965, p.1), which, like Sandy, had higher public sector additions than the national average (MHLG quarterly).

an example. It only began to prepare plans for new dwellings for the elderly in 1956, although the year before conversations with elderly people had led to the conclusion '... they do not want council houses and they do not want to be removed from their accustomed surroundings. It is therefore felt that their conditions should be much improved and their happiness ensured by the process of acquiring existing cottage properties'.[150] With general needs subsidies closed off, dwellings for the elderly at least brought an annual £10 subsidy and potentially vacated family homes. By early-1959, bungalows had been added in four settlements with plans for six more. By 1961, the Council's building was largely restricted to one-bedroom bungalows,[151] although progress was slow due to a shortage of builders.[152] Nevertheless, numbers crept up, such that by 1968 the Council had 319 one-bedroom bungalows.[153] As with Smallburgh, councils weighted housing programmes towards bungalows. In 1962, Smallburgh's bid for 88 new dwellings had all bar two as bungalows,[154] with 30 bungalows of the 32 applied for in 1963.[155] In 1968, 36 dwellings were planned, all bungalows, then 66 out of 73 in 1969, with calls for more right up to the end of the Council's existence.[156] Typical of Walsingham's bids was a 1957 request for 20 dwellings for the elderly, 25 as slum clearance and 17 to replace former military hutments.[157]

Only in Biggleswade was the general needs programme still important. Here, the council was advantaged by having so many pre-1939 dwellings (Table 3.10). This placed it in a similar position to the large cities that caused 1950s' governments so much heartache, given HRA surpluses meant they relied less on Treasury funding.[158] Biggleswade considered utilising HRA surpluses to build extra houses in 1958; seemed to accept the idea then backed off.[159] High interest rates were the deterrent (Table 4.15), with some schemes already suspended due to them.[160] Activity around this time was limited to slum clearance and rehousing,[161] but there

---

[150] BRO RDAR8/36 ARDCMOHar 1955, p.16; BRO RDAM2/22 ARDCHCM 13 December 1956; BRO RDAR8/37ARDCMOHar 1956, p.16.

[151] BRO RDAR8/42 ARDCMOHar 1961, p.15.

[152] *WR&WSR* 4 December 1962, p.1.

[153] BRO RDAM1/24 'Ampthill Abstract of Accounts for the Year Ending 31 March 1968' (with stock numbers from MoH-MHLG quarterly). By 1968, 17 one-bedroom aluminium bungalows were left standing from the original 130 erected in the late-1940s, while 36 two-bedroom bungalows had been built after 1956. So bungalows constituted 28.2% of new council homes post-1945 (21.6% of those standing in 1968) and 54.1% of the post-1956 equivalent.

[154] NRO DC22/2/27 SmRDCM 13 March 1962, p.947.

[155] NRO DC22/2/29 SmRDCM 12 March 1963, p.81.

[156] NRO DC22/2/29 SmRDCM 22 April 1968, p.573; 16 September 1969, p.700; NRO DC22/2/30 SmRDCM 23 January 1973, p.249.

[157] *D&FT* 25 January 1957, p.1.

[158] For example, TNA T227/808 'Housing Memo R.W.B.C. to Sir Edward Bridges', 25 August 1955.

[159] *WR&WSR* 1 April 1958; BRO RDBwM1/29 BiRDCM 9 April 1958, p.63.

[160] BRO RDBwM1/28 BiRDCM 23 October 1957, p.223; *BC&BG* 15 August 1958, p.11.

[161] *BC&BG* 12 September 1958, p.11; 9 January 1959, p.12.

was growing disquiet about younger people not getting homes, many of whom were employed in towns.[162] It was hoped bigger projects in larger villages might lessen costs to mitigate this effect, so general needs building re-started.[163] Helping the Council reach this decision, a survey of applicants found 'about 80%' would pay required rents for dwellings.[164] When the Treasury pressed for reductions in council-building,[165] Biggleswade responded by reviving its 1930s' practice of erecting no-subsidy homes (Chap. 3). In 1960, the Council approved a programme of 60 general needs additions and 19 slum clearance replacements, although the Ministry turned this into 63 dwellings of which 18 had to be old person's dwellings.[166] In 1962, this turned into 60 completions, with only 10 bungalows for the elderly and six to replace slum demolitions. The figures were 88, 17 and 16, respectively, for 1963 and 74, 14 and seven for 1964 (Biggleswade RDC 1963, p.17; 1964, p.17; 1965, p.17). Other councils, such as Walsingham, considered the same route, but tenant (in)capacities to pay, alongside a less healthy HRA, worked against progress. Little surprise Biggleswade completions were high, at the national average unlike the other investigated districts (Table 6.11). Of course, under the 1961 Housing Act, subsidies were re-introduced for general needs, albeit with meagre support save for the poorest councils (Table 6.5). So slim was the support that in 1965 Braughing stopped building for general needs as this required higher rents for existing tenants to cover costs.[167]

Even with a government sympathetic to council provision, in the late-1960s the investigated rural districts complained about low allocations and finance-limiting activities.[168] These were the cries of those wanting to secure more council provision, not blocking it. Characterising the mood, when rent increases were proposed for Newport Pagnell RDC homes, '... mainly so that new homes in the district can continue to be built', concern over increases was rebutted with the statement: 'People living in older council houses may say they don't want new building. But this is a community service and people must be prepared to pay what it costs today'.[169] Recall that compared to the past rural districts were seeing more private building than the nation as a whole (Table 6.11). Had councils been content to leave

---

[162] *BC&BG* 9 January 1959, p.12; 27 February 1959, p.1. By 1959, for instance, there were 200 council houses in Potton, with 80% of tenants working elsewhere (*BC&BG* 6 November 1959, p.1).

[163] *BC&BG* 15 August 1958, p.11; 27 February 1959, p.1; 27 March 1959, p.1.

[164] *BC&BG* 24 April 1959, p.1.

[165] TNA HLG118/298 'Memo to the PM from Henry Brooke', 25 February 1960.

[166] *BC&BG* 12 February 1960, p.1; BRO RDBwM1/32 BiRDCHECM 8 June 1960, p.41.

[167] HRO RDC3/1/15 BrRDCECM 8 April 1965, p.6502.

[168] NRO DC22/2/29 SmRDCM 21 September 1965, p.341; NRO DC13/5/33 ERDCM 28 March 1967, para.153; NRO DC19/6/31 WRDCM 17 May 1967, p.193; HRO RDC7/1/42 HtRDCHCM 5 December 1967, p.577; HRO RDC3/1/18 BrRDCECM 13 February 1968, p.7273.

[169] *WR&WSR* 5 September 1967, p.1. This was followed by an explanation: 'If we are to continue demolishing houses, new ones must be built. People must accept the economic facts as they are. They don't usually refuse a home because of the rent and if house building doesn't go on villages will be strangled'.

matters to the private sector, they were in a good position to do so. That they continued to press for more council-building, and showed adaptability in achieving this aim, bears witness to their assessment that council provision was essential for the working-classes. The 1960s was different from the 1950s, when private building was limp in most districts (Table 6.11). Characteristic was the reaction in Erpingham, which continued to build council homes despite the lower standards the government imposed on them: 'They were having to build houses because there were no private investors who could afford to build houses for rents which tenants could afford to pay and from all quarters the local authorities had been under pressure to provide them'.[170]

Further insight can be gleaned by comparing household numbers in public sector tenancies (as in Table 6.9) with the number of council dwellings erected (Table 6.11). For 1961–1971, these do not overlap exactly as computation dates are close but not the same. Nonetheless, the values obtained enable comparisons. Hatfield was unusual here as its construction volumes did not reach 45% of council tenancy increases. The main reason was the peculiarity of Hatfield's ability to place applicants in New Town dwellings. Another peculiarity was Walsingham. The government allowed councils to take over former military bases after the Second World War to use as temporary accommodation. At the 1951 peak, some 25,909 families were living in 1023 camps. By 31 December 1960, all camps were planned to have closed, except for those adapted so they could be part of the general stock. These then housed 2896 families on 140 camps (MHLG 1961a, pp.37–38). Walsingham still had 88 families in such hutments at the end of 1959,[171] with occupation extending for some at least until 1967, although references to these hutments was ephemeral at best, so their eventual closure date was unclear.[172]

Accommodation in camps raises a wider consideration, namely, the role of temporary homes. With most local authority dwellings built after 1919, property ages under this tenure were more recent than the norm. Given associations between property age and degrees of unfitness,[173] this means few council dwellings should have been targeted for demolition.[174] As a result, while demolition replacements generally did not add to the housing stock, they did increase the number of public sector tenants. The main council-owned demolitions were temporary dwellings, such as camp hutments and 1945–1951 prefabricated dwellings. Prefabs were often intended

---

[170] *NNN* 29 April 1955, p.9.

[171] NRO DC19/6/68 WRDCHCM 30 November 1959, p.185.

[172] References on their continued occupation include *D&FT* 19 April 1963, p.3; NRO DC19/6/31 WRDCM 26 April 1967, p.183.

[173] The first Housing Condition Survey found 97% of dwellings unfit for human habitation were built before 1919, so one-third of this age were unfit (TNA HLG118/767 'National Housing Condition Survey 1967', May 1967). The national investigation into reconditioning rural homes found more rural workers living in dwellings built before 1914 than in towns (MoH 1947b, p.7).

[174] Exceptions included the demolition of six council homes in Hatfield to make way for a new police station (Hatfield RDC 1968, p.36). Such actions typified the tendency for council-house demolitions to be for unusual reasons rather than deterioration.

to have a lifespan of 10 years, but most saw extended service. Ampthill proposed removing its 130 aluminium bungalows in 1961, received Ministry agreement that rapid action was needed in 1964 and in 1966 had 'demolish and replace' in the Council's programme.[175] Similarly, Walsingham took steps to remove temporary dwellings in 1960, Hatfield in 1961 and Smallburgh in 1962, with Biggleswade having to wait until 1968 to receive County planning permission to build replacements.[176] The point of significance, especially given Ampthill, Biggleswade and Hatfield had more than 100 temporary prefabs each, is that demolition and replacement should not have changed council tenant numbers. Yet, council-building volumes reveal that, for all seven investigated rural districts, the increase in council tenancies from 1961 to 1971 was more than council new-build (minus demolished temporary prefabs).

This indicates additions other than new-build. One route was the conversion of existing dwellings into smaller units. This was encouraged after 1945 if extra dwellings resulted,[177] although some councils, like Ampthill, initially found no suitable possibilities.[178] This soon changed. Policy-wise, there was no negativity towards conversions, with Ampthill looking to divide large houses into flats for the elderly under the 1949 Housing Act.[179] Others had already started, as with Erpingham seeking to convert a hotel and a chapel.[180] One-off references to such actions appeared irregularly in council minutes, with little sense of their magnitude, nor often if initiatives came to fruition. Sometimes there were systematic commitments to conversion. Braughing illustrated this, after requests from Cottered residents to convert dwellings into old people's units. The Council investigated, decided 1936 Act houses were unsuitable (too small), but 1919 Act homes could be adapted successfully, resulting in a programme to change 1919 Act properties into flats. With recognition that the existing stock might be adapted to meet housing demand, the Council went further in 1963 by recognising that single women often could not get a mortgage, so they should be allowed onto the housing waiting list for the first time, with this commitment accompanied by the decision to buy houses that could be converted into smaller units, as well as to acquire small cottages then modernise them.[181]

---

[175] *WR&WSR* 5 December 1961, p.5; BRO RDAM1/20 ARDCHPByCM 12 November 1964, p.411; BRO RDAM1/22 ARDCHPByCM 13 October 1966.

[176] NRO DC19/6/68 WRDCHCM 29 February 1960, p.211; HRO RDC7/1/29 HtRDCHCM 5 December 1961, p.324; NRO DC22/2/27 SmRDCM 13 March 1962, p.947; *BC&BG* 29 November 1968, p.1. Braughing and Erpingham did not have temporary prefabricated dwellings, although they did have non-traditional permanent ones, like Airey and Unity dwellings.

[177] HCH 28 May 1946, Vol.423, col.960–61.

[178] BRO RDAM2/22 ARDCHCM 11 February 1946.

[179] BRO RDAM2/22 ARDCHCM 14 April 1949.

[180] *T&WT* 18 January 1947, p.7; NRO DC13/5/21 ERDCM 22 August 1949, para.75.

[181] HRO RDC3/1/5 BrRDCM 3 February 1955, pp.252–53; HRO RDC3/2/11 BrRDCEMCM 14 August 1955, p.2863; HRO RDC3/1/6 BrRDCHCM 12 December 1957, pp.3645–46; HRO RDC3/1/13 Braughing Tenant Selection Committee Meeting 4 April 1963, p.5808.

In short, councils were adapting their existing stock to meet needs, as well as adding to the stock other than through new-build.

Faced with growing demand for council housing (Chap. 3), alongside national funding and priority regimes that made progress difficult, rural councils enhanced their offer through purchase. The 1955 responses of Ampthill's elderly residents led the Council to purchase and refurbish deficient homes. Council minutes revealed regular discussion on this point, at times in response to owner enquiries, otherwise on the Council's initiative. This led to action over individual homes but also to proposals for bulk purchase, as with 16 Maulden dwellings in 1950, 11 Marston cottages in 1955, 25 at Westoning in 1957 and eight at Pulloxhill in 1968.[182] Hatfield signalled its intention to use purchasing powers in 1960, by employing compulsory purchase orders to acquire homes from landlords charging exorbitant rents, while Biggleswade engaged in bulk buying, as with 10–20 Cambridge Road, Dunton in 1974.[183] But by 1974 the policy environment had changed. Under the 1972 Housing Finance Act, the Conservative government had imposed rent increases on council tenants, to encourage more to move out of the tenure (Harloe 1995, p.290; Jacobs et al. 2003). A year later, the oil crisis hit the national economy, with rises in public spending resulting (Perkin 1989, p.505). One dimension of this was government money to buy unsold speculative builder homes (even second-hand owner-occupied dwellings) to shore-up the construction industry.[184] By 30 September 1974, 13,600 dwellings had been purchased.[185] These acquisitions came just after RDCs were abolished, but this was the kind of opportunity councils made use of to provide homes for local residents. Such actions generally saw public sector tenancy growth outpace new-build numbers.

6.2   Building Styles

A key question in council house-buying, as in house-building, was the trade-off between quantity and quality. This was most vividly exposed in the 1945–1954 period, when the case for quality was made by Aneurin Bevan. He applied principles from the foundation of the National Health Service to housing, with quality not ability to pay the guiding ethic (Francis 1997, p.116). For Bevan, cutting standards was 'the coward's way out' (Foot 1973, p.86). He captured the immediate post-war mood:

---

[182] This is a selection of the initiatives to buy blocks of dwellings (BRO RDAM2/22 ARDCHCM 25 January 1950; 21 February 1957; BRO RDAR8/36 ARDCMOHar 1955, p.16; BRO RDAM1/24 ARDCM 12 December 1968).

[183] HRO RDC7/1/27 HtRDCHCM 5 July 1960, p.177; BRO RDBwM1/45 BiRDCHCM 9 January 1974, pp.530–531.

[184] This pattern was repeated in the early-1990s. After more than a decade of efforts to reduce social housing (Forrest and Murie 1988), the government released substantial funds for housing associations to acquire private dwellings (Hoggart and Silva 1997, pp.11–13).

[185] HCH 6 December 1974, Vol.882, col.658W–60W.

> The wartime periods had emphasised the priorities of equality, social cohesion, the break-
> ing down of old time-worn class barriers … The very idea of 'fair shares', Labour's master
> concept in 1945–50, exalted the virtues of common sacrifice and communal effort, as
> opposed to private gain or selfish, commercial exploitation. (Morgan 1984, pp.296–97;
> Hennessy 1992; Kynaston 2007)

As in 1919, when better standards were promoted based on 1918 Tudor Walters
recommendations (Addison 1924, p.215; Burnett 1986, p.227), Bevan drew on official 1944 Dudley Committee calls for 17% more space, the provision of outbuildings, better fittings and a second WC for homes for five persons (MoH 1944c). Such
expectations, while targeted at council dwellings, had knock-on effects, since those
building for private-owners tended to be influenced by council standards, even '…
though their houses were usually less well constructed and had smaller rooms than
council houses' (Pugh 2008, p.62). Official standards were not accepted universally,
and meeting them imposed costs that raised eyebrows. Thus, Dudley standards were
estimated to add 36% to the average cost of a 1938–1939 dwelling. Given inflation
since 1939, this meant houses cost 227% more, which would have been only 140%
greater without improvements (Bowley 1949, pp.148–49). Not happen-chance that
there were often delays in the implementation of new standards. Thus, costs meant
many Tudor Walters recommendations were not introduced in 1919 Act dwellings
(Addison 1924), while 1961 Parker Morris recommendations were not made mandatory until 1969 (Darke and Darke 1979). Even then, homes for private-owners
were less effectively regulated, with poor quality often resulting, as with the strings
of cheaply erected inter-war bungalows along north Norfolk's rivers (Wade-Martins
and Williamson 2008, p.155) or the swaths of urban fringe speculations in counties
like Essex (Gayler 1970; Hardy and Ward 1984).[186] But the enforcement of new
standards was not just about cost. Also significant were dissimilar views on 'acceptable' accommodation. In Ampthill, for example, the 1920 Medical Office of Health
was clear that: 'All that is wanted by the agricultural labourer is a single large room
on the ground floor, with a rather large scullery, where all the cooking could be done
when necessary, as in the summer months'.[187] Echoing complaints from elsewhere,
Biggleswade Town debates over the 1919 Act were punctuated by claims dwellings
were too lavish for the working-classes.[188] Overlain by electoral considerations,
such attitudes were fundamental to 1951–1955 government strategy (Jones 2000),
when a population tired of rationing was offered a 1951 Election contrast between
more slowly growing numbers of high-quality homes or more homes.

---

[186] For instance, in 1926, 507 rural districts had adopted (at least minimal) building regulations,
whereas 140 had none (HCH 15 April 1926, Vol.194, col.470). The government refused to urge
councils to adopt building bye-laws, arguing this was a local matter (HCH 22 April 1926, Vol.194,
col.1364–65). Only in the late-1930s was the National House Builders' Registration Council set-
up to arrange '… the inspection of houses by its own staff at all important stages of construction in
order to ensure the observance of the standards which it has laid down, and, if satisfied that the
construction of the building accords with these standards, issues a certificate to the builder' (HCH
1 December 1938, Vol.342, col.594).

[187] BRO RDAR8/1 ARDCMOHar 1920, p.7.

[188] For example, *NBC* 2 July 1920, p.3.

The 1951 Conservative strategy was unusual in supporting more public sector building, even if lower quality construction was common under the Party (Darke 1991, p.159). In the 1920s and 1930s, this was seen in encouragement to build the cheapest houses (Bowley 1945, p.45; Holmans 1987, p.309), with regular messages that dwellings would not be approved unless size was reduced,[189] or reductions imposed on the '… the standard of convenience, comfort and amenity of the houses'.[190] As Darke (1991, p.164) observed, 'It is instructive to compare the 1949 Housing Manual, which illustrates this [Bevan's priority on quality], with its successors of 1952, 1953 and 1958, in which the only sparks of creative thought are devoted to ever more ingenious ways to save costs'. The strategy had been developed in the run-up to the 1951 Election, when the Party exploited dissatisfaction with rationing and austerity (Zweiniger-Bargielowska 1994), playing not just on middle-class discontent (Morgan 1990, p.82) but on renewed shortages when the Korean War started in 1951, with the promise to build 300,000 new homes a year capturing the public imagination (Hennessy 2006, p.192). To achieve this goal, the new housing minister, Harold Macmillan, explained to the Cabinet that: 'In the execution of our housing policy I propose to take the following action … To encourage the building of smaller houses by Local Authorities'.[191] Moreover, as private-owners preferred brick homes, councils were pressed to build 'new tradition' cement dwellings: '… we want to keep as much of the local authorities programmes in new tradition as possible – this is to avoid increasing the demand for bricks'.[192] A proposed inducement was to count 'new tradition' units as half allocations, so doubling possible construction volumes, although councils were not told this.[193] When application numbers fell below gov-

---

[189] For instance, BRO UDA6/1 AUDCHBCM 12 November 1931; BRO RDBwM1/10 BiRDCM 16 December 1931; NRO DC13/5/73 ERDCHCM 13 January 1932, p.2. In all these cases, the Ministry insisted on dwellings of 760 sq.ft., which rural councils thought unnecessarily restrictive (TNA HLG37/44 'Evidence of Neville Hobson, RDCA Executive Council Member', undated c1936, p.7).

[190] Ampthill provided an example of insistence outbuildings be dispensed with (W&DR 5 March 1932, p.1). Such reductions were opposed by local authority associations, as made clear to the Ministry: '… the Committee wish to re-emphasize their view that the reduction in standards should be prevented at all costs' (TNA HLG101/812 Letter from Association of Municipal Corporations to S.F. Wilkinson, MHLG, 11 May 1953).

[191] TNA CAB129/48 C(51)23 'Housing Programme', 19 November 1951, p.1. There is some dispute over how far building smaller units contributed to attaining the 300,000 target. Macmillan claimed the new homes only used 10% less materials (TNA CAB129/53 C(52)241 'Housing 1953', 15 July 1952, p.2), with Turner (1994, p.82) placing weight on 'wringing' more resources from other sectors of the economy than lowering standards. Although some criticised 'over-investment' in social programmes like housing for Britain's developing economic problems (e.g. Barnett 2001), others noted much social spending received contributory payments (National Insurance, rents, etc.), with social spending below the levels of other nations, unlike defence (Cairncross 1996, pp.5–6), while others focused on weak economic policies, as for competition (Broadberry and Crafts 1996).

[192] TNA HLG101/505 'Housing Programme. Tenders for New Tradition Houses', 2 July 1953.

[193] TNA HLG72/2 28/52 'Expansion of Housing Programme. Non-Traditional Houses', 6 March 1952; TNA HLG101/505 'Tenders for New Tradition Houses', 2 July 1953. That councils were

ernment wishes, councils were told it was '… essential that a large number of new tradition houses should be built'.[194] Not that accepting these homes removed difficulties with the Ministry. Braughing discovered this when bidding for 18 new tradition Unity dwellings. The Ministry's Principal Regional Officer had already told the Council its dwellings were favourably regarded but expensive.[195] Consistent with this, the Ministry disallowed Braughing's application as too costly, suggesting savings be made by removing cupboards and fittings. The Council rejected the proposal, which required new plumbing arrangements and created unacceptable dwellings for the Council.[196] In doing so, Braughing probably saved itself from future grief. In line with many of the new building approaches the government forwarded, these new tradition dwellings became troublesome for councils. In Erpingham, 17 of the 18 residents of the Elizabeth Road Unity houses in Holt petitioned the Council in 1959 about excessive dampness, inadequate heating and draughtiness.[197] Similar problems emerged with other non-traditional structures. Thus, Biggleswade's aluminium prefabricated homes had serious condensation problems.[198] Little surprise Walsingham's Housing Officer advised caution over agreeing to any non-traditional system, noting that the Netherlands had tried 120 different systems since 1945 but only four had survived to 1963.[199]

If councils wanted to build in small numbers across their villages, problems intensified. For the Ministry, targeting 300,000 new homes a year: 'The most effective results and the best prices are likely to be secured by building large groups of houses and so giving the contractors reasonably long and certain production runs'.[200] This was despite homes for agricultural workers being a high priority so recently. The type of entanglement that could result was illustrated by Brixworth RDC. This Council had met or surpassed building targets in previous years. It had shifted priorities onto homes for private-owners, which should have pleased the government.

---

impacted by these messages was clear. Braughing, for example, shifted its programme towards non-traditional dwellings as a result (HRO RDC3/2/12 BrRDCHCM 24 April 1956, p.3078; H&EO 11 May 1956, p.6), while Biggleswade was allocated an additional 30 dwellings after changing its application from traditional to new tradition (BRO RDBwM1/25 BiRDCM 9 June 1954, p.148).

[194] NRO DC19/6/66 WRDCHCM 26 October 1953, pp.23–24.

[195] HRO RDC3/2/8 BrRDCPHHCM 18 September 1952, p.2134.

[196] H&EO 5 October 1956, p.4.

[197] NNN 30 January 1959, p.4.

[198] BC&BG 6 March 1959, p.13; BC&BG 1 January 1965, p.12.

[199] NRO DC19/6/69 WRDCHCM 10 June 1963, p.104. Diacon (1991, p.45) provides a further reason for questioning the government's efforts to impose non-traditional dwellings on councils, which was much higher costs in later years. Thus, based on a mid-1980s' DoE survey, Diacon provided figures showing that 80.5% of traditionally built homes required repair work if built over 1919–44, compared with 100% erected non-traditionally, with costs per dwelling at c£6300 and c£9500, respectively. The relevant costs for 1945–64 dwellings were c£3900 and c£7200 and for post-1964 c£2000 and c£3500.

[200] TNA HLG72/2 28/52 'Expansion of Housing Programme. Non-Traditional Houses', 6 March 1952.

Once the lid on private building was eased, it sought more than 100 private licences and less council dwellings. The Council appealed for a few additional council numbers to start a small slum replacement scheme. The Ministry's reaction revealed its priorities:

> This Local Authority have not been willing to take New-Traditional houses. Their allocation for 1954 must therefore come out of the reduced pool for traditional houses. They are an authority much committed to the building in every parish and have since 1945 and since the War developed or are building on 32 different sites with a total of 512 houses ... If you feel like making a gesture, another 10 would probably satisfy them, *if you can spare that from the kitty.*[201]

Immediately after 1951, no undue pressure was imposed to adopt the smaller, cheaper designs the government favoured.[202] This allowed councils like Hatfield to reject suggestions floor areas be reduced.[203] But over time, the Ministry pressed for lower costs and finishing standards. As Walsingham was told in 1953:

> Economy in the design of houses can keep the cost of housing down by, for example, the construction of dining-kitchen plus living room types in lieu of the three ground floor room types, the reduction of the pitch of roofs, omission of bay windows and timber surrounds to steel windows, and by the use of terrace blocks as far as possible.[204]

These suggestions did not go unchallenged, as with the Norfolk Women's Housing Council putting forward a 'fundamental observation' that larger kitchens were required. But the trend was one way. Average floor space for three-bedroom council houses fell from 1051 sq.ft. in 1947–1949 to 902 sq.ft. in 1957–1959.[205]

These shifts were national in scope, but they were layered onto poorer inter-war rural standards, with national and some local officials assuming rural homes should be inferior to urban. We see this in assertions that 'urban housing standards' should not be imposed on the countryside.[206] We see the sentiment in 1919 Housing Commissioner messages that road-making for rural sites was unnecessary; economy was more important.[207] It arose on a wider front in recurring tussles between rural councils and the Ministry over building parlour or non-parlour houses. Expressing a common view on rural councils, in 1919 the Biggleswade Medical

---

[201] TNA HLG101/812 Letter to Beddoe from MHLG Nottingham Regional Office on Brixworth RDC, 7 December 1953.

[202] TNA HLG68/78 [Principal Regional Officers'] Housing Minutes Appendix 31, 8 January 1952.

[203] HRO RDC7/1/16 HtRDCM 10 June 1952, p.18. Even in 1955, Biggleswade Town rejected low-cost designs, due to their poor standard (*BC&BG* 16 September 1955, p.1).

[204] NRO DC19/6/65 WRDCHCM 11 May 1953, p.224 (similarly HRO RDC3/2/8 BrRDCPHHCM 18 September 1952, p.2134). Smallburgh looked to save £33 on a two-bedroom house by removing cupboards, removing fibre glass quilting to ceilings, changing from oak to metal entrance gates, changing from brick to concrete coal bunkers and substituting a rain water tank with soakaway drainage (NRO DC22/2/27 SmRDCM 2 October 1956, p.442).

[205] HCH 26 July 1960, Vol.627, col.119W.

[206] As with the Central Landowners' Association submission to the Rural Housing Sub-Committee (MoH 1937b, p.33).

[207] NRO DC13/5/82 ERDCHCM 29 September 1919, p.35.

Officer of Health recommended every new dwelling had a parlour, a living room, a scullery with sink and copper and water laid on, a larder, a bathroom and wash-basin combined, storage for coal and fuel, and three bedrooms, one of which should be large enough for a double bed and cot to fit comfortably.[208] This reflected 1919 Act hopes of reducing political disquiet by showing the state cared: 'By building the new houses to a standard previously reserved for the middle-classes, the government would demonstrate to the people just how different their lives were going to be in the future' (Swenarton 1981, p.86). But Whitehall accepted rural houses should be different, regularly asserting a parlour was unnecessary.[209] This was rejected by many rural councils[210] and by key players in Labour's housing strategies, like John Wheatley, who asked that:

> ... we remember that today [1926] we are building for the people of 60 years hence and are laying down the standard and conditions under which they will live, [so] it is difficult to understand the mind of a gentleman [Neville Chamberlain] who, with some little knowl-edge of modern tendencies, thinks that the people of this country, half a century from now, will want a lower standard of houses than those we are building under the Acts to which he has referred.[211]

Facing 'reality', many councils concluded inadequate subsidies made new homes unaffordable for the low-paid. Even in cities like Birmingham, some council dwell-ings were as small as 572 sq.ft., so as to keep costs down yet qualify for 1923 Act subsidies by two square feet.[212] Given rural–urban wage differentials, many rural councils parked preferences and built smaller. In some cases, this was forced on them, as in Hatfield, which countered 1933 Ministry instructions to leave construc-tion in villages to the private sector by signalling local builder fixation on parlour houses, which left growing demand for small homes unanswered.[213]

During the Second World War, attitudes changed. Whitehall messages now car-ried tones of regret over 1930s' practices, suggesting a determination to make improvements. As put by the Rural Housing Sub-Committee: 'It is imperative that the relative inferiority of rural and particularly agricultural housing should not be allowed to persist after the War' (MoH 1944a, p.17). Lower quality homes were not

---

[208] NBC 8 August 1919, p.3. As Gardiner (2010, p.61) put it, no parlour '... was disquieting to working-class sensibilities, which required a "best room" for occasional family celebrations, for-mal entertaining, and laying out the dead'.

[209] For example, NRO DC22/2/45 SmRDCHCM 17 December 1919; or for Biggleswade Town, NBC 18 June 1920, p.3. This message was transmitted regularly in the 1930s also, as to Erpingham (NRO DC13/5/73 ERDCHCM 5 March 1932, p.8) and Ampthill (W&DR 2 April 1932, p.1).

[210] For example, NRO DC13/5/6 ERDCM 4 June 1923, p.23, on supporting a Neath RDC resolu-tion rejecting national pressure to restrict rural building to non-parlour homes, and opposition in Smallburgh to the Ministry's desire for non-parlour homes under the 1931 Housing (Rural Authorities) Act, although 'reality' intervened with the Council producing plans to improve space without a parlour (NRO DC22/2/14 SmRDCM 5 July 1932, p.337).

[211] HCH 2 December 1926, Vol.200, col.1407–08.

[212] HCH 26 May 1926, Vol.195, col.447W.

[213] TNA HLG48/872 Letters between Hatfield RDC Clerk and MoH, 27 September 1933; 22 November 1933; 29 November 1933; 22 February 1934; 27 February 1934.

portrayed as cheaper but as little different cost-wise from superior dwellings, especially given lower maintenance charges (Ministry of Works and Planning 1942, p.49). Bold instructions were forthcoming:

> The size of house desired is the three bedroomed parlour house, containing parlour, large living room – kitchen, scullery and WC on the ground floor, and three bedrooms and bathroom upstairs. There is some demand for the alternative of a living room, and a large kitchen – scullery. This demand requires the enlargement of the pre-War standard area possibly to 825 to 850 square feet for non-parlour to 900 to 950 square feet for a parlour type house. (This area does not include out-houses).[214]

These sentiments penetrated Whitehall corridors, with officials empathising with rural needs:

> The recent decision to increase the size of council houses from a range of 800-900 square feet to one of 900-950 square feet for a three-bedroom house will be of special benefit to rural areas where space in the house is specially valuable and it will also enable Rural District Councils to use again the plans of their agricultural cottages. These were designed by some of the best architects and are some of the most attractive cottages in the country ... But the decision of previous Governments to limit the size made it impossible to continue to use most of these plans.[215]

In line with this statement, local authorities wanted to build better homes and have discretion to build sympathetically with the local environment, rather than following bland, monotonous 1930s' national templates (MoH 1944c).

With widespread approval for improved living conditions for the working-classes, pre-1939 dwellings left much to be desired. Right after 1945, little was done, as the focus was on increments to the housing stock. Yet even in the late-1940s, councils were noting inter-war dwellings needed upgraded. There were significant shortfalls in electricity, gas, water and sewer systems (Chap. 5), but many more issues needed intention. Solving them was often expensive, which meant programmes were spread across years. The alterations needed included removing asbestos,[216] providing felt underlays for roofs,[217] adding damp courses or damp proofing[218] alongside extensive replacement of kitchen ranges, coal coppers, sinks, doors, ceilings and windows.[219] As late as 1959, Biggleswade reported 1000 coun-

---

[214] TNA HLG37/50 'Statement by Rural House Design Panel', undated c1943. This was communicated to councils in a 15 November 1945 circular (TNA CAB129/5 CP(45)330 'Progress Report on Housing', 6 December 1945).

[215] TNA HLG40/50 'Memo for House of Commons Agricultural and Food Group Meeting', 28 November (no year c1945), pp.1–2. In contrast with this space allocation, the Ministry had recommended three-bedroom homes of 760 sq.ft. in the 1930s (e.g. MoH 1935, p.156). In the mid-1930s, 72% of council homes were reported to be three-bedroom (MoH 1936, p. xxiii).

[216] HRO RDC7/9/1 HtRDCHCM 7 September 1948, p.419.

[217] As in Hatfield (*H&PBG* 19 September 1952, p.1) and Newport Pagnell (*WR&WSR* 15 November 1966, p.2).

[218] In Biggleswade 800 dwellings needed this action (*BC&BG* 30 January 1959, p.13; 22 May 1959, p.1), a significant load given a Council stock of 1057 pre-1939 homes. In Sandy this was still a problem in 1971 (BRO UDSM1/12 SaUDCM 29 March 1971).

[219] As in Biggleswade (*BC&BG* 4 February 1955, p.1).

cil homes needed major repairs.[220] Many dwellings with piped water had no hot water facility[221] or bathroom installed.[222] Giving a sense of what confronted councils, Walsingham's 1960 report on its pre-1939 homes indicated that 60 had modern facilities, 148 could be brought to modern standards with a hot water system, new fittings and minor structural alterations, 94 had sewerage and mains water available but needed major structural work, 107 had extreme difficulty with drainage requiring major alterations, and 20 had no water mains or drainage available and needed major structural work.[223] In the same year, Smallburgh reported it had 499 dwellings with no sinks and a further 14 with sinks draining into buckets.[224] Apart from the discomfort households were put through by inadequate initial design and construction, alongside the cost of bringing dwellings to a 'reasonable standard',[225] councils did not have a smooth ride with tenants over modernisation. Rents rose, while the installation of a bath often meant the loss of a third bedroom, which many opposed.[226] Wheatley's stricture that homes built in the 1920s needed to be fit for 1980s' families brings to the fore the consequences of poor builder practices and impoverished inter-war design standards. Building cheaply had significant long-term costs (Diacon 1991). This has been emphasised in recent decades by the shoddy construction of high-rise flats in the 1950s and 1960s (e.g. Dunleavy 1977; Portsmouth City Council 2011; Matthews 2019), but problems of inferior design and construction have a long history, as well as particular rural manifestations. Following 1980s' demolitions of dwellings erected in the 1950s and 1960s due to defects making them uneconomic to maintain, fierce criticism of 1950s–1960s' practices was lev-

---

[220] *BC&BG* 22 May 1959, p.1.

[221] The first year's reconditioning programme for Braughing involved 102 dwellings, providing bathrooms, WCs and drainage but no hot water (HRO RDC3/2/11 BrRDCECM 12 May 1955, pp.2783–84).

[222] There were common delays as water or sewer connections were missing, as for Biggleswade (BRO RDBwM1/26 BiRDCM 6 July 1955, p.153; *BC&BG* 30 January 1959, p.13; 11 March 1960, p.11; 17 January 1964, p.17), Newport Pagnell RDC (*WR&WSR* 12 January 1960, p.1), Braughing (HRO RDC3/1/12 BrRDCFCM 16 January 1962, pp.5386–90), Erpingham (NRO DC13/5/32 ERDCM 1 October 1964, p.6304) and Smallburgh (RDC 1967, p.27). Elsewhere, as in Biggleswade Town, baths were added once water-sewer systems arrived (*NBC&BR* 29 May 1951, p.4).

[223] *D&FT* 22 January 1960, p.1.

[224] NRO DC22/2/27 SmRDCM 17 January 1960, pp.832–33.

[225] Before standard improvement grants, council applications appear not to have been entertained by the Ministry (e.g. BRO UDSM1/4 SaUDCM 28 July 1952, p.196). With these awards in place, councils like Braughing proceeded with caution to ensure tenants could pay for improvements through rent rises (e.g. HRO RDC3/1/10 BrRDCECM 8 December 1960, p.4978; HRO RDC3/1/12 BrRDCFCM 4 January 1961, p.5364; 16 January 1962, p.5389).

[226] For instance, when this was proposed to 20 householders in Langford (Biggleswade), 16 did not want to be deprived of the third bedroom (*BC&BG* 29 July 1955, p.1), leading to solutions like that of Smallburgh, which modernised 56 three-bedroom dwellings in Hoveton but only converted half to two-bedroom (NRO DC22/2/29 SmRDCM 6 April 1965, p.292). This option was considered by Biggleswade in 1955, where retaining a third bedroom added an estimated cost of £800, which was built-into future rents (*BC&BG* 29 July 1955, p.1).

elled against governments and councils (e.g. Coleman 1985). More nuanced examination placed more weight on government action, given feeble regulation of the construction industry, alongside the advantages well-resourced corporations had in cajoling and manipulating small, under-funded councils into contracts (Dunleavy 1981).

Those who could not afford home ownership were constrained by the options governments and councils structured for them. If they were not stuck in poor-quality private rental (Table 6.13), they lived-out the tension between quality and affordability. The modernisation of council dwellings was merely a forerunner of what was to come later in the 1960s when the government decided to implement Parker Morris standards. Appearing first in 1961, these were considered a desirable minimum by the 1964 government,[227] in a move that shifted council-building towards the quality-first tone of 1945–1950. One change came in space expectations. The basis of comparison here changed, with three-bedroom homes replaced in statistics by five-bedspace dwellings in the late-1960s, but trends were clear, with the average square footage for this category of dwelling at 1050 in 1950, 914 in 1955, 897 in 1960, 930 in 1965, then a mandatory 960 in 1969.[228] The impacts were obvious. Biggleswade concluded that Parker Morris standards increased the cost of three-bedroom houses from £2021 to £2739, largely because square footage was increased from 790 to 1015.[229] Unlike Braughing, which pooled rents across all council dwellings, Biggleswade charged tenants the cost of homes they occupied. Tension arose

Table 6.13 Percentage of English households with exclusive use of basic household amenities, 1951–1971

	Households in tenure in 1971			All households		
	Owner-occupied	Public sector	Private Rental	1971	1961	1951
County boroughs	85.5	90.1	46.2	78.6	66.2	52.2
UDCs – boroughs	91.1	93.4	61.3	85.6	67.1	55.6
Rural districts	91.3	93.3	74.0	85.7	70.6	45.6
England	89.4	92.0	55.9	82.7	69.4	52.8

Source: Computed from county reports of the population censuses
Note: These percentages are not strictly equivalent over time. They reflect official interpretations of what were 'acceptable' basic amenities at each census. For 1951, this meant piped water, a cooking stove, a kitchen sink, a WC and a fixed bath. In 1961, it was cold and hot water taps, a fixed bath and a WC. By 1971, it was a hot water supply, a fixed bath or shower and an inside WC

---

[227] TNA HLG118/467 'Admissible Expenditure for New Aggregate Cost Subsidies: Note on Meeting of 10 November 1965'.

[228] TNA HLG118/948 'Revised Draft on Parker Morris Standards. Appendix I', undated c1970.

[229] BRO RDBwM1/40 BiRDCHCM 4 December 1968, p.527. Comparisons of costing for council-building was always difficult, especially over time, as dwellings were built to differing specifications. For instance, New Towns generally built homes nearly 70 sq.ft. larger than councils near them, while 'New Towns also build to full Parker Morris standards, whereas their neighbours so far only achieve these standards for about 50% of their dwellings' (TNA HLG69/995 Letter from Dr. H.S. Phillips, MHLG, to L.J. Sharpe, Royal Commission on Local Government, 19 January 1968). Yet, a year later, the government believed that '… in the public sector about

over moving families from soon-to-be demolished slums or prefabricated dwellings into Parker Morris standard homes, for rents rose from £1/11/6d or £1/18/6d to £4 after relocation.[230] Only 36% of tenants who replied to a Council survey were prepared to meet these rents. This was anticipated, as the Housing Manager had already expressed alarm over difficulties letting new homes.[231] Further: 'From inspection of the figures the highest number of applicants prepared to pay these rents reside in the more urban parts of the district'.[232] One expression of this was only three of 39 tenants agreeing in Dunton (1971 population 464). The Council had planned building 19 more council homes in the parish, but shelved the idea.[233]

Following the introduction of cost yardsticks under the 1967 Act, difficulties getting project approval increased. A 1971 Biggleswade Engineer and Surveyor report was characteristic, in warning that the Council's plan to erect 60% of dwellings as one- or two-bedroom would not work, as they cost more than the yardstick. Unless re-considered, the housing programme might have to halt.[234] As the National Federation of Building Trades' Employers spelt out in 1968: 'The provision of single storey old people's homes is an urgent problem with many local authorities yet it requires only a small proportion of such dwellings within a development to make the whole scheme virtually impossible within the existing cost yardsticks'.[235] The new policy had teething problems. Amendments were made, as in 1972 when the government was '… prepared to grant special yardstick allowances for individual schemes in areas of particular stress where local market conditions make this necessary'.[236] As Biggleswade testified, insufficient allowance for lower density schemes had particular rural applicability. Rural proposals repeatedly failed the yardstick when lower densities were proposed, until repeated complaints secured a higher allowance.[237] Building delays resulted, as they did when regional costings were recalibrated. Here Hatfield did benefit, with its yardstick raised in 1971 from an 8% to a 28% supplement, which was accompanied by revised costings for dwellings for the elderly.[238] Unfortunately, even then, the Council's largest development

---

92% of the houses being built today comply with the Parker Morris recommendations for space and heating, and that about 70% are to full Parker Morris standards' (HCH 6 May 1969, Vol.783, col.58W–59W).

[230] BRO RDBwM1/40 BiRDCHCM 13 November 1968, p.452.

[231] BRO RDBwM1/40 BiRDCHCM 14 May 1969, p.1033; BC&BG 4 July 1969, p.23; 6 March 1970, p.11.

[232] BRO RDBwM1/39 BiRDCHCM 13 September 1967, p.279.

[233] BRO RDBwM1/39 BiRDCHCM 8 November 1967, p.472.

[234] BRO RDBwM1/42 BiRDCHCM 13 January 1971, p.616; BRO RDBwM1/43 BiRDCHCM 29 March 1972, p.985.

[235] TNA HLG118/945 Letter from National Federation of Building Trades' Employers Director to MHLG Permanent Secretary, 15 November 1968.

[236] HRO RDC7/1/52 HtRDCHTPCM 5 December 1972, p.838.

[237] BRO RDBwM1/42 BiRDCHCM 14 April 1971, p.918.

[238] HRO RDC7/1/48 HtRDCHTPCM 6 April 1971, p.1191.

could not secure tenders below the yardstick.[239] Permission to build below Parker Morris standards was refused.[240]

The interchange between quality and quantity generally created friction. Particularly influential in such deliberations were costs. All governments wanted the discipline of cost guidelines, since this enabled higher output for the same resources, perhaps not within sector but certainly across sectors. But cost guidance could easily slip into cost-cutting, with substandard outcomes resulting.[241] For most of the public, governments are expected to show a lead in promoting improved living standards. Difficulties arise when targeted improvements result in unaffordable demands on citizens. If decisions are forced between standards and high prices, personal circumstances might dictate improvements are foregone, potentially even current arrangements are abandoned in favour of less pricey options. In a housing context, beyond council housing, for most of the twentieth-century, the main alternative was inferior private rental (Table 6.13). For new-build, exiting this dilemma could be achieved in the longer term by more technically proficient and productive companies erecting dwellings at lower cost, as happened elsewhere (Barlow and Duncan 1994; Golland 1998). Alternatively, it could arise from abandoning the low-wage emphasis the British 'establishment' has favoured for the economy (Brittan 1964; Lash and Urry 1987), replacing it with technologically based, research-driven innovation that yields wages enabling more citizens to afford decent housing. An emphasis on the former lies behind the poor performance of the building sector, while a stress on the latter should bring improvement to the industry (Smyth 1985; Wellings 2006). But perhaps less prominence should be allotted to new-build and more weight to enhancing the existing stock?

6.3   Reconditioning the Stock

At the turn of the twentieth-century, the reconditioning of working-class dwellings was enabled under the 1875 Artisans' and Labourers' Dwellings and Improvement Act. The Act was never extended to rural districts (English et al. 1976, p.16). It was not until the 1926 Housing (Rural Workers) Act that grant-aid was available to improve rural dwellings. Introducing this Act, which was not extended to towns, Chamberlain argued that rural housing was different because

---

[239] HRO RDC7/1/49 HtRDCHTPCM 19 October 1971, p.496.

[240] BRO RDBwM1/39 BiRDCHLCM 27 March 1968, p.900; BRO RDBwM1/40 BiRDCHCM 4 December 1968, p.527.

[241] Councils did not have to accept lower standards. Thus, when Biggleswade Town inspected lower cost houses in Lincolnshire, they '… thought the houses worse than the old type parlour houses' (*BC&BG* 16 September 1955, p.1; *WR&WSR* 20 September 1955, p.5). But given the Ministry could refuse permission to borrow funds for new dwellings (viz. loan sanction), the alternative, as with the Town's decision to defer, could be fewer dwellings.

... in the country districts we have a population which is, generally speaking, stationary, if not declining, and consequently you have not there the problem which you have in the towns of having to provide for a constantly increasing number of families. The other feature is that even in pre-war times the agricultural labourer was never expected, and, as a matter of fact, was never in a position, to pay an economic rent for his house ... [and] although many things are cheaper in the country than in the towns, that cannot be said of new houses, for the position in the country makes house-building there actually more expensive than it is in the towns.

Moreover,

... in many districts, particularly near the large towns, there has been an invasion of the country by the town dwellers ... who can afford to pay a higher rent, [and] have frequently taken possession of the new accommodation in the villages and have thus deprived the agricultural workers of the opportunity of getting improved houses.

Charging that new rural homes under the 1924 Act cost the Exchequer £220 each, with an additional £80 from the council, Chamberlain stressed the expense of new-build, drawing attention to the aesthetic merit of old cottages:

Our country villages contain a great deal that is characteristic of old England in style and material and in the architecture of their cottages. To look at cottages, such as you may see in the Cotswold district in Gloucestershire, or in East Kent, where I was the other day, is a constant pleasure, not only to country dwellers, but to town dwellers too, and I must say that it seems to me it would be something like an act of vandalism if we were to destroy these reminders of an older and more picturesque world in order to replace them with buildings which, though they may be sensible, are of a different style and cannot be said to harmonise with their surroundings.[242]

Cabinet had concerns over the Act, in part because of feared political 'noise' if grants were paid to landlords.[243] In his introductory speech, Chamberlain noted this concern, asking why public money should be used to induce landlords to act as they should anyway? His response was that many landlords had limited resources, while '... the benefits arising out of this use of public money must go practically entirely to the tenants and not to the landlords'.[244] The Act thereby limited rent increases if agricultural labourers inhabited grant-aided dwellings, with restraint lasting 20 years.

This provision was a weakness. Whether close to its passing or years later, the 1926 Act was graded a disappointment. Progress under the Act was slow (e.g. MoH 1930a, p.80), which matched Chamberlain's musings, with his diary entry for 19 November 1927 reading: '... I think the only way to stimulate them is to get the District Councils to make themselves disagreeable to the owners' (Self 2006, p.429). Commentary on weak take-up in Whitehall often blamed councils for not publicising the Act,[245] but the real problem lay with property-owners. Two contem-

---

[242] HCH 3 August 1926, Vol.198, col.2839, col.2840 and col.2841 for the three citations.

[243] TNA CAB27/309 CP30(26) Committee on Rural Housing and Slum Areas, 1926.

[244] HCH 3 August 1926, Vol.198, col.2842.

[245] TNA HLG37/42 Rural Housing Sub-Committee Minutes, 26 February 1936, p.2, while ministers laid the charge publicly (e.g. HCH 10 December 1936, Vol.318, col.2153).

porary commentators were particularly critical of the consequences. Pedley (1942, p.90), for example, rejected the idea that poor use of Act was due to landlord ignorance, asserting'… the real reason would appear to be that landlords no longer have the interest on their estates and tenants which existed before the Great War'. Shears (1936, p.6) offered a more economically self-interested version, noting that cottage owners did not want employee tenants, as rents were then controlled by the Agricultural Wages Acts. They preferred to let to non-farm workers who could be charged a higher, more rapidly rising rent. As the Aylesbury RDC Clerk wrote to the Minister of Health:

> One of the real causes which is the root of the matter is that property-owners will not tie themselves for 20 years to the restrictions which have to be observed should they take advantage of the Act. They have to undertake that the letting of the house for that period, only be to one class of person and a restricted rent, and failure to observe these conditions means repayment of the amount advanced with compound interest as well as periodical inspection by the Council's officer …[246]

Over time, Ministry interpretations came to acknowledge landlord 'apathy', while highlighting how the 'energy and enthusiasm' of local officials or councillors could cajole reluctant landlords to act.[247]

This conclusion matched Linsley's (2005, pp.215–31) Norfolk investigation, which revealed dissimilar performances by neighbouring districts. Ministers and officials often spoke positively about high take-up in Devon, which received more grants than any other English county.[248] But numbers were low everywhere, which some blamed on the 1930 and 1936 Acts encouraging demolition and rebuild rather than reconditioning.[249] Official reports still pressed the case that the Act would increase housing supply, alongside messages that rural new-build was not a priority:??

> An important difference between reconditioning in rural districts and similar work undertaken in urban districts is that in rural districts it is practicable and not uncommon to increase the existing accommodation by the addition of extra bedrooms as part of the work of reconditioning. Our recommendation, therefore, in regard to new building to abate overcrowding in the acquired houses in urban areas need not be extended to rural areas, where the same result can be achieved by an enlargement of the reconditioned house for which subsidy under the Housing (Rural Workers) Acts is available. (MoH 1933b, p.44)

The Ministry foresaw increased activity under the Act after 1933, with the withdrawal of general needs subsidies.[250] This happened but numbers were meagre. Annually, applications rose from an average of 1570 (with 1055 approved) before 1933 to 2559 from then until 1936 (with 1864 approved; CHAC 1936, p.3). Place these against Tilley's (1947, p.43) estimate that less than 5% of agricultural tied

---

[246] TNA HLG29/179 Letter from Aylesbury RDC Clerk to Minister of Health, 10 July 1931.

[247] TNA HLG52/759 'Minute Sheet to Mr. Rucker', 7 May 1935.

[248] HCH 21 November 1928, Vol.222, col.1739W–40W.

[249] TNA HLG37/50 'CPRE Submission on Rural Housing', undated c1943.

[250] TNA CAB24/234 CP386(32) 'Housing Policy', 27 January 1933, p.4.

cottages were reconditioned under the Act. For sure there was evidence of council reluctance to offer grant-aid to landlords, with North-East England identified as a particular 'culprit',[251] but the bigger picture was of twice the total take-up in Scotland as in England. The list of English counties with more than 500 applications in the first 10 years of the Act suggested a 'peripherality' effect (CHAC 1936, p.17). Cornwall, Cumberland, Devon, Norfolk, Shropshire, Southampton, Somerset, Suffolk East, Wiltshire and Worcestershire comprised the list, with counties attracting more urban interest often having little take-up. In the case of Bedford, Berkshire, Buckingham, Northamptonshire, Oxford and Peterborough, for example: 'The reconditioning of houses for agricultural labourers is discouraged by the opportunities for obtaining high prices for weekend cottages'.[252] Ten years later, the RDCA reported that landlords were repaying improvement grants, for by eliminating the Act's restrictions refurbished dwellings could be sold (Chap. 2).[253]

Some commentators preferred demolition and replacement to rehabilitation (e.g. Tilley 1947, p.47). An advantage of demolition was removing the possibility that wrecked dwellings found new life as substandard residences. Mackintosh (1936, p.40) fretted over this, noting how Northamptonshire dwellings deemed unsatisfactory were promoted as desirable for the aged. Such an ascription perturbed Mackintosh, for in many such properties '… the stair is so steep that it would require the agility of a sailor to manage it', with water supply far away down muddy lanes. Yet, as 1945 approached, an extension to the Housing (Rural Workers) Act was promoted (as happened in 1931 and 1938; Martin 1938), in part because rural builders were believed to be better suited to reconditioning than new-build;[254] although increased financial support was deemed necessary.[255] The new government was not convinced.[256] With labour shortages acute, Bevan's priorities were clear:

> I want first to canalise all the available rural labour into the building of new houses. Later on, when we can see how the problem develops, I hope to come to Parliament to ask for an Act to enable cottages to be reconditioned … I have no prejudice in this matter. All I want is for labour to go first to the best places in the immediate emergency.[257]

---

[251] TNA HLG37/43 'Investigation by General Inspectors 1934', undated c1936, p.31.

[252] TNA HLG37/43 'Investigation by General Inspectors 1934', undated c1936, p.5.

[253] TNA HLG37/51 Rural Housing Sub-Committee Minutes, 11 April 1946, p.3.

[254] This view was challenged where rural building firms were so sparse reliance had to be placed on companies in surrounding towns (e.g. TNA HLG37/54 Letter from the Kent Joint Advisory Rural Housing Committee Clerk to Rural Housing Sub-Committee Secretary, 15 November 1945).

[255] TNA HLG37/50 'Memorandum of Oxfordshire County Council', 23 November 1943; 'Land Agents' Committee Supplementary Statement on Rural Housing', undated c1943; 'CPRE Submission on Rural Housing', undated c1943; TNA MAF234/7 'NFU Document on Rural Housing', Cyclo 1490/45, 28 September 1945.

[256] An exception was repairing war-damaged dwellings. By mid-1951 the government announced 775,000 such homes had been repaired by local authorities but could not give figures for the private sector. This local government total was close to the combined new-build and war-damaged replacement number of 865,409 (HCH 31 July 1951, Vol.4 91, col.168W).

[257] HCH 17 October 1945, Vol.414, col.1228. See his explanation for this priority when working to re-introduce grants to upgrade existing homes (TNA MAF234/16 'Grants for Reconditioning

This approach drew criticism from farmers, although farm-worker unions worried reconditioning would perpetuate the 'evils' of tied cottages.[258] How far Bevan's decision was based on concern reconditioned cottages would not improve living conditions sufficiently is unclear. What was certain was he wanted to preserve country cottages:

> … many of these cottages which have been reconditioned ought to be preserved. Many of them have great architectural value. It would be a disaster if they fell into ruin. Their facade, their exteriors, are often quite charming and ought to be preserved. The interiors, of course, have to be brought up to date.[259]

The Rural Housing Sub-Committee was charged to investigate reconditioning (MoH 1947b), after which Bevan made good his commitment to support reconditioning in the 1949 Housing Act (MoH 1949). The innovation of this Act was that assistance was offered both to rural and urban areas.

In one respect, the early months of this new legislation reflected what was to come in the next 25 years, for initial awards were made to 204 rural dwellings but to only 93 in the rest of England and Wales.[260] Towns began to catch up, but nowhere near their population share. Thus, one 1960 report cited 57.2% of approved grants for conversions and improvements going to RDCs from 1949 up to 1954, after which the number fell annually to around 41% by 1959–1960.[261] These numbers were achieved even though tied cottages were excluded until 1952 (Baker 1953, p.190). As under the 1926 Act, the Ministry reported owners were reluctant to 'untie' cottages by accepting improvement aid, despite Ministry assurances they could obtain possession of 'untied cottages' if needed for business.[262] Although investigators found more grant usage on tied cottages than other private rental (e.g. Giles and Cowie 1960; Fletcher 1969), rural awards continued to decline proportionately (below 30% by the mid-1960s).[263] This was still above the RDC population share, but some councils found the 16-point requirements needed for grant approval onerous.[264] Irritation also resulted from the necessity of obtaining Ministerial approval before awarding grants, with officers often perturbed by

---

Rural Cottages', 25 February (no year, c1949)).

[258] TNA HLG101/213 Letter from NFU Warwickshire Branch to W.J. Brown MP, 15 November 1945; TNA HLG37/55 Letter from Bedfordshire County Council Clerk to T. Hauff, Rural Housing Sub-Committee, 27 February 1946; TNA HLG37/51 Rural Housing Sub-Committee Minutes, 21 February 1946, p.1; TNA HLG37/53 Rural Housing Sub-Committee. 'Minority Report by Jennie Lee', undated c1946, pp.1–2.

[259] HCH 17 October 1945, Vol.414, col.1228.

[260] HCH 19 October 1950, Vol.478, col.2 65W.

[261] TNA MAF186/86 'Brief by R.J.E. Taylor for the Parliamentary Secretary', 14 September 1960.

[262] TNA HLG101/582 'Agricultural Housing Subsidies and Improvement Grants. Note for Discussion Between Ministers on 17 January 1952. Suggested Amendments', 12 January 1952.

[263] TNA HLG118/767 'Note to Mr. Williams from T.A. Doughty', 27 September 1967.

[264] Rev. Lingwood at Walsingham claimed asking for the Act to be applied made applicants feel like criminals (*D&FT* 22 May 1953, p.1).

conditions imposed by the Ministry.[265] Yet the context of grant-making had changed. The 1959 House Purchase and Housing Act introduced 'standard grants' to enable provision of five basic amenities in dwellings of sound condition. This increased interest substantially. For council-owned dwellings, 11,136 grants were approved in the first half-year of standard awards (compared to 5077 for conversions or discretionary improvements for all 1959), which rose to 33,138 in 1960 (plus 9372 conversion-discretionary awards). For private-owners, numbers were even higher, with comparable figures of 21,295 (40,848) and 49,681 (38,641) (MHLG 1962, p.34). This tendency was encouraged by rises in interest rates in the late-1950s (Table 4.15), which discouraged new-build. Rural districts responded well. Reporting on 1958, ministers listed 108 English councils that were not making improvement grants, out of which only five were rural. At the time, there were just over 400 RDCs, with a few more than 450 urban authorities. In 1961, the contrast remained. All rural authorities now awarded discretionary grants, but 54 English urban councils abstained.[266] Although data for RDCs were not plentiful, Ministry documents for the mid-1960s pinpointed divergences. First, rural districts accounted for 28.5% of 1965 awards in England and Wales, which broke down as 20.7% for council dwellings and 31.9% for privately owned homes.[267] Within these numbers, the rural share of standard grants for council dwellings was just 11.7% compared with 29.3% for private-owners. For discretionary awards, which allowed higher payments,[268] 39.7% of national awards were for RDC-owned dwellings, whereas private-owners took up 37.2%.[269] Further, discretionary payments were higher in rural than in urban areas, with receipts per dwelling around 20% more for conversions and 20–60% greater for discretionary awards for 1957–1963.[270]

There are a number of trends to note here. First, after the 1949 Act, neither Labour nor Conservative governments were initially energetic in promoting improvement grants, even if maximum awards rose in 1952 from £100 to £200, and ministers were verbally supportive.[271] Compared with an electorally sensitive new-build target of 300,000 homes a year, for 1949–1953 grant-aid produced only 3000 improved dwellings, with 700 conversions creating new dwellings (MHLG 1953, p.15). Take-up rates were lower than under the Housing (Rural Workers) Act, even though the 1926 Act only applied to rural areas. Changes came as limitations on materials and labour eased, alongside 1950s' government desires to widen private

---

[265] For example, BRO RDAM2/22 ARDCHCM 21 January 1954; or on Smallburgh complaints, *NNN* 25 February 1955, p.3.

[266] HCH 4 February 1958, Vol.581, col.145W–47W; HCH 5 December 1961, Vol.650, col.135W–37W.

[267] TNA HLG118/767 'Note to Mr. Williams from T.A. Doughty', 27 September 1967.

[268] Even by 1968 standard grants had not risen above their initial £155 maximum, while discretionary awards had an upper limit of £400 (MHLG 1968a, p.4).

[269] TNA HLG118/767 'Improvement Grants in RDs', 20 September 1967.

[270] TNA HLG118/316 'Possible Rise in the Limit of Discretionary Grant', undated c1964.

[271] TNA T229/476 Letter from J.C. Wrigley, MHLG, to F.F. Turnbull, The Treasury, 25 August 1952; HCH 3 March 1953, Vol.512, col.19W.

sector choice.[272] Under the 1954 Housing Repairs and Rents Act, the grant winning process was simplified, with post-improvement rent restraint weakened. There was also recognition that meeting the 16 points in locales without piped water was difficult (MHLG 1954). Easing conditions had an immediate impact. Compared to a cumulative total of just 10,667 improvement and 1206 conversion awards before the 1954 Act, by 31 January 1956 an additional 43,312 improvement and 3538 conversion grants had been awarded. The 1959 House Purchase and Housing Act gave a further boost, with the government reiterating CPRE messages from the 1930s,[273] that the national emphasis on slum clearance should not detract from saving as many 'charming old country cottages' as possible.[274] Awards hit an annual average above 110,000 for 1966–1969, of which more than 80,000 went to private-owners, with assistance for standard amenities around two-thirds of the volume (ONS annual). With disproportionately high improvement awards and growing private new-build (Tables 6.11 and 6.14), the trend in the countryside was towards better housing conditions.

This positive tendency did not come without anxiety. Most evident were fears grants would be awarded to weekenders or for holiday homes. Ministry officials made clear councils had leeway over eligibility for discretionary awards but cautioned there was reluctance to impose conditions on dwelling use after improvement, questioning the legality of this action.[275] This flexibility allowed some councils, like Blofield and Flegg and Erpingham,[276] to reject applications for holiday homes (Coleman 1982). More broadly, a 1972 survey of around 50 RDCs found '… 21 per cent do not rule out the possibility of giving grants for second homes but would do so with varying degrees of reluctance. About 7 per cent treat each case on its merits and have no predisposition either way. Nineteen per cent definitely do not give grants'.[277] Council inaction had various origins. One was the caution of poorly resourced institutions. This was captured in a 1966 survey of East Anglian districts, which reported: 'Most of the councils although very willing to give improvement grants, adopt a passive role – i.e. they wait for applications to come in. These councils argue that they are so short of staff that they do not want to encourage more work'.[278] That local rate contributions encouraged reluctance was suggested as early as the 1949 Act (Association of County Sanitary Officers 1952, p.9) but was ongo-

---

[272] TNA HLG68/83 Memo 'Housing Act, 1949: Improvement Grants', undated c1954.

[273] TNA HLG47/702 Letter to G.H. Jack, CPRE, from J.C. Wrigley, MoH, 2 December 1936; TNA HLG37/50 'CPRE Submission on Rural Housing', undated c1943.

[274] These words are those of the MHLG Permanent Secretary, Evelyn Sharp, at the RDCA conference at Torquay (*WR&WSR* 29 July 1958, p.2).

[275] TNA HLG117/146 Letter from Lord Hastings, MHLG, to the Earl of Harrowby, 20 May 1963; HCH 18 July 1963, Vol.681, col.713; HCH 9 May 1968, Vol.764, col.130W.

[276] TNA HLG118/558 'Improvement Report Eastern Counties', October 1966; NRO DC13/5/35 ERDCM 22 December 1970, para.90.

[277] HCH 27 November 1972, Vol.847, col.157–58.

[278] TNA HLG118/558 'Area Improvement. Follow-up in Eastern Counties. Housing Improvement', undated c1966, pp.1–2.

ing.[279] Visible in this regard were rural slow-downs and even terminations of programmes as interest rates rose.[280] While councils knew reconditioning raised
property values, and so revenue, they were concerned about burdens on the rates.[281]
Additionally, councils like Penistone RDC and Tickhill UDC were reluctant to 'load
the rate fund' to help landlords make improvements they could afford themselves.[282]
Others, like Honiton RDC, did not act against unfit dwellings but encouraged reconditioning when they fell vacant, although not by awarding full grant-aid'... especially to people coming from elsewhere'.[283] This deliberate stance was at odds with
vagueness elsewhere, like Burnham on Couch, which '... decided long ago against
grants but cannot say what reasoning lay behind the decision'.[284] Such uncertainty
did not characterise another batch of councils, which, like Hemsworth and
Sawbridgeworth, claimed never to have received 'serious' applications, or, as with
West Mersea, felt they had '... few properties which are out of date'.[285] To this kaleidoscope of rationalities can be added owners and tenants resisting improvement.
Amongst tenants, in Biggleswade and Hatfield, this was noted especially for the

---

[279] For example, in 1969 Wolverton UDC charged that standard grants imposed sufficient burden
on the rates and would not countenance discretionary awards (TNA HLG118/576 Telephone
Conversation with Wolverton UDC Clerk (ref H6/33/41), 13 February 1969). Ampthill Town first
agreed to make awards on the Chair's casting vote (BRO UDA9/2 AUDCHBCM 14 October 1954,
p.225), then reversed the decision and resisted giving grants (BRO UDA9/6 AUDCM 9 June 1958,
p.10; WR&WSR 24 November 1959, p.15; BRO UDA9/7 AUDCM 9 November 1959, p.79). In
1969 the Council had made no discretionary awards.

[280] Under the 1949 Act, councils had to find 25% of the cost of improvement grants, generally raising funds through 20-year loans. Interest rate rises produced regular interruptions to grant awards
in Ampthill (BRO RDAM2/22 ARDCHCM 19 April 1956; WR&WSR 30 October 1956, p.10;
BRO RDAM2/23 ARDCHCM 21 November 1957; WR&WSR 31 July 1962, p.8), and occurred in
Biggleswade (WR&WSR 15 October 1957, p.14; 10 June 1958, p.15), Erpingham (NNN 15
September 1961, p.1), Hatfield (RDC 1963, p.54) and Wells-next-the-Sea (D&FT 10 January
1958, p.1). That interest rates were a general local authority concern was appreciated in Whitehall
(e.g. TNA HLG101/582 Letter to Private Secretary to Heathcoat Amory MP from P.I. Wolf,
MHLG, 4 November 1957; TNA HLG31/24 HI19/57 'Improvement Grants. Housing Act 1949',
undated c1957).

[281] Newport Pagnell RDC, for example, computed that grants awarded by 1958 cost £412 a year on
the rates but brought in £164 in extra revenue following higher property valuations (WR&WSR 23
September 1958, p.1). This did not satisfy Councillor Hawkins, who held that cost to the RDC was
too high and it was not right '... that people "with plenty of this world's goods" should have public
money in this way' (WR&WSR 3 January 1961, p.19).

[282] TNA HLG118/576 'Discretionary Grants', 3 July 1962. This view was also recorded inter-war,
not necessarily in councils leaning to the political Left (TNA HLG37/43 'Housing (Rural Workers)
Acts', undated c1936, p.3), but in pro-private enterprise districts like Smallburgh (NWP&ENS 5
August 1932, p.1). Indeed, Labour-leaning Easington was prepared to offer aid but found little
demand (TNA HLG37/43 'Investigation by General Inspectors 1934', undated c1936, p.32).

[283] TNA HLG118/1392 'Unfit Houses in Rural Districts', undated c1970.

[284] TNA HLG118/576 'Memo from H.A.M. Cruickshank to Miss Williams' (ref H1/B/772), 6
July 1962.

[285] TNA HLG118/576 'Memo L. Whitaker to Mr. Cowley, Mr. Blackshaw and Mr. Niven:
Discretionary Grants', 3 July 1962; TNA HLG118/576 'Memo from H.A.M. Cruickshank to Miss
Williams' (ref H1/B/772), 6 July 1962.

elderly and young married couples, who were concerned about rent rises, while Thingoe RDC found tied cottage tenants reluctant to seek improvements for fear of losing their jobs. Thingoe also noted property-owners avoided applications lest this restricted future rent hikes.[286] Similar tendencies were reported elsewhere, as with Cosford RDC, where owners obtained vacant possession, improved buildings, then sold them without grant assistance.[287]

Of course, in the 1960s 'suburbanisation' to commuter villages accelerated (Crichton 1964; Connell 1978; Bell 1994), as did smaller flows into urban-distant locales (e.g. Dean et al. 1984; Bolton and Chalkley 1990; Cross 1990). That these inflows introduced many wealthy managers and professionals to rural living is evident from the literature, as with Dunn and associates (1981, p.145) finding one-quarter of professional households in their Cotswolds survey lived in dwellings occupied by manual or agricultural workers within the previous five years. Such householders were not restricted to seeking homes in good condition. Indeed, with land-use planning favouring new-build in larger villages (Cloke 1979), those moving into 'key' villages were more likely to occupy new homes than those going to smaller places (Herington and Evans 1979). Poorer physical fabric did not appear to perturb buyers, especially where land-use designations were tight. Hence, in Hatfield:

> ... old cottages in Green Belt areas, however poor, are in great demand, for once demolished, planning consent to re-build even on the same site must be refused, except in very exceptional circumstances ... [so] a great many persons are prepared to 'convert' the shell of a cottage into a modern home at high cost. (Hatfield RDC 1972, p.40)

Previous failures to improve rural housing conditions now played into the hands of the better paid (Radford 1970). Grant allocations nevertheless brought into highlight urban expectations, as in Ampthill, Chesterton and Newmarket RDCs, where the geography of awards followed the completion of drainage and sewer schemes;[288] although, sometimes new residents pressed for services after arrival.[289] So, while the volume of improvements rose, reconditioned homes outnumbered grants awarded. Unfortunately, councils lack information on unaided dwellings.

That said, council contributions to dwelling improvement were significant. Again offering numerical indicators is not easy, as council minutes and newspapers are commonly imprecise, not simply on the addresses of grant applicants but often over application numbers. Nevertheless, local gains were evident in awards to landed estates. For the Duke of Bedford's properties, for example, we pick up a growing number of applications by the Bedford Settled Estate from 1958 up to 1970, with 65 dwellings, described as more than 100 years old and generally well below modern

---

[286] TNA HLG118/558 'Improvement Report Eastern Counties', July 1966; October 1966; Hatfield RDC (1969, p.41).

[287] TNA HLG118/558 'Improvement Report Eastern Counties', August 1966; 'Follow-up in Eastern Counties. Housing Improvement', undated c1966, p.1.

[288] TNA HLG118/558 'Improvement Report Eastern Counties', July 1966; October 1966.

[289] WR&WSR 2 March 1965, p.12.

standards, put forward for grant-aid in January 1970.[290] Smaller portfolios were evident when minutes listed residences, as with two grants for Mrs. H. Barnes of Aspley Heath and two for Mrs. M. Agate of Hulcote in 1962.[291] However, in no district was reporting consistent in information or coverage to draw convincing conclusions on award recipients. Nevertheless, it was clear awards made a substantial imprint on local housing. Take Erpingham as an example. This district had a population of 18,704 in 1971. These residents lived in 7130 dwellings. Of these, 1200 privately owned and 380 council-owned dwellings had benefited from improvement grants by 1971.[292] Surprisingly, in the mid-1960s, some councils believed demand for improvement grants would fall. By 1966, for instance, Dunmow RDC had given 990 improvement grants for its 4346 pre-1945 private houses, with the Clerk holding that the stage had come when applications were likely to cease.[293] This view was not shared by Depwade RDC and Walsingham,[294] but coincided with ideas circulating in Whitehall. Here, debate on forward strategy raised doubts about rehabilitation, as with the view: 'There is little point in spending large sums on improving old houses if in less than a generation there is to be no demand for old housing, even if structurally sound and improved with all the standard amenities'.[295] It followed that, despite rural council reservations about second homes, some in Whitehall welcomed them. Hence, reports in 1966 of more slums in rural East Anglia than in more densely settled areas like Essex and Hertfordshire met with the response: 'Fortunately, houses in the country and in the villages of East Anglia are now much in demand as second homes'.[296]

If Whitehall mandarins were gearing up for lower spending on dwelling improvements, economic shocks following the 1967 sterling devaluation changed perspectives. A £300 million public spending cut was planned for 1968–1969, followed by £416 million for 1969–1970 (Wilson 1971, p.483). Ministry circulars made clear priorities had shifted from new-build onto slum replacement and conserving structurally sound old houses (see MHLG 1968a).[297] With the government committed to improving housing, reconditioning was a cheap option. The 1969 Housing Act eased regulations on sale after grant-aided rehabilitation and allowed developers into the process (Dugmore and Williams 1974). Financial incentives rose signifi-

---

[290] For 1958–62, mentions of Bedford Settled Estate applications were found at: BRO RDAM2/23 ARDCHCM 18 December 1958; 22 January 1959; 12 March 1959; 23 April 1959; 22 October 1959; 19 May 1960; 20 October 1960; 17 November 1960; 15 December 1960; 16 February 1961; 18 May 1961; 22 June 1961; 20 July 1961; 19 October 1961; 23 November 1961; and 15 February 1962. Further applications were recorded between 1962 and 1970, with the 1970 bid at BRO RDAM1/25 ARDCHPBuCM 15 January 1970.

[291] BRO RDAM2/23 ARDCHCM 15 February 1962.

[292] NRO DC13/5/35 ERDCM 29 June 1971, para.24.

[293] TNA HLG118/558 'Improvement Report Eastern Counties', July 1966.

[294] TNA HLG118/558 'Follow-up in Eastern Counties. Housing Improvement', undated c1966, p.1.

[295] TNA HLG118/413 'The Housing Programme in the 1970s', undated c1966.

[296] TNA HLG118/558 'Follow-up in Eastern Counties. Housing Improvement', undated c1966, p.1.

[297] BRO RDAM1/24 ARDCHCM 16 January 1969.

cantly. This was almost a re-run of the late-1950s, when policy change was also provoked by national economic difficulties, with adjustments to reconditioning support emerging as if an after-thought in housing policy.[298] The result was the same nevertheless. Similar to experiences identifying unfit dwellings (Chap. 2), when provoked to investigate further, councils found ever more buildings needing attention. In Hatfield, the White Paper *Old Houses into New Homes* (MHLG 1968a) led to a survey which identified 99 houses lacking major amenities (Hatfield RDC 1969, p.41). After the 1969 Act, a follow-up found an additional 131 homes needing attention (Hatfield RDC 1970, p.42). Similarly, in 1972, Biggleswade estimated that 14.1% of council dwellings and 13.7% of private homes did not meet satisfactory standards.[299] Contrary to mid-1960s' assertions that demand for reconditioning was falling, the 1969 Act boosted action. For Merrett (1982, p.38), the impact of the Act was dazzling. Take this with a little caution, as the Environment and Home Office Sub-Committee of the House of Commons Expenditure Committee found many developers would have proceeded without grants (Hamnett 1973, p.261), even if it was vital for some (Dugmore and Williams 1974, p.160). Much early gentrification was associated with 'pioneering' households, with developers largely excluded by tighter regulations pre-1969 (Dugmore and Williams 1974). The 1969 Act heralded a new geography of grant-aid, as the involvement of development companies rose, with a concomitant shift in take-up away from the countryside towards cities, albeit the rural portion only fell to just above its population quota by 1972 (Table 6.14). Overall, improvement grants made a deep impression on the countryside, but rural councils were not vigorous proponents of their use. The same can be said of governments, no matter what their political hue. National agencies could have introduced more positive, energetic, sympathetic policies if they were determined to bring effective improvement to rural housing. They could have made reconditioning the stock a priority, rather than an option to turn to when cash was tight. Without enduring constructive contributions from the centre, many rural dwellings deteriorated. For a long time, policies for grant-aid encouraged decline, so stocking the pool from which wealthier urban in-migrants fished. Rural areas

Table 6.14 Discretionary improvement grants in England and Wales, 1969–1972

	Dwellings with grants approved	Percentage of dwellings in all grants approved				
		London	County boroughs	Non-county boroughs	Urban districts	Rural districts
1969 (quarter 4)	13,241	9.7	25.0	12.5	20.1	32.5
1970	87,398	13.1	27.6	14.6	19.0	25.5
1971	137,608	14.4	29.3	14.6	17.9	23.7
1972	260,007	9.1	31.3	15.5	22.4	21.6

Source: HCH 12 April 1973, Vol.854, col.327W–28W

---

[298] For a Parliamentary commentary on this, see HCH 23 April 1970, Vol.800, col.163W–64W.

[299] BRO RDBwM1/44 'Biggleswade Chief Public Health Inspector's Report', 11 October 1972, p.393.

secured more reconditioning awards than urban, but national rehabilitation policies did a disservice to countryside inhabitants.

6.4   That Urban Focus

Offering a perspective on the inter-war decades that was as valid 30 years after 1945, Aneurin Bevan captured key issues in rural housing neglect by governments:

> Was it not a fact that the overwhelming majority of houses built in rural areas before the War were built for urban dwellers and for well-to-do people? The fact is that although the rural population fell from 20 per cent of the total population in 1919 to 17 per cent in 1938 rural housing, although it should have been practically 20 percent of the total housing, was only 13 per cent, because the rural district councils were often not permitted to build houses, or were not stimulated to build them.[300]

This charge was based not only on the specificities of legislation that encumbered responses but also on the worldviews of Westminster politicians and Whitehall mandarins. Bevan's indictment repeated the accusation of Arthur Greenwood, an earlier Minister of Health, who blamed policies for their minimal contribution to house-building for the rural poor, emphasising the strength of his critique with the line: 'No Tory Act of any kind has ever done anything special for the rural areas'.[301] This harsh judgement draws on the fact that both the 1924 and 1930 Housing Acts made special provision for building in the countryside, whereas the major Conservative legislation of the era, the 1923 Act, did not. It also drew on early Conservative assertions that urban problems were the most acute and took precedence.[302] Adding lustre to such accusations, the minority Labour government's proposal to build 40,000 new rural homes under the 1931 Housing (Rural Authorities) Act was shrunk to less than 2000 units under the Conservative-dominated National government.[303] But ascribing restrictive possibilities for rural districts on one political party does not stand scrutiny. It is the case that slum clearance campaigns in both the 1930s and the 1950s–1960s were associated with Conservative governments. But the 1930 Housing Act was Labour legislation. Thus, it was Labour's stipulation that only places of more than 20,000 inhabitants had to furnish five-year slum

---

[300] HCH 17 October 1945, Vol.414, col.1227.

[301] HCH 10 July 1931, Vol.254, col.2444. Other Greenwood attacks include: HCH 2 August 1926, Vol.198, col.2849; HCH 1 May 1929, Vol.227, col.1582–83; HCH 7 February 1933, Vol.274, col.116–18; HCH 28 February 1933, Vol.275, col.205–06.

[302] For example, Alfred Mond, then Minister of Health (HCH 3 August 1921, Vol.145, col.1389) or in internal communications (e.g. TNA HLG48/697 'Report by E.R. Forber on Slum Clearance Schemes', 24 May 1922).

[303] TNA MAF48/208 'Plan for 40,000 dropped'. *Daily Herald*, 15 March 1932. The rationale was outlined in TNA HLG40/30 Letter from Hilton Young to Chancellor of the Exchequer, 1 December 1931. The instigator of the 1931 Act agreed the cuts were better than suspending the scheme (TNA HLG40/30 'Minute of Meeting with Sir Tudor Walter', 14 December 1931).

removal and replacement programmes (MoH 1930b, p.2). This Act also gave subsidy rates that were disadvantageous to rural districts (MoH 1944a, pp.11–12; Chap. 4). Little surprise RDCs made less use of the 1930 Act than urban centres, for the regulations hardly enticed responses. Did such partialities have applicability for other policy instruments?

From the outset of substantive, direct national intervention in housing markets, policy deliberations demonstrated a tenor separating rural and small urban districts from larger towns and cities. Leading up to the 1919 Act, for example, proposals from the Local Government Board excluded rural districts and towns of under 20,000 population from housing responsibilities.[304] The potential for rural neglect under county council administration became apparent later, when Ministry officials found urban county councillors reluctant to support investment in rural water and sewer supply.[305] Similar frictions were seen in Ministry of Agriculture frustrations over Ministry of Health failure to appreciate rural housing issues.[306] These frictions exemplified Ashford's (1982, p.41) warning that '… tension between town and country was, and in many respects remains, at the very root of tensions with the British subnational system'. Perhaps lack of understanding helps account for disappointing inter-war interventions to ameliorate funding shortcomings that weakened rural outcomes. After all, the 1926 Housing (Rural Workers) Act did little to improve the stock, while the 1931 Housing (Rural Authorities) Act was emasculated, with seven years needed before governments were jolted to re-introduce rural-friendly legislation in the form of the 1938 Housing (Financial Provisions) Act. Then, as in the 1950s (and 1960s), proclamations by ministers and officials largely emphasised how the main housing needs were in cities.[307] Indeed, Whitehall messages not infrequently implied rural problems required little attention, as in a 1939 communication on unfit dwellings:

---

[304] TNA RECO1/592 'Memorandum of LGB President on Housing of the Working-Classes After the War', undated c1918. This bias was repeated when only towns over 20,000 were asked to prepare slum clearance plans under the 1930 Act (MoH 1930b, p.2) and when RDCs could not apply for temporary post-1945 dwellings until urban centres had ordered 150,000 dwellings (HCH 1 February 1945, Vol.407, col.1624).

[305] TNA HLG50/188 'Note on RDCA Executive Council Meeting of 7 June 1944 with the Minister and John Wrigley'; TNA HLG127/116 Letter (and attached memo) from F.L. Edwards 'Rural Water Supply, Sewerage and Sewage Disposal. New Scheme of Grants', 29 April 1959.

[306] For example, TNA MAF234/10 'Notes of a Policy Meeting', 14 November 1945. This tension induced calls for greater coordination between ministries (TNA HLG125/10 'Notes on Meeting Between TS2(C) and Research Section, Land Services Department, MAF', 27 April 1950), although there was little movement in this direction (e.g. as early as 1946, Prime Minister Attlee rejected bringing disparate housing functions into one ministry; HCH 18 July 1946, Vol.425, col.1379). Strain was evident earlier, as illustrated by complaints over the Ministry's 'feverish activity' in pushing slum clearance compared with its 'apathy' towards rural housing (TNA HLG40/16 'Memorandum by Jonah Walker-Smith', undated c1931).

[307] An early indication was MoH (1920a, p.6). This tendency increased after 1951 (e.g. MHLG (1953, p.12); TNA HLG125/42 SRT56/28 'Slum Clearance', January 1956; HCH 24 November 1959, Vol.614, col.30W; HCH 18 May 1961, Vol.640, col.169W; HCH 2 May 1963, Vol.676, col.1325; HCH 30 October 1969, Vol.790, col.3W–4W).

The statistics in relation to unfit houses show that in the overwhelming majority of cases, houses in regard to which proceedings have been taken by Local Authorities on the ground that they were unfit for human habitation and not capable at reasonable expense of being rendered fit have subsequently either been made fit by the owners or have become the subject of operative Demolition Orders without any suggestion either from the owner or anyone else that demolition was not the most appropriate method of dealing with the house.[308]

Around 15 years later, ministers were claiming rural slums would be gone by 1960,[309] that few dwellings were becoming unfit owing to improvement grants and the ability of landlords to charge higher rents,[310] and that demand for rural social housing had waned,[311] a hollow message given large-scale unmet demand 30 years later (Clark 1992; Rural Development Commission 1993; Bevan et al. 2001).[312] The new 1964 government at least recognised that better information was needed to make policy, but until it arrived, '… first priority will be given to relieving the acute shortage of houses to rent in the conurbations – especially in areas which attract newcomers including immigrants from the Commonwealth – and to clearing the great concentrations of slums'.[313] By 1967, relevant data were available, showing assumed unfitness differences between conurbations, other urban areas and rural districts were illusory.[314] Like redirecting a super tanker, the effect of this knowledge did not adjust policy easily. Allocations for new council-building had already been distributed based on visions of deficiency concentrations in cities. Indeed, the view persisted that: 'Unfitness in country areas is perhaps not the greatest of our problems'.[315] The core of this sentiment, as well as elements of its flaws, can be traced over time through provisions in national policies.

Take, for example, actions to alleviate overcrowding under the 1935 Housing Act. Excluding London, official figures on this gave overcrowding rates of 4.2% for cities, 3.0% for urban districts and 2.9% for rural districts, with significant regional variation in all categories (MoH 1936). London's score was particularly high, at 6.8% for private residences and 10.5% for council-owned dwellings. But stating

[308] TNA HLG47/1 MoH Circular 1762. 'Housing Act 1936. Demolition of Individual Unfit Houses in Rural Areas', 26 January 1939. The Ministry was not alone in thinking this way, as the following Walsingham extract indicates: 'A large majority of the houses condemned as unfit for habitation are in such a bad condition that they will automatically demolish themselves, as many have done already. (NRO DC19/6/15 WRDCM 10 October 1928, p.69).

[309] TNA HLG101/748 'Notes for the Parliamentary Secretary on Slum Clearance, for Institute of Housing's 25th Annual Conference at Scarborough', undated c1956–57.

[310] HCH 16 November 1959, Vol.613, col.93W.

[311] TNA HLG117/19 CHAC Minutes, 9 January 1959, p.9.

[312] Derounian (1993, p.141) claimed that six to nine affordable homes were needed in each of England's 8000 villages to meet demand for low-cost homes.

[313] TNA CAB129/123 C(65)151 'Housing Programme 1965–70. Draft White Paper', 12 November 1965, p.25.

[314] TNA HLG118/767 'National Housing Condition Survey 1967', May 1967.

[315] TNA HLG118/1392 Letters to Regional Officers 'Clearance in Rural Areas', 18 March 1970. A more general sense of priorities was given in TNA HLG118/413 'The Housing Programme 1966–70'.

numbers so boldly does a disservice to the inexact measurements yielding this pattern.[316] For one, the survey undertaken did not use a consistent definition of what a working-class dwelling was, with varied interpretations resulting (Jennings 1971, p.130). For another, in assessing overcrowding, the Act counted rooms other than bedrooms in computations (Marshall 1968, p.196).[317] As Gardiner (2010, p.262) noted, quite apart from reducing 'recorded incidences' of overcrowding by implying people should sleep in kitchens and living rooms, the government reduced its commitment to act by defining 'overcrowded dwellings' as having more than two persons per room. This did not stop national officials proclaiming rural overcrowding was minor and manageable by councils (e.g. MoH 1937a, p.118). The issue is not a quibble over inaccuracy but the fundamental issue of whether funding criteria discriminated against rural districts. In a nutshell, were rural districts given reasonable access to resources to address housing deficiencies or were they 'arbitrarily' excluded from opportunities. After all, funding criteria rarely encompassed the whole population that required attention, especially for new arenas of government engagement; monetary comfort commonly reached only a slice of the distress meriting attention. As a 1933 Buntingford housing survey noted:

> … a pedantic and literal application of the terms of the [1930] Act would involve the demolition and replacement of most of the houses, as well as cottages, in the rural area. It is obvious, therefore, that any schemes for clearances village by village, and parish by parish, should be governed by discretion, a sense of proportion, and good judgement.[318]

Put another way, were 'common-sense' criteria for specific programmes 'rigged' to the detriment of the countryside?

Adding insult to injury, when allowing additional subsidies for relieving overcrowding amongst agricultural labourers, procedures under the 1935 Act implied little trust in rural councils. With contributions of between £2 and £8 a year for new dwellings, the Ministry emphasised how varied rural circumstances meant '… a flat rate of subsidy would not equitably meet the needs of the case' (MoH 1935, p.160). Hence, the Rural Housing Sub-Committee was asked to decide subsidy levels. This added layer of officialdom was imposed despite the expectation that the Committee's '… work will largely consist in recommending the maximum subsidy for a number of small applications, and if they look at this work in isolation they may feel that it is hardly worth the while of busy men'.[319] Matching expectations, by 1939, applications had arrived from only 108 RDCs, with the full £8 subsidy granted for 1865 of the 2073 dwellings applied for (MoH 1939, p.96). This extra funding barely encouraged the building of more homes, despite severe rural shortfalls. Was this because subsidy levels were potentially too low, because of the added bureaucracy (for little

---

[316] For a contemporary account of difficulties 'measuring' overcrowding, see Connor (1936, p.29). White (1977) offered a more recent analysis.

[317] For a RDC critique, see TNA HLG37/43 'Memorandum by Depwade RDC Housing Committee', undated c1936, p.2.

[318] HRO RDC4/1/9 BuRDCM 10 August 1933, p.14.

[319] TNA HLG40/2 'Memo to the Minister from J.W.', 30 September 1936.

return) or a combination of the two? That the 1935 Act produced few new homes was illustrated by cases like Ampthill, where 70% of identified overcrowding cases were settled without new-build.[320] This was not because other solutions were easy to find. As in London, council dwellings were more overcrowded (3.7% and 2.8% in council and private homes in RDCs; MoH 1936, p.xxi), as councils were obliged to respond to major housing needs, which led to overcrowded families being moved into council dwellings. As three-bedroom dwellings dominated previous building rounds, many councils explored erecting larger dwellings.[321] This did not circumvent affordability issues, with the Ministry pressing councils to offer homes at lower than normal rents rather than build new.[322] Other solutions included adding rooms using Housing (Rural Workers) Act funding,[323] removing lodgers (Nixon 1935, p.151)[324] or breaking up families, as with the two daughters who were moved to their grandmother's to abate overcrowding in Buntingford.[325] Rural councils were confronted with limited opportunities to add to the council stock, while districts away from urban commuter belts saw continued reluctance amongst builders and landlords to erect new homes[326] or utilise home improvement opportunities under the Housing (Rural Workers) Act (Pedley 1942, p.86).

Unsurprisingly, private rental harboured the poorest housing conditions (e.g. Table 6.13). One manifestation was the sharing of household accommodation (Table 6.15). By 1971, only 3.9% of households in England shared a dwelling, a major drop from 14.2% in 1951. Distribution-wise, rural districts had few households affected. Figures rose up the urban hierarchy, with official documents in the mid-1950s drawing attention to housing shortages in big towns, where they reported '… many thousands of families with children still living in shared accommodation'.[327] Ministers latched onto the idea of ameliorating housing problems where conditions were worst, citing big houses in city neighbourhoods like north Kensington as the priority.[328] As Richard Crossman explained in 1965:

> … quite literally those unable to afford owner-occupation and not eligible for council houses are being herded together in worse and worse quarters, more and more in multi-

---

[320] *W&DR* 4 January 1938, p.6.

[321] As with Hatfield (*H&PBG* 27 March 1936, p.6), Biggleswade (BRO RDBwM1/13 BiRDCM 7 April 1937, p.15), Ampthill (under Ministry pressure, *W&DR* 22 June 1937, p.7), Braughing, Depwade, Ely, Erpingham, Smallburgh and Ware (all TNA HLG40/3 'Applications Under Sec.108, Housing Act 1936. Notes on Financial Recommendations Made', undated c1937).

[322] BRO RDBwM1/13 BiRDCM 15 December 1937, p.190.

[323] NRO DC13/5/73 ERDCHCM 7 September 1936, p.254.

[324] BRO RDBwM1/13 BiRDCM 15 December 1937, p.190; BRO RDAM2/22 ARDCHCM 10 February 1944.

[325] *B&NEHG* 2 September 1938, p.4. This was not a new solution for rural councils (e.g. BRO RDAR8/6 ARDCMOHar 1925, p.8).

[326] For example, NRO DC19/6/62 WRDCHCM 11 December 1934, p.67.

[327] TNA HLG101/618 'Housing Subsidies', 14 July 1955.

[328] TNA HLG118/298 'Memo to PM from Henry Brooke', 25 February 1960.

Table 6.15 Percentage of English households sharing a dwelling by local authority category, 1951–1971

	1971	1961	1951
England	3.9	6.1	14.2
London	13.4	24.5	40.4
County boroughs	3.4	5.6	13.6
UDCs – Boroughs	1.7	2.8	9.1
Rural districts	0.5	0.5	3.6

Source: Computed from data in county reports of the population censuses and Registrar-General (2002)

Note: The values for London are for Greater London in 1971 but in 1961 and 1951 for the counties of London and Middlesex, so they are not strictly equivalent. The same applies for county boroughs and UDCs-boroughs, since some that were outside London and Middlesex counties in 1961 had become part of Greater London by 1971. Over this time period, of course, other councils changed status as well and many lost or gained territory. The table thereby only captures general trends in differences by local government category

> occupation. The 1963 tenant inquiry showed that four out of five of the boys and girls who had not married when the [1957] Rent Act was passed were living in multi-occupation.[329]

In the 1950s and the 1960s, eliminating multi-occupation intensified as a policy goal, with councils given more effective authority to regulate such dwellings,[330] while reducing overcrowding and multi-occupation entered the lexicon of housing policy priorities (MHLG 1969, p.2). This seemed to occur without much analysis of living conditions. Yet, as early as 1931, Nixon (1935, p.152) found the assumption that shared dwellings meant poor living conditions could be false, as investigation showed families sharing dwellings occupied more rooms than non-sharing families. Moreover, the basis on which 'sharing' was assessed was not secure. The 1951 Census, for instance, offered no guidance on whether a shared dwelling meant a common living room or eating at the same table, while person counts were expected to include in-laws but not lodgers.[331] Quite apart from definitional issues, question marks existed over the substance of the problem. Nationally, multi-occupation was not a dominant theme in housing conditions. Compared with the absence of basic facilities, this was a lesser problem (compare Table 6.13 with Table 6.15). Yet, in policy terms, multi-occupation projected messages that housing distress was concentrated in cities, justifying more investment there. Directing attention to a single indicator was reminiscent of the Inter-Department Committee on Rent Restrictions report, which promoted overcrowding as 'the indicator' for housing shortage (MoH 1937b, p.27). With lower overcrowding in the countryside (e.g. Table 2.5), had this recommendation been adopted, it could have deprived rural areas of even more inter-war investment.

---

[329] HCH 22 March 1965, Vol.709, col.78.

[330] HCH 11 March 1969, Vol.779, col.251W–52W; HCH 25 March 1969, Vol.780, col.246W.

[331] TNA WORK45/269 Draft Memo 'Future Demand for Housing and Land', October 1959.

Set against inter-war patterns, 1945–1951 seemed to offer new wind for rural prospects. It certainly started that way, with priority in the period given to housing agricultural (and mining) workers.[332] But favouring agriculture was soon questioned. On the one hand, dispersed agricultural dwellings required small schemes, when large projects were deemed more effective.[333] On the other hand, '... the term 'priority' is becoming somewhat meaningless these days. Whatever is said, not much can be done without direction of labour to fulfil any absolute promises of priority', so special attention for rural areas was constrained.[334] By October 1947, the Minister was suggesting that '... by the end of 1948 there would be more new agricultural houses in the rural areas than farm workers to occupy them',[335] although two years later the message was still that '... outstanding demand for houses from agricultural workers without a separate home of their own would be met in 14 months from now'. The semblance of rural priority had narrowed to

> ... only in districts where there is a large outstanding demand from agricultural workers without a separate home, or where the Minister of Agriculture is of opinion that there is a need for a substantial increase in the amount of labour required for agriculture in the district and that houses are required for new recruits or transfers from other districts.[336]

With the new 1951 government, the tone changed. Ministry documents now noted RDCs had done well from post-1945 building. The argument rural building was needed to compensate for inter-war neglect was no longer trumpeted. More emphasis was placed on falling farm-worker numbers.[337] With a bravado that would astound later commentators (e.g. Clark 1992; Bevan et al. 2001; Satsangi et al. 2010), by 1961 the government was proclaiming that '... there are many rural areas and small towns where most cases of acute housing need that require local authority assistance have already been met, or very nearly so' (MHLG 1961b, p.5). Faced with government neglect, a returned emphasis on slum clearance, private rental deterioration or sale, and rising demand for countryside bolt-holes, the post-1945 housing prospects tightened for rural inhabitants unable to afford home ownership. Despite showing more sensitivity to rural deprivation than during the inter-war years (Griffiths 2007), Labour in the 1960s continued centralising housing into cities through priority allocations. This was despite non-priority zones being more energetic in promoting house-building, as when 1964 comparisons showed allocation take-up was running at 80% in non-priority areas in contrast with 40% for priority authorities.[338] Four

---

[332] TNA T229/473 'Memo for Cabinet IPC(WP)(49)', 13 January 1949, p.2.

[333] TNA T229/473 'Memo for Cabinet IPC(WP)(47)', 23 August 1947.

[334] TNA HLG40/56 'Housing for Rural Workers. Prepared for Parliamentary Debate on 25 March 1947'.

[335] TNA HLG36/30 CHAC Minute Book, 24 October 1947 Meeting, pp.370–71.

[336] Both quotations from TNA T227/159 'Joint Memorandum by Minister of Health and Minister of Agriculture and Fisheries LP(49)58', 12 July 1949.

[337] TNA MAF255/112 'Agricultural Housing Subsidies and Improvement Grants. Note for Discussion Between Ministers, 17 January 1952'; TNA MAF234/18 'NFU Memo on Rural Housing', 7 February 1952.

[338] TNA HLG117/172 'Housing. Rate of Approvals', 23 July 1964.

years later, the Ministry remarked on regional differences in take-up, noting that priority authorities in Yorkshire and Humberside had not used half their allocation in three years, with shortfalls across the board expected for 1967 and 1968.[339] That priority authorities continued to be favoured, even following the 1967 Housing Condition Survey, signified how information did not determine policy.

6.5   An Information Deficit

Accusations of urban bias in policymaking need handling with care. One can imagine such claims being rejected on the grounds that decisions were made with limited information, with consequences and effects not readily appreciated. A former MHLG head made this point, noting the absence of coherent government policy towards housing, excusing this on the grounds the Ministry had inadequate information (Sharp 1969, p.71). This was excuse-making. Like the scale of inter-war economic inequities (Scott 2007), the breadth and magnitude of rural distress was too great to sustain claims of ignorance. There were too many reports to ministries and by ministry officials to make claims of non-awareness credible. Inaction might be excused by some as the outcome of a fiscally conservative mindset that so constrained politicians and officials they saw little prospect of addressing obvious societal distress (Perkin 1989; Cairncross 1996; Scott 1996). But, in democratic systems, citizens have an expectation that governments treat people equally, rather than with deliberate bias. This is not straightforward, as appreciated in recent decades as concern over unconscious bias has grown. Analysis has already revealed overly middle-class gains in social policies (Le Grand 1982), with demands that national policies be 'rural proofed' to mitigate continuing disbenefits for countryside dwellers testifying to the currency of such considerations (Countryside Agency 2002; Fahmy et al. 2004). But addressing either overt or hidden inequities relies on accessing quality information to evaluate policy impacts. Failure to even question the need for data to assess policy implementation signifies adherence to higher priorities than responding to democratic principles or the needs of the country.

Even a cursory examination of the evidential grounding of policymaking in the years investigated reveals major shortcomings. This is not a commentary on more difficult concepts of housing, such as 'shortage' or 'need', whose assessment inevitably draws on a series of assumptions that bear heavily on conclusions (e.g. Bradshaw 1972). Rather, it relates to ministers side-stepping explanations for policy priorities and impacts by pleading lack of information. Measurable statistical evidence might be expected if governments base policies on more than hunch and innuendo. This was rarely found. Take a basic consideration, like the cost of housing. Repeatedly, ministers revealed to Parliament that they could not provide information on this question. One reason was that, while councils passed on tender price

---

[339] TNA HLG118/934 'Memo to Mr. R.C. Jones from Mr. Brain', 9 February 1968.

data, no information on final costs was transferred upwards. There could be significant divergence between the two (Chap. 5). Moreover, ministers disputed tender price information merited attention (save to accept or reject proposals), since they had no data on the composition of building programmes, making average figures meaningless as they were based on uneven bundles by dwelling size and building type (number of bedrooms, parlour or non-parlour, flats or bungalows, etc.).[340] Similarly, apart from differences arising when councils used unemployed workers as a social measure (Ryder 1984), comparison between direct labour and private contractor building was not easy to assess as they built different dwellings.[341] Even asking how many dwellings had been built by each city, town or rural district took the questioner beyond the knowledge of the Ministry in the early years of council housing.[342] At least under the 1919 Act, the Treasury covered the giant share of the state's costs, so it had a vested interest in knowing what rents were paid, resulting in detailed reports.[343] After this, right up to the 1972 Housing Finance Act, when Westminster again sought to impose tight national direction on local rents (Minns 1973), ministers lived without submissions from councils on rent levels or policies.[344] As for what kind of buildings people were living in, in the inter-war period at least, non-traditional buildings existed in unknown numbers, even if approval totals were known (not completions).[345] Post-1945, these lapses eased, with the *Housing Return for England and Wales* (MoH-MHLG quarterly), plus circulations of printed pages for councils (some filtering through to county record offices),[346]

---

[340] HCH 9 October 1924, Vol.177, col.739W–40W; HCH 20 July 1939, Vol.350, col.738W; HCH 13 February 1947, Vol.433, col.505–06.

[341] HCH 19 July 1966, Vol.732, col.49W.

[342] HCH 5 July 1922, Vol.156, col.393W; HCH 14 March 1923, Vol.161, col.1542; HCH 28 February 1924, Vol.170, col.735W.

[343] National figures can be found at HCH 4 July 1922, Vol.156, col.215W–18W; HCH 22 February 1923, Vol.160, col.1050W–52W; 20 March 1924, Vol.171, col.1344–46. Examples of figures for councils (largely urban) include: HCH 9 July 1923, Vol.166, col.946W–48W; HCH 5 March 1924, Vol.170, col.1406W–08W.

[344] HCH 2 December 1926, Vol.200, col.1402–03; TNA HLG101/17 'Note to the Minister from J. Wrigley', undated c1938, p.20; HCH 4 February 1960, Vol.616, col.165W; HCH 6 November 1962, Vol.666, col.781–782; HCH 22 February 1963, Vol.672, col.104W; HCH 16 November 1965, Vol.720, col.44W. This did not mean no rent information was gathered. There were recordings for Treasury purposes, which focused on HRA impacts rather than burdens on tenants (TNA HLG101/17 Letter to John Chown, MoH, from B.W. Gilbert, The Treasury, 23 April 1936).

[345] HCH 12 February 1925, Vol.180, col.341; HCH 15 November 1926, Vol.199, col.1538.

[346] Walsingham minutes, for example, periodically listed returns for all rural districts in Norfolk, although mostly post-1945 (NRO DC19/6/19 5 August 1931, p.38; NRO DC19/6/63 16 February 1949, p.218; NRO DC19/6/67 11 February 1957, p.121; NRO DC19/6/68 9 February 1959, p.123; NRO DC19/6/69 4 March 1963, p.84; 8 March 1965, p.221). Of the other councils investigated, such reports were few and far between, although Braughing provided some figures from Annual Reports of the East Hertfordshire Combined Districts Medical Officer of Health (e.g. HRO RDC3/28/12, p.13; HRO RDC3/28/17, p.12). Newspapers occasionally offered tabular data, largely on house-building numbers, but sometimes including demolitions (e.g. *H&EO* 16 January 1926, p.6; *NBC&BR* 7 January 1947, p.4; *T&WT* 11 February 1955, p.10; *WR&WSR* 17 May 1955,

offering regular reports. But it was not until the 1964–1970 government that note-worthy efforts were made to raise data standards to those needed for effective policymaking.[347]

The slight data grip on public sector activity paled beside knowledge of the private sector. Information on items like building society loans, sales prices or dwelling upgrades (whether to landlords or private-owners) was poor over most years investigated.[348] Understandably, some questions, like new home numbers for rent or sale, were difficult to measure, given purpose could shift between commissioning and completion.[349] But even basic information, like the number of dwellings built for private-owners, was not collected until October 1922 (MoH 1926, p.57), while assessing availability for the working-classes only came after 1933–1934, when new dwellings rated at less than £13 (regarded as working-class homes) were registered (MoH 1934, p.151). Later, partial insight was available in independent reports, as with Co-operative Building Society accounts of mortgagees' purchase prices and loans. This enhanced the shallow imagery gained from samples of Inland Revenue stamp duty payments. Such superficiality was common in Westminster's knowledge bank. Even in 1971, questions on average sales prices of three-bedroom houses drew a blank, even for London.[350]

The list of similar 'holes' in Whitehall's knowledge was long, and extended in surprising ways into the 1970s. Today, lapses over the decades seem remarkable. For instance, having obtained agreement with the building industry that, in return for a long-term building programme under the 1924 Housing Act, the sector agreed to employ more workers and train more apprentices (Clarke 1924), two years later the government admitted it had no record of apprentices admitted over the past three years.[351] Despite the problems created by starting a major house-building programme in 1919 with insufficient knowledge of the capacity and regulatory conditions needed for programme achievement, years later annual outputs of basic building ingredients like bricks were unknown.[352] Irrespective of the volume of dwellings recognised (no matter how loosely defined), ministers had no accurate knowledge of how many condemned buildings were lived in, nor of actual demolitions, save for those undertaken under the Ministry's own programmes (i.e. not by

---

p.18; *D&FT* 15 August 1958, p.7). Inter-war, councils provided frequent, if irregular, reports on house-building across parishes, but data covering the same time period and including comparable content across councils were rare.

[347] One statement on this is at HCH 24 January 1967, Vol.739, col.228W, with recognition less burdensome and more effective data gathering was needed at HCH 29 April 1968, Vol.763, col.775.

[348] HCH 3 April 1924, Vol.171, col.2422; TNA HLG101/17 'Minute Sheet 92004/1/P6 Note to Mr. Wrigley from E.O.', undated c1938, p.34; HCH 7 November 1961, Vol.648, col.40W.

[349] HCH 25 March 1926, Vol.193, col.1360.

[350] HCH 1 May 1958, Vol.587, col.549–50; HCH 20 March 1961, Vol.630, col.94W; HCH 18 July 1963, Vol.681, col.716; HCH 29 April 1971, Vol.816, col.186W.

[351] 18 February 1926, Vol.191, col.2148W.

[352] HCH 21 June 1927, Vol.207, col.1675.

councils through Public Health Acts).[353] As for information on which local demands for dwellings could be assessed, ministers and officials regularly debunked the value of waiting lists, holding there were different local practices without questioning whether some uniformity could raise the quality of allocation processes.[354] For rural issues, ministers were unable to indicate new-build numbers in agricultural parishes, even when special subsidies were available for these places (e.g. MoH 1927, p.58). Even in the 1970s, there were no official estimates of the number of farm-workers living in tied cottages.[355]

The list goes on and on. But let us shift attention to the question of whether these deficiencies were recognised. The simple answer is: they were. In 1926, for instance, the Ministry itself noted that: 'The dearth of trustworthy statistics with regard to existing water undertaking has long been a source of weakness in the handling of the various problems of water supply' (MoH 1926, p.44). More broadly, the Committee on Local Expenditure asserted that: 'One of the most potent means of securing more effective administration lies in the proper use of statistical returns and costing systems' (MoH 1932, p.18). Reflecting the failure of government agencies to respond to this call, by 1937 the Ministry was challenging its own estimates of dwellings needed to clear slums or abate overcrowding, noting a lack of surety over estimates.[356] This confirmed the view of the Rural Housing Sub-Committee, that there was a lack of accurate data for policy purposes.[357] It also became evident that information from one Ministry had limited value for others, as with complaints that Ministry of Labour data were only valuable for that Ministry.[358] Post-1945, there were similar laments, as when estimating demand for housing and land, about which '… our knowledge of the present situation is so limited'.[359] Seeking more substantive responses to current housing difficulties, by the mid-1960s it was estimated that about a million private rental units had been lost since the 1957 Rent Act, the Act ministers had proclaimed was the saviour of private rental,[360] but this was only a guesstimate which exposed the lack of information on this and other key housing questions.[361] At this time, the stated intention was to address major housing

---

[353] HCH 27 July 1950, Vol.478, col.112 W; HCH 3 April 1962, Vol.657, col.26W; HCH 3 March 1971, Vol.812, col.448W.

[354] TNA HLG101/417 'Housing Application Lists', 3 June 1948; TNA HLG31/16 HI26/49 'Housing Applications', undated c1949; HCH 4 December 1956, Vol.561, col.104W; TNA HLG118/933 'Memo to Mr. Grimshaw from J.M. Thompson', 2 May 1966; HCH 7 May 1973, Vol.856, col.12.

[355] HCH 11 December 1975, Vol.902, col.628.

[356] TNA HLG48/685 'Minute Sheet. J.C.W. to the Minister', 1 February 1937.

[357] TNA HLG37/43 'Supplement to Second Report of the Rural Housing Sub-Committee Paper M13', pp.1–2.

[358] HCH 28 July 1937, Vol.326, col.3146.

[359] TNA WORK45/269 'Future Demand for Housing and Land', October 1959.

[360] HCH 30 June 1959, Vol.608, col.26W; HCH 9 February 1960, Vol.617, col.201; HCH 18 June 1963, Vol.679, col.26W.

[361] HCH 29 June 1965, Vol.715, col.295.

problems, recognising that housing conditions were worse and needs more acute in some places than others but that work on identifying the realities of local and regional housing needs required 'a great deal of work'.[362]

Again, a long list to demonstrate the extensiveness of official awareness of data shortfalls could be provided. But the point has been made. What has not been highlighted so far are responses to this awareness. These came in a number of forms. One was to proclaim that housing was a local issue, so it was up to councils to collect useful data. It was not the role of the government to interfere (despite its widespread interjections across housing policy spheres).[363] This rationale began to break down when councils produced information governments did not like. When farmworker dwelling needs were estimated for the 1931 Housing (Rural Authorities) Act, the Great Depression was uppermost in government minds, not responding to housing need (Committee on National Expenditure 1931; MoH 1932). With ministers gearing up to cut the Act's building programme, one might expect antagonism unless local estimates were meagre. So it proved. For Norfolk, Ministry officials asserted that

> ... the number of houses asked for considerably exceeds the number of houses really required and I have definite private information that this is true of the applications from Norfolk. It seems that the applicant Authorities have followed the old army policy of assuming that their applications would be drastically cut down and therefore asking for much more than they hoped to get.[364]

Norfolk County Council was not alone in being subject to the accusation that: '... It is impossible to believe that the County have given the matter sufficiently detailed consideration'.[365] More generally:

> The reports made by the Inspectors show that the applications, as was to be expected, are based on widely different forms of data and in some instances, it would appear, merely on a general impression of the situation. The general effect of the inquiries made is to show that the urgent need for houses is approximately 60 per cent of the number for which applications have been received, i.e. for (in round figures) about 4,000 houses.[366]

Reliance on guesswork, innuendo and a few inspectors was made necessary because the Ministry of Health had cut the regional staff that used to work with councils on housing under the 1919 Act.[367] Sat in an information vacuum, official reactions to 1931 Act bids had the hallmarks of not liking the message, so shoot the messenger. At the time, the proponent of the Act was certain applications did not meet

---

[362] TNA CAB129/123 C(65)151 'Housing Programme 1965–70. Draft White Paper', 12 November 1965, p.8.

[363] Demonstrating unity of views across governments on this are two illustrations from 1964, the first under the Conservatives, the second under Labour: HCH 21 April 1964, Vol.693, col.1066–67; HCH 24 November 1964, Vol.702, col.1074.

[364] TNA HLG40/19 Letter to A.P. Hughes-Gibb from Rural Housing Advisory Committee Secretary, 24 October 1931.

[365] TNA HLG40/19 Letter to F. Collin Brown, 24 October 1931.

[366] TNA HLG40/20 'Secretary's Memorandum', 1 January 1932 position.

[367] TNA HLG47/11 'Memo to Arthur Lowry', 2 March 1933.

requirements.[368] If ministers and officials were convinced, councils were not up to providing valid information, solutions were in their own hands. After all, councils were forced to undertake rapid overcrowding surveys for the 1935 Housing Act. This showed national agencies could require quick data collection if they prioritised basing policy on evidence.[369] Rural councils faced difficulties with such surveys, owing to a lack of skilled staff (Chap. 5), but there were ways around this, as with Islington responding to high local unemployment by using 52 out-of-work assistants to undertake preliminary 1935 Act surveys, with skilled workers taking detailed measurements (White 1977). For sure, rural councils might have shied away from such a step on cost grounds. The solution was again in the government's hands, as it and its predecessors had contrived a revenue regime that lacked flexibility and substance to fund local services effectively compared with other nations (Rhodes 1976; Karran 1988). The government could also have made targeted payments to cover costs or used professional surveys to derive reliable data for national policy.[370]

As for unevenness in the data provided, poor definition or understanding of concepts and their measurement should have been addressed by better Ministry instructions, training and verification, but as the sad experience of ever-growing estimates of dwellings unfit for habitation showed (e.g. Parker and Mirrlees 1988, p.368), national policymakers were unwilling to take this step. When they were, as with the 1967 Housing Condition Survey, it revealed previous assumptions on unfitness were misplaced. Had the conclusion been reached that council staff lacked professional standards or the resources for such work, again the solution was at hand, as with establishing Royal Commissions to recommend how to modernise local government in London and the rest of England and Wales in 1957 and 1966 (Sharpe 1960; Royal Commission on Local Government in England 1969). Of course, a Royal Commission was set up to look into local government reform in the 1920s (Royal Commission on Local Government 1925, 1928), and changes were made (MoH 1929; Registrar-General 1929), but the mindset of the then government was restricted, with financial considerations rather than performance receiving foremost attention. This was readily apparent in the innumerable occasions when ministers cast aside requests for information about housing with the objection that obtaining evidence cost too much, put an undue load on officials or would be of no value.[371]

Of course, there could be political advantage in obfuscation, which the absence of comprehensive, accurate statistical information aids. This applied both to the

---

[368] TNA HLG40/20. 'Notes by J. Tudor Walters for the Committee', undated c1932.

[369] This does not detract from the valid criticism of the 1935 surveys, although critiques have centred more on definition, which primarily sprang from political orientation, than data deficiencies.

[370] The 1967 Housing Condition Survey showed sample surveys using small groups of skilled technicians could produce powerful evidence to support policy (MHLG 1968b); powerful at least if politicians and mandarins cared to take on board the evidence furnished.

[371] There were many examples of this, even restricting attention to *Hansard*: HCH 11 March 1925, Vol.181, col.1323; HCH 4 July 1934, Vol.291, col.1909W–10W; HCH 1 February 1955, Vol.536, col.96W; HCH 22 January 1957, Vol.563, col.16.

local and the national realms. Illustrative of the latter, in 1956 the MP for Epping was perturbed by the basis of the industrial dispersal policy in the London County Council Development Plan, which Ruth Glass's research had shown was not based on evidence, but upon impressions of London's growing congestion.[372] What came across too often was a sense that policymakers knew what they wanted and did not want evidence lest it contradicted their prejudices.[373] At a local level, we see this in a 1952 account by the Medical Officer of Health for Biggleswade, whose visits found tenants in older houses living in terrible conditions. His request for a survey to establish how widespread such conditions were was rejected by the Council, with the view expressed that 'little purpose would be served by such a survey'.[374] The tone is reminiscent of Keith Joseph's comment that: 'I have no comprehensive information about rent increases in the last twelve months; but I am quite sure that municipal rents are not generally beyond the means of tenants'.[375] All was well it seems, not because data showed this but because the Minister wanted it to be so. Along similar lines, Harold Macmillan's 1953 wish to squash reports that dwelling deteriorations were as great as new-build numbers essentially came down to the statement: 'No figures have ever been given to me to confirm this, and I am sure that it is not true'.[376] Ultimately, what lay behind sentiments of this kind were failings of the British political elite. These inflame those who lament the nation's continued relative economic decline, around which they identify the heavy imprint of short-term, over-grandiose, dithering governments (Allen 1976; Barnett 1972, 1986, 1995, 2001; Brown 2017). With a 'muddling through' approach to governance (Lindblom 1959; Hennessy 1996), a fundamental difficulty has been the lack of vision over how local government should make effective contributions to society:

> At no stage of English history has any government held a consistent and logical policy on the range and limits of municipal services. Local government was not evolved to provide a coordinated system of administration for a logically defined range of services; it emerged, piecemeal, in answer to a succession of separate needs and demands. (Keith-Lucas and Richards 1978, p.35)

References

Addison C (1924) Politics from within 1911–1918, including some records of a great national effort: volume two. Herbert Jenkins, London

---

[372] HCH 9 July 1956, Vol.556, col.84.

[373] Not that commentators find much has changed today, as an editorial in *The Sunday Times* recently argued: 'Yes, there's dysfunction, Gove. It starts with you. Ministers who ignore data and their own mistakes are doomed to fail' (5 July 2020, p.23).

[374] *NBC&BR* 30 September 1952, p.2.

[375] HCH 6 November 1962, Vol.666, col.781.

[376] HCH 4 November 1953, Vol.520, col.174.

Addison C (1934) Four and a half years: a personal diary from June 1914 to January 1919. Hutchinson, London

Addison P (1994) The road to 1945: British politics and the Second World War, rev edn. Pimlico, London

Allen GC (1976) The British disease: a short essay on the nature and causes of the nation's lagging wealth. Hobart Paper 67. Institute of Economic Affairs, London

Ashford DE (1982) British dogmatism and French pragmatism: central-local policy-making in the welfare state. Allen & Unwin, London

Association of County Sanitary Officers (1952) Housing: second interim report on the housing survey in rural areas (England and Wales). Norwich

Baker WP (1953) The English village. Oxford University Press, London

Ball M (1983) Housing policy and economic power: the political economy of owner occupation. Methuen, London

Barlow J, Duncan SS (1994) Success and failure in housing provision: European systems compared. Pergamon, Oxford

Barnett C (1972) The collapse of British power. Eyre Methuen, London

Barnett C (1986) The audit of war: the illusion and reality of Britain as a great nation. Macmillan, London

Barnett C (1995) The lost victory: British dreams, British realities 1945–1950. Macmillan, London

Barnett C (2001) The verdict of peace: Britain between her yesterday and the future. Macmillan, London

Bell MM (1994) Childerley: nature and morality in a country village. University of Chicago Press, Chicago

Bevan M, Cameron S, Coombes M, Merridew T, Raybould S (2001) Social housing in rural areas. Chartered Institute of Housing, Coventry

Biggleswade Rural District Council (1952) Annual report of the medical officer of health and sanitary inspector 1951. Biggleswade

Biggleswade Rural District Council (1963) Annual report of the medical officer of health and sanitary inspector 1962. Biggleswade

Biggleswade Rural District Council (1964) Annual report of the medical officer of health and sanitary inspector 1963. Biggleswade

Biggleswade Rural District Council (1965) Annual report of the medical officer of health and sanitary inspector 1964. Biggleswade

Bolton N, Chalkley B (1990) The rural population turnaround: a case study of north Devon. J Rural Stud 6:29–43

Bowley M (1945) Housing and the state 1919–1944. Allen & Unwin, London

Bowley M (1949) Housing and the economic crisis in Great Britain. Int Labour Rev 59:127–153

Bradshaw J (1972) The concept of social need. New Society, 30 March, pp 640–643

Bramley G, Smart G (1995) Rural incomes and housing affordability. Rural Development Commission, Salisbury

Brittan S (1964) The Treasury under the Tories 1951–1964. Penguin, Harmondsworth

Broadberry SN, Crafts NFR (1996) British economic policy and industrial performance in the early post-war period. Bus Hist 38:65–91

Brown T (2017) Tragedy and challenge: an inside view of UK engineering's decline and the challenges of the Brexit economy. Matador, Kibworth Beauchamp

Burnett J (1986) A social history of housing 1815–1985, 2nd edn. Methuen, London

Cairncross A (1996) Managing the British economy in the 1960s. Macmillan, Basingstoke

Campbell J (1987) Nye Bevan: a biography. Hodder & Stoughton, London

Central Housing Advisory Committee (1936) Rural housing. HMSO, London

Clapson M (1998) Invincible green suburbs, brave new towns: social change and urban dispersal in postwar England. Manchester University Press, Manchester

Clark DM (1990) Affordable rural housing: challenge for the nineties. Rural Development Commission, Salisbury

Clark DM (1992) Rural social housing – supply and trends: a 1992 survey of affordable new homes. Rural Development Commission, Salisbury

Clarke JJ (1924) The new Housing Act, 1924. Town Plan Rev 11(2):119–127

Cloke PJ (1979) Key settlements in rural areas. Methuen, London

Coleman R (1982) Second homes in north Norfolk. In: Moseley MJ (ed) Power, planning and people in rural East Anglia. University of East Anglia Centre for East Anglian Studies, Norwich, pp 97–117

Coleman AM (1985) Utopia on trial: vision and reality in planned housing. Hilary Shipman, London

Committee on National Expenditure (1931) Report. Cmd 3920. HMSO, London

Connell J (1978) The end of tradition: country life in central Surrey. Routledge & Kegan Paul, London

Connor LR (1936) Urban housing in England and Wales. J R Stat Soc 94:1–65

Council for Research on Housing Construction (1934) Slum clearance and rehousing: the first report of the Council for Research on Housing Construction. P.S. King, London

Countryside Agency (2002) Rural proofing 2001/2: a report to government by the Countryside Agency. Cheltenham

Crichton RM (1964) Commuters' village: a study of community and commuters in the Berkshire village of Stratford Mortimer. David & Charles, Dawlish

Cross DFW (1990) Counterurbanization in England and Wales. Avebury, Aldershot

Crossman R (1975) The diaries of a Cabinet Minister: volume one – Minister of Housing 1964–66. Hamish Hamilton and Jonathan Cape, London

Cullingworth JB (1959) Overspill in south-east Lancashire: the Salford-Worsley scheme. Town Plan Rev 30:189–206

Darke J (1991) Local political attitudes and council housing. In: Lowe S, Hughes D (eds) A new century of social housing. Leicester University Press, Leicester, pp 159–174

Darke J, Darke R (1979) Who needs housing? Macmillan, London

Daunton MJ (1984) Introduction. In: Daunton MJ (ed) Councilors and tenants. Leicester University Press, Leicester, pp 1–38

Daunton MJ (1996) How to pay for the war: state, society and taxation in Britain, 1917–24. Engl Hist Rev 111:882–919

Dean KG, Shaw DP, Brown BJH, Perry RW, Thorneycroft WT (1984) Counterurbanisation and the characteristics of persons migrating to west Cornwall. *Geoforum* 15:177–190

Derounian J (1993) Another country: real life beyond rose cottage. National Council for Voluntary Organizations, London

Diacon D (1991) Deterioration of the public sector housing stock. Avebury, Aldershot

Doling J (1997) Comparative housing policy: government and housing in advanced industrialized countries. Macmillan, Basingstoke

Dresser M (1984) Housing policy in Bristol 1919–30. In: Daunton MJ (ed) Councillors and tenants. Leicester University Press, Leicester, pp 156–216

Dugmore K, Williams P (1974) Improvement grants. Area 6:159–160

Dunleavy PJ (1977) Protest and acquiescence in urban politics. Int J Urban Reg Res 1:193–218

Dunleavy PJ (1981) The politics of mass housing in Britain 1945–75. Clarendon, Oxford

Dunn MC, Rawson M, Rogers A (1981) Rural housing: competition and choice. Allen & Unwin, London

Eatwell R (1979) The 1945–1951 Labour government. Batsford, London

English J, Madigan R, Norman P (1976) Slum clearance: the social and administrative context in England and Wales. Croom Helm, London

Fahmy E, Cemlyn S, Gordon D (2004) Rural proofing and best practice in neighbourhood renewal. University of Bristol Townsend Centre for International Poverty Research, Bristol

Fletcher P (1969) The agricultural housing problem. Soc Econ Adm 3:155–166

Foot M (1973) Aneurin Bevan: a biography – volume two 1945–1960. David-Poynter, London

Forrest R, Murie A (1988) Selling the welfare state: the privatisation of public housing. Routledge, London

Francis M (1997) Ideas and policies under Labour 1945–1951: building a new Britain. Manchester University Press, Manchester

Francis M (2012) 'A crusade to enfranchise the many': Thatcherism and the 'property-owning democracy'. Twent Century Br Hist 23:275–297

Frazer WM (1935) Overcrowding and the Housing Act, 1935. Public Health 49(November):50–56

Gardiner J (2010) The thirties: an intimate history. Harper Press, London

Gay O (1987) Pre-fabs: a study in policy-making. Public Adm 65:407–422

Gayler HJ (1970) Land speculation and urban development: contrasts in south-east Essex, 1880–1940. Urban Stud 7:21–36

Giles AK, Cowie WJG (1960) Some social and economic aspects of agricultural workers' accommodation. J Agric Econ 14(2):147–169

Golland A (1998) Systems of housing supply and housing production in Europe: a comparison of the United Kingdom, The Netherlands and Germany. Ashgate, Aldershot

Griffiths CVJ (2007) Labour and the countryside: the politics of rural Britain 1918–1939. Oxford University Press, Oxford

Grundy E (1987) Retirement migration and its components in England and Wales. Ageing Soc 7:57–82

Halliday J, Coombes M (1995) In search of counterurbanisation: some evidence from Devon on the relationship between patterns of migration and motivation. J Rural Stud 11:433–446

Hamnett CR (1973) Improvement grants as an indicator of gentrification in inner London. Area 5:252–261

Hardy D, Ward C (1984) Arcadia for all: the legacy of a makeshift landscape. Mansell, London

Harloe M (1995) The people's home? social rented housing in Europe and America. Blackwell, Oxford

Harris R (2012) 'Ragged urchins play on marquetry floors': the discourse of filtering is reconstructed, 1920s–1950s. Hous Policy Debate 22:463–482

Hatfield Rural District Council (1952) Annual report of the medical officer of health and public health inspector 1951. Hatfield

Hatfield Rural District Council (1963) Annual report of the medical officer of health and public health inspector 1962. Hatfield

Hatfield Rural District Council (1964) Annual report of the medical officer of health and public health inspector 1963. Hatfield

Hatfield Rural District Council (1965) Annual report of the medical officer of health and public health inspector 1964. Hatfield

Hatfield Rural District Council (1966) Annual report of the medical officer of health and public health inspector 1965. Hatfield

Hatfield Rural District Council (1968) Annual report of the medical officer of health and public health inspector 1967. Hatfield

Hatfield Rural District Council (1969) Annual report of the medical officer of health and public health inspector 1968. Hatfield

Hatfield Rural District Council (1970) Annual report of the medical officer of health and public health inspector 1969. Hatfield

Hatfield Rural District Council (1972) Annual report of the medical officer of health and public health inspector 1971. Hatfield

Hennessy P (1992) Never again: Britain 1945–1951. Vintage Books, London

Hennessy P (1996) Muddling through: power, politics and the quality of government in postwar Britain. Victor Gollancz, London

Hennessy P (2006) Having It so good: Britain in the fifties. Allen Lane, London

Henson AE (1957) Rural housing. In: British housing and planning yearbook 1957. National Housing and Town Planning Council, London, pp 103–110

Herington J, Evans DM (1979) The spatial pattern of movement in 'key' and 'non-key' settlements. Working Paper 3. Loughborough University Department of Geography, Loughborough

Hertfordshire County Council (1961) Building in the green belt. Hertford

Hinton J (1988) Self-help and socialism: the squatters' movement of 1946. Hist Work J 25:100–126
Hoggart K, Silva CN (1997) Gain and pain in housing association expansion in London. Occasional
    Paper 45. King's College London Department of Geography, London
Holmans AE (1987) Housing policy in Britain: a history. Croom Helm, London
Horne A (1988) Macmillan 1894–1956: volume one of the official biography. Macmillan,
    Basingstoke
Jacobs K, Kemeny J, Manzi T (2003) Privileged or exploited council tenants? the discursive
    change in Conservative housing policy from 1972 to 1980. Policy Polit 31:307–320
James L (2006) The middle class: a history. Little Brown, London
Jennings JH (1971) Geographical implications of the municipal housing programme in England
    and Wales 1919–39. Urban Stud 8:121–138
Jones H (1991) New tricks for an old dog? the Conservatives and social policy, 1951–55. In: Gorst
    A, Johnman L, Lucas WS (eds) Contemporary British history 1931–1961: politicians and the
    limits of policy. Pinter, London, pp 33–43
Jones H (2000) 'This is magnificent!': 300,000 houses a year and the Tory revival after 1945.
    Contemp Br Hist 14:99–121
Karran TJ (1988) Local taxing and local spending: international comparisons. In: Paddison R,
    Bailey S (eds) Local government finance: international perspectives. Routledge, London,
    pp 53–84
Keith-Lucas B, Richards PG (1978) A history of local government in the twentieth century. Allen
    & Unwin, London
Kynaston D (2007) Austerity Britain 1945–51. Bloomsbury, London
Lash S, Urry J (1987) The end of organized capitalism. Polity, Cambridge
Lemon A (1973) Retirement and its effects on small towns. Town Plan Rev 44:254–262
Lindblom CE (1959) The science of 'muddling through'. Public Adm Rev 19(2):79–88
Linsley B (2005) Homes for heroes: housing legislation and its effects on housing in rural Norfolk
    1918–1939. PhD thesis University of East Anglia
Mackintosh JM (1936) Rural housing. Northamptonshire County Council, Northampton
Macmillan H (1969) Tides of fortune 1945–1955. Macmillan, London
Marshall JL (1968) The pattern of housebuilding in the inter-war period in England and Wales.
    Scott J Polit Econ 15:184–205
Martin JG (1938) Memorandum upon the Housing (Rural Workers) Acts 1926 to 1938. National
    Housing & Town Planning Council, London
Matthews C (2019) Homes and places: a history of Nottingham's council houses, 2nd edn.
    Nottingham City Homes, Nottingham
Merrett S (1979) State housing in Britain. Routledge & Kegan Paul, London
Merrett S (1982) Owner-occupation in Britain. Routledge & Kegan Paul, London
Ministry of Health (1920a) First annual report, 1919–1920: part II – housing and town planning.
    Cmd 917. HMSO, London
Ministry of Health (1920b) Grants to private persons or bodies of persons constructing houses
    under the Housing (Additional Powers) Act, 1919. HMSO, London
Ministry of Health (1921a) Second annual report, 1920–1921, Cmd 1446. HMSO, London
Ministry of Health (1921b) Report of the departmental committee on the high cost of building
    working class dwellings, Cmd 1447. HMSO, London
Ministry of Health (1922) Third Annual Report, 1921–1922. Cmd 1713. HMSO, London.
Ministry of Health (1924) Fifth annual report, 1923–1924. Cmd 2218. HMSO, London
Ministry of Health (1925) Sixth annual report, 1924–1925. Cmd 2450. HMSO, London
Ministry of Health (1926) Seventh annual report, 1925–1926. Cmd 2724. HMSO, London
Ministry of Health (1927) Eighth annual report, 1926–1927. Cmd 2938. HMSO, London
Ministry of Health (1929) General circular on the Local Government Act, 1929. Circular 1000.
    HMSO, London
Ministry of Health (1930a) Eleventh annual report, 1929–1930. Cmd 3667. HMSO, London
Ministry of Health (1930b) Housing Act, 1930. Circular 1138. HMSO, London

Ministry of Health (1932) Report of the Committee on Local Expenditure (England and Wales). Cmd 4200. HMSO, London

Ministry of Health (1933a) Housing Act, 1930: part I. Circular 1331. HMSO, London

Ministry of Health (1933b) Report of the departmental committee on housing. Cmd 4397. HMSO, London

Ministry of Health (1934) Fifteenth annual report, 1933–1934. Cmd 4664. HMSO, London

Ministry of Health (1935) Sixteenth annual report, 1934–1935. Cmd 4978. HMSO, London

Ministry of Health (1936) Housing Act, 1935: report on the overcrowding survey in England and Wales 1936. HMSO, London

Ministry of Health (1937a) Eighteenth annual report, 1936–1937. Cmd 5516. HMSO, London

Ministry of Health (1937b) Reports of the Inter-Departmental Committee on the Rent Restrictions Acts. Cmd 5621. HMSO, London

Ministry of Health (1939) Twentieth annual report, 1938–1939. Cmd 6089. HMSO, London

Ministry of Health (1944a) Rural housing: third report of the Rural Housing Sub-Committee of the Central Housing Advisory Committee. HMSO, London

Ministry of Health (1944b) Private enterprise housing: report of the Private Enterprise Sub-Committee of the Central Housing Advisory Committee of the Ministry of Health. HMSO, London

Ministry of Health (1944c) Design of dwellings: report of the Central Housing Advisory Committee. HMSO, London

Ministry of Health (1947a) Report of the Ministry of Health for the year ended 31st March 1946. Cmd 7119. HMSO, London

Ministry of Health (1947b) Reconditioning in rural areas: fourth report of the Rural Housing Sub-Committee of the Central Housing Advisory Committee. HMSO, London

Ministry of Health (1949) Housing Act, 1949. Circular 90/49. HMSO, London

Ministry of Health (1950) Report of the Ministry of Health for the year ended 31st March 1949. Cmd 7910. HMSO, London

Ministry of Health (1951) Report of the Ministry of Health for the year ended 31st March 1950. Cmd 8342. HMSO, London

Ministry of Health. (quarterly) Housing return for England and Wales (From 1951 Ministry of Housing & Local Government) HMSO, London

Ministry of Housing & Local Government (1953) Houses: the next step. Cmd 8996. HMSO, London

Ministry of Housing & Local Government (1954) New homes for old: improvements and conversions. HMSO, London

Ministry of Housing & Local Government (1955) Slum clearance (England and Wales): summary of returns including proposals submitted by local authorities under section I of the Housing Repairs and Rents Act, 1954. Cmd 9593. HMSO, London

Ministry of Housing & Local Government (1956) Report of the Ministry of Housing and Local Government for the Year 1955. Cmd 9876. HMSO, London

Ministry of Housing & Local Government (1959) Report of the Ministry of Housing and Local Government 1958. Cmnd 737 HMSO, London

Ministry of Housing & Local Government (1961a) Report of the Ministry of Housing and Local Government 1960. Cmnd 1435. HMSO, London

Ministry of Housing & Local Government (1961b) Housing in England and Wales. Cmnd 1290. HMSO, London

Ministry of Housing & Local Government (1962) Report of the Ministry of Housing and Local Government 1961. Cmnd 1725. HMSO, London

Ministry of Housing & Local Government (1963) Report of the Ministry of Housing and Local Government 1962. Cmnd 1976. HMSO, London

Ministry of Housing & Local Government(1964) Report of the Ministry of Housing and Local Government 1963. Cmnd 2338. HMSO, London

Ministry of Housing & Local Government (1965) Report of the Committee on Housing in Greater London. Cmnd 2605, Milner-Holland Report. HMSO, London

Ministry of Housing & Local Government (1967) Report of the Ministry of Housing and Local Government 1965 and 1966. Cmnd 3282. HMSO, London

Ministry of Housing & Local Government (1968a) Old houses into new homes. Cmnd 3602. HMSO, London

Ministry of Housing & Local Government (1968b) Housing condition survey: England and Wales, 1967. Econ Trends, 175, 87–99

Ministry of Housing & Local Government (1969) Report of the Ministry of Housing and Local Government 1967 and 1968. Cmnd 4009. HMSO, London

Ministry of Housing & Local Government. (quarterly) Housing return for England and Wales (Before 1951 Ministry of Health.) HMSO, London

Ministry of Works (1948) Temporary housing programme. Cmd 7304. HMSO, London

Ministry of Works & Planning (1942) Report of the Committee on Land Utilisation in Rural Areas. Cmd 6378. Scott Report. HMSO, London

Minns R (1973) The significance of Clay Cross: another look at district audit. Policy Politics 2:309–329

Morgan KO (1984) Labour in power, 1945–1951. Clarendon, Oxford

Morgan KO (1990) The people's peace: British history 1945–1989. Oxford University Press, Oxford

Morgan KO, Morgan J (1980) Portrait of a progressive: the political career of Christopher, Viscount Addison. Clarendon, Oxford

Muchnick DM (1970) Urban renewal in Liverpool: a study of the politics of redevelopment. Occasional Paper in Social Administration 33. Bell , London

Newton K (1976) Second city politics: democratic processes and decision-making in Birmingham. Oxford University Press, Oxford

NHBC Foundation (2015) Homes through the decades: the making of modern housing. Milton Keynes.

Nixon JW (1935) The size, constitution and housing standards of the family in England and Wales, 1911 to 1931. *Revue de l'Institut International de Statistique /Rev Int Statistical Institute* 3:142–162

Office of National Statistics. (annual) Annual abstract of statistics. HMSO, London

Parker J, Mirrlees C (1988) Housing. In: Halsey AH (ed) British social trends since 1900, 2nd edn. Macmillan, Basingstoke, pp 357–397

Pedley WH (1942) Labour on the land: a study of the developments between the two great wars. P.S. King & Staples, London

Perkin H (1989) The rise of professional society: England since 1880. Routledge, London

Phillips DR, Williams AM (1982) Rural housing and the public sector. Gower, Farnborough

Portsmouth City Council (2011) A history of council housing in Portsmouth. Portsmouth

Pugh M (2008) 'We danced all night': a social history of Britain between the wars. Bodley Head, London

Radford E (1970) The new villagers: urban pressure on rural areas in Worcestershire. Frank Cass, London

Ravetz A (2001) Council housing and culture: the history of a social experiment. Routledge, London

Registrar-General (1929) Local Government Act, 1929: part VI and the second, third, fourth and fifth schedules. Memorandum LGA 17. HMSO, London

Registrar-General (2002) 1971 Census aggregate data. UK Data Service. https://doi.org/10.5257/census/aggregate-1971-1

Rhodes G (1976) Local government finance 1918–1966. In Committee of Inquiry into Local Government Finance, Local government finance: appendix six. HMSO, London, pp 102–173

Rollings N (2001) Whitehall and the control of prices and profits in a major war, 1919–1939. Hist J 44:517–540

Royal Commission on Local Government (1925) First report: constitution and extension of county boroughs. Cmd 2506. HMSO, London

Royal Commission on Local Government (1928) Second report. Cmd 3213. HMSO, London

Royal Commission on Local Government in England (1969) Report. Cmnd 4040, Redcliffe-Maud report. HMSO, London

Rural Development Commission (1993) The rural housing problem. Salisbury

Ryder R (1984) Council house building in County Durham 1900–39. In: Daunton MJ (ed) Councillors and tenants. Leicester University Press, Leicester, pp 40–100

Satsangi M, Gallent N, Bevan M (2010) The rural housing question. Policy Press, Bristol

Scott P (1996) The worst of both worlds: British regional policy, 1951–64. Bus Hist 38:41–64

Scott P (2007) Triumph of the south: a regional economic history of early twentieth century Britain. Ashgate, Aldershot

Self RC (2006) Neville Chamberlain: a biography. Ashgate, Aldershot

Sharp E (1969) The Ministry of Housing and Local Government. Allen & Unwin, London

Sharpe LJ (1960) The politics of local government in Greater London. Public Admin 38:157–172

Shears RT (1936) Housing the agricultural worker. J R Agric Soc Engl 97:1–12

Simmonds AGV (2002) Raising Rachman: the origins of the Rent Act. Hist J 45:843–868

Simon ED (1933) The anti-slum campaign. Longmans, Green, London

Smallburgh Rural District Council (1957) Smallburgh RDC medical officer of health annual report 1956. Stalham

Smallburgh Rural District Council (1958) Smallburgh RDC medical officer of health annual report 1957. Stalham

Smallburgh Rural District Council (1967) Smallburgh RDC medical officer of health annual report 1966. Stalham

Smith HL (1992) The politics of Conservative reform: the equal pay for equal work issue, 1945–55. Hist J 35:401–415

Smyth H (1985) Property companies and the construction industry in Britain. Cambridge University Press, Cambridge

Standing Committee on Prices and Trusts (1920a) Profiteering Acts, 1919 and 1920: interim report on the prices, costs and profits of the brick trade. Cmd 959. HMSO, London

Standing Committee on Prices and Trusts (1920b) Profiteering Acts, 1919 and 1920: findings and decisions of a sectional committee appointed by the building materials sub-committee of the standing committee on prices and trusts to investigate the prices, costs and profits at all stages of timber. Cmd 985. HMSO, London

Standing Committee on Prices and Trusts (1920c) Profiteering Acts, 1919 and 1920: interim report on cement and mortar. Cmd 1091. HMSO, London

Standing Committee on Prices and Trusts (1921a) Profiteering Acts, 1919 and 1920: report on light castings. Cmd 1200. HMSO, London

Standing Committee on Prices and Trusts (1921b) Profiteering Acts, 1919 and 1920: final report on stone, brick and clayware trades. Cmd 1209. HMSO, London

Standing Committee on Prices and Trusts (1921c) Profiteering Acts, 1919 and 1920: report on pipes and castings. Cmd 1217. HMSO, London

Stevenson J, Cook C (1977) The slump: society and politics during the depression. Jonathan Cape, London

Sutcliffe AS, Smith R (1974) Birmingham 1939–1970: history of Birmingham volume three. Oxford University Press, London

Swenarton M (1981) Homes fit for heroes: the politics and architecture of early state housing in Britain. Heinemann, London

Swenarton M (2007) Houses of paper and brown cardboard: Neville Chamberlain and the establishment of the Building Research Station at Garston in 1925. Plan Perspect 22:257–281

Tilley MF (1947) Housing the country worker. Faber & Faber, London

Turner J (1994) Macmillan. Longman, Harlow

Wade-Martins S, Williamson T (2008) The countryside of East Anglia: changing landscapes 1870-1950. Boydell, Woodbridge

Warnes AM (1991) London's population trends: metropolitan area or megalopolis? In: Hoggart K, Green DR (eds) London: a new metropolitan geography. Edward Arnold, London, pp 156–175

Wellings F (2006) British housebuilders: history and analysis. Blackwell, Oxford

White J (1977) When every room was measured: the overcrowding survey of 1935–36 and its aftermath. Hist Workshop J 4:86–94

Willetts D (1992) Modern Conservativism. Penguin, Harmondsworth

Wilson H (1971) The Labour government, 1964–1970: a personal record. Weidenfeld & Nicolson and Michael Joseph, London

Zweiniger-Bargielowska I (1994) Rationing, austerity and the Conservative Party recovery after 1945. Hist J 37:173–197

Chapter 7
Rural Implementation: Frustration, Challenge and Compromise as Housing Realities

Abstract Targeting local responses to national policies, this chapter explores the allocation of new-build numbers to councils, pulling out its rather arbitrary nature and potential openness to lobbying. Characteristic of detailed interventions over dwelling numbers were Whitehall's intrusive directions as regards the design and appearance of dwellings, which were subject to criticism for their lack of sensitivity to local landscapes. Similar interventions punctuated council attempts to secure sites for house-building, which were already complex owing to site problems, acquisition difficulties and added costs supplying services. Government and construction industry preferences for building many homes on single sites saw rural councils pushed in this direction to secure more dwellings. Tension between centralisation pressures and council desires to serve local populations resulted in dissimilar geographies of council-building between districts. High levels of landed estate provision did reduce council-building, but not so as to justify claims estate homes were of sufficient quality council intervention was unnecessary. The chapter concludes by examining the seven investigated districts over the first three-quarters of the century, drawing out how housing priorities changed, but not always in the same way, with national priorities unevenly adapted for local gain.

Keywords Housing allocations · Dwelling appearance · Building sites · Centralisation pressures · Intra-district house-building

A multitude of council minutes and newspaper reports provide transparent evidence of restricted rural council scope for action. For one, while councillors were supportive of private sector solutions, they were regularly faced with private inaction or substandard performance. For many, this confirmed the necessity of council intervention. This was muted if 'imposing' on property-owners was involved. Often this created policy failure, like allowing tenants to live in appalling conditions because owners would not improve substandard dwellings. The hurdles councils had to overcome were heightened by being hemmed in by low wages and poor housing conditions. Limited in what they could achieve, councils were confronted with (commonly unsympathetic) national imperatives. For sure, at times local vested

© Springer Nature Switzerland AG 2021   407
K. Hoggart, *A Contrived Countryside*, Local and Urban Governance,
https://doi.org/10.1007/978-3-030-62651-8_7

interests manipulated council actions: whether as local employers or in-migrant
service-class seekers of a bucolic, imagined past. These were not central drivers of
rural housing change. In this chapter, this is illustrated by exploring attempts to
increase housing numbers, in the design of new dwellings and even in their location.
For each, the experience of rural councils provides a tale punctured by hindrances
and frustrations.

For context, recall that councils were placed under obligations in 1919 to survey
local housing conditions and respond to deficiencies (e.g. MoH 1944b, pp.5–7):

> The housing authority have a general statutory responsibility for providing accommodation
> to meet the housing needs of their district. So long as a need exists, it is their duty to con-
> tinue with the provision of accommodation by building new houses or by acquiring, and
> when necessary converting, existing houses or other buildings which can be made suitable
> for the housing needs of their district.[1]

Characteristically, this call to action was couched so councils had wiggle-room
should they not want to act, as the same document explained: 'These obligations are
of a general character. They do not place on the authority any direct obligation to
satisfy the immediate needs of an individual family in urgent need of accommodation'. This framework justified ministerial claims that the formulation and implementation of housing policy was in local authorities' hands.[2] Indeed, in a centralised
state system, ministries found it difficult to force councils to act if they were disinclined (Dunleavy and Rhodes 1983, p.115). Inaction worked against effective
implementation, which was reinforced through shallow Whitehall knowledge of
local behaviour and circumstances, a factor made more prominent by a huge number of local government units compared to Whitehall staff complements (Cross and
Mallen 1978). Numerous analysts confirm that this gave councils leeway in day-to-
day activities. Thus, for a primary national directive for local action, namely ministry circulars, Shipp and Harris (1977, p.8) reported that '… central government does
not know how successful its circulars have been until months after the policies have
(or have not) been implemented'. Delay and obfuscation in implementation provided councils with space to enact their own preferences. Dearlove (1973) provided
an exquisite exposition of this, showing how Kensington and Chelsea used national
circulars to justify policies it favoured while ignoring messages it disliked. Sutcliffe
and Smith (1974, p.100) gave a more ideological tone, when noting how
Birmingham's Conservatives championed local autonomy in the 1940s but '…
abandoned this cry almost completely when their own party took power at

---

[1] TNA HLG31/30 Enclosure to HI37/50 'Accommodation for Homeless Families', undated c1950.
[2] As expressed by former housing ministers, John Wheatley (HCH 14 May 1924, Vol.173,
col.1383W–85W), Neville Chamberlain (HCH 19 February 1925, Vol.180, col.1275; HCH 22
April 1926, Vol.194, col.1365), Arthur Greenwood (HCH 18 July 1929, Vol.230, col.644W),
Hilton Young (HCH 25 May 1933, Vol.278, col.1255), Aneurin Bevan (HCH 9 November 1950,
Vol.480, col.1112–13), Harold Macmillan (HCH 27 November 1951, Vol.494, col.1097), Henry
Brooke (HCH 25 March 1958, Vol.558, col.20W), Richard Crossman (HCH 24 May 1966, Vol.729,
col.246), Anthony Greenwood (HCH 26 March 1968, Vol.761, col.1143) and Julian Amery (HCH
27 October 1971, Vol.823, col.1704).

Westminster'. Expressed in broader terms, for Jackman (1978, p.273): 'There is little doubt that the legislative and administrative apparatus could allow central government very great control over local authorities, sufficient to reduce them to its agents. But detailed study of the process suggests that this potential is not in fact exercised'. In policy-makers' terms, Harold Macmillan (1969, p.375) described the MHLG as '… a department concerned with guidance, advice, supervision, sometimes even warning and reproof, but never with positive action', while Evelyn Sharp (1969, p.26) claimed the MHLG was apologetic if it felt it necessary to instruct a council.

Yet national officials in the inter-war decades disliked local 'independence' (Pugh 2008, p.419), with Ministry efforts to restrict local actions formulated as early as 1922 (Ward 1984, p.348). Tension in central-local relations were not helped by limited Ministry capabilities. As Simon (1933, p.64) put it, the inter-war Ministry of Health's Housing Division lacked an effective machinery for control or management, especially as its staff complement was 'ludicrously small'. By 1939, local government did not have high prestige (Gay 1987), with electricity, gas and hospitals relocated to new national agencies post-war. Yet, despite the opposition of his officials, Bevan was an enthusiast for local authority engagement with housebuilding (Malpass 2003, p.656). By contrast, the Conservative 'tradition' was suspicious of local government (Young 1975; Rhodes 1984), although Party factions wedded to tradition slowed change. This resulted in poor governance, as Whitehall was badly equipped and staffed to provide effective leadership or support to more than 1000 councils. Pressure for fewer, larger local units, with more unified responsibilities, led Enoch Powell to propose transforming the London County Council area into just seven boroughs in 1955 (Young 1975). His proposal failed to gather support, but two years later, a Royal Commission was established to recommend changes to London government (Sharpe 1960; Foley 1972). Nothing was done about the rest of the country until Richard Crossman established a 1966 Royal Commission on his own initiative, making the announcement when the MHLG's most senior civil servant was on holiday (Keith-Lucas and Richards 1978, p.211). But while the recommendations of these Commissions would lead to structural change, they did not address core Westminster desires for local government to do its bidding (MacLeod 1968; Rhodes 1976; Ball 1980).[3] A sense of this urge was displayed in internal 1968 communications over approving council-building:

> The present system, whereby the Department passively records as 'approvals' tenders which the authority has accepted weeks (or even months in some cases) beforehand is incompatible with an adequate control of the programme. Ministers decide how many

---

[3] When national authorities were concerned council spending might be extravagant or inefficient (TNA HLG52/1344 'Financial Position of Local Authorities 1922–25'; Branson 1979) or when councils were lethargic in following government policy (as with action against Bedford Town over implementing the 1919 Housing, Town Planning Etc. Act; HCH 22 April 1920, Vol.128, col.594W–95W).

houses may be approved for tender each year and therefore it must be the Department, and not the authorities, who do the approving.[4]

With small Whitehall staff numbers giving limited scope for positive action, the lack of legal sanctions that accompanied the polite fiction of local autonomy meant ministers had to proceed cautiously or risk political controversy (Cullingworth 1979, p.10).[5] Collaboration with ministries was encouraged, but councils were too numerous for close relationships or the development of trust. Most ministries were reluctant to widen the scope for local action (Keith-Lucas and Richards 1978, p.41), while rural councils were generally too short-staffed for detailed attention to their responsibilities (e.g. Wade-Martins and Williamson 2008, p.159).

The social distance between the public school – Oxbridge tenor of the civil service's upper echelons (Brittan 1964; Scott 1982; Theakston and Fry 1989) and, the often aged, petit bourgeois world of rural councillors generated a further separation. This found expression in national complaints that small councils lacked quality elected members or officials (Harrison and Norton 1967; MHLG 1967). Not surprisingly, the local–central relationship mixed guidance with direction:

> The Ministry's general function is to give guidance … We exercise a more direct control at three points. First, we settle each local authority's programme; this is their share of the national programme and must depend on the resources available nationally and locally. Second, we approve the tender price of each contract; this financial control is necessary in view of our responsibility for paying Exchequer subsidies and for sanctioning applications for permission to borrow the money required to build. Third, we exercise control on space standards.[6]

Councils were not treated equally. Larger authorities had more scope for action than smaller ones (Rhodes 1967), not simply owing to their greater resources but also from the circumscription of responsibilities, as signalled in proposals to exclude RDCs from 1919 Act implementation[7] and 1930 Act instructions to county councils to overview rural housing conditions (Clarke 1931). From the mid-1960s even more flexibility was given to cities, as with the announcement that: '… the authorities in the principal industrial towns have been given three-year programmes limited only by their capacity to build',[8] a status no rural council was conferred with. Whether

---

[4] TNA HLG150/7 'P.F. Grant Memo to Mr. Fowler', 13 September 1968.

[5] Dearlove (1973, p.20), for example referred to '… advice or guidance which in law the central government has no strict authority to give and no legal power to enforce'. Most especially as regards house-building, the most effective measure was the sanctioning of loans, which Evelyn Sharp (1969, p.29) took to be the MHLG's 'most powerful weapon' but which lost potency when councils were able to 'finance out of revenue', for which they did not need Ministry approval. Yet, controlling through loan sanction was politically uncomfortable, as it was '… an extension of the original intention of these powers, which was to prevent local authorities over-borrowing' (TNA T227/809 'Memo P.R. Baldwin to Mr. Thorley', 31 May 1956).

[6] TNA HLG101/812 Letter from MHLG Private Secretary, to Chair of National Union of Conservative and Unionist Associations, 16 August 1954.

[7] TNA CAB24/72 GT6556 'Housing Scheme. Suggestions by Mr. Chamberlain', 25 December 1918.

[8] HCH 1 November 1966, Vol.735, col.228.

through lobbying or collaboration, larger authorities were more likely to be listened to. This fostered a particular colouring to housing policy.[9]

7.1 New-Build Allocations

Implementing the 1919 Act caused alarm in Westminster given delays, 'especially in rural districts', were believed to have 'deplorable' consequences.[10] This was unfair, as rural districts had submitted better housing schemes than others (Table 7.1). Further cause for aggravation was reported in local newspapers, which condemned Whitehall, claiming: 'The local councils are not permitted to have any opinions of their own – they may select sites for a Housing Commissioner to approve or disapprove, but beyond that they seem to have no power'.[11] Contributing to heavy-handedness were four drivers: first, the cost of the programme was largely Treasury borne; second, there was fear of revolutionary agitation if nothing was done (Chap. 2); third, progress was slow in councils worried about rent affordability, whose inaction might undermine the 'homes fit for heroes' programme;[12] and, fourth, new programme teething problems were obvious. Yet, the Act was in preparation well before the 'Great War' ended, at a time when government actions penetrated virtually all aspects of life, when rapid action to avert difficulty and disaster should have been commonplace. If the government prioritised house-building, it had the know-how and the muscle to introduce and amend arrangements to smooth processes.

Table 7.1 The grading of new-build programme submissions under the 1919 Housing, Town Planning, Etc. Act by local government category in England and Wales, 1920

Percent of submissions graded	City of London and Metropolitan Boroughs	County Boroughs	Boroughs and UDCs	Rural districts
Satisfactory	31.0	36.6	53.0	57.8
Satisfactory as an instalment	51.7	59.8	41.9	37.9
Not satisfactory	10.3	3.7	1.7	2.5

Source: MoH (1920, p.12)
Note: The totals within categories do not add to 100 as responses that were 'doubtful' or 'not received' were not included. Only nine councils failed to make submissions (two were RDCs)

---

[9] Illustrative indications cover the 1924 Act (HCH 18 January 1924, Vol.169, col.433–34), the 1930 Act (HCH 14 April 1931, Vol.251, col.39–40) and slum clearance in cities (HCH 27 February 1962, Vol.654, col.121W).

[10] TNA CAB24/88 GT8144 'Report on Revolutionary Organisations in the UK', 11 September 1919, p.127–3.

[11] *BC&BG* 23 April 1920, p.2.

[12] As with Bedford (HCH 22 April 1920, Vol.128, col.594W–95W; *BC&BG* 23 April 1920, p.2), Cromer (*FakPost* 17 September 1920, p.7) and Saffron Walden RDC (*H&EO* 23 April 1921, p.3).

This did not happen. Rural councils were not alone in being antagonised by the government's failure to establish conditions for a successful programme. The response of Smallburgh gave a sense of the frustration:

> …it is impossible to fix a date for completion of the [Council's housing] Scheme, or even to state definitely the number of houses which would be erected this year, inasmuch as the results attained would largely depend upon whether the necessary money and materials were available as required, and there was also the labour question to consider.[13]

The Ministry's rejection of Sheringham's scheme, although based on Ministry plans, generated a more pointed reaction:

> After the long experience of the methods of the Ministry of Health in hindering the Housing Scheme which was to be part of the new world promised by the grateful Government to the men and women who fought and worked for the country at a time of crisis, no one will be surprised to hear that the Sheringham Urban District Council is also prevented from going on with its plans for the erection of working-class dwellings to meet the needs of the locality … Future historians reviewing this decade will say that the people asked for houses and were given *red tape* … The subsidies offered as an incentive to enterprise are of little avail when the State controls the materials necessary for the operations …[14]

Such complaints extended beyond rural districts, as exemplified by the MP for Peebles and Southern's account of Woolwich's difficulties building under the Act.[15] This account had notable similarities with the 1946–1950 traumas of Finsbury (Bullock 1989). The commonalty was the stifling impact of national decisions.

Beyond proximity to the world wars, there was little let-up in rural despair. This was evident in new-build approvals, with minutes punctuated with protests against allocation and stipulations, or, more resignedly, disappointment over them. At the tail-end of the 1919 Act, councils became used to seeing building numbers diluted, as with Ware RDC's cut from 200 to 128.[16] Little changed under the 1924 Act, with Blofield RDC shrunk from 225 to 50, despite a new factory increasing demand for housing (alongside 300 houses condemned as uninhabitable).[17] More commonly, the Ministry did not announce cuts but questioned proposals in a manner suggesting little respect for local determination. Responses were frequently influenced by shortfalls in labour and materials, which were signposted in official reports, even years after post-war turbulence (e.g. MoH 1924a, p.54, p.65; 1926, p.59; 1950a, p.124; MHLG 1961a, p.31; 1963, p.12). For sure, governments could have responded more effectively to under-performance in the building trade (Barlow and Duncan 1994; Wellings 2006), but leaving this to one side, labour and material shortcomings were outweighed by a deeper motivation in Ministry interventions. One aspect of

---

[13] NRO DC22/2/45 SmRDCHCM 11 May 1920. This response was to the Housing Commissioner asking when stages in the housing scheme would be completed.

[14] *FakPost* 21 May 1920, p.5.

[15] HCH 15 July 1920, Vol.131, col.2658–65.

[16] *H&EO* 16 April 1921, p.3.

[17] *NWP&ENS* 19 December 1924, p.5.

this was cost, with Ministry officials regularly questioning tender prices or seeking site or design changes to lower costs. These continued across the decades, with Whitehall officials often pronouncing on local circumstances they knew little about. As a Ministry inspector spelled out in 1931:

> I am of opinion that both Newmarket and Linton need help about as much and about as little as any RD in East Anglia, and that we cannot with any staff which have at our disposal, or which could without administrative extravagance be allotted to the job, form any fair judgement differentiating the relative neediness of one RD from another RD.[18]

Detailed interventions nonetheless occurred, with Whitehall's red-tape raising workloads on under-staffed RDC and Ministry offices, as well as impacting on efficient state operations, as the RDCA pointed out in 1967:

> There is a general criticism of the time occupied by staff in dealing with the complicated forms produced by the Department. There is no doubt that the scheme is causing considerable increase in the amount of administrative expenditure. Another criticism is the time taken in arguing about relatively small matters. An example has been given that due to delays on the part of the Department in clearing questions relating to expenditure of only £400, between six and eight weeks good building weather was lost earlier this year. The consequential loss of rent will have exceeded the amount at issue.[19]

Excuses might be made that governments must be judicious with public money. No question on this score, even if much waste in government can be placed at the door of ideological blindness or flights of fantasy amongst national politicians (e.g. Hall 1980; Hennessy 1996). The issue is not whether good practice should be followed but what produces efficient, effective operations. There are multiple means by which aims can be achieved. Whitehall hoped for consensual collaboration but overlaid this with detailed reviews, without providing themselves (or councils) with the tools for successful outcomes. This constituted a nit-picking approach to central overview (Chaps. 5 and 6), which worked against a fundamental necessity for quality performance in bureaucracies, namely trust (Breton and Wintrobe 1982).

Characteristic of the instructions councils received was one to Walsingham. Proposing 24 new homes in 1927, the Housing Committee provided the Council with information on tenant applicants. The Council had specifically asked parish councils for surety there were '… reliable applicants for Council houses at inclusive rents not exceeding 4/6d', following which one parish was eliminated. The Ministry response was characteristically blunt:

> … in the first instance, he [the Minister] will be glad to be informed whether the Council are satisfied:
>
> 1. That the houses will meet a genuine working-class need.
> 2. That they cannot be erected without the aid of financial assistance.
> 3. That the proposed subsidy of £12.10.0 per house per annum is the minimum required.

---

[18] TNA HLG40/19 Letter from W.D. Bushell, General Inspector, to E.C.H. Salmon, MoH, 10 November 1931.

[19] TNA HLG118/805 Letter from RDCA Secretary to W.O. Ulrich, 14 December 1967.

Hardly surprisingly for a low-waged agrarian area, the Council response was that the proposed subsidy was required, although even '… with this subsidy the houses will not be a paying proposition'.[20] This response could have been laid at the Ministry's door by many rural councils in any of the 55 years after 1918. More important was the Ministry questioning 'demand' for new homes, despite the Council's application including data to convince on this point. This was a common reaction to council submissions. It highlighted traits in national thinking. In 1930, for instance, Smallburgh sought approval for 36 additional homes in Hoveton. The Parish Council had had 60 applications for homes and supplied a list of 36 workers in boat building who wanted new homes as they lived far from Hoveton due to local housing shortages. The Ministry was unimpressed. It delayed a decision by requesting more evidence, then in 1932 ruled that, because there were no unfit or overcrowded dwellings in the parish, no new homes could be entertained.[21] While this was going on, Smallburgh applied for 66 farm-worker homes under the 1931 Act. The County Council concurred with this number and at least 46 were deemed necessary by the Ministry's Inspector. The Council was allocated 20 (and non-parlour not the requested parlour). When it pressed for 24 more, the Ministry concluded it did not need assistance under the Act at all but could build with lower subsidies under the 1924 Act.[22] We see the driving force of economy in these transactions, both in reduced allocations and in substituting non-parlour for parlour homes. We also see a Ministry showing scant regard for the local economy, for this area had buoyant boat building activity. Similar denials of permission to erect homes for non-agricultural workers were reported elsewhere, as at Bakewell RDC, which had the added twist that the Council sought to build without subsidies.[23] Five years later, Smallburgh proposed no-subsidy homes for Hoveton, as the Ministry would otherwise refuse permission, and there was a long list of applicants for homes. Eventually, in 1937, 24 non-assisted Hoveton homes were approved.[24] Delayed provision at a time when the industry was well toned for construction was telling. The homes approved fell short of numbers required and arrived late. Workers in thriving industries who could not afford home ownership fell through policy cracks, with the

---

[20] NRO DC19/6/14 WRDCM 30 March 1927, p.121; TNA HLG48/379 Letter from J.N. Dark, MoH, to Walsingham RDC Clerk, despatched 13 May 1927; Letter from Walsingham RDC Clerk to MoH Secretary, 19 May 1927.

[21] NWP&ENS 21 March 1930, p.15; 13 June 1930, p.1; FakPost 8 August 1930, p.5; NRO DC22/2/14 SmRDCM 5 July 1932, p.5.

[22] NWP&ENS 4 September 1931, p.5; TNA HLG40/20 'Secretary's Memorandum', 1 January 1932; TNA HLG40/17 'List of Applications Received at 4 January 1932'; T&WT 20 February 1932, p.10; NRO DC22/2/14 SmRDCM 5 July 1932, p.337; TNA HLG40/20 'Particulars of Tenders Received and Approved by 26 November 1932'; NRO DC22/2/46 SmRDCHCM 17 October 1933, p.76.

[23] TNA HLG37/43 'Report on Local Investigations in Wiltshire, Bedfordshire, Derbyshire and Anglesey', undated c1936, p.31.

[24] NM&PWJ 20 April 1935, p.6; T&WT 21 December 1935, p.8; NRO DC22/2/47 SmRDCHCM 25 May 1937, p.588.

knock-on effect that shortage of affordable housing kept many in unsatisfactory accommodation for want of an alternative.

Inter-war, when Ministry action focused less on promotion and more on controlling local initiative, there was an unwillingness to accept local knowledge on housing need. Illustrative were challenges to council requests for homes with bedroom numbers outside the 'norm',[25] instructions to build non-parlour not parlour homes,[26] restricting old people's homes to one-bedroom[27] or challenging demand for extra dwellings.[28] Ministry officials habitually requested further evidence on demand, interrogated evidence provided and disagreed with local assessments.[29] That this provoked irritation locally was illustrated when a Ministry official investigated council tenant complaints in Bessingham (Erpingham) in 1924. These homes had been inspected by Council staff and found satisfactory, leading to the criticism the Ministry visit was costly and showed a lack of trust in the Council.[30] Little surprise Bakewell complained in 1936 '… that they had not been allowed sufficient freedom of action by the Ministry of Health', while the 1947 Chair of the Biggleswade's Housing Committee charged '… the Council today had practically no power at all in connexion with house-building'.[31] Official accounts reached the same conclusion, arguing that, while the Ministry was promotional over the 1919 and 1924 Acts, and after 1933 for the 1930 Act, otherwise its actions were largely those of control and checking, rather than stimulating and promoting initiative (MoH 1944a, p.28).[32]

This led to wasted effort, as councils, occasionally on demand but frequently at their request, had to meet Ministry officials to press cases. Council minutes were

---

[25] This might be because councils did not feel farm-workers could afford rents for larger houses, as in Ampthill (*W&DR* 25 September 1926, p.1) and Smallburgh (*NWP&ENS* 2 September 1932, p.4). Sandy similarly had bungalows approved, but only if it guaranteed they would go to aged persons (BRO UDSM1/1 SaUDCM 27 July 1931, p.402). Very occasionally the reverse occurred, as with Ampthill being pressed to build four-bedroom homes for overcrowded families (*W&DR* 22 June 1937, p.7).

[26] NRO DC13/5/73 ERDCHCM 13 January 1932, p.2; 5 March 1932, p.8.

[27] TNA HLG49/393 Letter from J.N. Dark, MoH, to Sandy UDC Clerk, 11 January 1932; BRO UDSM1/1 SaUDCM 21 March 1932, p.457; NRO DC22/2/14 SmRDCM 2 August 1932, p.359.

[28] BRO UDA6/1 AUDCHBCM 7 January 1932.

[29] Examples include: TNA HLG48/872 Letter from the Hatfield RDC Clerk to MoH, 16 December 1932; Reply, 16 January 1933; BRO RDBwM1/11 BiRDCM 15 February 1933; HRO RDC4/1/9 BuRDCM 22 February 1934, p.60.

[30] *HMC&WP* 6 June 1924, p.1.

[31] TNA HLG37/43 'Report on Local Investigations …', undated c1936, p.31; *NBC&BR* 16 September 1947, p.9.

[32] Rural councils also complained about the time it took to make decisions. Approval might come so late the summer building period was largely missed (HCH 14 July 1950, Vol.477, col.1822). Delays caused by dotting the 'i's and crossing the t's were problematic before building started. In one Biggleswade case, a builder and nine workmen turned up one morning to start a Henlow project but could not because confirmed tender specifications, etc. had not arrived from the Ministry. Following 'gingering up' action by the Council, approval arrived and work started the next morning (*NBC&BR* 24 April 1951, p.9).

replete with references to such meetings or attempts to arrange them. Rebuffs were often sharp, as Biggleswade found in 1926 when told '… there was not the slightest possibility of the Minister varying his decision in respect of the incidence of the estimated loss in building further houses'.[33] Sandy received a similar response a few years later, although this at least offered prospects for written persuasion:

> I am directed by the Minister of Health to state that the necessity for an interview at the present stage is not appreciated, and he would be glad to learn in the first instance what steps the Council have taken on the lines suggested in his letter of the 21st July to reduce the cost of the one-bedroomed bungalows proposed to be built for aged persons, and with what result.[34]

Seeking meetings with Ministry officials persisted long after 1945. One reason for face-to-face approaches was a belief they yielded results. In Chap. 6, the 1963 example of Hatfield securing higher subsidies for new flats following a meeting was noted. Another visible signal was a 1928 Erpingham meeting, which led to near complete acceptance of its housing programme.[35] But, as evidence for farmers' organisations shows, influencing national policy-makers was strengthened by collective clout rather than individual action (e.g. Self and Storing 1962; Wilson 1977). Unfortunately for rural districts, when compared with the electoral and economic influence of cities, or indeed of statutory geographical groupings (such as for Wales),[36] representative organisations like the RDCA exerted slight pulls on Ministry consciousness. The outcome, for Adonis and Pollard (1997, Ch7), was that national housing policy was largely 'rural blind'.

The importance of this was apparent after 1945 when governments were more directing towards local housing. This was obvious under the 1945–1951 government, given strictures imposed by shortages of labour and materials, alongside economic hangovers from the 1939–1945 conflict, all of which focused minds on national priorities (Eatwell 1979; Morgan 1984). In differing form, when government objectives primarily targeted slum clearance and support for home ownership, it was equally apparent under 1950s Conservative then 1960s Labour regimes. Yet, the basis on which national strategy was determined owed more to negotiation than evidence. As the new 1951 government found in discussion with local government associations: '… the 'facts' on which the subsequent discussions will be based are not the product of simple arithmetic … [instead] they owe [much] to hard bargaining on both sides'.[37] This heralded 'flexible' building allocations, as a minister for housing explained in 1953:

---

[33] BRO RDBwM1/9 BiRDCM 21 April 1926.

[34] TNA HLG49/393 Letter from C.R. Kerwood to Sandy UDC Clerk, 15 August 1932. When a request for more than slum clearance or overcrowding was rebuffed, the UDC sought support from its MP and the UDCA (BRO UDSM1/2 SaUDCM 26 October 1936, p.885).

[35] HRO RDC7/1/32 HtRDCM 9 April 1963, p.672; NRO DC13/5/72 ERDCHCM 28 March 1928, p.100.

[36] On expecting pressure from Welsh MPs if allocation cuts affected the Principality, see TNA HLG117/172 Letter to W.A. Wood, HMLG, from J. Davey, Welsh Office, 3 September 1964.

[37] TNA T227/823 'Memo to Mr. J.G. Owen from D.J, Mitchell', 20 December 1951.

You write to me on 21ˢᵗ July asking how we arrived at the figures for approving tenders for individual local authorities. You asked whether it was done by means of a percentage reduction on all local authorities or what was the basis. The answer isn't a simple one, because we have no universal rule or simple formula - we are not so rigidly bureaucratic as that: What we try to do is to give each local authority its appropriate programme in the light of all the circumstances, within the framework of the national programme as a whole.[38]

Expanding the point, Duncan Sandys, a housing minister in 1955, claimed that: 'My regional officers are instructed to treat each local authority's building programme individually'.[39] This was a heroic goal with 1000 plus councils to deal with, alongside dismally small Whitehall staff numbers, but its intention was cast in less positive light by Sandys' explanation that: 'In many cases authorisations are made before the receipt of any application. In others, the building programme is settled through informal discussion between the regional representatives of my Ministry and the local authorities concerned'.[40] Hence: 'The issue of allocations is an informal arrangement'.[41] This might seem to have ended a few months later, when the government informed councils it was bringing the system of housing allocations to an end (MHLG 1956, p.9).[42]

But the economic traumas of 1950s governments did not go away. Interest rate rises and searches to cut public spending stifled the policy agenda, and saw governments dampen council-building. Slower loan sanctions were proposed. This did not meet ministerial approval:

I agree that in the present circumstances we must keep the rate [of new-build] as low as we reasonably can. I do not, however, like the method you suggest of approving tenders more slowly, which would give local authorities an impression of general incompetence. Instead, as I mentioned, I propose that we should exercise an even more strict control than hitherto over tenders generally to achieve the same end.[43]

There was a de facto return of allocations. Braughing was told plans must be approved before going to tender. Ampthill was informed there was no value in making submissions unless proposals were for slum replacement. Newport Pagnell RDC was given an explicit maximum of 10 new homes a year.[44] It might not be called an allocation but if it looked, smelled and tasted like one, surely it was one? The 1960s emphasis on greater shares of new-build going to priority authorities reinforced emergent trends (Chap. 6). As expressed by the MHLG (1956, p.9): 'Many councils, more especially in the industrial districts, were still faced with a considerable shortage of houses, quite apart from slum clearance … Accordingly,

[38] TNA HLG101/812 Letter to Irene Ward MP from Ernest Marples, MHLG, 11 August 1953.
[39] HCH 2 March 1955, Vol.537, col.296W.
[40] HCH 12 July 1955, Vol.543, col.156W.
[41] HCH 26 July 1955, Vol.544, col.562.
[42] This was noted locally (BRO RDAM2/22 ARDCHCM 17 November 1955; HRO RDC3/2/11 BrRDCPHHCM 17 November 1955, p.2942).
[43] TNA T227/809 Letter to Chancellor of the Exchequer from Duncan Sandys, MHLG, 8 June 1956.
[44] HRO RDC3/1/6 BrRDCHCM 12 December 1957, pp.3645–46; WR&WSR 4 March 1958, p.1; 6 May 1958, p.1.

bigger allocations of houses to be started in 1955 were given to local authorities in industrial areas'. The interchange over Brixworth RDC, which revealed a 'kitty' of allocations that could be distributed as officials chose,[45] was indicative of 'loose' allocation practices, which Biggleswade benefited from:

> On condition they put them in hand immediately and that actual building started before the end of the year, an offer was made to Biggleswade Rural Council last week of 'ten or twelve' houses on top of their 1955 allocation. The offer was made by the Principal Regional Officer of the Ministry of Housing to the Clerk ...[46]

While allocations exceeding expectations were rare, there were hikes in awards at short notice if this suited the Ministry. Examples included 12 added houses for Erpingham in 1933, an extra 35 for Biggleswade Town in 1948 and Biggleswade's hike of 10–12 in 1955, with the failure of priority areas to meet targets producing the following invitation to Ampthill: 'If therefore your Council wish to add to the agreed further schemes – even for general need – in 1969 I should be pleased to consider any proposals'.[47] This 1969 offer was shelved a month later with an announcement all additional allocations would go to priority areas.[48] This reflected a tendency for placing extra allocations towards strategic goals, as with 1948 help to increase farm-worker dwellings and 1950 gains for places with dollar-earning industries.[49] But the driving force behind additional allocations might be to maintain the Ministry's standing in departmental budget allocations (especially when the Treasury was bearing down on housing expenditure, as under 1950s governments). This oriented additional permissions to where the building sector could respond rapidly. As seen in Chap. 5, this did not favour rural districts,[50] but some cities saw major rises.[51]

Even if addition numbers were rarely offered, the prospect of gaining advantage from slack in allocation processes helps explain why councils regularly sought

---

[45] TNA HLG101/812 Letter to Beddoe from MHLG Nottingham Regional Office on Brixworth RDC, 7 December 1953.

[46] *WR&WSR* 11 October 1955, p.11.

[47] NRO DC13/5/73 ERDCHCM 27 March 1933, p.64; *NBC&BR* 24 August 1948, p.1; *WR&WSR* 11 October 1955, p.9; BRO RDAM1/24 ARDCHCM 10 April 1969. To the chagrin of the Minister, 20 cities or London boroughs failed to meet targets in 1969 (HCH 30 October 1969, Vol.790, col.3W–4W).

[48] HCH 18 November 1969, Vol.791, col.238W.

[49] Both Biggleswade (*NBC&BR* 27 April 1948, p.2) and Braughing (HRO RDC3/2/4 BrRDCPHHCM 20 May 1948, p.1233) received invitations for increments. Allocations to support dollar-earning industries were signalled in HCH 19 October 1950, Vol.478, col.265W.

[50] On many occasions rural councils were frustrated by slow building. This was especially so for 1946–1955, when demand for new-build was particularly high, as in Biggleswade, which still had problems in the early-1960s (*NBC&BR* 23 May 1950, p.2; *BC&BG* 26 May 1961, p.12) and Walsingham (TNA MAF147/1 'Survey of Additional Houses for Agricultural Workers. Walsingham').

[51] As an illustration, Sheffield saw its initial 1951 allocation rise from 1200 to 1709 (HCH 1 May 1951, Vol.487, col.993).

face-to-face meetings.[52] Councils made sure local MPs were aware of their disquiet.[53] At times, this proved cathartic. In 1954–1955, for example, councils were energised over the Ministry's refusal to countenance extra building when general housing needs were high. In Biggleswade Town '… the words "mockery", "hypocrisy", and "disgraceful" were freely used by [council] members', once informed the Ministry would not give an allocation of council dwellings to rehouse people in slum properties.[54] Similar sentiments were expressed by Newport Pagnell RDC's award of only 20 new homes, over Biggleswade receiving just 20–30 permissions and Smallburgh's allowance being halved.[55] Yet, Ampthill's allocation rose from 20 to 70 when its local Conservative MP intervened.[56]

Of course, as analysts of English society have charged, there have long been tight networks of 'connected people', who have not been embarrassed to intervene to secure desired goals (Scott 1982; Adonis and Pollard 1997; Jones 2014). One notes Newby and associates' observation that mainstream farmers looked to influence policy through organisations like the National Farmers' Union, while the 'grandees' of large-scale farming went directly to a minister (Newby et al. 1978, p.130). Reference to such intercessions, as expected, was not plentiful in publicly accessible documents, at least not for the period investigated. Nevertheless, there were hints of their force. Take the case of Clutton RDC, which applied on 28 July 1926 to erect working-class housing. This stirred a Ministry letter to the Mines Department on 20 August asking about coal mining prospects in the area (they were mixed). How the coal mining industry addressed housing supply in this district was not clear but nationally 15% of coal miners were estimated to live in accommodation tied to their employer at the start of the century (Benson 1989, p.84), with a 1950 Ministry estimate of 140,000 tied homes still occupied by coal mine, coastguard, dock, fire brigade, forestry, police and water workers.[57] Whatever the local circumstances, mine owners were interested in the Council's proposal. As an internal memo of 27 October put it:

---

[52] As seen regularly for Biggleswade (BRO RDBwM1/20 BiRDCM 23 February 1949, p.28; BRO RDBwM1/21 BiRDCM 22 February 1950, p.58; HCH 30 November 1950, Vol.481, col.171W–72W; BRO RDBwM1/24 BiRDCM 28 October 1953, p.227; NBC&BR 15 June 1954, p.2; BRO RDBwM1/26 BiRDCM 31 August 1955, p.201; BRO RDBwM1/27 BiRDCM 14 March 1956, p.51; BC&BG 14 September 1956, p.1), with other examples from the same era for Biggleswade Town (BC&BG 21 January 1955, p.1), Cromer (NorfChron 18 February 1955, p.1; 17 June 1955, p.5), Hatfield (HRO RDC7/1/18 HtRDCM 3 September 1952, p.120) and Smallburgh (HCH 30 November 1950, Vol.481, col.171W–72W; NNN 15 August 1952, p.5).

[53] As with Ampthill (WR&WSR 20 January 1948, p.1), Biggleswade (NBC&BR 23 May 1950, p.2), Biggleswade Town (BC&BG 28 January 1955, p.1) and Braughing (HRO RDC3/2/2 BrRDCPHHCM 18 November 1943, p.630).

[54] BC&BG 28 January 1955, p.1.

[55] WR&WSR 23 November 1954, p.1; BRO RDBwM1/25 BiRDCM 24 November 1954, p.301; NNN 3 December 1954, p.1

[56] BRO RDAM2/22 ARDCHCM 21 January 1954; 17 June 1954.

[57] TNA HLG40/50 'Motion. Cottage Certificate Procedure', 22 February 1950, p.1.

> Lord Strachie has telephoned to me in a great state of excitement about an application of the
> Clutton Rural District Council for permission to build another 100 houses. He is satisfied
> that there is no case for this. The money is not available and the population of the district is
> likely to diminish than to increase ...

A handwritten note to John Wrigley on 28 October revealed that Lord Strachie had raised the issue three months earlier, leading to a review of proposals. This culminated in a letter to the RDC on eight December stating that the Minister '... does not think that the position at the moment is sufficiently clear to justify him in assenting to the erection of these houses at the present time'.[58] How far the poor performance of some mines bore on this outcome cannot be assessed. Dispute existed about at least one mine over miners wanting an eight-hour working day, and there were flooding and financial problems in others. Set against this, the documentation mentioned collieries with reserves for many decades, and requests were being submitted for more miners' cottages. But it is the manner in which Lord Strachie's intervention induced the Ministry to review the case that was compelling. It suggested certain 'lobbyists' received 'special treatment'.

This practice was evident years later, when Henry Upcher wrote on behalf of Erpingham expressing concern that the onset of World War hostilities might block completion of 10 cottages for farm-workers. Internal communications between the Ministry and the Treasury made obvious a positive response to the enquiry was encouraged, for Upcher was described by the Treasury to be '... an important man in Norfolk and for whose opinion Sir Samuel [Hoare] has a great respect, and to say that he hopes it will be possible to do what Mr Upcher desires'. Approval was granted within six weeks of the letter being sent.[59] Eight years later, the now-knighted, Upcher was frustrated; yet, his intervention again elicited energy in the Ministry's response:

> Sir Henry Upcher feels that little or no useful purpose would be served by his attending a
> meeting such as that suggested by Mr Rowell ... He is, of course, Chairman of the Erpingham
> Rural District Council ... His Council have recently applied for permission to build a con-
> siderable number of additional houses for agricultural workers, their application being
> made after full consultation with my Committee but they have now been informed by the
> Ministry of Health that they can this year build practically none at all ... I fear that all Rural
> Councils in this County are being treated in very much the same way. As a result they are
> suffering from a feeling of real frustration and helplessness.[60]

Officials urged that: 'We should also do everything possible to persuade them [RDCs] to submit schemes in the near future for the erection of houses in those

---

[58] TNA HLG48/297 'Clutton RDC. Housing General Scheme 1919–1926'.

[59] TNA HLG48/868 'Erpingham RDC. Letter from H. Upcher, Sheringham Hall, to Samuel Hoare, The Treasury, 22 February 1940; Letter from A.S. Hutchinson, The Treasury, to S.F. Wilkinson, MoH, 23 February 1940; Letter from S.F. Wilkinson to A.S. Hutchinson, 8 March 1940; Note, 8 April 1940. Sir Samuel Hoare was a leading Conservative, holding the posts of Secretary of State for Air, Secretary of State for India, Foreign Secretary, First Lord of the Admiralty and Home Secretary up to 1940.

[60] TNA MAF147/1 Letter from J. Christie to D.D. Barnard, 28 February 1948.

parishes where the demand is most urgent'.[61] People like Upcher were not alone in pressing for extra farm-worker homes at the time. Lobbying had occurred repeatedly before his letter was received.[62] His intervention was not determining but Ministry reactions draw a light on sub-surface inputs into policy processes.

More generally, obtaining permissions made for uncomfortable rural experiences. Soon after entering the MHLG, Harold Macmillan (1969, p.376) summarised the ministry as having: '… no urgency or drive; no production organisation central or local; no progress offers; no machinery for identifying and breaking "bottlenecks". The Ministry was in no sense a Production Department'. Indeed, shortly after taking office, Macmillan faced regions for which over-allocating council numbers was the norm, so as to achieve required volumes, while private licences were being returned '… because the holders were not yet ready or could not afford to proceed', with builders needing assurances of continuity '… before they were prepared to acquire and service large sites'.[63] Such assurances were forthcoming, at first through significant increases in private licences, then in the mid-1950s by council allocation cuts to release resources for private building.[64] Before these reductions were signalled, rural councils were squeezed so private building was not overheated. Hence, even though council-building was increasing (Fig. 6.2), Ampthill's 1953 programme was limited owing to demands from 'other forms of building'.[65] With weak performance in the construction sector, problems did not go away. By 1962, the Council Chair was apportioning joint blame on the Ministry and builder shortages for lethargy in the council programme, with Ministry insistence on programme cuts in 1964 likewise due to industry problems.[66] The Ministry then rejected the Council's 1965 programme on the grounds it wanted to build more homes than in 1964.[67] No wonder Alderman Harry Bonner interpreted such interventions as the RDC 'losing ground'.[68] Process-wise, the government might claim the formal quota

---

[61] TNA MAF147/1 Letter from C.W. Rowell, Provincial Land Commissioner, MAF Cambridge, to D.D. Barnard, 19 March 1948.

[62] Instances include pressure from Lord Addison (TNA HLG40/56 'Memo to John Wrigley from H Symon', 30 April 1947), county and national NFU appeals (HRO RDC7/9/1 HtRDCM 13 May 1947, p.302) and meetings between ministers, officials, unions and farmers' organisations (*NBC&BR* 20 May 1947, p.5), which combined to influence Cabinet policy, resulting in rural allocations concentrating on agricultural needs (TNA CAB129/20 CP(47)249 'Priority of Housing for Miners, Agricultural Workers and Key Workers in the Development Areas', 5 September 1947; TNA MAF234/12 Letter to RDCs and Selected Urban Housing Authorities from MoH, October 1947).

[63] TNA HLG68/78 Principal Regional Officers' Meeting. 'Appendix to Housing Minutes', 8 January 1952, p.1, p.3.

[64] Especially around 1954–55, as for Smallburgh (*NNN* 3 December 1954, p.1) and Ampthill (BRO RDAM2/22 ARDCHCM 17 March 1955).

[65] *WR&WSR* 3 November 1953, p.2.

[66] *WR&WSR* 4 December 1962, p.1; 5 May 1964, p.16.

[67] BRO RDAM1/21 ARDCHCM 9 September 1965, p.228.

[68] *WR&WSR* 5 May 1964, p.16. He was not alone with this sentiment. Almost exactly the same expression was used in 1955 by Cromer in a failed attempt to have an allocation raised. Here hous-

system of the late-1940s had gone, but most RDCs saw little change from 1951, when Ampthill's Surveyor summarised the mood of frustration:

> From time to time statements have been made by the Ministers that authorities who have made good progress would receive a further allocation, but in practice this has not resulted. Our experience has been that where works have been advanced so that applications for additional consents have been lodged there has been instability by the Government departments, tenders have been held up pending the next quota period and we have been told we have exceeded our allowance. In addition, we are given our quota six months at a time. We receive this figure possibly two months before the end of a period and as this figure now approximates to 50 houses per half year, out of which number the private licences must be deducted, it means very little time is given to get contracts going if the allocation is split into a large number of different parts and it is easier to get a contract going for a large number of houses than it is to put into operation a large number of smaller contracts.[69]

Contrast this account with assertions made within the Ministry that six-month allocations did not stop councils planning ahead, as rural councils with limited resources '… needed constant encouragement and the half-yearly allocation gave them this'.[70] Based on the materials covered for this book, this explanation demonstrated little understanding of rural council proclivities. These drew on visible demand for council-building (Chap. 3), a desire to respond as others were not (Chap. 4), and frustration over direct and indirect government action that generated delay, raised costs and failed to ensure the alignment of building and supply capacities (Chap. 6). Set within a tight framework for allocating building numbers, these difficulties were especially difficult for rural districts, given the small, scattered size of most projects, alongside added complications from poor resources, low tenant paying capacities and inadequate water and sewer systems. Beside which, the playing field on which allocations were made was not level, with cities treated more favourably because their residents were wealthier and they had greater political clout through their ability to embarrass the government or to call on connections to extract concessions (Chap. 6).

7.2 Dwelling Design and Appearance

Interventions retarding rural house-building were not the only arena of frustration. Similar impacts were found for the design and external appearance of dwellings. This is not the place to investigate the causes of such impacts. These have been explored for 1909–1983 by Punter (1986, 1987), whose conclusion highlighted cross-cutting imperatives characterising so much national policy-making:

---

ing applications were rising faster than additions to the stock (*NorfChron* 18 February 1955, p.1).

[69] *WR&WSR* 31 July 1951, p.10.

[70] TNA HLG68/78 Principal Regional Officers' Meeting. 'Appendix to Housing Minutes', 8 January 1952, p.2. It was explained that, while six-month allocations did disadvantage some large towns, the system was not rigidly applied.

Over the 75 years it is difficult to decide whether central government advice on aesthetic control has been a defeatist orthodoxy in the gifted amateur tradition, a bureaucratic convenience to improve the efficiency of the planning and particularly the appeal system, or a convenient smokescreen to allow commercial interests the freedom to fashion the built environment to their own ends. The orthodoxy of control has consistently reflected administrative convenience, interest group lobbying, and confusion about the nature of design, perhaps in that order. (Punter 1987, p.58)

Yet, when planning council houses under the 1919 Act, positivity surrounded dwelling design and site layout. In the Biggleswade countryside, the plan was for three-bedroom houses with a bathroom upstairs, built in twos, threes or fours but not in rows. There were limitations imposed by lack of piped water and sewage disposal in various villages but large gardens were proposed, not just to provide opportunities for vegetable and other product growth but also for dispersing household waste.[71] Proposing no more than eight dwellings an acre, this aligned with national guidelines for rural areas, with 12 the maximum for towns.[72] This early confluence of ideas was soon disabused, with national Housing Commissioners insisting on detailed, unwelcome changes to local proposals. For Biggleswade, such interventions led to a redesign of cottages into blocks of four with bathrooms downstairs.[73] Ministry calls for more dwellings on a site were common, as Walsingham experienced at the start of its programme.[74] More generally, councils were instructed to comply with fine-grained demands. Take, for example, one Housing Commissioner's directions to Ely Town:

1. Omit allotments at west end of the site. These are not large enough to be worthwhile.
2. In place of circular road put 30ft. x 30ft. turning space. The circular grass plot would be particularly liable to be trodden down.
3. Keep fences along cul-de-sac road back from road leaving a grass margin about 8ft. wide.
4. Omit diagonal paths from turning space. The doors of the houses are near the centres of the blocks, and paths running out square would be more convenient.
5. Omit curbing and channelling at side of road. This is not required in a road of this description.
6. Put rodding eyes every 100ft. along drains for cleaning purposes.
7. Take new sewer in road into existing sewer about 100ft. further down road.[75]

Quite apart from the delay caused by altering plans, alongside arranging meetings with officials to debate changes, such requirements stoked resentment. This

---

[71] *NBC* 1 August 1919, p.6.

[72] *NBC* 8 August 1919, p.3; Ministry of Reconstruction (1918, p.7); HCH 2 May 1918, Vol.105, col.1736; MoH (1920, p.17).

[73] *BC&BG* 21 November 1919, no page number.

[74] *NWP&ENS* 10 October 1919, p.5.

[75] TNA HLG47/341 Letter from the Housing Commissioner to Ely UDC Clerk, 10 March 1920. These stipulations were for layout only. A series of further demands were made for house plans.

particularly applied when changes in design and equipment meant homes would be more poorly provided than councils were comfortable with. A 1934 Fakenham example illustrated the detail. This involved 40 slum replacement homes, which the Ministry held were at '… a price higher than the Minister is now approving for houses of comparable types and sizes'. Amongst the long list of cost-cutting measures were some the Council resisted. These included omitting: dressers, saving £80; 100 gallon corrugated iron water cisterns and taps, saving £55; clothes posts, 7/6d; bedroom ventilator and fittings, 5/8d; one layer of tiles to chimney pots, 9/−; water service and taps to empty over wash boilers, £18/9/0d; and a four-inch drain from the well station to the nearest manhole, saving £2/17/6d. Then there were reduced provisions, like: grates to cost 10/− less each; using a two gallon rather than three-gallon WC cistern, 2/6d each; reducing gate prices by 1/6d each; using creosoted weather boarding rather than Lichgate Wood Shingler, £6/18/6d; and reducing contingencies per house from £5 to £2/10/0d.[76] All this over the design of dwellings, which is only part way there, as many problems arose during construction.

Chapters 5 and 6 highlighted rural concerns over building standards due to builder (in)action. Rural councils knew these shortcomings, as in Biggleswade, where red brick shortages led contractors to ignore agreed specifications and use white brick or rough cast instead, but they did not see builders as solely responsible.[77] Many councillors added material suppliers to the miscreants, with government inaction over ensuring sufficient materials also blamed. Even six years after the First World War, official reports called for the use of more traditional materials, like stone, because brick supplies were insufficient (National House Building Committee 1924, p.26). These shortages reappeared as later housing problems, as with dampness caused by porous brick walls in Walsingham, which Ministry officials blamed on the use of (inferior) local bricks owing to earlier general shortages.[78] That the use of substandard materials was known in the Ministry but not in the Council added weight to criticisms the government was a key contributor to deficits. In this regard, Ware RDC was far from alone in blaming shortcomings in council homes on the way '… the Government had cut down the specifications for the sake of economy'.[79]

This did not mean that 'economy' was undesirable. 'Good economy' was critical to rural councillors, as more expensive dwellings meant unaffordable rents. Hence, council leaders often asked for new homes without frills that '… are not pretentious, but they are well built and commodious'.[80] On this, there were mixed Ministry messages over layout plans. On the one hand, construction economies were required regularly, as in Ministry advice not to draw up bills of quantities for proposals so as

---

[76] NRO DC19/6/62 WRDCHCM 23 October 1934, p.55.

[77] BC&BG 12 November 1920, p.5.

[78] FakPost 24 January 1930, p.1; H&FP 2 September 1932, p.5.

[79] H&EO 19 January 1924, p.8.

[80] The quote was from the Ampthill Chair (W&DR 3 March 1928, p.3) but the sentiment was common, as in Erpingham (FakPost 23 September 1927, p.3).

to lower costs[81] or, more explicitly in times of economic turmoil like the early-1930s, when the Ministry told councils it '… could not approve plans which were not designed with due regard for the strictest principles of economy'.[82] This announcement drew attention to the Janus-head of the Ministry, for a short time before this communication the Ministry had asserted '… the importance of securing designs satisfactory in appearance and suitable to the locality', wanting the design, construction and repair of dwellings to match standards laid out centrally.[83] This instruction had legislative force, as councils had a duty under '… Section 38 of the Housing Act, 1930, to have regard to the beauty of the landscape or countryside and the other amenities of the locality' (MoH 1933a, pp.4–5), which meant employing an architect or seeking advice from advisory panels of the Council for the Preservation of Rural England (CPRE). Yet, when rural building expansion was expected under the 1938 Housing (Financial Provisions) Act, alarm was expressed over rural capacities to access (and pay for) qualified architectural assistance,[84] with the Ministry strengthening its architectural staff to assist local proposals. To promote better design, templates were also issued to councils.[85] Further, if designs were deemed unacceptable, direct intervention resulted, as in 1957 when Southam RDC was told to employ an architect rather than relying on its Sanitary Inspector for dwelling plans.[86]

As early as 1919, the Ministry supported construction using local materials, like stone, even if this meant more expense.[87] The added cost was revealed in periodic reports on house-building tenders, as with the 1931 Act, when prices ranged from £244 a house in the Isle of Axholme (Lindsey) to £341 for West Ward stone houses (Westmorland).[88] Extra allowance for using traditional materials was not formalised, being dependent on local enquiries,[89] until the 1949 Housing Act introduced a standard subsidy for such building, which was retained in the 1950s even when other subsidies were cut.[90] These payments were still subject to Ministry approval. Moreover, they were limited in scope, with few rural districts accessing them. Tucked within internal reports on this aid were references to their availability in

---

[81] NRO DC13/5/72 ERDCHCM 31 May 1926, p.2. Potentially, this made it difficult for builders to tender, although small rural builders often worked this way.

[82] This illustrative instruction was to Walsingham (*FakPost* 8 July 1932, p.5).

[83] TNA HLG48/379 Letter from J.C. Wrigley, MoH, to Walsingham RDC Clerk, despatched 11 February 1929.

[84] TNA HLG40/32 'Preservation of Amenities in the Building of New Houses', undated c1938.

[85] *NBC&BR* 18 December 1951, p.1; *WR&WSR* 25 December 1951, p.1.

[86] TNA HLG31/24 'Discussions with Local Authorities on Layouts, Tenders, Etc. Note on Meeting of 1 January 1957'.

[87] HCH 17 December 1919, Vol.123, col.396.

[88] TNA HLG40/16 'Housing (Rural Authorities) Act 1931. Advisory Committee Report', undated c1931, p.10.

[89] HCH 11 December 1947, Vol.445, col.223W.

[90] A £5 per year subsidy for houses built of stone was retained (TNA HLG71/2377 'Revised Housing Subsidies', undated c1955.)

areas like the Cotswolds '… to preserve the amenities of the district'.[91] Put simply, much of rural England (or Wales) was not regarded as sufficiently 'special' to merit these payments. Hence, for most of rural England building in traditional materials mirrored the inter-war practice, whereby '… the cottage styles recommended bore limited resemblance to any vernacular tradition' (Sherwood 1996, p.55; also Macdonald 2017, p.298). Not surprisingly, in the first four years of 1949 Act subsidies, just 1411 awards were made.[92] Over the same period, around 130,000 council houses were built in rural England and Wales.[93] Council-building that helped preserve the character of a locality, it seems, was merited for less than 1% of dwellings. Outside favoured areas, councils might encourage local inputs, but not always with success. In 1929, for example, Smallburgh wanted to use Norfolk hand-made tiles but was thwarted by high prices and supply lapses. Only one pair of cottages was finished with the tiles.[94]

Many rural councillors wanted more resources for design and layout. Although often restricted by scant revenues, and by an economic philosophy limiting public spending, many favoured quality-built, aesthetically pleasing homes. References in council minutes to inspections of new dwellings bear testament to this.[95] Also notable were reactions to medals for the best regional housing projects, lists of which reveal high percentages of rural entries and awards.[96] There was pride when an award was won, as when Braughing's Buntingford homes were deemed best in the Eastern Region in 1951,[97] and disappointment with failure, as with Biggleswade's loss by one vote on its Ickwell site.[98] Within what they saw as their capabilities, councils searched for better designs and layouts. This was indicated in different ways. Ampthill worked for many years with Professor Albert Richardson (UCL Architecture).[99] When county branches of the CPRE were formed, councils quickly

---

[91] TNA HLG101/748 Abolition of Housing Subsidies. 'Untitled document', undated c1955–1958. English RDCs benefiting from the subsidy included North Cotswold, Shepton Mallett, Cheltenham, Chapel-en-le-Firth, Tintwistle and Buxton (TNA HLG101/241 'Increased Subsidy for Houses Constructed to Preserve the Character of the Surroundings', undated file covers 1949–1961).

[92] HCH 22 March 1954, Vol.525, col.81W–82W.

[93] TNA MAF186/86 'Brief by R.J.E. Taylor for the Parliamentary Secretary', 14 September 1960.

[94] NRO DC22/2/11 SmRDCM 22 January 1929, p.308. Some 20 years later, Biggleswade wanted to render houses at Southill externally and colour-wash them cream to harmonise with other dwellings but decided to use light coloured facing bricks once the cost of colour-washing was known (BRO RDBwM1/20 BiRDCM 13 July 1949, p.154). However, as the County Planning Officer wanted colour-washing, the Council had to reverse its decision after the Ministry indicated it had omitted this provision when granting approval (BRO RDBwM1/20 BiRDCM 12 September 1949, p.226).

[95] For example, HRO RDC3/1/5 BrRDCM 3 December 1953, p.152.

[96] For example, TNA HLG36/31 CHAC Minute Book, 25 July 1950, pp.484–87.

[97] HRO RDC3/1/5 BrRDCM 5 June 1952, p.32.

[98] BRO RDBwM1/26 BiRDCM 16 February 1955, p.55.

[99] Not always without controversy, as some councillors were less committed to the designs he favoured; see WR&WSR 1 March 1960, p.2.

appointed representatives to them.[100] This drew more attention to the appearance of dwellings. One outcome was CPRE complaints about districts close to towns, which were held to be negatively influenced by 'urban-minded' councillors imposing inappropriate bye-laws on the countryside,[101] as with sanctioning dwellings from a set design that carried a 'council house stamp'.[102] Growing calls were made for authorities to respond positively to the architectural, artistic or historic value of properties.[103] Despite these efforts, there was discontent at council and Ministry levels over the appearance of dwellings, with Ministry technical officers holding '... that it is in the unsympathetic architectural handling of rural houses that the greater fault lies. The fact that many rural surveyors have been trained in urban offices may account for their bias towards urban type of houses'.[104] This offers one answer to a question raised at a 1948 Erpingham meeting, namely '... whether any action could be taken to relieve the monotony in design which enabled one to pinpoint Council houses in practically any part of the country'?[105]

A key to this dreariness was cost pressure. Ministry demands for reductions in the size and equipment of dwellings were common. Instructions regularly specified precise changes, like Biggleswade being told to omit fire places in second bedrooms and ensure joists and rafters were 14 inches apart.[106] Despite Ministry calls for good design (MoH 1937a, p.119; 1938, p.110), councils were pushed towards actions they deemed inconsistent with providing quality accommodation. Ministry requests for cheaper designs under the 1931 Act brought Walsingham frustrations to the forefront. Warnings were given that economy measures would soon make the new homes 'nothing more than slums', when the Council 'wanted to build houses, not hovels'.[107] This sentiment reared its head frequently as councils and the Ministry tussled over standards. Illustrative was tension over Battle RDC's 1949 rejection of Ministry instructions to use cheaper materials, which exposed Ministry frustration over this council's 'prejudice' for 'better than average' designs and inputs.[108] Over a longer time frame, terraced housing gave insight on councils acting against their preferences. Terraces favoured concentrated homes in fewer villages, which

---

[100] As with Hadham (HRO RDC6/1/6 HaRDCM 6 June 1929, p.221) and Buntingford (HRO RDC4/1/8 BuRDCM 12 September 1929, p.186) once the Hertfordshire branch was formed in 1929. In Norfolk the county branch came in 1933 but its focus was mostly on advertising, litter and hedgerow loss until after 1945, when it gave attention to council housing, so we see later engagement with rural councils like Erpingham (NRO DC13/5/20 ERDCM 26 July 1948, p.43).

[101] TNA HLG47/702 Letter from CPRE Secretary to J.C. Wrigley, MoH, 16 March 1936.

[102] As with Wayland RDC (*T&WT* 28 August 1937, p.10).

[103] HRO RDC3/1/1 BrRDCM 2 March 1939, p.403.

[104] TNA HLG37/47 RH1 'Notes on Scott Committee on Land Utilisation in Rural Areas', undated c1943, p.3.

[105] NRO DC13/5/20 ERDCM 28 June 1948, p.34.

[106] BRO RDBwM1/11 BiRDCM 31 August 1932.

[107] *FakPost* 8 July 1932, p.5.

[108] TNA HLG101/213 'Memo to Mr. Bilbey from Terry Powell, Regional Architect, on Battle RDC', 30 September 1949.

countered policies to build in all parishes. Yet, by 1937, Braughing planned to build in blocks of six,[109] despite knowing terraces were not liked by tenants, who wanted detached or semi-detached dwellings.[110] But Ministry demands to save money pushed councils towards terraces, although some resisted, as with Romney Marsh RDC, even in the war years.[111] After 1945, restrictions on resources, then an emphasis on economising, continued to impact on housing styles. As early as 1948, for example, Smallburgh opposed a Ministry proposal to build terraces, citing their urban character, their long, narrow gardens and the crowding of families in small areas.[112] When the North Mymms Ratepayers' Association protested against proposed terraces, Hatfield responded that blocks were necessary to meet Ministry cost guidelines.[113] This dislike of terraces extended to many residents, although they did not always receive a sympathetic hearing from councillors. Thus, when Brookmans Park inhabitants complained over Hatfield's proposed sandwiching of terraces between detached and semi-detached homes, they were accused of 'inverted snobbery', given private jerry-builders had done their worst in the area.[114] This exasperation mimicked Ministry responses to the CPRE two decades earlier: '... The Society for the Preservation of Rural England have sometimes placed picturesqueness above the health of the occupiers and many rural councillors and owners eagerly grasp all opportunities for delays following representations from this and other societies'.[115] Such tensions would grow over the decades as councils reacted to housing need while inhabitants (including councillors) found new developments 'too urban' (e.g. Buller and Lowe 1982; Lowe et al. 1995). Such tension over terraced housing continued into the 1960s.[116] Capturing friction from competing demands, in 1959 debates in Swaffham RDC, the point was made, on one side, that: 'We build our nasty, terrible little jerry-built houses all over the place and they are potential slums', with the counter claim that: 'We build houses to try and suit the pockets of the people who are going to live in them. We are trying to give the working-class people in this area a good, modern house at a reasonable cost'.[117]

Adding to the angst, rural councils felt hemmed-in by an inability to influence private building styles. This was particularly apparent in the 1930s, as in Blofield RDC, which was worried about jerry-building and insufficient council control over standards. This led to the claim that: 'Houses were undoubtedly being put up which

---

[109] B&NEHG 2 July 1937, p.4.

[110] TNA HLG37/48 Rural Housing Sub-Committee. 'National Federation of Women's Institutes Evidence', October 1942.

[111] TNA HLG40/27 Draft Memo '3000 Agricultural Cottages', undated c1943.

[112] NRO DC22/2/48 SmRDCHCM 30 March 1948, p.3399; 22 June 1948, p.3501.

[113] H&PBG 24 June 1949, p.1.

[114] H&PBG 20 February 1953, p.1.

[115] TNA HLG37/43 'Investigation by General Inspectors 1934', undated c1936.

[116] Illustrative reports on Biggleswade include: BC&BG 1 March 1957, p.12; 22 July 1960, p.15; 28 October 1960, p.14; 17 February 1961, p.14; BRO RDBwM1/35 BiRDCHECM 13 May 1964, p.810.

[117] T&WT 23 January 1959, p.1.

would not be very satisfactory in the fairly near future'.[118] This was seen as a recent problem, arising when 'outside builders arrived'. The claim matched alarm over the spread of inferior inter-war rural building to meet urban recreational demands (Gayler 1970; Hardy and Ward 1984). More widely, 'tasteless and dreary' were descriptions of privately owned suburban and semi-suburban homes of the 1930s (MoH Town and Country Planning Advisory Committee 1938, p.5), which corresponded with Blofield's disquiet over inadequate controls. Yet, the fact homes for private-owners were suspect, and so merited scrutiny, did not absolve councils from the accusation their own homes were 'ugly'.[119] Organisations with an interest in rural property, such as the Land Agents' Society, noted the impoverishing impact of cost-cutting on the appearance and content of rural council homes (MoH 1937b, p.28). These perturbations did not go away after 1945. In the mid-1950s, for instance, Biggleswade councillors complained that new RDC dwellings at Caldecote were an'... absolute eyesore which is going to remain for a life-time'. Words like 'slums' and 'an absolute disgrace' decorated debate on these mid-1950s homes.[120] Similar complaints were made about Northill's new terraced cottages, which were equated with 'barracks or a huge barn'.[121] Such complaints grew as more slimmed down dwellings were constructed as part of early-1950s Ministry impositions. But this was a step down a slope rather than an end-point. Tracing changes in single councils reveals pressure from the Ministry to put ever more homes on sites, so breaking the long-held rule of thumb of eight an acre. Complaints arrived from parish councils that densities were not in keeping with villages, with a sense of the changes occurring seen when a 1965 project agreed a density reduction to 15 an acre.[122] The introduction of cost-yardsticks intensified pressures, with contractors proposing higher densities in order to dip under yardstick targets.[123]

In some cases, startlingly so for South Oxfordshire, where Larkin (1979, p.75) found 10% of permanent dwellings were caravans, shortages saw more households seeking this accommodation. In the investigated districts, caravans were much less significant. Smallburgh had the most regular council discussions on them, in part because it sought to limit their visual and other impacts, and in the early-1930s experienced unwelcome problems with unofficial occupation of beach huts and chalets at Bacton and Sloley.[124] Smallburgh saw residential caravans rise from 44 to 92 between 1961 and 1970, which meant they comprised around 1% of the residential stock at the end of the decade. For the Council, the bigger challenge came from holiday caravans and chalets, given their combined number was 10 times greater

---

[118] *NM&PWJ* 9 March 1935, p.7.

[119] HCH 10 February 1937, Vol.320, col.470–71; TNA HLG37/45 Rural Housing Sub-Committee. 'County Councils' Association Submission', undated c1937.

[120] *BC&BG* 3 June 1955, p.6.

[121] *WR&WSR* 11 October 1955, p.14.

[122] *BC&BG* 2 June 1961, p.17; 25 January 1963, p.13; 23 April 1965, p.18.

[123] TNA HLG118/945 Letter from National Federation of Building Trades' Employers Director to MHLG Permanent Secretary, 15 November 1968.

[124] *T&WT* 28 November 1931, p.7; 26 December 1931, p.7; *NWP&ENS* 10 June 1932, p.1.

than residential caravans (Smallburgh Rural District Council 1962, p.25; 1971, p.29). As for the usage of holiday lets for winter residences, numbers were not clear. The practice surfaced occasionally in council minutes, as with complaints over Erpingham using nine East Runton caravans for this purpose in 1956.[125] Walsingham was also troubled by the possibility, although its part of the north Norfolk coast was less pressured by caravan site demands as so much land was owned by landed estates like Holkham (Wade-Martins and Williamson 2008, p.113). Even so, when a residential licence renewal application for stationary caravans was made in 1957, Walsingham instructed occupants to move elsewhere, as '… the Council were most concerned at the continued practice of caravans being used as permanent accommodation'.[126] This contrasted with South Oxfordshire, where caravans were integral to council housing policy. Rather than agitation over residential use, substantive concerns focused on landscape impacts, especially for caravan concentrations close to the coast. After 1945, there were intense housing shortages but, as the 1950s progressed, councils sought to eliminate or upgrade inter-war coastal huts, shacks and caravan sites. Although the economic benefits of tourism were welcomed, coastal holiday camps and caravan parks were resisted.[127] That councils were less effective in mitigating these intrusions was captured by Yaxley (1977, p.119), who described the 1970s 'horrors' of brash estates, gaggles of bungalows and regiments of caravans on the coast from Sheringham to Yarmouth (viz. all coastal Smallburgh). Adding to landscape pressure was house-building for private-owners, which councillors saw as neglecting inland sites.[128] Such tendencies point to an uneven within district distribution of house-building.

7.3   Securing Building Sites

The literature on housing construction in cities provides regular messages that acquiring housing sites was difficult (e.g. Muchnick 1970; Sutcliffe and Smith 1974; Dale 1980). This issue was less central to the private sector, as builders were drawn to low-cost suburban sites close to arterial roads (Jackson 1973; Pugh 2008, p.68). City councils, by contrast, met the joint force of construction firms resisting council incursions beyond their territories (e.g. Yelling 1992, p.103), alongside Conservative Party fears that council tenants would weaken their electoral prospects in the shires (Sutcliffe and Smith 1974, p.231; Young and Kramer 1978).[129] In

---

[125] *NNN* 25 May 1956, p.3.

[126] *D&FT* 18 April 1957, p.5.

[127] As in Erpingham (*NNN* 9 January 1953, p.1; 20 March 1964, p.1), Smallburgh (*NNN* 5 November 1954, p.1; *NorfChron* 25 February 1955, p.6) and Walsingham (see text).

[128] Examples from the three Norfolk districts at different times are: NRO DC19/6/11 WRDCM 16 May 1923, p.20; *EDP* 6 June 1935, p.7; *NNN* 3 April 1964, p.3.

[129] This lay behind the Conservative government ignoring the Royal Commission on Local Government in England (1969) by bringing in the boundaries of metropolitan areas, so conurba-

combination, this makes Newton's (1976, p.201) evaluation of Birmingham under-standable: 'What appears to have determined the city's house-building rate more than anything else was the availability of large sites for big housing projects'. Such statements might leave the impression rural sites were 'easy' to come by. This was not the case.

One reason was the difficulty of building on farmland. Even before the Second World War raised the priority of food production, councils could need permission from the Board of Agriculture before land was transferred from farm usage.[130] Such inter-war interventions paled beside those after 1939, when Ministry officials agreed farmland protection made acquiring rural sites difficult.[131] These complications should not be belittled. It was regularly reported that housing needs in villages could not be met because land was not available, with building often shifted to villages with sites at hand.[132] This might be because landowners did not want to sell,[133] or if

---

tions were 'given over' to Labour, while the Conservatives dominated non-metropolitan districts. This led to accusations of gerrymandering (Jennings 1977, p.24; Sharpe 1978), with Dunleavy (1980) estimating that, under then current voting patterns, more than three-quarters of English and Welsh people lived in areas that would see no change in political party control (58% coming under the Conservatives and 20% under Labour). Conservative inclinations to promote social segregation for political purposes were also evident in high council dwelling allocations to cities, '... while reductions were made for those areas where private enterprise builders were undertaking a large house-building programme' (MHLG 1956, p.9).

[130] As with acquiring land at Wiveton (NRO DC19/6/8 WRDCM 15 October 1919, p.9) and using common land (NRO DC13/5/16 ERDCM 8 February 1926, p.186).

[131] TNA HLG79/5 'Note from H. Heady to Mr. Beaufoy', 19 October 1945.

[132] In Erpingham sites were an early problem in Holt, Mundesley and Runton (FakPost 20 February 1920, p.2; 3 September 1920, p.7; 28 August 1925, p.3), as for Little Heath and Essendon in Hatfield (HRO RDC7/1/9 HtRDCM 25 September 1924, p.39; HA&SAT 28 July 1933, p.11) and Gravenhurst in Ampthill (W&DR 17 July 1926, p.1), while Smallburgh's complaints to North Walsham over too many Town applicants for its homes generated the response North Walsham had no land for building (YarmInd 5 November 1927, p.2). Parliamentary questions reveal many RDCs had difficulties securing sites, even with strong Ministry support. Examples from the late-1940s include Downham, Basford, Calne and Chippenham, and Clitheroe (HCH 25 February 1947, Vol.433, col.364W–65W; HCH 22 May 1947, Vol.437, col.313W; HCH 11 December 1947, Vol.445, col.1167–68; HCH 15 December 1949, Vol.470, col.304W). Instances of building reloca-tions included shifting Erpingham homes from Aylmerton to Cley (HMC&WP 9 July 1926, p.5; NRO DC13/5/73 ERDCHCM 27 March 1933, p.64) and from Salthouse to Southrepps (HMC&WP 15 January 1926, p.4). In Smallburgh failure to build or shifting venues were common, as at Sutton and East Runton (NRO DC22/2/10 SmRDCM 11 January 1927, p.202; T&WT 16 April 1932, p.7), then two years later at Sutton rather than Stalham (NRO DC22/2/11 SmRDCM 22 January 1929, p.307). Newspapers reported the same on a wider front, as in Biggleswade (Old Warden to Shefford, BC&BG 20 January 1922, p.5) and Aylsham and Loddon RDCs (FakPost 17 June 1927, p.4; T&WT 1 July 1933, p.2). These are a few of many examples. The pattern persisted after 1945.

[133] Examples across the decades include: Hatfield (HRO RDC7/1/8 HtRDCM 16 August 1923, p.351); Braughing (H&EO 5 September 1936, p.10; HRO RDC3/1/21 BrRDCHCM 21 December 1971, p.8940); Erpingham (NRO DC13/5/75 ERDCHCM 18 September 1945, p.19a); Ampthill (BRO RDAM1/26 ARDCHPBuCM 17 December 1970, p.392); and, Biggleswade (BRO RDBwM1/45 BiRDCHCM 11 July 1973).

asking prices rose when owners knew the land was for housing.[134] With Ministerial approval, councils could compulsorily purchase, but, like their reluctance to close unfit dwellings, they hesitated when an owner's capital was in property; although, this was no reason for mitigation in the Ministry's mind (MoH 1933b, p.9).[135] Taking their role as guardians of the (local) public purse seriously, when building under the 1919 Act ended and the national government instructed councils to sell-off unused land bought for the Act,[136] RDCs were second only to county councils in having used most of the land they had acquired (county boroughs and boroughs had the lowest usage).[137] When the 1923 Act was passed, the government wanted to help private builders by making the remaining 1919 Act land available to them.[138] Rural councils again responded, selling proportionately more land than the national average.[139] Overall, this was creditworthy, since demand for land amongst private buyers was often weak. In Walsingham, attempts to sell, even in Fakenham, found no takers. Ampthill first looked to sell back to original owners and Smallburgh explored parish council purchases, before Ampthill shifted to public auctions when original owners were not interested, while both Smallburgh and Walsingham drifted towards finding private builders.[140] A few months later, the issue was irrelevant. Before Biggleswade Town could secure a definitive response from the Ministry over whether it could let 1919 Act land for market gardening, the 1924 Act brought new instructions to build on unsold sites (MoH 1924b, p.18). Previously sold sites were now re-acquired.[141] Weak demand from private builders reduced sales potential but problems securing sites meant councils built on what they could get.

---

[134] As in Smallburgh (NRO DC22/2/45 SmRDCHCM 29 June 1920; *NWP&ENS* 10 August 1928, p.11), Sheringham (*FakPost* 12 October 1928, p.5), Ampthill (BRO RDAR8/11 ARDCMOHar 1930, p.12), Biggleswade Town (TNA HLG49/952 Letter from Biggleswade UDC Clerk to MoH Secretary, 31 December 1935) and Biggleswade (BRO RDBwM1/17 BiRDCM 26 March 1947, p.337).

[135] Often, this message was implicit, indicated by action rather than words, but occasionally, it was articulated explicitly, as in discussion at Smallburgh (*NWP&ENS* 23 January 1931, p.5).

[136] TNA HLG68/29 'Closing Down of Addison Scheme', 10 August 1922.

[137] RDCs had used 49.3% of the land they had acquired when the government undertook a survey in 1923, which was 10% above the England and Wales average (TNA HLG48/687 Letter to Edgar Harper, Valuation Offices, from E.R. Forber, 13 June 1923).

[138] TNA HLG68/29 'Closing Down of Addison Scheme', 10 August 1922.

[139] RDCs had sold 15.1% of the area bought by the time of the government survey. This placed them ahead of the 11.2% national average (TNA HLG48/687 Letter to Edgar Harper, Valuation Offices, from E.R. Forber, 13 June 1923).

[140] On Walsingham NRO DC19/6/9 WRDCM 5 October 1921, p.232; NRO DC19/6/11 WRDCM 17 October 1923, p.69 in binding; on Ampthill *W&DR* 4 February 1922, p.1; on Smallburgh NRO DC22/2/45 SmRDCHCM 23 May 1922, where Ludham Parish Council indicated an inability to buy but wanted the land for housing, saying it would reconsider if the RDC must sell (the RDC decided to retain, despite having two offers on the land), and *NWP&ENS* 26 October 1922, p.5.

[141] *BC&BG* 21 July 1922, p.3; 19 January 1923, p.6; *NBC* 23 February 1923, p.7; BRO UDBwM1/7 BiUDCM 18 September 1923, p.3; 16 September 1924, p.324; 18 November 1924, p.340.

Problems getting sites did not go away. Even after the end of hostilities in 1945, War Agricultural Executive Committee approval was needed for land with food production potential. Objections on agricultural grounds became common, both for farmland and allotments.[142] This constraint extended into the 1950s, even though a less rigid interpretation accepted housing on acreages with inferior yields in 1947.[143] Although this measure was promoted by Whitehall,[144] the Cabinet worried over farmland losses.[145] Hence, in the 1950s building boom, ministers '... urged local authorities to make use of every practicable alternative to agricultural land'.[146] This created friction locally, when site acquisitions were turned down on agricultural grounds. The frustration caused was captured by the 1958 comments of Ampthill's Clerk: 'If you only sneeze on a bit of agricultural land there is an objection. It is so sacrosanct today you must not touch a piece of agricultural land'.[147] The strength of this sentiment might have varied with land quality, but its potency was real. As early as 1913, for instance, government inspectors were reporting that practically all available land in Biggleswade was under market gardening.[148] Decades later, when the government supported extending compulsory acquisition,[149] even prioritised areas like Hatfield had difficulties getting sites in country neighbourhoods, while Smallburgh looked to relocate new houses to parishes with less land in wheat production.[150] Such effects were intensified by war and after-war pressures; yet, even by the early-1960s, Hatfield had only one compulsory land purchase for dwellings outside Old Hatfield.[151]

Site problems were not limited to council-building. In Biggleswade, for example, Arlesey village had only seven private homes built in the 10 years after 1945

---

[142] Examples included: Ampthill (*WR&WSR* 30 October 1945, p.1; BRO RDAM2/22 ARDCHCM 22 November 1956); Biggleswade (BRO RDBwM1/15 BiRDCM 28 March 1945, p.431; BRO RDBwM1/23 BiRDCM 16 April 1952, p.40); Braughing (TNA HLG79/5 'Note from T. Williams, MAF, to L. Silkin, MT&CP, 9 November 1945); Erpingham (*NM&PWJ* 25 October 1947, p.3); Sandy (*WR&WSR* 28 September 1954, p.9); and, Smallburgh (TNA MAF147/6 'Agricultural Housing. Smallburgh RDC', file covers 1946–1953).

[143] TNA HLG71/580 'Notes of a Meeting with the Ministry of Agriculture', 13 February 1947.

[144] TNA HLG71/582 'Memo on Rural Planning for First Discussion with Ministry of Agriculture, Local Authority Associations and Town Planning Institute', 13 December 1948; TNA HLG52/1228 'Memo to Agricultural Land Service', undated c1948–49.

[145] TNA CAB132/11 15 July 1949, p.5.

[146] HCH 24 March 1953, Vol.513, col.636.

[147] *WR&WSR* 14 January 1958, p.15.

[148] TNA HLG1/845 'Report of Inquiry by Mr. Harry Stewart', 7 July 1913. The importance of market gardening to Biggleswade is captured in various accounts (e.g. Chambers 1917; Beavington 1975). Kennett (1978, p.118) claimed so little agricultural land was taken for housing in Bedfordshire that the M1 motorway and Luton Airport took more.

[149] HCH 8 June 1943, Vol.390, col.530.

[150] HRO RDC7/9/1 HtRDCM 16 April 1943, p.30; *NNN* 2 September 1949, p.1.

[151] HRO RDC7/66/1 'Hatfield Particulars of Compulsory Purchase Orders Made', undated c1962.

owing to site difficulties.[152] This problem extended even to the outskirts of large towns, as with St Albans, where the 17 firms of the St Albans Allied Builders Ltd. appealed against St Albans RDC's refusal to allow development on a site owing to agricultural and green belt objections. A key claim of the builders was that there were only three plots available for housing in the district for 1962.[153] Planning strictures were not the only limitation. Around Bishop's Stortford the private sector created the shortage, with two builders having a near monopoly on ownership of potential sites, on which they only built themselves (whether privately or for councils).[154]

Yet the shift in national priorities onto slum clearance in the late-1950s favoured the private market. For one, unfavourable financial and regulatory regimes reduced council-building. For another, there were challenges acquiring sites for slum clearance. Difficulties arose when councils looked to rehouse occupants before demolishing unfit dwellings. With relatively small housing stocks, rural councils had few options unless they acquired new sites. This generated situations like that in Biggleswade, where 1963 demolition orders could not be acted on for 26 unoccupied units as they were in the middle of terraces, and the terraces could not go because no local building sites (or council homes) were available for relocations.[155] Site difficulties for rural slum clearance plagued councils.[156] The RDCA drew the Ministry's attention to associated problems, as with this submission in 1959–1960: 'The operation of slum clearance arrangements in rural areas will create some very ugly gaps in village streets. Some of the vacant sites will be small or of irregular shape and some will be in the ownership of more than one person'.[157] Added to which, infill sites might involve several conveyances, with an architect having to change elevations to blend with existing homes, whereas 'peripheral' sites usually required one conveyance with contractors preferring all houses on one site (Henson 1957, p.106).

Although possibilities were restricted, most rural councils did not want to forego potential housing gains, so council-owned land was often made available to private builders. When this occurred in the 1920s, it was at times under sufferance. Yet, even when council-building was a national priority, some explored site sales to private builders. In the late-1940s, this arose partly from councils seeking to encourage private investment at a time when their building volumes were restricted.[158] So,

---

[152] *BC&BG* 11 February 1955, p.7.

[153] *Herts Advertiser* 24 February 1961, p.1.

[154] *H&EO* 8 January 1954, p.1.

[155] *BC&BG* 24 May 1963, p.9.

[156] Examples of difficulties securing sites included: Buntingford (HRO RDC4/1/8 BuRDCM 24 March 1931, p.399), Loddon RDC (*T&WT* 1 July 1933, p.2) and Smallburgh (NRO DC22/2/46 SmRDCHCM 5 February 1935, p.251).

[157] TNA HLG37/128 'Evidence of the Rural District Councils' Association 1959–60', p.10.

[158] There were references to limits on building for private-owners as 'going against the grain'. Councils protesting over restrictions included: Biggleswade (BRO RDBwM1/18 BiRDCM 8 October 1947, pp.502–03), Erpingham (*NM&PWJ* 7 June 1947, p.5; NRO DC13/5/21 ERDCM 12

when private-owner quotas could be raised to 50% of construction totals, many rural councils went straight to the maximum.[159] Selling plots for private homes accompanied this step.[160] Sites for private housing nevertheless remained a challenge into the 1960s, despite government claims of no shortages.[161] Processes offering a better supply of sites had existed for some time,[162] with combined requirements for private and public building formalised in 1968 when local planning authorities were instructed to ensure future land supplies (DoE 1970).[163] Visible signs of improvement came quickly, with recorded availability at then current building rates of 5¼ years for Hertfordshire and 6½ years for south Bedfordshire.[164] Other initiatives, with a longer impact, included pressure to re-use derelict land. This received scant attention in Parliament before 1964. Yet, over 1964–1971, 20,471 acres were reclaimed or landscaped in England, with the total rising above the annual average of 2559 acres to reach 4792 in 1972. Over the same period, 36,600 acres of farmland

December 1949, para.148), Hatfield (HRO RDC7/1/14 HtRDCM6 June 1950, p.15), Sandy (BRO UDSM1/3 SaUDCM 19 December 1949, p.617) and Smallburgh (NRO DC22/2/49 SmRDCHCM 8 November 1949, p.3960). The generality of this view was demonstrated by protests elsewhere, as at St Faith's and Aylsham RDC (*NNN* 18 November 1949, p.5), Watford RDC (HRO RDC7/9/1 HtRDCM 10 January 1950, p.i1000) and Wayland RDC (*T&WT* 30 March 1951, p.1).

[159] As in Ampthill Town (BRO UDA9/2 AUDCHBCM 14 February 1952, pp.133–34), Braughing (HRO RDC3/1/4 BrRDCM 6 December 1951, p.373) and Hatfield (HRO RDC7/1/15 HtRDCM 4 December 1951, p.214). The sentiment was not universal, with Ampthill not fixing a quota (*WR&WSR* 25 December 1951, p.1) and non-local private applications questioned in Erpingham (*NNN* 2 May 1952, p.1).

[160] One example was Biggleswade (BRO RDBwM1/23 BiRDCM 19 March 1952, p.5; 9 July 1952, p.127), which by 1954 was advertising plots for sale (BRO RDBwM1/25 BiRDCM 1 September 1954, p.217). Sales to encourage private building also occurred in Braughing (HRO RDC3/1/5 BrRDCM 4 September 1952, p.48), Ampthill (BRO RDAM2/22 ARDCHCM 23 July 1953) and Biggleswade Town (*NBC&BR* 8 September 1953, p.7). Council and newspaper sources suggest little activity of this kind in Norfolk, where private demand was less intense. The first record I found of this being considered in Walsingham led to a decision not to sell, as the land might be needed in the future (NRO DC19/6/68 WRDCHCM 14 October 1958, p.103), although sales were later agreed in Swaffham RDC (*T&WT* 20 February 1959, p.1) and Smallburgh (NRO DC22/2/27 SmRDCM 22 November 1960, pp.818–819). Demand for private homes was not the only consideration, with Biggleswade Town reversing its decision to sell (*BC&BG* 4 December 1959, p.21) and with reluctance and opposition in Wells-next-the-Sea and Erpingham on account of site shortages for council-building (*D&FT* 5 August 1960, p.1; *NNN* 30 March 1961, p.4).

[161] As reported for Norfolk and Suffolk by Keith Joseph (*D&FT* 10 March 1961, p.13). Keith Joseph's assertion was accompanied by statements supporting constraint on urban sprawl (HCH 20 November 1959, Vol.613, col.1559–67), although he argued land was needed beyond green belts and within towns (HCH 28 June 1960, Vol.624, col.104W–05W; 22 November 1962, Vol.667, col.1396), leading to an examination of green belt boundaries (TNA CAB129/110 C(62)145 'Housing', 2 October 1962), followed by selective release of green belt land (TNA T224/711 'Memo from Keith Joseph to the PM', 13 January 1964).

[162] As with Circular 24/50 asking for forward planning on land for three years (MoH 1950b).

[163] TNA CAB129/123 C(65)151 'Housing Programme 1965–70', 12 November 1965; HCH 20 February 1968, Vol.759, col.61W.

[164] TNA HLG150/5 'Land Commission Reports on Land Availability Situation', November 1968.

were lost to 'urban uses',[165] which was compensated somewhat as cleaned derelict land had a minor housing impact at this time, with most going for open space or agriculture.[166]

All that noted, there was periodicity in site difficulties. One element was the willingness of councils to act decisively. It was notable that compulsory purchases were more common shortly after both world wars,[167] when housing policy had particular significance for the public and for political party manifestos (Social Market Foundation 2013).[168] The real surge in compulsory orders came when slum clearance was prioritised, when governments supported their use to remove unfit dwellings with no compensation if dwellings were 'unfit'.[169] Thus, compared to 204 local government orders in the first year of the 1919 Act, there were 296 under the 1930 Act in 1934–1935, of which 251 were confirmed by the Ministry. A total of 1661 orders had been confirmed by March 1938, despite slow progress until 1934 (MoH 1935, p.151; 1938, p.99). How far rural districts contributed to these totals is unclear. Blair's (1972) investigation of farmland loss in Essex concluded that little use was made of compulsory purchase, with cases largely focused on specific parts of urban fringes. Intensity also varied over time, as in Hatfield, where only three compulsory land purchases were recorded between 1945 and the early-1960s; yet there were seven in 1965, followed by eight in 1966.[170] This, of course, was a district experiencing rapid expansion (Table 4.7). But it was also a district that had reduced growth in the 1960s, when these purchases occurred. Notably, many acquisitions were of small plots, with council minutes indicating a continuous search for sites into the 1970s, of a kind whereby '… many of our schemes must be classified as the scrapings of the bottom of the barrel, reflecting that our special problems appear to be appreciated by us and by us alone'.[171] Even so, compulsion was limited compared to open market purchases, suggesting a

---

[165] HCH 28 March 1973, Vol.853, col.329W.

[166] HCH 31 July 1974, Vol.878, col.306W.

[167] After 1945, the government supported compulsory purchase for site acquisition, but a court ruling made public hearings necessary if the owner objected (TNA HLG31/13 HI46/46 'Compulsory Purchase Orders for Land', undated c1946).

[168] Under the 1919 Act, compulsory orders were numerically small but large compared with the past (MoH 1921, pp.65–66).

[169] As expressed by housing ministers (e.g. HCH 15 November 1934, Vol.293, col.2127; HCH 13 December 1955, Vol.547, col.1007). The general rule was to offer only site value as compensation for demolished dwellings, although councils were empowered to make payments if demolished or closed dwellings had been well maintained despite their defects (MHLG 1959, p.55). After 1957, full market value was allowed if properties had been owned for less than 15 years (MHLG 1968, p.10).

[170] HRO RDC7/66/1 'Hatfield Particulars of Compulsory Purchase Orders', undated c1962; HRO RDC7/29/1 'Hatfield Register of Loan Sanctions', undated c1973.

[171] HRO RDC7/1/51 HtRDCH&TPCM 6 June 1972, p.64.

wider applicability of Blair's conclusion that councils believed compulsory orders raised prices.[172]

Even when sites were offered for free, they might be unsatisfactory or have unacceptable conditions attached.[173] Alternatively, physicality might make propositions expensive. One example was Udimore in Battle RDC, which sat in characteristic Weald territory of ridges and steep slopes. Here, Ministry policies encouraged feelings of discrimination:

> My Council was very disappointed that under the recent Housing Act further subsidies are granted to towns where the cost of land is very exceptional, but no extra subsidy is granted in the country, where the Council has to provide water and sewerage and make excavations in steep slopes in order to build the houses at all.[174]

The Ministry acknowledged that rural site acquisition raised 'special difficulties', with increased administrative loads arising from dispersed sites.[175] Particular problems arose when the Ministry pressed for larger contracts for builders, which, if spread over multiple sites, meant all plots had to be acquired before work commenced, even though '… protracted negotiations are often necessary before conveyances can be completed'.[176] Not surprisingly, there were calls for streamlined processes (MoH 1944a, p.40). This was not easy to achieve, especially after land-use planning procedures tightened. This applied even before the 1947 Town and Country Planning Act came into force.[177] Illustrative were the verdicts of the Ministry's regional planning officer on Biggleswade's proposed 1945 sites. Objections included agricultural impacts (Arlesey, Potton and Stotfold), bad drainage (Hatch), ribbon development (Henlow), road improvements (Langford) and isolation from a main settlement (Edworth and Wrestlingworth). The list could have been longer, but the Air Ministry withdrew its objections to Ickwell and Everton.[178] Such challenges often saw councils pushed towards larger sites as no smaller ones

---

[172] As reported for Biggleswade Town (*NBC&BR* 23 October 1951, p.2).

[173] Biggleswade RDC (1931) reported no site difficulties in 1930, but in 1929 it did not accept a seller's conditions for a Henlow site, had an Arlesey owner refusing to sell site frontage onto the road and another asking an unacceptabe price, while the District Valuer would not agree a price for any Blunham site (BRO RDBwM1/10 BiRDCM 17 April 1929; 15 May 1929). By 1932, substantial difficulties existed over sites at Campton, Meppershall, Mogerhanger and Potton (BRO RDBwM1/11 BiRDCM 12 April 1932; 8 June 1932; 6 July 1932; 31 August 1932; 28 September 1932; 26 October 1932; 23 November 1932).

[174] TNA HLG101/213 Letter from Battle RDC Clerk to MoH Secretary, 7 September 1949.

[175] TNA HLG37/50 'RDCA Submission on Rural Housing', undated c1943.

[176] TNA HLG40/19 'Report on the Possibility of Cooperative Action by Local Authorities in the Norfolk and East Suffolk Areas', undated c1931.

[177] The Ministry warned councils to consult planning authorities (and the MAF) for all site proposals as early as 1943 (e.g. HRO RDC3/2/2 BrRDCPHHCM 18 November 1943, p.629). An increase in site rejections followed, as exemplified by the Ministry's Cambridge region (TNA HLG40/56 Letter to J.H. Hare MP from L.J. Edwards, MoH, 16 April 1946). When Biggleswade had five sites rejected by County planners, it decided to have a County officer at future site inspections (*NBC&BR* 4 March 1947, p.4).

[178] BRO RDBwM1/15 BiRDCM 3 January 1945, p.377.

were available. But Ministry inquisitions were fuelled by a rule that any purchased land surplus to immediate requirements had to be used within 10 years, which might work in larger villages but created difficulties in smaller places.[179] Hardly surprisingly, when sites were difficult to find, suboptimal locations were proposed, with objections following.[180] Over time, pressure on councils grew because land prices were rising, with private developers better able to cover price inflation, given tight Ministry overview of costs. As happened at Shillington (Ampthill), sites that councils spurned as too pricey were snapped up by private developers, leaving councils with more problems responding to housing pressure.[181] By 1970, price surges in Walsingham led to a retraction of aspirations, with future development largely restricted to council-owned sites.[182] This was not a strategy that encouraged positive responses to housing need, for the 1970–1974 government soon instructed councils to dispose of surplus land to private builders.[183] This contributed to sharp falls in council-building after 1970 (Fig. 6.2); although, this was not the only cause. As the 1972 Ampthill Surveyor's report summarised:

> In the early post-war years land was cheap and readily available and sufficient was acquired to meet the requirements of most of the parishes for a long period. The stock of land held by the Council is now rapidly diminishing and in many of the parishes has been fully used ... Land values have risen to an unprecedented rate during the past 12 months and it would appear that the overall cost of a dwelling will have doubled over a very short period.[184]

There are many aspects to site acquisition that would add more flesh to the storyline above, but core messages would not change. What is worth emphasising is the way site difficulties not only created delay, but also redirected and even thwarted projects. The significance of delay has been touched on before, as regards Ministry intervention, labour and material shortages, water and sewer supply deficiencies, and builder (in)action. A range of causes created delays over sites, including personal interventions. In 1945, for instance, a minister intervened over a proposed development in Buntingford, asserting the site was a bad choice. Investigation led to embarrassment, as abandoning the site was out of the question, given the Ministry had already approved buying two of its portions, while the third was compulsorily

---

[179] Examples from the mid-1930s included: HRO RDC4/1/9 BuRDCM 14 June 1934, p.92; NRO DC19/6/62 WRDCHCM 11 December 1934, p.68; TNA HLG49/952 Letter from Biggleswade UDC Clerk to MoH Secretary, 31 December 1935; Letter from J.M.K. Hawton, MoH, to Biggleswade UDC Clerk, 9 January 1936.

[180] Two examples from 1937 in Smallburgh were Witton on isolation grounds (*YarmInd* 13 March 1937, p.9) and Stalham as the site overlooked private housing (*T&WT* 31 July 1937, p.9). Other districts had similar experiences. In Braughing, site proposals were rejected on the grounds of isolation at Westmill, dampness alongside bad smells from a brook at Furneux Pelham (HRO RDC3/2/2 BrRDCPHHCM 21 September 1944, pp.691–692; 19 October 1944, p.698), road and pavement deficiencies at Much Hadham (*H&EO* 15 May 1959, p.7) and retention of open space at Buntingford (HRO RDC3/1/21 BrRDCHCM 4 April 1972, p.8621).

[181] BRO RDAM1/26 ARDCHPBuCM 17 December 1970, p.392.

[182] NRO DC19/6/32 WRDCM 20 May 1970.

[183] HCH 8 April 1971, Vol.815, col.311W; HCH 28 July 1971, Vol.822, col.104W.

[184] BRO RDAM1/28 ARDCHPBuCM 14 June 1972, p.9.

purchased with only the price to be determined. Nevertheless, pressure was exerted and Braughing scaled back the proposed development, resulting in fewer new homes.[185] This example reached resolution relatively quickly but prolonged negotiations, sometimes involving site changes, could extend over many months. Such delays compounded the impact of other slowdowns (Chaps. 5 and 6). Given the rapidity with which governments changed policy emphasis, funding arrangements and regulations, rural council ambitions were often thwarted as projects did not start soon enough. We see this in disappointment when councils were told to cut building volumes or when national subsidy changes forced programme reductions (including ending payments early). Delays had an enduring impact. They were more than short-term slow-downs. National politicians were well aware that building programmes commonly had a sluggish start or were likely to be squeezed or closed early, leading to shortfalls in programme aims.[186] Rural councils were particularly disadvantaged, given their weaker resource base, small, less qualified staff complements, poorer infrastructure (like water and sewers), legislation that often lacked countryside-friendly nuances and, to top this list off, difficulties securing workable sites. Added to which, pressure from varied sources pushed councils towards building in locations over which their citizens were cautious, if not antagonistic.

7.4   Within District Housing Provision

Across the decades, within district tension existed between district-wide and parish-specific housing interests. Prior to the 1919 Act, strain was mitigated somewhat by the expectation parishes made rate fund contributions to new council houses. Little council-building took place, for, without national subsidies, few residents could afford consequential rents.[187] In addition, parishioners were reluctant to pick-up costs not covered by rents, which in many cases would stretch ratepayers' wallets, given their slim resources. The 1919 Act removed this constraint, with national subsidies and rate contributions spread across whole districts. But a district-wide levy created friction in Biggleswade and Hatfield. Perhaps surprisingly, in both cases, the district council argument was this lowered building volumes. In the case of Hatfield, confrontation with the Ministry ensued in 1922–23, focused on the Council's desire

---

[185] This saga was played out in internal communications (TNA HLG79/5 'Note from H. Heady to Mr. Beaufoy', 19 October 1945; 'Note from W.T. Jeffries to Mr. Heady and Mr. Elliott, 12 November 1945; 'Note to Mr. Beaufoy from H. Heady', 11 January 1946).

[186] We see this in reactions to 1919 legislation (TNA CAB24/59 GT5282 'Housing of the Working Classes After the War', 1 August 1918, p.1), the 1923 Act (HCH 2 December 1926, Vol.200, col.1401), the 1930 Act (TNA CAB24/247 CP12(34) 'Housing Policy', 1 February 1934, p.1), the 1956 Act (TNA HLG101/778 'Memo to Mr. Beddoe from P.P.B. Rickard', 10 July 1957) and even in increased council-building in 1963 (TNA CAB129/113 C(63)80 'White Paper on Housing Policy', 10 May 1963, p.1).

[187] TNA HLG1/845 'Report of Inquiry by Harry Stewart', 7 July 1913.

to erect more dwellings in Old Hatfield.[188] Biggleswade's concerns came a few years later, but again when exploring possibilities under Housing Acts. Then, pointing to the Council's 611 dwellings under the 1919 Act (so it could hardly be accused of penny-pinching), the Council's case was the same as Hatfield's. Potential tenants and some parish ratepayers, as in Potton, Sandy and Stotfold in Biggleswade's case, could afford parish charges but it would be unfair to impose them elsewhere, as this would hit poorer agricultural parishes hard.[189]

This symbolises the often complex relationship of parishes and councils. It provides nuance to the often-held view that districts were artificial constructs, for it was the parish and the county that attracted residents' affections and commitments (e.g. Baker 1953, p.182). Hence, parishes took an active interest in district decisions. Especially for council-building and allocating tenancies, they regularly demanded action and favour. Parishes frequently argued they should decide council tenancies. These requests were generally rebuffed, although parish council input in selections was common, and councillors from relevant parishes were usually involved in allocation decisions. As Connell (1978) identified, such close engagement carried the risk of personal values and economic interests intervening. Often this came in seeking assurance on rent-paying capabilities. Thus, in the 1930s, the Rural Housing Sub-Committee reported that some RDCs were '… most unwilling to accommodate in their new houses persons who they suspect will prove bad tenants or be unable to pay the full rent', while in 1970 the Central Housing Advisory Committee (CHAC) cautioned against moral tones in allocations, whereby '... a 'clean' rent book sometimes seemed to be essential qualifications for eligibility – at least for new houses'.[190] While not denying the potential for discriminatory practices, a critical issue for parishioners was a commitment to localism. Hence, whether looking at the early-1920s or the early-1970s, there was strong support for those 'of the parish' obtaining accommodation. Council minutes habitually signalled that applicants from the same parish were favoured.[191] Providing a quantitative measure of this was not easy, given the ephemeral nature of entries on allocations. Two insights from the late-1950s and 1960s show the tenacity of the tendency. The first was Biggleswade's 1956–1962 allocation of new homes to those displaced by action against unfit

---

[188] HRO RDC7/1/8 HtRDCM 21 December 1922, p.267; 15 February 1923, p.290; *HM&CP* 17 February 1923, p.12.

[189] *NBC&SN&DN* 14 August 1925, p.1; 9 October 1925, p.1; BRO RDBwM1/9 BiRDCM 7 October 1925.

[190] TNA HLG37/43 'Report on Local Investigations …', undated c1936, p.5; BRO RDBwM1/41 BiRDCHCM 14 January 1970, pp.666–72. A case in Walsingham illustrated the point (*FakPost* 12 July 1929, p.5).

[191] An early illustration was the allocation of a Sculthorpe home. This had been turned down by two parishioners (rent too high, etc.), with the only other applicant living in Fakenham, which, while a neighbouring parish, was deemed unacceptable. A fresh call for applications was made (*NWP&ENS* 29 October 1920, p.8). Lament over no bona fide local applicants for new homes characterised discussion in many councils (as for Smallburgh, *NWP&ENS* 24 October 1924, p.5).

dwellings. Here, 89.5% of those relocated moved to homes in the same parish.[192] This was despite a shortage of sites at the time, leading the Council to restrict new-build to villages with sites immediately available.[193] For four of the six parishes that did not provide homes to all relocated persons (out of 15 villages with allocations), options were limited as county plans restricted development to infilling or rounding-off.[194] Some settlements were subject to explicit notice they could not take more dwellings, as with Blunham.[195] Faced with this prospect, Everton residents informed the Council they would wait until homes could be provided rather than move else-where.[196] The second demonstration came from Ampthill, where minutes gave near monthly lists of allocations from December 1966 until May 1970. During this period, 85.4% of new council tenancies went to residents of the same parish. Size of settlement made a marginal impression on this figure, with 80.4% for parishes with more than 2000 inhabitants, 88.6% for those with 1000–1999 residents and 100% for smaller places (the last with under a tenth of allocations). The closest compara-tor from other districts was for Cottered, Little Hadham and Much Hadham in Braughing, where late-1960s allocations to the larger Hadhams (both over 1000 residents) saw 40.0% of dwellings going to tenants from the same parish, while Cottered (570 inhabitants) had a 75% local allocation.[197] Tenant priorities and lim-ited vacancies will have produced different impacts across councils; yet there was a commitment to housing people where they wished to be, even if this was in small places, which neither government policies nor builder priorities favoured (Chaps. 5 and 6). That such inclinations persisted into the 1970s was demonstrated, with frus-tration, in a 1971 statement by the Ampthill Medical Officer of Health: 'There is still a great demand for council accommodation in this area both from young cou-ples and the elderly. It is noticeable however that refusal of offers are increasing due to selectivity of applicants. There is still a somewhat parochial attitude prevalent in the district'.[198]

Localism traits were less apparent in places subject to large-scale urban spillover. Well before new town designation, or de Havilland moved there, London-based interests marked the Hatfield housing scene, as evinced in its demographic growth (Table 4.7). Supporting local economic activity meant accommodation expansion even if this fed concerns the Council was building for anyone.[199] In less pressured

[192] BRO RDBwH6/1 'Biggleswade Housing Subsidies Act 1956. Displacement Register (Unfit Houses)', undated c1963.

[193] *WR&WSR* 20 September 1955, p.5; 5 May 1959, p.14.

[194] BRO RDBwM1/32 BiRDCTPCM 15 March 1961; *BC&BG* 17 November 1961, p.12.

[195] *BC&BG* 24 April 1959, p.1.

[196] *WR&WSR* 15 March 1960, p.10. The same was reported by Smallburgh Rural District Council (1958), p.22, with the RDCA (1966, p.8) reporting a general reluctance of those born in a village to move away from it.

[197] HRO RDC3/1/19 BrRDCECM 9 December 1969, p.7755; HRO RDC3/1/20 BrRDCECM 26 February 1971, p.8148.

[198] BRO RDAR8/52 ARDCMOHar 1971, p.16.

[199] *HA&SAT* 25 September 1926, p.7.

districts, it was common for RDCs to provide homes only for those working (or living) in the district.[200] Put more flamboyantly, 1947 debates in Biggleswade Town centred on the banner 'Biggleswade people for Biggleswade houses', with opposition to 'foreigners' getting council homes leading to separate waiting lists: one for those who neither worked nor lived in the Town (portrayed as having no hope until all residents were satisfied) and 'locals'.[201] Even in Hatfield, localism carried some weight. For the Council's non-parlour homes, for example, the 366 tenants of 1936 comprised 244 with one or both adults working locally and with a prior local residence, 33 with a previous local home, 78 working locally and 21 widows. Only 10 of the 366 did not fall into one of these categories.[202] There was serious questioning if localism was ignored, with criticism when 1946 allocations saw persons from Chelmsford and Northumberland offered tenancies, even though they had worked locally for years but had families living away.[203] But pressure to open-up allocations rose. In the 1930s, this was seen when offers of replacement dwellings following slum clearance were turned down, often due to higher rents, with councils filling vacancies with residents from other parishes in a district.[204] After 1945, lobbying by the British Legion and others to prioritise ex-service personnel gathered pace, while the troubled next few decades for the British economy intensified demand for allocations to workers in export industries (Chap. 3).[205] Localism sentiments did not go away but parish-based emphases diminished over time, as typified by a 1967 Biggleswade policy statement: '... while the attitude towards the letting of houses must be based on priority that should not necessarily mean that priority be given to housing or rehousing of a person within his own parish'.[206]

To appreciate the drive behind the dilution of localism, three 'centralisation' trends merit attention, namely demand for rural homes; expectations of improved

---

[200] As in Erpingham (*FakPost* 8 April 1927, p.3), which ruled homes only went to those working in the district given demand from neighbouring districts (NRO DC19/6/16 WRDCM 10 October 1928, p.69).

[201] *NBC&BR* 28 January 1947, p.2; 25 February 1947, p.4.

[202] HRO RDC7/3/1 Hatfield Housing Urgency Committee Meeting 29 April 1936, p.319.

[203] *H&PBG* 1 March 1946, p.1.

[204] For example, BRO RDBwM1/12 BiRDCM 10 April 1935.

[205] British Legion actions included: Braughing (*H&EO* 15 December 1945, p.3; 15 June 1946, p.3); Biggleswade Town (*NBC&BR* 27 August 1946, p.3); and, both Ampthill and Bletchley UDC (*WR&WSR* 21 January 1947, p.1; 18 February 1947, p.1).

[206] BRO RDBwM1/39 BiRDCHLCM, 16 October 1967, p.395. Change could come quickly, with Erpingham objecting to granting a private licence to a non-resident in 1950 (*NNN* 28 July 1950, p.1), but rejecting a motion to restrict tenant allocations to those living in the RDC two years later (NRO DC13/5/23 ERDCM 28 April 1952, para.228). However, the pace of change varied. Sheringham opposed applications from outside the Town in 1952 (*NNN* 18 July 1952, p.1), Braughing objected to a council home going to an incoming local teacher in 1953 (*H&EO* 9 January 1953, p.5), with Ampthill regularly refusing to reserve council dwellings for public sector workers (e.g. BRO RDAM2/22 ARDCHCM 24 August 1950; 19 October 1950; 18 November 1954; 17 February 1955; 21 July 1955) and there were rows in Cromer over a council home going to a non-resident in 1966 (*NNN* 14 January 1966, p.1). Yet Biggleswade Town reserved large tranches of new housing for 'dollar workers' (*NBC&BR* 13 October 1953, p.7).

amenities; and, for public sector dwellings, national direction. For the first, rural councils generally assumed virtually all parishes would be blessed with better housing. Anguish over private sector failings did not diminish convictions the sector should do more, yet councils responded with noteworthy commitments to alleviating housing deficits (Chap. 6). Proposals were commonly dispersed across parishes. By 1921, for example, Biggleswade had built Addison houses in 19 of its 26 parishes, with the largest parish with no new dwelling having only 102 inhabitants (Biggleswade RDC 1922, p.7). Similar patterns were recorded elsewhere, across a range of Housing Acts. Thus, the 1919 programme for Hitchin RDC covered 27 villages and hamlets across 21 parishes, Dunmow RDC wanted to respond to unanimous parish calls for housing in 1925, while Depwade looked to provide 44 new homes in 13 parishes under the 1931 Housing (Rural Authorities) Act.[207] Slip forward a few decades and little had changed. In 1943, Braughing wanted new council homes in all but two of its parishes, including four in a parish with a 1951 population of 139 (the parishes missing out had less), while post-war Ampthill had built in 23 of its 29 parishes by 1960.[208]

Not all was plain sailing. Councils were often rebuked by parish councillors for not providing homes in specific locales. At times, explanations were easy, as with Briston in 1927 and Aspley Guise in 1939, neither of which had parish requests tabled for accommodation.[209] This was probably a relief for the district council, as calls for more homes came in thick and fast from parishes (Chap. 3). More worrying were parish councils asking for more homes when there were no identified applicants. In Walsingham, a 1955 debate was stirred by this, when no homes were proposed for Wood Norton, provoking the claim it was futile to put names on a waiting list that offered no chance of a home.[210] With slow turnover of rural tenancies (Pacione 1980; Forrest and Murie 1992), and despite Whitehall restricting council-build to slum replacement or old people's homes, the strength of disquiet was revealed in the 20 to 7 victory for Wood Norton, with the decision not to build referred-back.[211] These concerns stretched into the 1960s, as in worries Weybourne (Erpingham) would become a place only for old people owing to housing shortages, with 132 applicants reported when a single dwelling became available.[212] These anxieties exemplified tension over council house distribution. The 1955 Chair of Walsingham's Housing Committee was adamant the Council had to build homes where people wanted them, urging his colleagues that: 'Housewives seemed to prefer to live in houses which were in the centre of population rather than in the vil-

[207] *Hertfordshire Express and Hitchin, Letchworth and Stevenage Gazette* 8 March 1919, p.3; *H&EO* 30 May 1925, p.6; TNA HLG40/16 'Housing (Rural Authorities) Act 1931. Advisory Committee Report', undated c1931, pp.11–12.

[208] HRO RDC3/2/2 BrRDCPHHCM 22 April 1943, p.580; BRO RDAR8/41 ARDCMOHar 1960, p.15.

[209] *FakPost* 11 February 1927, p.3; *W&DR* 28 February 1939, p.3.

[210] *NorfChron* 24 June 1955, p.1.

[211] *D&FT* 24 June 1955, p.1.

[212] *NNN* 27 October 1967, p.1.

lages', concerning which they should: 'Look at the number of agricultural cottages vacant in the district'.[213] Strain here was three-way. First, there was an absolute shortage of affordable, 'fit' dwellings. Second, demand for better services drew householders to larger settlements. Third, farmers (in particular) called for homes near dispersed workplaces. Housing shortages for working populations were poignantly highlighted in claims accommodation shortages were driving young people from villages.[214] This assertion merits handling with caution, as it could embed narrow conceptions of 'local housing need'. Younger residents might have wanted a 'local' home but in a 'local centre' with a better array of services than their birth parish (Ministry of Works & Planning 1942; Association of County Sanitary Officers 1952; Martin 1965; Jones 1999). Employment change potentially produced more departures than housing deficits (e.g. Drudy 1978).[215]

7.4.1   An Impetus Towards Centralisation

That noted, given accommodation scarcity, the charge new houses were built in the 'wrong places' needs investigating. Such claims characterised debate early in the century. In 1927, for example, Councillor Roy ruffled feathers in Smallburgh by asking why houses were built where they were not wanted (agricultural parishes), while places focused on the boating industry had unmet housing demand.[216] New homes not finding tenants in agricultural parishes occurred elsewhere,[217] although complaints over this tendency induced counter critiques of concentrating building in service centres.[218] Friction between housing initiatives supporting agriculture and

---

[213] *NorfChron* 24 June 1955, p.1.

[214] Illustrations were: BRO RDAR8/11 ARDCMOHar 1930, p.12; HRO RDC3/2/1 BrRDCPHHCM 22 December 1938, p.311; BRO RDBwM1/20 BiRDCM 23 March 1949, p.49; NRO DC19/6/66 WRDCHCM 22 November 1954, p.96; HRO RDC7/1/22 HtRDCHCM 6 November 1956, p.238.

[215] To exemplify, by 1952 Hatfield had built 60 houses under agricultural workers' provisions in Housing Acts, of which 42 originally had farm-worker occupants but this number had dropped to 24 (HRO RDC7/1/16 HtRDCM 10 June 1952, p.22).

[216] *NWP&ENS* 11 February 1927, p.3. Recall that some Smallburgh parishes, like Felmingham, had homes built that could not be let locally, with resulting tenants claimed to be from North Walsham, to the annoyance of Smallburgh councillors (see *NWP&ENS* 4 November 1927, p.1; 2 November 1928, p.5); although others claimed tenants only worked in North Walsham (*EDP* 1 November 1928, p.5).

[217] This was notable under the 1919 Act and inter-war generally (Chap. 4), but applied post-1945 (e.g. TNA MAF147/4 Letter from Erpingham RDC Clerk to F.G. Wicks, Norfolk Agricultural Executive Committee, 17 September 1951). In some cases, as in St Faith's and Aylsham RDC, tenants were only found months after dwellings were finished (*NNN* 30 September 1949, p.1). Homes in agricultural parishes often went to tenants without a farm link (even in war-time, see TNA HLG48/868 Letter from Erpingham RDC Clerk to the MoH Secretary, 24 April 1941).

[218] As with West Beckham (NRO DC13/5/73 ERDCHCM 14 August 1933, p.86). The charge Walsingham built too many homes in Fakenham and the adjoining village of Hempton, leaving too few for farm-workers in small villages, was countered by pointing out that 281 of 549 waiting list

those with a broader socio-economic remit grew as the years progressed. In part, this was because councils increasingly moved away from dispersing new-build, with even the RDCA arguing scattered development should be limited.[219] One impetus driving this view was the emergence of lobby groups favouring landscape conservation (e.g. Lowerson 1980; Sheail 1981; Punter 1986), which drew suste-nance from the unregulated private development that scarred the countryside with ribbon expansion and the shacks, shanties and unmade roads of plotlands (Gayler 1970; Hardy and Ward 1984). The 1930s governments promoted 'freedoms' for private companies, but were pressured to control the spread of petrol stations and advertising boards, then ribbon development (Clarke 1936), followed by green belt preservation (Munton 1983). It is not unreasonable to hold that by 1939 the essen-tials of the British land-use planning system were established (Booth 1999, p.280). Yet, planning lacked regulatory teeth, with uneven implementation of powers to intercede in development decisions, and councils left to steer a course between the public interest (e.g. not loading private costs onto the public purse) and the interests of landowners and developers.[220] Trends nonetheless were moving in one direction. Regulation grew post-war, in functional depth and complexity, in geographical cov-erage and down the settlement hierarchy (Green 1971; Davidson and Wibberley 1977; Cloke 1983). One explanation is offered by public choice theory. This por-trays greater state regulation almost as a grand conspiracy by bureaucrats seeking to enrich their wealth, power and status. But public choice analysts stumble when trying to account for citizen support for environmental regulation (Pennington 2000), while government failure to take responsibility for driving positive change in the rural environment further casts doubt on public choice principles (e.g. Punter 1987). Whatever the reasons, the English public has long been supportive of rural landscape preservation (Young 1988; Countryside Commission 1997), even if this provided a shield for NIMBYism (Buller and Lowe 1982; Herington 1984; Lowe et al. 1995), as well as a convenient smokescreen for the farm lobby's desire to limit 'interference' in its activities (Bishop 1998; Booth 1999).

The bundle of attachments and interests associated with such sentiments found expression in a land-use planning system that spelt the message 'urban' should be separated from 'rural' (Gilg 1978; Murray 2012). That land-use planning was not the primary driver behind this emphasis was transparent in inter-war trends towards

---

applicants were from these places, which had 51 'farm people' on their lists (*D&FT* 5 November 1954, p.1; 3 December 1954, p.1).

[219] TNA HLG37/44 'Evidence of Neville Hobson, RDCA Executive Council Member', undated c1936, p.5. This view was reported across many rural organisations in MoH (1937b), with the Minister of Health offering his endorsement (HCH 15 February 1938, Vol.331, col.1739).

[220] TNA HLG37/43 'Sporadic Development', undated c1936. For Addison (1994, p.174) a good reason for timidity was the cost of compensating private-owners for refusing development. Even in the 1950s, when the government was looking to shift house-building away from the public sector to private-owners, the Ministry was clear that private enterprise would largely build in fringe areas, due to the cost of sites in towns, so that: 'In the long term private housing, which is inevitably more scattered and less planned that municipal, is apt to prove very wasteful in the provision of public services' (TNA T229/680 'Housing Memo on Meeting at The Treasury', 2 December 1953, p.3).

concentrating housing in fewer settlements, when the planning system lacked teeth. As a 1942 Women's Institute submission made clear, it was increasingly unacceptable for families to be too far from schools, shops, churches and workplaces.[221] This view was supported by official agencies:

> The defects of the inter-war house have been particularly marked in rural areas. Council cottages have frequently been built in remote places where no public services can readily be made available. Because the country household is compelled to be more self-sufficient than the urban household, the lack of out-buildings and storage space has been a serious deprivation. The internal plan of many inter-war rural cottages has not been adapted to the mode of life of their occupants, and their outward appearance has been singularly inappropriate to their surroundings. (MoH 1944c, p.17)

The sense that rural provision was badly handled by inter-war governments was exposed in inspections of council-building proposals. Examine the case of Iping in Midhurst RDC. The reaction on its inspection was pointed: '... my impression was one rather of astonishment that anybody should propose to put houses at Iping, which seemed to me to be only a very small hamlet. Can you tell me exactly what was in the mind of the Rural District Council when initially they proposed to put houses at Iping?'.[222] The local response was equally sharp, with the RDC strongly dissenting '... from the view that Iping is a village "in a state of disintegration", and would like to know what grounds there are for this statement'.[223] Parallel illustrations of dissonance in interpretation were plentiful. For St Faith's and Aylsham RDC, the Ministry's 1949 rejection of housing tenders for small villages raised fears of social disintegration unless council homes were permitted. The issue was still alive 12 years later, when the RDC's acceptance of geographically focused council-building was deemed 'largely responsible' for decaying villages.[224] De-prioritising small villages might have been predicted for the 1945–1951 government, given Labour Party suspicions the rural landscape was largely valued for urban recreation (Griffiths 2007, p.309), alongside farm-worker union (NUAW) pressure to end tied cottages. Indeed, the government initially favoured larger settlements for although '... one-third of the really rural population [is estimated to] live in isolated houses, one-third in small villages, and one-third in large. Our policy [on

---

[221] TNA HLG37/48 Rural Housing Sub-Committee. 'National Federation of Women's Institutes Evidence', October 1942, p.3. Half a mile away was deemed reasonable for rural England but not beyond this. Access to good transport extended the range. Worth noting here Pacione's (1980) findings on a Scottish village, where even in the 1970s two-thirds of council tenants lived within two miles of their workplace, compared to 10% for private tenants and 5% for owner-occupiers.

[222] TNA HLG71/581 Letter from E.S. Hill, MTCP, to H.R. Wardill, MCTP Regional Planning Officer Tunbridge Wells, 17 April 1946.

[223] TNA HLG71/581 Letter from H.R. Wardill, MTCP Regional Planning Officer Tunbridge Wells, to E.S. Hill, MCTP, 7 May 1946.

[224] NNN 16 December 1949, p.7; 6 January 1961, p.9. At the time fears were expressed that Erpingham was too 'urban minded' by refusing to build in smaller villages (NNN 30 March 1961, p.4). This sentiment intensified when the RDC proposed placing old people's homes in larger villages (NNN 1 December 1961, p.1).

dwelling numbers] hitherto has aimed at one-sixth, one-sixth, two-thirds'.[225] But with balance of payments deficits causing alarm, the position shifted, leading to NUAW disenchantment over failure to abolish tied cottages.[226] Early messages that subsidies should not go to tied cottages[227] came with recognition of the '… acute clash between business needs and human feelings, both of which have got to be satisfied if we are to keep agriculture and the countryside as a whole alive and effective'.[228] That farmers were likely favoured in this dispute was suggested by Tom Williams, Labour's agriculture minister, being known within the Party as 'the farmer's chum', with the 1947 Agriculture Act attacked because its sole unequivocal beneficiary was the farmer, not the consumer, the farm-worker or the government (Chase 1993). Support was also visible in the 1947 Town and Country Planning Act, which gave widespread development control exemptions to farming (Self and Storing 1962; Gilg 1978). Despite official recommendations that new dwellings should be erected where services were available (MoH 1944c), homes in isolated rural locales were built.[229] Indeed, the NUAW complained about 'flagrant' (mis)use of public money erecting dwellings '… on farmers' land, and presumably well away from any amenities such as would apply in villages'.[230] This outcome owed something to lobbying by farmer groups at the local level.[231]

Nationally, whatever the official view on scattering new-build, 1947 balance of payments problems encouraged a sympathetic hearing for farmers. Early in the 1939–1945 War, the Cabinet confirmed that at the end of hostilities new houses, 'particularly in rural areas', would be the second housing priority (after repairing war-damaged dwellings).[232] By 1947, the government was moving resources to

---

[225] TNA HLG71/581 'Siting of New Houses in the Country', 23 October 1946.

[226] The NUAW expressed a strong preference for building in villages with amenities, believing dwellings on farms offered justification for tied cottages (e.g. TNA HLG71/580 Letter from Alfred Dann, NUAW General Secretary, to L. Silkin, MTCP, 11 November 1946; TNA MAF234/12 Letter from Alfred Dann to A.R. Manktelow, MAF, 14 October 1947).

[227] TNA HLG107/181 'Housing Subsidies. Housing (Financial and Miscellaneous Provisions) Act, 1946', 13 June 1946, with this message communicated widely in MoH Circular 118/46 (see also MoH 1946, p.3).

[228] TNA HLG71/580 Letter to A.M. Lowe, MAF, from Herbert Gatliff, MoH, 21 November 1946.

[229] Not without difficulty, with some RDCs, like Biggleswade, reporting builder problems securing labour for small sites; leading to consideration of larger projects (NBC&BR 8 January 1946, p.1).

[230] The quote concerned Much Wenlock RDC (TNA HLG71/580 Letter from Dann to Aneurin Bevan, 24 July 1947). Reports on wider application of this practice included TNA MAF234/3 Minute Sheet, 17 December 1947.

[231] Illustrations of local lobbying included: HRO RDC3/2/3 BrRDCPHHCM 17 April 1947, p.1035; HRO RDC7/9/1 HtRDCM 13 May 1947, p.302; NBC&BR 20 May 1947, p.5. In Hatfield, concern farming was not receiving appropriate consideration extended to suggesting the largely farming parish of Essendon be transferred to Hertford RDC, with which Essendon was felt to 'have much more in common' (HRO CP35/6/2 Letter to Essendon Parish Council Chair from David Freemantle of Bedwell Lodge, Essendon, 28 September 1946).

[232] TNA CAB65/42 War Cabinet 170(42) Meeting Conclusions, 17 December 1942.

farming and mining areas so new dwellings were erected faster.[233] Given general economic turmoil at the time, councils were told that Principal Housing Officer approval was needed for all new houses except war-damage replacement, with special consideration for homes for farm-workers (MoH Circular 137/47).[234] Many farm-worker homes went to small parishes. In Walsingham, for example, 56.2% of all dwellings erected under the 1946 Housing (Financial and Miscellaneous Provisions) Act went to parishes with less than 500 residents – a proportion higher than the population share of these parishes. However, as the impact of war receded and better economic circumstances emerged, agricultural interests lost potency. With 1950s promises of increased new-build volumes, the attraction of small housing projects withered. By 1952, the Ministry was referring to 'small clusters' of council houses as having at least eight properties, with higher building costs for small groups weakening support for special rural subsidies.[235] Extra support became discretionary, and, with farm-worker wages having risen to attract workers to the land, the argument was marshalled that rural districts no longer needed support.[236] Needless to say, farm-worker wages quickly fell relative to others with little debate in Westminster over ability to pay council rents,[237] which had risen considerably in rural districts (Table 4.20).

In the late-1940s into the 1950s pressure grew for larger building projects using more industrialised methods (Chap. 6). The sense that 'the future' demanded better access to facilities was keenly felt. Commentators like Tilley (1947) argued that settlements of 600–800 inhabitants were required to maintain services and

---

[233] TNA CAB129/20 CP(47)249 'Priority of Housing for Miners, Agricultural Workers and Key Workers in the Development Areas', 5 September 1947.

[234] BRO RDBwM1/18 BiRDCM 10 September 1947, p.479.

[235] Farmers' groups continued to lobby. Whitehall's reaction was typified in responses to Clun RDC, whose high costs were blamed on the isolated character of district, including the need to provide water schemes, sewerage, etc., so annual losses per house on a four dwelling project amounted to £14/3/9d per dwelling (TNA MAF234/1 Letter from NFU to C. Holland Martin MP, 29 January 1952).

[236] TNA HLG31/19 Housing Instructions HI40/52 'Housing Act 1952'; TNA MAF255/112 'The Special Subsidy for Rural Houses', undated c1952. Within Whitehall the message was that farm-worker minimum weekly wages had risen sharply, from 32/– in 1937 to 65/– in 1944 then to 94/– in 1949, making them comparable with other rural workers (postmen 90/– at age 21 and 98/– at 25, railway porters 92/6d and building labourers 95/4d; TNA HLG101/582 'Draft Paper from John Wrigley to Mr. Beddoe', 17 June 1949). This message was still promoted in 1952, even in MAF, as farm-worker minimum wages had grown faster than manufacturing wages since 1939 (e.g. TNA MAF255/112 AWB4752 'Agricultural Wages Board: Memorandum by the MAF', undated c1952). Questions over special subsidies for farm-worker homes were raised as early as 1943 (TNA HLG37/46 Rural Housing Sub-Committee Meeting Minutes, 4 March 1943).

[237] Even in 1949, the Central Office of Information's Social Survey found those interviewed compared agriculture unfavourably with other rural jobs, given working hours and wages (TNA RG23/132 'Recruitment to Agriculture 1949'). By 1956, the NUAW was told that wives were 'sick of making do' with farm-workers' wages (*D&FT* 13 July 1956, p.7). In the 1960s, wages for those 21 years or older hovered around, but often fell below, 70% of average earnings in manufacturing (HCH 3 March 1972, Vol.832, col.197W–98W).

amenities for a modern age. Around the same time, the Minister of Town and Country Planning reportedly '… expressed the view that the smallest village in which any further development would be authorised, at any rate for the time being, would be one incorporating as a minimum, 1000 people'. Cross-examined, the precision of this articulation was disputed but the Minister emphasised the benefits of size.[238] Small villages and hamlets were to be turned over to agriculture, not housing (as articulated in county plans; e.g. Bedfordshire County Council 1952). This view was central to North Hertfordshire Joint Planning Committee proposals to place the whole of Hitchin RDC into a restricted rural zone, which would prohibit people living there who were not related to agriculture. This was promoted '… because of the danger that they might be turned into dormitories', with the minister holding that those who wanted to live in villages should show they had a reasonable need to be there. In contrast, the RDC Chair '… felt strongly that people should not be stopped from living in a village simply because they did not wish to follow the plough'.[239] The abrasive interaction of these views was notable in the late-1940s (and later). Supporting the perspective of many RDCs, the Rural Housing Sub-Committee held that '… rural districts and rural counties are often too poor to tackle rural housing and its necessary water supplies and sewerage with reasonable efficiency', so RDCs should accept small industrial units. But county councils, in preparing new development plans, were drawn to Scott Committee messages on land utilisation (Ministry of Works & Planning 1942). As understood in Bedfordshire, this was that '… if suitable industry were to be introduced into the countryside then small towns from 2000 to 5000 population were more suitable than the small villages' (Bedfordshire County Council 1952, p.71). This matched Whitehall sentiments, as reflected in a 1945 communication to Biggleswade over Stotfold:

> It is understood that a large percentage of the population of this village travels to industrial work in Letchworth, Baldock and Hitchin. This being so, I would suggest that your Council re-consider whether it is good planning to erect so many houses in what should be an essentially agricultural village, having particularly valuable agricultural land.[240]

For the MAF, stringent conditions were required for manufacturing in the countryside, with small towns not villages its 'proper place'.[241]

Land-use plans embedded settlement categorisations to reflect this understanding. Hence, in Biggleswade, parishes were deemed to have:

> No reason for further development except agriculture (11 parishes)
> Requiring consolidation (three parishes)
> No development envisaged (five parishes)
> Plots restricted though development could occur (two parishes)
> Unsuitable for further housing but industry might be suitable (two parishes)
> Requiring the careful preservation of its character (one parish)

---

[238] TNA HLG71/581 Letter from J. Phillips, NFU, to Basil Engholm, MAF, 25 February 1946; Reply, 19 March 1946.

[239] *Hertfordshire Express and Bedfordshire Express* 18 May 1946, p.5.

[240] BRO RDBwM1/15 BiRDCM 3 January 1945, p.377.

[241] TNA HLG71/581 Letter from A.M. Lowe, MAF, to Muriel Jenkins, MCTP, 29 June 1948.

No ribbon development to be allowed (two parishes)
Development expected (six parishes)[242]

Significantly, for the six parishes where development was expected, four had populations below the touted 2000 minimum (two under 1000, one under 500). At ground level, the realities of rural life were more complex than Westminster's image of a countryside given over to agriculture. As the 1951 Ampthill Medical Officer of Health spelt out, there were already villages with heavy outward daily commuting and substantial non-agricultural employment in brick-making, manufacturing, the military, education and traditional small-scale production (like brush works and timber yards).[243] In investigated Bedfordshire RDCs, 56.8% of parishes had more than 10% of employed heads of household in agriculture in 1971, compared with 75% in Erpingham, 84.2% in Braughing, 86.5% in Walsingham and 94.3% in Smallburgh.[244] Generally, smaller places relied more on farming. Thus, in the three north Norfolk districts, parishes with fewer than 500 inhabitants had 38.5% of 1971 heads of household in paid employment in agriculture (22.3% for parishes with 500–999 inhabitants), with 29.0% (19.5%) in Hertfordshire and 25.0% (18.4%) in Bedfordshire.[245] Given this was 20 years after post-war county plans were formulated, 'exclusivity' for farming in smaller settlements still carried weight (Davidson and Wibberley 1977; Blunden and Curry 1985).

But if there is one thing the literature on land-use planning teaches us, it is that slippage occurs between plans and outcomes. Davies and associates summarised the realities cogently: 'Development control, far from being simply a regulatory process for implementing a development plan, can be a bargaining process in which the plan becomes no more than the benchmark for starting negotiations' (Davies et al. 1986, p.11). Hence, analyses of development control decisions find weaker than expected regulatory impacts on new-build locations even under enhanced landscape protections (e.g. Blacksell and Gilg 1977; Anderson 1981; Preece 1981; Buller and Hoggart 1986; Gilg and Kelly 1997). Even those who supported concentrating housing into key settlements were disappointed by the implementation of the policy (Green 1971), with too many places designated to make the policy effective (Cloke 1979), and much new-build going to places with no development designation (Woodruffe 1976; Gilder 1979; Herington and Evans 1979). Quite apart from localism priorities, there might be good reasons for seeing housing in smaller settlements. Hence, while preferring to see new farm-worker homes in villages, the 1947

---

[242] *WR&WSR* 12 August 1952, p.2. Biggleswade debated categories with parish councils before the Housing Committee formulated building plans (BRO RDBwM1/23 BiRDCM 19 March 1952, p.5). The categorisation was revised later, producing fewer classes (e.g. BRO RDBwM1/32 BiRDCTPCM 15 March 1961).

[243] BRO RDAR8/32 ARDCMOHar 1951, p.3.

[244] Computations for socio-economic groups excluded parishes with less than 10 workers in the 10% sample used for the 1971 Census reports. Only one of the four Hatfield parishes (Essendon) had more than 10% working in agriculture.

[245] Apart from Essendon (population range 500–999) the Hertfordshire computations relied solely on Braughing parishes.

NUAW General Secretary persuaded Whitehall's agricultural mandarins that size should not be the prime criterion but placement.[246] This message had parallels with later academic research, showing new-build was most efficiently located where services had spare capacity, which often was not larger settlements (Moseley 1974; Owens 1984).

Settlement size was nevertheless expected to impact on dwelling availability, given pressures to centralise provision. Although centralisation impulses waned at times, they never went away. Sherwood (1996, p.55) captured this for inter-war Northamptonshire, where: '… most of the suggestions for [council] schemes incorporated a minimum of 20 houses, quite inappropriate in scale for the majority of villages', while in the 1960s into the 1970s larger sites, encouraged by cost yardsticks, land-use plans, plus builder and government preferences, reinforced council-building in larger settlements in South Hams.[247] How far did these pressures translate into house-building outcomes? When exploring this question over a 50-year period, certain data sources, like planning applications, are not available. A paucity of relevant information at the parish level is striking. House-building numbers providing a solid base for assessing trends would have been a delight, if they existed. Growth in dwellings was thereby estimated using households numbers. These the census recorded for parishes.[248] Across the seven RDCs investigated, persons living in households on average accounted for more than 99% of district populations. Deviations from totals arose principally from residential institutions, like boarding schools, hospitals, hotels and prisons, alongside military installations (Table 4.6). Available data does not distinguish households by tenure over the 50 years explored, although some councils offered partial information and national trends were clear (Figs. 6.1 and 6.2). Exemplifying local trends, 66.2% of new dwellings in Ampthill were for private-owners for 1921–1929, with this proportion rising to 79.4% for 1930–1938.[249] Confirming this 1930s density, the 1932–1939 Hatfield private-owner share was 91.2%. Of course, not all councils had such high percentages. Given the energetic manner in which Biggleswade approached the 1919 Act, it is no

---

[246] TNA HLG71/580 'Notes of a Meeting with the Ministry of Agriculture', 13 February 1947.

[247] Phillips and Williams (1982a, p.74, p.81, p.95) reported 51.3% of council homes in the four largest settlements, compared with 39% of waiting list applicants.

[248] If many households lived in single dwellings this could exaggerate dwelling number change but this effect was generally minor in rural districts, given low multi-occupation (Table 6.15). With definitional change across censuses, figures indicate trends not precise occurrences. This applies as much to households as population totals (e.g. Walford 2001, 2005). In 1921, for example, the census date was shifted from Spring to June, with population counts based on place of residence on the census night (Abbott 1922). As a result, places attracting holiday-makers had high volumes that year, as evinced in 1931 census commentaries noting 1921 populations were inflated.

[249] The figures, as for Biggleswade and Hatfield, are from medical officer of health annual reports. In the case of Ampthill and Biggleswade values were only available from 1921, with 1937 missing from the Ampthill records searched. No information on 1939 was found. Hatfield sources were poorer, with only two years found in the 1920s and with 1930s information starting at 1932 (and ending as a half-year for 1939). The Biggleswade and Hatfield reports were published. Those for Ampthill were recorded in council papers (the BRO RDAR8 series).

surprise that only 22.6% of its new dwellings were for private-owners for 1921–1929, although restrictions on council-building saw the balance shift to a 59.2% private-owner share over 1930–1938. No precise data existed on inter-war trends in the north Norfolk districts, although, as for the districts listed above, post-1945 they largely paralleled the national trend of building for private-owners growing over post-war decades (Table 7.2).

For overall growth, patterns over the decades were clear (Table 7.3). Expansion occurred sooner and more forcefully closer to London. This confirms earlier studies pointing to growth spreading out from London before 1939 (Hooson 1958; Burchardt 2012). The second obvious trend was the impact of parish size, with more populous parishes having higher growth rates, often significantly so, almost universally over time. The most notable exception was in Hertfordshire, although the investigated districts provided a special case, with dissimilar experiences for each. The larger parish populations were all in Hatfield, with nowhere in Braughing climbing above 2000 inhabitants until 1971. Yet, even the London-infused environment of Hatfield saw parishes with dissimilar trajectories. Hatfield 'Old Town' boasted 5695 residents in 1921, grew to 21,019 by 1961 and then to 25,990 in 1971. At the other extreme, Essendon retained an essentially agricultural character, with 500–999 inhabitants in every decade. Lying closer to London, North Mymms, with 2021 residents was the only Hertfordshire parish investigated in the 2000–2999 band in 1921, but had 5458 inhabitants by 1951 and 12,522 in 1971. The pace of 1931–1951 growth in North Mymms was surpassed by the other southerly parish, Northaw, which outstripped its 94.2% population increase with a 176.9% hike. This effect is muted in Table 7.3 because Northaw shared the 1931 population category of 1000–1999 inhabitants with Braughing's Much Hadham, which only grew by 13.2%. Northaw had 694 inhabitants in 1921, reached 3214 in 1951, went over 5000 by 1961, then saw slower change to 1971 (5946). This was indicative of two points: first, that expansionary pressures from London were intense across southern Hatfield inter-war, with only the more agricultural, more northerly parish not seeing substantial growth; and, second, in southern Hertfordshire, where green belt restrictions were sharpest (Hertfordshire County Council 1961), planning changed the geography of house-building. Illustrative of this was Much Hadham, which grew in the late

Table 7.2 Percent of all new houses built for private-owners in investigated rural districts, 1945–1974

	1945–1861	1962–1974
Hatfield	51.0	51.6
Braughing	34.0	87.5
Ampthill	42.2	78.7
Biggleswade	34.1	74.0
Erpingham	40.2	91.9
Smallburgh	41.5	90.1
Walsingham	29.2	73.5
England and Wales	36.5	61.6

Source: Computed from MoH-MHLG (quarterly)

Table 7.3 Percent change in households by parish population in investigated rural districts, 1921–1971

Parish population	Census period			
	1921–1931	1931–1951	1951–1961	1961–1971
	Hertfordshire			
Over 3000	25.5	128.0	81.2	13.0
2000-2999	69.1			
1000-1999	14.8	107.0	11.3	59.6
500–999	14.9	32.5	1.2	9.4
Under 500	2.9	11.7	4.5	1.1
	Bedfordshire			
Over 3000	26.1	69.9	47.6	30.9
2000-2999	18.7	27.6	26.3	36.6
1000-1999	11.0	37.6	18.7	40.1
500–999	10.6	34.5	12.5	37.0
Under 500	14.2	18.4	8.9	23.2
	Norfolk			
Over 3000			14.5	18.3
2000-2999	6.4	20.6	37.2	12.8
1000-1999	10.0	31.1	26.9	10.8
500–999	8.9	21.5	4.4	8.1
Under 500	6.5	20.3	2.0	1.7

Source: Computed from county reports of the population censuses
Note: The population size categories were determined by the parish population at the start of the census period; hence, the number of parishes in each category changed slightly between census periods. Blank entries indicate no parish fell into the size category

nineteenth-century with the arrival of the railway but without the urgency of commuter-fed development in the west of the county (Bailey 1978; Smalley 1995). The closure of the railway in 1965 was symbolic of the village's new standing, for although it was the only settlement in Braughing with more than 1000 residents up to the 1951 Census, it fell behind Buntingford when the latter alone was designated for further housing expansion. Thus, while Much Hadham was larger than Buntingford even in 1961 (1946 compared to 1557 inhabitants), with restrictions on the former and growth encouragement for the latter, this had reversed by 1971 (1823 compared to 3814, respectively). The 'free-for-all' of the inter-war decades had been replaced by directed development. Overlying this was disparity between Braughing and Hatfield, associated with less 'urban' development pressures in the 'traditional' rurality of Braughing (Table 1.1), whose poorer transport links and greater distance from London shielded it from intense inter-war and post-war private development (Fig. 1.1).

In Table 7.3, we see reduced rates of household expansion in 1961–1971 in Hertfordshire, save for the spurt associated with Buntingford's designation. Suggestive of waves of development moving outward from London (Warnes 1991), by the 1960s growth was higher in the Bedfordshire districts. The county was expected to see major expansion from the 1960s into the 1970s, which caused

disquiet amongst parish councils fearing increments out of character with local villages.[250] Yet county planners regularly held that '... closely knit development is
appropriate to the character of Bedfordshire villages and that the development that
has been allowed should satisfactorily fit into the character'.[251] Whether local residents thought it fitted or not, there was substantial (relative) household growth in
smaller parishes in the 1960s compared with the 1950s, as indeed there was on a
lesser scale for smaller parishes in Norfolk (Table 7.3). One possibility, which is
difficult to assess without exploring planning applications in detail, is that demand
for small village life led to more in-filling and the upgrading of uninhabited properties. The only information to offer glimpses on this came from Bedfordshire's
Ampthill, which documented improvement grant applications and awards for
1959–1969. These records lack clarity on some items, including distinguishing
between standard and discretionary awards.[252] They also do not indicate if applications were for uninhabited or occupied buildings. The patterns revealed were nonetheless instructive. Taking 'successful' applications only, parishes with more
approvals than household shares were the very smallest and those with 1000–1999
inhabitants (Table 7.4).[253] With planning restrictions intended to limit growth in the
smallest villages, the possibility of service-class gentrification lying behind these
patterns merits consideration (Phillips 2005).

What might have contributed to this effect was building conversions, either from
more to less units (or vice-versa), or from non-residential to residential. These were
more numerous in smaller places. Hence, 38.6% of original buildings in conversion
applications were for parishes with less than 500 residents, with 36.8% in parishes
with 500–999 inhabitants.[254] But conversions accounted for a small share of total

---

[250] BRO RDAM1/24 ARDCHCM 13 February 1969, p.537; BRO PC Clophill 1/6 Parish Council
Meeting 20 June 1974; BRO PC Lidlington 1/4 Parish Council Meeting 23 March 1976.

[251] BRO PC Houghton Conquest 18/13. A broader discussion of links between growth expectations
for Bedfordshire and the need to preserve villages is at BRO RDAM1/22 ARDCHPByCM 14
July 1966.

[252] Prior to 1954, grants were available for improvement or conversion as long as the total cost was
under £600, then £800, with awards of up to 50% of costs. The 1954 Housing Repairs and Rents
Act restricted awards to £400 per dwelling. Awards were discretionary. In 1959 'standard grants'
were introduced for structurally sound buildings that lacked basic amenities (bath, hot water, WC,
etc.). Applicants could claim standard grants as a 'right'. Maximum payments changed over time,
with lower provisions for standard grants (£150–£200), while discretionary awards rose to a maximum of £1000 by the late-1960s (Hamnett 1973; English et al. 1976, p.43).

[253] The records show a rejection rate of only 3.2%. Some 2.8% of approved applications resulted in
no improvement. The reasons were missing for half the records. For others, for 46.2% this was
because the property was sold before work started, for 38.5% as households moved and for 15.4%
an applicant's death.

[254] The 38.6% of dwellings in conversion applications in the smallest parishes produced 28.6%
post-conversion numbers, as most merged units. Even this underplays slightly as 'change of use'
applications counted zero under 'original dwellings' but one after transformation. Under 500 population parishes, alongside those of 2000–2999 inhabitants were the only categories for which
conversions reduced dwelling numbers. The biggest rise in accommodation was for parishes with
500–999 residents, which moved from 36.8% (before) to 51.0% (after) of dwellings grant-aided.

awards (3.6% of applications and 5.4% of original buildings involved). Mitigating the prospect these trends indicate service-class impacts is the role of landlords. The Bedford Settled Estate alone covered 9.5% of all approved applications, with the Estate and two local brick companies in combination covering 18.3%. These three institutions were particularly active in providing worker accommodation in smaller villages. When their inputs were discounted, any appearance of disproportionate improvement in smaller villages disappeared (Table 7.4). Add to these three employers other companies, charities, trusteeships, etc., and the total share of successful applications rose to 35.8%. Amongst these numbers, a few owners were from outside the district but intimately involved with it. One example was the Diocese of St Albans, whose territory still covers Bedfordshire, which improved properties it owned. Even counting these agencies, applicants from outside the district had a minor role, accounting for just 4.6% of all approved applications. Even then, proposals tended to come from nearby, as migration theory predicts, with many from small places just beyond Ampthill's boundaries. The largest urban inputs were from Greater London, Luton-Dunstable and Leighton Buzzard, which covered 2.3% of applications. Further suggesting growth owed little to service-class inflows, the 1971 census statistics for Ampthill's parishes revealed that only 3.9% of heads of household in the smallest parishes had service-class occupations, with not much over 10% in larger. More substantial service-class inflows were to follow but by 1971 the service-class imprint on rural Bedfordshire was not strong.[255]

Table 7.4 Percent of all dwellings with successful home improvement grants in Ampthill by parish population, 1959–1969

	Parish population size category, 1961				
	Under 500	500– 999	1000- 1999	2000- 2999	Over 3000
% Households in 1961	10.9	30.3	24.4	20.4	14.2
% Dwellings approved for improvement	12.5	26.0	31.4	19.5	10.6
% Dwellings approved without three key employers	10.4	20.0	32.7	23.9	13.0

Source: Computed from the six files BRO RDAR9/1 to RDAR9/6
Note: The three key employers applying for the most grants were the Duke of Bedford's Estate (the Bedford Settled Estate), the London Brick Company and the Marston Valley Brick Company. A 'successful' improvement grant was taken to be an approved application that was not later withdrawn

---

[255] Service-class representation was lower in Biggleswade and north Norfolk, where values well under 10% were common. In each case, percentages were lower in smaller parishes. In Hertfordshire service-class shares were closer to 15% in Braughing and more like 20% in Hatfield, even with new town impacts (Table 1.1).

7.4.2   Estates and Coasts

Local actors were instrumental in much stock improvement in Ampthill, but the low-paid still faced significant handicaps in securing homes. The trajectory for rural private rental was downward (Chap. 2), with options for rural residents increasingly narrowing onto home-ownership or council tenancy. For England as a whole, relatively few new private rental homes were built after the 1920s, despite increases in the late-1940s for farm-workers and miners. Even so, in the 1970s private rental had a significant presence in smaller parishes (Table 7.5). Owner-occupation was on the low side in these places, with council provision about the same as in parishes up to 2000 residents. The closeness of figures for council tenancy was notable, especially given very low provision in some parishes. Hence, excluding parishes with under 50 dwellings, 11.8% of parishes in the seven rural districts had less than one-tenth of households in council accommodation. These places existed in all seven districts. For six of these parishes, the dominant tenure was home ownership but in 14 it was private rental. Here private rental was so dominant, owner occupation was also often under 10%. Mostly these places were part of large landed estates, such as Holkham in Walsingham (Earl of Leicester) or Ridgmont and Woburn in Ampthill (Duke of Bedford), although many former estate villages, like Old Warden in Biggleswade, had high private rental despite having passed from landed estates to other owners (shifting from the Ongley family to the Shuttleworths, who put it into a charitable trust). Case studies inform us that some estate villages at this time had poor housing and limited opportunities for residents (e.g. Kendall 1963; Bird 1982; Short and Godfrey 2007), although tenants might see improvements with new property owners or if former tenants left (Bowler and Lewis 1987; Spencer 1995). Consistent with Bowler and Lewis's Northamptonshire conclusions, parishes with high private rental densities tended to be smaller, so usually coming under 'limited growth' planning objectives. But even before land-use restraints were formalised, rural councils were inclined to exclude such places from building plans if landowners erected satisfactory dwellings. This occurred for Holkham and Old Warden in 1919, with Smallburgh assuming no need to build in 'estate' parishes, although major landowners were asked about their housing intentions.[256] Another impact arose when estates blocked construction by others, as reported for the Cuffley Estate (Hatfield) in 1923 and for the Duchy of Cornwall (repeating incidences told in academic studies; Kendall 1963; Dunn et al. 1981; Spencer 1995).[257] Perhaps most importantly estates structured the socio-political environment of housing decisions. As Councillor

---

[256] NRO DC19/6/8 WRDCM 19 March 1919, p.272; BRO RDBwM1/7 BiRDCM 23 July 1919, p.290; NRO DC22/2/45 SmRDCHCM 4 November 1919.

[257] HRO RDC7/1/8 HtRDCM 16 August 1923, p.351; TNA HLG37/43 'Report on Local Investigations …', undated c1936, p.12. Although some estates were in financial difficulty, reports of medical officers of health regularly noted their better accommodation (e.g. NRO DC19/6/14 WRDCM 26 May 1926, p.20; BRO RDAR8/11 ARDCMOHar 1930, p.12). This was not universal, as attested by Braughing's experience with Lord Mexborough's Estate, with many examples of the RDC chasing the Estate to improve dwellings and issuing demolition orders (e.g. HRO RDC3/1/1 18 June 1935, p.44; HRO RDC3/2/1 22 July 1936, p.127). At the same time, Lord Mexborough donated land for RDC house-building (HRO RDC3/1/1 BrRDCM 6 May 1937, p.233) and erected a few dwellings for Estate workers (e.g. *B&NEHG* 3 September 1937, p.4).

Table 7.5 Housing tenure in investigated rural districts by parish population, 1971

Percent of households

1971 parish population	Hertfordshire			Bedfordshire			Norfolk		
	Owner-occupiers	Public sector tenants	Private rental tenants	Owner-occupiers	Public sector tenants	Private rental tenants	Owner-occupiers	Public sector tenants	Private rental tenants
3000 plus	43.1	46.5	10.4	49.3	27.2	19.5	47.1	27.9	24.9
2000–2999				60.8	25.2	14.0	51.6	26.0	22.4
1000–1999	48.3	22.3	29.3	48.8	22.5	28.8	56.8	19.8	23.4
500–999	40.0	33.4	26.6	51.5	21.6	27.0	49.9	19.5	30.6
Under 500	40.7	23.1	36.2	29.5	21.8	48.7	41.1	20.9	38.0

Source: Computed from county reports of the 1971 population census

Note: Blank entries indicate no parish fell into the size category. In Hatfield (Hertfordshire), some 'council tenants' lived in new town accommodation under nomination agreements with the Development Corporation. There was only one parish in each of the two categories with over 2000 inhabitants in Norfolk

Thornton described planning for house-building in Milton Bryant (Ampthill) after the Second World War: '… we are in a difficult position, as all the land is in the hands of His Grace the Duke of Bedford'.[258]

With data on landownership not readily available, investigators like Bowler, Lewis and Spencer combined an array of sources to indicate 'estate' parishes. In their analysis, Bowler and Lewis found a high percentage of households in private rental was a serviceable proxy for estate-dominated villages. Like them, in this investigation, council papers, publications on landed estates (e.g. Grayson 1992; Barnes 1993; Wade-Martins 1994) and other materials were used to check proxy measures. The cut-off here was 60% of households in private rental, which was taken to signifying a strong likelihood of large estate holdings.[259] This expectation aligns with evidence that, when faced with fiscal discomfort, large estates sold peripheral estates or outlying plots to preserve core territory (Howkins 1991, p.279; Spencer 1995, pp.168–69; Beckett and Turner 2007, p.287; Horn 2013, pp.28–29), with concentrated private rental resulting. Offering some leeway for prior sales, the 60% cut-off was high enough to draw attention to 'core' villages, where, if they chose, estate owners could resist house-building by 'outsiders', while councils might view intervention as unnecessary. As Table 7.6 shows, where private rental volumes were high, this was associated with tepid household expansion up to 1961. Readers might object that the 1951–1961 pattern for larger Norfolk parishes suggests the contrary, but there was a specific story to tell here. There were only two Norfolk 'estate' parishes in the 1000–1999 range in 1951 (Raynham and Scottow). Both were affected by large military establishments bringing growth then retrenchment in the 1950s and 1960s (Table 4.6). These apart, the general trend was for low growth or decline in estate parishes, at least up to 1961 and even later in Norfolk. Bedfordshire in the 1960s presented a somewhat different story, for there were significant growth surges in estate parishes over the decade, even for the smallest places. While this might seem counterintuitive, it should be noted that much of Ampthill and Biggleswade fell outside green belt restrictions centred on Bedford and Luton. These two districts comprised the 'other rural' zones of Bedfordshire (e.g. Table 4.9). They saw much higher household growth in the 1960s than districts abutting Bedford and Luton, especially in owner-occupation (Table 6.9). As in Hertfordshire, the urge to preserve green belts is suggested by this pattern. What can be said is that, up to the end of the 1950s, 'estate' parishes saw less house-building than others, generally

---

[258] *WR&WSR* 7 September 1943, p.1.

[259] Using any cut-off introduces an element of arbitrariness. Bowler and Lewis used 80% but this was too restrictive for the districts investigated. Wade-Martins (1980, p.190), for example, noted that, on the Earl of Leicester's Holkham Estate, the Estate owned at least 50% of cottages in only one parish. The 60% limit offers an indicative compromise, which captured many well-known estate villages that would be missed by an 80% figure. In general, whatever the ownership of previous decades, by 1971 many estates had sold or closed properties such that their share of local accommodation had fallen (Havinden 1999, pp.210–13).

Table 7.6 Percent change in household numbers in 'estate' and non-estate parishes in Bedfordshire and Norfolk investigated rural districts, 1921–1971

		Percent change in household numbers			
		1921–1931	1931–1951	1951–1961	1961–1971
		Parishes with 1000–1999 inhabitants			
Norfolk	'Estate'	2.1		147.1	−20.3
	Not 'estate'	13.8	31.1	17.2	9.9
		Parishes with 500–900 inhabitants			
Bedfordshire	'Estate'		3.0	−0.7	25.5
	Not 'estate'	10.6	41.2	14.8	41.9
Norfolk	'Estate'		−4.5	1.3	−6.4
	Not 'estate'	8.9	22.6	6.0	8.8
		Parishes with under 500 inhabitants			
Bedfordshire	'Estate'	3.5	24.8	−1.9	46.6
	Not 'estate'	9.1	19.0	12.4	12.8
Norfolk	'Estate'	2.9	8.4	5.1	0.5
	Not 'estate'	7.2	23.4	1.3	5.2

Source: Computed from county reports of the population censuses
Note: 'Estate' parishes were defined as having more than 60% of households in private rental in 1971. The population size categories were determined by the start of the census period; hence, the number of parishes in categories changed slightly between census periods. Blank entries indicate no parish fell into the size category. Hertfordshire had only one parish with 60% households living in private rental, so it was excluded. Bedfordshire was not shown for 1000–1999 inhabitants as it only had one relevant parish for 1921 and none for other census dates. The particularly high value in 1951–1961 Norfolk 'estate' villages with 1000–1999 inhabitants was because only two parishes fell into this category with both experiencing military base impacts as exemplified in Table 4.6

irrespective of parish size. In the 1960s, this pattern was disrupted in Bedfordshire but not in Norfolk (Table 7.6).

A potential input into the spatial patterning of household expansion was the claim made on many occasions in Norfolk that growth was occurring along the coast but not elsewhere. Inter-war, for example, medical officer of health accounts noted new private development was chiefly along the coast, involving small-scale holiday cottages,[260] along with new homes built for the very wealthy (Wade-Martins and Williamson 2008, p.91). Similar expansion of second homes was reported in the early-1960s (Coleman 1982).[261] Erpingham was not alone in claiming only coastal villages were not experiencing depopulation pressure in the 1960s,[262] as exemplified in commentary at a 1962 Walsingham Council meeting: 'Blakeney and many other villages along the coast are virtually dead. The only time they come to life is for a

---

[260] NRO DC19/6/11 WRDCM 16 May 1923, p.20 in binding; *EDP* 6 June 1935, p.7.

[261] As in Walsingham (*NNN* 26 October 1962, p.1), Smallburgh (*EDP* 6 June 1935, p.6) and Erpingham (*NNN* 3 April 1964, p.3).

[262] *NNN* 3 April 1964, p.3. Similar laments over the potential disappearance of Norfolk villages were voiced elsewhere at this time (as with Mitford and Launditch; *D&FT* 23 February 1962, p.2; 6 March 1964, p.1).

fortnight or three weeks in a year when the moneyed people go down and occupy cottages for which they have paid the earth'.[263] Councillors held that coastal villages were 'ghost towns' for much of the year.[264] Yet, as the 1960s progressed, some comfort was gained when local firms built bungalows for-migrant retirees in Norfolk's small towns and villages (Lemon 1973; Coles 1982). Exploring the effects of coastal location had to be limited to places of fewer than 2000 residents, since no coastal parish had more than 1536 inhabitants even in 1971. Where comparison could be made was with the three coastal UDCs (Cromer, Sheringham and Wells-next-the-Sea), whose 1971 populations ranged from 2343 to 5376. Perhaps surprisingly, there was little to distinguish rural coastal parishes with over 1000 residents from these UDCs. Thus, increases in household numbers for the rural group were 13.8% 38.7%, 31.5% and 7.6% over the census periods examined (Table 7.7), which was little different from the UDCs (13.4%, 29.2% 16.7% and 9.7%). Rural coastal areas even grew faster than inland parishes with more than 2000 inhabitants up to 1951, then inland centres expanded more. Amongst smaller coastal parishes, by the 1960s there was a breakdown in settlement hierarchy effects, with the highest growth in the smallest places. More notable though was the tendency for coastal parishes to growth more than those inland. Hence, for the nine census period coastal-non-coastal contrasts before 1961, seven saw higher growth in coastal zones (Table 7.7). The sharpest exception was for the smallest parishes over 1931–1951 but this inland group contained various military bases that expanded rapidly in the 1930s, as well as places on the Norfolk Broads that saw tourism expansion (e.g. Hoveton).

Table 7.7 Percent change in households in investigated rural districts in Norfolk coastal and inland parishes, 1921–1971

	Percent change in household numbers			
	1921–1931	1931–1951	1951–1961	1961–1971
Parishes with 1000–1999 inhabitants				
Coastal	13.8	38.7	31.5	7.6
Inland	2.1	26.4	24.9	9.8
Parishes with 500–900 inhabitants				
Coastal	3.4	30.6	13.1	8.2
Inland	10.6	19.0	1.6	8.1
Parishes with under 500 inhabitants				
Coastal	8.1	8.8	3.5	13.5
Inland	6.3	20.0	1.8	−0.6

Source: Computed from county reports of the population censuses
Note: The population size categories were determined by the start of the census period; hence, the number of parishes in categories changed slightly between census periods. 'Coastal' refers to parishes adjacent to the north Norfolk coast

[263] *NNN* 26 October 1962, p.1.

[264] *NNN* 9 December 1949, p.1; 26 October 1962, p.1.

A point to note, which applied across the decades, was the mismatch between changes in population and household numbers. These bring to the fore remonstrations, like those of Grafton (1982) and Weekley (1988), over the paradox of demographic losses hiding stable or positive demographic tendencies. For example, while coastal parishes with fewer than 500 inhabitants saw resident losses of 6.3% for 1951–1961, household numbers increased by 3.5%. Indeed, for all the size categories shown in Table 7.7, the populations of coastal parishes fell in at least two of the four census periods, whereas household numbers rose consistently. This suggests a shift in household composition towards fewer residents in each home. One measure of this was the share of populations that were retired. Here the proportion in parishes increased as parish size rose in coastal areas but not in inland zones. For the latter, the retired percentage stood at around 10%–12% in 1971 in the three population categories in Table 7.7. On the coast, the values were 15.6% for the smallest parishes, 17.1% for the middle group and 24.7% for places with 1000–1999 inhabitants. Confirmation the retired contributed to north Norfolk's household expansion came from data on retired in-migrants over 1966–1971. Here, there was a sharp contrast between those moving into parishes within the same rural district and those coming from outside. Those who moved from within a district had minor impacts on parish populations, whether coastal or inland. The largest component of local populations coming from intra-district in-migrants was only 2.7% for coastal parishes of 500–1999 residents. The lowest addition was 1.1% for the smallest coastal parishes and for mid-sized inland parishes. By contrast, 9.2% of residents in coastal parishes with more than 1000 residents were in-migrant retirees from outside the district. On the coast, parishes with fewer than 500 inhabitants had the smallest population increments from 'outsider' retirees (at 4.8%) but this was higher than any inland parish category.[265] That these migrant flows were directed more to larger centres would be consistent with builder activity, which tended to favour small towns and larger villages (Lemon 1973). Significantly, retired in-migrants made up more than 30% of all inflows into coastal parishes with more than 500 inhabitants (whether from inside or outside a district). Movement into inland places made a significantly smaller imprint, with the share of retirees in these moves generally not far from 10%. Both for the elderly and for those coming from outside, the coast was an attraction, as was settlement size. As Table 7.3 indicates, there was a centralisation of household growth, which even the attractions of coastal locations only mitigated marginally. How far was this tendency repeated for council homes?

---

[265] These computations were made from the Registrar-General (2002). This source takes the retired population as those above the then state pension age, so 65 years for men and 60 years for women.

7.5   Intra-District Council-Building

Trends favouring house-building in large centres and on the coast were disrupted somewhat by land-use planning policies after 1947 and, with more localised effects, by major institutional interventions like military bases (Table 4.6). Overall, though, size counted. In previous chapters, a similar effect was shown for council-building, whether urged by government, builder action (or inaction), changed house-building methods or land-use plans. However, so far this propensity has been signalled as a tendency rather than an actuality. Divergence between policy intention and implementation always needs evaluation (Pressman and Wildavsky 1984; Rocke 1987; Gilg and Kelly 1997). As regards the provision of social housing, this merits particular attention, for while economics permeates policy action, a core value for council housing is its social purpose. This distinguishes council-building from construction for private-owners, for which the primary motivation is builder profit. The question therefore needs asking, whether council-building followed private sector trends or charted its own path. Signalling prospects of divergence, when a rural coalition sought to block house-building in Highmoor, Oxfordshire, only 38 dwellings were added in 43 years, with almost all council-owned (Spencer 1995, p.169). If council-building embedded dissimilar locational criteria from private construction, shifts in the balance of public and private building should produce dissimilar geographies (Table 7.2). Put another way, when building for private-owners accounted for the vast majority of new dwellings (Figs. 6.1 and 6.2), this might have disguised a smaller, distinct path in public sector completions.

Council papers offered few glimpses of such inclinations within districts, largely because systematic reports on new-build at parish level were rare. The most extensive data found were for Biggleswade (Table 7.8). These demonstrated key propensities in council-building. For one, the smallest parishes tended to be under-represented in building volumes relative to their share of district households.[266] Indeed, five parishes did not see a single council dwelling built over the 50-year period examined. This is not without precedent. Phillips and Williams (1982b, pp.308-09), for instance, found three parishes in South Hams (Devon) with no council homes, with a further 18 having less than 15 (only two out of 25 with council dwellings in Biggleswade had fewer than 15). Likewise, Read (2003, p.108) observed that Henley RDC did not build in all parishes, while 29 of 80 Lake District parishes lacked local authority homes (Shucksmith 1981, p.114; also Beazley et al. 1980 on South Oxfordshire).

---

[266] Computations for council-building used 1971 parishes, for a consistent geographical framework across the decades. In Biggleswade (and Ampthill) this had no effect on results, since these districts were barely touched by parish reorganisations. Walsingham on the other hand had 54 parishes at the 1921 census but 39 by the 1971 census, despite numbers being enhanced by the transfer-in of some parishes from other districts. The reduction resulted from mergers. These merged parishes were used in computations here. Few mergers changed the population category of the initial or resulting parishes.

Table 7.8   Percentage of new-build council dwellings in Biggleswade under different Housing Acts by parish population, 1913–1971

Parish population at relevant census	Percentage completed on the termination of building under the Housing Act of													
	1890–1909	1919	1924	1925	1930	1931	1936	1938	1946	Temp-orary	1956–1958 with subsidy	1956–1958 without subsidy	1961	1967
3000 plus	0.0	11.1	22.6	20.8	3.7	0.0	9.1	13.6	24.4	5.9	26.6	27.4	45.4	38.3
2000-2999	0.0	19.7	38.2	52.8	11.1	0.0	36.4	18.2	24.3	37.0	30.4	42.5	14.6	0.0
1000-1999	100.0	26.6	17.2	9.4	18.5	50.0	0.0	40.9	36.4	42.2	36.7	30.1	14.6	48.6
500-999	0.0	12.0	11.3	11.3	25.9	33.3	9.1	0.0	4.2	14.8	1.3	0.0	10.4	12.2
Under 500	0.0	30.6	10.8	5.7	40.7	16.7	45.5	27.3	10.8	0.0	5.1	0.0	14.9	0.9
Number built under act	20	549	372	106	54	36	22	44	936	135	158	113	355	161

Percent of households in district by population size for relevant census date

Relevant census	1921	1931	1951	1961
3000 plus	9.5	12.5	22.4	40.4
2000-2999	19.5	18.5	23.6	18.0
1000-1999	28.3	38.3	31.5	17.9
500-999	10.4	14.7	8.6	11.9
Under 500	16.1	16.0	13.9	11.7

Source: Computed from data in Biggleswade RDC (1923, p.7) and BRO RDBwH2/1 to RDBwH2/8, which are registers of houses provided under different Housing Acts, plus, for the 1931 Act, BRO RDBwM1/11 BiRDCM 17 February 1932

Note: The parishes used in computations were those at the 1971 census. To interpret the table, read down the column. For instance, the only council homes built under the 1890 Act were 20 at Langford (1921 population 1205), so the size category 1000–1999 covered 100% of completions under the Act. The RDC built 611 dwellings under the 1919 Act but 62 were in Sandy, which became a separate UDC in 1927. These 62 were excluded from this table. 'Temporary' refers to prefabricated dwellings erected from 1946–48. These were included because they only began to be vacated from 1967. In all, 55.5% of temporary dwellings had not been vacated by the end of 1971 (BRO RDBwH2/4 'Register of New Temporary Houses 1946–1948'). Taking 1967 Act figures as net rather than absolute (viz. as built minus vacated temporary dwellings), the net percentage of homes added across the population categories were 38.5%, −13.7%, 63.4%, 10.6% and 1.2%, reading downwards. Taking the number of vacated temporary dwellings away from the total listed above gives 3061 dwellings by 1971, with 3095 council tenancies reported in the 1971 Census. Some of this difference will be because temporary dwellings were vacated between the census date and the end of 1971. Another cause for divergence was council purchases of dwellings, as with calls to buy overcrowded properties to alleviate distress (e.g. NBC&BR 4 February 1947, p.7). There were no data on acquisition numbers or locations. The percentage of households in proximate censuses indicates the census against which population categories were determined, as well as offering a base for assessing the proportionality of provision. Reading down the size column, at the 1971 census the percentages of all council tenants in the population categories were 49.6%, 23.3%, 11.1%, 8.7% and 7.4%

Before taking this as indicative of poor provision for smaller places, note that even as late as 1971 four of the five Biggleswade parishes so afflicted had more than 70% of their households, and as high as 98.8%, in private rental. The fifth had a 1971 population of only 35 (47 in 1921). Recall also that Biggleswade was an aggressive builder under the 1919 Act, and under this Act, as with the farm-worker oriented Acts of 1931 and 1938, small parishes were over-represented in building numbers (Table 7.8). These Acts surpassed even the 1946 Act, despite its extra funds for farm-worker homes, perhaps because of the emphasis on locating new-build near services under this Act. Counter-balancing this, most inter-war no-subsidy homes were erected under the 1925 Act, for which building in larger centres dominated, which signified the weaker ability of workers in smaller villages to pay 'economic rents'. Perhaps surprisingly, inter-war slum clearance (1930 and 1936 Acts) saw higher returns in small parishes. Given rural councils negative views on funding under these Acts, and a general rural council reluctance to impose on property owners, this seems unexpected. Yet Biggleswade pressed for the removal of unfit housing across the decades, declaring even in the late-1960s that small parishes had the most urgent need for slum removal.[267] In its commitment to addressing poor housing, Biggleswade adjusted tactics to achieve all-round housing gain. Thus, in 1944 when the Ministry indicated councils were unlikely to benefit from post-war housing schemes unless they '… contemplate acquiring sites of over five acres in extent',[268] with large contractors who grouped schemes to be favoured, the Council responded by seeking 200 temporary prefabricated dwellings, looking to place 50 each in its four largest settlements.[269] Adaptability was again seen in 1954, when the Council was disconcerted by a low allocation from the Ministry. Its response was to concentrate building geographically, trusting rapid completions would elicit higher future allocations.[270] Three years later, Biggleswade denied Stotfold (its largest village) extra housing because Arlesey could immediately accept the larger building batches the then sparse subsidy regime made necessary to ensure rent affordability.[271] With national pressure to limit council-building, the RDC Clerk declared in 1960 that smaller villages had 'no chance' of new council homes.[272] This view was expressed elsewhere in the 1960s, as with Braughing's conclusion that industrialised methods '… would necessitate the construction of houses in comparatively large groups, probably in terraces. With land prices, building costs, and rates of interest at their present levels, the building of further houses in small groups and of

---

[267] BRO RDBwM1/40 BiRDCHCM 14 May 1969, p.1033.

[268] BRO RDBwM1/15 BiRDCM 29 March 1944, p.217.

[269] NBC&BR 9 January 1945, p.3. The Ministry offered 70 rather than 200 (BRO RDBwM1/15 BiRDCM 28 March 1945, p.432). Despite an ongoing preference for permanent over temporary homes (NBC&BR 11 December 1945, p.2; 30 April 1946, p.4), the Council pressed for more prefabs to address shortfalls, erecting 137 eventually.

[270] NBC&BR 16 November 1954, p.14.

[271] BC&BG 10 May 1957, p.12. This was despite Stotfold having a longer waiting list than Arlesey.

[272] BC&BG 15 January 1960, p.11.

traditional materials would have to be abandoned'.[273] Comparing new-build and household shares, tendencies away from the smallest places increased in Biggleswade after 1945 (Table 7.8).

The relationship of new-build and parish size was not linear across rural districts (Tables 7.8 and 7.9). In broad terms, after 1945 government initiatives favoured building in larger places, as cost pressures encouraged bigger projects in single locations. Ministry support for industrialised building intensified this impetus, as did the introduction of Parker Morris standards, because both raised building costs (and so rents), so discouraging tenant take-up where wages were lower.[274] The introduction of cost yardsticks was not sympathetic to small settlements, with the Ministry acknowledging its effects pinched too tightly.[275] But village size was not a determinant of the availability of housing sites. As an example, Ampthill was running out of building plots by 1972, with Ministry cost restrictions decreasing prospects of securing more. By this date, the RDC estimated it needed another 78 acres for house-building, but only owned 20.5. Of these only 5.5 were in parishes with more than 2000 residents, which by 1971 accounted for almost three-fifths of the district's households. More than half the available land was in parishes of 1000–1999 inhabitants (23.7% of households) and almost as much in parishes of 500–999 residents as for those with more than 2000.[276] Five years earlier almost 40 acres had been available, out of which the largest parishes held around half, with just over 30% and 20%, respectively, for smaller parishes (those with fewer than 500 residents had a combined availability of under an acre at both dates).[277] The significance of this arose from a 1955 decision, which was reaffirmed periodically, to focus building primarily on land the Council owned.[278] This was so projects were not

Table 7.9 Percent of new-build council dwellings in Ampthill by parish population, 1964–1969

Population size in 1961	Under 500	500–999	1000-1999	2000-2999	Over 3000
% of council new-build in RDC	6.5	28.8	25.9	21.6	17.3
% of 1961 district households	10.9	30.2	24.4	20.4	14.2

Source: Computed from BRO RDAM1/20 and RDAM1/25 'Ampthill Annual Abstract of Accounts'

---

[273] HRO RDC3/1/16 BrRDCECM 6 February 1966, p.6724.

[274] In 1969 the Biggleswade Housing Manager reported extreme difficulty letting new houses in the 'more rural' parts of the district, with little chance tenants would voluntarily leave low rent (potentially unfit) accommodation, even with rent rebates (BRO RDBwM1/40 BiRDCHCM 14 May 1969, p.1033).

[275] TNA HLG118/945 'Review of the Housing Cost Yardstick. Meeting with Local Authority Associations', 13 December 1968.

[276] BRO RDAM1/28 ARDCHPBuCM 14 June 1972, p.10.

[277] BRO RDAM1/23 ARDCHPBuCM 17 July 1967.

[278] BRO RDAM2/22 ARDCHCM 3 February 1955; *WR&WSR* 30 June 1964, p.27; BRO RDAM1/21 ARDCM 11 November 1965, p.369; BRO RDAM1/24 ARDCHCM 8 October 1968, pp.261–262; BRO RDAM1/29 ARDCHPBuCM 3 September 1973, pp.250–251.

held-up by acquisition delays or disputes over taking farmland, which had created delay for earlier schemes. But the distribution of house-building was not simply a matter of land availability. Ampthill also experienced delays because it could not secure builders for its contracts. This applied in specific parishes in the early-1950s, when the house-building programme was in full swing, as when firms shied away from council-building in the Duke of Bedford's prime village of Woburn.[279] By the early-1960s the problem had spread, with new-build shelved as builders were not available.[280] Despite these handicaps, and national centralisation trends, in the late-1960s Ampthill had a new-build distribution that reasonably matched parish household numbers (Table 7.9). The gains accruing to smaller parishes were reminiscent of Ampthill's performance from 1945–60, when 23 of its 29 parishes had new council homes.[281] Indeed, even when limited by low Ministry allocations, this RDC sought to distribute dwellings across many villages, as with the 11 parishes sharing a 1962 allocation of 75, 12 having a slice of 120 in 1963 and the 120 for 1964 being divided between nine parishes.[282] In each case, small parishes were targeted. They were not offered large projects, as seen by four dwellings for Milton Bryan in 1962, but this was to a parish with only 48 (1961) households, with Hulcote-Salford matching its four in 1963 (69 households). These apportionments indicate Ampthill responded to housing needs across the settlement hierarchy. Records on actual allocations before the 1960s were poor, although 1919 Act completions had a comparable distribution to 1964–1969.[283] After the 1919 Act, however, council minutes suggest smaller places attracted less activity. With subsidy cuts in the 1930s in particular, there were regular messages that rents were non-affordable for farm-workers. Building in smaller agricultural parishes dwindled.[284]

Walsingham resonates with a comparable message. Here systematic information on parishes did not extend beyond the 1946 Act, which, like the agriculture-focused 1938 Act, stood apart in this district for small parish gains (Table 7.10). Stripped of the enthusiasm Biggleswade demonstrated for the 1919 Act, Walsingham saw meagre returns for smaller places, even with special 1924 Act funding for agricultural

[279] WR&WSR 1 April 1952, p.1. When a builder was eventually found the prices quoted were too rich for the Ministry, so the project faltered (WR&WSR 1 July 1952, p.1). Council records and newspapers were too fleeting to grasp if the problem was specific to Woburn or extended to other parishes dominated by the Bedford Settled Estate.

[280] WR&WSR 4 December 1962, p.1.

[281] BRO RDAR8/41 ARDCMOHar 1960, p.15.

[282] BRO RDAM2/23 ARDCHCM 18 January 1962; BRO PC Houghton Conquest 18/13 26 July 1962; BRO RDAM1/18 ARDCHPByCM 23 October 1962, p.287; BRO RDAM1/19 ARDCHPByCM 10 October 1963, p.242.

[283] Six houses were built in a parish of less than 500 residents out of 48 erected, so 12.5% of the total, when this parish group accounted for 16.1% of RDC households in 1921 (BRO RDAR8/2 ARDCMOHar 1921). These 48 new homes exclude Toddington, which was transferred to Luton RDC shortly afterwards.

[284] For example, W&DR 26 August 1933, p.7; 6 July 1935, p.1.

parishes.[285] Walsingham typified rural Norfolk with many households in small parishes, and a bias towards agricultural occupations (Tables 1.1 and 1.2). It occupied a dissimilar context from the wealthier, more mixed economy of rural Bedfordshire. Yet, despite the limited time-run for the Walsingham data, trends were clear. Where funding was less advantageous for farming areas, as for the 1919 and 1930 Acts, building volumes focused on settlements with more non-farm work, with council reports indicating non-affordability for farm labourers was critical (Chap. 4). Even in agricultural parishes, 1919 dwellings often went to non-farm tenants.[286] Note that Walsingham had difficulty persuading local builders to engage with the 1919 Act, leading to a reliance on external firms quoting (locally) high prices.[287] Charges were further elevated by material shortages,[288] with dispute with Whitehall over rent expectations. Citing tenancy application withdrawals, the Council applied for lower rents even for the 'market town' of Fakenham.[289] In the end, building was delayed until prices fell, even though the Council feared this might induce the Ministry to claim it was defaulting on its responsibilities.[290] This helps explain patterns in Table 7.10. When prices did fall, it was too late, as 1919 Act approvals terminated in 1921. Walsingham had to wait for Treasury aid to restart, and for more generous support for farm worker dwellings, under the 1924, 1938 and 1946 Acts, to stimulate action. Then, even given the sluggish local economy, efforts were made to address needs in all settlements.

This should not distract from the frequently made point that those unable to afford owner-occupation were poorly served by British housing regimes (Berry 1974; Bassett and Short 1980). But this story is nuanced. There was a petit bourgeois mind-set underscoring many rural council decisions on rate-paying and service provision but there was also a commitment to serve the community. There was a poverty of provision alongside struggles against generally unfriendly government policies. Patterns of housing supply and improvement were complex. Take, for example, the distribution of council dwellings within rural districts. Publications on rural England have regularly drawn attention to the manner in which council dwellings were built on the fringes or even isolated from villages, sometimes, like Crichton, with a condemning tone suggesting the location was intentional (Crichton 1964, p.82; Connell 1978, p.77; Robin 1980, p.242). Deliberate social segregation

---

[285] Of the 35 Walsingham 'parishes' for which data were available for Table 7.10, six had no council homes when building under the 1946 Act ended. Four of them were heavily dependent on estate cottages. 'Parishes' is in inverted commas because two 'parishes' were aggregations in the data source. Little and Great Ryburgh were presented as the Ryburghs. They were recorded with council homes up to and including the 1946 Act, but by 1971 Little Ryburgh still had no council dwelling. In 1971, only three parishes were without council homes, the other two dominated by landed estates.

[286] NRO DC19/6/9 WRDCM 22 December 1920, p.149.

[287] NRO DC19/6/8 WRDCM 26 November 1919, p.23.

[288] *FakPost* 5 December 1919, p.1; NRO DC19/6/9 WRDCM 29 June 1921, p.207.

[289] NRO DC19/6/9 WRDCM 1 June 1921, p.196; 29 June 1921, p.208.

[290] NRO DC19/6/9 WRDCM 15 June 1921, p.203.

Table 7.10 Percentage of new-build council dwellings in Walsingham under different Housing Acts by parish population, 1919–1953

Parish population at relevant census	Percentage erected on termination of building under Housing Act of				
	1919	1924	1930	1938	1946
2000-2999	64.5	18.9	41.6	0.0	13.6
1000-1999	0.0	12.3	5.8	0.0	18.5
500–999	25.8	32.8	21.9	0.0	9.9
Under 500	9.7	27.9	9.5	100.0	56.2
Number built under Act	31	244	137	4	314
	Percent of households in district by population size for				
Relevant census	1921		1931		1951
2000-2999	17.5		18.0		20.4
1000-1999	21.9		16.3		18.6
500–999	23.6		32.4		21.8
Under 500	50.7		48.2		39.2

Source: For the 1919 Act NRO DC19/6/9 WRDCM 18 May 1921, p.192 in binding. For the Acts of 1924, 1930, 1938 and 1946 NRO DC19/4/1 – DC19/4/3 Registers of Houses Provided under Housing Acts

Note: The parishes used in computations were those at the 1971 census. The percentage of households for proximate censuses indicates the census against which population categories were determined, as well as offering a base to assess the proportionality of provision. The percentage of households by population group differs in this table from other computations because council house numbers for Great and Little Walsingham were aggregated in this data source, so these parishes were combined for this exercise, which involved these two parishes being placed under the 1000–1999 bracket, when individually they fell below this level. Building under the 1931 Housing (Rural Authorities) Act was not included owing to a lack of clarity in council records on where dwellings were built. This RDC had 22 dwellings initially approved under the 1931 Act and was granted permission to build a further 10, but where the initial 22 were built was not clear, nor was whether the final 10 were ever erected. The information that was clear was that four of the final 10 were proposed for Helhoughton (1931 population 304), while Sculthorpe (531 inhabitants) was to have six (NRO DC19/6/21 WRDCM 19 April 1933, p.10)

is implied, geared around middle-(and upper-)class fears, as seen in a particularly notorious example in the leafy urbanity of Oxford, when a wall was erected to block working-class access to the middle-class end of the same road (Collison 1963). Two points should be made about this image. The first is that social segregation exists in villages without physical barriers. Numerous studies report a sparsity of middle-class interactions with longer-standing working-class villagers (Pahl 1965; Harris 1974; Connell 1978; Pacione 1980; Strathern 1982). Second, there is no doubt council homes were sometimes deliberately located away from villages, as when 'the squire' insisted on this outcome in East Clandon in Surrey (Connell 1978, p.77). Yet, as shown earlier in this chapter, and as Robin (1980, p.242) reported for Elmdon, peripheral sites could be the only viable option. This was despite the fact that, in many cases, sites were rejected due to their 'isolation', alongside political opposition to them (Griffiths 2007, p.294). Then again, if we lift our attention away from the countryside for a moment, we find similar tales of peripherality, accompanied by lack of services, added costs for inhabitants and social isolation, in city council estates, especially inter-war (e.g. Bayliss 2001). Indeed, Gardiner (2010, p.273) asserted that 90% of inter-war council estates were suburban, which Brighton, Bristol, Leeds, Liverpool, London, Manchester and Nottingham bear witness to, both as regards location and the difficulties they created for their tenants (Thomas 1966; Dale 1980; Dresser 1984; Finnigan 1984; Yelling 1992; Pooley 1996; Olechnowicz 1997; Jones 2010).

Apart from proximity to village cores, another aspect of intra-district positioning was placement across settlements. Here we find the literature more silent than it should be. There are some glimpses, as with Phillips and Williams (1983, p.507) noting that non-classified (restricted growth) settlements in South Hams had approximately half the total population, but little more than a quarter of the council stock or Cloke (1979) identifying loose coincidence of key settlements and council house-building (also Sillince 1986). Significantly, such insights tend to explore local government after its 1974 reorganisation, when former urban districts were merged with rural ones (Dearlove 1979). These new groupings combined formerly distinct councils, with different regimes for funding and service provision. Notably, the proportion of 1971 households in council dwellings in England was considerably higher in UDCs and Boroughs (28.8%) than in the RDCs they merged with (22.1%). As such, after merger, it was likely rural components of new authorities had fewer council dwellings. The more important question for the new regime was whether 'urban values' and urban trajectories were pressed on the countryside after merger, which was one rural fear about reorganisation (RDCA 1966), with complaints of adverse urban impacts on rural housing stretching back to inter-war decades.[291] But when we look before 1974, despite some quality investigations (e.g. Jennings 1971; Sherwood 1996), comments tend to emphasise shortcomings at the district level, where limited rural building rears negative evaluations (e.g. Baker 1953, p.186). Little has been revealed about intra-district provision. Table 7.11 contributes an antidote.

What the top third of Table 7.11 shows is that the accumulation of council-building and dwelling purchases to 1971 produced relatively few council homes in smaller parishes. The exception was north Norfolk. This, however, owed much to the lopsided demography of these districts, for while places with fewer than 500 inhabitants had 41.3% of council homes in Walsingham, they also had 41.8% of households. Figures for Smallburgh were similar, with 26.5% and 29.9%, respectively, although for Erpingham the household share (42.9%) was smaller than for council dwellings (48.9%). These figures alone provide two surprises. The first is the relatively high presence of council homes in smaller villages. This was not what the literature leads us to expect. The second is the narrowness of the gap between household and council dwelling shares, suggesting rural councils placed homes in response to population demand rather than settlement size. This is reinforced by the

---

[291] TNA HLG47/702 Letter from CPRE Secretary to J.C. Wrigley, MoH, 16 March 1936; MoH (1937a, p.24).

middle third of Table 7.11, which shows that the percentage of all households living in council accommodation did not vary much by parish size. Where it did, places with proportionately more council homes were not always the larger ones. A slight bias towards larger parishes was there but it was weak in some cases (Biggleswade, Walsingham) and non-existent in others (Braughing, Smallburgh). The only district that fits the image of smaller places having conspicuously lower provision was Ampthill. Viewed alongside the presence of manual workers and farm labourers, Ampthill again scores poorly, as its smaller parishes had relatively few council homes compared with complements in this worker category. In this regard, as the bottom part of Table 7.11 suggests, Walsingham again scored well. Yet, compared to the other districts investigated, Walsingham built relatively few council dwellings (e.g. Tables 3.10 and 6.11); although compared to occupational and demographic structures, its performance was credible (Tables 7.10 and 7.11).

Except for household amenities, there was little evidence on the quality of the housing stock on which to make comparisons between the districts. Exploring whether exclusive access to basic facilities might cast light on council-building activity, the sector most likely to draw focused council attention was private rental (Table 7.12). This shows that, for the smallest parishes, two of the three councils with the highest proportions in council dwellings (Biggleswade and Braughing) had relatively high-quality private rental amenities. These two councils offered substantive opportunities for council accommodation down the settlement hierarchy even though local private rental units were not particularly poor in quality (relatively speaking). By contrast, Ampthill and Erpingham had relatively low council provision (Table 7.11), even though private rental was more suspect (Table 7.12). Smallburgh sits somewhat uncomfortably in a similar position, with less generous supplies of council dwellings in smaller places, alongside poorer provisioned private rental. Walsingham's pattern was more complex but did indicate responsiveness to local housing difficulties, with most council provision in the one parish in the 1000–1999 dwelling range (Table 7.11), which also had particularly poor private rental provision (Table 7.12), while the thinnest council offerings (the 500–999 population range) were in parishes with the best provided privately rented dwellings.

Bringing Walsingham into the spotlight draws attention to another issue, which is the role of landed estates. In Walsingham just shy of 18% of the district's 1971 households lived in parishes dominated by private rental. A consequence of councils not building where large estates dominated is demonstrated in Table 7.13. This shows that 'estate' villages had low rates of council provision for their size. Hence, figures in the mid-section of Table 7.11 need treating with a little caution. Note for example the contrast between 'estate' and other parishes in Biggleswade. For the smallest parishes, the already high value of 30.3% of all households who occupied council homes breaks down into just 3.2% in 'estate' parishes and 38.0% elsewhere. This 38.0% was considerably higher than the score for the largest parishes (32.6%). Accept for the moment that councils were justified in assuming local landowners provided high-quality homes. Most councils reported higher standards on estate cottages when considering locations under the 1919 Act, and if estates sold

Table 7.11   Council tenancy shares in investigated rural districts by parish population, 1971

	Population size in 1971				
	Under 500	500–999	1000-1999	2000-2999	Over 3000
Rural District Council	Percent of council tenancies within the RDC				
Braughing	26.1	19.3	29.6		25.1
Ampthill	2.6	13.2	25.4	19.2	39.7
Biggleswade	7.5	8.6	11.1	23.3	49.6
Erpingham	48.9	17.4	15.1	18.7	
Smallburgh	26.5	44.5	29.1		
Walsingham	41.3	19.7	8.8		30.3
	Percent of all households living in council housing by population strata				
Braughing	23.1	29.3	22.3		19.4
Ampthill	10.4	17.9	22.4	21.4	22.6
Biggleswade	30.3	28.1	22.6	28.3	30.3
Erpingham	19.0	12.9	11.4	26.0	
Smallburgh	20.7	24.6	24.2		
Walsingham	23.3	16.8	29.6		27.9
	Percent of heads of household with manual or farm-worker occupations				
Braughing	57.0	43.9	40.9		42.7
Ampthill	54.9	52.8	54.5	46.7	48.7
Biggleswade	57.4	44.3	32.6	46.9	51.1
Erpingham	62.8	55.9	36.2	41.4	
Smallburgh	58.4	49.4	42.8		
Walsingham	55.6	40.3	71.0		49.2

Source: Computed from county reports of the 1971 population census
Note: Hatfield was excluded from this list as it had so few parishes, with three of the four having more than 5000 residents in 1971. Blanks represent categories for which there were no relevant parishes. In Walsingham, the manual worker representation in parishes of 1000–1999 was particularly high as this category comprised a single parish, Briston, which housed many workers from the railway repair works at Melton Constable (Wrottesley 1970)

peripheral holdings to maintain core possessions, then parishes with high 1971 private rental might reasonably be expected to have had superior estate accommodation. Moreover, some, like Ampthill, saw standards rise following landlord applications for home improvement grants in the 1950s and 1960s (Table 7.4). Yet, even if estates provided good quality homes, council provision looked weak in some districts. For small non-estate parishes, for example, only in Biggleswade was the rate of council supply above the national average of 28.0% in 1971, albeit Walsingham came close. Mostly, for small non-estate parishes, the districts hovered around the English RDC average of 22.1% of all 1971 households living in council dwellings (with Ampthill lower; Table 7.13). A difficulty arises if you relax the assumption landlords provided good quality homes, especially given evidence of landowner failures to maintain estates' cottages (Kendall 1963; Mingay 1990). Using exclusive access to basic household amenities as a proxy for housing quality stretches interpretive bounds somewhat, but insofar as it helps capture quality differences, the impact of extensive private rental was mixed (Table 7.14). As expected, compared to council and owner-occupied homes, private rental was poorly equipped. Yet, in the smallest parishes, there was no clear pattern of better or worse private rental amenities for 'estate' and non-estate areas. In Ampthill, the smallest 'estate' parishes had poorer amenities; yet, virtually all 'estate' parishes had Bedford Settled Estate ties (e.g. Battlesden, Husborne Crawley, Millbrook, Milton Bryan, Potsgrove). But so did Ridgmont and Woburn, two slightly larger settlements, where amenities were superior to non-estate equivalents. This signals that rural reliance on high-quality homes being offered by large private landlords was questionable. This was despite little separating such parishes as regards improvement grant activity (Table 7.4). Thus, while Ridgmont and Woburn accounted for 62.9% of the Estate's successful improvement grant applications over 1959–1969, they also had 66.1% of private rental households in Ampthill's 'estate' parishes (for 1961, 65.8% for 1971). As for the notion that 'peripheral' possessions might receive less favour, this looks difficult to sustain with all Bedford Settled Estate parishes adjacent to one another. Besides which, when the Estate sold land it did so even in its heartland of Woburn,[292] sold properties occupied by Estate workers and pensioners, as with 81 put up for sale in 1961, of which 45 were in Ridgmont,[293] and demolished cottages in Woburn and elsewhere.[294] Overall, private rental conditions in 'estate' parishes were not sufficiently distinguished from other parishes, especially for the least populated areas, for councils to assume quality provision. Yet, the variety displayed between

Table 7.12 Percent of all households in private rental in the investigated rural districts with exclusive use of basic household amenities by parish population, 1971

Rural District Council	Population size in 1971				
	Under 500	500–999	1000-1999	2000-2999	Over 3000
Braughing	85.2	76.3	75.8		86.9
Ampthill	50.4	71.4	64.0	58.4	58.5
Biggleswade	73.7	65.6	84.6	49.1	69.1
Erpingham	47.7	50.7	73.9	68.2	
Smallburgh	60.5	61.1	76.3		
Walsingham	57.1	76.3	29.8		68.5

Source: Computed from Registrar-General (2002)
Note: Hatfield was excluded from this list as it had so few parishes, with three of the four having more than 5000 residents in 1971. Blanks represent categories for which there were no relevant parishes. The household amenities used for this computation were a hot water supply, a fixed bath or shower and an inside WC

---

[292] BRO RDAM2/23 ARDCHCM 18 February 1960; BRO RDAM1/20 ARDCHPByCM 11 February 1965, p.631.

[293] *WR&WSR* 6 June 1961, p.1.

[294] *WR&WSR* 4 December 1962, p.22. Evidence on the Earl of Leicester's Holkham Estate was more ephemeral in Walsingham records, although there were inter-war commitments to build new and improve existing Estate cottages with public subsidies (NRO DC19/6/14 WRDCM 31 August 1926, p.48; NRO DC19/6/16 WRDCM 12 September 1928, p.56).

Table 7.13 Percent of households in investigated rural districts as council and private rental tenants in 'estate' and other parishes, 1971

	Council tenants			Private rental tenants		
	'Estate' parishes	'Non-Estate parishes'	% households in population category in this tenure	'Estate' parishes	'Non-Estate parishes'	% households in population category in this tenure
Parishes with under 500 inhabitants						
Ampthill	9.4	11.2	10.4	72.8	44.2	57.3
Biggleswade	3.2	38.0	30.3	78.9	30.3	42.2
Erpingham	9.6	21.2	19.0	69.4	32.7	39.5
Smallburgh	7.0	21.7	20.7	83.4	30.9	32.4
Walsingham	9.8	25.9	23.3	70.7	35.1	40.8
Parishes with 500–999 inhabitants						
Ampthill	16.4	18.5	17.9	72.8	17.0	33.3
Walsingham	3.4	26.3	16.8	79.1	31.4	51.2

Source: Computed from Registrar-General (2002)
Note: 'Estate' parishes were taken to be those with greater than 60% of households in private rental in 1971. Only Ampthill and Walsingham had more than one parish in the 500–999 'estate' category in 1971

districts, both across parish sizes (Table 7.12) and tenure (Table 7.14), points to broader influences on housing quality than new-build or improvement policies.

Perhaps it is no surprise councils did not 'interfere' with large landowner estates, given previous evidence of a deferential tenor towards the local gentry (Lee 1963; Johnson 1972). Arguably, this was akin to general diffidence in petit bourgeois dominated rural communities towards 'interference' with property ownership. Even so, RDCs often responded to housing needs more sympathetically than given credit in the literature. One aspect of this was finding ways to secure extra homes for smaller settlements. It has been noted already that the slum clearance focus of the 1930s, 1950s and 1960s restricted general needs house-building. Even with a broader remit, as in the 1960s, prior years of inattention, whether in the form of lethargic house-building drives, as with inter-war Ampthill (Table 5.2), or meagre provision of basic infrastructure, like sewers and water,[295] rural programmes were pushed towards criteria esteeming geographical centralisation. One countervailing force was provision for the elderly. Their importance was heightened by low construction numbers in earlier decades, when councils were encouraged to concentrate on three-bedrooms (e.g. MoH 1935, p.156). Hence, inter-war, council proposals for the elderly were commonly criticised as too costly (e.g. MoH 1934, p.153). By contrast, in the 1960s, 'old people's homes' received a more favourable reception (e.g. MHLG 1961b, p.5). With few smaller homes available, single persons or couples had little option but to stay in accommodation they and others might regard as

---

[295] For example, in 1967, Salford was removed from Ampthill's building programme because the Ministry would not sanction a mains sewer scheme (*WR&WSR* 1 August 1967, p.1).

Table 7.14 Percent of households in investigated rural districts with exclusive use of basic household amenities in 'estate' and other parishes by tenure, 1971

	Private rental households		Council house tenants		Owner-occupied households	
	'Estate' parishes	'Non-estate parishes'	'Estate' parishes	'Non-estate' parishes	'Estate' parishes	'Non-estate' parishes
Parishes with under 500 inhabitants						
Ampthill	44.1	59.2	84.1	74.2	88.9	91.0
Biggleswade	71.1	75.7	68.0 [a]	89.8	83.5 [a]	89.4
Erpingham	45.5	48.7	57.0	66.3	73.2	78.5
Smallburgh	52.1	61.8	100.0 [a]	83.7	83.9 [a]	73.4
Walsingham	64.0	54.5	83.3	75.6	50.9	72.8
Parishes with 500–999 inhabitants						
Ampthill	74.4	66.0	89.4	89.7	87.4	90.5
Walsingham	80.3	69.2	87.8 [a]	71.4	78.2	72.7

Source: Computed from Registrar-General (2002)
Note: 'Estate' parishes were taken to be those with greater than 60% of households in private rental in 1971. Only Ampthill and Walsingham had more than one parish in the 500–999 'estate' category in 1971. The basic household amenities used for this computation were a hot water supply, a fixed bath or shower and an inside WC
[a]These entries drew on computations of less than 25 households

too big (and costly), whereas small units might free-up family accommodation and satisfy elderly aspirations. The pressure on councils to respond to unmet demand was such that some debated compulsory relocations of elderly tenants into smaller homes.[296] Offering a rural twist to voluntary moves were regular refusals by elderly residents to vacate properties if this meant changing their village of residence; building small meant building locally.[297]

Councils responded to the opportunity offered when national policy encouraged building for the elderly. Ampthill, Braughing, Erpingham and Walsingham all proposed old people's accommodation soon after 1945, often looking to build in every parish. Yet, government cost strictures, shortages of family-sized dwellings and high levels of dwelling unfitness pushed councils to prioritise larger dwellings.[298]

---

[296] *BC&BG* 3 March 1967, p.10.

[297] This can be illustrated by how often this issue arose. Take Biggleswade to illustrate (*BC&BG* 3 November 1967, p.16; BRO RDBwM1/40 BiRDCHCM 9 October 1968, p.384; 14 May 1969, p.1033). As reported in the 9 October 1968 Biggleswade Meeting, of 1977 three-bedroom council houses, 1003 had three occupants or less, with 1403 out of the Council's 2777 dwellings deemed 'under-occupied' (p.384). By the late-1960s, under-occupation was considered the biggest district housing problem by some councillors (*BC&BG* 6 March 1970, p.11).

[298] HRO RDC3/2/3 BrRDCPHHCM 22 November 1945, p.815; BRO RDAM2/22 ARDCHCM 29 May 1947; 6 May 1948; 16 September 1948; NRO DC13/5/20 ERDCHCM 2 March 1947; TNA MAF147/3 'Housing for Agricultural Workers. Walsingham RDC', 3 March 1948; *D&FT* 22 June 1951, p.6.

This did not lessen desires to build more small homes.[299] Such intentions received a minor boost in the early-1950s, when the government was more open to smaller dwellings as a means of achieving its building targets. Post-1955, this positive stance was retained. Outside of slum clearance and urban overspill, a £10 subsidy for one-bedroom bungalows was the primary vehicle through which council-building secured funding support. Ampthill engaged with this process early,[300] working with the County Council to combine housing with welfare services. By 1959, it had bungalows in four villages and in 1961 had the first warden-serviced old people's residences in rural Bedfordshire. From the mid-1950s into the early-1960s, it reasserted that its housing programme would be comprised solely of bungalow-building, plus some slum clearance,[301] and warden-centred facilities for the elderly. But Ampthill was not particularly generous towards smaller settlements. Perhaps this was to be expected for warden-serviced facilities,[302] but Ampthill also concentrated bungalows and small houses in larger villages (Table 7.15). More widely, council minutes suggest, sometimes through failed applications, otherwise in the patterning of applications, less populated villages were slower to receive smaller dwellings than elsewhere. This was encapsulated in Biggleswade, which provided the only systematic data on the building of smaller dwellings over time. Table 7.16 shows this Council's shift in completions, with smaller parishes initially receiving few bungalows or two-bedroomed houses but increasing their share over time. Worth noting that the Biggleswade Housing Committee did not favour bedsit accommodation and considered one-bedroom units insufficient for the district's residents,[303] given two-bedroomed units increased tenancy possibilities for young couples. Significantly, though, at a time when smaller dwellings were increasingly provided in smaller settlements (Table 7.16), Biggleswade decided that 60% of its new-build should be one- or two-bedroomed.[304] What building small dwellings gave this and other councils was the opportunity to place dwellings down the settlement

---

[299] For Braughing, *H&EO* 15 June 1946, p.3; HRO RDC3/1/14 BrRDCECM 12 November 1964, p.6349; HRO RDC3/1/20 BrRDCECM 8 September 1970, p.7957. For Erpingham, NRO DC13/5/75 ERDCHCM 2 March 1948; *NNN* 1 December 1961, p.1; 4 October 1963, p.11. In Smallburgh inter-war applications to build old people's homes failed to receive Ministry sanction (NRO DC22/2/14 SmRDCM 2 August 1932, p.359) but the Council came back with proposals after 1945 (NRO DC22/2/48 SmRDCHCM 23 July 1946, p.2723), looking to build in virtually all parishes (NRO DC22/2/27 SmRDCM 7 September 1954, p.224), with proposals put to the Ministry regularly after this (as with 30 bungalows sought for seven parishes in 1963; NRO DC22/2/29 SmRDCM 12 March 1963, p.81).

[300] BRO RDAM2/22 ARDCHCM 13 December 1956.

[301] BRO RDAR8/40 ARDCMOHar 1959, p.14; BRO RDAR8/42 ARDCMOHar 1961, p.15; BRO RDAM1/18 ARDCHPByCM 23 October 1962, p.287.

[302] Like Ampthill, many councils wanted warden-serviced residences, with the proviso they might only be justified in larger settlements: *NorfChron* 4 February 1955, p.7 (for Erpingham); NRO DC19/6/67 WRDCHCM 18 July 1955, pp.14–15; HRO RDC3/1/7 BrRDCHCM 2 October 1958, p.4008; BRO RDBwM1/33 BiRDCHECM 14 March 1962, p.520.

[303] BRO RDBwM1/42 BiRDCHCM 10 June 1970, p.22.

[304] BRO RDBwM1/42 BiRDCHCM 13 January 1971, p.616.

hierarchy. This seemingly contravened land-use plans, national prioritisation of industrialised building and the economics of large projects. In this regard, rural councils were able to secure more dwellings for smaller places, so producing distributions for council homes more evenly spread than national policy encouraged (Table 7.11).

7.6   Contributing to Contrivance

The performance of rural district councils in housing provision should be assessed against a backdrop of none too flattering commentaries on their performance. Without pressing detail too far, these have been captured in assessments like Bennett's (1914, p.118) claim they were 'farmers' clubs', Springall's (1936, p.94) reference to them as the 'rural House of Lords' and Harrison and Norton's (1967, p.49) reminder that they experienced difficulties getting anyone to stand for office. The academic literature on rural housing follows suit with a dark picture, with weight placed on Newby et al.'s (1978) East Anglian research, with its emphasis on farmer-dominated RDCs deliberate deflation of council-building to strengthen control over farm-workers (Rose et al. 1976; Saunders et al. 1978). All this in a context in which 1919 saw rural districts thrown into a policy world with expectations they would be pro-active rather than reactive, even though they '… were innocent of knowledge of house-building, yet they were suddenly given the awesome responsibility of carrying out the most important' government reconstruction (Morgan and Morgan 1980, p.107). Fifty some years down the line there was sharp criticism of RDCs, both for building fewer council dwellings than their urban counterparts and for concentrating construction in larger centres rather than for local needs (Phillips and Williams 1982a; Shucksmith and Henderson 1995; Sherwood 1996). Numerically there is little basis for questioning these conclusions, even if exceptions existed (Ryder 1984). The research undertaken here elicits a more sympathetic hearing for RDCs. This sees wisdom in Larkin's (1978, p.15) assessment that: 'The old rural district council may have been inefficient and their building programmes abysmally small, but they did at least respond to the most obvious housing need in the villages'.

Table 7.15 Percent of smaller council dwellings in Ampthill by parish population, 1968

Population size in 1961	Under 500	500– 999	1000- 1999	2000- 2999	Over 3000	Number of dwellings
% Bungalows	1.1	12.6	28.0	22.6	37.1	377
% Two-bedroom houses	3.2	0.0	27.4	9.7	59.7	62
% District households in 1961	10.9	30.2	24.4	20.4	14.2	

Source: Computed from BRO RDAM1/24 Ampthill Abstract of Accounts for the Year Ending 31 March 1968, p.323

Note: The computations are for council-owned dwellings only

Table 7.16 Percent of smaller council dwellings in Biggleswade by parish population, 1957–1967

	Percent of small dwellings built under the Housing Acts of						
	1956	1958	1961	1956	1958	1961	
Parish population in 1961	Bungalows			Two-bedroom houses			% 1961 RDC households in population category
Over 3000	37.5	55.6	18.2	49.0	35.7	47.1	40.4
2000-2999	50.0	33.3	18.2	22.4	33.3	10.1	18.0
1000-1999	12.5	0.0	18.2	16.3	21.4	13.8	17.9
500–999	0.0	11.1	36.4	4.1	4.8	11.1	11.9
Under 500	0.0	0.0	9.1	8.2	4.8	18.0	11.7
Dwellings built under the Act	32	49	36	42	22	189	

Source: Computed from the three files BRO RDBwH2/5 to RDBwH2/7. Biggleswade Register of New Houses Erected under the 1956, 1958 and 1961 Housing Acts
Note: The computations are for council-owned dwellings only

Put in the context of government policy, builder rationales and wider socio-economic trends, rural councils operated at the tail-end of the state apparatus. Being generally small-scale, under-resourced institutions, with limited authority, they were subjected to innumerable interventions that demonstrated a lack of trust in them. This was not restricted to rural councils, for the 'fiction' of an autonomous local government has long been part of the British state. When councils were compliant and towed the national line, they were able to operate under over-generalised national supervision. If they challenged national prerogative, they could be eliminated. It might be politically embarrassing to do so but the dust would soon settle (Branson 1979; O'Leary 1987). Less influential electorally and economically than cities, small councils were rarely at the forefront of such challenges, with a few noteworthy exceptions (Minns 1973; Macintyre 1980). This generally limited their confrontations with governments to administrative matters. Such issues were nonetheless charged with political motives. Sillince (1986) offers a good example, without needing to trouble the politically charged atmosphere of Westminster and Whitehall. Taking Warwickshire as a case study, Sillince outlined how the county council adjusted key settlement policy to move from controlling potentially discomforting trends to removing themselves from new embarrassment. Thus, when political controversy centred on growing in-migration to the countryside, the county council promoted key settlement policies to control village growth. But, when controversy shifted onto the decline of rural services, the county council proclaimed, against the evidence, that the policy was a failure, and downloaded responsibility onto districts in order to avoid controversy over items like school and library closures. Comparable patterns pertain for relationships between the centre and the county councils, with national authorities transferring services and responsibilities as best suited their purpose, with lower tiers in the state hierarchy having little scope for resistance or realignment (Saunders 1985). Within the British state, the mirage called local autonomy existed within the frameworks governments allowed councils to operate. Then, set inside this window of opportunity, national agencies and ministries made uneven allowances for local capacities. At the top of the hierarchy was London, which had numerous exemptions from ministry overview (Rhodes 1976; Keith-Lucas and Richards 1978; Young and Garside 1982). More generally: 'The balance between central and local government is more even when a ministry has to deal with a few large authorities than it is when it has to work with a large number of small authorities' (Layton 1961, p.33). Hence, at the bottom of the pile were under-resourced small urban and rural councils, which were subjected to extensive and intensive, if not particularly informed (Chap. 6), oversight and intervention.

This chapter has demonstrated the impact of the lack of trust that came with this framework. Forget for now that governments had the capability to alter operational environments so rural councils could access superior resources, better information and more professional staff, but failed to act. Despite its multitude of inequities and abuses, the local government system in the USA clearly demonstrates the many ways in which small councils can operate efficiently and effectively; provided there are safeguards against their capture by vested interests (Hoggart 1991). But in the tradition-bound world of English local government, what rural councils were left with was the imposition of policy intentions designed to promote national political objectives rather than respond to local needs. In Chap. 6 this was seen primarily through impacts on construction volumes, building standards, construction methods and dwelling upgrades. This chapter has explored how far councils could achieve building aims, design preferences and locational priorities. The backcloth for this chapter has been shifting national priorities, from housing expansion to cost-cutting, from building for all to residualisation, and from building for local needs to centralisation. Built within processes of state involvement, this chapter has shown a multitude of interventions by national agents that boxed-in local initiative. Constant questions were raised with councils on whether new-build was needed, whether costs were justified, whether locational decisions were right and whether designs were appropriate. In some cases, interventions were supportive, given the weak staffing, expertise and revenue of rural councils. These, however, could have been strengthened in more locally responsive ways. More commonly, the blocking or watering down of local proposals, or national agents overriding them as they pushed standard designs, construction methods and assumptions on 'best' sites or locations, weakened local imprints on the housing scene: in its volume, in its appearance, in its composition and in its geography. Despite this, rural councils imposed themselves on local housing circumstances when fulfilling a primary responsibility, namely responding to local housing needs.

In Chap. 3, a key element in local divergence was identified through drawing attention to the dissimilar performances of Biggleswade and Smallburgh. Along with Hatfield, which was distinguished by growth impulses associated with its new town designation, these districts had the highest 1971 council tenancy rates amongst the investigated rural districts (Table 1.3), Biggleswade with more in council homes than the average share in England and Smallburgh above that of English RDCs. Taking advantage of the 1919 Act, Biggleswade implemented a house-building programme that exceeded those of many large cities. This early intervention was a foretaste of what was to follow, for Biggleswade took cognisance of government policy evolutions to find new ways to address housing needs: at one time utilising possibilities of no-subsidy construction to cater for better-paid workers, at others pushing smaller dwellings (Table 7.16), and so on. Responding to possibilities might mean giving attention primarily to a single social group at a time, but each helped towards the goal of general housing advancement. In Smallburgh the situation was very different. Like its fellow north Norfolk councils, Erpingham and Walsingham,[305] Smallburgh at first came across a bit like a rabbit in the headlights. Traumatised by the cost of 1919 Act dwellings, plus shortages of labour and materials, its 1919 programme was small and ended early. Like the other councils, there was keenness to build homes, and to encourage private builders to do the same, with farmers in the area advocating more council-building.[306] Where Smallburgh differed from the others was in aggressively utilising the Council's authority to promote housing for the agricultural economy. Small, poorly equipped dwellings were built, so farm-workers could afford rents, while reluctance was shown towards building outside agricultural parishes. Eventually pushed into serving a wider clientele, the Council, which already charged above 'normal rents',[307] moved forward largely because it could charge 'economic rents'. Its contributions to housing from the rates constituted a minor element in property tax calls (Chap. 5), with the RDC often levying no rate charge across its services. Within this context, Smallburgh was active in inter-war council-building. Erpingham and Walsingham, by contrast, built relatively few dwellings (Table 3.10). Even with subsidies for slum clearance, Erpingham looked to demolish half or less the dwellings Smallburgh was removing after 1933.[308] Smallburgh championed new houses for agricultural workers provided it cost the Council and its ratepayers little. The strength of fiscal conservativism in this pro-farmer stance was readily apparent after 1945, when councils could not avoid rate subsidies for council-build.[309] Inter-war to post-1945, Smallburgh

---

[305] NRO DC13/5/82 ERDCHCM 19 April 1921, p.106; NRO DC22/2/8 SmRDCM 18 January 1921, p.17; NRO DC19/6/9 WRDCM 29 June 1921, p.207.

[306] Chapter 3 or, for Erpingham, NRO DC13/5/6 ERCM 12 January 1925, p.115; *FakPost* 11 February 1927, p.3.

[307] NRO DC22/2/47 SmRDCHCM 21 July 1936, p.261.

[308] Whereas the Erpingham programme was for 16 removals in 1934 and 26 in 1935, Smallburgh targeted 36 in 1934 and made reference to a possible 49 replacements in 1935 (NRO DC13/5/73 ERDCHCM 18 June 1934, p.137; 17 June 1935, p.188; NRO DC22/2/46 SmRDCHCM 6 February 1934, p.131; 28 May 1935, p.292). Council minutes gave little information on Walsingham's programme, except to note it had 119 dwellings recommended for clearing and wanted to proceed with 42 in mid-1934, after which it was in dispute with the Ministry over costs and further reference to the scheme was not found (NRO DC19/6/21 WRDCM 27 September 1933, p.60; NRO DC19/6/62 WRDCM 14 August 1934, p.32; 23 October 1934, p.55; 11 December 1934, p.67).

[309] Smallburgh still reported surpluses on its housing revenue account by 1958, which it wanted to use to fund capital projects (NRO DC22/2/27 SmRDCM 18 February 1958, p.565). Biggleswade was in a similar position but was more explicit over using surpluses to subsidise general needs homes (*WR&WSR* 1 April 1958, p.14). With no large pre-1939 housing stock to generate a surplus (Tables 3.10), but with a commitment to build more homes (Table 6.11), Ampthill was carrying a £4000 deficit on its HRA around this time (*WR&WSR* 24 March 1959, p.1). A decade later, under

shifted from an energetic house-building programme (Dickens et al. 1985), to a weak performer (Table 5.2). So Biggleswade and Smallburgh were two energetic providers of new homes, but of a different character: one pushing vested farmer interests, much as Newby and colleagues found, but where the 'solution' was build many not few (Saunders et al. 1978), the other responding to the breadth of accommodation shortcomings.

By contrast, Braughing, Erpingham and Walsingham appear at first sight as caricatures of the traditional, risk averse rural societies that formerly frequented the pages of academic publications (e.g. Redfield 1947; Fischer 1975). The vision conjured up in such presentations would carry within it truths about these councils but also embed falsehoods. What was clear was that each place had limited economic prospects. They might be favoured by public sector investment for a time, as with defence installations surrounding the Second World War (e.g. Wade-Martins 1994, pp.174–75), but their economies were largely dependent on low-wage agricultural output and services (Eastwood 1951; Allison 1961; Bailey 1978). Inter-war, their council minutes decried the absence of private investment, especially in north Norfolk. After 1945 private building was at first constrained but when the chains were taken off, these three districts saw relatively slow growth in private new-build. It was not until the late-1960s that numbers rose to anything comparable with the other investigated districts (albeit Smallburgh was slow as well; Table 3.4). Even by the 1970s, in Walsingham private building was still low for an English rural district (Table 7.2).

The first caution to note before ascribing traditional rurality to these places derives from their uneven size. If you take 1951 as an indicative year, given this was after the machinations of local government reorganisation in the 1930s, we find most of the districts investigated of roughly similar size, Braughing apart. Biggleswade was slightly bigger, at 26,427, and Smallburgh slightly smaller at 18,429, but in essence six of the seven districts were around 20,000 inhabitants (even Hatfield was only 23,334 then). Braughing by contrast had 10,415. So, when viewing figures like those in Table 3.10, with absolute building numbers, a doubling of Braughing values aids assessments of equivalence. Go back to 1921 and the two councils that brought most territory to the Braughing of 1951 only had 5019 (Buntingford) and 5795 residents (Hadham). This was a district where no settlement had even 2000 residents until late in the 1960s. There was little scope for gains from centralising housing investment. Inflows of London-centred residents at the southern end of the district gave an unusually high service-class component for an essentially agricultural area (Table 1.1), which helped promote rural private-owner building. Yet, experience with the 1923 Act revealed a primary commitment to local residents and civic duty, not promoting private options. In Hadham, for example, it was decided: 'Having regard for the impossibility of building cottages under the 1923 Housing Act to let to the Labouring Classes at a rent which they can afford to

---

new funding arrangements and cost squeezes, Smallburgh ceased making contributions to its HRA (NRO DC22/2/29 SmRDCM 25 June 1968, p.596), whereas Biggleswade continued its subsidies (BRO RDBwM1/40 BiRDCHCM 12 February 1969, p.794).

pay, this Council does not feel justified in granting assistance to private enterprise'.[310] This decision was later rescinded, and Hadham followed Buntingford in approving subsidies to private-owners, but only if properties were not of an expensive kind.[311] As for addressing local needs, here Braughing responded to inter-war localism by building in every parish. Comparing estimated 1943 populations with council house placements, 33.2% of dwellings were located in places with more than 1000 people, 21.6% for those with 500–999 inhabitants and 45.3% in the smallest parishes. Population shares for these groups were 42.1%, 26.1% and 31.7%.[312] A further glimpse of Braughing's push to address local needs was seen post-1945, when, despite its small size, it had built 305 council homes by March 1951 (MoH quarterly): more than any of the three Norfolk districts, only around 60 less than Biggleswade and just 120 shy of Hatfield. Indeed, by 1953, it was '… felt that the housing needs of most of the outlying Parishes had been met and it might be as well to consider' concentrating building on centres with most services.[313]

But changing national priorities led to conflict with Braughing over its high building standards.[314] These had been noted by Ministry officials for some time.[315] With relatively few properties meriting demolition (as in the late-1960s; Table 6.10), save for 20 replacements sought for former military hutments at High Wych,[316] the Council had a reduced capacity to erect dwellings in the 1950s and early-1960s (Table 3.4). It nonetheless provided more old people's bungalows, despite their cost, with the first 31 built at Buntingford, Braughing village and High Wych costing '… almost as much as the former rate fund contribution to the Housing Revenue Account in respect of all of the Council's houses',[317] which in 1961 numbered more than 800. Despite growing pressure on waiting lists (Chap. 3), the Council further committed to attending local needs by accepting single people on its list.[318] This was aided by Braughing having close to or above average property tax resources for an English rural district, whereas the other investigated districts tended to fall slightly below that average (Chap. 5; MoH 1939; DoE 1974). Nevertheless, even if disposed to commit to local housing needs, restrictions on council-building took their toll. By 1965, it was decided the district was falling behind, prompting councillors to call

---

[310] HRO RDC6/1/5 HaRDCM 6 December 1923, p.294.

[311] HRO RDC4/1/7 BuRDCM 13 December 1923, p.226; HRO RDC6/1/5 HaRDCM 7 May 1925, p.374.

[312] For the location of council dwellings and official 1943 population estimates, see HRO RDC3/2/2 BrRDCPHHCM 22 April 1943, p.580.

[313] HRO RDC3/2/9 BrRDCHCM 12 May 1953, p.2286.

[314] H&EO 5 October 1956, p.4; 9 November 1956, p.8.

[315] H&EO 12 September 1952, p.1; HRO RDC3/2/8 BrRDCPHHCM 18 September 1952, p.2134. They were also noted when the Council's old people's homes were compared with other districts (e.g. HRO RDC3/1/10 BrRDCM 1 September 1960, p.4859).

[316] Entries on the High Wych Camp up to its closure in 1960 punctuated the five files HRO RDC3/1/6 to RDC3/1/10.

[317] HRO RDC3/1/11 BrRDCFCM 24 January 1961, p.5026.

[318] HRO RDC3/1/13 Braughing Tenant Selection Committee Meeting 4 April 1963, p.5808.

for a general needs programme to be reinstated. This possibility was stymied by the high cost of building, which would put rents beyond potential tenants reach, and, with a slowing down of programmes outside 'priority councils', a great deal of Braughing's activity from the late-1960s was again directed at old people's dwellings.[319] This was a council with perhaps less energy than Biggleswade, and with less scope for addressing housing need given its less-buoyant demographic trajectory (Tables 4.5 and 4.7), but it demonstrated positive reactions to local housing needs and, despite building in many small villages, secured a council share of local tenancies above the English RDC average. This might be low compared to the urban average, but places like Braughing did not benefit from policies that favoured larger projects in towns and cities.

The same applied to Erpingham and Walsingham, both of which had bottom-heavy settlement hierarchies (Tables 1.2 and 7.10). Both had large agrarian workforces, which worked against tenants affording council homes (Table 1.1). They were equally slow starters in instigating council-building, given difficulties implementing the 1919 Act and securing tenants for dwellings built under it. In many ways, these two districts demonstrated the same tendencies. They built close to the same number of council dwellings inter-war (Table 5.2), even if Walsingham got off to a slower start and Erpingham slowed down (Table 3.10). In the first decade after 1945, they erected roughly the same housing numbers (Table 5.2) and in the late-1950s into the early-1960s their demolitions exceeded new dwelling numbers (Table 6.7). In the 1940s and early-1950s, the two of them had Ministry allocations lower than they wanted.[320] Erpingham's 1952 and 1953 allocations were half its capacity. Walsingham received a meagre allocation because the area's resources were deemed low and was unable to secure an uplift after the government's figures supporting this conclusion were found to be erroneous.[321] Seeing the government favouring non-traditional building, both accepted concrete Unity dwellings, hoping to secure higher allocations.[322] Likewise, both focused their 1930s then 1950s attention on slum replacement (and for the latter decade old people's dwellings).[323] In a nutshell, they both towed the national line. Where differences emerged were in outcomes. By 1971, Walsingham had secured sufficient council dwellings that its occupancy level was above the English RDC average, whereas Erpingham was well below it (Table 1.3). This occurred even through Walsingham had more private

---

[319] HRO RDC3/1/18 BrRDCECM 13 February 1968, p.7273; 12 March 1968, p.7306; HRO RDC3/1/20 BrRDCECM 8 September 1970, p.7957; 13 October 1970, p.7980; HRO RDC3/1/21 BrRDCHCM 25 January 1972, p.8534; HRO RDC3/1/22 BrRDCHCM 13 February 1973, p.9014.

[320] On which some Whitehall officials agreed (e.g. TNA MAF147/1 Letter from J. Christie to MAF Secretary, 16 December 1947).

[321] NNN 7 March 1952, p.1; 6 March 1953, p.1; NRO DC19/6/66 WRDCHCM 26 October 1953, pp.23–24; 22 November 1953, p.21.

[322] NNN 17 October 1952, p.1; NRO DC19/6/66 WRDCHCM 15 March 1954, p.49.

[323] NRO DC19/6/62 WRDCHCM 1 May 1934, p.5; NRO DC19/6/67 WRDCHCM 3 December 1956, p.114; NRO DC13/5/29 ERDCM 2 December 1958, para.108; NRO DC19/6/68 WRDCHCM 30 January 1961, p.271.

rental accommodation. Potentially, this hints at a key difference. In every decade investigated Erpingham had a superior demographic performance and swifter household expansion than Walsingham (Tables 4.5 and 4.7). This was accompanied by less private house-building in Walsingham, even in the 1960s and early-1970s (Table 7.2). Economically, Walsingham was more 'inward looking' than Erpingham, with only 18.8% of its 1971 resident workers employed outside the district, compared to Erpingham's 40.3% (Table 1.1). It had to rely more on its own devices. With almost 40% of its households in private rental, it also faced more serious housing difficulties, given this tenure had seen a shrinking stock with many units drifting towards dereliction (Harloe 1985; Bevan and Sanderling 1996). A survey of council minutes indicated a greater sense of urgency in Walsingham. In deliberations with the Ministry they '... emphasised the poverty of both owners and tenants',[324] they were more inclined to complain when the Ministry diluted dwelling specifications[325] and were prone to envisage longer term needs, as in suggesting 673 more homes were needed in 1948, whereas Erpingham discussions focused more on the next year's allocation.[326] Walsingham was also more likely to lament the neglect of general needs provision when slum clearance was a government priority, as in the 1930s and 1950s–1960s.[327] A sense of greater urgency was translated into forthright requests for higher dwelling allocations, as with seeking 88 as against 66 under the 1931 Housing (Rural Authorities) Act, or requests for 200 rather than Erpingham's 136 in 1946, or the 76 then 85 asked for in 1969 and 1970 when Erpingham minutes were silent over bids.[328] Not that the minutes needed to reveal much, given Walsingham built 145 new council homes between 1971 and the Council's demise in the first quarter of 1974 when Erpingham only built 39 (Table 6.10).

In subdued colours, the experience of Walsingham in raising its head above the parapet of a decision-making world constrained by lack of resources, weak authority and lack of dynamism in the private sector had parallels with Ampthill. Like the Norfolk councils, Ampthill approached the 1919 Act with caution. Following the national abandonment of the Act in 1921, no council homes were added until 1927. In approach, Ampthill was guarded. Its homes were inspected by Biggleswade in 1927, as they were erected at lower cost, but declared too poor in quality to be copied.[329] New-build was concentrated in the largest settlements. Thus, by 1928, while 51.3% of households lived in parishes with 1000–1999 people, some 73.1% of

---

[324] TNA HLG40/19 'Report on Applications for Special Assistance Received from RDCs in Norfolk and East Suffolk', undated c1931, p.20.

[325] For example, NRO DC19/6/20 WRDCM 6 July 1932, p.31.

[326] NRO DC19/6/63 WRDCHCM 2 September 1948, p.181.

[327] *EDP* 9 May 1935, p.5; *NM&PWJ* 3 June 1939, p.7; NRO DC19/6/69 WRDCHCM 10 December 1962, p.73.

[328] TNA HLG40/19 'Report on Applications for Special Assistance Received from RDCs in Norfolk and East Suffolk', undated c1931, p.12, p.20; NRO DC19/6/63 WRDCHCM 20 February 1946, p.35; NRO DC13/5/75 ERDCHCM 14 August 1946, p.69; NRO DC19/6/32 WRDCM 28 May 1969; 20 May 1970.

[329] *NBC&SN&DN* 27 March 1927, p.3.

council homes had been built there. With just under 20% of households, parishes with fewer than 500 inhabitants saw 9.6% of council-building.[330] When national emphases transitioned towards slum clearance and the relief of overcrowding, Ampthill complied meekly, rejecting the possibility of a no-subsidy programme, only seeking additional homes for farm-workers once the 1938 Act was passed.[331] The Council seemed constrained by the often minuted message that farm-workers could not afford council rents,[332] with the holding of council tenancies ascribed to family members working in the better-paid brick-making industry[333] Of all the districts investigated, it had the least inter-war completions, comfortably surpassed by Braughing, which was less than half its size (Table 3.10). After the Second World War, this Council was transformed. In 1942, it began surveying housing needs in the district. By 1943, it was grouping parishes so sewerage and town planning were catered for and, more importantly, to support agriculture:

> In these days much was heard about agriculture but they were not going to get the best type of men on farms unless they were given the best conditions with the amenities of electricity, gas, water, and sewerage. The need for houses was well established. They had to assume that the Government and politicians would redeem the pledges which had been given for agriculture. One could not have redeemed agriculture unless one had a contented countryside.[334]

The tone implied negative memories of failed post-1918 government actions in providing 'homes fit for heroes'. This was further suggested in the Council's full support for Uxbridge Councils' proposal '… that the housing of the people should have absolute first priority for attention after the War'.[335]

Reflective of its new emphasis, Ampthill wanted to erect 385 new dwellings in the first post-war year, more than it achieved in the 20 years to 1939.[336] Like Biggleswade, seeking to secure good allocations, it proposed building on a few sites, with 50 dwellings on each.[337] It engaged with local employers, to see how the totality of housing provision could be improved, and with local builders to coordinate and encourage all-out effort.[338] It engaged with new methods of construction, like Airey houses, as another opportunity to secure more homes.[339] Underlying this new vigour was a desire to aid agriculture, with at least 206 dwellings slated for

---

[330] Computed from a list of completed council dwellings in *W&DR* 3 March 1928, p.3. These numbers include Toddington, as it did not leave the RDC until 1933.

[331] BRO RDAM2/20 ARDCHCM 2 July 1934; 9 July 1935; *WR&WSR* 28 February 1939, p.3.

[332] For example, BRO RDAR8/11 ARDCMOHar 1930, p.12.

[333] TNA HLG37/43 'Report on Local Investigations …', undated c1936, p.24.

[334] BRO RDAM1/13 ARDCM 26 November 1942; citation by the Housing Committee Chair from *W&DR* 23 February 1943, p.2.

[335] BRO RDAM2/22 ARDCHCM 25 October 1943.

[336] *WR&WSR* 30 November 1943, p.1.

[337] BRO RDAM2/22 ARDCHCM 13 March 1944.

[338] BRO RDAM2/22 ARDCHCM 17 April 1944; 21 August 1945; *WR&WSR* 22 April 1947, p.1; 6 September 1949, p.3.

[339] BRO RDAM2/22 ARDCHCM 25 August 1947.

farm-workers in 1946 and extra points for farm-workers on the waiting list, both spurred by a 75% reliance on foreign workers in agriculture, as English workers could not be attracted due to a shortage of homes.[340] By 1955, they had more post-war completions than any investigated RDC, having built more than three times their total inter-war output (Table 5.2). They maintained commendable new-build numbers throughout the 1950s and effectively retained the same output in the 1960s, when most councils saw falls in council-building (Table 6.11). As national policy tightened around slum clearance, the Council shifted to building one-bedroom bun-galows for the elderly (maintaining slum removal).[341] Between 1957 and the end of 1967 Ampthill raised 590 additional dwellings, with 360 as one- or two-bedroom bungalows by early-1968.[342] Embedded within this performance, the Council prided itself on building in most parishes; yet, the grouping of parishes and the early post-war concentration on a few larger projects carried weight, with the Council deciding in 1955: 'That with view to speeding up building, priority be given in the first instance to building on sites where services including main drainage are available, but that it be clearly understood that such houses are not for the particular parish in which the houses are built, but for the area'.[343] Priority was given to more houses. Their distribution took second place, with small parishes losing out compared with other districts (Table 7.11). Up to the reorganisation of local government in 1974, Ampthill went on building in significant numbers (Table 6.10). The lethargy of the inter-war years was over. Looking at statistics for 1971, you would not know this. The arousal from slumber would be lost in the bald message that by 1971 Ampthill had fewer households in council tenancies than the national RDC average, despite home-ownership only being at that average (Table 1.3). Ampthill looked like it could be paraded as a characteristically under-performing rural district. It was not. Its history reveals two distinct eras, revealing again how, despite unaccommodating tendencies in national policy, local imprints did make impressions on rural housing histories.

The same point can be made about Hatfield, which looked like a traditional rural area pre-1939, save perhaps for it having a larger central settlement than most rural districts (Old Hatfield had 5695 of the RDC's 9072 inhabitants in 1921). Hatfield began its council programme slowly. No council dwellings were erected under Acts prior to 1914,[344] with 1919 Act efforts criticised for not addressing the depth of housing need; the Ministry grudgingly accepted its programme only as 'an

---

[340] BRO RDAM2/22 ARDCHCM 30 May 1946; *WR&WSD* 10 June 1947, p.6; 2 September 1947, p.2.

[341] BRO RDAM2/23 ARDCHCM 17 October 1957; BRO RDAR8/40 ARDCMOHar 1959, p.14; BRO RDAM2/23 ARDCHCM 21 July 1960; BRO RDAR8/42 ARDCMOHar 1961, p.15.

[342] BRO RDAM1/18 ARDCHPByCM 23 October 1962, p.287; BRO RDAM1/24 'Ampthill Abstract of Accounts for the Year Ending 31 March 1968', p.323. Included in the 1968 total were 17 aluminium bungalows erected in the late-1940s.

[343] BRO RDAM2/22 ARDCHCM 3 February 1955.

[344] TNA HLG14/1 'RDC Register of Instruments, Consents, Etc., 1892–1919'.

instalment'.[345] Where Hatfield differed from other rural districts was in the attention it received from London. Thus, even under the 1919 Act, Hatfield engaged with the London Housing Board to enable the Board to erect dwellings at Essendon, Little Heath and Stanborough, about which the RDC '… are most anxious that the houses proposed in this district should be erected'.[346] From an early stage, the Council was outward oriented. The tenor was characteristic of local growth machines (Molotch 1976), where councils become integral to business efforts to boost the local economy. Despite accounts of 'the scandal of slum housing' in Old Hatfield, alongside Medical Officer of Health reports that unfit dwellings could not be closed as there was nowhere for the people to go,[347] the Council shunned the 1924 Act, under which only rented properties were allowed, thereby foregoing the prospect of future sales,[348] instead building 1923 Act dwellings for commuters like clerks.[349] Hatfield found it could not avoid building for the working-classes, as private builders showed little inclination to erect homes the working-classes could afford. But with the low subsidies of the 1923 Act, rents were unaffordable for many, especially agricultural labourers.[350] With buoyant demand from outside the district, the Council built strongly in the 1920s, but private building dominated the 1930s (Table 3.10). In 1939, the Hatfield Chamber of Trade charged that the RDC's programme needed speeding up; de Havilland had moved in, the economy was growing and there were not enough homes.[351] But the Council continued to leave action to private builders. So, in its proposal for the first post-war year, Hatfield asked for a programme of 184 new homes.[352] This was 200 less than Ampthill, although they were comparable in size, and sat uncomfortably beside the Medical Officer of Health's 1945 estimate that 2400 dwellings were required within the next two years (Hatfield RDC 1947, p.8). But with the declaration of a new town within its territory, Hatfield was to transition into a new world of government direction, with opportunities for accommodating workers unavailable to other districts through new town nominations. Growth saw programme expansion, with 980 new homes for the Old Town announced in 1955.[353]

---

[345] TNA HLG48/324 Letter from A. Peters, Office of the Housing Commissioner, to Hertfordshire County Council, 25 November 1919; Letter to Hatfield RDC Clerk, 20 January 1920; Reply, 21 January 1920; TNA HLG48/324 Hatfield RDC. Housing General Scheme 1919–1926. 'Memo Signed W.McG.E.', 22 January 1920.

[346] HRO RDC7/1/7 HtRDCM 26 August 1920, p.428; HRO RDC7/1/8 HtRDCM 30 June 1921, p.108; 21 July 1921, p.115 (the last the source of the quotation).

[347] HRO RDC7/96/1 *Herts Record* 27 October 1922; 19 January 1923.

[348] As early as 1922, the RDC asked the Ministry for permission to sell dwellings it had erected (HRO RDC7/1/8 HtRDCM 15 June 1922).

[349] HRO RDC7/1/9 HtRDCM 25 September 1924, p.39.

[350] *HA&SAT* 28 August 1931, p.7.

[351] HRO RDC7/1/12 HtRDCM 16 March 1939, p.29.

[352] HRO RDC7/9/1 HtRDCHCM 19 October 1943, p.52; HRO RDC7/1/13 HtRDCM 21 September 1944, p.15. When the Ministry raised the prospect of temporary prefabricated dwellings, 75 were added (HRO RDC7/9/1 HtRDCHCM 18 April 1945, p.111).

[353] *Welwyn Times and Hatfield Herald* 7 January 1955, p.16.

Attributes often associated with towns became regular. On the Council, debates took a stronger party political tone, as in 1955 charges that the new Conservative administration had no policies save those in motion under the previous Labour group.[354] But the major change was in housing tenure. While the RDC was separate from the New Town Corporation, it had a public sector pallor. By 1969, only 19% of residents in the RDC were in council tenancies, but a further 27% lived in Corporation homes. Adding a further twist, 24% of those living in the new town area rented RDC homes.[355] The character of the area had changed, with as many in flats in the RDC as in the new town. Tenures had altered and the driver behind change had forceful national direction.

Reviewing the actions of the seven rural districts brings to mind Niner's (1975, p.87) conclusion that apparently similar council policies can produce different results: 'It would be virtually impossible to infer from any given result which detailed policies had been in operation. Local policies are just one strand in a whole range of factors affecting housing performance'. Viewed in reverse, similarities in the end-products of council actions can emanate from divergent policy intentions. What this tells us is that councils do not have free-will to determine outputs but do have agency influencing housing change. How far this contributed to the contrived countryside that evolved in England partly depended on how assertive and creative they were in imposing themselves on change processes. Concerning the first 75 years of the twentieth-century, the rural literature has not been prone to draw out forceful local state responses. Local agents tended to be portrayed as adopting laissez-faire or deferential stances, to be acted upon rather than acting (Hoggart and Buller 1987); often after 1945, this was associated with a rurality allied to petit bourgeois values and limited resources (e.g. Vidich and Bensman 1968). Yet, within the constraints they faced, in places that had significant agricultural ties, policy diversity characterised districts. Inter-war Hatfield and Smallburgh displayed leadership approaches embedded with fundamental economic drivers. Smallburgh was not pursuing growth but leaders did pursue vested interests. In some cases, rural leaders favoured growth, in others they resisted (Caird and Moisley 1961; Kendall 1963). This should not be confused with institutions being boxed-in by perceived structural constraints (Hodge and Whitby 1981), like inter-war Ampthill, Erpingham and Walsingham, where local leaders saw few opportunities for change. The transition of Ampthill from slumber to action, the forceful exploitation of openings by Biggleswade and the quiet, small-scale incremental impacts of Braughing, all point to ways out of the shackles leaders imagined enclosed them. Rather than taking the easy way out, of doing little and hoping the private sector would 'solve' their problems, these councils demonstrated a sense of civic duty; of recognition that democratic states have responsibilities to all citizens, not just those who can afford to pay, that structures embed within themselves discriminations against some citizens more than others, so firm but sympathetic action is required to help the less fortunate

---

[354] *H&PBG* 6 January 1956, p.5.
[355] HRO RDC7/1/44 HtRDCH&TPCM 14 January 1969, p.703.

(LeGrand 1982; Hoggart 1991). These seven councils responded in different ways to these challenges. In their diversity they demonstrated both the limitations of local action and its capacity to make a difference.

References

Abbott E (1922) The English census of 1921. J Polit Econ 30:827–840

Addison P (1994) The road to 1945: British politics and the Second World War, rev edn. Pimlico, London

Adonis A, Pollard S (1997) A class act: the myth of Britain's classless society. Hamish Hamilton, London

Allison KJ (1961) Industrial and agricultural. In: Norwich and its region. British Association for the Advancement of Science Local Executive Committee, Norwich, pp 119–126

Anderson MA (1981) Planning policies and development control in the Sussex Downs AONB. Town Plan Rev 52:5–25

Association of County Sanitary Officers (1952) Housing: second interim report on the housing survey in rural areas (England and Wales). Norwich

Bailey BJ (1978) Portrait of Hertfordshire. Robert Hale, London

Baker WP (1953) The English village. Oxford University Press, London

Ball ID (1980) Urban investment controls in Britain. In: Ashford DE (ed) National resources and urban policy. Croom Helm, London, pp 115–142

Barlow J, Duncan SS (1994) Success and failure in housing provision: European systems compared. Pergamon, Oxford

Barnes P (1993) Norfolk landowners since 1880. University of East Anglia Centre of East Anglian Studies, Norwich

Bassett KA, Short JR (1980) Housing and residential structure. Routledge & Kegan Paul, London

Bayliss D (2001) Revisiting the cottage council estates: England, 1919-39. Plan Perspect 16:169–200

Beavington F (1975) The development of market gardening in Bedfordshire 1799–1939. Agric Hist Rev 23:23–47

Beckett JV, Turner ME (2007) End of the old order? F.M.L. Thompson, the land question, and the burden of ownership in England, c1880–c1925. Agric Hist Rev 55:269–288

Bedfordshire County Council (1952) County development plan 1952: written analysis. Bedford

Bennett EN (1914) Problems of village life. Williams & Norgate, London

Benson J (1989) The working class in Britain, 1850–1939. Longman, Harlow

Berry F (1974) Housing: the great British failure. Charles Knight, London

Bevan M, Sanderling L (1996) Private renting in rural areas. University of York Centre for Housing Policy, York

Biggleswade Rural District Council (1922) Annual report of the medical officer of health and sanitary inspector 1921. Biggleswade

Biggleswade Rural District Council (1923) Annual report of the medical officer of health and sanitary inspector 1922. Biggleswade

Biggleswade Rural District Council (1931) Annual report of the medical officer of health and sanitary inspector 1930. Biggleswade

Bird SE (1982) The impact of private estate ownership on social development in a Scottish rural community. Sociol Rural 22:43–55

Bishop KD (1998) Countryside conservation and the new right. In: Allmendiger P, Thomas H (eds) Urban planning and the new right. Routledge, London, pp 186–210

Blacksell M, Gilg AW (1977) Planning control in an area of outstanding natural beauty. Soc Econ Adm 11:206–215

Blair AM (1972) Compulsory purchase: a neglected factor in the agricultural land loss debate. Area 12:183–189

Blunden JR, Curry N (1985) The changing countryside. Croom Helm, London

Booth P (1999) From regulation to discretion: the evolution of development control in the British planning system 1909-1947. Plan Perspect 14:277–289

Bowler IR, Lewis GJ (1987) The decline of private rented housing in rural areas: a case study of estate villages in Northamptonshire. In: Lockhart D, Ilbery BW (eds) The future of the British rural landscape. Geo Books, Norwich, pp 115–136

Branson N (1979) Poplarism 1919–25: George Lansbury and the councillors' revolt. Lawrence & Wishart, London

Breton A, Wintrobe R (1982) The logic of bureaucratic conduct. Cambridge University Press, Cambridge

Brittan S (1964) The Treasury under the Tories 1951–1964. Penguin, Harmondsworth

Buller HJ, Hoggart K (1986) Nondecision-making and community power: the case of residential development control in rural areas. Prog Plan 25:133–203

Buller HJ, Lowe PD (1982) Politics and class in rural preservation: a study of the Suffolk Preservation Society. In: Moseley MJ (ed) Power, planning and people in rural East Anglia. University of East Anglia Centre for East Anglian Studies, Norwich, pp 21–41

Bullock N (1989) Fragments of a post-war utopia: housing in Finsbury 1945-51. Urban Stud 26:46–58

Burchardt J (2012) Historicizing counterurbanization: in-migration and the construction of rural space in Berkshire (UK), 1901–51. J Hist Geogr 38:155–166

Caird JB, Moisley HA (1961) Leadership and innovation in the crofting communities of the outer Hebrides. Sociol Rev 9:85–102

Chambers CG (1917) Bedfordshire. Cambridge University Press, Cambridge

Chase M (1993) 'Nothing less than a revolution?': Labour's agricultural policy. In: Fyrth J (ed) Labour's high noon: the government and the economy 1945–51. Lawrence & Wishart, London, pp 78–95

Clarke JJ (1931) Slums and the Housing Act, 1930. Town Plan Rev 14(3):163–193

Clarke JJ (1936) Restriction of Ribbon Development Act, 1935. Town Plan Rev 17(1):11–32

Cloke PJ (1979) Key settlements in rural areas. Methuen, London

Cloke PJ (1983) An introduction to rural settlement planning. Methuen, London

Coleman R (1982) Second homes in north Norfolk. In: Moseley MJ (ed) Power, planning and people in rural East Anglia. University of East Anglia Centre for East Anglian Studies, Norwich, pp 97–117

Coles R (1982) Retirement in rural north Norfolk. In: Moseley MJ (ed) Power, planning and people in rural East Anglia. University of East Anglia Centre for East Anglian Studies, Norwich, pp 119–136

Collison P (1963) The Cutteslowe Wall: a study in social class. Faber & Faber, London

Connell J (1978) The end of tradition: country life in central Surrey. Routledge & Kegan Paul, London

Countryside Commission (1997) Public attitudes to the countryside. Countryside Commission, Cheltenham

Crichton RM (1964) Commuters' village: a study of community and commuters in the Berkshire village of Stratford Mortimer. David & Charles, Dawlish

Cross M, Mallen D (1978) Local government and politics. Longman, Harlow

Cullingworth JB (1979) Essays on housing policy. Allen & Unwin, London

Dale J (1980) Class struggle, social policy and state structure: central-local relations and housing policy, 1919–1939. In: Melling J (ed) Housing, social policy and the state. Croom Helm, London, pp 194–223

Davidson J, Wibberley G (1977) Planning and the rural environment. Pergamon, Oxford

Davies HWE, Edwards D, Rowley AR (1986) The relationship between development plans, development control and appeals. Planner 72(10):11–15

Dearlove J (1973) The politics of policy in local government. Cambridge University Press, Cambridge

Dearlove J (1979) The reorganisation of British local government. Cambridge University Press, Cambridge

Department of the Environment (1970) Land availability for housing. Circular 10/70. HMSO, London

Department of the Environment (1974) Rates and rateable values in England and Wales 1973–1974. HMSO, London

Dickens P, Duncan SS, Goodwin M, Gray F (1985) Housing, states and localities. Methuen, London

Dresser M (1984) Housing policy in Bristol 1919–30. In: Daunton MJ (ed) Councillors and tenants. Leicester University Press, Leicester, pp 156–216

Drudy PJ (1978) Depopulation in a prosperous agricultural region. Reg Stud 12:49–60

Dunleavy PJ (1980) Social and political theory and the issues in central-local relations. In: Jones GW (ed) New approaches to the study of central-local government relationships. Gower, Aldershot, pp 116–136

Dunleavy PJ, Rhodes RAW (1983) Beyond Whitehall. In: Drucker H, Dunleavy PJ, Gamble A, Peele G (eds) Developments in British politics. Macmillan, London, pp 106–133

Dunn MC, Rawson M, Rogers A (1981) Rural housing: competition and choice. Allen & Unwin, London

Eastwood T (1951) Industry in the country towns of Norfolk and Suffolk. Oxford University Press, London

Eatwell R (1979) The 1945–1951 Labour government. Batsford, London

English J, Madigan R, Norman P (1976) Slum clearance: the social and administrative context in England and Wales. Croom Helm, London

Finnigan R (1984) Council housing in Leeds 1919-1939: social policy and urban change. In: Daunton MJ (ed) Councillors and tenants. Leicester University Press, Leicester, pp 102–153

Fischer CS (1975) Toward a subcultural theory of urbanism. Am J Sociol 80:1319–1341

Foley DL (1972) Governing the London region. University of California Press, Berkeley

Forrest R, Murie A (1992) Change on a rural council estate: an analysis of dwelling histories. J Rural Stud 8:53–65

Gardiner J (2010) The thirties: an intimate history. Harper Press, London

Gay O (1987) Pre-fabs: a study in policy-making. Public Adm 65:407–422

Gayler HJ (1970) Land speculation and urban development: contrasts in south-east Essex, 1880-1940. Urban Stud 7:21–36

Gilder IM (1979) Rural planning policies: An economic appraisal. Prog Plan 11:213–271

Gilg AW (1978) Countryside planning. David & Charles, Newton Abbot

Gilg AW, Kelly M (1997) Rural planning in practice: the case of agricultural dwellings. Prog Plan 47:75–157

Grafton DJ (1982) Net migration, outmigration and remote rural areas: a cautionary note. Area 14:331–318

Grayson WC (1992) Chicksands: a millenium history. Shefford Press, Shefford

Green RJ (1971) Countryside planning: the future of the rural regions. Manchester University Press, Manchester

Griffiths CVJ (2007) Labour and the countryside: the politics of rural Britain 1918–1939. Oxford University Press, Oxford

Hall PG (1980) Great planning disasters. Weidenfield & Nicolson, London

Hamnett CR (1973) Improvement grants as an indicator of gentrification in inner London. Area 5:252–261

Hardy D, Ward C (1984) Arcadia for all: the legacy of a makeshift landscape. Mansell, London

Harloe M (1985) Private rented housing in the United States and Europe. Routledge, London

Harris C (1974) Hennage: a social system in miniature. Holt, Rinehart & Winston, New York

Harrison M, Norton A (1967) Local government administration in England and Wales. Maud Committee report on the management of local government volume five. HMSO, London

Hatfield Rural District Council (1947) Report of the medical officer of health 1946. Hatfield

Havinden MA (1999) Estate villages revisited. University of Reading Rural History Centre, Reading

Hennessy P (1996) Muddling through: power, politics and the quality of government in postwar Britain. Victor Gollancz, London

Henson AE (1957) Rural housing. In: British housing and planning yearbook 1957. National Housing and Town Planning Council, London, pp 103–110

Herington J (1984) The outer city. Harper & Row, London

Herington J, Evans DM (1979) The spatial pattern of movement in 'key' and 'non-key' settlements. Working Paper 3. Loughborough University Department of Geography, Loughborough

Hertfordshire County Council (1961) Building in the green belt. Hertford

Hodge I, Whitby MC (1981) Rural employment: trends, options, choices. Methuen, London

Hoggart K (1991) People, power and place: perspectives on Anglo-American politics. Routledge, London

Hoggart K, Buller HJ (1987) Rural development: a geographical perspective. Croom Helm, London

Hooson DJM (1958) The recent growth of population and industry in Hertfordshire. Trans Inst Br Geogr 25:197–208

Horn P (2013) Country house society: the private lives of England's upper class after the First World War. Amberley Publishing, Stroud

Howkins A (1991) Reshaping rural England: a social history 1850–1925. Harper Collins Academic, London

Jackman R (1978) Issues in financial allocation. In: Davies RL, Hall PG (eds) Issues in urban society. Penguin, Harmondsworth, pp 268–299

Jackson AA (1973) Semi-detached London: suburban development, life and transport, 1900–39. Allen & Unwin, London

Jennings JH (1971) Geographical implications of the municipal housing programme in England and Wales 1919-39. Urban Stud 8:121–138

Jennings RE (1977) Education and politics: policy-making in local education authorities. Batsford, London

Johnson RW (1972) The nationalisation of English rural politics: Norfolk South West, 1945-1970. Parliam Aff 26:8–55

Jones A (1999) No cardboard boxes, so no problem? young people and housing in rural areas. In: Rugg J (ed) Young people, housing and social policy. Routledge, London, pp 145–158

Jones B (2010) Slum clearance, privatization and residualization: the practices and politics of council housing in mid-twentieth-century England. Twent Century Br Hist 21:510–539

Jones O (2014) The establishment: and how they get away with it. Allen Lane, London

Keith-Lucas B, Richards PG (1978) A history of local government in the twentieth century. Allen & Unwin, London

Kendall D (1963) Portrait of a disappearing English village. Sociol Rural 3:157–165

Kennett DH (1978) Portrait of Bedfordshire. Robert Hale, London

Larkin A (1978) Rural housing - too dear, too few and too far. Roof 3:15–17

Larkin A (1979) Rural housing and housing needs. In: Shaw JM (ed) Rural deprivation and planning. Geo Books, Norwich, pp 71–80

Layton E (1961) Building by local authorities. Allen & Unwin, London

Lee JM (1963) Social leaders and public persons: a study of county government in Cheshire since 1888. Clarendon, Oxford

LeGrand J (1982) The strategy of equality: redistribution and the social services. Allen & Unwin, London

Lemon A (1973) Retirement and its effects on small towns. Town Plan Rev 44:254–262

Lowe PD, Murdoch J, Cox G (1995) A civilised retreat? anti-urbanism, rurality and the making of an anglo-centric culture. In: Healey P, Cameron S, Davoudi S, Graham S, Madani-Pour A (eds) Managing cities. Wiley, Chichester, pp 63–82

Lowerson J (1980) Battles for the countryside. In: Gloversmith F (ed) Class, culture and social change: a new view of the 1930s. Harvester, Brighton, pp 258–280

Macdonald P (2017) Rural settlement change in East Suffolk, 1850-1939. PhD thesis University of East Anglia

Macintyre S (1980) Little moscows: communism and working-class militancy in inter-war Britain. Croom Helm, London

MacLeod RM (1968) Treasury control and social administration: a study of establishment growth at the Local Government Board 1871–1905. Occasional Paper in Social Administration 23. Bell, London

Macmillan H (1969) Tides of fortune 1945–1955. Macmillan, London

Malpass P (2003) Private enterprise in eclipse? a reassessment of British housing policy in the 1940s. Hous Stud 18:645–659

Martin EW (1965) The shearers and the shorn: a study of life in a Devon community. Routledge & Kegan Paul, London

Mingay GE (1990) The rural slum. In: Gaskell SM (ed) Slums. Leicester University Press, Leicester, pp 92–143

Ministry of Health (1920) First annual report, 1919–1920: part II – housing and town planning. Cmd 917. HMSO, London

Ministry of Health (1921) Second annual report, 1920–1921, Cmd. 1446. HMSO, London

Ministry of Health (1924a) Fifth annual report, 1923–1924, Cmd 2218. HMSO, London

Ministry of Health (1924b) Circular to local authorities on the Housing (Financial Provisions) Act, 1924. Circular 520. HMSO, London

Ministry of Health (1926) Seventh annual report, 1925–1926. Cmd 2724. HMSO, London

Ministry of Health (1933a) Housing (Financial Provisions) Act, 1933. Circular 1334. HMSO, London

Ministry of Health (1933b) Report of the departmental committee on housing. Cmd 4397. HMSO, London

Ministry of Health (1934) Fifteenth annual report, 1933–1934. Cmd. 4664. HMSO, London

Ministry of Health (1935) Sixteenth annual report, 1934–1935. Cmd. 4978. HMSO, London

Ministry of Health (1937a) Eighteenth annual report, 1936–1937. Cmd. 5516. HMSO, London

Ministry of Health (1937b) Rural housing: second report of the Rural Housing Sub-Committee of the Central Housing Advisory Committee. HMSO, London

Ministry of Health (1938) Nineteenth annual report, 1937–1938. Cmd 5801. HMSO, London

Ministry of Health (1939) Rates and rateable values in England and Wales 1938–1939. HMSO, London

Ministry of Health (1944a) Rural housing: third report of the Rural Housing Sub-Committee of the Central Housing Advisory Committee. HMSO, London

Ministry of Health (1944b) Private enterprise housing: report of the Private Enterprise Sub-Committee of the Central Housing Advisory Committee of the Ministry of Health. HMSO, London

Ministry of Health (1944c) Design of dwellings: report of the Central Housing Advisory Committee. HMSO, London

Ministry of Health (1946) Housing (Financial and Miscellaneous Provisions) Act, 1946. Circular 118/46. HMSO, London

Ministry of Health (1950a) Report of the Ministry of Health for the year ended 31st March 1949. Cmd 7910. HMSO, London

Ministry of Health (1950b) Housing – revised procedure for submission of proposals to the Ministry of Health. Circular 24/50. HMSO, London

Ministry of Health (quarterly) Housing return for England and Wales. [From 1951 Ministry of Housing & Local Government.] HMSO, London

Ministry of Health Town & Country Planning Advisory Committee (1938) Report on the preservation of the countryside 1938. HMSO, London

Ministry of Housing & Local Government (1956) Report of the Ministry of Housing and Local Government for the year 1955. Cmd 9876. HMSO, London

Ministry of Housing & Local Government (1959) Report of the Ministry of Housing and Local Government 1958. Cmnd 737 HMSO, London

Ministry of Housing & Local Government (1961a) Report of the Ministry of Housing and Local Government 1960. Cmnd 1435. HMSO, London

Ministry of Housing & Local Government (1961b) Housing in England and Wales. Cmnd 1290. HMSO, London

Ministry of Housing & Local Government (1963) Report of the Ministry of Housing and Local Government 1962. Cmnd 1976. HMSO, London

Ministry of Housing & Local Government (1967) Management of local government, Maud Committee report. HMSO, London

Ministry of Housing & Local Government (1968) Old houses into new homes. Cmnd 3602. HMSO, London

Ministry of Housing & Local Government (quarterly) Housing return for England and Wales. [Before 1951 Ministry of Health.] HMSO, London

Ministry of Reconstruction (1918) Housing in England and Wales: memorandum by the advisory housing panel on the emergency problem. Cd 9087. HMSO, London

Ministry of Works & Planning (1942) Report of the Committee on Land Utilisation in Rural Areas. Cmd 6378. Scott report. HMSO, London

Minns R (1973) The significance of Clay Cross: another look at district audit. Policy Polit 2:309–329

Molotch H (1976) The city as a growth machine. Am J Sociol 82:309–332

Morgan KO (1984) Labour in power, 1945–1951. Clarendon, Oxford

Morgan KO, Morgan J (1980) Portrait of a progressive: the political career of Christopher, Viscount Addison. Clarendon, Oxford

Moseley MJ (1974) Growth centres in spatial planning. Pergamon, Oxford

Muchnick DM (1970) Urban renewal in Liverpool: a study of the politics of redevelopment. Occasional Paper in Social Administration 33. Bell, London

Munton RJC (1983) London's green belt: containment in practice. Allen & Unwin, London

Murray PJ (2012) The Council for the Preservation of Rural England, suburbia and the politics of preservation. Twent Century Br Hist 23:25–37

National House Building Committee (1924) Report on the present position in the building industry, with regard to the carrying out of a full housing programme, having particular reference to the means of providing an adequate supply of labour and materials. Cmd 2104. HMSO, London

Newby HE, Bell C, Rose D, Saunders P (1978) Property, paternalism and power. Hutchinson, London

Newton K (1976) Second city politics: democratic processes and decision-making in Birmingham. Oxford University Press, Oxford

Niner P (1975) Local authority housing policy and practice – a case study approach. Occasional Paper 31. University of Birmingham Centre for Urban & Regional Studies, Birmingham

O'Leary B (1987) Why was the GLC abolished? Int J Urban Reg Res 11:193–217

Olechnowicz A (1997) Working class housing in England between the wars. Clarendon, Oxford

Owens SE (1984) Energy and spatial structure: a rural example. Environ Plan A16:1319–1337

Pacione M (1980) Differential quality of life in a metropolitan village. Trans Inst Br Geogr 5:185–206

Pahl RE (1965) Urbs in rure: the metropolitan fringe in Hertfordshire. Geographical Paper 2. London School of Economics, London

Pennington M (2000) Public choice theory and the politics of urban containment: voter-centred versus specific-interest explanations. Eviron Plann C Gov Policy 18:145–162

Phillips M (2005) Differential productions of rural gentrification: illustrations from north and south Norfolk. Geoforum 36:477–494

Phillips DR, Williams AM (1982a) Rural housing and the public sector. Gower, Farnborough

Phillips DR, Williams AM (1982b) Local authority housing and accessibility: evidence from South Hams, Devon. Trans Inst Br Geogr 7:304–320

Phillips DR, Williams AM (1983) Rural settlement policies and local authority housing: observations from a case-study of South Hams, Devon. Environ Plan A15:501–513

Pooley GC (1996) Local authority housing: origins and development. The Historical Association, London

Preece RA (1981) Patterns of development in the Cotswolds area of outstanding natural beauty. Research Paper 27. University of Oxford School of Geography, Oxford

Pressman JL, Wildavsky A (1984) Implementation: how great expectations in Washington are dashed in Oakland; or, why it's amazing that federal programs work at all, this being a saga of the Economic Development Administration as told by two sympathetic observers who seek to build morals on a foundation. University of California Press, Berkeley

Pugh M (2008) 'We danced all night': a social history of Britain between the wars. Bodley Head, London

Punter J (1986) A history of aesthetic control, 1909–1953: the control of the external appearance of development in England and Wales. Town Plan Rev 57:351–381

Punter J (1987) A history of aesthetic control, 1953–1985: the control of the external appearance of development in England and Wales. Town Plan Rev 58:29–62

Read B (2003) Henley rural: the history of a rural district council in Oxfordshire 1894–1932. ELSP, Bradford-on-Avon

Redfield R (1947) The folk society. Am J Sociol 52:293–308

Registrar-General (2002) 1971 census aggregate data. UK Data Service. https://doi.org/10.5257/census/aggregate-1971-1

Rhodes G (1967) Town government in South-East England. Greater London Paper 12. London School of Economics, London

Rhodes G (1976) Local government finance 1918-1966. In: Committee of Inquiry into Local Government Finance, Local government finance: appendix six. HMSO, London, pp 102–173

Rhodes RAW (1984) Continuity and change in British central-local relations: the 'Conservative threat' 1979-83. Br J Polit Sci 14:261–283

Robin J (1980) Elmdon: continuity and change in a north-west Essex Village 1861–1964. Cambridge University Press, Cambridge

Rocke T (1987) Implementation of rural housing policy. In: Cloke PJ (ed) Rural planning: policy into action? Harper & Row, London, pp 164–184

Rose D, Saunders P, Newby HE, Bell C (1976) Ideologies of property. Sociol Rev 24:699–730

Royal Commission on Local Government in England (1969) Report. Cmnd 4040, Redcliffe-Maud report. HMSO, London

Rural District Councils' Association (1966) Evidence of the Rural District Councils' Association to the Royal Commission on Local Government in England. HMSO, London

Ryder R (1984) Council house building in county Durham 1900-39. In: Daunton MJ (ed) Councillors and tenants. Leicester University Press, Leicester, pp 40–100

Saunders P (1985) The forgotten dimension of central-local relations: theorising the 'regional state'. Eviron Plann C Gov Policy 3:149–162

Saunders P, Newby HE, Bell C, Rose D (1978) Rural community and rural community power. In: Newby HE (ed) International perspectives in rural sociology. Wiley, Chichester, pp 55–85

Scott J (1982) The upper classes: property and privilege in Britain. Macmillan, Basingstoke

Self P, Storing HJ (1962) The state and the farmer. Allen & Unwin, London

Sharp E (1969) The Ministry of Housing and Local Government. Allen & Unwin, London

Sharpe LJ (1960) The politics of local government in Greater London. Public Adm 38:157–172

Sharpe LJ (1978) Reforming the grass roots: an alternative analysis. In: Halsey AH, Butler DE (eds) Policy and politics. Macmillan, London, pp 82–110

Sheail J (1981) Rural conservation in inter-war Britain. Clarendon, Oxford

Sherwood KB (1996) Housing provision and population change in the countryside 1919-1939: some evidence from Northamptonshire. East Midland Geogr 19(2):43–58

Shipp PJ, Harris R (1977) Communications between central and local government in the manage-
    ment of local authority expenditure. Report HR5032. Social Science Research Council, London
Short BM, Godfrey J (2007) 'The Outhwaite controversy': a micro-history of the Edwardian land
    campaign. J Hist Geogr 33:45–71
Shucksmith M (1981) No homes for locals? Gower, Farnborough
Shucksmith M, Henderson M (1995) A classification of rural housing markets in England.
    HMSO, London
Sillince J (1986) Why did Warwickshire's key settlement policy change in 1982? Geogr J
    152:176–192
Simon ED (1933) The anti-slum campaign. Longmans, Green & Co., London
Smallburgh Rural District Council (1958) Smallburgh RDC medical officer of health annual report
    1957. Stalham
Smallburgh Rural District Council (1962) Smallburgh RDC medical officer of health annual report
    1961. Stalham
Smallburgh Rural District Council (1971) Smallburgh RDC medical officer of health annual report
    1970. Stalham
Smalley B (1995) A Short history of Much Hadham. self-published volume, Much Hadham
Social Market Foundation (2013) The politics of housing. National Housing Federation, London
Spencer D (1995) Counterurbanization: the local dimension. Geoforum 26:153–173
Springall LM (1936) Labouring life in Norfolk villages 1834–1914. Allen & Unwin, London
Strathern M (1982) The village as an idea: constructs of village-ness in Elmdon, Essex. In: Cohen
    AP (ed) Belonging: identity and social organization in British rural cultures. Manchester
    University Press, Manchester, pp 247–277
Sutcliffe AS, Smith R (1974) Birmingham 1939–1970: history of Birmingham volume three.
    Oxford University Press, London
Theakston K, Fry GK (1989) Britain's administrative elite: permanent secretaries 1900-1986.
    Public Adm 67:129–147
Thomas CJ (1966) Some geographical aspects of council housing in Nottingham. East Midland
    Geogr 4:88–98
Tilley MF (1947) Housing the country worker. Faber & Faber, London
Vidich AJ, Bensman J (1968) Small town in mass society: class, power and religion in a rural com-
    munity, 2nd edn. Princeton University Press, Princeton
Wade-Martins P (1994) An historical atlas of Norfolk, 2nd edn. Norfolk Museums Service, Norwich
Wade-Martins S, Williamson T (2008) The countryside of East Anglia: changing landscapes
    1870–1950. Boydell, Woodbridge
Walford NS (2001) Reconstructing the small area geography of mid-Wales for an analysis of popu-
    lation change 1961-1995. Int J Popul Geogr 7:311–338
Walford NS (2005) Connecting historical and contemporary small-area geography in Britain: the
    creation of digital boundary data for 1971 and 1981 census. Int J Geogr Inf Sci 19:749–767
Ward SV (1984) List Q: a missing link in inter-war public investment. Public Adm 62:348–358
Warnes AM (1991) London's population trends: metropolitan area or megalopolis? In: Hoggart K,
    Green DR (eds) London: a new metropolitan geography. Edward Arnold, London, pp 156–175
Weekley IG (1988) Rural depopulation and counterurbanisation: a paradox. Area 20:127–134
Wellings F (2006) British housebuilders: history and analysis. Blackwell, Oxford
Wilson GK (1977) Special interests in policy-making: agricultural policies and politics in Britain
    and the United States. Wiley, Chichester
Woodruffe BJ (1976) Rural settlement policies and plans. Oxford University Press, Oxford
Wrottesley AJ (1970) The Midland and Great Northern Joint Railway. David & Charles,
    Newton Abbot
Yaxley D (1977) Portrait of Norfolk. Robert Hale, London
Yelling JA (1992) Slums and redevelopment: policy and practice in England 1918–45, with par-
    ticular reference to London. UCL Press, London

Young K (1975) The Conservative strategy for London, 1855-1975. London J 1(1):56–81

Young K (1988) Rural prospects. In: Jowell R, Witherspoon S, Brook L (eds) British social attitudes. Gower, Aldershot, pp 155–174

Young K, Garside PL (1982) Metropolitan London: politics and urban change 1837–1981. Edward Arnold, London

Young K, Kramer J (1978) Strategy and conflict in metropolitan housing: suburbia versus the Greater London Council 1965–1975. Heinemann, London

Chapter 8
The Political Economy of English Rural Housing

Abstract This chapter provides a framework for appreciating the contrived nature of the English countryside. This is not based on a series of deliberate acts, targeted toward a particular vision of what the countryside should be. Rather it derives from identifying how public policy across many legislative enactments and policy instruments, stretching across the decades, set the tone that made today's outcomes more likely. A few national decisions were fundamental to the evolution of the countryside, such as the introduction of rent restrictions in 1915 and the instigation of mass municipal housing in 1919. None of these were determining. They could have been pulled back from. This chapter explores dominant features in English society that made such reversals unlikely. These include proclivities toward amateurism, muddling through rather than visionary policy, status infused top-down hierarchies, poor productivity, discriminations that left certain economic sectors in low-wage purgatory, including agriculture, inflexible, slow changing, under-resourced and highly constrained rural governments, and predilections toward urban favouritism. The chapter draws links to place the rural housing scene within the context of these fundamental characteristics of the state.

Keywords A conservative nation · Laissez-faire priorities · Top-down direction · Rural diversity · Local autonomy

8.1 The Political Economic Context

Conceptualising the countryside as a contrived product might give the impression of deliberation; of a targeted 'campaign' to produce a desired end-product. This is not the meaning laid on the term here. For the housing landscape of rural England to be directed in this way would require more forethought, vision and commitment than the nation's leaders should be credited with. As comparative investigations of public policy reveal, Britain has long been distinguished by its political ethos. In Ashford's (1986, p.307) words: 'Continents argue about definition of the state, while the

© Springer Nature Switzerland AG 2021   497
K. Hoggart, *A Contrived Countryside*, Local and Urban Governance,
https://doi.org/10.1007/978-3-030-62651-8_8

British more likely argue about whether there is a state'. The mindset is not one of purpose and direction but of cautious, incremental change, of 'muddling through' (Lindblom 1959; Hennessy 1996); urged on by 'pragmatism' that affords little weight to political radicalism or imagination. Hence, even though the inter-war decades saw a fulcrum realignment in political opposition within this 'Conservative Nation' (Gamble 1974), '… Labour could replace the Liberals with barely an institutional tremor' (Ashford 1986, p.306). Despite media attempts to stir public reaction with exaggerated claims of political extremism (Curran and Seaton 1988), transitions from one governing party to another have tended towards business as usual. Nationally, this was exemplified when the Conservatives furthered the previous Labour administration's housing policies in the early-1950s, with Labour returning the compliment in the mid-1960s, both for council-building and in accepting owner-occupation as the premier housing tenure (Harloe 1995, p.287). Locally, it was seen in slight political disagreement on councils, even in large cities with established political party regimes (e.g. Blondel and Hall 1967; Jones 1969; Sutcliffe and Smith 1974; Stacey et al. 1975). Perhaps influenced by the backcloth of Britain's declining economic and international influence, politicians like Willetts (1992, p.18) downplay the dominance of Conservative governance in the twentieth-century. Yet even Willetts (1992, p.6) portrays the Conservatives as the party of the silent majority. Providing an analytical rather than aspirational emphasis, Gamble and Walkland (1984, p.87) put flesh on the caricature of the 'Conservative Nation' by portraying actions by powerful Conservative supporters as seeking to set the political tone irrespective of ruling party: '… the system of adversary politics as it has been developed and perfected in the last sixty years was actually one of the most successful creations of Conservative statecraft and helped to prevent the creation of a truly radical alternative to Conservativism'. This has parallels with Benedict Anderson's (1983) conceptualisation of nationalism as an imagined community, built around a cohesive 'elite' (Urry 1986), which colludes to promote and perpetuate values to maintain its ascendancy (Bulpitt 1983).[1] The long-term success of the strategy was visible long ago, as Hobsbawm (1968) concluded, noting that by 1867, the British working-class could no longer be considered revolutionary. It finds expression today in working-class support for established institutions of the British state (e.g. Owen 2007; McKibbin 2010). Critical for our purpose, what did this mean for rural housing?

At heart, a key message is that to understand the rural realm, you need to start by looking at its national setting. This means more than acknowledging or exploring national policies; it requires understanding frameworks that produced one policy regime rather than another. At one level, this means stepping outside a particular national context, to appreciate the peculiarities of national groundings through comparative analysis, as I have sought to explore in political (Hoggart 1991) and rural

---

[1] On cohesion, Anthony Sampson (1982, p.35) claimed: 'The Tory Party is run by about five people who all treat their followers with disdain. They're mostly Etonians, and Eton is good for disdain'. Consistent with this image, others note how in times of stress national elite consensus emerges quickly (Ashford 1981; Gamble and Walkland 1984).

contexts in the past (Hoggart et al. 1995). At another level, it involves locating villages and rural districts 'horizontally', amidst a cacophony of rural and regional diversity (Hoggart 1988, 1990; Murdoch et al. 2003; Hodge and Monk 2004), and 'vertically' as regards national power relationships and mindsets. Despite ups and downs concomitant on specific Acts of Parliament, the first 75 years of the twentieth-century shared threads across multiple policies with substantial consequences for the countryside. Put another way, claims by politicians, and academic researchers, that the policies they introduce (or study) are innovative, unique or fundamental, need approaching with pinches of salt. The purpose of this concluding chapter is to highlight how persisting tendencies in the English policy environment set the tone for change in the countryside.

8.1.1   A Radical Alternative?

With Britain often cited as the home of Parliamentary democracy, we should start by asking how far governments generated change dynamics. That weight is placed on 'change' is self-evident, given the foundation for political rule in England in earlier centuries was the landowning classes, for which, up to late in the nineteenth-century: 'The Conservative Party was, *par excellence*, the party of the landed interests' (Cannadine 1990, p.65). Central to those interests were core conservative values, which theorists and would-be theorists seem to agree '… centre upon the propensity to use and to enjoy what is available rather than to wish for or to look for something elsewhere … What is esteemed is the present … on account of its familiarity' (Oakeshott 1975, p.23). Set within this attachment to tradition and aversion to change is an inner drive. As Richard Rose (1965, p.143) articulated it:

> Of all the features of the Conservative Party, the intense concern with winning elections and holding office is its most notable. So strongly do Conservatives seem to wish to hold office (perhaps as the result of childhood expectations acquired through socialisation) that commitment to a particular set of policies is not deep. The Party principles are extremely vague, and can be used to legitimate a very wide range of policy alternatives.

Hence, 'Conservatives are wary of grand statements of principles and beliefs' (Willetts 1992, p.3). Even what some see as a distinctive philosophy in Thatcherism, although dismantled in many forms by Party grandees more recently, was downplayed by Willetts (1992, Ch4) as embodying little more than a One Nation Conservative pamphlet. Change under Conservative regimes has been inclined to come from reversion to past practices or in response to 'threats' to the status quo, not from a strategy for national advancement. Yet maintaining 'control' required electorally popular policies, including sweeping incursions into opposition territory (Smith 1992; Jones 2000).

Large-scale council-building was first proposed under a war-time coalition. The leading proponents were Addison, a self-proclaimed radical, and a lifelong Tory (Lord Salisbury), with strong support coming from the Conservative Party leader

(Bonar Law), but with opposition from Hayes Fisher, the Conservative Local Government Board President (Addison 1934, p.494). Mainstream thought in the 1920s was that housing difficulties were a temporary aberration; that private building would bounce back from its war-time depression (Bowley 1945, p.15). No surprise, Chamberlain's 1923 Housing Act was intended to show private enterprise was better than council-building (Lyman 1957, p.110; Self 2006, p.91). Suggestions that this marked a distinctive Conservative approach were confounded when the short-lived 1924 Labour government was replaced and Chamberlain, despite personal antagonism towards the 1924 Housing Act (Self 2000, 2006), did not repeal it. The legislation of 1923 and 1924 overlapped little in take-up (Table 6.1) but operated side by side (Fig. 4.1). The Liberals were soon a spent force (Seaman 1966, p.10), but Labour offered little that was distinctive. As an alliance between trade unionists and political socialists, Labour was bathed in tension (Cole 1948; Beavan 2006). The unions wanted to squeeze economic gains from employers, but lacked a political philosophy (Seaman 1966, p.171), whereas the Independent Labour Party, which offered core values to the political socialists, '… was undogmatic, fraternal, a secular church with a powerful overlay from late-Victorian revivalist nonconformity. It was a movement founded on the ideal of comradeship, and on ethical rather than economic considerations' (Morgan 1984, pp.9–10). So, when Ramsey Macdonald formed the 1929 Labour government, its aim was not socialism but showing the public that Labour possessed competent administrators (Taylor 1965; Guttsman 1968; Griffiths 2007). A lack of tangible benefits for the working-classes under the 1929–1931 government drew attention to the electoral necessity of material gains (Addison 1994, p.16), which marginalised 'socialist' inclinations in the party (Miliband 1961). When Clement Attlee became Labour leader in 1935, middle-of-the-road politicians were firmly in control (Saville 1993, p.xvi), with the party shedding ideologically grounded policies aligned with owning the means of production (e.g. Tichelar 2003).

In the mindset of the Conservative Establishment, however, Labour was a troubling 1930s' challenger, although the majority of manual workers never voted Labour, not even trade union members (Taylor 1965, p.177). Indeed, Labour had insufficient support to form a government until well into the 1939–1945 War, when views shifted largely due to distrust of Conservative intentions (Fielding 1992; Mortimer 1993; Kynaston 2007). Exaggerated Conservative fears were commonplace, with roots in the mythologies the Party spun about the electorate, wherein: '… the Conservatives' stereotype of their own natural supporters suggested the largely unpolitical citizen liable to doze off while capitalism collapsed around him, [while] the typical socialist supporter was seen as politicised to the point of fanaticism' (Jarvis 1996, p.78).[2] More realistically, Labour's cautious, pragmatic politics

---

[2] Articulations of extremism directed at Labour politicians have been common. Ingham (1984, p.37) noted how Harold Wilson's moderate proposals for economic management were branded dangerous socialism by the City of London and within the Conservative Party. Revelations Wilson was investigated by security service agents signalled traits in the 'Establishment' when disturbed by even minor challenges (Wright 1987).

emerged from divisions within the Party and its supposed natural supporters. The Party could draw on no groundswell of radicalism, for the working-classes were themselves socially divided (Pahl 1985), with strong attachments to traditional institutions and practices (Owen 2007), alongside a culture of defensiveness and deference (Newby 1975; McKibbin 2010). Perhaps some amongst the middle-class 'socialists' had more radical inclinations (Morgan 1984, p.9), but such empha-ses were not embraced by the trade unions or the working-classes (Cole 1948; Pelling 1963; James 2006). Even solid working-class communities, like those of coal mining, offered shallow support for Labour at this time (e.g. Dennis et al. 1956). By contrast, aided by middle-(and upper-)class alarm following the Bolshevik Revolution, the Conservatives encouraged the middle-classes to come together in anti-working-class alliances (McKibbin 2010, p.91). These efforts were openly vis-ible well after 1945 in Conservative–Liberal alliances to keep councils out of Labour hands (e.g. Beith 1973). Little wonder, Labour policies tended to be cautious. Hence, while commonly portrayed as dogma by the political Right, the 1940s' nationalisations of economic and welfare sectors were for pragmatic reasons, with nationalisation attracting much Conservative support, as with Churchill endorsing railway nationalisation as early as 1918 and Baldwin pushing through airline and electricity nationalisation in 1927 (Morgan 1990, p.115; Willetts 1992, p.29). In tidying up private company failures, the Party's non-ideological approach was so 'mainstream' that only road haulage and iron and steel were sufficiently contentious to elicit de-nationalisation after 1951 (Calder 1969, p.584).[3] From then until 1974, Labour only had a Parliamentary majority from 1964 to 1970, during which time, problems left by the previous government saw Labour make its mark largely by intensifying the existing housing drive, then pushing for improved quality, rather than ploughing a distinctive path (Chap. 6). Inter-war and post-1945, politicians of the main parties huffed and puffed, were pious and pontificated, but little differenti-ated them. If you make allowance for the disruptive influence of the immediate post-war years, alongside the trauma of the Great Depression, then add the tendency of governments to carry forward predecessor policies, the 1918–1974 years con-tained only two periods associated with 'undiluted' party rule, namely 1933–1939 and 1955–1963, in both cases when Conservative ascendancy stretched into second terms.[4] In this regard, Willetts' (1992) claim of few years of 'unadulterated' Conservative rule in the Century holds true. Unless politicians pushed forcefully for innovative policies, they would be carried along by deep-seated tendencies in the state apparatus, with little to separate one government from another except tinkering at the edges.

---

[3] Arguments for nationalisations were poor management and lack of investment. For slum clear-ance, these criteria led to minimal compensation (viz. land value). This did not apply to 1940s nationalisations. These takeovers cost the '… equivalent of around 25% of the value of annual GDP (though the cost was spread over several years), paid to the previous owners of nationalised industries in the form of government stock' (Rhodes et al. 2018, p.6).

[4] In 1931, the Conservatives won 473 out of 615 Parliamentary seats, followed by 432 in 1935, while in 1955, 344 out of 630 were secured with 365 gained in 1959 (Butler and Freeman 1963).

8.1.2   Mainstream Urges

The British housing scene has attracted widespread criticism. The tone of assessments is captured in Berry's (1974) book title reference to 'the great failure'. This sentiment was shared with Bellman (1928, p.21), who was sanguine: 'If we have a Housing problem today it is because for half a century the authorities in this country have been supine and the people indifferent'. Others went farther, seeing feebleness as inherent in government: 'The problem is not that the civil service is too strong and creative in devising public policy, but that politicians are too weak and not creative enough' (Heclo and Wildavsky 1974, p.378). Such critiques embody long-held attacks on the British state. One aspect of these appraisals is shallow appreciation of specialists in leadership circles (Barnett 2001; Brown 2017). Politicians reflect this. Note the appointments of Harold Macmillan and Richard Crossman, two of the more successful ministers for housing. Both were surprised to lead a housing ministry and humbled by their inadequacies for the role. When Macmillan (1969, p.363) was offered the post: 'I was rather taken aback by this proposal. I knew nothing whatever about the housing problem except that we had pledged ourselves to an enormously high figure, generally regarded by the experts as unattainable'. Expecting to be offered Education, Crossman (1975, p.12) was similarly stunned: 'About this job I knew virtually nothing'. That ministers could nevertheless stamp their mark on housing direction was made clear by Wheatley's 1924 Act, which was a personal rather than a Labour Party initiative (Taylor 1965, p.210).[5] Yet, as Heclo and Wildavsky suggest, we should not assume that dynamic ministers were the norm (irrespective of what memoirs say). Morgan (1984, p.85), for example, debunked claims from the political Left that 1945–1951 government reforms were undermined by a right-wing civil service by pointing out that weaker ministers, as in Education, Labour and Supply, were susceptible to civil service dictation but the determined, like Bevan in Health, were not. Added to which, politicians functioned within a well-established ministry *modus operandi*, which gave their operational style different colours. Griffith (1966) characterised these from a local government perspective as promotional (Education), regulatory (the Home Office) or laissez-faire (Health, when without housing). Irrespective of personality, persuasiveness or propensities to bully, ministers faced dissimilar frameworks within which to make their mark.

On this, Heclo and Wildavsky (1974, p.379) gave food for thought when noting that: 'Bureaucracy would only be frustrating party government if there were something there to frustrate'. In the context of analysts (and politicians) characterising the British polity by its 'Conservative' nature, it is perhaps fitting that theoretical perspectives from the political Right provide an explanation for this. It comes in the form of public choice theory, particularly elements that conceptualise politicians as constantly seeking votes to ensure they stay in office, so their actions lack principle,

---

[5]Like Crossman on local government reorganisation in 1966 (Keith-Lucas and Richards 1978, p.211).

supporting whatever populist cause might bring out the voters (Downs 1957). Some might attribute the defeats of 1945 and 1964 to Conservative leaders losing touch with the British electorate rather than Labour responding to public opinion, but we can readily trace Downsian-type actions in the 1997 victory of Labour (Wickham-Jones 2005). Also important is another dimension of public choice theory, which relates to the role of public bureaucracies. In what reportedly reflected Mrs Thatcher's views of the civil service, the public choice account of bureaucracies portrays officials as prisoners to a desire to increase the size of their agency so as to enhance salaries (more underlings), prestige (more responsibility) and power (Downs 1967; Niskanen 1971). These hypotheses merit attention, although they fall short of adequate explanation. For one, long-term Conservative aims have been directed towards promoting agendas and story-lines that draw voters towards worldviews supportive of the Party, rather than slavishly following public opinion (Jarvis 1996; Weiler 2000; Jacobs et al. 2003; Davies 2013). Similarly, the Blair government's strategy was not to regulate markets but to '… bend the population to the logic of the market' (Faucher-King and Le Galès 2010, p.xii). Likewise, while there is considerable evidence of bureaucratic influence over the formulation and implementation of public policies (Page 1985), there is insufficient support for the view that officials consistently exert significant, independent impacts. For one, officials, like politicians, are not generally carved from the dynamic, forceful, intellectual mould implied in many images of leaders. By way of illustration, take Macmillan's view of Thomas Sheepshanks, the 1946–1955 Permanent Secretary for planning and (1951–1955) housing, as '… "sweet" but not an effective figure. "Small" in every sense of the word … Poor S[heepshanks] w[oul]d have made a fine canon, or even archdeacon – but Permanent Secretary of the Ministry of Housing – oh no!' (Catterall 2003, p.161). Hugh Dalton, Labour's 1950–1951 Minister for Housing and Planning, concurred, noting Sheepshanks '… will never miss a catch and never hit a six' (Pimlott 1986, pp.515–16). As Dunleavy (1985) articulated when dismantling public choice ideas, alongside officials not necessarily being forceful advocates, they commonly share professional interests across governmental tiers, with national ministries often favouring new responsibilities and staffing at lower tier levels (Laffin 1986; Smith 1989). Shared interests across tiers within professional communities promotes a fundamental prerequisite for efficient bureaucratic operations, namely trust (Breton and Wintrobe 1982). Adding lustre to misgivings about assumed growth fetishes amongst bureaucrats, Lowe (1984) showed how the inter-war Treasury exerted influence to limit, not encourage, Whitehall department expansion, so, from a public choice perspective, working against its own best interests. The key point is that powerful interests can gain more from structuring possibilities than chasing specific targets.

Understanding the networks that construct prospects for others within national government draws attention to the Treasury. Relations with the Treasury are not the same as with other departments. For sure, there has been tension between ministries at any point in time. One example was the Ministry of Works, which promoted technological advancement in building during the Second World War, but owing to inter-ministry jealousies was side-lined as house-building expanded post-1945 (Gay 1987). Crossman's and Macmillan's diaries provided regular insight on 'fights' to ward-off competing claims that would deny their department resources. The Treasury had a more central role. From 1919, for instance, its Permanent Secretary was recognised as head of the civil service, with a right to advise the Prime Minister on all senior appointments, and with no policy involving new expenditure going to Cabinet without prior reference to the Treasury (Lowe 1978). Yet principles of ministerial responsibility meant the Treasury could not direct or work positively with ministries. It exerted influence primarily through vetoing other's plans (Pemberton 2004). This negativity matched traditional economic worldviews on the role of the state. The Treasury pursued dear money policies inter-war (and after 1945), which raised interest rates and investment costs in pursuit of a return to the gold standard. In this, it was spurred by a vision that the prestige of British capitalism was synonymous with the fortunes of financial markets and the City of London (Morgan and Morgan 1980; Ward 1988). Hence, faced with the Great Depression, the Treasury rejected New Deal style policies that helped revive the US economy, in favour of cutting costs and balancing the books (Perkin 1989), so generating increased poverty and greater inequality (Martin 1988; Dunford 1995; Scott 2007), although the absence of outlets for investment fortuitously provided cash for mortgages for the better paid (Seaman 1966; Jackson 1973; Morgan 1990; Green 1991). A pursuit of nineteenth-century fiscal rules brought blacklists for councils that prioritised addressing local deprivations (Ward 1984), while support for finance over other economic sectors led onto the stop-go policies of the 1950s–1960s, alongside inadequate attention to manufacturing efficiency (e.g. Morgan 1984, p.134). Hence, rather than investing the bounty of Marshall Aid in infrastructure or improving manufacturing productivity, as in France and Germany, Britain sunk its gold and foreign currency reserves into shoring up the nation's status as a financial power (Barnett 1995, pp.367–9).

The central relationship for any ministry was with the Treasury. Crossman (1975, p.333) referred to '… the all-pervasive Treasury influence in every spending department', while, for those aspiring to senior administrative posts, Permanent Secretaries have increasingly had to spend time in central coordination and planning agencies, like the Treasury (Theakston and Fry 1989, p.146). This reinforced tendencies within elite social networks, for: 'Treasury influence rests not on hard-nosed interpretation of formal powers but in personal networks, sensitive bargaining, and up-to-date information that operate to create habits of mind leading to anticipation of Treasury reaction' (Heclo and Wildavsky 1974, p.380; Lowe 1984). As the focal point of Whitehall networks, two elements in Treasury behaviour penetrated policy-making. The first was the way the Treasury typified, in concentrated form, the centrality of trust and connections in policy processes. These relationships were summarised by Ham (1981, p.41):

> The small, exclusive social world of the Treasury mandarin is part of a larger civil service cocoon for the administrative elite. A successful career at a private school followed by three years at Oxford or Cambridge, reading an arts subject, leads to entry into that cadre which the 'young flyer' will not leave for forty years or so. During this lifetime of learning his way round Whitehall, never specialising too much in anything, he may well have developed enough contacts to be picked out as a useful adornment to the board of some large financial institution … he will have been aware that, while political masters come and go, the Treasury influence is permanent. (also Brittan 1964; Theakston and Fry 1989)

As Bulpitt (1983, p.157) caricatured the world of senior Whitehall mandarins: 'It was run by "chaps", "sound chaps" in London, who did their best to get on with equally sound, but sometimes socially suspect "chaps", in the periphery'. Presaging a pattern that persists today, Ashford (1986, p.24) drew out an important aspect of this London mindset when noting how early social policy was based on the peculiar problems of London labour markets, even though pivotal worker difficulties were in the North. The 1950s'–1960s' emphasis on shared dwellings as a primary indicator of housing distress testified to the enduring strength of this tendency, for it captured city distinctiveness (Table 6.15), which fed into housing investment priorities (Chap. 6), but did not match physical unfitness patterns (MHLG 1968), nor absence of facilities (Table 2.7).

Further constraining the official imagination was a lack of technical ability. For Brittan (1964, p.29): 'Whitehall in general and the Treasury in particular are in rather a mixed-up mood about specialists … it is still maintained that for the bulk of its work the Treasury needs professional administrators rather than experts in any particular subjects'. Little surprise, no professional economists were employed in a central economic department in 1939, with only 25 in the Treasury by the early-1960s (Brittan 1964, p.28; Cairncross and Watts 1989, p.343). This compared with close to 400 in the Government Economic Service by the late-1980s (Cairncross and Watts 1989, p.344). As for housing, the Ministry of Health staff complement was only 49 in 1930, although this rose with post-war house building to 877 by 1950 (119 technical officers).[6] No pun intended, but the national administration of housing in the inter-war period looked like a cottage industry.[7] The Treasury might be viewed the same way. John Maynard Keynes reportedly 'inveighed' against Treasury officials, who he saw as incapable and incompetent (Hennessy 1992, p.199). The 1945–1951 Labour government promoted technical improvement (Morgan 1984, p.85), but in an environment favouring non-specialists, the lack of technical ability was telling. The deficiencies that existed, inter-war and early post-war, were captured by Booth (2001, p.357), who noted how: 'Treasury men were apt to change their mind very quickly and to clothe their arguments in whatever intellectual mantle gave the greatest likelihood of acceptance'. The Treasury floundered, with policies not working, without the originality to investigate Keynes's ideas (Brittan 1964, p.49; Ham 1981, pp.67–68), and boxed-in by the 'super careful finance' principles of Chancellors like Neville Chamberlain and Philip Snowden (Seaman 1966, p.246; Miller 1976, pp.473–4; Self 2006, p.224). Analysts find scant improvement after 1945, as précised in Sharpe's (1982) lament that, while the Treasury failed to manage the economy (or get estimates right), this did not diminish its belief that it should have more control, especially over the public sector. This applied even in

---

[6] HCH 20 March 1930, Vol.236, col.2102; HCH 20 July 1950, Vol.477, col.192W.

[7] I found no comparable indications of housing section staffing after this, but figures for the MHLG tantalise (although the Ministry had wider responsibilities). Over 1951–1964, employee numbers fell by almost 200, whereas they rose by more than 1000 over 1964–1968 with an expanded house-building programme and more attention to evidence-based policy.

fields outside the immediate orbit of the Treasury, like local government (Layton 1961; Ball 1980).

The framework within which local housing advancement was sought offered the joint restraints of intrusive detailed intervention by ministries combined with the directing hands of 'amateurs', whose appearance in policy-making circles owed little to their leadership capacity or technical abilities, but derived more from family background, alongside the school and university they attended. Deficiencies were evident not merely in personnel but also in operational structures. Chapter 5 explored the latter as regards the difficulties rural councils faced. Hemmed in by modes of organisation that perpetuated insufficiency and non-elasticity in revenue sources and staffing complements, rural councils were starved of capabilities to respond to housing requirements. Compared to other countries, there was inflexibility (e.g. Karran 1988; Hoggart 1991). Some structural constraints were relieved through national intervention, as with expanding central grants (Rhodes 1976), but rather than addressing outdated local government structures, these mediations embedded core vices within the system, namely while relief was offered in the short-term, constraints on council operations were not alleviated, nor local initiative encour- aged. These national interventions left priorities in the hands of ministries (Ashford 1982), thereby reinforcing urban bias and rural neglect (Chaps. 6 and 7). With little vision over an appropriate role for local government (Keith-Lucas and Richards 1978, p.35), sectors like housing operated without coherence and with insufficient coordination with other government actions, as those running ministries admitted (e.g. Sharp 1969, p.71; also Self 2006, p.71). Up to 1974, and well after given later abolitions, reinstatements, mergers, unitary authority designations and metro-wide mayoral elections, governments used local authorities for their own, often short- lived, political ends. Viewed in this light, we need to interpret the causes of rural outcomes carefully. The rather localised character of the rural literature would ben- efit from a wider appreciation of the national scene. Rather than attributing blame for poor rural homes on councils, attention '… must fall also on the policies of the central government' (Shucksmith 1981, p.37). This book concurs, although this view does not go far enough. It is not just individual policies that merit investiga- tion, but the whole apparatus structuring, massaging, cajoling and bullying local agents towards outcomes. These merit exploring as part of a wider state impetus that sees commonalty stretch across policy enactments. Key messages emerge more in trends over time across policy fields than in outputs from single (or a few) poli- cies. In England, what has been critical is the peculiar character of the state, with its inherent social discriminations:

> The view is very much one of the population from the top down rather than the bottom up; the public is all those people whom the state and its Establishment wish to address or acknowledge as their own … In a social sense 'the public' is clearly coterminous with something like 'polite society'. Whether or not one is of the elect of the polite, responsible or respectable is, of course, a matter of judgement by one's betters. (Johnson 1985, p.233)

Politically, a small, cohesive 'centre' based in London might have required electoral verification to occupy the seat of government, but the core strength of this cohesive group meant the absence of a majority did not disrupt key strands in policy direction.

8.1.3 Geographical Discriminations

Starting before the twentieth-century, Britain declined economically and in its international influence (Gamble 1981; Sked 1987; Robbins 1993). Explanations share many features. Irrespective of political perspective, a key fault economically was poor productivity (Allen 1976; Brown 2017).[8] As Thompson (2001, p.6) noted, theorising what made British 'entrepreneurs' tick has largely been left to social and cultural historians, so it is no surprise that accounts draw attention to socio-cultural dispositions; viz. prioritising social standing, landed estates, knighthoods and peerages over improving enterprise (Wiener 1981; Tylecote 1982; Robbins 1993). These 'elite' values percolated downwards:

> The tradition of snobbism was transmitted intact to the new wealthy families of industrialists who rose on the tide of Britain's manufacturing supremacy in the Nineteenth-Century. They too delighted to play the sedulous ape to the landed gentry. Their ambition to adopt the habits and manners of their betters … (Allen 1976, p.36)

One feature of cultural explanations is portrayals of a 'unique' political economy, distinguished by a separation of financial and manufacturing arms of the capitalist class (Ingham 1984). As Massey (1986, p.47) summarised: 'In no other metropolitan country is international capital as overwhelmingly politically powerful. In no other country, perhaps, is non-international industrial capital so backward and undynamic'. A history of empire and aristocratic antipathy to manufacturing (although not by all; Thompson 2001), helped by declining returns from the land, drew major landowners to the finance sector (Perkin 1989; Rothery 2007; Horn 2013). As Britain's manufacturing lead waned, the interests of finance and industrial capital diverged: 'Paradoxically the very process which weakened British production – the rise of new industrial powers, the enfeeblement of the British competitive power – reinforced the triumph of finance and trade' (Hobsbawm 1968, p.152). This separation was mutually reinforcing. As Cairncross (1995, p.24) pointed out, a shortage of finance was rarely a problem for manufacturers, while low demand from manufacturing helped promote short-term horizons in financial institutions. The priority afforded to finance was evident in inter-war struggles to return to the gold standard, which manufacturing opposed but the Treasury, the Bank of England and the City of London supported (Seaman 1966; Ham 1981; Booth 1987; Ward 1988). It was apparent when the 1945 and 1964 governments took over ailing balance of

---

[8] The House of Commons Library (2020) reported the UK's 2016 productivity was 16% below the average for G7 nations.

payments conditions,[9] with concerns over finance sector impacts slowing effective responses (Morgan 1984; Newton 2009). The victory of the sector required national economic needs be subordinated to foreign currency markets, which critics claim no country except Britain has been prepared to allow (e.g. Leys 1986). Maintaining so overtly an internationalist stance drew Britain towards overseas engagements, with commitments to defence in particular diverting resources away from productive activities (Taylor 1989; Hennessy 2006, p.549). For some theoreticians, Britain was a conundrum: 'The continued political weakness of British industrial capital is at the core of orthodox Marxism's difficulties with the British case' (Ingham 1984, p.37).

This weakness impacted on national development and the internal geography of opportunity. This was expressed in intensified form during the 1930s Depression, the stop-go economies of the 1950s–1960s and the enforced deflation and its aftermath of the 1980s. In each case, regional inequality increased, with the most severe downturns and most sluggish revivals in regions dependent on primary industries and manufacturing (Martin 1988; Townsend 1993; Dunford 1995; Scott 2007). London and the greater South-East, with a long history of minor, specialist manufacturing and an international specialisation in finance and trade (Green 1991), saw their fortunes rise. The pattern persists today. As a consequence, by the 1970s, there was a distinctive geography within the countryside. Rural districts that were London-distant, and intra-regionally city-distant, tended to be agrarian-centred, smaller and resource poorer, compared with those better integrated into the externally oriented economies of cities and the South East (Table 2.9). These 'more traditional' rural areas generally presented worse accommodation than places in city commuter fields (Table 2.11). Low levels of owner-occupation testified to their lack of appeal to private investors over most of the twentieth-century (Table 2.13).

This differentiation of the rural realm began intensifying inter-regionally and intra-regionally inter-war. The dominant tendency for inter-war governments was the pursuit of Baldwin's 'New Conservativism', which Self (2006, p.132) articulated as social idealism tied to sound finance. The latter dominated. Efforts to bring about a revival of Britain's position in global financial markets led to positive government interventions in only a few arenas, as when private sector inefficiency or ineffectiveness was particularly troubling, as with air transport and electricity. This left many sectors short of investment and encouragement until 'rescued' by foreign investment or 'saved' by rearmament. Chamberlain, with Treasury support, thought 'sound finance' a better defence than rearmament (Ham 1981, p.11). His and other senior ministers' dislike of positive action left regions and rural areas abandoned, with social programmes as sticking plasters to ameliorate the consequences of a philosophy that '… the only certain solution of the problem of the workless areas was the assisted transference of unemployed workers to areas with work' (Self

---

[9] In 1945, days after hostilities ended, the USA ended lend-lease arrangements with Britain, adding to the strain of having lost £4,000 million in external disinvestments, with external earnings from shipping down 30%, physical exports down 40% and civilian industries physically run-down (Calder 1969, p.586).

2006, p.222). This resulted in a deliberate disregard and suppression of embarrassing reports of physical suffering and health deterioration in distressed regions (Self 2006, p.133). Indeed: 'The only major stimulus the Government provided for the economy was the rearmament programme from 1936 onwards' (Seaman 1966, p.235). National recovery after 1933 was fuelled by a fall in global commodity prices, which provoked growth in banking and finance but further damaged regions dependent on primary products and established manufacturing (Ward 1988). The economic distress metered out by laissez-faire policies had longer term consequences. Workers were agitated lest mass unemployment returned, resulting in post-1945 opposition to skills dilution to expand the workforce and resistance to scrapping restrictive practices (Calder 1969, p.129). Combined with a raft of collusive agreements between companies, prospects of a new economic dynamism were weakened (Broadberry and Crafts 1996, p.77). This position was reinforced in the 1950s when government policy ignored evidence of growing regional imbalances and failed to encourage productivity gains in depressed areas even though full employment made conditions favourable for a long-term approach (Scott 1996). As in the 1930s and 1950s, the orthodox economic antipathy towards intervening to promote long-term economic improvement reinforced inequities and drained capacities for national advancement.

8.2   The National Conditioning of Rural Housing

The above offers a hurried journey through the national political economy. Implicit within this abbreviated account are tendencies that had major effects on rural housing. These extended beyond the particularities of single legislative actions. There is no wish to downplay the significance of specific Acts of Parliament or legislative instruments. As revealed for Biggleswade (Table 7.8) and for Walsingham (Table 7.10), when comparison is made across Housing Acts, different outcomes can be identified even for the same district. Moreover, looking at single Housing Acts provides insight into the motivations and consequences of political decisions, as revealed by council-building alone disguising legislative imprints unless demolition totals are noted, as for Norfolk over 1956–1964 (Table 6.7). Yet this book affirms that core tendencies weave through and across individual legislative actions. Built within the accumulation of legislation were biases that conditioned the capacity of rural councils to respond to local housing needs. These partialities might be hidden in the detail of legislation, but played out in its implementation, as in the 1930 Housing Act giving higher subsidy rates to agricultural parishes, yet larger payments per dwelling to towns (Chap. 4). They might be overt through inaction, as with the extended time gap between rural-friendly legislation following the decimation of the 1931 Housing (Rural Authorities) Act and the passing of the 1938 Housing (Financial Provisions) Act or indeed in disregarding features of the 1930 and the 1956 Acts that limited rural slum clearance. To bring together insights on partial orientations like these, the analytical approach needed is akin to investigations of social class, such as LeGrand's (1982) articulation of how even social policy embeds biases favouring the middle-classes. Put more generally, for Savage (2000, p.159), such investigations expose: '… the brute realities of social inequality and the extent to which these are constantly effaced by a middle-class, individualised culture that fails to register the social implications of its routine actions'. At times deliberately, but also through the accumulated consequences of seemingly disconnected individual actions, aggregated public policy effects have geographical implications. These apply particularly in nations like England with dominant socio-political inclinations. For rural housing, four primary features of English Establishment practices merit drawing out.

8.2.1   Prioritising Home Ownership

At the start of the twentieth-century, the overwhelming majority of homes were privately rented (DoE 1977, p.38). Predispositions favouring the continuance of this tenure were strong, but dictates of political self-preservation were stronger, with state intervention to quell social unrest soon leading to the political abandonment of the landlord class (Merrett 1982; Daunton 1984). Building new private rental was verbally supported but without effective action, so new inter-war private homes were mostly owner-occupied (MoH 1938, p.114),[10] with private rental additions vastly outnumbered by demolitions and sales into home ownership (Table 2.2). This trend continued after 1945, with just over half of English households home owners in 1971 (Table 1.3). There was no inevitability about this tenure evolution. The introduction of the state as a major player in housing provision emerged in the midst of private sector failure and government fears of revolution. But problems of economic disruption and political unrest were not unique to Britain, whereas the solution of large-scale state housing was more unusual (Harloe 1995; Doling 1997; Golland 1998). Initially seen as a temporary intrusion, by 1924, it had become clear that ongoing state involvement was required to alleviate housing distress. The 1923 Act provided a foundation for reviving private building, such that by early-1928 rural districts in England and Wales had seen 64,935 new council dwellings under all Housing Acts, whereas the private sector had built 84,514 using 1923 Act subsidies alone (102,825 with subsidies under all Acts).[11] As building costs fell,

---

[10] Only 28.3% of inter-war private new-build in England and Wales was rented in 1939 (MoH 1944c, pp.51–52). For properties below £20/10/0d in rateable value, which was commonly assumed appropriate for the working-classes in London (although £13 was used outside London, which the data source omits), new private rental was only 37.4% of new council dwelling numbers.

[11] HCH 17 February 1928, Vol.213, col.1095W-96W. By 1930, 160,620 privately owned homes had been erected in RDCs without state assistance against 120,061 with (MoH 1930, p.80, p.247). Building without subsidy was rising in importance at the time, with 55.5% of post-1918 private-owner dwellings so constructed by 1930 (MoH 1930, p.80), 75.5% by 1936 (TNA HLG37/43 'Rural Districts. Number of Houses Completed Since the Armistice', August 1936) and 80.9% by 1943 (MoH 1944a, p.64).

especially relative to the cost of living (Fig. 3.2), the necessity of subsidies was perceived to have waned. Chamberlain argued that subsidies kept prices high, so his 1927 cuts would yield lower building costs.[12] This was political messaging, as costs had begun to fall in 1925, before his cuts (MoH 1944b, p.51). Here, we see a politician's sleight of hand, which often characterised Westminster's promotion of housing initiatives. Note, for example, that when the 1919 Act was passed, the coalition government offered no definition for the intended occupants for houses, supposedly the working-classes. This did not change until the 1930s; yet, by then, the housing scene had been transformed by falling building costs and private construction occurring largely without subsidy. This suited the 'sound finance' mindset of the then government, with ministers seeing little except cuts in public spending and wages as the route to economic gain.[13] But the idea this was a non-interventionist government is a misnomer. With investment funds seeking safe havens in the face of economic recession (Richardson 1967, p.161),[14] government legislation like the 1933 Housing (Financial Provisions) Act provided structured opportunities to enhance the finance sector. Building society operations changed sharply with bigger loans available, longer repayment periods allowed and council guarantees of mortgage repayments extended.[15] Low interest rates were promoted and tax concessions offered to societies (Pugh 2008, p.63). The scene was set for building societies to expand aggressively (Bellman 1928; Humphries 1987; Scott and Newton 2012). Accompanied by thin council-building subsidies, the high of 113,274 grant-aided new council homes in 1927 fell to 32,685 in 1935.[16] Building societies not surprisingly laid claim to having funded three-quarters of all houses erected in the 1930s (Mowat 1955, p.460). For rural districts, the numbers were startling: 86,271 council dwellings were added between 1930 and 1943 compared with 410,822 for private owners (MoH 1930, p.80; MoH 1944a, p.64).

Those who could secure a mortgage found it easy to acquire a home. Those who could not were left behind. There was a 'surplus' of private homes in the countryside. Many private units were on the path to dereliction, but numerically homes were available. Few additions came from private builders, except near towns or tourist destinations (Table 4.9 and Table 7.3). Further, while rural councils added 47,739 new dwellings to their stock over 1933–1939, 58.5% were slum

---

[12] HCH 2 December 1926, Vol.200, col.1405.

[13] For Taylor (1965, p.239), 'Baldwin expressed the general view when he said on 30 July 1925: "All the workers of this country have got to take reductions in wages to help put industry on its feet".' Little had changed in Conservative (or Treasury) thinking by the 1950s, when it was claimed competitiveness depended not on entrepreneurship, innovation and investment, but on controlling labour costs (Baines and Johnson 1999; Booth 2000).

[14] The Depression brought embarrassment for building societies, as the lack of alternative high-yielding securities threatened them with capital they could not utilise (Yelling 1992, p.88).

[15] Building societies had lent up to 70% of a purchase price, which was raised to 90%, with repayment extended from 20 to 30 years, with interest charged at 1% below the prevailing rate, subject to a minimum of 3% (MoH 1933b, pp.2–3).

[16] HCH 11 February 1948, Vol.447, col.93W-94W.

replacements, so not enhancing housing availability (MoH 1934, p.302; MoH 1939, p.251). Although building societies became more willing to lend to those on lower incomes or with less secure employment than the salaried (Richardson 1967, pp.161–162), rural employment suffered not just from low wages but also irregular work (Hussey 1997). As with post-1945, cost alone was not a central issue for home ownership, as was plain from government figures showing rental was more expensive than owner-occupation. Table 8.1 gives a flavour for 1952–1953, showing that rural home owners paid less for housing by income category, save the very wealthiest and those with the lowest incomes, with home owners only paying more than renters in cities. Without geographical markers or income band information, Table 6.8 offers a similar vision for 1969, although here rental is broken down to reveal lower rents in council dwellings than in housing associations or private rental, with tax relief placing home buyers in an intermediate position. This marked a notable change from the inter-war years, when high council rents meant many tenants were middle-class (Chap. 4). No surprise, ministers gave no definition of 'the working class' under the 1919 Act. But by the 1930s, mortgage repayments cost no more than many council rents (Mowat 1955, p.460), with investigators like O'Carroll (1996a) noting that leaving a council tenancy for home ownership could save money or secure better accommodation (also Scott 2008, p.9). The government message now proclaimed council housing should be restricted to the poorest in the working-classes (MoH 1932, p.99; 1933a, p.88). This limited accommodation options for those not counted as the poorest. Despite associations with respectability (Benson 1989, p.76; Pugh 2008, p.63), many in the working-classes were reluctant to become home owners, as this involved debt (Scott 2008, p.10; Gardiner 2010, p.307), while building society loan criteria still hesitated or rejected loans for older buildings, single people, lower income neighbourhoods or those in blue collar jobs (Ford 1975; Duncan 1976; Williams 1978; Paris and Blackaby 1979). Added to this was

Table 8.1 Weekly housing expenditure by household income, tenure and settlement category, 1953–1954

	Weekly household income at least						
	£20	£14 but under £20	£10 but under £14	£8 but under £10	£6 but under £8	£3 but under £6	Under £3
	Rural districts						
Unfurnished rented	0.92	0.80	0.73	0.65	0.53	0.49	0.37
Owner-occupied	1.12	0.72	0.60	0.49	0.45	0.44	0.42
	Urban under 100,000 population						
Unfurnished rented	1.43	0.98	0.84	0.78	0.77	0.72	0.68
Owner-occupied	1.07	0.93	0.89	0.81	0.74	0.65	0.50
	London and urban over 100,000						
Unfurnished rented	1.25	0.99	0.86	0.80	0.73	0.65	0.56
Owner-occupied	1.45	1.07	0.91	0.82	0.80	0.78	0.47

Source: Ministry of Labour and National Service (1957, pp.187–201)
Note: The original presentations of these numbers as pounds, shillings and pence have been converted to whole and decimal portions of pounds to ease comparison

the possibility that wages were less important than the availability of dwellings for sale (O'Carroll 1996b). This last aspect would be consistent with more recent evidence on working-class home purchase. Council tenants in the 1980s were commonly attracted by Right-to-Buy provisions for pragmatic reasons. The shortage of council homes was telling, as this restricted tenant choice, leading to ownership being considered, especially, like their inter-war counterparts (O'Carroll 1996a), when homes were sold at heavily discounted prices (Forrest and Murie 1990). Opportunities taken up were often short-term, with Chaney and Sherwood (2000) finding many were sold after a few years. Formerly rural council dwellings became service-class homes.

Set within the ideological bubbles of English politicians, it is no surprise housing tenure has been assumed to influence voting behaviour (Williams et al. 1987; Davies 2013), even if empirical research is less confirmatory (Heath et al. 1985). Added to any hoped-for electoral gain, the dominant policy stance for the council stock was constrained supply. The 2020 announcement by the Chair of the National Infrastructure Commission that the government needed to ditch ideology and start large-scale council building to avoid the continuance of housing shortages,[17] confirms the enduring tendency to push private building rather than a balanced housing portfolio. One component of this imbalance was marginalising council tenants. Beyond 'crisis' periods like after the world wars, council tenancies were deemed to be for the low-paid. Ignoring subsidies and policy support for home ownership (e.g. Table 6.8), politically inspired messages played on populist prejudices, of multitudes able to afford higher rents, of council tenants owning Jaguars (Jarvis 1996; Weiler 2000; Jacobs et al. 2003; Davies 2013; Smyth and Robertson 2013). The imagery was of a council sector festooned with the 'undeserving'; implying there was less need for 'genuine' council provision, so distracting attention from national housing shortfalls. The impression given was of a highly subsidised council sector, even though subsidy regimes were variable, with those in older dwellings commonly paying more than the cost of their home, as well as expected to help fund council new-build and cover 'losses' on rent rebates. Of course, contributions from the Treasury and from ratepayers were made, with the 1919 and 1946 Acts requiring local contributions, even if, as in 1956, this stipulation could be removed to encourage shifts into private ownership. Adding to the marginalisation of the sector, government policy in the 1930s and 1950s promoted inferior council accommodation, culminating in the much disliked high-rise programme of the late-1950s (Darke 1991). Subsidies for this programme were high but this owed more to government and construction industry priorities than council preferences (Dunleavy 1981). A two-(or three-)tier housing system developed, overladen with social stigma, making public support for council-building insecure (especially amongst home owners). Yet, given generally low wages in rural districts, the private sector did not offer solutions to housing distress amongst the low-paid. Private landlords were commonly overseeing deterioration in their stock. Private builders were unable or unwilling to

---

[17] 'Council houses "only way to reach 300,000 homes goal" ', *The Times* 8 July 2020, p.2.

erect dwellings at prices most rural residents could afford. The council sector held out the best prospect of home improvement, but council actions were largely hamstrung by government prioritisation of owner-occupation.

8.2.2   Structuring a 'Laissez-Faire' Economy

State actions structured options to favour owner-occupation through assistance to funding institutions (building societies) and to buyers (mortgage tax relief, capital gains exemptions, etc.). In the same way, while generally promoting images of a 'free' market, the state structured the economy to favour some sectors (especially finance) and discriminate against others. Governments have shown remarkable willingness to abandon economic sectors, as with much manufacturing and staple industries in the 1930s (Ward 1988). In this regard, agriculture occupies a particular place in the nation's economic history. This arose in part as income-earning possibilities through manufacturing and trade encouraged more open trading polices which induced falls in food import restrictions. Pressures to open up the electoral base also made an impression, as this gave urban voters more political influence, with politicians anticipating electoral rewards from cheap food. In the late-nineteenth-century, food imports flooded in, with significant consequences for the nation's economic geography, for the landed classes, and for finance and trade (Perry 1974; Cannadine 1990; Thompson 2001). The impact on rural areas was harsh, with significant falls in capital for investment, alongside pressure on farm-worker wages. The First World War offered some respite, with increased food output encouraged, but soon after the War, government support was abruptly cut (Whetham 1974; Penning-Rowsell 1997). Inter-war government fixation on maintaining good relations with the Empire, in order to secure exports (Smith 1989), meant accepting more food imports. Expectations of another war, then conflict itself, promoted a new emphasis on farm output growth, but post-1945, state support was conditioned by comparison with world commodity prices, which was disliked by farmers, whose lobbying over 1960–1964 saw protectionism return (Bowers 1985; Chase 1993). Farm-workers were less politically powerful. They struggled to secure even a minimum wage settlement (Howkins and Verdon 2009), with stipends controlled by locally dominated wage boards until a national system was established after 1945. The brief prioritisation given to farm-workers in the 1940s produced little but a temporary bump in a wage trend that paralleled inter-war levelling beneath industrial figures (Fig. 3.3; Newby 1977; Danziger 1988). By contrast, many farmers' incomes bounced back from early-1920s' decline relatively rapidly (Penning-Rowsell 1997; Howkins 2003; Wade-Martins and Williamson 2008), with lobbying by farmers' organisations later securing significant farmer income gains and protections (Self and Storing 1962; Wilson 1977; Smith 1989). Farm-worker pay did not reflect change in the sector's fortunes. Rather, the combination of lobbying for protection from international competition and continued low worker wages meant the sector reflected wider economic drivers, wherein: 'British capital simply sought to keep wages as low as possible rather than to develop a high wage and high productivity economy' (Lash and Urry 1987, p.183). Even today, the nation's poor productivity is difficult to dispute (Brown 2017; House of Commons Library 2020). Herein lay a fundamental cause of poor housing in rural districts. With farm work comprising large tranches of the rural workforce,[18] low payments to farm-workers had knock-on effects on general rural wages. Many could not afford council homes, unless built particularly meanly, while private tenant rents offered landlords insufficient slack for dwelling upgrades. Other countries, like Germany, had seen success in employer rather than municipal housing, but this was largely in growing industries, not in financially constrained ones like agriculture (Harloe 1995).

Cross-national comparisons also reveal how low productivity in English business played out in poor construction standards and high dwelling prices (MoH 1921; Reiner and Broughton 1953; Barlow and Duncan 1994; Construction Task Force to the Deputy Prime Minister on the Scope for Improving the Quality and Efficiency of UK Construction 1998). Rural residents faced lower wages and inflated prices. This double-whammy was intensified by government policies. Grounded in an orthodox economic mindset that pushed the 'sound finance' of balancing budgets rather than investing productively, for most of the century, the nation's leaders adopted what they proclaimed was a non-interventionist strategy, so the private sector could 'perform'. This meant little was done to coordinate investment or productive activity. Take the immediate post-war years to illustrate. Lessons had been learnt by 1945–1951 compared with 1919–1922, but neither period was approached on the war-footing Attlee thought essential (Campbell 1987, p.159). Demobilisation of troops was slow (Pugh 2008, p.62), material supplies insufficient (Catterall 2003, p.143) and private builders were drawn to luxury dwellings, not meeting key housing needs.[19] In both cases, after about two years, programmes were sharply cut in the face of fiscal problems. After 1918, no serious effort was made to incentivise the building industry to engage with house-building priorities until 1924 (National House Building Committee 1924), then Bevan's insistence on building where demand existed – which was everywhere – dissipated resources after 1945 (Francis 1997). Move away from the near war years and there might be change in form but not substance. Shortages of supplies and skilled labour continued in most post-1945 years, while prioritising 'sound finance' over investment saw many rural areas unable to secure new housing as they lacked water and sewer systems.

The exercise of power is as much about securing compliant behaviour without having to act as it is about persuading or forcing actions on others (Lukes 1974). It is expressed as much in not acting, like not investing out of pique when a government is elected you disfavour, as in making commitments. Placed in a comparative international setting, analysts have shown that low productivity in Britain can be traced to short-term investment horizons, a general lack of investment, insufficient

---

[18] For the seven RDCs investigated, Hatfield had the least of all paid workers in agriculture in 1921 (23.7%), with Smallburgh the highest (48.6%).

[19] HCH 28 October 1919, Vol.120, col.495W-96W; HCH 27 April 1920, Vol.128, col.1043-44; HCH 5 August 1920, Vol.133, col.395; Francis (1997, p.117).

commitments to productive infrastructure, inadequate training, fragile management capacities, poor labour relations, lagging competitiveness, slow transmission of invention into innovation and weak coordination of activities (Allen 1976; Gamble 1981; Sked 1987; Robbins 1993; Barnett 2001). In other words, the nation's problems arise from action and inaction. National governments, corporate executives and the mass media have commonly projected an almost mystical image of good governance that places high esteem on 'free' markets and 'laissez-faire' approaches. Indeed, government action is commonly spurned, with fingers pointed at great failures in government interventions in planning, technology and markets (e.g. Hall 1980; Hennessy 1996). Yet such interventions have made positive impacts in other countries (Harris 1986; Chowdhury and Islam 1993; Schwartz 1994). This suggests the problem is less to do with the principle of intervention, or to rephrase with business, labour and the state apparatus working in a coordinated manner, than with the particular manifestations of intervention in Britain, where leaders are drawn to amateurish, status-consciousness and a sense of entitlement (Guttsman 1968; Scott 1982; Jones 2014). The consequences of these national failings are played out in poor housing conditions, high housing costs, insufficient buying power and feeble policy implementation. Hiding behind proclaimed 'laissez-faire' economic policies disguises the reality of sectors being favoured or disfavoured as an outcome of power politics, where the exertion of influence is not simply about achieving short-term aims but also about bending public opinion to perpetuate established practices. The mindsets of government and business, which have overseen the decline of the nation, showed a rigidity that weakened prospects of effective national planning and progress, with locally grounded outcomes all too evident. These were seen particularly in biases within policy circles that contrived to maintain a low-wage economy. They were seen in fundamental productivity deficits that forced housing costs beyond capacities to pay, requiring municipal housing not just for the lowest paid but for large tranches of the working population, so making the council sector more of an enforced subsidy for employers, given their failure to stay internationally competitive.

8.2.3 Intervention for Continuity

In Punter's (1986, 1987) review of aesthetic control in land-use planning, his final section has the pointed heading 'A flawed orthodoxy and a lack of leadership'. For Punter, the impetus behind government intervention was difficult to establish. He asked whether government advice reflected the 'defeatist orthodoxy in the gifted amateur tradition', was a 'bureaucratic convenience' to improve planning efficiency, or a 'convenient smokescreen to allow commercial interests the freedom to fashion the built environment to their own ends' (Punter 1987, p.58). From this volume, the answer could be all three. They operate at different 'levels' or penetrate policy processes and outcomes in different ways, but traces of all three are visible in Establishment preferences for generalists, dislike of evidence-based policy, in imposing national views with little regard for local diversity and in an overly optimistic faith in private solutions to housing deficiencies. These inputs to policy interweaved in ways that make it difficult to attribute specific weights to them. It is not just that their influence came in dissimilar forms, expressed unevenly across policy spheres. Underscoring interchanges between the diverse forces acting on policy deliberation was the absence of vision, principles and values. Given leader inclinations to 'muddle through', it comes as no surprise that analysts like Orbach (1977, p.46) highlight how housing has been driven by 'emergency' actions, with temporary 'solutions' becoming intrinsic to long-term policy emphases.

Such enduring temporary 'fixes' were evident in the introduction of rent restrictions in 1915 and in the mass council housing programme of 1919. The consequences of these actions were profound, for they fuelled decline in private rental, made the public sector a major player, and provoked policies to under-write expansion in owner-occupation. What this stumbling approach failed to provide was a positive vision for housing improvement across tenures. Thus, in 1919, when the government was discomforted by political discord, it was not troubled if 'working-class' accommodation went to those with strong middle-class chords backed by the best-paid artisans.[20] Yet, by 1933, when the government had little economic initiative save to pump-prime building societies, the political advantage was not to see the middle-classes in council homes but to encourage all but the poorest to buy a home. The residualisation of the council sector had begun. This went into abeyance when 1930s' policies provoked an electoral backlash, to which failed housing policies contributed much (Francis 1997, p.115). Post-1945, housing for the most needy replaced class-based delineations of council tenancy, at least for a time. But the attractions of owner-occupation, through tax and other incentives, alongside politically charged social discriminations against other tenures (Jarvis 1996; Jacobs et al. 2003; Jones 2010), was a bedrock of electioneering. The manner in which this was used in later decades has been well documented (Forrest and Murie 1988; Weiler 2000; Davies 2013), but its particular rural manifestation is worth pondering. This was more recently evident under the Right-to-Buy policy of the 1980 Housing Act. With heavily discounted sales of council homes to tenants, the Act offers a telling example of how national policies impacted negatively on rural working-class prospects. In all, 130 (post-1974) 'rural districts' applied to be exempt from sales, but only 20 were granted relief from losing social housing units (Gilg 1982, p.22). Councils were quick to respond, seeking measures to ensure district inhabitants could access homes, as with local residency requirements in planning policies. These were repeatedly refused or challenged by national government (Gilg 1982, p.37; 1985, p.6; 1986, p.12). The initial fears of the 130 applying councils were confirmed. The best houses in the most socially sought-after villages were

---

[20] HCH 5 May 1919, Vol.115, col.630W; HCH 25 June 1919, Vol.117, col.165-66; HCH 30 June 1919, Vol.117, col.721; HCH 5 November 1919, Vol.120, col.1526W. The definition of the working-classes was left to local authorities, with the recommendation that they '... bear in mind the special claims of ex-Service men in selecting tenants for their houses' (HCH 19 November 1919, Vol.121, col.943W).

purchased (Beazley et al. 1980; Phillips and Williams 1981), with their re-sale down the line to service-class in-migrants (Clark 1990; Chaney and Sherwood 2000).[21] Meanwhile, under the auspices of housing associations, which became the main social housing provider after the 1988 Housing Act, structures and regulations governing operations perpetuated and even intensified the lack of rural social housing availability (Gallent and Bell 2000; Bevan et al. 2001; Hoggart and Henderson 2005).

Whether in times of crisis or to secure political advantage, the rural consequences of interventions have been significant. This is not to say they were always intended, nor that there was not public support and strong arguments in favour of intervention. In inter-war decades, for example, there was public discomfort over private 'freedoms' to exploit the countryside. These were seen in the development of plotlands, in ribbon development, in the visual intrusion of advertising billboards, etc. These energised activists through organisations like the CPRE. They introduced formalised attention to architecture and design in rural dwellings and led to numerous Acts of Parliament to control 'urban intrusions' into the countryside (Lowerson 1980; Booth 1999). Planning restraint added value to rural residences owing to supply constraints, which endowed advantages on larger house-builders, who could secure land with development potential (Rydin 1986; Adams and Watkins 2002), and secured rural middle-class support (Popplestone 1967; Cloke and Thrift 1990). But while land-use planning focused development on larger settlements, so securing higher price premiums for places with 'no-growth' designations (Cloke 1979), it would be stretching the imagination to credit land-use planning with the service-class gains identified today (Marsden et al. 1993; Murdoch and Marsden 1994). The issue is not whether particular Acts or government instructions favoured one group or another, but whether such predispositions were recognised and responded to. If not, the question rearing its head is what this tells us about national governance.

Here, a focus for attention is urban preference. There are a number of reasons why governments favoured larger cities over other places in policy-making. For one, as regards London, Westminster MPs and Whitehall mandarins, alongside a multitude of lobbyists, think tanks and affiliated agencies, plus the headquarters of corporate UK, have long been centred there (Westaway 1974). This came alongside an evolving professionalisation of the city's workforce (Hamnett 2003), which produced a particular London 'bubble' of familiarity, infused with a highly articulate, organised, attention-seeking population concentration. This had knock-on effects, as seen in South-East England, with corporations keeping new product development and technical innovation close to head offices, while governments favoured research and development units close by for related reasons (Hymer 1975; Hall et al. 1987). In combination these tendencies fuelled the South-East economy as more dynamic enterprises located there, with service industries attracted to the region's buying power (Martin 1988; Dunford 1995; Scott 2007). On a broader

---

[21] After purchasers moved, former council homes in cities tended to have a high turnover, which worked against Right-to-Buy proponents hoped-for increases in social stability (Wilson 1999).

front, cities benefited from large voting blocs, with proximity easing political action. At times, this appeared detrimental, as concentrations of social deprivation helped generate civil disturbance. But such flashpoints drew attention to the need for political action. The isolation of rural workers meant that pressures for improvement commonly fell flat, as effective lobbies were difficult to organise (Newby 1975), whereas city civil unrest attracted policy responses (Taylor 1984; Keith 1989). In these circumstances, national policy-makers were disposed to view housing problems through a city lens. Whether by deliberately ignoring deprivation elsewhere, myopically assuming national uniformity or being shielded within politico-bureaucratic processes that were 'too much effort' to change, makes no difference. Government action, and lethargy over changing, acknowledging and responding to biases in direction, demonstrated greater attention to cities. This was readily visible in pronouncements on major Acts of Parliament. Outside housing legislation in the near war years, like 1919, 1923, 1924 and 1946, the tone of housing policy was city-centred, emphasising overcrowding, slum concentrations, multi-occupancy and high-rises. Added to which, governments were tepid in working to alter operational environments that might benefit rural districts. Rather than viewing water and sewer systems as essential like the postal service, rural provision was denigrated as not paying its own way. No such claims were made when exorbitantly priced, poor-quality high-rise flats were built on prime city sites (Dunleavy 1981). Rural councils were damned for not using ratepayers' funds to ensure sufficient council construction, when these institutions had few resources, built to lower specifications, and were unable to charge higher rents owing to low pay scales, thanks to policies favouring urban consumers. All in all, this was a classic case of blaming the victim. It was easier for governments not to ask fundamental questions, as they might provoke disquieting answers.

8.2.4   A Top-Down Worldview

Investigators of local government have condemned the lack of philosophy or underlying principles attached to the English system (e.g. Cross and Mallen 1978; Keith-Lucas and Richards 1978; Ashford 1982). What has emerged is a system geared around national interests. In the case of the Treasury, this has meant opposing local government access to funding mechanisms valued by national agencies (Rhodes 1976). The question has not been what local government needs but what the Treasury wants. National reviews of local funding were conveniently ignored when buoyant revenues were recommended (as with the Committee of Inquiry into Local Government Finance 1976). No wonder Sharpe (1978, pp.105–06) declared: 'If the structure of local government is also to be determined by the needs of central government then it is difficult to see the justification for a local government system as opposed to some form of decentralised local administration'. Dunleavy (1985) offered a rationale for current arrangements when noting how senior Whitehall mandarins preferred small, cohesive units to determine policy, with local government charged with implementation. This arrangement favoured the centre, which could distance itself from failure, with Whitehall appalled at the prospect civil servants might have to manage councils that seriously under-performed or defied a government (e.g. Parkinson 1985). As this volume has demonstrated, ministries do not require a visible local presence for detailed directing. It might be, as Punter (1986, 1987) claimed, that much intervention came through negativity rather than positively encouraging and enabling but the end-product of central control pervaded.

Apart from short-term policy horizons and a vacuum over local government principles, a fundamental divide in the state apparatus arose in social standing. Serious commentaries on the English, as well as more populist accounts (Cooper 1979), acknowledge the unusual importance attached to social distinction amongst its nationals. As John Stuart Mill wrote in 1858:

> The English, of all ranks and classes, are at bottom, in all their feelings, aristocrats. They have the conception of liberty, and set some value on it, but the very idea of equality is strange and offensive to them. They do not dislike to have many people above them as long as they have some below them, and therefore they have never sympathised and in their present state of mind never will sympathise with any really democratic or republican party ... (Elliot 1910, p.205)

Mill was pointing to more than the upper classes lording it over the middle-classes who lord it over the working-classes,[22] signifying a multifaceted diversity of distinctions. Studies of English society dwell on these separations, alongside the manner in which those of lower standing copy (and become advocates of) the behaviour of their 'betters'. The upper-class dinner parties so avidly imitated by middle-class householders offers one example (James 2006, p.436),[23] with intra-class differentiation between the 'respectable' (wealthier, closer to white-collar) and 'rough' working-classes another (Perkin 1989, p.107). Less has been written about hierarchies in the state apparatus, but its presence is entrenched, as Johnson (1985, p.132) observed: 'The British political culture is quite actively anti-egalitarian and, indeed, in some ways almost anti-democratic. This fact permeates British behaviour and thought at every level. The British "know their place" '.

There has been a persistent social distance between Parliament and local government. That the precincts of Westminster and Whitehall have long been imbued with the atmosphere of an old boys' club was illustrated by the backgrounds of those occupying its senior echelons. Key aspects of this were outlined above but the comparators need emphasising. In Whitehall the proportion of all Permanent Secretaries drawn from Oxbridge was pretty constant for a century, running at around 75%, with this percentage also enduring for membership of private clubs (Theakston and Fry 1989). Amongst elected members, since 1945, 70–80% of Conservative MPs

---

[22] For rural articulations, see Bourne (1912) and Bell (1994).

[23] The importance of social distinction, especially for the socially cohesive upper-classes, and its impact on British politics and the economy, has been the subject of various studies (e.g. Allen 1976; Wiener 1981; Tylecote 1982; Thompson 2001). Those pointing to detrimental consequences have come from the political Left and Right.

had been educated at public schools, with over 50% going to Oxbridge (Scott 1982, p.163). Labour numbers were 18% and 21%, respectively, for 1979, compared with then Conservative values of 73% and 49% (Audickas and Cracknell 2020, p.13). Figures are less readily available for local government, but some insight is gained from surveys. Thus, even after 1974 reorganisation introduced many younger councillors, McGrew and Bristow (1984) found that only 27% of Conservative councillors had a degree, even in metropolitan areas (the 1979 figure for MPs was 68%), with 42% for Labour (59%). Moreover, while two-thirds of Conservative MPs held a business directorship while they sat in the House (Scott 1982, p.175), large-scale employers had withdrawn from local government well before the 1960s (Bealey et al. 1965; Morris and Newton 1970, 1971; Olney 2007). Even so, social distinction was rife amongst lower tiers of the state. Even post-reorganisation, some non-metropolitan county councils retained an aristocratic flavour (Newton 1979), although this was more embedded pre-1974 (e.g. Lee 1963; Johnson 1972). This separated counties from districts, which were more inclined to be small business dominated (Springall 1936; Moss and Parker 1967; Newton 1979), as exemplified in Bennett's (1914, p.118) observation that it is '... scarcely an exaggeration to describe them [RDCs] as "farmers' clubs"'. Parish councils stretched into wider social horizons, as working-class participation was enabled because agricultural labourers and others could attend meetings without wage losses (Pedley 1942, p.133).[24] This was identified in Maud Committee research as fundamental to social distinctions between government tiers, as the '... time of meeting was a principal determinant of the composition of membership' (Harrison and Norton 1967, p.55). Hence, 'Only with the security of well-established self-employment or employment by a local authority is a councillor in a safe position to live out the nineteenth-century myth, the myth of the part-time amateur character of the city's councillor's job' (Heclo 1969, p.200). Unlike MPs, councillors had no salary. Despite recommendations that they receive payment, even allowances for expenses took time coming, with many councillors resigning from councils for work-related reasons (Moss and Parker 1967; Heclo 1969). With younger councillors reporting damage to careers due to council commitments, and little compensation for time on council work, it was little wonder councillors were unduly drawn from the retired. Policy determination came to be centred on a small group of elected members, while most others focused on their constituency (Heclo 1969; Muchnick 1970; Corina 1974; Axford 1978).

As Johnson (1985) noted, top-down approaches to governance owe much to social distinctions drawn by national 'elites'. As the 'periphery' of the nation state, those in local government were barely trusted (Griffith 1966, p.511), as they were different social animals, not working-class in the main but not from social circles dominated by public schools, Oxbridge and London clubs. While mistrust of the local sphere owed much to difficulties controlling spending (Ball 1980),

---

[24] Around the turn of the century, Green (1920, p.124) found that 91 of 140 parish councillors elected in Warwickshire were farm labourers.

government reports emphasised the low quality of local policy-makers, policy debate and interactions with constituents (MHLG 1967) or drew attention to insufficient technical and administrative capacities (Royal Commission on Local Government in England 1969). Yet, following the reorganisation of local government in 1974, which supposedly equipped councils for these tasks, it was soon evident their new freedoms were illusory. National interventions were still more detailed than for nationalised industries (Corden and Curley 1974). View this experience, plus evidence in this book, alongside Clark's (1985, p.6) definition of local autonomy '… as the capacity of local governments to act in terms of their interests without fear of having every decision scrutinised, reviewed, and reversed by higher tiers of the state'. In this light, it is not difficult to appreciate Young's (1975, pp.32–33) conclusion that: 'The theory of local democracy rests upon certain premises concerning the autonomy of local institutions, the particularity of local circumstances, and the distinctiveness of local political behaviour. These premises are today no longer well-founded'. Barely a decade after 1974, the government abolished councils it deemed 'too independent' (Flynn et al. 1985; Wheen 1985; O'Leary 1987). Like the 1974 reorganisation, when Royal Commission recommendations were ignored in favour of Conservative Party gains (Sharpe 1978; Dunleavy 1980),[25] national governments treated councils as administrative outliers. Interventions were shielded behind the façade of local democratic accountability. As comparative investigations show, a feature of the British system is '… how easily national policy-makers can act without careful consultation with local government, and how easily national objectives are imposed on this vast subnational structure' (Ashford 1981, p.68). This has been expressed through major restructuring, as in the 1930s, the 1960s and the 1980s, the end-products owing much to political party considerations (Branson 1979; O'Leary 1987). It found expression in incremental steps that circumscribed local authority action. At one level, this occurred in the piecemeal removal of single functions, arguably for service efficiency but politically inspired as well (Saunders 1985; Hampton 1987), as with termination of council-building programmes under the 1988 Housing Act (Pryke and Whitehead 1995). At another level, it resulted from actions against challenges to national policies, as with rate-capping in the 1980s (Grant 1986) or the whittling away of council responsibilities by diluting control through exclusions, like 'enterprise zones, 'free' schools and Right-to-Buy provisions (Forrest and Murie 1988; Hoare 1985; Clarke and Cochrane 1987). Little wonder McGrew and Bristow (1984) found that almost four-fifths of

---

[25] Before losing office in 1970, the Labour government accepted most Royal Commission proposals. Major deviations were introduced by the incoming Conservatives (Cross and Mallen 1978; Dearlove 1979), repeating the pattern, more dramatically, of London government reform (Young 1975; Young and Garside 1982). One reason the Conservatives are associated with action of this kind is that they have had majorities or dominated coalitions over much of the twentieth-century. This included long stretches in office, which enabled core values to come to the fore, as well as failings. For the Labour Party only 1997–2010 compared with such Conservative eras but 'New Labour' actions centred on adapting to the neoliberal world order while transforming the Party to broaden its support, given a declining working-class electorate (Wickham-Jones 2005; Faucher-King and Le Galès 2010).

councillors thought national control over local authorities was greater than desirable, nor that academics have investigated *Half a Century of Municipal Decline* (Loughlin et al. 1985).

Additional limitations were placed on councils' ability to act independently, such as being denied access to resources to carry out functions, living with administrative and electoral envelopes unsuited to demands placed on them (Chap. 5) and interacting with ministries that chopped and changed policies with little regard to local consequences (Chap. 6), while engaging in detailed interventions (Chap. 7). Fallibilities in the frameworks local government operated within were known long before 1974 (e.g. Rhodes 1976). The national response to deficits was puny. Not prepared to upset their supporters, national politicians tinkered with the system rather than confronting its deficiencies and making it fit for purpose. Maintaining small, under-funded local units, confronted by substantial demands for improved living conditions, national authorities handicapped possibilities for positive action by failing to remove constraints. Worse, by depriving councils of capacities to acquire the skill sets needed for their work, by limits on their authority and via funding regimes dependent on government largesse, councils relied heavily on national support to implement programmes. But with more than 1000 local authorities, ministries were incapable of understanding individual council needs. At the most basic level, a way of alleviating the problem was to secure accurate information to better understand local needs. In 1964, the MHLG did set out a basis on which uniform cost records for housing could be maintained by councils (MHLG 1965, p.20). Such initiatives were few and far between. As we saw in Chap. 2 for dwelling unfitness and in Chap. 3 for council waiting lists, ministries were keener to ignore local assessments or discredit local tabulations than to seek quality evidence to support policy. A litany of information needed for effective decision-making was poor quality or not collected (Chap. 6). There were many good reasons for informed, effective overview of local actions. We should not assume local agents were less slothful, inept or self-seeking than their national counterparts; they might have sung with a different pitch, but they were just as capable of questionable practices. But what distinguished them was their scope for action. Local and particularly rural councils had such circumscribed autonomy that whatever imprint they made on the local housing scene was necessarily limited. Central control worked against decisive, fundamental or innovative local action.

8.3 Those Local Inputs

One theme in rural studies has been the failure of rural councils to generate sufficient quality homes. With a legal responsibility to survey their territories for housing needs, and respond to them, blame for deficits has been attributed to councils. The bigger picture in this tale of woe directs us to the national level. Rural failures sit in the midst of fundamental national shortcomings. Even excluding limitations placed on rural councils, had they sought to use it, rural authorities had limited scope to insist on action by others. Restricted building programmes were accompanied with weak demand for council dwellings, as rents were beyond many residents. Enforcing improvement on privately owned dwellings was akin to climbing a greasy pole, for acceptable accommodation to put displaced households into was uncomfortably rare, while owners could close properties or sell rather than improve. Perhaps with innovative inducements owners might have upgraded more. But such incentives would be in the hands of national not local officials, as they controlled the legislative agenda and the purse strings to fund all but minimal programmes. Of course, change need not have come through housing programmes. Had rural workers been paid better, this might have encouraged property owners to build and upgrade, so attracting a broader, more financially secure base for housing improvements. Change of this sort rested in national not local hands. None of this detracts from the culpability of rural leaders who did not do enough or deliberately thwarted housing gains in support of vested interests (Rose et al. 1976).

What this investigation has demonstrated is that rural responses to housing disorder were varied. Confirming the conclusions of Niner (1975), looking at the end-products, or outputs, of local policy implementation does not reveal a great deal about processes. Similar destinations can be reached via different routes, while parallel journeys can lead to dissimilar terminals. Both cases reveal the potency of local inputs, even if freedom of action was constrained. To extend an analogy from earlier in this volume, rural councils might (or might not) have wanted to drive housing programmes from the front seat of a new Audi Q7, but national authorities saddled them with a clapped-out 1993 Ford Mondeo. That they still had wheels and used them differently was evident in diverse policy scenarios. In Ampthill, house-building levels were measly inter-war, with arousal from the cautious approach of that era seeing a transformation post-1945, when construction and housing improvement rose significantly (Table 5.2). Even so, post-1945 efforts did not bring Ampthill provision up to the 1971 English RDC average (Table 1.3). Contrast this with its neighbour, Biggleswade, which had a similar economic base (Table 1.1), but drove council commitments with force, not just inter-war but post-1945, and with adaptability in utilising policy instruments to maximise housing gains. Biggleswade reached 1971 with proportionately more council homes than the RDC and England average. So did Hatfield, although its trajectory was distinctive. Its buoyant local economy supported an inter-war strategy of encouraging private building, being dragged into council provision when speculative builders failed to erect smaller dwellings. Post-war, its housing path was effectively usurped by national authorities, following the designation of a new town in its terrain. The entanglement of its inter-war strategy with local business interests was similar to Smallburgh, which diverged from Hatfield by commitments to agriculture. Rather than restricting council provision, more homes were sought and built cheaply, so farm labourers might match rent demands. Within the Smallburgh strategy were similar themes to Newby et al.'s (1978) insight on restricting council-building, namely the prioritisation of farmer interests, which for Smallburgh meant building more but hesitantly for non-farm workers. This orientation came with an aspiration to keep property taxes low, which led to a downturn in building rates after 1945 as demands on the tax base

grew and HRA surpluses fell (Table 5.2 and Table 6.11). The importance of property tax bases was also evident for Braughing, Erpingham and Walsingham. In the
case of the former with an inclination to see better quality homes for residents, with
a willingness to put council resources (when the Ministry allowed) towards this
purpose. But Erpingham and Walsingham were consistently at the low end of the
property wealth spectrum; not devastating poor but sufficiently lacking to characterise these councils as spending inhibited due to asset paucity.

This reinforces a key message from this text. For much of the twentieth-century,
private builders had limited interest in rural districts. Only Hatfield's urban spillover
attractions provided an exception throughout the decades. Contrary to twenty-first-
century images of private owners outbidding local inhabitants to dominate rural
landscapes, for much of the twentieth-century, rural districts struggled to attract
private investment. Post-1945, only in the 1960s did homes for private owners start
to outweigh public sector additions to the stock (Table 6.11). In terms of cumulative
post-1945 numbers, the first of the RDCs investigated with more private than public
sector additions was Hatfield in 1961. The other districts reached the milestone at
roughly one a year until 1967 when Braughing arrived (MoH-MHLG quarterly).
This left Walsingham at the tail, with a larger stock of post-1945 public sector
dwellings than private until 1972. Inter-war figures on private and council-building
were more difficult to come by, as there were few accounts of private completions
save for the odd single year. Two exceptions were Ampthill, with its slight inter-war
council programme, and Biggleswade, with a significant one (Table 3.10). In
Ampthill's case, between the 1921 census and 1939, the district added 305 council
dwellings alongside more than 1100 private ones, with figures of 1064 and around
700, respectively, in Biggleswade.[26] Elsewhere, evidence was patchy but, excepting
Hatfield, confirmed rural council statements of slight inter-war private building,
save for bungalows and holiday homes on the north Norfolk coast and Norfolk
Broads (Wade-Martins and Williamson 2008, p.115).[27] However, if these councils

---

[26] Ampthill totals excluded Toddington from 1921 census numbers and estimated council dwelling
numbers when it left the RDC, with comparison made for 1939 counts for the housing stock and
council totals (BRO RDAR8/20 ARDCMOHar 1939, p.1; BRO RDAR8/40 ARDCMOHar 1959,
p.15). For Biggleswade, annual new-build was more accessible. One caveat was Sandy leaving the
RDC in 1927, with the council dwellings it took with it known but 1919–1927 privately built
homes unknown. In all, 742 private homes were erected in Biggleswade over 1921–1938, with 158
for 1921–1927. This would give Sandy 26 new private homes for the period if dwellings were
distributed evenly.

[27] For Hatfield, annual data were available for 1928 and 1929, showing 200 new council dwellings
and 176 private, which government restrictions on new-build, plus the arrival the de Havilland factory, helped to transform into annual 1932–1939 completions of 28 council and 290 private dwellings (figures from Hatfield Medical Officer of Health annual reports). Data for Braughing only
covered 1936 and 1937, when 80 council and 64 private homes were built. At this time, the rural
districts in east Hertfordshire saw roughly equivalent volumes of council and private new-build
(Ware RDC exactly 50:50, Hertford RDC 57.5% private, but four of the five urban districts were
private sector dominated; HRO RDC3/28/1-2 Annual Reports for the East Hertfordshire Combined
Districts Medical Officer of Health). The only comparators for the Norfolk districts, except for
single, isolated years, were for Walsingham. Information in council minutes was ephemeral but for

were similarly placed as regards the rest of rural England, then owner-occupation took up less of the household budget than renting (Table 8.1). Even so, building for private owners was sparse. In this context, it is no surprise councils bewailed ministry restrictions on their house-building and the paucity of national funding. A useful comparator on the importance of local inputs is the breakdown of social class as a predictor of voting behaviour, with the working-classes prone to vote Conservative in areas benefiting from a contrived national economy that pushed growth towards the South-East and other 'suburban' tracts (Martin 1988; Dunford 1995, Scott 2007), while the middle classes often voted Labour in areas left behind (Warde 1986). Put simply, local contexts matter. With petit bourgeois-dominated rural councils, and poor resources, *a priori* predictions might favour little spending by rural councils on working-class housing. This has been assumed by many commentators, who appear to read-off this assessment from the fact that rural councils provided fewer council homes than cities. This image does not do justice to variety in rural council actions; when they were allowed to, many rural councils responded to private sector inaction.

Throughout this investigation, one feature of rural council activity that came across strongly was a desire to work for the benefit of the local citizenry. Yes, in Hatfield and Smallburgh, there was an assertion of business interests, but a general desire to serve was evident across districts. The tone of many local approaches was exemplified by Newport Pagnell RDC in 1967. Here, a decision was made to raise council rents '… mainly so that new homes in the district can continue to be built', with a rent rebate scheme for those who could not afford to pay. As the Clerk put the position: 'People living in older council houses may say they don't want new building. But this is a community service and people must be prepared to pay what it costs today'. The RDC was asking for tenants to pay more rent, but there was also a charge to the rates for every home built (100 under construction, with 300 more planned), while the HRA deficit was predicted to rise substantially. The justification was expressed by Councillor Bedchambers as: 'They don't usually refuse a home because of the rent and if house-building doesn't go on villages will be strangled'.[28] This cameo offers an expression of the desire to respond to local needs. Acting on such desires was not always straightforward, especially in places with poor resources, which struggled over commitments. Often, this was not due to housing as such but other demands, as with water and sewer systems in the 1950s, at a time when the government had deliberately reduced grants for rural schemes. Thus, there were times when seemingly committed authorities gave no rate funding for housing, as with Newport Pagnell RDC from the late-1950s when no new council dwellings were built, with HRA deficits returning when new-build restarted.[29] We also see

---

six reported years over 1920–1930, the district added 113 council and 77 private dwellings. The Council's building programme then was weaker than in the 1930s (Table 3.10).

[28] *WR&WSR* 5 September 1967, p.1.

[29] No-build in the late-1950s was associated with Ministry restrictions on development owing to national failure to invest in adequate water provision (Eley 1973; *WR&WSR* 13 March 1956, p.1; 15 November 1960, p.1; 5 March 1963, p.1).

differences in councils thinking innovatively to secure more homes, to use a further Newport Pagnell example, as in 1949 when the RDC considered selling council homes to tenants to gain funding for more council building.[30]

Whatever the initiative shown, councils were hemmed in by national direction. This was evident in changes in housing tenure in the 1960s (Table 8.2). Most consistent in this regard was the continuing contraction of private rental. For council provision, the most notable features of the era were increases in Ampthill, Biggleswade and Hatfield above the national RDC average, with the latter two above the England average, which Ampthill hovered around. The differentiator for Ampthill and Biggleswade came from their willingness to adapt strategy. For the council sector, this was outlined in Chap. 7. For private ownership, it was seen in encouraging private building. Both made 1953 decisions to offer council land to applicants building their own homes.[31] Shortly after, both widened the policy to include developers, as well as acquiring and advertising land for private use. This policy was toned down when there was a shortage of sites for council-building, as with Biggleswade in the late-1960s,[32] although revived in the early-1970s when MHLG Circular 10/70 requested councils dispose of surplus land to help private building.[33] Both councils responded to government requests to ease private-owner access to land, but refused to acquiesce to government pressure to sell council houses.[34] Responsiveness to local housing demands permeated council action. But other

Table 8.2 Percent change in household numbers in investigated rural districts by tenure, 1961–1971

	Owner-occupiers	Council-New Town tenants	Private rental tenants
Hatfield	25.7	36.8	−28.2
Braughing	86.6	17.8	−16.1
Ampthill	94.5	32.5	−24.4
Biggleswade	100.9	36.5	−7.6
Erpingham	53.1	7.5	−23.1
Smallburgh	63.7	14.6	−21.8
Walsingham	50.2	11.2	−23.4
All English RDCs	57.0	30.2	−23.4
England	34.1	32.9	−28.0

Source: Computed from county reports in the population censuses

[30] WR&WSR 20 September 1949, p.1.

[31] BRO RDAM2/22 ARDCHCM 23 July 1953; WR&WSR 1 December 1953, p.1; 2 March 1954, p.4; NBC&BR 4 August 1953, p.2.

[32] NBC&BR 3 August 1954, p.2; BC&BG 16 August 1957, p.12; WR&WSR 2 December 1958, p.12; BRO RDBwM1/41 BiRDCHCM 8 October 1969, p.421.

[33] BRO RDAM1/27 ARDCHCM 7 September 1971, p.196; BRO RDBwM1/45 BiRDCHCM 11 July 1973; 10 October 1973.

[34] BRO RDBwM1/42 BiRDCM 28 October 1970, p.406; BRO RDBwM1/43 BiRDCHCM 9 February 1972, p.769; 12 April 1972, p.904; BRO RDBwM1/44 BiRDCHCM 12 July 1972, p.125. BRO RDAM1/28 ARDCHPBuCM 17 May 1973, p.961.

councils were less advantageously placed. For council-building, they continued to press for more new homes but their efforts were constrained by government interventions, as seen in cuts in council programmes in the late-1950s (Table 3.4) and in negative net contributions to the housing stock once demolitions gathered pace (Table 6.7). Not until the late-1960s did more 'traditionally rural' councils (Braughing, Erpingham, Smallburgh and Walsingham) experience surges in private owner-building (Table 3.4). With strong recreational appeal, as in Smallburgh, the rise was particularly sharp, although the poorest district (Walsingham) lagged behind. These patterns provoke two thoughts. First, recall Topham's (1970) stricture that councils cannot make private investors act. If the national government did not generate an environment conducive to attracting private building to localities, councils had few powers to overturn their disadvantage. Not being able to draw on private sector support, arguably, such councils needed more government support, not less, assuming governments were committed to improving the nation's housing stock. Second, noting the lateness of private investment in 'peripheral' areas, if a key to rural dynamics was service-class inflows, then much of the countryside was untouched by these intrusions until the late-1960s; earlier than this, the service-class was largely absent or highly concentrated in a few locales (Hoggart 1997).

Putting a further piece in the jigsaw draws attention to the distinction between new-build numbers and changes in owner-occupation. For the investigated RDCs, except Smallburgh, 1960s' absolute increases in owner-occupation were above new-build volumes for private owners.[35] Although disparities varied, the absolute divergence was generally mopped up by falls in privately rented dwellings, without having to count reductions in vacant dwellings and the like. In Smallburgh's case, private new-build was higher than growth in owner-occupation, an indication perhaps of the importance of second homes near the Norfolk Broads and on the coast (Coleman 1982; Wade-Martins and Williamson 2008). The wider message is that, while 'outside' demand for rural owner-occupied residences was evinced in private building (Table 3.4), private rental decline was critical to owner-occupied additions. This left those who were unable to achieve owner-occupied status with few places to go except the council. But in the 1960s, rural councils faced growing waiting lists (Chap. 3), with housing stocks limited and national policies discriminating against rural needs (Chaps. 6 and 7).

8.4   Contrivance

The charge in this book is that shortages in affordable rural housing for those who could not become home owners have a long gestation. The housing shortfalls we see today were not inevitable. But dominant tendencies within the state made the

---

[35] This statement can be made with conviction as absolute differences between changing household and new-build numbers were greater than a full year's new-build at the time.

affordable rural housing deficits of today more likely, not necessarily due to deliberate acts but because forces driving the national political economy predisposed towards this outcome. Although specific Acts of Parliament raised hopes of improvement, propensities within the state apparatus, linked intricately to social status infused economic and political hierarchies (Guttsman 1968; Sampson 1982; Scott 1982; Jones 2014), dragged 'deviations' back to the smothering centralist path of urban prioritisation. As many others have explored and articulated better than I am able, the British polity presents a confusion of moves to ensure the continued dominance of a small Establishment, mixed with a knee-jerk fear of challenges to dominant tendencies, resulting in a cacophony of initiatives to maintain the upper-hand while buying-off electoral support (Adonis and Pollard 1997; James 2006). A central theme in this peculiar articulation is directionless leadership, derived from ideas that decry coordinated action, look to old, trusted ways rather than innovation, favour short-term reactionary responses rather than planning and working towards a visionary future that offers broadly based national advancement (Allen 1976; Barnett 2001; Brown 2017). Critically, if core tendencies in the political economy are left to one side, interpretations of poor rural housing performance are restricted to understanding what happened within existing structures and everyday sociopolitical relationships, when key difficulties were grounded in structural relationships. This is evident for a local government system in which councils operated in a top-down, socially discriminatory environment, fuelled by distrust at the centre, depreciating minority interests (like rural councils) and perpetuating archaic fiscal, functional and organisational practices rather than standing back to ask how democracy and living standards should be enhanced. As so many have asserted, there are strong anti-democratic tendencies amongst the nation's powerful, outcomes from which include weak subnational institutions (limiting challenge to the centre), inward-looking national frames of reference (limiting awareness of poor national performance), libertarian economic values extolling business 'freedom' (shielding under-performance from criticism) and orthodox economic interpretations of the state's role (emphasising low taxes rather than productive investment). Put simply, individual acts did not need to be intentionally designed to produce poor rural housing outcomes, as key local players in the rural drama were tightly constrained. They could make local impressions but their capacities would never challenge nationally conjured predispositions.

A characteristic outcome of such predilections was the blame game. Local councillors and their officials were considered inferior, not serious and not capable, with local government not attracting the 'right sort of people' (e.g. MHLG 1968). Less so publicly perhaps, but in the corridors of Westminster and Whitehall, rural councils were chastised for their reluctance to act, with this disinclination espoused as the primary cause of rural housing deficits.[36] Culpability was pinpointed at the outset of state involvement in housing provision:

---

[36] TNA MAF48/206 'Minutes of Deputation', 9 March 1926; TNA HLG40/30 Untitled report (memo behind it suggests for Ernest Strohmenger), 20 April 1931; TNA HLG40/2 'Memo to Mr George', 12 February 1936; TNA HLG101/258A 'Postponement of Demolition of Unfit Houses.

> The failure of Rural District Councils to rise to the duty of providing houses is easily under-
> stood. The Councils have little vision; they distrust, because they do not understand, the
> Government's system of loan and subsidy, and in any case they cannot build in an
> economical and seemly way because they do not employ skilled architects to design and
> superintend the work.[37]

For the government, it seems, if there was a rural housing problem, the fault lay with
rural disinclinations to build, to remove unfit units, to spend money and to realise
opportunities to improve housing. All this from national authorities whose economic orthodoxy saw little scope for state action save cutting investment and wages
and hoping the private sector would respond (Perkin 1989; Cairncross 1996), from
a string of governments that prolonged the life of a local government system so
devoid of responsibilities virtually no citizens knew who their councillors were or
what their councils did, which left potential councillors reluctant to engage with an
enterprise seemingly irrelevant to daily lives, with local elections decided largely on
national issues beyond council authority (Hampton 1970; Green 1972). Under an
almost continuous agricultural policy emphasis that relegated rural areas to a low-
wage economy (Hodge and Whitby 1981; Hill and Ray 1987), councils addressing
working-class rural needs were confronted with deciding to build homes few could
afford or dwellings below acceptable standards. The list could go on, bringing in
such issues as failures to invest in water and sewer systems, inaction over low
builder productivity, unwillingness to provide councils with buoyant revenue channels, and so on. So much could have been done by governments, but so little was.
National leaders failed to grasp the significance of the downward trend in the
nation's international standing, economically and politically (Gamble 1981; Sked
1987; Taylor 1989; Pemberton 2004), devoting massive resources in attempts to
maintain the nation's role in financial markets, with seemingly scant regard for negative impacts on the wider economy. This revealed a shallow understanding of how
sustaining international standing requires drawing on a firm base of productive
national activity (Barnett 1972, 1986, 1995, 2001).

Whether transferring resources from subsidising the finance sector into more
beneficial activities would have made a difference, given entrenched dispositions
towards amateurism, social status, short-termism and lack of coherent vision, is a
moot point. After all, a fundamental feature of rural housing decline was the reflex
1915 response to political dissent that placed private rental under 'temporary' rent
restrictions lasting more than 40 years (arguably longer). Without a coherent strategy, immediate problems tended to be responded to quickly, with apparently little
appreciation of long-term consequences, and had a habit of staying fixed for genera-
tions. All in all, there was lethargy in the national polity that mitigated against
reversing trends. This stupor resulted in policies lingering, not simply well past any
conceivably appropriate sell-by date, but also without originality in addressing
intrinsic weaknesses. Allowing private rental to decline so markedly over the

---

Circular 2090. Note of Interview', 27 March 194; TNA HLG118/1392 'Unfit Houses in Rural
Districts', undated c1970.

[37] TNA CAB24/93 CP122 'Housing in Agricultural Districts', 14 November 1919, p.1.

decades is a visible indicator of wasteful regard for the nation's resources. Ossified ancient cottages might have become ripe prospects for the dream 'rose cottages' of the incoming service-classes, but the degradation of this housing stock was bought at the price of appalling living conditions for many low-paid workers over the decades. Its broader impact was thousands more properties of the same ilk disintegrating beyond repair. Many of these units did not need to disappear for, despite government claims to the contrary, general demand for rural living persisted, even in the early decades of the century.

The introduction of council housing to counter dereliction made its own mark on the landscape. Enacted within national mind-frames that prioritised cost over quality, council dwellings transplanted a codified architecture of blandness and uniformity onto a diverse countryside. The few places national leaders admired for their chocolate box appeal, like the Cotswolds, managed to secure limited funding to avoid the telling council house stamp. Onto a withering landscape of vernacular architecture, larger villages added private-owner estates, seemingly transplanted intact from city suburbs (Radford 1970; Ambrose 1974). This was made easier by national failure to address private rental problems, by lack of imagination over council provision (or other mechanisms for securing better homes) and by the free-for-all of 1930s' policies that convinced activists, and eventually the government, that restrictions on building were required (Gilg 1978; Lowerson 1980). Land-use planning controls were less rigid than often portrayed (Bishop 1998; Booth 1999), making policy enactments jagged at the edges (Buller and Hoggart 1986; Sillince 1986; Gilg and Kelly 1997); yet restrictions on small settlements did divert house-building towards larger places (Table 7.3). This helped to maintain an 'exclusive' environment for those who could afford it. But there was a wider picture to this social exclusivity. This arose from inter-district disparities in house-building. Layered on top of biases towards cities in the allocation of council dwellings were social discriminations. Whether politically intentional or not, these complied with other political party actions to socially engineer districts for political advantage (Sharpe 1978; Young and Kramer 1978). Glimpses of this were seen in admissions that council-building was deliberately supressed in areas 'given over' to owner-occupation, as in 1955, when: '… bigger allocations of houses to be started in 1955 were given to local authorities in industrial areas, while reductions were made for those areas where private enterprise builders were undertaking a large house building programme'. They were also evinced in politicians fretting over the political (party) ineptitude of Whitehall officials in imposing Treasury cuts on allocations to electorally marginal constituencies, as with Richard Crossman's (1975, p.332) horrified reaction to 1965 reductions. Academics regularly note the socially divisive consequences of development control restrictions on villages, but too rarely note inter-district processes that help further cocoon the well-to-do in a socially exclusive comfort blanket.

When pondering the contrived nature of the British rural housing landscape, it would be foolhardy not to acknowledge that under different circumstances, aspects of today's rurality would persist. An idealisation of the countryside has been a persistent feature of English society (Lowenthal and Prince 1965; Williams 1973;

Keith 1984). Roots might be traced back to middle-class adherence to unattainable upper crust sensibilities, but whatever rationale is employed, a wealth of evidence exists on the draw of country living for the service-classes (Bolton and Chalkley 1990; Halfacree 1994; Halliday and Coombes 1995); viz. of those with the economic muscle to secure desired rural abodes. Given changing patterns of work and communication, amongst other considerations, the service-classes have become more residentially open-minded, such that their increasing presence in the countryside might be anticipated under any regime, as suggested by other countries (e.g. Perry et al. 1986; Dam 2000; Paniagua 2002). The idea that past policies contrived to enable the service-class capture of the countryside consequently comes down not to individual actions but to the broad sweep of rural dynamics. Fundamentally, these were embedded in a persistently low-wage economy, which limited capabilities to act, encouraged working-class flight and shrunk perceptions of what might be feasible. They were rooted in constraints on rural council actions, owing to limited resources, weak authority and continuing detailed impositions by national agencies. These circumstances were then constrained by national regimes predisposed towards eschewing performance in favour of social status and connections, innovation in favour of stability, autonomy in favour of control, and broadly based interventions in favour of promoting private interests. Added to this, the lingering impact of predilections towards amateurism in national leadership circles culminated in a policy environment devoid of an information base suitable for effective policy implementation.[38] Even had national leaders wished to treat rural districts equitably, they operated in a socio-political milieu that worked against achieving this end.

References

Adams D, Watkins C (2002) Greenfields, brownfields and housing development. Blackwell, Oxford

Addison C (1934) Four and a half years: a personal diary from June 1914 to January 1919. Hutchinson & Co., London

Addison P (1994) The road to 1945: British politics and the Second World War, rev edn. Pimlico, London

Adonis A, Pollard S (1997) A class act: the myth of Britain's classless society. Hamish Hamilton, London

Allen GC (1976) The British disease: a short essay on the nature and causes of the nation's lagging wealth. Hobart Paper 67. Institute of Economic Affairs, London

---

[38] Those interested in traits across spheres, with similar outcomes of national under-performance, might find insight from sport instructive. For cricket, Williams' (2012) exposition is well written and instructive, as exemplified in how into the 1960s most county cricket governing bodies still adhered to the practice of insisting only amateurs, no matter how ill-qualified, captain teams, since professional players could not be relied on to 'act like gentlemen'. Instructively for these representatives of English Establishment priorities, such amateurs commonly received 'expenses' significantly higher than salary and other payments to professional players. This system failed in the 1960s under the weight of its own contradictions.

Ambrose PJ (1974) The quiet revolution: social change in a Sussex village 1871–1971. Chatto & Windus, London

Anderson B (1983) Imagined communities: reflections on the origins and spread of nationalism. Verso, London

Ashford DE (1981) Policy and politics in Britain: the limits of consensus. Blackwell, Oxford

Ashford DE (1982) British dogmatism and French pragmatism: central-local policy-making in the welfare state. Allen & Unwin, London

Ashford DE (1986) The emergence of the welfare states. Blackwell, Oxford

Audickas L, Cracknell R (2020) Social background of MPs 1979–2020. Briefing Paper CBP7483. House of Commons Library, London

Axford B (1978) Charles Selwyn and Mark Woodnutt, political leaders on the Isle of Wight. In: Jones GW, Norton A (eds) Political leadership in local authorities. University of Birmingham Institute of Local Government Studies, Birmingham, pp 81–100

Baines D, Johnson P (1999) In search of the 'traditional' working-class: social mobility and occupational continuity in interwar London. Econ Hist Rev 52:692–713

Ball ID (1980) Urban investment controls in Britain. In: Ashford DE (ed) National resources and urban policy. Croom Helm, London, pp 115–142

Barlow J, Duncan SS (1994) Success and failure in housing provision: European systems compared. Pergamon, Oxford

Barnett C (1972) The collapse of British power. Eyre Methuen, London

Barnett C (1986) The audit of war: the illusion and reality of Britain as a great nation. Macmillan, London

Barnett C (1995) The lost victory: British dreams, British realities 1945–1950. Macmillan, London

Barnett C (2001) The verdict of peace: Britain between her yesterday and the future. Macmillan, London

Bealey F, Blondel J, McCann WP (1965) Constituency politics: a study of Newcastle-under-Lyme. Faber & Faber, London

Beavan B (2006) Challenges to civic governance in post-war England: the peace day disturbances of 1919. Urban Hist 33:369–392

Beazley M, Gavin D, Gillon S, Raine C, Staunton M (1980) The sale of council houses in rural areas: a case study of South Oxfordshire. Working Paper 44. Oxford Polytechnic Department of Town Planning, Oxford

Beith AJ (1973) The anti-labour caucus: the case of the Northumberland Voters' Association. Policy Polit 2:153–165

Bell MM (1994) Childerley: nature and morality in a country village. University of Chicago Press, Chicago

Bellman H (1928) The silent revolution: the influence of the building societies on the modern housing problem. Methuen, London

Bennett EN (1914) Problems of village life. Williams & Norgate, London

Benson J (1989) The working class in Britain, 1850–1939. Longman, Harlow

Berry F (1974) Housing: the great British failure. Charles Knight, London

Bevan M, Cameron S, Coombes M, Merridew T, Raybould S (2001) Social housing in rural areas. Chartered Institute of Housing, Coventry

Bishop KD (1998) Countryside conservation and the new right. In: Allmendiger P, Thomas H (eds) Urban planning and the new right. Routledge, London, pp 186–210

Blondel J, Hall R (1967) Conflict, decision-making and the perceptions of local councillors. Polit Stud 15:322–350

Bolton N, Chalkley B (1990) The rural population turnaround: a case study of north Devon. J Rural Stud 6:29–43

Booth A (1987) A managed economy? Econ Hist Rev 40:499–522

Booth P (1999) From regulation to discretion: the evolution of development control in the British planning system 1909–1947. Plan Perspect 14:277–289

Booth A (2000) Inflation, expectations and the political economy of Conservative Britain, 1951–64. Hist J 43:827–847

Booth A (2001) New revisionists and the Keynesian era in British economic policy. Econ Hist Rev 54:346–366

Bourne G [pseudonym for Sturt G] (1912) Change in the village, 1955 edn. Duckworth, London

Bowers JK (1985) British agricultural policy since the Second World War. Agric Hist Rev 33:66–76

Bowley M (1945) Housing and the state 1919–1944. Allen & Unwin, London

Branson N (1979) Poplarism 1919–25: George Lansbury and the councillors' revolt. Lawrence & Wishart, London

Breton A, Wintrobe R (1982) The logic of bureaucratic conduct. Cambridge University Press, Cambridge

Brittan S (1964) The Treasury under the Tories 1951–1964. Penguin, Harmondsworth

Broadberry SN, Crafts NFR (1996) British economic policy and industrial performance in the early post-war period. Bus Hist 38:65–91

Brown T (2017) Tragedy and challenge: an inside view of UK engineering's decline and the challenges of the Brexit economy. Matador, Kibworth Beauchamp

Buller HJ, Hoggart K (1986) Nondecision-making and community power: the case of residential development control in rural areas. Prog Plan 25:133–203

Bulpitt JG (1983) Territory and power in the United Kingdom. Manchester University Press, Manchester

Butler D, Freeman J (1963) British political facts 1900–1960. Macmillan, London

Cairncross A (1995) The British economy since 1945, 2nd edn. Blackwell, Oxford

Cairncross A (1996) Managing the British economy in the 1960s. Macmillan, Basingstoke

Cairncross A, Watts N (1989) The economic section 1939–1961: a study in economic advising. Routledge, London

Calder A (1969) The people's war: Britain 1939–1945. Pimlico, London

Campbell J (1987) Nye Bevan: a biography. Hodder & Stoughton, London

Cannadine D (1990) The decline and fall of the British aristocracy. Yale University Press, New Haven

Catterall P (ed) (2003) The Macmillan diaries: the Cabinet years, 1950–1957. Macmillan, London

Chaney P, Sherwood K (2000) The resale of right to buy dwellings: a case study of migration and social change in rural England. J Rural Stud 16:79–94

Chase M (1993) 'Nothing less than a revolution?': Labour's agricultural policy. In: Fyrth J (ed) Labour's high noon: the government and the economy 1945–51. Lawrence & Wishart, London, pp 78–95

Chowdhury A, Islam I (1993) The newly industrialised economies of East Asia. Routledge, London

Clark GL (1985) Judges and cities: interpreting local autonomy. University of Chicago Press, Chicago

Clark DM (1990) Affordable rural housing: challenge for the nineties. Rural Development Commission, Salisbury

Clarke A, Cochrane A (1987) Investing in the private sector: the enterprise board experiment. In: Cochrane A (ed) Developing local economic strategies. Open University Press, Milton Keynes, pp 4–22

Cloke PJ (1979) Key settlements in rural areas. Methuen, London

Cloke PJ, Thrift NJ (1990) Class and change in rural Britain. In: Marsden TK, Lowe PD, Whatmore SJ (eds) Rural restructuring: global processes and their responses. David Fulton, London, pp 165–181

Cole GDH (1948) A history of the Labour Party from 1914. Routledge & Kegan Paul, London

Coleman R (1982) Second homes in north Norfolk. In: Moseley MJ (ed) Power, planning and people in rural East Anglia. University of East Anglia Centre for East Anglian Studies, Norwich, pp 97–117

Committee of Inquiry into Local Government Finance (1976) Report. Cmnd 6453. The Layfield Committee. HMSO, London

Construction Task Force to the Deputy Prime Minister on the Scope for Improving the Quality & Efficiency of UK Construction (1998) Rethinking construction. Department of the Environment, Transport & the Regions, London

Cooper J (1979) Class: a view from middle England. Corgi, London

Corden IA, Curley JM (1974) Control over the capital investment of local authorities. Public Financ Account 1:231–233

Corina L (1974) Elected representatives in a party system: a typology. Policy Polit 3:69–87

Cross M, Mallen D (1978) Local government and politics. Longman, Harlow

Crossman R (1975) The diaries of a Cabinet Minister: volume one – Minister of Housing 1964–66. Hamish Hamilton and Jonathan Cape, London

Curran J, Seaton J (1988) Power without responsibility: the press and broadcasting in Britain, 3rd edn. Routledge, London

Danziger R (1988) Political powerlessness: agricultural workers in post-war England. Manchester University Press, Manchester

Darke J (1991) Local political attitudes and council housing. In: Lowe S, Hughes D (eds) A new century of social housing. Leicester University Press, Leicester, pp 159–174

Daunton MJ (1984) Introduction. In: Daunton MJ (ed) Councillors and tenants. Leicester University Press, Leicester, pp 1–38

Davies A (2013) 'Right to buy': the development of a Conservative housing policy, 1945–1980. Contemp Br Hist 27:421–444

Dearlove J (1979) The reorganisation of British local government. Cambridge University Press, Cambridge

Dennis N, Henriques F, Slaughter C (1956) Coal if our life: an analysis of a Yorkshire mining community. Eyre & Spottiswoode, London

Department of the Environment (1977) Housing policy: technical volume 1. HMSO, London

Doling J (1997) Comparative housing policy: government and housing in advanced industrialized countries. Macmillan, Basingstoke

Downs A (1957) An economic theory of political action in a democracy. J Polit Econ 45:135–150

Downs A (1967) Inside bureaucracy. Little Brown, Boston

Duncan SS (1976) The allocation of mortgages and the formation of housing sub-markets. Area 8:307–316

Dunford M (1995) Metropolitan polarization, the North-South divide and socio-spatial inequality in Britain: a long-term perspective. Eur Urban Reg Stud 2:145–170

Dunleavy PJ (1980) Social and political theory and the issues in central-local relations. In: Jones GW (ed) New approaches to the study of central-local government relationships. Gower, Aldershot, pp 116–136

Dunleavy PJ (1981) The politics of mass housing in Britain 1945–75. Clarendon, Oxford

Dunleavy PJ (1985) Bureaucrats, budgets and the growth of the state. Br J Polit Sci 15:299–328

Eley AW (1973) The passing of independence: the story of a rural district council. Occasional Paper 1. Bradwell Abbey Field Centre for the Study of Archaeology, Natural History & Environmental Studies, Milton Keynes

Elliot HSR (1910, ed) The letters of John Stuart Mill: volume one. Longman, Green & Co., London

Faucher-King F, Le Galès P (2010) The New Labour experiment: change and reform under Blair and Brown. Stanford University Press, Stanford

Fielding S (1992) What did 'The people' want? The meaning of the 1945 General Election. Hist J 35:623–639

Flynn N, Leach S, Vielba C (1985) Abolition or reform? the GLC and the metropolitan county councils. Allen & Unwin, London

Ford J (1975) The role of the building society manager in the urban stratification system: autonomy versus constraint. Urban Stud 12:295–302

Forrest R, Murie A (1988) Selling the welfare state: the privatisation of public housing. Routledge, London

Forrest R, Murie A (1990) A dissatisfied state? consumer preferences and council housing in Britain. Urban Stud 27:617–635

Francis M (1997) Ideas and policies under Labour 1945–1951: building a new Britain. Manchester University Press, Manchester

Gallent N, Bell P (2000) Planning exceptions in rural England: past, present and future. Plan Pract Res 15:375–384

Gamble AM (1974) The conservative nation. Routledge & Kegan Paul, London

Gamble AM (1981) Britain in decline: economic policy, political strategy and the British state. Macmillan, Basingstoke

Gamble AM, Walkland SA (1984) The British party system and economic policy, 1945–83: studies in adversary politics. Clarendon, Oxford

Gay O (1987) Pre-fabs: a study in policy-making. Public Adm 65:407–422

Gilg AW (1978) Countryside planning. David & Charles, Newton Abbot

Gilg AW (1982) Countryside planning yearbook three. Geo Books, Norwich

Gilg AW (1985) Countryside planning yearbook six. Geo Books, Norwich

Gilg AW (1986) Countryside planning yearbook seven. Geo Books, Norwich

Gilg AW, Kelly M (1997) Rural planning in practice: the case of agricultural dwellings. Prog Plan 47:75–157

Golland A (1998) Systems of housing supply and housing production in Europe: a comparison of the United Kingdom, The Netherlands and Germany. Ashgate, Aldershot

Green FE (1920) A history of the English agricultural labourer 1870–1920. P.S. King & Co., London

Green G (1972) National, city and ward components of local voting. Policy Polit 1:45–54

Green DR (1991) The metropolitan economy: continuity and change 1800–1939. In: Hoggart K, Green DR (eds) London: a new metropolitan geography. Edward Arnold, London, pp 8–33

Griffith JAG (1966) Central departments and local government. Allen & Unwin, London

Griffiths CVJ (2007) Labour and the countryside: the politics of rural Britain 1918–1939. Oxford University Press, Oxford

Guttsman WL (1968) The British political elite. MacGibbon & Kee, London

Halfacree KH (1994) The importance of 'the rural' in the constitution of counterurbanization: evidence from England in the 1980s. Sociol Rural 34:164–189

Hall PG (1980) Great planning disasters. Weidenfield & Nicolson, London

Hall PG, Breheny M, McQuaid R, Hart D (1987) Western sunrise: the genesis and growth of Britain's major high tech corridor. Allen & Unwin, London

Halliday J, Coombes M (1995) In search of counterurbanisation: some evidence from Devon on the relationship between patterns of migration and motivation. J Rural Stud 11:433–446

Ham A (1981) Treasury rules: recurrent themes in British economic policy. Quartet, London

Hamnett CR (2003) Unequal city: London in the global arena. Routledge, London

Hampton W (1970) Democracy and community: a study of politics in Sheffield. Oxford University Press, Oxford

Hampton W (1987) Local government and urban politics. Longman, London

Harloe M (1995) The people's home? social rented housing in Europe and America. Blackwell, Oxford

Harris N (1986) The end of the third world: newly industrializing countries and the decline of an ideology. Penguin, Harmondsworth

Harrison M, Norton A (1967) Local government administration in England and Wales. Maud Committee report on the management of local government volume five. HMSO, London

Heath A, Jowell R, Curtice J (1985) How Britain votes. Pergamon, Oxford

Heclo HH (1969) The councillor's job. Public Adm 47:185–202

Heclo HH, Wildavsky A (1974) The private government of public money. Macmillan, London

Hennessy P (1992) Never again: Britain 1945–1951. Vintage Books, London

Hennessy P (1996) Muddling through: power, politics and the quality of government in postwar Britain. Victor Gollancz, London

Hennessy P (2006) Having it so good: Britain in the fifties. Allen Lane, London

Hill BE, Ray D (1987) Economics for agriculture: food, farming and rural economics. Macmillan, Basingstoke

Hoare AG (1985) Dividing the pork-barrel: Britain's enterprise zone experiment. Polit Geogr Q 4:29–46

Hobsbawm EJ (1968) Industry and empire. Penguin, Harmondsworth

Hodge I, Monk S (2004) The economic diversity of rural England: stylised fallacies and uncertain evidence. J Rural Stud 20:263–272

Hodge I, Whitby MC (1981) Rural employment: trends, options, choices. Methuen, London

Hoggart K (1988) Not a definition of rural. Area 20:35–40

Hoggart K (1990) Let's do away with rural. J Rural Stud 6:245–257

Hoggart K (1991) People, power and place: perspectives on Anglo-American politics. Routledge, London

Hoggart K (1997) The middle classes in rural England 1971–1991. J Rural Stud 13:253–273

Hoggart K, Henderson SR (2005) Excluding exceptions: housing non-affordability and the oppression of environmental sustainability? J Rural Stud 21:181–196

Hoggart K, Buller HJ, Black R (1995) Rural Europe: identity and change. Arnold, London

Horn P (2013) Country house society: the private lives of England's upper class after the First World War. Amberley Publishing, Stroud

House of Commons Library (2020) Productivity. Economic Indicators Paper 02791. London

Howkins A (2003) The death of rural England: a social history of the countryside since 1900. Routledge, London

Howkins A, Verdon N (2009) The state and the farm worker: the evolution of the minimum wage in agriculture in England and Wales, 1909–24. Agric Hist Rev 57:257–274

Humphries J (1987) Inter-war house building, cheap money and building societies: the housing boom revisited. Bus Hist 29:325–345

Hussey S (1997) Low pay, underemployment and multiple occupations: men's work in the inter-war countryside. Rural Hist 8:217–235

Hymer S (1975) The multinational corporation and the law of uneven development. In: Radice H (ed) International firms and modern imperialism. Penguin, Harmondsworth, pp 37–62

Ingham G (1984) Capitalism divided? The city and industry in British social development. Macmillan, Basingstoke

Jackson AA (1973) Semi-detached London: suburban development, life and transport, 1900–39. Allen & Unwin, London

Jacobs K, Kemeny J, Manzi T (2003) Privileged or exploited council tenants? the discursive change in Conservative housing policy from 1972 to 1980. Policy Polit 31:307–320

James L (2006) The middle class: a history. Little Brown, London

Jarvis D (1996) British Conservatism and class politics in the 1920s. Engl Hist Rev 111:59–84

Johnson RW (1972) The nationalisation of English rural politics: Norfolk South West, 1945–1970. Parliam Aff 26:8–55

Johnson RW (1985) The politics of recession. Macmillan, Basingstoke

Jones GW (1969) Borough politics: a study of Wolverhampton town council, 1888–1964. Macmillan, London

Jones H (2000) 'This is magnificent!': 300,000 houses a year and the Tory revival after 1945. Contemp Br Hist 14:99–121

Jones O (2014) The establishment: and how they get away with it. Allen Lane, London

Karran TJ (1988) Local taxing and local spending: international comparisons. In: Paddison R, Bailey S (eds) Local government finance: international perspectives. Routledge, London, pp 53–84

Keith WJ (1984) The rural tradition: a study of non-fiction prose writers on the English countryside. University of Toronto Press, Toronto

Keith M (1989) Riots as a 'social problem' in British cities. In: Herbert DT, Smith DM (eds) Social problems and the city, 2nd edn. Oxford University Press, Oxford, pp 289–306

Keith-Lucas B, Richards PG (1978) A history of local government in the twentieth century. Allen & Unwin, London

Kynaston D (2007) Austerity Britain 1945–51. Bloomsbury, London

Laffin M (1986) Professional communities and policy communities in central-local relations. In: Goldsmith M (ed) New research in central-local relations. Gower, Aldershot, pp 108–121

Lash S, Urry J (1987) The end of organized capitalism. Polity, Cambridge

Layton E (1961) Building by local authorities. Allen & Unwin, London

Lee JM (1963) Social leaders and public persons: a study of county government in Cheshire since 1888. Clarendon, Oxford

LeGrand J (1982) The strategy of equality: redistribution and the social services. Allen & Unwin, London

Leys C (1986) The formation of British capital. New Left Rev 160:114–120

Lindblom CE (1959) The science of 'muddling through'. Public Adm Rev 19(2):79–88

Loughlin M, Gelfand MD, Young K (1985, eds) Half a century of municipal decline. Allen & Unwin, London

Lowe R (1978) The erosion of state intervention in Britain, 1917–24. Econ Hist Rev 31:270–286

Lowe R (1984) Bureaucracy triumphant or denied? The expansion of the British civil service, 1919–1939. Public Adm 62:291–310

Lowenthal D, Prince HC (1965) English landscape tastes. Geogr Rev 55:186–222

Lowerson J (1980) Battles for the countryside. In: Gloversmith F (ed) Class, culture and social change: a new view of the 1930s. Harvester, Brighton, pp 258–280

Lukes S (1974) Power: a radical view. Macmillan, London

Lyman RW (1957) The first Labour government 1924. Chapman & Hall, London

Macmillan H (1969) Tides of fortune 1945–1955. Macmillan, London

Marsden TK, Murdoch J, Lowe PD, Munton RJC, Flynn A (1993) Constructing the countryside. UCL Press, London

Martin RL (1988) The political economy of Britain's north-south divide. Trans Inst Br Geogr 13:389–418

Massey DB (1986) The legacy lingers on: the impacts of Britain's international role on its internal geography. In: Martin RL, Rowthorn B (eds) The geography of de-industrialisation. Macmillan, Basingstoke, pp 31–52

McGrew T, Bristow S (1984) Candidate to councillor: a study of political recruitment. In: Bristow SL, Kermode D, Mannin M (eds) The redundant counties? G.W. & A. Hesketh, Ormskirk, pp 69–100

McKibbin R (2010) Parties and people: England 1914–1951. Oxford University Press, Oxford

Merrett S (1982) Owner-occupation in Britain. Routledge & Kegan Paul, London

Miliband R (1961) Parliamentary socialism: a study in the politics of Labour. Merlin Press, London

Miller FM (1976) The unemployment policy of the National government, 1931–1936. Hist J 19:453–476

Ministry of Health (1921) Report of the departmental committee on the high cost of building working class dwellings, Cmd 1447. HMSO, London

Ministry of Health (1930) Eleventh annual report, 1929–1930. Cmd 3667. HMSO, London

Ministry of Health (1932) Thirteenth annual report, 1931–1932. Cmd 4113. HMSO, London

Ministry of Health (1933a) Fourteenth annual report, 1932–1933. Cmd 4372. HMSO, London

Ministry of Health (1933b) Housing (Financial Provisions) Act, 1933. Circular 1334. HMSO, London

Ministry of Health (1934) Fifteenth annual report, 1933–1934. Cmd 4664. HMSO, London

Ministry of Health (1938) Nineteenth annual report, 1937–1938. Cmd 5801. HMSO, London

Ministry of Health (1939) Twentieth annual report, 1938–1939. Cmd 6089. HMSO, London

Ministry of Health (1944a) Rural housing: third report of the Rural Housing Sub-Committee of the Central Housing Advisory Committee. HMSO, London

Ministry of Health (1944b) Private enterprise housing: report of the Private Enterprise Sub-Committee of the Central Housing Advisory Committee of the Ministry of Health. HMSO, London

Ministry of Health (1944c) Valuation for rates 1939. HMSO, London

Ministry of Health (quarterly) Housing return for England and Wales [From 1951 Ministry of Housing & Local Government]. HMSO, London

Ministry of Housing & Local Government (1965) Report of the Committee on Housing in Greater London. Cmnd 2605, Milner-Holland report. HMSO, London

Ministry of Housing & Local Government (1967) Management of local government. Maud Committee report. HMSO, London

Ministry of Housing & Local Government (1968) Housing condition survey: England and Wales, 1967. Econ Trends 175:87–99

Ministry of Housing & Local Government (quarterly) Housing return for England and Wales [Before 1951 Ministry of Health]. HMSO, London

Ministry of Labour & National Service (1957) Enquiry into household expenditure 1953–54. HMSO, London

Morgan KO (1984) Labour in power, 1945–1951. Clarendon, Oxford

Morgan KO (1990) The people's peace: British history 1945-1989. Oxford University Press, Oxford

Morgan KO, Morgan J (1980) Portrait of a progressive: the political career of Christopher, Viscount Addison. Clarendon, Oxford

Morris DS, Newton K (1970) Profile of a local political elite: businessmen as community decision-makers in Birmingham 1838–1966. New Atlantis 1(2):111–123

Morris DS, Newton K (1971) The social composition of a city council: Birmingham 1925–1966. Soc Econ Adm 5(1):29–33

Mortimer J (1993) The changing mood of the working people. In: Fyrth J (ed) Labour's high noon: the government and the economy 1945–51. Lawrence & Wishart, London, pp 243–254

Moss L, Parker SR (1967) The local government councillor. Maud Committee report on the management of local government volume two. HMSO, London

Mowat CL (1955) Britain between the wars, 1918–1940. Methuen, London

Muchnick DM (1970) Urban renewal in Liverpool: a study of the politics of redevelopment. Occasional Paper in Social Administration 33. Bell, London

Murdoch J, Marsden TK (1994) Reconstituting rurality. UCL Press, London

Murdoch J, Lowe PD, Ward N, Marsden TK (2003) The differentiated countryside. Routledge, London

National House Building Committee (1924) Report on the present position in the building industry, with regard to the carrying out of a full housing programme, having particular reference to the means of providing an adequate supply of labour and materials, Cmd 2104. HMSO, London

Newby HE (1975) The deferential dialectic. Comp Stud Soc Hist 17:139–164

Newby HE (1977) The deferential worker: a study of farm workers in East Anglia. Allen Lane, London

Newby HE, Bell C, Rose D, Saunders P (1978) Property, paternalism and power. Hutchinson, London

Newton K (1979) The local political elite in England and Wales. In: Lagroye J, Wright V (eds) Local government in Britain and France. Allen & Unwin, London, pp 105–113

Newton S (2009) The two sterling crises of 1964 and the decision not to devalue. Econ Hist Rev 62:73–98

Niner P (1975) Local authority housing policy and practice: a case study approach. Occasional Paper 31. University of Birmingham Centre for Urban & Regional Studies, Birmingham

Niskanen WA (1971) Bureaucracy and representative government. Aldine, Chicago

O'Carroll A (1996a) The sale of council housing in the inter-war period. Hous Stud 11:527–541

O'Carroll A (1996b) The influence of local authorities on the growth of owner occupation: Edinburgh and Glasgow 1914–1939. Plan Perspect 11:55–72

O'Leary B (1987) Why was the GLC abolished? Int J Urban Reg Res 11:193–217

Oakeshott M (1975) On being conservative. In: de Crespigny A, Cronin J (eds) Ideologies of politics. Oxford University Press, London, pp 23–51

Olney R (2007) Squire and community: T.G. Dixon at Holton-le-Moor, 1906–1937. Rural Hist 18:201–216

Orbach LF (1977) Homes for heroes: a study of the evolution of British public housing 1915–1921. Seeley Service & Co., London

Owen N (2007) MacDonald's parties: the Labour Party and the 'aristocratic embrace', 1922–31. Twent Century Br Hist 18:1–53

Page EC (1985) Political authority and bureaucratic power. Harvester, Brighton

Pahl RE (1985) Divisions of labour. Blackwell, Oxford

Paniagua A (2002) Counterurbanization and new social class in rural Spain: the environmental and rural dimension revisited. Scott Geogr J 118:1–18

Paris C, Blackaby B (1979) Not much improvement: urban renewal policy in Birmingham. Heinemann, London

Parkinson M (1985) Liverpool on the brink: one city's struggle against government cuts. Policy Journals, Hermitage

Pedley WH (1942) Labour on the land: a study of the developments between the two great wars. P.S. King & Staples, London

Pelling H (1963) A history of British trade unionism. Penguin, Harmondsworth

Pemberton H (2004) Relative decline and British economic policy in the 1960s. Hist J 47:989–1013

Penning-Rowsell EC (1997) Who 'betrayed' whom? power and politics in the 1920/21 agricultural crisis. Agric Hist Rev 45:176–194

Perkin H (1989) The rise of professional society: England since 1880. Routledge, London

Perry PJ (1974) British farming in the great depression 1870–1914. David & Charles, Newton Abbott

Perry R, Dean K, Brown B (1986) Counterurbanisation: international case studies of socio-economic change in rural areas. Geo Books, Norwich

Phillips DR, Williams AM (1981) Council house sales and village life. New Society, 26 November, pp 367–368

Pimlott B (ed) (1986) The political diary of Hugh Dalton, 1918–40, 1945–60. Jonathan Cape, London

Popplestone G (1967) Conflict and mediating roles in expanding settlements. Sociol Rev 15:339–355

Pryke M, Whitehead C (1995) Private sector criteria and the radical change in provision of social housing in England. Environ Plann C Gov Policy 13:217–252

Pugh M (2008) 'We danced all night': a social history of Britain between the wars. Bodley Head, London

Punter J (1986) A history of aesthetic control, 1909–1953: the control of the external appearance of development in England and Wales. Town Plan Rev 57:351–381

Punter J (1987) A history of aesthetic control, 1953–1985: the control of the external appearance of development in England and Wales. Town Plan Rev 58:29–62

Radford E (1970) The new villagers: urban pressure on rural areas in Worcestershire. Frank Cass, London

Reiner WJ, Broughton HF (1953) Productivity in house-building: second report. Department of Scientific & Industrial Research, Building Research Station, National Building Studies 21. HMSO, London

Rhodes G (1976) Local government finance 1918–1966. In: Committee of Inquiry into Local Government Finance, Local government finance: appendix xix. HMSO, London, pp 102–173

Rhodes C, Booth L, Brown J, Butcher L, Harari D, Keep M, Mor F, Potton E (2018) Public ownership of industries and services. Briefing Paper CP8325. House of Commons Library, London

Richardson HW (1967) Economic recovery in Britain 1932–39. Weidenfeld & Nicolson, London

Robbins K (1993) The eclipse of a great power: modern Britain 1870–1975. Longman, Harlow

Rose R (1965) Politics in England. Faber, London

Rose D, Saunders P, Newby HE, Bell C (1976) Ideologies of property. Sociol Rev 24:699–730

Rothery M (2007) The wealth of the English landed gentry, 1870–1935. Agric Hist Rev 55:251–268

Royal Commission on Local Government in England (1969) Report. Cmnd 4040, Redcliffe-Maud report. HMSO, London

Rydin Y (1986) Housing land policy. Gower, Aldershot

Sampson A (1982) The changing anatomy of Britain. Hodder & Stoughton, London

Saunders P (1985) The forgotten dimension of central-local relations: theorising the 'regional state'. Environ Plann C Gov Policy 3:149–162

Savage M (2000) Class analysis and social transformation. Open University Press, Buckingham

Saville J (1993) Introduction. In: Fyrth J (ed) Labour's high noon: the government and the economy 1945–51. Lawrence & Wishart, London, pp xv–xxxviii

Schwartz HM (1994) States versus markets. St. Martin's Press, New York

Scott J (1982) The upper classes: property and privilege in Britain. Macmillan, Basingstoke

Scott P (1996) The worst of both worlds: British regional policy, 1951–64. Bus Hist 38:41–64

Scott P (2007) Triumph of the south: a regional economic history of early twentieth century Britain. Ashgate, Aldershot

Scott P (2008) Marketing mass home ownership and the creation of the modern working-class consumer in inter-war Britain. Bus Hist 50:4–25

Scott P, Newton LA (2012) Advertising, promotion, and the rise of a national building society movement in interwar Britain. Bus Hist 54:399–423

Seaman LCB (1966) Post-Victorian Britain, 1902–1951. Methuen, London

Self RC (2000, ed) The Neville Chamberlain diary letters: volume two, the reform years, 1921–27. Ashgate, Aldershot

Self RC (2006) Neville Chamberlain: a biography. Ashgate, Aldershot

Self P, Storing HJ (1962) The state and the farmer. Allen & Unwin, London

Sharp E (1969) The Ministry of Housing and Local Government. Allen & Unwin, London

Sharpe LJ (1978) Reforming the grass roots: an alternative analysis. In: Halsey AH, Butler DE (eds) Policy and politics. Macmillan, London, pp 82–110

Sharpe LJ (1982) The Labour Party and the geography of inequality: a puzzle. In: Kavanagh D (ed) The politics of the Labour Party. Allen & Unwin, London, pp 135–170

Shucksmith M (1981) No homes for locals? Gower, Farnborough

Sillince J (1986) Why did Warwickshire's key settlement policy change in 1982? Geogr J 152:176–192

Sked A (1987) Britain's decline. Blackwell, Oxford

Smith MJ (1989) Changing agendas and policy communities: agricultural issues in the 1930s and the 1980s. Public Adm 67:149–165

Smith HL (1992) The politics of Conservative reform: the equal pay for equal work issue, 1945–55. Hist J 35:401–415

Smyth J, Robertson D (2013) Local elites and social control: building council houses in Stirling between the wars. Urban Hist 40:336–354

Springall LM (1936) Labouring life in Norfolk villages 1834–1914. Allen & Unwin, London

Stacey M, Batstone E, Bell C, Murcott A (1975) Power, persistence and change: second study of Banbury. Routledge & Kegan Paul, London

Sutcliffe AS, Smith R (1974) Birmingham 1939–1970: history of Birmingham volume three. Oxford University Press, London

Taylor AJP (1965) English history 1914–1945. Clarendon, Oxford

Taylor S (1984) The Scarman report and explanation of riots. In: Benyon J (ed) Scarman and after. Pergamon, Oxford, pp 20–34

Taylor PJ (1989) Britain's century of decline: a world-systems interpretation. In: Anderson J, Cochrane A (eds) A state of crisis: the changing faces of British politics. Hodder & Stoughton, London, pp 8–26

Theakston K, Fry GK (1989) Britain's administrative elite: permanent secretaries 1900–1986. Public Adm 67:129–147

Thompson FML (2001) Gentrification and the enterprise culture: Britain 1780–1980. Oxford University Press, Oxford

Tichelar M (2003) The Labour Party, agricultural policy and the retreat from rural land nationalisation during the Second World War. Agric Hist Rev 51:209–225

Topham N (1970) Housing authorities and the investment decision. Manch Sch Econ Soc Stud 38:285–302

Tylecote AB (1982) German ascent and British decline 1870–1980: the role of upper class structure and values. In: Friedman E (ed) Ascent and decline in the world-system. Sage, Beverly Hills, pp 41–67

Urry J (1986) Class, space and disorganised capitalism. In: Hoggart K, Kofman E (eds) Politics, geography and social stratification. Croom Helm, London, pp 16–32

van Dam F (2000) Revealed and stated preferences for rural living: evidence from the Netherlands. In: Haartsen T, Groote PG, Huigen PPP (eds) Claiming rural identities. Van Gorcum, Assen, pp 80–91

Wade-Martins S, Williamson T (2008) The countryside of East Anglia: changing landscapes 1870–1950. Boydell, Woodbridge

Ward SV (1984) List Q: a missing link in inter-war public investment. Public Adm 62:348–358

Ward SV (1988) The geography of interwar Britain: the state and uneven development. Routledge, London

Warde A (1986) Space, class and voting in Britain. In: Hoggart K, Kofman E (eds) Politics, geography and social stratification. Croom Helm, London, pp 33–61

Weiler P (2000) The rise and fall of the Conservatives' 'grand design for housing', 1951–64. Contemp Br Hist 14:122–150

Westaway J (1974) The spatial hierarchy of business organizations and its implications for the British urban system. Reg Stud 8:145–155

Wheen F (1985) The battle for London. Pluto Press, London

Whetham EH (1974) The Agriculture Act, 1920 and its repeal – the 'great betrayal'. Agric Hist Rev 22:36–49

Wickham-Jones M (2005) Signalling credibility: electoral strategy and New Labour in Britain. Polit Sci Q 120:653–673

Wiener MJ (1981) English culture and the decline of the industrial spirit 1850–1980. Cambridge University Press, Cambridge

Willetts D (1992) Modern Conservativism. Penguin, Harmondsworth

Williams R (1973) The country and the city. Chatto & Windus, London

Williams P (1978) Building societies and the inner city. Trans Inst Br Geogr 3:23–34

Williams CCP (2012) Gentlemen and players: the death of amateurism in cricket. Weidenfeld & Nicolson, London

Williams NJ, Sewel J, Twine F (1987) Council house sales and the electorate: voting behaviour and ideological implications. Hous Stud 2:274–282

Wilson GK (1977) Special Interests in policy-making: agricultural policies and politics in Britain and the United States. Wiley, Chichester

Wilson W (1999) The right to buy. Research Paper 99/36. House of Commons Library, London

Wright P (1987) Spy Catcher. Viking Penguin, New York

Yelling JA (1992) Slums and redevelopment: policy and practice in England 1918–45, with particular reference to London. UCL Press, London

Young K (1975) The Conservative strategy for London, 1855–1975. Lond J 1(1):56–81

Young K, Garside PL (1982) Metropolitan London: politics and urban change 1837–1981. Edward Arnold, London

Young K, Kramer J (1978) Strategy and conflict in metropolitan housing: suburbia versus the Greater London Council 1965–75. Heinemann, London

Index

Note: The study districts have so many entries in the text, they are not included in the index

© Springer Nature Switzerland AG 2021
K. Hoggart, *A Contrived Countryside*, Local and Urban Governance,
https://doi.org/10.1007/978-3-030-62651-8

---

[1] The seven RDCs securing most attention in this book are referred to so numerously across the chapters, that they have not been included in the Index.

Printed by Printforce, the Netherlands